1987

Introduction to Moral Reasoning

Introduction to
Moral Reasoning

Applying Basic Moral Principles to Selected Readings

R A L P H W. C L A R K

WEST PUBLISHING COMPANY
St. Paul New York Los Angeles San Francisco

Copyediting—Gregory Smith
Design—Paula Shuhert
Composition—Boyer & Brass, Inc.
Cover Design—Taly Design Group
Cover Art—Lee Anne Dollison, *Icy Waters*

Library of Congress Cataloging-in-Publication Data

Clark, Ralph W.
  Introduction to moral reasoning.

  Bibliography: p.
  Includes index.
  1. Ethics. I. Title.
BJ1025.C55 1986   170   85-22565
ISBN 0-314-93161-9

For Tommy, Jeff, and Eric

C O N T E N T S

CHAPTER 10

Preface

This book is intended to be much more accessible to its readers than other texts that are similar to it. It is needed because readings in philosophy by their very nature are difficult, especially for students who are taking introductory courses. Readings in philosophy are difficult, because necessarily they are filled with careful and often technical distinctions and with complex analyses of concepts and arguments. Philosophical readings should be contrasted with philosophical *questions*, which in most areas of philosophy are quite accessible. Philosophical questions readily invite discussion and thought, while the writings of philosophers place obstacles in the student's path.

Nowhere is this more true than in the area of current moral problems. Moral questions regarding the family and friendship, love and sex, euthanasia, the rights of women and minorities, future generations, the world of business, and so on, are in themselves very inviting and interesting. What is needed, therefore, is a textbook that gives its readers as much help as possible in understanding and evaluating what philosophers have said about these questions and others. To serve that purpose, the present book contains the following features:

1. An introductory chapter that provides an orientation to moral philosophy. Chapter 1 is intended to provide students with an understanding of basic moral principles and how they may be applied in trying to find defensible answers to moral questions. It is written in a way that is intended to be memorable and clear and also fair to a diversity of moral viewpoints. It is also intended to reach out to its readers in a sympathetic way: to draw upon their own perspectives—which may, for example, be either religious or nonreligious—as a starting point in philosophical inquiry.

2. Opening essays for chapters 2 through 10 that tie the readings together while also directing students to additional work that is relevant to each chapter. Much attention has been paid to making these essays readable and clear.

Some of the essays contain summaries of factual and legal material that is needed as background for discussing the moral questions in those chapters.

3. Reading selections that have been chosen and edited so as to be interesting and accessible *in addition* to being fair representations of diverse viewpoints.

4. Comments and questions following each reading selection that (a) stimulate the student's thinking and (b) clarify, when necessary, difficult points in the reading selections.

5. Helpful "extras," such as an essay on writing papers for philosophy classes, a glossary that contains historical references and illustrative examples, bibliographies and brief biographical sketches.

6. A choice of topics that is contemporary and reflects current interest in such areas as children's rights and business ethics, as well as interest in the more traditional areas of medical ethics, punishment, job discrimination, world hunger, and so on.

Many people have helped in preparing this book. I would like especially to thank: the students who over the years have taken my current moral problems courses and have told me what they liked and did not like about them, my colleagues Henry Ruf and Mark Wicclair for their helpful comments on earlier versions of chapter 1, my wife Suzanne for discussing nearly everything in the book with me, and J. B. Yowell and M. Margaret Adams of West Publishing Company for their encouragement and consistently very helpful editorial advice. Most importantly, I would like to thank the following reviewers: Joan Callahan of Louisiana State University, Jon Moran of Southwest Missouri State University, Robert Corrington of The Pennsylvania State University, and Jim Stone of the University of New Orleans. Finally, thank you to the secretaries in my department, Myrtle Dodge and Kellie Vankirk, who have typed and retyped everything quickly and accurately.

Writing Papers For Philosophy Classes

Many of the characteristics of good philosophical writing are also characteristics of good writing in other disciplines. Clarity, vigor, conciseness, smoothness, the capacity to generate and sustain interest—all of these characterize good writing wherever it may be found. But good philosophical writing has certain additional characteristics that are for the most part unique to it. In the present essay I will discuss what they are. Very often, they are responsible for giving students problems in writing papers for philosophy classes.

Please bear in mind that my purpose is not to define *the* way to write a good paper. One person's writing style may be quite different from another's, and one person's perspective on philosophy may be quite different from some other person's perspective. Therefore, there is no single, unique way to write a good philosophical paper.

I should mention also that there are many different kinds of philosophical papers: critical essays, historical interpretations, reviews of books, papers that are restricted to clarifying concepts or analyzing the logical structure of arguments, and others. I will discuss only one kind of paper—the critical essay on a controversial topic. Any of the moral issues covered in this book would be appropriate subjects for such a paper, as would a great variety of topics in other areas of philosophy such as the theory of knowledge or metaphysics.

In writing a critical essay you need to do some philosophizing of your own. You need to determine what *you* believe is the correct position on some controversial topic, and you then need to present arguments in defense of your position. But doing this cannot take place in a vacuum: It is absolutely essential for you to include a presentation of the most important things that other writers have said on the topic for your paper. Your instructor will probably give you some idea as to how extensive this section of your paper should be. For a relatively short paper on, let us say euthanasia, it might be sufficient for you to summarize the major points in the articles from the present book, or a similar collection, which deal with euthanasia. For a longer paper you would need to find additional material on euthanasia.

If you are writing on a topic that is covered in the textbook for the course for which the paper is assigned, then you *absolutely must* take into account the assigned readings in the text that are relevant to your paper. Moreover, you absolutely must take into account any additional arguments bearing upon your topic that have been presented in class lectures or discussion. You should prepare careful notes for all this material and any additional readings, and only after you have assembled your notes should you decide what to include in the paper.

There are special requirements for writing a good critical essay: fairness and open-mindedness are very important, but so also is a certain degree of personal commitment to the position that you are defending. You need to be open-minded in order to see what the opposing viewpoints are. At the same time, you need to have some commitment to what you believe is correct in order to make the assignment worthwhile to you and also to help you make your presentation compelling to those who read it.

At the heart of any critical essay is the tension between opposing viewpoints. Philosophers do not at all shy away from conflicts of ideas, but do insist upon clarity and fairness in presenting conflicts. As philosophers see it—and they are of course not unique in this regard—the way to reach the truth, or at least to make progress toward reaching it, is to begin by presenting both sides to a controversy as fairly and completely as possible, and only then to set about discussing the strengths and weaknesses of each side. You cannot determine how strong your own position is without examining opposing positions and seeing how yours stacks up against them. There is a famous quotation from the nineteenth century philosopher John Stuart Mill that very aptly sums up this viewpoint: "He who knows only his own side of the case knows little of that."

The following are general guidelines for writing philosophical papers.

Rule #1. You must state very clearly and precisely what the goals and limitations of your paper are. It could be said that good philosophical writing is self-conscious in a way that is not as true of writing in other areas. You must think very deliberately about exactly what you intend to cover in your paper, and then do your best to tell the reader what that is. I don't mean that you need to follow the old rubric: "Say what you are going to say, say it, then say what you have said." Some professors may suggest that you follow this guideline, particularly for longer compositions, but other professors may tell you not to follow it. For short papers—say anything under six pages or so—there will probably not be space enough for you to follow this guideline.

What I mean here is that you must set very clear limits to your topic and your treatment of it. For example, in a paper on euthanasia, after you have defined the word "euthanasia," you will need to say whether or not you are going to discuss euthanasia for people of all ages or only for young or only for old people. Also, you will need to make clear how your discussion of euthanasia will tie in with a discussion of broader issues such as the meaning of "human life," the question of whether or not anyone ever has a right to take any human life, and so on. All of this should of course be done as concisely as possible.

There are some shortcut methods for specifying the scope of a paper, but it is sometimes difficult for a person who is just beginning the study of philosophy to use them. For example, professional philosophers often set the scene in their papers by referring to recent philosophical work in books or journals: "My intention in this paper is to comment on the controversy between Smith and Jones in their recent articles on euthanasia. I shall give a new argument to show that Jones can after all defend himself against the objections raised by Smith." You need to be very cautious in using this procedure to delimit your topic because its success requires that you have a somewhat extensive knowledge of the books and articles bearing upon your topic. You need to know that the controversy between Smith and Jones is still open, and you need to know that Smith and Jones have particularly important things to say.

When you are letting the reader know at the beginning of your paper exactly what its goals and limitations are, it is important that you say *why* your presentation matters. It is important that you motivate the reader to be interested in the outcome of your paper.

Rule #2. Everything in your paper must be tied together into a logically coherent whole. Almost everything in a good philosophical paper plays a role in the logical presentation of ideas. Therefore, practically nothing should be present that is not (a) part of the statement of some philosophical position or question, or (b) part of an argument for or against some philosophical position or answer to a question. This means that you should omit or very much minimize, for example, remarks about the lives of philosophers or about the times in which they lived. Aside from the logical irrelevance of most such material, in the typical paper for a philosophy class there is no room for anything extraneous since so much space is needed to say precisely and completely what must, as a bare minimum, be included in the paper.

Whenever possible, use *conclusion indicators* such as "therefore," "consequently," and, "it follows that," and *premise indicators* such as "since," "for," "because," and "the reason for this is." Conclusion indicators and premise indicators tell the reader very explicitly that you are presenting an argument. For example, if I say, "Even toxic chemicals that are buried deep in the earth may eventually seep into ground water and *therefore* they are dangerous," the statement that precedes the word "therefore" is the premise of a brief argument and the statement that follows the word "therefore" is the conclusion. The word "therefore" tells the reader that the conclusion of an argument is about to be given. Whenever possible, it is helpful to telegraph to the reader what you are doing in the paper.

Now, I could have said, "Even toxic chemicals that are buried deep in the earth are dangerous *because* they may eventually seep into the ground water." Here the word because tells the reader that a premise for an argument is about to follow. Most arguments in your papers will be more complex than this one since they will have more than one premise giving reasons as to why the conclusion should be accepted. Moreover, it is very often the case that arguments are tied together into *argument chains* where the conclusion of one argument will be a premise in another. Conclusion indicators and premise indicators will help to let the reader know exactly how an argument chain has been put together.

Rule #3. When you are criticizing a position, be sure to state it as clearly, persuasively, and sympathetically as you can. It is unfair to state someone's position in a way that makes it weaker than it actually is, and then to attack *your* statement of the position as though it were adequate. Philosophers call this *attacking a straw man* (a substitute for the true man, that is, the true argument). It is difficult to give a brief example of the contrast between a straw man and an adequate statement of someone's position just because the way to avoid presenting a straw man is *not to be too brief* in describing a position that you are about to attack. For example, if you were going to attack the views of William Earle in chapter 10, you would need first to give *all* of his arguments in defense of war. You would need to describe war the way *he* describes it. If you were to say only that Earle defends war because he believes it to be heroic, that would not be adequate; that would be a straw man.

Rule #4. Whatever you say you should put in your own words, but you should always give credit where it is due for the ideas that you include in your paper. You should use direct quotes very sparingly and then only if they are short. If you do quote something directly, then you need to give a citation for the quote—either in the body of the paper by indicating the author, work, and page number(s), or in a footnote at the bottom of the page or at the end of the paper that contains the same information. Your instructor may tell you which form is required for your class.

If you are stating a position that is associated with the name of some philosopher, then you should mention the name. For example, "I will now discuss Karl Marx's theory of the alienation of workers." However, mentioning a name should never be a substitute for stating clearly what is at issue. For example, the reader may not know what Marx said about the alienation of workers. Moreover, it may well be that what Marx said is not entirely clear anyway, even to someone who knows Marx; and therefore it will be necessary for you to say what *you* believe Marx said.

Whenever you use someone else's ideas—whether or not you quote directly from that person—you need in *some way* to indicate the source of the ideas. This can be done by means of a citation in a footnote or in the body of a paper, or it can sometimes be accomplished in a less formal way. For example, you could say in the body of the paper: "I will now summarize the views of Mary Anne Warren on abortion from the assigned paper in the course textbook." Or you could say: "In raising objections against the position of Steven Goldberg on the death penalty I have drawn heavily upon the work of Arthur Koestler." Books and articles that you have made use of in writing your paper should be listed in a bibliography at the end of the paper.

Rule #5. Good philosophical writing almost always requires that a paper be rewritten at least once. Doing philosophy is difficult for everyone; there are no easy formulas for doing it and no shortcut methods. Since it is practically impossible to get your paper right the first time, you will almost surely need to write a second draft. Be sure to keep a xeroxed copy of the *final* draft. Often students will keep their rough drafts and hand in the only copy of the final draft. But then a lot of work would need to be done over if the paper somehow got lost.

In preparing to write a second draft, you should read through the first draft slowly and carefully. Is the paper free of mistakes in spelling and grammar? Does it read smoothly? Have you defined all important words whose meanings are not clear and obvious? Will the reader easily see why each sentence follows the one before it? Why each paragraph follows the one before it? Is your presentation fair? Is it complete enough? Have you used enough examples to make clear what you mean and especially to make clear how general ideas are to be applied in specific cases? In stating your own views, or your evaluations of someone else's views, have you given good reasons in defense of what you say? In answering the last question, you need not be concerned as to whether or not the reader of your paper will be convinced by what you say. All you need to do is to present arguments that should *appear from some reasonable perspective* to carry some weight. The instructor for your class—or whoever else is assigned to read your paper—may of course not share your perspective on a particular topic. But this should not matter at all since your job is to demonstrate that you know what *sort* of thing a good defense is.

You may be wondering when and how it is appropriate to seek help in writing your paper. Your instructor may give you somewhat different guidelines, but the general rule here is that the first draft of your paper should be *entirely* your own work. That is, the actual writing of the first draft should be entirely your own work. It is, of course, permissible for you to discuss with others the topic of your paper before you sit down to write it. Discussing your topic with others is in fact a very good idea. As for the second draft of your paper, it is permissible to receive the *appropriate* kind of help. It is permissible to ask someone to read your first draft and make comments on it, which you can then respond to in writing the second draft. Remember that in the final analysis, all philosophy is a cooperative enterprise between people who respond to each other's arguments and counterarguments.

Introduction to
Moral Reasoning

The Basic Moral Principles
and How to Apply Them

T he purpose of this book is to help you, the reader, to draw from within yourself your own moral feelings and ideas and to reason about them in a systematic way, and to tie them together into a coherent order and see where they lead. Our starting point is the belief that nearly everyone—that is, at least, nearly everyone who is likely to read this book—has a basic moral outlook on life. Nearly everyone wants to be moral and nearly everyone who has reached the point of taking a course in ethics has a commitment to the "basic ingredients" of a moral life.

But it is one thing to have a basic moral outlook and something else again to have mastered the complexities of moral reasoning. There are several factors that account for the complex nature of moral reasoning. One of the most important is that making moral decisions usually involves finding a balance among different values that conflict in some way. Consider for example the punishment of criminals. The punishment given for a particular crime needs to be harsh enough for it to function as a deterrent, but at the same time the rights and interests of the criminal need to be considered and balanced against the deterrent value of the punishment. Furthermore, penal programs that are designed both to punish and, if possible, to rehabilitate criminals are always expensive. The cost must be borne by society, but if the cost is too great it will place an excessive burden upon honest taxpayers. Again, a balance needs to be achieved so that enough money is spent on penal programs, but not too much. Conflicts of values that arise in regard to punishment are typical of value conflicts that are to be found in all areas of life.

One of the reasons why there are so many value conflicts in the world is that the world is a complex place, containing many different individuals and groups of individuals whose interests and perspectives diverge. Another reason is that *basic*

1

moral values themselves sometimes conflict, or at least they very often appear to conflict. For example, the protection of individual rights is one of the most basic moral values. But so also is justice in society, which may conflict, or appear to conflict, with the protection of individual rights. For example, someone who owns a business would appear to have a right of free choice in regard to who is hired to work in the business. But if this right is exercised in a racially or sexually discriminatory fashion, then the just treatment of people who apply for jobs may be threatened.

A later section of this chapter will examine in some detail what appear to be the most important conflicts among basic moral values, each of which will be stated as a *basic moral principle*. Your major task in reading the present chapter will be to think about each moral principle and how it might be applied in answering moral questions. Put another way, your major task will be to think about the role that moral principles play in moral reasoning.

A. Moral Pluralism

The approach to moral reasoning taken in this book places special emphasis on the conflicts that appear to occur among basic moral principles. I say "appear to occur" because philosophers do not all agree as to the extent of conflict among basic moral principles. There is a different approach to moral reasoning that is found in some other ethics textbooks: namely, an emphasis on the need to determine which is the *single* most important moral principle. Perhaps a single basic moral principle could be found that would in some way include within it all of the moral values that there is reason to believe are important; but showing in a convincing way that one particular principle is the most important is a very difficult, if not impossible task.

The approach taken in this book can be called *moral pluralism*. It is based upon the assumption that there is no single basic moral principle, or at least that there is no single basic moral principle that can readily be defended. The approach taken in this book presupposes that *each one* of several different basic moral principles has a certain plausibility about it, and that a moral person ought not to ignore any of the basic moral principles. Rather, the task is to find the proper balance among them. Moral pluralism is presented here as a way to ensure that no one of the generally recognized and important moral values will be ignored in the discussions of specific moral questions that this book is intended to generate.

The focus of this book is on current moral issues such as capital punishment, abortion, preferential treatment for women and minorities, nuclear deterrence, and so on. This book is intended to be an exercise in the *application* of moral reasoning; it is not intended to be an examination of moral principles or moral theories for their own sake. Consequently, it will not address questions about the ultimate nature and origin of morality. Do all moral values come ultimately from God? Or are they instead produced entirely by social processes? Is there perhaps some other answer that is best? Questions such as these are very important in courses dealing with ethical theory, philosophy of religion, issues in sociology, and so on. However, in preparing this book, I have been guided by a belief that I think is very important: namely, that a person can live an admirably moral life *regardless* of what he or she may suppose is the ultimate nature and origin of morality. Therefore, this book is addressed equally to those who believe and to those who do not believe that morality has a religious basis. It is addressed equally to those who accept what is called the "divine command" theory of morality (according to which morality is dependent in some way upon God's commands)[1] and to those who reject the divine command theory of morality.

B. Concern for Others and Respect for Oneself

While this book does not address questions about the ultimate nature and origin of morality, it does address questions about the essential *content* of morality. What is it that makes a moral act moral? What is it that makes a moral person moral? What is morality all about?

In attempting to answer such questions it will be helpful to begin by saying what morality is *not* about. It will be helpful to distinguish between morality, on the one hand, and related areas of interest on the other. Morality, of course, has to do with questions of right and wrong. But there are other kinds of "rightness" and "wrongness" in addition to the moral kind. For example, we sometimes say that a person did the wrong thing because what he or she did was *illegal*. Laws establish criteria for what is right and wrong, but those criteria are not exactly like moral criteria since laws are sometimes morally indefensible. There used to be many more examples of such laws in the U.S.—most notably, laws that were passed before the civil rights movement had made its impact upon society and which unjustly restricted the rights of blacks and other minorities. Of course, it is usually the case that what is morally right is also legal, but there are exceptions. Laws can always be subjected to moral scrutiny. Therefore, we can say that morality provides a "higher" or more important level of rightness and wrongness than does any set of laws.

Likewise, morality provides a higher level of rightness and wrongness than is provided by a consideration of purely practical, or *prudential*, values. For example, in many lower echelon executive positions in business, it is wrong in a prudential sense to object too strongly to practices established by the boss. If you do object too strongly, you may not be promoted or may even be transferred or fired. Your career may suffer. Nevertheless, we can easily imagine a case where the *morally* right thing to do would be to object very strongly to a policy that could endanger others—people, let us say, who might end up buying a dangerous product that your company is planning to manufacture.

Despite the fact that we can separate moral questions, on the one hand, from both legal and practical questions, on the other hand, many of the moral issues discussed in this book do have important legal and practical dimensions. For example, the abortion controversy involves the question of whether or not abortion should be legal, along with the question of whether or not abortions are moral, even if legal. And nearly all of the controversies in business ethics have practical implications as well as moral ones. But finding the legal answer or finding the prudential answer to a question is not necessarily to find the morally correct answer.

Let us return to the question, what is morality all about? A partial, essentially negative answer has been given by distinguishing moral rightness and wrongness from legal and prudential rightness and wrongness. A positive, but very general answer can be given by saying that morality means *concern for others and respect for oneself.*

Let us examine the first half of this answer first: that morality entails concern for others. This means that morality in some way stands in opposition to selfishness. Are there any moral feelings or ideas that are common to everyone, or nearly everyone? The answer to this question would seem to be yes. One of the common moral ideas is the belief that a person is immoral if he or she is selfish, or selfish a good deal of the time. The idea of selfishness is a somewhat vague idea, of course. I don't mean to say that everyone, or nearly everyone, has a clearly thought out idea of what being selfish is; instead, they feel that *somehow* a person cannot be moral and also be essentially selfish. People have the right idea, but they may not have thought it through completely. One of the purposes of this book is to help its readers to think through what selfishness is.

As a starting point, I want to say that a person is selfish when he or she always, or usually, acts solely for the sake of self-interest. Most people believe that this is wrong. For example, a child is likely to feel guilty for taking another child's toys since the child may know that he was thinking only of himself when he took them. Likewise, for the same reason, a manufacturer will very likely know that she was wrong to cover up a defect in one of her products so as to increase her own profits. The same is true for anyone who injures or kills someone, or steals, lies, or cheats for selfish reasons. I am not saying that it is wrong for a person ever to do something primarily for himself or herself. What is wrong is to devote the greater part of one's energy to doing such things. We morally condemn people who consistently put themselves ahead of everyone else—that is, people who steal, cheat, deceive, etc., or who are prepared to steal, cheat, or deceive if they can get away with it.

In the history of moral thought many different concepts and phrases have been used to capture the idea that it is wrong to be selfish. The most famous perhaps are "love thy neighbor as thyself" and "do unto others as you would have them do unto you." In addition, there is the rule that we should treat other people as ends in themselves, never merely as means to satisfy our own interests and desires.[2] Put another way, this means that it is wrong to use, or to exploit, other people. Another relevant concept is that of respect for others. There is also the idea that every person has a certain inherent dignity just in being a person. There are other such concepts as well.

Someone may object that if morality requires not being selfish, then very few people are moral; instead, most people really are selfish, since when they help another person they are in reality doing it for themselves and not for the sake of the other person. It may be claimed that fear of being caught and punished is what keeps most of us from lying, cheating, stealing, etc.

The doctrine that people generally do everything they do for selfish reasons is called *psychological egoism.*[3] The best argument against psychological egoism is that a great many people must not be selfish since they consistently do not take advantage of chances to help themselves at the expense of other people. Take the matter of throwing litter on the highway, which is probably the easiest way to dispose of trash when you are traveling. If you are driving on a highway that is not close to where you live, you won't ever need to look at the trash that you throw out, and if there are no other cars around there is practically no chance at all that you will be caught. Yet there are a great many people who would never think of throwing litter on the highway. Likewise, they would never think of shoplifting, even in a situation where they can be reasonably certain of not getting caught. They respect the rights of other people and that is why they would not do things to harm other people.

Someone who defends psychological egosim may persist by saying that people who do not take advantage of chances to help themselves at the expense of others are still selfish, since they get a great deal of satisfaction from respecting other people's rights or would feel guilty if they did not. Respecting other people's rights is simply their way of doing what they feel is best for themselves. The defender of psychological egoism would say, for example, that parents who help their children do so for their own (the parents') sake: helping the children is what makes the parents feel good, and therefore it is a selfish thing for the parents to do.

But notice what this means: if doing something for the satisfaction that it gives me is a selfish reason for acting, then it would seem that *every possible* act that I do voluntarily is selfish. If I choose voluntarily to do something, it is presumably because I feel I will get some satisfaction from doing it. It is what I want to do.

Now, the defender of psychological egoism may want to say that every possible voluntary act is selfish. But that is a very strange and indefensible thing to say since we really don't know what is meant in saying it. If every possible voluntary act is selfish, then we don't know what a nonselfish act could possibly be like. Consequently, the claim that every voluntary act is selfish is a meaningless claim. This is because we don't know what the contrast is between being selfish and not being selfish, which the claim makes reference to. This point can be illustrated by comparing the claim made by the psychological egoist to other sorts of claims. For example, to call something green makes sense because we know what it is like for a thing not to be green; the same is true for every claim that a thing has a certain property or characteristic. We must be able to think what it would be like for something not to have that property. But if the defender of psychological egosim says that every possible voluntary act is selfish, then we cannot even imagine what a nonselfish voluntary act would be like.

The situation is very different when we describe one person as being selfish and another person as being not selfish in, for example, the efforts made by each to save a drowning child. We know that the person who saves a drowning child only because of the expectation of a reward is acting selfishly because we know that if there were no expectation of a reward then the person would let the child drown. In contrast, the person who would save the child regardless of whether or not a reward was expected is not acting selfishly. Both of these people presumably would feel a lot of satisfaction in doing what they did; but the second person would feel satisfaction just because he or she had done something that was not selfish. What counts, therefore, is not the satisfaction received but the reason for the satisfaction. The important moral distinction is not between whether or not a person feels happy about doing something; it is between the *kinds* of acts that make a person feel happy—whether these acts are selfish or not.[4]

Morality, we have said, in part means having concern for others. It does not follow from this that people are always more moral the less they do things simply to help themselves. They should not do everything to help others and nothing to help themselves. After all, the whole point of helping others is that there are things that are good *for them*, which will increase their well-being for themselves. Therefore, if one believes that helping others is a good thing, then one must believe that it is right for a person to enjoy things for himself or herself. If it is right to give help, then it is right to receive help. Then it must also be right for me to help myself since people are very often in a better position to help themselves than is anyone else.

Everyone, or nearly everyone, would agree that people have "duties to themselves"—that is, obligations to help themselves when it is possible to do so while not disregarding the interests of other people. This brings us back to the statement made earlier, that morality means concern for others *and* respect for oneself. When there is a conflict between self-interest and concern for others, being moral means finding a proper balance between the two. Exactly how that balance is to be achieved is a difficult question. An answer to it—or at least a partial answer—will be provided through an examination of the basic moral principles that are discussed below in the section of this chapter entitled "Rights, Justice, and the Common Good."

C. Concern for Others—Two Necessary Conditions

Suppose that the ruler of a small country is a fanatical table tennis player who believes that table tennis is the most important thing in life. As a consequence, he decrees that all the people in his country must devote most of their energy to developing their table tennis skills. Building houses, growing food, making highways—all such things will be allowed only to the minimal degree needed to keep people alive and healthy so that they can play table tennis. The ruler of the country really believes that he is doing what is best for the people in his country, and he is willing to make very great personal sacrifices so as to promote table tennis. As he sees it, he is not being selfish at all. He has been told that many people in his country hate table tennis, but he ignores this because he is a fanatic. Can we say that he truly has concern for the people in his country?

The answer must surely be that the ruler does not really have concern for the people in his country. He has the wrong attitude toward them. Specifically, what is wrong is that he does not consider at all what the people want for themselves. He argues that the people do not know enough to determine what is really good for them; but because he believes this he does not treat them *as persons*—as being capable of making at least some important choices for themselves regarding what is good for them. In saying that morality means (in part) concern for others, we should have said concern for others *as persons*. We should have said that being moral requires treating others as *autonomous*—not merely as extensions of ourselves, but as individuals in their own right.

The repeated failure of people to do this is no doubt what has given "doing good" a bad name. There is a well-known passage in *Walden* where Henry David Thoreau says, "If I knew for a certainty that a man was coming to my house with the conscious design of doing me good, I should run for my life."[5] Thoreau had in mind the attitude of the meddling do-gooder whose pushiness makes it impossible for any true help to be given.

Doing good would not have a bad name if people understood that concern for others always means considering two things: (1) what the person to be helped believes is best for him or her and (2) what *you* believe is best for that person. There is no hard-and-fast rule regarding how much weight we should give to each of these factors, but it is always wrong to ignore either one of them. In parent-child relationships, the second of these conditions will usually need to be emphasized. In caring relationships between adults, the ideal is probably to give much greater weight to the first of the two conditions. This is because each person has what could be called privileged access to his or her own desires, hopes, fears, sense of obligation, and so on. Usually, he or she knows most about these things and almost certainly spends more time thinking about them than anyone else does. Also, being allowed to make one's own choices—even if they are wrong—may help to build a person's character. At the same time, a person can be very seriously mistaken regarding what he or she believes to be best for himself or herself, and someone who truly cares for that person will sometimes want to protect that person from his or her own mistakes.

D. Rights, Justice, and the Common Good

Thus far, in saying that morality requires concern for others as persons, we have not addressed the question of *which others* one needs to have a concern for. Suppose that the ruler of the small country who wanted to make everyone play table tennis became convinced of the error of his ways and gave up his campaign to promote table tennis. Suppose that he became a very enlightened ruler to his subjects, treating them all as autonomous individuals. His behavior could still be morally objectionable if he were to become a good ruler to his own subjects but to no one else. For example, suppose that he decreed that whenever his soldiers encountered people from nearby countries they should be captured and then killed or made into slaves. Even though such a ruler might be concerned for others (within his own country) as persons, his concern would be very *selective*, which is clearly wrong.

Another kind of selective, immoral concern for others focuses on the present time. For example, it is wrong to defend nuclear power as a relatively cheap energy source for people living now if we ignore the dangers to future generations from buried radioactive nuclear waste. (I am not saying that the use of nuclear power *is* wrong, only that it is wrong to defend it in a shortsighted way.) Likewise, it is wrong to pay for a great many social services at the present time by increasing the national debt by billions of dollars each year and passing on this constantly growing debt to future generations.

Another example of selective, immoral concern would be parents who are so generous to their children that they treat people outside their family unfairly. There are many other ways that people can behave immorally, even when they are not concerned only for themselves, such as practicing religious or political intolerance, acting in a prejudiced way against certain minorities, or exhibiting sexist attitudes.

Should we conclude that being moral means having concern for *all* other people and ignoring the interests of no one? The problem with saying this is that, while it is correct, it will leave open as many questions as it will answer. This is because there are several different apparently conflicting ways to have concern for other people and care for one's fellow human beings. In the history of moral philosophy these are represented by the three great principles of Rights, Justice, and the Common Good. Needless to say, these principles have been stated in many different ways by different philosophers. What follows is an attempt to state them in such a way that the most important conflicts among basic moral values will easily be seen.

1. According to the *Principle of Rights*, we ought to protect the individual freedom and well-being of every person. In a classic formulation of this principle, found in the Declaration of Independence, everyone is said to have a right to life, liberty, and the pursuit of happiness.[6] Whether or not these are the most important rights is a very controversial question that cannot, of course, be resolved here. As regards the relationship between rights and moral pluralism, the most important point to keep in mind is that what we are calling the Principle of Rights puts equal stress on protecting the freedom and well-being of each and every individual person. Young or old, rich or poor, healthy or sick, law-abiding or criminal—all are said to have the same basic rights. As specified by the Principle of Rights, concern for others should in some way embrace all people *as individuals*.

   By itself, the Principle of Rights is inadequate because there are many situations where doing the morally correct thing seems to violate someone's rights. Take the example of eminent domain, the power that the government has to take a person's property in order to build a highway, power line, or something else intended to serve the public good. Eminent domain requires that a person's right to his or her property be infringed upon: his or her property may hold a great deal of meaning (perhaps it has been in the family for generations) and he or she may be very unwilling to give it up for the "fair market value" that is supposed to be paid for it. The reasoning in defense of eminent domain is that in special cases the public good may outweigh the good of the individual, and when it does the individual should sell the property regardless of how strongly he or she will feel the loss of it. The principle of eminent domain can be abused, and often has been abused, but the reasoning behind it seems to be sound: sometimes it is right to require an individual to give up something in order to serve the common good.

   Consider also the morality of punishment. Ideally, punishment would always rehabilitate the person punished, resulting in a better person, preventing further crimes from being committed, and also deterring other potential criminals. In the real world, unhappily, that ideal seems most often impossible to achieve, especially when the punishment in question is a long prison sentence. The person who is punished is too often not helped by it. The person's chances for happiness are diminished by the punishment, and often he or she ends up more committed than before to a life of crime because of his or her association in prison with other criminals. But we still believe that punishment is justified for the sake of the public welfare. There are other examples in addition to eminent domain and the morality of punishment that show that the Principle of Rights has limitations. Some of these will be discussed in later sections of this chapter.

2. The *Principle of the Common Good* has been formulated so as to avoid problems inherent in the Principle of Rights. The Principle of the Common Good is the basic principle of the philosophy of utilitarianism, which is probably the most influential moral theory in the recent history of western philosophy. It received its classic formulation in the nineteenth century by two British philosophers, Jeremy Bentham[7] and John Stuart Mill.[8] According to utilitarianism, being moral means doing what will bring about the greatest good for the greatest number of people. Everyone must be considered; then the moral thing to do is what is most helpful overall to the greatest number. According to the Principle of the Common Good, concern for others means concern for other people taken all together as a collective whole.

Like the Principle of Rights, what we are calling the Principle of the Common Good is inadequate by itself because there are many possible situations where bringing about the greatest good for the greatest number would seem to be morally wrong. For example, the Principle of the Common Good would appear to make possible under the right circumstances the defense of slavery: where a small minority is enslaved, if this really does make the greater number of people happy, and there is no other social policy that would make them as happy, then slavery would be morally right. But most people would say that slavery is wrong, in and of itself, and that serving the common good is not a sufficient defense of slavery. According to Bentham and Mill, slavery is wrong because it never would actually serve the common good, but their claim is questionable.

What essentially is wrong with slavery? One answer must be that it violates people's rights. We saw above that the Principle of Rights is not adequate by itself since it does not allow that *sometimes* an individual should sacrifice his or her own good, or at least some part of it, for the common good. In the same way, the Principle of the Common Good is not adequate by itself since it does not allow that sometimes bringing about the greatest good for the greatest number must be abandoned in order to protect individual rights.

3. According to the *Principle of Justice*, we ought to help those people the most who are the most in need of help.[9] That is, concern for others is to be understood in terms of a variable scale, where the greatest concern is to be addressed to those who have the greatest needs. For example, if a person is born crippled, he or she should be given the extra help needed to be happy by those of us who are best able to give help. Another example is the "Robin Hood" principle that is part of the justification for a graduated income tax. The idea is that money from the rich should be given to the poor in order to make people more nearly equal in how well off they are. Also, according to the Principle of Justice, if a person is naturally gifted as a physician, say, or a craftsman, or a composer, then that person should willingly use his or her talents to help others; one should not work *only* for the sake of the money that he or she will earn from the work.

Please bear in mind that the word "justice" can have meanings that are different from the meaning that is encompassed by what we are here calling the Principle of Justice. The meaning of "justice" that is focused on in this chapter is the one that appears to conflict in the sharpest way with the Principle of Rights and the Principle of the Common Good.

The Principle of Justice is a necessary part of moral pluralism because neither the Principle of Rights nor the Principle of the Common Good contain a guarantee that justice (in the sense that we understand it here) will be served. The idea behind the Principle of Rights is that we ought to protect the good of each individual as much as possible regardless of what that good is. We ought to protect what people have—their lives, liberty, and chances for happiness. But the natural inequalities among human beings are very great and it is immoral to ignore them.

As regards the Principle of the Common Good, there is no assurance that bringing about the greatest good for the greatest number will bring about a just distribution of goods—as can be seen from considering the example of slavery that was discussed above. Slavery, we should say, is wrong, not just because it violates one's rights to liberty and the pursuit of happiness; it is wrong also because it provides for very unequal treatment of human beings.

We can imagine a society where rights to life, liberty, and the pursuit of happiness are protected and where the greatest good for the greatest number is also achieved, but which also has great inequalities in wealth, social status, and happiness. Economic history over the past two centuries indicates that the most efficient economic system is one that is relatively free of governmental restraints and where individual rights are protected. Under such a system, there are strong incentives for productive work and for investment in productive industries, and there is also a very effective system for the distribution of materials, finished goods, and services to those who are able to pay for them. Free enterprise makes a country much richer, with the result that the overall well-being of the people in the country will increase a great deal. There will be strong economic incentives for developing new labor-saving machines, medicines, better ways to grow food, and so on.[10] However, there will be no guarantee that the abundance in the country will be distributed in a just way. Hence, justice is something that the society needs to take into consideration in addition to its protection of rights and its concern for the overall well-being of people in the society. The Principle of Justice should be seen as placing certain limits on the principles of Rights and the Common Good, and not, of course, as replacing them.

We should conclude from the above discussion of the three principles that all of them—Rights, Justice, and the Common Good—are essential to morality. They delineate three different ways to have concern for others: individually, in relation to one another, and collectively. If there were just two people in the world, morality would be relatively simple, since the main thing you would need to do would be to balance your own interests against the interests of the other person. But since there are a great many people in the world, morality is very complicated.

We said above that being moral means having concern for others and respect for oneself. Then we said that concern for others can be expressed in several different ways, depending upon which of the three principles—Rights, Justice, or the Common Good—is being emphasized. In order to include respect for oneself in an account of basic moral values, a fourth principle must be added to the list: the Principle of Self-Interest. Morality is complicated because it requires not only balancing Self-Interest, on the one hand, against Rights, Justice, and the Common Good, on the other hand; it also requires balancing Rights, Justice and the Common Good against each other.

It may be helpful to compare morality to the way parents should care for their children. If there is only one child, what the parents need to do is to weigh the child's interests against their own. But suppose the family has several children. Of course, the parents should care for all of them. But what does this entail? In order for one of the parents to get a better job and thus be able to better provide for the entire family, the family may, let us say, move to a different state. The parents may choose this option, even though it presents a very real hardship to one of the children who must leave behind close friends or perhaps a school that is especially well suited to his or her needs. This particular child may not benefit at all from the move, and may even be harmed by it. Yet, because the parents really do care for their children, it may be the best thing for them to do. What the parents will be doing is applying on a small scale the Principle of the Common Good.

What is important is that the interests of one child not be sacrificed *too much* for the overall well-being of the family. Each child must be thought of as having a certain worth and dignity that could never be sacrificed for the good of the other children. That is, the parents must also apply on a small scale the Principle of Rights. Each child must be cared for individually and at the same time they must all be cared for collectively. These are two of the ways that parents should care for their children.

The third way has to do with justice in the sense that we are understanding it here, that is, giving the most help to the child who needs the most help. Sensitive parents recognize that they should follow the Principle of Justice in raising their children—but again only up to a point. They may spend more money on the education of a child who has special talents even though that child already has an advantage over the other children in possessing special talent. In the interests of justice, the parents won't carry this too far. They won't try to make everything equal among their children, simply more nearly equal than would be the case if they cared for their children only individually and collectively.

E. Making Moral Decisions

It is not the purpose of this book to provide definite, final answers to any specific moral question. Each of you who reads this book must find answers for yourself. The purpose of this book is to provide a framework within which a discussion of moral questions can take place. The framework provided in this chapter for defending one's answer to a moral question consists of the following principles and guidelines for applying them. Together, they constitute the basis for the sort of moral pluralism that the present book is dedicated to.

I. Protecting the individual freedom and well-being of everyone is a basic moral value. (The Principle of Rights.)

II. Bringing about the greatest good for the greatest number is a basic moral value. (The Principle of the Common Good.)

III. Helping the most those who most need help is a basic moral value. (The Principle of Justice.)

IV. Paying attention to one's own self-interest is a basic moral value. (The Principle of Self-Interest.)

Each of these principles states a value that may (but of course often does not) conflict with the other values. Being moral requires that no one of the four principles ever be neglected; but in any given situation one of them may be emphasized more than the others. Moral questions that are difficult to answer are often those that involve conflicts among the four principles. It is fair to say that moral sophistication and maturity lie in the ability to balance skillfully these principles against each other.

Chapters 2–10 of this book contain reading selections addressed to specific moral problems. Each chapter deals with a single problem or a cluster of related problems. Your job is to read each selection carefully and then ask yourself several important questions about it: Does the author clearly understand all of the facts relevant to his or her position? Do the conclusions given in the selection appear to follow from the reasons given for them? Most important, is the author's position morally defensible in terms of basic moral principles? That is, has the author given adequate consideration to the four principles—Rights, Justice, the Common Good, and Self-Interest? Regarding some of the selections, it will be relatively easy for you to decide. Regarding other selections, you will very likely have some difficulty deciding whether or not each of the principles has been given adequate consideration. This may be the case, for example, regarding the selection in chapter 4 from Peter Singer on the moral obligations that people in relatively rich countries have to people in poor countries.

You may find that you disagree with what some other students in the class say about a particular selection, or that you disagree with what the instructor says. When this happens, remember that for the moral problems covered in this book, there is room for sincere disagreement even among people who have become thoroughly familiar with what is involved in each of the moral problems and who have thought carefully about them. Your responsibility is to be sure that the moral views that you hold are based upon a good-faith effort to consider all of the relevant facts and to apply the basic moral principles to the particular moral issue under discussion.

In order to illustrate the way in which the principles of Rights, Justice, the Common Good, and Self-Interest are to be applied in moral reasoning, let us examine briefly the issue of the military draft. Should a country ever have a military draft? If so, under what conditions?

If we consider only the Principle of Rights, then it is difficult to see how the military draft could ever be defended morally. The basic rights of life, liberty, and the pursuit of happiness are threatened or sharply curtailed when a person is drafted. According to the Principle of Rights (when it is appealed to by itself), as far as possible every individual should be given *equal* protection of basic rights. But the draft, of course, is very selective: not everyone is called, but only those who are, as it is supposed, best able to serve.

Perhaps you will say that the draft simply is immoral. Many people do feel that way. But many other people believe that the draft can be defended under certain circumstances: when there is a *bona fide* and very serious threat from a hostile foreign power, when the draft is not used as a means to avoid paying people in the armed forces a proper salary, and when it appears that the draft really will be the most effective way to ensure that the country will be protected. Those who defend the draft would appeal primarily to the Principle of the Common Good, arguing that sometimes the welfare of society as a whole should be allowed to outweigh the protection of rights.

The Principle of Justice appears to cut both ways in regard to the draft. On the one hand, the draft appears to be unjust since very often the men (and the same could be true for women) who are drafted are the poorer and less well educated people who already have somewhat deprived lives. On the other hand, it has also been argued at various times in history that the people who are most in need of protection from a conquering enemy—children, older people, those who are ill, and so on—are the least able to defend themselves and therefore should be protected by the more able-bodied among the citizens of a country.

Where the Principle of Self-Interest falls in regard to the draft will depend upon whose self-interest is considered. For those likely to be drafted, self-interest will constitute a reason to oppose the draft; for those likely not to be drafted but instead to be protected by those who are drafted, self-interest will constitute a reason to endorse the draft.

The position that you take on the draft will reflect the way in which you believe the basic moral principles should be balanced against each other. It is not my purpose to suggest how you should do this, beyond spelling out the following guidelines:

1. If you were to give weight only to the Principle of Self-Interest, then your stand would not be a moral one since concern for others would not be a part of it.

2. If you were to give no weight at all to any one or two of the three principles of Rights, Justice, and the Common Good, then your position would be difficult to defend. It would reflect concern for others, but not in a balanced fashion since you would be ignoring one (or possibly two) of the important ways that concern for others can be manifested. For example, suppose that someone were to say the following when faced with any hesitation on the part of a person who has been drafted: "His country needs him and that is reason enough for him to serve and not complain about it. Nothing more needs to be said." Regardless of whether or not we ourselves favor the draft, we should object to this and insist that the draft resister does have a case. Whether or not the draft resister's case is stronger than the opposing case would be another question.

3. You need to keep in mind that the Principle of Justice has to do with what is called *distributive justice*. There is another type of justice called *procedural justice*. Distributive justice, as its name implies, has to do with the ideal goal of distributing fairly to everyone the good things in life—such as education, medical care, housing, clothing, food, leisure time, etc. But procedural justice has to do with correctly following legal or customary procedures in deciding what people deserve. A person on trial for robbery is accorded procedural justice if he or she is given a fair trial in which all the laws and customs

governing trials are followed. A person in need of welfare payments is treated with procedural justice if, again, all the laws and customs are followed regarding eligibility for welfare assistance.

4. You should also keep in mind that moral judgments can be of several different sorts. Do not be misled in regard to this by the fact that the present book is concerned primarily with questions about the morality of *issues*—euthanasia, obligations of friends, etc.—and not as much with questions about the morality of persons. You should at least bear in mind that there is an important distinction between what is called *act morality* and what is called *agent morality*. Agent morality has to do with the overall assessment of whether or not a person is moral, while act morality has to do with the moral assessment of the kinds of acts that a person does. Unquestionably, a person can properly be said to be moral even while occasionally doing something that is not morally correct. Being moral does not require being perfect.

Also, being a moral person is to a large degree (the exact measure of which is somewhat controversial) a matter of what someone *intends* to do, whether or not successful. In contrast, the question of whether or not a particular kind of act (such as withholding treatment for a terminally ill person) is moral is determined for the most part independently of judgments about the intentions of particular individuals who may do the sort of act that is in question.

F. Are Moral Values Relative?

If this chapter were being given as a lecture rather than as something for you to read, it would be apprpriate at this point for the lecturer to stop and ask if there were any questions. One of them might well be this: Are we to accept the four basic moral principles—Rights, Justice, the Common Good, and Self-Interest—as being true for everyone? What about the fact that people come from very different sorts of cultures or backgrounds? Why should a person who was raised in, say, a traditional Eastern society have to accept the very same moral values as a person who was raised in a traditional Western society? And aren't there further differences among Eastern societies themselves that are morally relevant, and further differences among Western societies that are morally relevant?

The preceding questions have to do with the issue of *relativism* in moral reasoning. The most commonly defended version of moral relativism is called *cultural ethical relativism*. A typical statement of it would go as follows: there are no absolute moral principles that are true for everyone; instead, moral principles are relative to the beliefs of different cultures or societies. What is true for one society need not be true for another, and therefore, "When in Rome do as the Romans do."

Is there any reason to believe that cultural ethical relativism is correct? There may appear to be a good reason, namely, that being tolerant and accepting of people in different cultures is a good thing. If we reject cultural ethical relativism, then it may seem that we are imposing our values on others and that we are not accepting people in other cultures for what they are. That may seem to be intolerant and narrow-minded.

In the previous paragraph I said that there may *appear* to be a good reason to believe that cultural ethical relativism is correct. However, in actuality, the appearance is quite misleading. This can readily be seen if we consider exactly what it means to accept the Principles of Rights, Justice, the Common Good, and Self-Interest. Accepting them does *not* mean that everyone has to arrive at the very same answers to every moral question. Moral reasoning is not like that. It is not an exact science because, first, there are no hard-and-fast rules that tell us how to balance the basic moral values against each other; and second, there are no hard-and-fast rules for applying even a single moral principle to examples in the real world. Hence, in moral reasoning there is always some room for disagreement among even the most reasonable, well-informed, and morally sensitive people. (This is not, of course, to say that people do not sometimes make the wrong moral choices, since this happens frequently.)

Therefore, we *should* be on guard against being intolerant of others who may sometimes disagree with us in their answers to moral questions. It does not follow from this that we should be tolerant of someone who says, "I don't care at all about rights," or "I don't care at all about justice." But if cultural ethical relativism as stated above were true, then we would need to be tolerant of cultures or societies, such as Nazi Germany, that disregarded rights or justice; this is part of what it would mean to say that the principles of Rights and Justice were relative to a particular culture or type of culture.

The fact is that the sort of moral pluralism regarding basic moral principles that is adhered to in this book is already a flexible and open-ended approach to moral reasoning, and thus is not in need of being relativised any further to a variety of cultures. It is one thing to allow that reasonable and sensitive people—whether they are within a single society or live in very different societies—may disagree in a particular case on how best to achieve a balance of, say, rights and the common good. It is something else again to say that we should be accepting of someone who disregards altogether questions of rights or the common good.

Therefore, cultural ethical relativism as stated above should be rejected since it says that all moral positions are equally acceptable. We should not say that the principles of Rights, Justice, the Common Good, and Self-Interest are relative. Likewise, we should not say that the general characterization of morality given earlier in this chapter is relative. We said that morality means concern for others as persons and respect for oneself. There is no reason to say that this is true only for some cultures or societies and not for others.

Now suppose someone makes the following claim: "When I say that values are relative, what I mean is that things such as how a person dresses, what a person eats, what marriage customs are followed, and so on are relative to cultures. When in Rome do as the Romans do in regard to these matters. Be tolerant in regard to these matters, but not in regard to the acceptance or rejection of the basic moral principles."

Is this a defensible version of cultural ethical relativism? The answer must be that, while it is a very definite improvement over the version of cultural ethical relativism discussed above, nevertheless it is still not entirely acceptable. The problem with it is that customs regarding dress, marriage practices, etc., in different cultures or societies *may sometimes* reflect the fact that the people in a particular culture or society are not putting enough weight on one of the basic moral principles. For example, some presently existing societies, and a much larger number of societies throughout history, have had marriage practices in which the rights of women are almost totally disregarded. Many other examples of this kind could be found. Hence, the only rule that can be followed here is no rule at all: for many diverse cultural practices a relativistic approach is fine, but for many others it is not fine. Each case needs to be judged by itself.

Notes

1. See, for example, the moral writings of Saint Thomas Aquinas, particularly the *Summa Theologica*, ed. Anton C. Pegis (New York: Random House, 1944), 748–781, questions 91–94. Originally published in the thirteenth century.

2. For the best known statement of this rule see Immanuel Kant, *Groundwork of the Metaphysic of Morals*, chap. 2, ed. H. J. Paton (New York: Harper and Row, 1948), 95–96. First published in the late eighteenth century.

3. The most important philosopher in the history of philosophy who has supported psychological egoism is Thomas Hobbes, in *Leviathan* (Indianapolis: Bobbs-Merrill, 1958), 109–119. Hobbes's work dates back to the early seventeenth century.

4. A very good statement of this argument is found in the preface to Joseph Butler's *Five Sermons* (Indianapolis: Bobbs-Merrill, 1950) 3–18. First published in the eighteenth century.

5. Henry David Thoreau, *Walden* (Boston: Houghton Mifflin, 1960). First published in 1854.

6. The position taken in the Declaration of Independence stems from the writings of John Locke, in particular his *Treatise of Civil Government*, ed. Charles L. Sherman (East Norwalk: Appleton-Century-Crofts, 1937), 5–6. Originally published in the late seventeenth century.

7. In Jeremy Bentham *An Introduction to the Principles of Morals and Legislation*, ed. J. H. Burns and L. A. Hart (London: Athlone Press, 1970). First published in 1789.

8. In John Stuart Mill *Utilitarianism* (New York: Dutton, 1950). First published in 1861.

9. The classical sources for this principle are first, Christian ethical writings, in particular the story of the Good Samaritan (*Luke* 10:25–37) and second, the writings of Karl Marx, especially *Das Kapital*, trans. Ben Fowkes (New York: Vintage Books, 1977). First published in 1867.

10. The classical defense of free enterprise is to be found in Adam Smith's *An Inquiry into the Nature and Causes of the Wealth of Nations* (New York: Random House, Modern Library edition, abridged by Richard F. Teichgraeber, 1985.) Originally published in 1776. Smith is perhaps best known for having said that the private pursuit of wealth through free enterprise will be guided by an "invisible hand" to promote the interests of society as a whole (p. 225).

Sex, Love, and Marriage

any people believe that of all the important things in life, those that cause the most happiness are close, caring relationships: especially between wives and husbands, parents and children, and within enduring friendships. There are, of course, other important causes of happiness, such as achievement in one's work, appreciation and creation of art, attainment of knowledge, enjoyment of nature, and so on. But it is usually believed that the happiness derived from these sources is in some important way dependent upon human relationships, particularly close ones. Joy in these things needs to be shared or communicated; achievements in art, science, and business need people who will respond to them.

While it is widely believed that close human relationships are a very important source of happiness, it is also recognized by everyone, or nearly everyone, that these same relationships are the source of many moral problems. This is especially so regarding close human relationships that have a sexual component—which is the focus for the present chapter. (The following chapter addresses nonsexual relationships.)

The issues focused on in this chapter are: the morality of sex outside of marriage; the moral tie, if there is any, between sex and love; the question of whether marriage should be monogamous or should exist at all; the question of what love means or ought to mean in human relationships.

A good place to begin is with a discussion of marriage. Historically, the institution of marriage has been given protection in a variety of different ways. On the one hand, many laws have been passed for the purpose of channeling the human sex drive into marriage. Sex before marriage has been outlawed in many societies, and even more frequently adultery has been outlawed. Divorce has been banned. Marriage has almost universally been restricted to heterosexual couples, while homosexual sex has been made illegal. Contraception and abortion have been outlawed and a very serious social stigma has been attached to childbirth outside of marriage. Sex with prostitutes and even masturbation have been made illegal. On the other hand, many laws have been passed that give parents special rights over their children, that give husbands special rights over their wives, that require legitimate birth for inheritance, and so on.

At the present time in most western countries, very few of the above laws are in effect. Many have been repealed and the rest, for the most part, are not being enforced or are being enforced only in a very selective fashion. This means that a great many issues regarding marriage and sex are currently wide open in the sense that society has no established and widely accepted practices regarding these matters. Perhaps more than at any other time in history, the burden in finding answers to moral questions regarding marriage and sex falls upon the individual.

When questions about the value of marriage are considered, two perspectives need to be taken: first, each person needs to ask *for himself or herself* whether or not marriage, or marriage to a particular person, would be a good thing; and second, each person needs to ask whether or not the *institution* of marriage is a good thing for society. In answering the first question, the Principle of Self-Interest will be given an especially prominent role. In answering the second question, the Principle of the Common Good will be given an especially prominent role.

Two of the reading selections for this chapter are devoted to an extensive discussion of marriage. One of them, by Bertrand Russell, is a cautious defense of marriage as having significant value both for society as a whole and for most individuals—but only if a number of conditions are met. In particular, Russell advocates a much greater degree of freedom within marriage than is sometimes thought to be desirable: "Love can flourish only as it is free and spontaneous; it tends to be killed by the thought that it is a duty." The reading selection from John McMurtry is an attack upon the institution of marriage, which McMurtry believes is altogether too restrictive.

For both Russell and McMurtry, marriage in the traditional sense (monogamous marriage) is too restrictive regarding sex. Both of these writers maintain that sex outside of marriage does not have to be a bad thing. In contrast, Lewis B. Smedes defends the traditional Christian view that sex is morally wrong unless it is within marriage. He argues that sex outside of marriage is problematic for several different reasons, one of which is that it involves significant risks to oneself as well as to the other person. It is very easy for oneself to be hurt and also very easy to hurt someone else.

A discussion of marriage and sex would be incomplete if it did not include a discussion of love. But love can mean several different things. In its broadest sense, love is equivalent to moral concern for others. This is the sense in which it may be said that we have an obligation to love our fellow human beings. This sense of love is probably best understood in terms of those moral princples that apply universally to all human beings in the way that the principles of Rights and Justice apply to everyone.

In regard to marriage and sex, "love" needs to be given a much more restricted meaning, so that love for one person entails that restrictions be placed upon love for others. There is no doubt some truth to the idea that a person who is a friend to everyone is a friend to no one, and this is nowhere more true than in the area of romantic friendship or romantic love. But how exclusive should romantic love be? Should it be restricted to two persons (at a given time) only? The love of nonromantic friendship is, of course, much broader than that, with friends only needing to treat each other in some way that is special, without necessarily excluding everyone else.

As McMurtry sees it, the model for nonromantic friendship should be applied as well to romantic love. McMurtry rejects the traditional view that marriage, because of its exclusiveness, tends to preserve and to strengthen love between spouses. Russell, with some qualifications, accepts the traditional view of marriage.

Disagreement is also to be found in answers to the following question: Is it morally wrong to have sex with someone whom you do not love? The answer given by Smedes is yes, with some qualifications. The answer given by Albert Ellis, in the first of the reading selections in this chapter, is no. Ellis defends the idea that, while sex with love is usually better than sex without love, there is no essential moral connection between sex and love. Sex, says Ellis, is a good thing all by itself. It can add to the happiness of people who are not really capable of loving others. Such people ought not to be deprived of sex or made to feel guilty about their sex lives that are carried on in the absence of love and very often outside of marriage.

The topic of love is a much broader topic than either the topic of marriage or the topic of sex. In the second of the reading selections for the present chapter, Thomas Merton argues that love embraces everything that really matters in life: "Love is our true destiny. We do not find the meaning of life by ourselves alone—we find it with another." The "other," says Merton, can be a person or it can be God. The sense in which Merton is using the word love is apparently different from both "romantic love" and "moral concern for others."

Merton objects to the conceptual framework that has given us the expression "lovemaking": love, he argues, can be completely independent of sex and, moreover, love is not at all the kind of transaction that the expression "lovemaking" suggests. That is, love is not a "deal" that is arrived at for the satisfaction of mutual needs. Instead, says Merton, love is a sacrifice.

In the reading selections for this chapter there are other important topics in addition to the ones that have been mentioned above. Among these are questions about happiness and compatibility in marriage (discussed at some length by Russell), the idea that marriage is a form of ownership (taken up by both Russell and McMurtry), the role of marriage in childrearing (argued about by McMurtry—who defends the perhaps surprising idea that childrearing can best take place outside of marriage), and the distinction between immature and mature love (which is found in Merton).

A L B E R T   E L L I S

The Justification of Sex Without Love

A scientific colleague of mine, who holds a professorial post in the department of sociology and anthropology at one of our leading universities, recently asked me about my stand on the question of human beings having sex relations without love. Although I have taken something of a position on this issue in my book, *The American Sexual Tragedy*, I have never quite considered the problem in sufficient detail. So here goes.

In general, I feel that affectional, as against nonaffectional, sex relations are *desirable* but not *necessary*. It is usually desirable that an association between coitus and affection exist— particularly in marriage, because it is often difficult for two individuals to keep finely tuned to each other over a period of years, and if there is not a good deal of love between them, one may tend to feel sexually imposed upon by the other.

The fact, however, that the coexistence of sex and love may be desirable does not, to my mind, make it necessary. My reasons for this view are several:

1. Many individuals—including, even, many married couples—*do* find great satisfaction in having sex relations without love. I do not consider it fair to label these individuals as criminal just because they may be in the minority.

Moreover, even if they are in the minority (as may well *not* be the case), I am sure that they number literally millions of men and women. If so, they constitute a sizable subgroup of humans whose rights to sex satisfaction should be fully acknowledged and protected.

2. Even if we consider the supposed majority of individuals who find greater satisfaction in sex-love than in sex-sans-love relations, it is doubtful if all or most of them do so for *all* their lives. During much of their existence, especially their younger years, these people tend to find sex-without-love quite satisfying, and even to prefer it to affectional sex.

When they become older, and their sex drives tend to wane, they may well emphasize coitus with rather than without affection. But why should we condemn them *while* they still prefer sex to sex-love affairs?

3. Many individuals, especially females in our culture, who say that they only enjoy sex when it is accom-

Albert Ellis, who was in private practice in psychotherapy for many years, is Executive Director of the Institute for Rational-Emotive Therapy in New York City, and has written a great many books and articles on a wide range of psychological topics.

Albert Ellis, "The Justification of Sex Without Love," in *Sex Without Guilt* (New York: Lyle Stuart, 1958) pp. 66–75. Published by arrangement with Lyle Stuart.

panied by affection are actually being unthinkingly conformist and unconsciously hypocritical. If they were able to contemplate themselves objectively, and had the courage of their inner convictions, they would find sex without love eminently gratifying.

This is not to say that they would *only* enjoy nonaffectional coitus, nor that they would always find it *more* satisfying than affectional sex. But, in the depths of their psyche and soma, they would deem sex without love pleasurable *too*.

And why should they not? And why should we, by our puritanical know-nothingness, force these individuals to drive a considerable portion of their sex feelings and potential satisfactions underground?

If, in other words, we view sexuo-amative relations as desirable rather than necessary, we sanction the innermost thoughts and drives of many of our fellowmen and fellowwomen to have sex *and* sex-love relations. If we take the opposing view, we hardly destroy these innermost thoughts and drives, but frequently tend to intensify them while denying them open and honest outlet. This, as Freud (1924–50, 1938) pointed out, is one of the main (though by no means the only) source of rampant neurosis.

4. I firmly believe that sex is a biological, as well as a social, drive, and that in its biological phases it is essentially nonaffectional. If this is so, then we can expect that, however we try to civilize the sex drives—and civilize them to *some* degree we certainly must—there will always be an underlying tendency for them to escape from our society-inculcated shackles and to be still partly felt in the raw.

When so felt, when our biosocial sex urges lead us to desire and enjoy sex without (as well as with) love, I do not see why we should make their experiencers feel needlessly guilty.

5. Many individuals—many millions in our society, I am afraid—have little or no capacity for affection or love. The majority of these individuals, perhaps, are emotionally disturbed, and should preferably be helped to increase their affectional propensities. But a large number are not particularly disturbed, and instead are neurologically or cerebrally deficient.

Mentally deficient persons, for example, as well as many dull normals (who, together, include several million citizens of our nation) are notoriously shallow in their feelings, and probably intrinsically so. Since these kinds of individuals—like the neurotic and the organically deficient—are for the most part, in our day and age, *not* going to be properly treated and *not* going to overcome their deficiencies, and since most of them definitely *do* have sex desires, I again see no point in making them guilty when they have nonloving sex relations.

Surely these unfortunate individuals are sufficiently handicapped by their disturbances or impairments without our adding to their woes by anathematizing them when they manage to achieve some nonamative sexual release.

6. Under some circumstances—though these, I admit, may be rare—some people find more satisfaction in nonloving coitus even though, under other circumstances, these *same* people may find more satisfaction in sex-love affairs. Thus, the man who *normally* enjoys being with his girlfriend because he loves as well as is sexually attracted to her, may occasionally find immense satisfaction in

being with another girl with whom he has distinctly nonloving relations.

Granting that this may be (or is it?) unusual, I do not see why it should be condemnable.

7. If many people get along excellently and most cooperatively with business partners, employees, professors, laboratory associates, acquaintances, and even spouses for whom they have little or no love or affection, but with whom they have certain specific things in common, I do not see why there cannot be individuals who get along excellently and most cooperatively with sex mates with whom they may have little else in common.

I personally can easily see the tragic plight of a man who spends much time with a girl with whom he has nothing in common but sex: since I believe that life is too short to be well consumed in relatively one-track or intellectually low-level pursuits. I would also think it rather unrewarding for a girl to spend much time with a male with whom she had mutually satisfying sex, friendship, and cultural interests but no love involvement. This is because I would like to see people, in their 70-odd years of life, have maximum rather than minimum satisfactions with individuals of the other sex with whom they spend considerable time.

I can easily see, however, even the most intelligent and highly cultured individuals spending a *little* time with members of the other sex with whom they have common sex and cultural but no real love interests. And I feel that, for the time expended in this manner, their lives may be immeasurably enriched.

Moreover, when I encounter friends or psychotherapy clients who become enamored and spend considerable time and effort thinking about and being with a member of the other sex with whom they are largely sexually obsessed, and for whom they have little or no love, I mainly view these sexual infatuations as one of the penalties of their being human. For humans are the kind of animals who are easily disposed to this type of behavior (Grant, 1957).

I believe that one of the distinct inconveniences or tragedies of human sexuality is that it endows us, and perhaps particularly the males among us, with a propensity to become exceptionally involved and infatuated with members of the other sex whom, had we no sex urges, we would hardly notice. That is too bad; and it might well be a better world if it were otherwise. But it is *not* otherwise, and I think it is silly and pernicious for us to condemn ourselves because we are the way that we are in this respect.

We had better *accept* our biosocial tendencies, or our fallible humanity—instead of constantly blaming ourselves and futilely trying to change certain of its relatively harmless, though still somewhat tragic, aspects.

For reasons such as these, I feel that although it is usually—if not always—*desirable* for human beings to have sex relations with those they love rather than with those they do not love, it is by no means *necessary* that they do so. When we teach that it *is* necessary, we only needlessly condemn millions of our citizens to self-blame and atonement.

The position which I take—that there are several good reasons why affectional, as against nonaffectional, sex relations are desirable but not necessary—can be assailed on several counts. I shall now consider some of the objections to this position to see if they cannot be effectively answered.

It may be said that an individual who has nonloving instead of loving sex relations is not necessarily wicked but that he is self-defeating because, while going for immediate gratification, he will miss out on even greater enjoyments. But this would only be true if such an individual (whom we shall assume, for the sake of discussion, *would* get greater enjoyment from affectional sex relations than from nonaffectional ones) were *usually* or *always* having nonaffectionate coitus. If he were *occasionally* or *sometimes* having love with sex, and the rest of the time having sex without love, he would be missing out on very little, if any, enjoyment.

Under these circumstances, in fact, he would normally get *more* pleasure from *sometimes* having sex without love. For the fact remains, and must not be realistically ignored, that in our present-day society sex without love is *much more frequently* available than sex with love.

Consequently, to ignore nonaffectional coitus when affectional coitus is not available would, from the standpoint of enlightened self-interest, be sheer folly. In relation both to immediate *and* greater enjoyment, the individual would thereby be losing out.

The claim can be made of course that if an individual sacrifices sex without love *now* he will experience more pleasure by having sex with love in the future. This is an interesting claim; but I find no empirical evidence to sustain it. In fact, on theoretical grounds it seems most unlikely that it will be sustained. It is akin to the claim that if an individual

starves himself for several days in a row he will greatly enjoy eating a meal at the end of a week or a month. I am sure he will—provided that he is then not too sick or debilitated to enjoy anything! But, even assuming that such an individual derives enormous satisfaction from his one meal a week or a month, is his *total* satisfaction greater than it would have been had he enjoyed three good meals a day for that same period of time? I doubt it.

It may be held that if both sex with and without love are permitted in any society, the nonaffectional sex will drive out affectional sex, somewhat in accordance with Gresham's laws of currency. On the contrary, however, there is much reason to believe that just because an individual has sex relations, for quite a period, on a nonaffectional basis, he will be more than eager to replace it, eventually, with sex with love.

From my clinical experience, I have often found that males who most want to settle down to having a single mistress or wife are those who have tried numerous lighter affairs and found them wanting. The view that sex without love eradicates the need for affectional sex relationships is somewhat akin to the ignorance is bliss theory. For it virtually says that if people never experienced sex with love they would never realize how good it was and therefore would never strive for it.

Or else the proponents of this theory seem to be saying that sex without love is so greatly satisfying, and sex with love so intrinsically difficult and disadvantageous to attain, that given the choice between the two, most people would pick the former. If this is so, then by all means let them pick the former—with which, in terms of their greater and total happiness, they would presumably be better off.

I doubt, however, that this hypothesis *is* factually sustainable. From clinical experience, again, I can say that individuals who are capable of sex with love usually seek and find it; while those who remain nonaffectional in their sex affairs generally are not particularly capable of sex with love and need psychotherapeutic help before they can become thus capable.

Although, as a therapist, I frequently work with individuals who are only able to achieve nonaffectional sex affairs and, through helping them eliminate their irrational fears and blockings, make it possible for them to achieve sex-love relationships, I still would doubt that *all* persons who take no great pleasure in sex with love are emotionally deficient. Some quite effective individ-

uals—such as Immanuel Kant, for instance—seem to be so wholeheartedly dedicated to *things* or *ideas* that they rarely or never become amatively involved with people.

As long as such individuals have vital, creative interests and are intensely absorbed or involved with *something*, I would hesitate to diagnose them as being necessarily neurotic merely because they do not ordinarily become intensely absorbed with *people. Some* of these nonlovers of human beings are, of course, emotionally disturbed. But *all?* I wonder.

Disturbed or not, I see no reason why individuals who are dedicated to things or ideas should not have, in many or most instances, perfectly normal sex drives. And, if they do, I fail to see why they should not consummate their sex urges in nonaffectional ways in order to have more time and energy for their nonamative pursuits.

C O M M E N T S ■ Q U E S T I O N S

1. It should be noted that two of Ellis's key points can be accepted or rejected independently of each other: (a) Those people who are capable only of having sex without love and affection should not be made to feel guilty about their sex lives; (b) For those people who are capable of it, it may be best to have *both* sex with, and sex without, love and affection. Do you believe that it is important to accept or reject these points independently of each other? That is, to accept (a) but reject (b) or accept (b) but reject (a)?

2. Ellis is willing to allow that sex with love and affection is generally more desirable than sex without love and affection. But, he says, millions of men and women do in fact derive a great deal of satisfaction from sex without love. Indeed, some of them are incapable of love and affection, and therefore should not be made to feel guilty about their sex lives. Do you believe that people have a *right* to have sex without love and affection if they so choose?

3. Ellis does not discuss the phenomenon of emotional attachment,

which often develops between people having a sexual affair even when they do not consider themselves to be in love with each other. Because they have become emotionally attached to each other, one or both of them may feel very bad when the affair is broken off— as it is likely to be if what the people involved really want is sex *along with* love and affection. Do you believe that Ellis is wrong not to discuss this point?

4. Ellis also does not discuss problems associated with venereal disease, which increases among people who frequently change sex partners. Some researchers believe that a frequent change of sex partners may lead not only to a greater incidence of venereal disease, but also to other health problems as well. In evaluating the soundness of Ellis's arguments, how much weight do you believe should be given to a consideration of health risks? Also, how much weight do you believe should be given to a consideration of the risks of pregnancy?

THOMAS MERTON

Love and Need: Is Love a Package or a Message?

We speak of "falling in love," as though love were something like water that collects in pools, lakes, rivers, and oceans. You can "fall into" it or walk around it. You can sail on it or swim on it, or you can just look at it from a safe distance. This expression seems to be peculiar to the English language. French, for instance, does not speak of "*tomber en amour*" but does mention "falling amorous." The Italian and Spanish say one "enamors oneself." Latins do not regard love as a passive accident. Our English expression "to fall in love" suggests an unforeseen mishap that may or may not be fatal. You are at a party: you have had more drinks than you need. You decide to walk around the garden a little. You don't notice the swimming pool . . . all at once you have to

Thomas Merton is famous for his writings on spiritual and religious themes. From the age of 26 until his death in 1968 when he was 53 years old, he was a Trappist Monk. He was the author of a great many books and articles, several of which became best-sellers.

swim! Fortunately, they fish you out, and you are wet but none the worse for wear. Love is like that. If you don't look where you are going, you are liable to land in it: the experience will normally be slightly ridiculous. Your friends will all find it funny, and if they happen to be around at the time, they will do their best to steer you away from the water and into a nice comfortable chair where you can go to sleep.

Sometimes, of course, the pool is empty. Then you don't get wet, you just crack your skull or break your arm.

To speak of "falling into" something is to shift responsibility from your own will to a cosmic force like gravitation. You "fall" when you are carried off by a power beyond your control. Once you start you can't stop. You're gone. You don't know where you may land. We also speak of "falling into a coma" or "falling into disgrace," or "falling into bankruptcy." A thesaurus reminds us one can "fall into decay," "fall on the ear," and even "fall flat on the ear." A certain rudimentary theology regards the whole human race as "fallen" because Eve tempted Adam to love her. That is bad theology. Sex is not original sin. (A better view is that the love of Adam for Eve was originally meant as a communion and a diversity-in-oneness which reflected the invisible God in visible creation for "God is love.")

The expression to "fall in love" reflects a peculiar attitude toward love and toward life itself—a mixture of fear, awe, fascination, and confusion. It implies suspicion, doubt, hesitation, in the presence of something unavoidable—yet not fully reliable. For love takes you out of

yourself. You lose control. You "fall." You get hurt. It upsets the ordinary routine of life. You become emotional, imaginative, vulnerable, foolish. You are no longer content to eat and sleep, make money and have fun. You now have to let yourself be carried away with this force that is stronger than reason and more imperious even than business!

Obviously, if you are a cool and self-possessed character, you will take care never to *fall*. You will accept the unavoidable power of love as a necessity that can be controlled and turned to good account. You will confine it to the narrow category of "fun" and so you will not let it get out of hand. You will have fun by making others fall without falling yourself.

But the question of love is one that cannot be evaded. Whether or not you claim to be interested in it, from the moment you are alive you are bound to be concerned with love, because love is not just something that happens to you: *it is a certain special way of being alive.*

Love is, in fact, an intensification of life, a completeness, a fullness, a wholeness of life. We do not live merely in order to vegetate through our days until we die. Nor do we live merely in order to take part in the routines of work and amusement that go on around us. We are not just machines that have to be cared for and driven carefully until they run down. In other words, life is not a straight horizontal line between two points, birth and death. Life curves upward to a peak of intensity, a high point of value and meaning, at which all its latent creative possibilities go into action and the person transcends himself or herself in encounter, response, and communion with another. It is for this that we came into the world—this communion and self-transcendence. We do not become fully human until we give ourselves to each other in love. And this must not be confined only to sexual fulfillment: it embraces everything in the human person—the capacity for self-giving, for sharing, for creativity,.for mutual care, for spiritual concern.

Love is our true destiny. We do not find the meaning of life by ourselves alone—we find it with another. We do not discover the secret of our lives merely by study and calculation in our own isolated meditations. The meaning of our life is a secret that has to be revealed to us in love, *by the one we love*. And if this love is unreal, the secret will not be found, the meaning will never reveal itself, the message will never be decoded. At best, we will receive a scrambled and partial message, one that will deceive and confuse us. We will never be fully real until we let ourselves fall in love—either with another human person or with God.

Hence, our attitude toward life is also going to be in one way or another an attitude toward love. Our conception of ourselves is bound to be profoundly affected by our conception—and our experience—of love. And our love, or our lack of it, our willingness to risk it or our determination to avoid it, will in the end be an expression of ourselves: of who we think we are, of what we want to be, of what we think we are here for.

Nor will this be merely something that goes on in our head. Love affects more than our thinking and our behavior toward those we love. It transforms our entire life. Genuine love is a personal revolution. Love takes your ideas, your desires, and your actions and welds them together in one experience and one living reality which is a new *you*. You may prefer to keep this from happening. You may keep your thoughts, desires, and acts in separate compartments if you want: but then you will be an artificial and divided person, with three little filing cabinets: one of ideas, one of decisions, and one of actions and experiences. These three compartments may not have much to do with each other. Such a life does not make sense, and is not likely to be happy. The contents of the separate filing cabinets may become increasingly peculiar as life goes on. Our philosophy of life is not something we create all by ourselves out of nothing. Our ways of thinking, even our attitudes toward ourselves, are more determined from the outside. Even our love tends to fit into ready-made forms. We consciously or unconsciously tailor our notions of love according to the patterns that we are exposed to day after day in advertising, in movies, on TV, and in our reading. One of these prevailing ready-made attitudes toward life and love needs to be discussed here. It is one that is seldom consciously spelled out. It is just "in the air," something that one is exposed to without thinking about it. This idea of love is a corollary of the thinking that holds our marketing society together. It is what one might call a package concept of love.

Love is regarded as a deal. The deal presupposes that we all have needs which have to be fulfilled by means of exchange. In order to make a deal you have to appear in the market with a worthwhile product, or if the product is worthless, you can get by if you dress it up in a good-looking package. We unconsciously think of ourselves as objects for sale on the market. We want to be wanted. We want to attract customers. We want to look like the kind of product that makes money. Hence, we waste a great deal of time modeling ourselves on the images presented to us by an affluent marketing society.

In doing this we come to consider ourselves and others not as *persons* but as *products*—as "goods," or in other words, as packages. We appraise one another commercially. We size each other up and make deals with a view to our own profit. We do not give ourselves in love, we make a deal that will enhance our own product, and therefore no deal is final. Our eyes are already on the next deal—and this next deal need not necessarily be with the same customer. Life is more interesting when you make a lot of deals with a lot of new customers.

This view, which equates lovemaking with salesmanship and love with a glamorous package, is based on the idea of love as a mechanism of instinctive needs. We are biological machines endowed with certain urges that require fulfillment. If we are smart, we can exploit and manipulate these urges in ourselves and in others. We can turn them to our own advantage. We can cash in on them, using them to satisfy and enrich our own ego by profitable deals with other egos. If the partner is not too smart, a little cheating won't hurt, especially if it makes everything more profitable and more satisfactory for me!

If this process of making deals and satisfying needs begins to speed up, life becomes an exciting gambling game. We meet more and more others with the same needs. We are all spilled out helter-skelter onto a roulette wheel hoping to land on a propitious number. This happens over and over again. "Falling in love" is a droll piece of luck that occurs when you end up with another person whose need more or less fits in with yours. You are somehow able to fulfill each other, to complete each other. You have won the sweepstake. Of course, the prize is good only for a couple of years. You have to get back in the game. But occasionally you win. Others are not so lucky. They never meet anyone with just the right kind of need to go with their need. They never find anyone with the right combination of qualities, gimmicks, and weaknesses. They never seem to buy the right package. They never land on the right number. They fall into the pool and the pool is empty.

This concept of love assumes that the machinery of buying and selling of needs and fulfillment is what makes everything run. It regards life as a market and love as a variation on free enterprise. You buy and you sell, and to get somewhere in love is to make a good deal with whatever you happen to have available. In business, buyer and seller get together in the market with their needs and their products. And they swap. The swapping is simplified by the use of a happy-making convenience called money. So too in love. The love relationship is a deal that is arrived at for the satisfaction of mutual needs. If it is successful it pays off, not necessarily in money, but in gratification, peace of mind, fulfillment. Yet since the idea of happiness is with us inseparable from the idea of prosperity, we must face the fact that a love that is not crowned with every material and social benefit seems to us to be rather suspect. Is it really *blessed?* Was it really a *deal?*

The trouble with this commercialized idea of love is that it diverts your attention more and more from the essentials to the accessories of love. You are no longer able to really love the other person, for you become obsessed with the effectiveness of your own package, your own product, your own market value.

At the same time, the transaction itself assumes an exaggerated importance. For many people what matters is the delightful and fleeting moment in which the deal is closed. They give little thought to what the deal itself represents. That is perhaps why so many marriages do not last, and why so many people have to remarry. They cannot feel real if they just make one contract and leave it at that!

In the past, in a society where people lived on the land, where the possession of land represented the permanence and security of one's family, there was no problem about marriage for life: it was perfectly natural and it was accepted without even unconscious resistance. Today, one's security and one's identity have to be constantly reaffirmed: nothing is permanent, everything is in movement. You have to move with it. You have to come up with something new each day. Every morning you have to prove that you are still there. You have to keep making deals.

Each deal needs to have the freshness, the uniqueness, the paradisal innocence of closing with a brand-new customer. Whether we like it or not, we are dominated by an "ethic," or perhaps better, a "superstition" of quantity. We do not believe in a single lasting value that is established once

for all—a permanent and essential quality that is never obsolete or stale. We are obsessed with what is repeatable. Reality does not surrender itself all at once, it has to be caught in small snatches, over and over again, in a dynamic flickering like the successive frames of a movie film. Such is our attitude.

Albert Camus in one of his early books, *The Myth of Sisyphus*, praised Don Juan as a hero precisely because of his "quantitative" approach to love. He made as many conquests as he possibly could. He practiced the "ethic of quantity." But Camus was praising Don Juan as a "hero of the absurd" and his ethic of quantity was merely a reflex response to the "essential absurdity" of life. Camus himself later revised his opinion on this matter. The "ethic of quantity" can take effect not only in love but in hate. The Nazi death camps were a perfect example of this ethic of quantity, this "heroism of the absurd." The ethic of quantity leads to Auschwitz and to despair. Camus saw this and there was no further mention of the ethic of quantity in his books after World War II. He moved more and more toward the ethic of love, sacrifice, and compassion.

Anyone who regards love as a deal made on the basis of "needs" is in danger of falling into a purely quantitative ethic. If love is a deal, then who is to say that you should not make as many deals as possible?

From the moment one approaches it in terms of "need" and "fulfillment," love has to be a deal. And what is worse, since we are constantly subjected to the saturation bombing of our senses and imagination with suggestions of impossibly ideal fulfillments, we cannot help revising our estimate of the deal we have made. We cannot help going back on it and making a "better" deal with someone else who is more satisfying.

The situation then is this: we go into love with a sense of immense need, with a naive demand for perfect fulfillment. After all, this is what we are daily and hourly told to expect. The effect of overstimulation by advertising and other media keeps us at the highest possible pitch of dissatisfaction with the second-rate fulfillment we are actually getting and with the deal we have made. It exacerbates our need. With many people, sexual cravings are kept in a high state of high irritation, not by authentic passion, but by the need to prove themselves attractive and successful lovers. They seek security in the repeated assurance that they are still a worthwhile product. The long word for all this is narcissism. It has disastrous affects, for it leads people to manipulate each other for selfish ends.

When you habitually function like this, you may seem to be living a very "full" and happy life. You may seem to have everything. You go everywhere, you are in the middle of everything, have lots of friends, "love" and are "loved." You seem in fact to be "perfectly adjusted" sexually and otherwise with your partner(s). Yet underneath there may be a devouring sense that you have nevertheless been cheated, and that the life you are living is not the real thing at all. That is the tragedy of those who are able to measure up to an advertising image which is presented to them on all sides as ideal. Yet they know by experience that there is nothing to it. The whole thing is hollow. They are perhaps in some ways worse off than those who cannot quite make the

grade and who therefore always think that perhaps there is a complete fulfillment which they can yet attain. These at least still have hope!

The truth is, however, that this whole concept of life and of love is self-defeating. To consider love merely as a matter of need and fulfillment, as something which works itself out in a cool deal, is to miss the whole point of love, and of life itself.

The basic error is to regard love merely as a need, an appetite, a craving, a hunger which calls for satisfaction. Psychologically, this concept reflects an immature and regressive attitude toward life and toward other people.

To begin with, it is negative. Love is lack, an emptiness, a nothingness. But it is an emptiness that can be exploited. Others can be drafted into the labor of satisfying this need—provided we cry loud enough and long enough, and in the most effective way. Advertising begins in the cradle! Very often it stays there—and so does love along with it. Psychologists have had some pretty rough things to say about the immaturity and narcissism of love in our marketing society, in which it is reduced to a purely egotistical need that cries out for immediate satisfaction or manipulates others more or less cleverly in order to get what it wants. But the plain truth is this: love is not a matter of getting what you want. Quite the contrary. The insistence on always having what you want, on always being satisfied, on always being fulfilled, makes love impossible. To love you have to climb out of the cradle, where everything is "getting," and grow up to the maturity of giving, without concern for getting anything special in return. Love is not a deal, it is a sacrifice. It is not marketing, it is a form of worship.

C O M M E N T S ■ Q U E S T I O N S

1. It is wrong, says Merton, to think of love as a mutual exchange, or business transaction, where person A agrees to meet person B's needs if person B will meet person A's needs. If love were like this, then it would seem that one should make as many transactions as possible, so as to get the best deal. But to do so would not be to love anyone at all. Love is not getting, but giving. In saying these things, Merton appears to ignore entirely the Principle of Self-Interest. Is he wrong to do this? In answering this question, it may help to think of love in the context of marriage. Can two people have a successful marriage if they do not get from it a large part of what they want?

2. Love includes sexual fulfillment, but also much more—in fact, according to Merton, it really embraces everything of importance in our lives. The "secret of our lives," he says, can be understood only through love, which will transform a person's entire life. This is true both in the case where the one we love is another person and in the case where the one we love is God. Do you agree with Merton that love—as a value both for ourselves and for others—should be ranked as number one among all the values in life? If you disagree with Merton, then what value would you rank as number one?

3. Do you agree with Merton's claims that the imagery of popular advertising presents a very much distorted view of what love is? If Merton is correct, then is popular advertising harmful in this regard? (See chapter 8 for a general discussion of the morality of advertising.)

4. Does Merton say anything that directly contradicts any point made by Albert Ellis? Or do their discussions simply go off in different directions? That is, do the views of Ellis and Merton conflict or do they complement each other?

5. Does a religious account of love differ markedly from a psychological account? That is, is there a different "source" for our ability to love in the former account?

B E R T R A N D   R U S S E L L

Marriage and Morals

When we look round the world at the present day and ask ourselves what conditions seem on the whole to make for happiness in marriage and what for unhappiness, we are driven to a somewhat curious conclusion, that the more civilized people become the less capable they seem of lifelong happiness with one partner. Irish peasants, although until recent times marriages were decided by the parents, were said by those who ought to know them to be on the whole happy and virtuous in their conjugal life. In general, marriage is easiest where people are least differentiated. When a man differs little from other men, and a woman differs little from other women, there is no particular reason to regret not having married someone else. But people with multifarious tastes and pursuits and interests will tend to desire congeniality in their partners, and to feel dissatisfied when they find that they have secured less of it than they might have obtained. The Church, which tends to view marriage solely from the point of view of sex, sees no reason why one partner should not do just as well as another, and can therefore uphold the indissolubility of marriage without realizing the hardship that this often involves.

Another condition which makes for happiness in marriage is paucity of unowned women and absence of social occasions when husbands meet other women. If there is no possibility of sexual relations with any woman other than one's wife, most men will make the best of the situation and, except in abnormally bad cases, will find it quite tolerable. The same thing applies to wives, especially if they never imagine that marriage should bring much happiness. That is to say, a marriage is likely to be what is called happy if neither party ever expected to get much happiness out of it.

Fixity of social custom, for the same reason, tends to prevent what are called unhappy marriages. If the bonds of marriage are recognized as final and irrevocable, there is no stimulus to the imagination to wander outside and consider that a more ecstatic happiness might have been possible. In order to secure domestic peace where this state of mind exists, it is only necessary that neither the

Bertrand Russell, who died in 1970 at the age of 98, was one of the best known and most influential of twentieth century philosophers. He wrote a great many books on a wide variety of topics. Among the many honors which he received was the Order of Merit in 1949 and the Nobel Prize for Literature in 1950.

husband nor the wife should fall outrageously below the commonly recognized standard of decent behaviour, whatever this may be.

Among civilized people in the modern world none of these conditions for what is called happiness exist, and accordingly one finds that very few marriages after the first few years are happy. Some of the causes of unhappiness are bound up with civilization, but others would disappear if men and women were more civilized than they are. Let us begin with the latter. Of these the most important is bad sexual education, which is a far commoner thing among the well-to-do than it can ever be among peasants. Peasant children early become accustomed to what are called the facts of life, which they can observe not only among human beings but among animals. They are thus saved from both ignorance and fastidiousness. The carefully educated children of the well-to-do, on the contrary, are shielded from all practical knowledge of sexual matters, and even the most modern parents, who teach children out of books, do not give them that sense of practical familiarity which the peasant child early acquires. The triumph of Christian teaching is when a man and woman marry without either having had previous sexual experience. In nine cases out of ten where this occurs, the results are unfortunate. Sexual behaviour among human beings is not instinctive, so that the inexperienced bride and bridegroom, who are probably quite unaware of this fact, find themselves overwhelmed with shame and discomfort. It is little better when the woman alone is innocent but the man has acquired his knowledge from prostitutes. Most men do not realize that a process of wooing is necessary after marriage, and many well-brought-up women do not realize what harm they do to marriage by remaining reserved and physically aloof. All this could be put right by better sexual education, and is in fact very much better with the generation now young than it was with their parents and grandparents. There used to be a widespread belief among women that they were morally superior to men on the ground that they had less pleasure in sex. This attitude made frank companionship between husbands and wives impossible. It was, of course, in itself quite unjustifiable, since failure to enjoy sex, so far from being virtuous, is a mere physiological or psychological deficiency, like a failure to enjoy food, which also a hundred years ago was expected of elegant females.

Other modern causes of unhappiness in marriage are, however, not so easily disposed of. I think that uninhibited civilized people, whether men or women, are generally polygamous in their instincts. They may fall deeply in love and be for some years entirely absorbed in one person, but sooner or later sexual familiarity dulls the edge of passion, and then they begin to look elsewhere for a revival of the old thrill. It is, of course, possible to control this impulse in the interests of morality, but it is very difficult to prevent the impulse from existing. With the growth of women's freedom there has come a much greater opportunity for conjugal infidelity than existed in former times. The opportunity gives rise to the thought, the thought gives rise to the desire, and in the absence of religious scruples the desire gives rise to the act.

Women's emancipation has in various ways made marriage more difficult. In old days the wife had to adapt herself to the husband, but the husband did not have to adapt himself to the wife. Nowadays many wives, on grounds of woman's right to her own individuality and her own career, are unwilling to adapt themselves to their husbands beyond a point, while men who still hanker after the old tradition of masculine domination see no reason why they should do all the adapting. This trouble arises especially in connection with infidelity. In old days the husband was occasionally unfaithful, but as a rule his wife did not know of it. If she did, he confessed that he had sinned and made her believe that he was penitent. She, on the other hand, was usually virtuous. If she was not, and the fact came to her husband's knowledge, the marriage broke up. Where, as happens in many modern marriages, mutual faithfulness is not demanded, the instinct of jealousy nevertheless survives, and often proves fatal to the persistence of any deeply rooted intimacy even where no overt quarrels occur.

There is another difficulty in the way of modern marriage, which is felt especially by those who are most conscious of the value of love. Love can flourish only as long as it is free and spontaneous; it tends to be killed by the thought that it is a duty. To say that it is your duty to love so-and-so is the surest way to cause you to hate him or her. Marriage as a combination of love with legal bonds thus falls between two stools. Shelley says:

"I never was attached to that great sect
  Whose doctrine is, that each one should
    select
  Out of the crowd a mistress or a friend,
  And all the rest, though fair and wise,
    commend
  To cold oblivion, though it is in the code
  Of modern morals, and the beaten road

Which those poor slaves with weary
    footsteps tread,
Who travel to their home among
    the dead
By the broad highway of the world,
    and so
With one chained friend, perhaps a
    jealous foe,
The dreariest and the longest
    journey go."

There can be no doubt that to close one's mind on marriage against all the approaches of love from elsewhere is to diminish receptivity and sympathy and the opportunities of valuable human contacts. It is to do violence to something which, from the most idealistic standpoint, is in itself desirable. And like every kind of restrictive morality it tends to promote what one may call a policeman's outlook upon the whole of human life—the outlook, that is to say, which is always looking for an opportunity to forbid something.

For all these reasons, many of which are bound up with things undoubtedly good, marriage has become difficult, and if it is not to be a barrier to happiness it must be conceived in a somewhat new way. One solution often suggested, and actually tried on a large scale in America, is easy divorce. I hold, of course, as every humane person must, that divorce should be granted on more grounds than are admitted in the English law, but I do not recognize in easy divorce a solution of the troubles of marriage. Where a marriage is childless, divorce may be often the right solution, even when both parties are doing their best to behave decently; but where there are children the stability of marriage is to my mind a matter of considerable importance. (This is a subject to which I shall return in connection with the family.) I think that where a marriage is fruitful and both parties to it are reasonable and decent the expectation ought to be that it will be lifelong, but not that it will exclude other sex relations. A marriage which begins with passionate love and leads to children who are desired and loved ought to produce so deep a tie between a man and woman that they will feel something infinitely precious in their companionship, even after sexual passion has decayed, and even if either or both feels sexual passion for someone else. This mellowing of marriage has been prevented by jealousy, but jealousy, though it is an instinctive emotion, is one which can be controlled if it is recognized as bad, and not supposed to be the expression of a just moral indignation. A companionship which has lasted for many years and through many deeply felt events has a richness of content which cannot belong to the first days of love, however delightful these may be. And any person who appreciates what time can do to enhance values will not lightly throw away such companionship for the sake of new love.

It is therefore possible for a civilized man and woman to be happy in marriage, although if this is to be the case a number of conditions must be fulfilled. There must be a feeling of complete equality on both sides; there must be no interference with mutual freedom; there must be the most complete physical and mental intimacy; and there must be a certain similarity in regard to standards of values. (It is fatal, for example, if one values only money while the other values only good work.) Given all these conditions, I believe marriage to be the best and most important relation that can exist between two human beings. If it has not often been

realized hitherto, that is chiefly because husband and wife have regarded themselves as each other's policeman. If marriage is to achieve its possibilities, husbands and wives must learn to understand that whatever the law may say, in their private lives they must be free.

*   *   *   *   *

Most young men, in their early adult years, go through troubles and difficulties of a quite unnecessary kind in regard to sex. If a young man remains chaste, the difficulty of control probably causes him to become timid and inhibited, so that when he finally marries he cannot break down the self-control of past years, except perhaps in a brutal and sudden manner, which leads him to fail his wife in the capacity of a lover. If he goes with prostitutes, the dissociation between the physical and the idealistic aspects of love which has begun in adolescence is perpetuated, with the result that his relations with women ever after have to be either Platonic or, in his belief, degrading. Moreover, he runs a grave risk of venereal disease. If he has affairs with girls of his own class, much less harm is done, but even then the need of secrecy is harmful, and interferes with the development of stable relations. Owing partly to snobbery and partly to the belief that marriage ought immediately to lead to children, it is difficult for a man to marry young. Moreover, where divorce is very difficult, early marriage has great dangers, since two people who suit each other at twenty are quite likely not to suit each other at thirty. Stable relations with one partner are difficult for many people until they have had some experience of variety. If our outlook on sex were sane, we should expect university students to be temporarily married though childless. They would in this way be freed from the obsession of sex which at present greatly interferes with work. They would acquire that experience of the other sex which is desirable as a prelude to the serious partnership of a marriage with children. And they would be free to experience love without the concomitants of subterfuge, concealment, and dread of disease, which at present poison youthful adventures.

* * * * *

Power, sex and parenthood appear to me to be the source of most of the things that human beings do, apart from what is necessary for self-preservation. Of these three, power begins first and ends last. The child, since he has very little power, is dominated by the desire to have more. Indeed, a large proportion of his activities spring from this desire. His other dominant desire is vanity—the wish to be praised and the fear of being blamed or left out. It is vanity that makes him a social being and gives him the virtues necessary for life in a community. Vanity is a motive closely intertwined with sex, though in theory separable from it. But power has, so far as I can see, very little connection with sex, and it is love of power, at least as much as vanity, that makes a child work at his lessons and develop his muscles. Curiosity and the pursuit of knowledge should, I think, be regarded as a branch of the love of power. If knowledge is power, then the love of knowledge is the love of power. Science, therefore, except for certain branches of biology and physiology, must be regarded as lying outside the province of sexual emotions. As the Emperor Frederick II is no longer alive, this opinion must remain more or less hypothetical. If he were still alive, he would no

doubt decide it by castrating an eminent mathematician and an eminent composer and observing the effects upon their respective labours. I should expect the former to be nil and the latter to be considerable. Seeing that the pursuit of knowledge is one of the most valuable elements in human nature, a very important sphere of activity is, if we are right, exempted from the domination of sex.

Power is also the motive to most political activity, understanding this word in its widest sense. I do not mean to suggest that a great statesman is indifferent to the public welfare; on the contrary, I believe him to be a man in whom parental feeling has become widely diffused. But unless he has also a considerable love of power he will fail to sustain the labours necessary for success in a political enterprise. I have known many high-minded men in public affairs, but unless they had a considerable dose of personal ambition they seldom had the energy to accomplish the good at which they aimed. On a certain crucial occasion, Abraham Lincoln made a speech to two recalcitrant senators, beginning and ending with the words: "I am the President of the United States, clothed with great power." It can hardly be questioned that he found some pleasure in asserting this fact. Throughout all politics, both for good and for evil, the two chief forces are the economic motive and the love of power; an attempt to interpret politics on Freudian lines is, to my mind, a mistake.

If we are right in what we have been saying, most of the greatest men, other than artists, have been actuated in their important activities by motives unconnected with sex. If such activities are to persist and are, in their humbler forms, to become common, it is necessary that sex should not overshadow the remainder of a man's emotional and passionate nature. The desire to understand the world and the desire to reform it are the two great engines of progress, without which human society would stand still or retrogress. It may be that too complete a happiness would cause the impulses to knowledge and reform to fade. When Cobden wished to enlist John Bright in the free trade campaign, he based a personal appeal upon the sorrow that Bright was experiencing owing to his wife's recent death. It may be that without this sorrow Bright would have had less sympathy with the sorrows of others. And many a man has been driven to ab-stract pursuits by despair of the actual world. To a man of sufficient energy, pain may be a valuable stimulus, and I do not deny that if we were all perfectly happy we should not exert ourselves to become happier. But I cannot admit that it is any part of the duty of human beings to provide others with pain on the off chance that it may prove fruitful. In ninety-nine cases out of a hundred pain proves merely crushing. In the hundredth case it is better to trust to the natural shocks that flesh is heir to. So long as there is death there will be sorrow, and so long as there is sorrow it can be no part of the duty of human beings to increase its amount, in spite of the fact that a few rare spirits know how to transmute it.

C O M M E N T S ■ Q U E S T I O N S

1. "... the more civilized people become the less capable they seem of lifelong happiness with one partner ... a marriage is likely to be what is called happy if neither party ever expected to get much happiness out of it." Is Russell correct in saying this? If you disagree with Russell, would you say that perhaps Russell was correct one or two generations ago, but not at the present time? Or would you say that at the present time a realistic person should expect even less from marriage?

2. According to Russell, the following are some of the most important causes for unhappiness in marriage among civilized people: (a) Inadequate sexual education. (Russell had in mind particularly the Victorian attitudes of earlier generations.) (b) The instinctive tendency that most people have to want more than one sexual partner during their lifetimes. (c) The development of more nearly equal roles for men and women; that is, a decline in the tradition of male dominance, with the result that women are less inclined to adapt themselves to their husbands. (d) The fact that marriage has always tended to make love a duty, which is destructive of love. Has the women's liberation movement of the last twenty-five years affected the validity (or invalidity) of any of these points? Has the relatively recent research on sex, such as that

of Masters and Johnson, affected the validity or invalidity of any of these points?

3. Russell defends what is now called "open marriage"—where sexual relations with people outside the marriage are permitted. He sees this as the best path to be followed by couples who no longer have sexual passion for each other but who have children who could be hurt by a divorce. Does it make sense to say that an "open marriage" is still a marriage at all? Do you believe that Russell has adequately considered the harmful effects upon both parents and children when parents who would like to be divorced stay together just

for the sake of their children?

4. Do you believe that the Principle of the Common Good can best be followed by, as Russell suggests, viewing the need for sex as being on a par with the need for food? Would such an attitude help to protect people's rights? Or would it interfere with the protection of people's rights?

5. Given ideal conditions for marriage, Russell says, "I believe marriage to be the best and most important relation that can exist between two human beings." Do you agree? Does Russell give a complete list of the conditions needed to make a marriage ideal?

L E W I S   B.   S M E D E S

Christian Sexual Ethics

1. The Morality of Caution

Any reasonable single person trying to make a rational decision about his sexual activity will "count the cost." The first thing they may ask is: "Am I likely to get hurt?" Sexual intercourse has some risk along with certain possible rewards for unmarried people, and the cautious person will weigh the risks. The question of "getting hurt" has two parts: (1) how seriously can I get hurt, and (2) how

great is the risk of getting hurt? If the odds are not good and the possible hurt pretty serious, the cautious per-

Lewis B. Smedes is Professor of Theology and Ethics at Fuller Theological Seminary in Pasadena, California. He is on the editorial staff of The Reformed Journal, *to which he has frequently contributed. He has written or translated some twenty books.*

Lewis B. Smedes, "Christian Sexual Ethics," in *Sex for Christians* (Grand Rapids: Eerdmans, 1978), 115–130. Used by permission.

son may decide to wait until marriage, when the risk will be mostly eliminated.

The hurts that sexual intercourse could cause unmarried people are obvious enough. Getting pregnant, even in a permissive society, is a painful experience for an unmarried woman. Once pregnant, she has no way of escaping a painful decision: she can abort the fetus, she can give the baby up for adoption, or she can rear the child herself. Or, of course, she can get married—but this may not be an option for her. The route of abortion has been paved by liberalized laws. But no matter how easy it may be to get, and no matter what her intellectual view of abortion may be, she is likely to find out afterwards that it is a devastating experience for herself, especially if she is sensitive to the value of human life. Adoption is another route. Every child given up for adoption may be God's gift to some adoptive parents. This is a compensation. But giving up children nourished to birth inside their own bodies is something few young women can do without deep pain. Keeping the baby and rearing it may be easier than it used to be. Many communities no longer lash the unwed mother with their silent judgment: this may be only because the community does not care, but it still makes life easier for the mother. But rearing the baby alone is still heavy with problems for the unmarried mother in the most tolerant society. Some may have a chance at marriage; but marriage forced on two people is an invitation to pain. In short, pregnancy can cause considerable hurt.

While pregnancy still hurts, the risk of it is not threatening to many unmarried people. However, any notion that the risk has been eliminated is careless thinking. The contraceptive pill has cut the chances, but it has not removed the possibility. Unwanted children, both in marriage and out of it, testify that no birth control device known up to this point is fail-proof. And, of course, there is the risk of that accidental time when precautions were neglected. As a matter of fact, the majority of young people having intercourse for the first time do not use any preventive means at all. Many young women refuse to take precautions because they do not want to think of themselves as planning for intercourse; it must happen only as they are swept into it in a romantic frenzy. Still, all things considered, the risk of pregnancy may have become small enough so that the cautious person may decide it is worth taking.

The threat of disease is a real one, especially for the promiscuous person. Antibiotics, once heralded as a sure cure, have stimulated virus strains more potent than ever. And venereal disease is currently in a virtual epidemic stage. Still, for prudent and selective people the odds seem comfortably against infection.

The risk of threatening an eventual marriage by premarital sex is hard to calculate. A deeply disappointing sexual experience before marriage could, one supposes, condition a person against happy sex in marriage. But, of course, unmarried people considering intercourse do not plan on having a bad experience. Guilt feelings about a premarital experience can inhibit one's freedom of self-giving in marriage sex: for example, a woman's inability to experience orgasm in marriage is sometimes traceable to guilt about premarital sex. And promiscuity before marriage could possibly make extramarital sex easier to fall into should marriage sex be unrewarding. But all these threats depend too much on how individual people feel; they are not useful as blanket judgments. The question of threat to marriage has to be answered in terms of the individuals involved.

Jane, who believes religiously that sexual intercourse before marriage is a sin, runs a fairly strong chance of making marriage harder for herself by premarital intercourse, especially if she has sex with someone besides the man she marries. But Joan, who was reared in a moral no man's land, may not risk marriage happiness at all by having premarital sex, though she may risk it for much deeper reasons. All in all, the argument that sexual intercourse by unmarried people threatens their future marriage is a flimsy one; too much depends on the moral attitudes of the persons involved. This implies, of course, that one does not have to be one hundred percent moral to have a happy marriage, though it may help.

The morality of caution leaves us with no clear-cut decision. Christian morality cannot support a blanket veto of sexual intercourse for unmarried people on this basis. It all depends on how the risks are calculated in each person's situation. The morality of caution will lead prudent people to ask with whom, why, and when they are having intercourse. But it is not enough to tell them that they ought not do it. Following the morality of caution alone, sexual morality comes down to this: if you are reasonably sure you won't get hurt, go ahead.

The point to notice is that the morality of caution is concerned only with possible hurt to the person involved. It does not bother with questions about the kind of act sexual intercourse is; it does not ask whether unmarried people are morally qualified for it on the basis of either their relationship or the nature of the act. I do not suppose that many people, in their best moments, will decide on the basis of caution alone. But wherever it is snipped away from the other considerations, it works on the assumption that sexual intercourse as such has no more *moral* significance than a gentle kiss.

2. The Morality of Concern

Here we move beyond caution to a personal concern about the risk of causing hurt to others. The morality of caution asks: am I likely to get hurt? The morality of concern asks: am I likely to hurt someone else? The calculations of both moralities are roughly the same. The difference is that here concern is directed toward the other person. The crucial questions here will be how far one's concern reaches and how sensitive one is to the kinds of hurt he could cause. It may be that the concerned person will interpret the risks differently than the merely cautious person will.

For instance, a girl may be willing to take the risk of pregnancy as far as she is concerned. But if she considers the hurt that pregnancy may involve for the unwanted child, she may weigh the odds quite differently: the risk of pregnancy will be the same, but the possible hurt to others may count against having intercourse more heavily than if its pleasure is matched only against possible hurt to herself. If she gets pregnant, the girl may decide to abort or give the child up for adoption. The fetus has no choice. Here she is dealing with a potential person's right to exist. If she gives the child up for adoption, she is determining that the child will not be reared by its natural parents. And if she decides to keep the child, she may be forcing a situation of permanent disadvantage on another human being. This may sound as though only the woman is making the decision; but the same considerations must go into the thinking of her partner. By his act he may be risking severe disadvantages for another human being—or at least a potential human being—and giving that human being no choice in the matter. The unmarried couple may be able to opt for the risk; but the unwanted offspring is not given a chance to weigh the odds.

But again, the risk may seem small enough to take for the sophisticated person. And for some couples there is always a back-up emergency plan— marriage. But here again the element of concern is brought in: are the people involved reasonably sure that they won't hurt each other by getting married? The person with concern will ask the question and seek advice in answering it: but only he or she can give the answer for himself.

No person who makes decisions out of concern for others will run much risk of infecting another person with venereal disease. And a person who is truly concerned will be least likely to be a threat: he would not likely be a person who goes in for casual bed-hopping. The risk is not great for two people who are serious about sexual intercourse as an expression of deeply involved affection because the probability of promiscuity is not great. At any rate, the morality of concern would tell a person to be very careful, but it would probably not tell him to abstain from sexual intercourse entirely.

Personal concern looks a lot deeper than the risk of getting someone pregnant or spreading a disease.

A concerned person will wonder how sexual intercourse will affect his partner as a whole person, because each person's sexual experiences are a major theme in the symphony he is creating with his life. No one can take sex out at night and put it away until he wants to play with it again. What we do with sex shapes what we are; it is woven into the plot of a drama we are writing about ourselves. The person with whom we have sexual relations cannot let his sexual passions dance on stage, take a curtain call, and go back to some backstage corner to let the rest of the play go on. So a concerned person will ask how a sexual experience can fit into the total life—the whole future—of that other person. Where will it fit in his memories? How will it be digested in his conscience? What will it do to his attitude toward himself? How will it help create the symphony that he can make of his life? The morality of concern reaches out into the tender tissues of the other person's whole life; and it refuses to endorse any act that will stunt that person's movement into a creative, self-esteeming, and freely conscious life.

However, it also goes beyond the other person. It asks about the people around them—their friends, their families, and their community. A single, discreet, and very secret affair may not bring down the moral walls of Jericho. But a Christian person of concern will think beyond his own affair: he must universalize his action and ask what the effects would be if unmarried people generally followed his example.

Much depends, naturally, on the kind of sex he is thinking about. If he is thinking about casual sex, on the assumption that all two people need for good sex is to like each other, we have one set of problems. If he is thinking about sleeping only with the person he is planning to marry, we have another. If he is thinking of casual sex, he will have to ask about the burdens on society created by a considerable number of unwanted children, a formidable increase in venereal disease, and a general devaluation of sexual intercourse as an expression of committed love. But if he is thinking only of sex between two responsible people who are profoundly in love—though not legally married—the question is limited to what the effect on public morals would be if everyone in *his* position felt free to have sexual intercourse. He might respond by saying that if it *were* moral for him, it would be moral for others. Thus public morality would not be damaged if everyone did it; habits and customs might change, and moral *opinions* would change, but morality itself would be unscathed. And he would be right— on this basis.

Concern for the other person and his community sets the question within the perimeter of Christian love. It comes within the single blanket law that all of our decisions are to be made in responsible love. In the terms of this morality, sexual intercourse is morally neutral, and the question of its rightness or wrongness is answered only in relation to its consequences for other people. If the risk of harmful consequences is small enough, single people are free to go ahead. The morality of concern forces people to judge according to circumstances; for example, the answer to the question whether two mature retirees should refrain from sexual intercourse may be very different from that concerning two youngsters on a sexual high. Acting only out of loving concern, one puts aside the possibility that there may be something special about sexual intercourse that disqualifies everyone but married persons. It demands only that each person weigh the risks carefully and then make a responsible decision for his particular case.

3. *The Morality of Personal Relationships*

Two things set off the morality of personal relationships from the first two: first, its focus is on how intercourse will affect the *relationship* between the two persons; second, its concern is more positive. The clinching question is whether sexual intercourse will strengthen and deepen the relationship. If it can be a creative factor in the relationship, it is good—provided, of course, neither person gets hurt individually. Behind this way of deciding the right and wrong of intercourse lies a whole new understanding of human beings as persons-in-relationship. The view is that the individual comes into his own in relationship: the "I" is a truly human "I" only as it exists in an "I-You" relationship. The tender spot in human morality, then, is always at the point of personal contact with another. And this is why the effect sexual intercourse has on the relationship is the pivotal question.

The relationship can be creatively supported only when two people have regard for each other as ends to be served rather than as means to be used. When two people use each other in sexual intercourse, they hurt the relationship and corrupt the sexual act. They twist the relationship into a functional association. One has a functional relationship with a person whenever he concentrates on getting a service from him. What one wants from a plumber is to have his leaky faucet fixed; what he wants from a dentist is to have his toothache cured; what one may want from a sexual partner is to have his ego served or his sex drive satiated. In these cases one is after a functional association. But what someone wants in a personal relationship is to let the other person thrive as a person, to give him the regard and respect he merits as a friend, and to be privileged to grow into a relationship in which they will both desire no more from each other than mutual concern and enjoyment. In short, he wants the other person to be something along *with* him rather than merely to do something *for* him.

Now in most cases, two people in love treat each other in both functional and personal ways. There is constant tension between expecting one's friend to deliver the pleasures of friendship and respecting him only for what he is. In sexual love, the functional side often *tends* to shove the personal side into the background. The sex drive is so intense that it becomes a temptation to manipulate and even exploit the other person. To the extent that the functional is predominant in our sex lives, we treat the other person as a means and thus dehumanize him. When this happens sexual intercourse is immoral, not because it is sexual intercourse between two unmarried people but because it distorts and destroys a personal relationship.

Sexual intercourse can deepen and enrich a personal relationship only when it takes place within the reality of a personal relationship. This means that the preliminary questions two unmarried people must ask each other are: Do we already have a genu-

inely personal relationship that can be deepened and enriched? Do we have deep personal regard for each other? Do we treat each other now in integrity? Do we say no to any temptation to use each other? Did we accept each other as friends before sexual intercourse entered our heads? The possibility that sexual intercourse might be good for them travels with the answers to these preliminary considerations. Then they have to ask the clinching question: will sexual intercourse deepen and enrich or will it threaten and distort our relationship?

But how can they possibly know what it will do? First of all, each person has to examine himself. He or she will have to probe his/her own feelings and ask personal questions about them: Is he being exploitative? Is he pressing the other person to do something he/she may not want to do? Is he minimizing the other person's freedom and dignity? But these questions are about negative factors that could hurt the relationship. How does he know that sexual intercourse will actually strengthen the relationship? This exposes the Achilles' heel of the morality of personal relationships.

Furthermore, how can this standard be applied? How can two unmarried people know ahead of time whether sexual intercourse will enrich their relationship? They could probably try it and find out. But that would summarily throw the moral question out of court. And perhaps this is the only way out for the morality of personal relationships. At best, the decision has to be made on very uncertain personal insights: the people involved can only guess beforehand what will happen to their relationship after they have got out of bed. They can probe their readiness with all honesty and still not know for sure how they will feel toward each other afterward.

If we were talking about two people's date for dinner or a concert, almost any risk might be worth taking. But sexual intercourse opens trap doors to the inner cells of our conscience, and legions of little angels (or demons) can fly out to haunt us. There is such abandon, such explosive self-giving, such personal exposure that few people can feel the same toward each other afterward. And if one thinks he is ready, he cannot be sure the other person is. The problem is not just that one of the two will feel sour toward the other; the problem is that one of the partners may unleash feelings of need for the other that he/she had no inkling existed. He/she may thus be catapulted into a commitment that the other is not ready to take. And so the relationship can be injured by one person's making demands on it that the other is not ready for. And the person who is least committed is likely to withdraw inwardly from a relationship that demands more than he can give.

If we could somehow segregate people according to maturity, and if only people over fifty used the morality of personal relationships, we might have a workable standard. If, in addition to this, the decision were made with moral assistance from a community of friends and family, it might be a usable norm. And if the decision were made in the cool of the day, it would at least be manageable. But unmarried people moving toward sexual intercourse include many people whose experience in durable and creative relationships is almost nil. A decision concerning sex is often

made alone in the passions of the night, when every untested lust may seem like the promptings of pure love. Perhaps there is a moral elite who could responsibly use a moral guideline with as many loose ends as this one; but there is no way of knowing for sure who they are.

So we are back where we started. Each of the three moralities for sexual intercourse focuses on factors outside of the act itself. None of them assumes that sexual intercourse has a built-in factor that in itself would disqualify unmarried people for it. But Christian morality has traditionally believed that there is such a factor. For it has maintained that, even if nobody gets hurt and even if a personal relationship could be enriched by it, it is wrong for all but married people. It has taught that there is more to sexual intercourse than meets the eye—or excites the genitals. Sexual intercourse takes place within a context of what persons really are, how they are expected to fulfill their lives in sexual love, and how they are to live together in a community that is bigger than their private relationships. We now go on to ask about this special ingredient of sexual intercourse, for it stands behind the traditional Christian negative to unmarried people.

4. *The Morality of Law*

New Testament morality on this point is a morality of law. Some things were morally indifferent; Paul insisted on this. For some things there was no law except the law of love; and love flourished in freedom. But when people, as in Corinth, applied Christian freedom to sex, Paul put up fences. One of the fences was marriage. He made no distinctions between casual sex, sex between engaged couples, or sex between mature widowed people. The no was unqualified. The question is: Why?

Before getting into Paul's sexual morality, we must concede that the Old Testament gives him shaky support. Female virginity had a high premium; but male virginity was not all that important. And female virginity was demanded not so much for virginity's sake as for social reasons: the family line had to be guarded at all costs. And the male in particular had a right to be absolutely certain that his children were his own. The society had no place in it for the unmarried woman, no place except the brothel. So the rules said that if a woman had sexual intercourse before marriage, then tried to fake virginity with her bridegroom and was exposed by failure to produce a bloodied sheet, she would be executed forthwith (Deut. 22:13–21). However, this was probably not likely to happen. If a man slept with a virgin who was not betrothed, he was obligated to pay a dowry to her father and marry her (Deut. 22:28, 29). And the prospects for an unmarried girl who had lost her virginity were so bad that no woman was likely to keep quiet about the affair. She would at least tell her father, who, threatened with loss of dowry, would put the fear of God into a reneging sex partner. A man was in real trouble, however, if he slept with a virgin betrothed to another man; he was in trouble with her fiancé and with her father, for it was especially their rights that he had abused. He would be stoned to death; and if their act was discovered in the city, the woman would also be stoned—on the assumption that she failed to cry for help (Deut. 22:23–27). But if a man slept with a prostitute, nothing was said because nothing was lost. Casual sex between young people, however, was probably nonexistent. Once a boy slept with a girl, he was expected to marry her; and the girl was not likely to be noble about it and let him off the hook.

The Old Testament as a whole did not read the seventh commandment as a no to sexual intercourse between unmarried people. The morality of sexual intercourse did not rest with the character of the act as much as with its possible consequences. What was wrong was for a man's rights to be violated. Unmarried sex violated the command against stealing as clearly as it did the command against adultery.

The New Testament looks at the question from a very different standpoint. It has a blanket word for sexual immorality: *porneia*, translated as fornication in the older versions and as immorality in the newer. Fornication includes more than sexual intercourse between people who are not married. It does refer to breaking one's oath of fidelity to a husband or wife (Matt. 5:32; 19:9); but it could include a lot of other practices, like homosexual relations. And Paul makes clear that it also means sexual intercourse for unmarried people. In I Cor. 7 he concedes that to be both unmarried and a virgin is, under the circumstances, the best life. But "because of the temptation to immorality, each man should have his own wife and each woman her own husband" (I Cor. 7:2). Better to marry, he said, than to be ravished with unfulfilled desires. So he must have meant that "immorality" included sexual intercourse outside marriage. And if unmarried sexual intercourse was wrong, it was a serious wrong; it ought not even be talked about (Eph. 5:3). God's will is that we abstain from fornication, not giving way to "the passion of lust like heathen who do not know God" (I Thess. 4:6). Fornication is sin; intercourse by unmarried people is fornication; therefore, intercourse by unmarried people is sin.

We must now ask the crucial question about Paul's blanket rule. What is there about sexual intercourse that makes it morally improper for unmarried people? Surely not every instance of coitus by unmarried people is simply a surrender to lust "like the heathen." And if it is not in lust, and it hurts no one, why is it wrong? Did Paul assume that it would always be in lust or would always be harmful? And if some unmarried people's sex was not lustful, would it then be morally proper? Divine law, though often expressed in negative rules, is rooted in a positive insight. The law against adultery, for example, reflects a positive view of marriage and fidelity. And this view of marriage rests on an insight that God created men and women to live out their closest personal relationship in a permanent, exclusive union. We may suppose that behind Paul's vigorous attack on fornication is a positive view of sexual intercourse.

Sexual intercourse involves two people in a life-union; it is a life-uniting act. This is the insight that explains Paul's fervent comment on a member of Christ's body sleeping with a prostitute (I Cor. 6:12–20): "Do you not know that he who joins himself to a prostitute *becomes one body* with her?" (v. 16—italics mine). Of course, Paul is horrified that a prosti-

tute is involved: a Christian man is a moral clown in a brothel. But the character of the woman involved is not his basic point. Paul would just as likely have said: "Do you not know that he who joins himself to the prim housewife next door becomes one body with her?" And the incongruity would have been the same. Paul bases his remark on the statement in Genesis 2 that "the two shall become one." And he sees sexual intercourse as an act that signifies and seeks the intrinsic unity—the unbreakable, total, personal unity that we call marriage.

It does not matter what the two people have in mind. The whore sells her body with an unwritten understanding that nothing personal will be involved in the deal. She sells the service of a quick genital massage—nothing more. The buyer gets his sexual needs satisfied without having anything personally difficult to deal with afterward. He pays his dues, and they are done with each other. But none of this affects Paul's point. The *reality* of the act, unfelt and unnoticed by them, is this: it unites them—body and soul—to each other. It unites them in that strange, impossible to pinpoint sense of "one flesh." There is no such thing as casual sex, no matter how casual people are about it. The Christian assaults reality in his night out at the brothel. He uses a woman and puts her back in a closet where she can be forgotten; but the reality is that he has put away a person with whom he has done something that was meant to inseparably join them. This is what is at stake for Paul in the question of sexual intercourse between unmarried people.

And now we can see clearly why Paul thought sexual intercourse by unmarried people was wrong. It is wrong because it violates the inner reality of the act; it is wrong because unmarried people thereby engage in a life-uniting act without a life-uniting intent. Whenever two people copulate without a commitment to life-union, they commit fornication.

Thus Paul's reason for saying no to sexual intercourse for the unmarried goes a crucial step beyond all the common practical reasons. We can suppose that Paul would appreciate anyone's reluctance to risk getting hurt; we can be sure he would see a Christian impulse in a person's concern for the other person; and we may assume that he would endorse the notion that sexual intercourse ought to promote the personal relationship between the two partners. But his absolute no to sexual intercourse for unmarried people is rooted in his conviction that it is a contradiction of reality. Intercourse signs and seals—and maybe even delivers—a life-union; and life-union means marriage.

C O M M E N T S ■ Q U E S T I O N S

1. Smedes endorses, with some qualifications, the view of St. Paul in the New Testament according to which sex between unmarried people is morally wrong because it is a "life-uniting act without a life-uniting intent." One argument that has been made against the position of St. Paul is that sometimes two people do not know whether or not they want to commit themselves to "life-union" until *after* they have become sexual partners, and that therefore it may be morally acceptable for them to have sex before committing themselves to marriage. Do you believe that this is a good argument?

2. Do you believe that adhering to the ethical position outlined by Smedes is the best way to follow the Principle of the Common Good? What about the Principles of Rights and Self-Interest?

3. Is it possible for two people having sex to treat each other as ends, not merely as means to achieve their own gratification, even though they have no intention of marrying?

4. Is Smedes's "morality of caution" too cautious? Is his "morality of concern" an exaggeration? Is the position of Smedes perhaps not cautious or concerned enough?

5. How would you compare the views of Smedes to the views of Ellis, Russell, and Merton? Which, in your opinion, is the most moral? Is any one of them more idealistic than the others? Is it a good thing to be idealistic? Is any one of these views more realistic than the others?

J O H N   M c M U R T R Y

Monogamy: A Critique

*   *   *   *   *

II

"Monogamy" means, literally, "one marriage." But it would be wrong to suppose that this phrase tells us much about our particular species of official wedlock. The greatest obstacle to the adequate understanding of our monogamy institution has been the failure to identify clearly and systematically the full complex of principles it involves. There are four such principles, each carrying enormous restrictive force and together constituting a massive social control mechanism that has never, so far as I know, been fully schematized.

To come straight to the point, the four principles in question are as follows:

1. *The partners are required to enter a formal contractual relation:* (*a*) whose establishment demands a specific official participant, certain conditions of the contractors (legal age, no blood ties, etc.) and a standard set of procedures; (*b*) whose governing items are uniform for all and exactly prescribed by law; and (*c*) whose dissolution may only be legally effected by the decision of state representatives.

The ways in which this elaborate principle of contractual requirements are importantly restrictive are obvious. One may not enter into a marriage union without entering into a contract presided over by a state-investured official.[1] One may not set any of the terms of the contractual relationship by which one is bound for life. And one cannot dissolve the contract without legal action and costs, court proceedings and in many places actual legislation. (The one and only contract in all English-speaking law that is not dissoluble by the consent of the contracting parties.) The extent of control here—over the most intimate and putatively "loving" relationships in all social intercourse—is so great as to be difficult to catalogue without exciting in oneself a sense of disbelief.

Lest it be thought there is always the real option of entering a common law relationship free of such encumbrances, it should be noted that: (*a*) these relationships themselves are subject to state regulation, though of a less imposing sort; and (much more

---

1. Any person who presides over a marriage and is not authorized by law to do so is guilty of a criminal offense and is subject to several years imprisonment (e.g., Canadian Criminal Code, Sec. 258).

John McMurtry is Professor of Philosophy at the University of Guelph, Canada. He is the author of The Structure of Marx's World-View *and many articles in philosophical journals.*

Reprinted by permission of *The Monist* from Vol. 56, No. 2, 1972.

important) (*b*) there are very formidable selective pressures against common law partnerships such as employment and job discrimination, exclusion from housing and lodging facilities, special legal disablements,[2] loss of social and moral status (consider such phrases as "living in sin," "make her an honest woman," etc.), family shame and embarrassment, and so on.

2. *The number of partners involved in the marriage must be two and only two* (as opposed to three, four, five or any of the almost countless other possibilities of intimate union).

This second principle of our specific form of monogamy (the concept of "one marriage," it should be pointed out, is consistent with any number of participating partners) is perhaps the most important and restrictive of the four principles we are considering. Not only does it confine us to just *one* possibility out of an enormous range, but it confines us to that single possibility which involves the *least* number of people, two. It is difficult to conceive of a more thoroughgoing mechanism for limiting extended social union and intimacy. The fact that this monolithic restriction seems so "natural" to us (if it were truly "natural" of course, there would be no need for its rigorous cultural prescription by everything from severe criminal law[3] to ubiqui-

tous housing regulations) simply indicates the extent to which its hold is implanted in our social structure. It is the institutional basis of what I will call the "binary frame of sexual consciousness," a frame through which all our heterosexual relationships are typically viewed ("two's company, three's a crowd") and in light of which all larger circles of intimacy seem almost inconceivable.[4]

3. *No person may participate in more than one marriage at a time or during a lifetime* (unless the previous marriage has been officially dissolved by, normally, one partner's death or successful divorce).

Violation of this principle is, of course, a criminal offence (bigamy) which is punishable by a considerable

---

2. For example, offspring are illegitimate, neither wife nor children are legal heirs, and husband has no right of access or custody should separation occur.

3. "Any kind of conjugal union with more than one person at the same time, whether or not it is by law recognized as a binding form of marriage—is guilty of an indictable offence and is liable to imprisonment for five years" (Cana-

dian Criminal Code, Sec. 257, [1][a][ii]). Part 2 of the same section adds: "Where an accused is charged with an offence under this section, no averment or proof of the method by which the alleged relationship was entered into, agreed to or consented to is necessary in the indictment or upon the trial of the accused, nor is it necessary upon the trial to prove that the persons who are alleged to have entered into the relationship had or intended to have sexual intercourse."

(Here and elsewhere, I draw examples from Canadian criminal law. There is no reason to suspect the Canadian code is eccentric in these instances.)

4. Even the sexual revolutionary Wilhelm Reich seems constrained within the limits of this "binary frame." Thus he says (my emphasis): "Nobody has the right to prohibit his or her partner from entering a temporary or lasting sexual relationship with someone else. He has only the right *either to withdraw or to win the partner back.*" (Wilhelm Reich, *The Sexual Revolution,* trans. by T. P. Wolfe [New York: Farrar, Strauss & Giroux, 1970], p. 28.) The possibility of sexual partners extending their union to include the other loved party as opposed to one partner having either to "win" against this third party (or to "withdraw" altogether) does not seem even to occur to Reich.

term in prison. Of various general regulations of our marriage institution it has experienced the most significant modification: not indeed in principle, but in the extent of flexibility of its "escape hatch" of divorce. The ease with which this escape hatch is opened has increased considerably in the past few years (the grounds for divorce being more permissive than previously) and it is in this regard most of all that the principles of our marriage institution have undergone formal alteration. That is, in plumbing rather than substance.

4. *No married person may engage in any sexual relationship with any person whatever other than the marriage partner.*

Although a consummated sexual act with another person alone constitutes an act of adultery, lesser forms of sexual and erotic relationships[5] may also constitute grounds for divorce (i.e., cruelty) and are generally proscribed as well by informal social convention and taboo. In other words, the fourth and final principle of our marriage institution involves not only a prohibition of sexual intercourse per se outside one's wedlock (this term deserves pause) but a prohibition of all one's erotic relations whatever outside this bond. The penalties for violation here are as various as they are severe, ranging from permanent loss of spouse, children, chattel, and income to job dismissal and social ostracism. In this way, possibly the most compelling natural force towards expanded intimate relations with others[6] is strictly confined

within the narrowest possible circle for (barring delinquency) the whole of adult life. The sheer weight and totality of this restriction is surely one of the great wonders of all historical institutional control.

III

With all established institutions, apologetics for perpetuation are never wanting. Thus it is with our form of monogamous marriage.

Perhaps the most celebrated justification over the years has proceeded from a belief in a Supreme Deity who secretly utters sexual and other commands to privileged human representatives. Almost as well known a line of defence has issued from a conviction, similarly confident, that the need for some social regulation of sexuality demonstrates the need for our specific type of two-person wedlock. Although these have been important justifications in the sense of being very widely supported they are not—having other grounds than reasons—susceptible to treatment here.

If we put aside such arguments, we are left I think with two major claims. The first is that our form of monogamous marriage promotes a profound affection between the partners which is not only of great worth in itself but invaluable as a sanctuary from the pressures of outside society. Since, however, there are no secure grounds whatever for supposing that such "profound affection" is not at least as easily achievable by any number of *other* marriage forms (i.e., forms

---

5. I will be using "sexual" and "erotic" interchangeably throughout the paper.

6. It is worth noting here that: (*a*) man has by nature the most "open" sexual instinct—year-round operativeness and variety of stim-

uli—of all the species (except perhaps the dolphin); and (*b*) it is a principle of human needs in general that maximum satisfaction involves regular variation in the form of the need-object.

which differ in one or more of the four principles), this justification conspicuously fails to perform the task required of it.

The second major claim for the defence is that monogamy provides a specially loving context for child upbringing. However here again there are no grounds at all for concluding that it does so as, or any more, effectively than other possible forms of marriage (the only alternative type of upbringing to which it has apparently been shown to be superior is non-family institutional upbringing, which of course is not relevant to the present discussion). Furthermore, the fact that at least half the span of a normal monogamous marriage *involves no child-upbringing at all* is disastrously overlooked here, as is the reinforcing fact that there is no reference to or mention of the quality of child-upbringing in any of the prescriptions connected with it.

In brief, the second major justification of our particular type of wedlock scents somewhat too strongly of red herring to pursue further.

There is, it seems, little to recommend the view that monogamy specially promotes "profound affection" between the partners or a "loving context" for child-upbringing. Such claims are simply without force. On the other hand, there are several aspects to the logic and operation of the four principles of this institution which suggest that it actually *inhibits* the achievement of these desiderata. Far from uniquely abetting the latter, it militates against them. In these ways:

1. Centralized official control of marriage (which the Church gradually achieved through the mechanism of Canon Law after the Fall of the Roman Empire[7] in one of the greatest seizures of social power in history) necessarily alienates the partners from full responsibility for and freedom in their relationship. "Profound closeness" between the partners—or at least an area of it—is thereby expropriated rather than promoted, and "sanctuary" from the pressures of outside society prohibited rather than fostered.

2. Limitation of the marriage bond to two people necessarily restricts, in perhaps the most unilateral possible way consistent with offspring survival, the number of adult sources of affection, interest, material support and instruction for the young. The "loving context for child-upbringing" is thereby dessicated rather than nourished: providing the structural conditions for such notorious and far-reaching problems as (*a*) sibling rivalry for scarce adult attention,[8] and (*b*) parental oppression through exclusive monopoly of the child's means of life.[9]

3. Formal exclusion of all others from erotic contact with the marriage

---

7. "Roman Law had no power of intervening in the formation of marriages and there was no legal form of marriage. . . . Marriage was a matter of simple private agreement and divorce was a private transaction" (Havelock Ellis, *Studies in the Psychology of Sex* [New York: Random House, 1963], Vol. II, Part 3, p. 429).

8. The dramatic reduction of sibling rivalry through an increased number of adults in the house is a phenomenon which is well known in contemporary domestic communes.

9. One of the few other historical social relationships I can think of in which persons hold thoroughly exclusive monopoly over other persons' means of life is slavery. Thus, as with another's slave, it is a criminal offence "to receive" or "harbour" another's child without "right of possession" (Canadian Criminal Code, Sec. 250).

partner systematically promotes conjugal insecurity, jealousy and alienation by:

    a. Officially underwriting a literally totalitarian expectation of sexual confinement on the part of one's husband or wife: which expectation is, *ceteris paribus*, inevitably more subject to anxiety and disappointment than one less extreme in its demand and/or cultural-juridical backing;[10]

    b. Requiring so complete a sexual isolation of the marriage partners that should one violate the fidelity code the other is left alone and susceptible to a sense of fundamental deprivation and resentment;

    c. Stipulating such a strict restraint of sexual energies that there are habitual violations of the regulation: which violations *qua* violations are frequently if not always attended by (i) willful deception and reciprocal suspicion about the occurrence or quality of the extramarital relationship, (ii) anxiety and fear on both sides of permanent estrangement from partner and family, and/or (iii) overt and covert antagonism over the prohibited act in both offender (who feels "trapped") and offended (who feels "betrayed.")

---

10. Certain cultures, for example, permit extramarital sexuality by married persons with friends, guests, or in-laws with no reported consequences of jealousy. From such evidence, one is led to speculate that the intensity and extent of jealousy at a partner's extramarital sexual involvement is in direct proportion to the severity of the accepted cultural regulations against such involvements. In short such regulations do not prevent jealousy so much as effectively engender it.

The disadvantages of the four principles of monogamous marriage do not, however, end with inhibiting the very effects they are said to promote. There are further shortcomings:

1. The restriction of marriage union to two partners necessarily prevents the strengths of larger groupings. Such advantages as the following are thereby usually ruled out.

    a. The security, range and power of larger socioeconomic units;

    b. The epistemological and emotional substance, variety and scope of more pluralist interactions;

    c. The possibility of extra-domestic freedom founded on more adult providers and up-bringers as well as more broadly based circles of intimacy.

2. The sexual containment and isolation which the four principles together require variously stimulates such social malaises as:

    a. Destructive aggression (which notoriously results from sexual frustration);

    b. Apathy, frustration, and dependence within the marriage bond;

    c. Lack of spontaneity, bad faith and distance in relationships without the marriage bond;

    d. Sexual phantasizing, perversion, fetishism, prostitution and pornography in the adult population as a whole.[11]

Taking such things into consideration, it seems difficult to lend cre-

---

11. It should not be forgotten that at the same time marriage excludes marital partners from sexual contact with others, it necessarily excludes those others from sexual contact with marital partners. Walls face two ways.

dence to the view that the four principles of our form of monogamous marriage constitute a structure beneficial either to the marriage partners themselves or to their offspring (or indeed to anyone else). One is moved to seek for some other ground of the institution, some ground that lurks beneath the reach of our conventional apprehensions.

IV

The ground of our marriage institution, the essential principle that underwrites all four restrictions, is this: *the maintenance by one man or woman of the effective right to exclude indefinitely all others from erotic access to the conjugal partner.*

The first restriction creates, elaborates on, and provides for the enforcement of this right to exclude. And the second, third and fourth restrictions together ensure that the said right to exclude is—respectively—not cooperative, not simultaneously or sequentially distributed, and not permissive of even casual exception.

In other words, the four restrictions of our form of monogamous marriage together constitute a state-regulated, indefinite and exclusive ownership by two individuals of one another's sexual powers. Marriage is simply a form of private property.[12]

That our form of monogamous marriage is when the confusing layers of sanctity, apologetic and taboo are cleared away another species of private property should not surprise us.[13] The history of the institution is so full of suggestive indicators—dowries, inheritance, property alliances, daughter sales (of which women's wedding rings are a carry-over), bride exchanges, legitimacy and illegitimacy—that it is difficult not to see some intimate connections between marital and ownership ties. We are better able still to apprehend the ownership essence of our marriage institution, when in addition we consider:

(a) That until recently almost the only way to secure official dissolution of consummated marriage was to be able to demonstrate violation of one or both partner's sexual ownership (i.e., adultery);

(b) That the imperative of premarital chastity is tantamount to a demand for retrospective sexual ownership by the eventual marriage partner;

(c) That successful sexual involvement with a married person is prosecutable as an expropriation of ownership—"alienation of affections"—which is restituted by cash payment;

---

12. Those aspects of marriage law which seem to fall outside the pale of sexual property holding—for example, provisions for divorce if the husband fails to provide or is convicted of a felony or is an alcoholic—may themselves be seen as simply prescriptive characterizations of the sort of sexual property which the marriage partner must remain to retain satisfactory conjugal status: a kind of permanent warranty of the "good working order" of the sexual possession.

What constitutes the "good working order"

of the conjugal possession is, of course, different in the case of the husband and in the case of the wife: an *asymmetry* within the marriage institution which, I gather, women's liberation movements are anxious to eradicate.

13. I think it is instructive to think of even the nonlegal aspects of marriage, for example, its sentiments as essentially private property structured. Thus the preoccupation of those experiencing conjugal sentiments with expressing how much "my very own," "my precious," the other is: with expressing, that is, how valuable and inviolable the ownership is and will remain.

(d) That the incest taboo is an iron mechanism which protects the conjugal ownership of sexual properties: both the husband's and wife's from the access of affectionate offspring and the offsprings' (who themselves are future marriage partners) from access of siblings and parents;[14]

(e) That the language of the marriage ceremony is the language of exclusive possession ("take," "to have and to hold," "forsaking all others and keeping you only unto him/her," etc.), not to mention the proprietary locutions associated with the marital relationship (e.g., "he's mine," "she belongs to him," "keep to your own husband," "wife stealer," "possessive husband," etc.).

V

Of course, it would be remarkable if marriage in our society was not a relationship akin to private property. In our socioeconomic system we relate to virtually everything of value by individual ownership: by, that is, the effective right to exclude others from the thing concerned.[15] That we do so as well with perhaps the most highly valued thing of all—the sexual partners' sexuality—is only to be expected. Indeed it would probably be an intolerable strain on our entire social structure if we did otherwise.

This line of thought deserves pursuit. The real secret of our form of monogamous marriage is not that it functionally provides for the needs of adults who love one another or the children they give birth to, but that it serves the maintenance of our present social system. It is an institution which is indispensable to the persistence of the capitalist order,[16] in the following ways:

1. A basic principle of current social relations is that some people legally acquire the use of other people's personal powers from which they may exclude other members of society. This system operates in the workplace (owners and hirers of all types contractually acquire for their exclusive use workers' regular labour powers) and in the family (husbands and wives contractually acquire for their exclusive use their partner's sexual properties). A conflict between the structures of these primary relations—as would obtain were there a suspension of the restrictions governing our form of monogamous marriage—might well undermine the systemic coherence of present social intercourse.

2. The fundamental relation between individuals and things which satisfy their needs is, in our present society, that each individual has or

---

14. I think the secret to the long mysterious incest taboo may well be the fact that in all its forms it protects sexual property: not only conjugal (as indicated above) but paternal and tribal as well. This crucial line of thought, however, requires extended separate treatment.

15. Sometimes—as with political patronage, criminal possession, *de facto* privileges and so forth—a *power* to exclude others exists with no corresponding "right" (just as sometimes a right to exclude exists with no corresponding power). Properly speaking, thus, I should here use the phrase "power to exclude," which covers "effective right to exclude" as well as all nonjuridical enablements of this sort.

---

16. It is no doubt indispensable as well—in some form or other—to any private property order. Probably (if we take the history of Western society as our data base) the more thoroughgoing and developed the private property formation is, the more total the sexual ownership prescribed by the marriage institution.

does not have the effective right to exclude other people from the thing in question.[17] A rudimentary need is that for sexual relationship(s). Therefore the object of this need must be related to the one who needs it as owner or not owner (i.e., via marriage or not-marriage, or approximations thereto) if people's present relationship to what they need is to retain—again—systemic coherence.

3. A necessary condition for the continued existence of the present social formation is that its members feel powerful motivation to gain favorable positions in it. But such social ambition is heavily dependent on the preservation of exclusive monogamy in that:

(a) The latter confines the discharge of primordial sexual energies to a single unalterable partner and thus typically compels the said energies to seek alternative outlet, such as business or professional success;[18]

(b) The exclusive marriage necessarily reduces the sexual relationships available to any one person to absolute (nonzero) minimum, a unilateral promotion of sexual shortage which in practice renders hierarchical achievement essential as an economic and "display" means for securing scarce partners.[19]

4. Because the exclusive marriage necessarily and dramatically reduces the possibilities of sexual-love relationships, it thereby promotes the existing economic system by:

(a) Rendering extreme economic self-interest—the motivational basis of the capitalistic process—less vulnerable to altruistic subversion;

(b) Disciplining society's members into the habitual repression of natural impulse required for long-term performance of repetitive and arduous work tasks;

(c) Developing a complex of suppressed sexual desires to which sales techniques may effectively apply in creating those new consumer wants which provide indispensable outlets for ever-increasing capital funds.

5. The present form of marriage is of fundamental importance to:

(a) The continued relative powerlessness of the individual family: which, with larger numbers would constitute a correspondingly increased command of social power;

---

17. Things in unlimited supply—like, presently, oxygen—are not of course related to people in this way.

18. This is, of course, a Freudian or quasi-Freudian claim. "Observation of daily life shows us," says Freud, "that most persons direct a very tangible part of their sexual motive powers to their professional or business activities" (Sigmund Freud, *Dictionary of Psychoanalysis*, ed. by Nandor Fodor and Frank Gaynor [New York: Fawcett Publications, Premier Paperback, 1966], p. 139).

19. It might be argued that exclusive marriage also protects those physically less attractive persons who—in an "open" situation— might be unable to secure any sexual partnership at all. The force of this claim depends, I think, on improperly continuing to posit the very principle of exclusiveness which the "open" situation rules out (e.g., in the latter situation, x might be less attractive to y than z is and yet z not be rejected, any more than at present an intimate friend is rejected who is less talented than another intimate friend).

(b) The continued high demand for homes, commodities and services: which, with the considerable economies of scale that extended unions would permit, would otherwise falter;

(c) The continued strict necessity for adult males to sell their labour power and adult women to remain at home (or vice versa): which strict necessity would diminish as the economic base of the family unit extended;

(d) The continued immense pool of unsatisfied sexual desires and energies in the population at large: without which powerful interests and institutions would lose much of their conventional appeal and force;[20]

(e) The continued profitable involvement of lawyers, priests and state officials in the jurisdictions of marriage and divorce and the myriad official practices and proceedings connected thereto.[21]

---

20. The sexual undercurrents of corporate advertisements, religious systems, racial propaganda and so on are too familiar to dwell on here.

21. It is also possible that exclusive marriage protects the adult-youth power structure in the manner outlined on pp. 53–54.

VI

If our marriage institution is a linchpin of our present social structure, then a breakdown in this institution would seem to indicate a breakdown in our social structure. On the face of it, the marriage institution is breaking down—enormously increased divorce rates, nonmarital sexual relationships, wife-swapping, the Playboy philosophy, and communes. Therefore one might be led by the appearance of things to anticipate a profound alteration in the social system.

But it would be a mistake to underestimate the tenacity of an established order or to overestimate the extent of change in our marriage institution. Increased divorce rates merely indicate the widening of a traditional escape hatch. Nonmarital relationships imitate and culminate in the marital mold. Wife-swapping presupposes ownership, as the phrase suggests. The Playboy philosophy is merely the view that if one has the money one has the right to be titillated, the commercial call to more fully exploit a dynamic sector of capital investment. And communes—the most hopeful phenomenon—almost nowhere offer a *praxis* challenge to private property in sexuality. It may be changing. But history, as the old man puts it, weighs like a nightmare on the brains of the living.

C O M M E N T S ■ Q U E S T I O N S

1. In the institution of marriage, says McMurtry, "possibly the most compelling natural force towards expanded intimate relations with others (that is, sexual desire) is strictly confined within the narrowest possible circle for the whole of adult life. The sheer

weight and totality of this restriction is surely one of the great wonders of all historical institutional control." How would you compare the restrictions that are built into the traditional view of marriage with the restrictions that are built into other traditional roles, such as the role of a clergyman, lawyer, housewife, soldier, college student? Do you believe that human beings are generally better off with many or with few restrictions in their lives? (This is perhaps a somewhat vague question, but still it is worth thinking about since the issue of control versus freedom is one of the most important in life.)

2. One of the alternatives to monogamous marriage that McMurtry favors is "communal marriage"— where several men and several women live together. In your opinion, has McMurtry given adequate consideration to all of the emotional conflicts, insecurities, jealousies, and other problems in this kind of relationship?

3. In regard to bringing up children, there are, says McMurtry, many advantages to be found in larger personal/sexual groupings than those of monogamous marriage. Traditional, "extended families" (which often included grandparents, uncles or aunts, etc.) provide children a close association with several adults in addition to the children's parents. Many social commentators have mourned the decline of extended families for its bad effects upon child rearing. Do you believe that McMurtry describes an acceptable replacement for the extended family?

4. In light of the fact that monogamous marriage is found as much in socialist as in nonsocialist countries, can McMurtry's attempt to link together monogamy and capitalism be defended? That is, is McMurtry correct in saying that monogamous marriage is an objectionable form of private property?

5. According to McMurtry, there is little reason to believe that monogamous marriage promotes a "profound affection" between the partners. Instead, the many restrictions and the exclusiveness of monogamous marriage promote insecurity, alienation, frustration, and aggression between partners. Do you believe that this is likely to be true in most marriages? All marriages? Few marriages? Is it likely to be true for most marriages that fall short of meeting the conditons for an ideal marriage that are dis cussed by Russell? Is it more likely to be true for marriages where the spouses have had sex before marriage? Or no sex before marriage?

6. How would you compare the views of McMurtry to the views of the other authors in this chapter? Must we choose one among them as being the "most correct"? Is it possible to find something in each of the selections that appears to be correct and that could be combined with points from other selections to form a more complete picture of things than is to be found in any one of the selections by itself? Or do you believe that there is at least one of the reading selections that should be rejected altogether?

R E A D I N G S

Atkinson, Ronald. *Sexual Morality.* New York: Harcourt Brace Jovanovich, 1965.

Baker, Robert and Frederick Elliston. *Philosophy and Sex.* Buffalo, N.Y.: Prometheus Books, 1975.

Bertucci, Peter A. *Sex, Love and the Person.* New York: Sheed and Ward, 1965.

Fromm, Erich. *The Art of Loving.* New York: Harper & Row, 1956.

Gosling, J. H. *Marriage and the Love of God.* New York: Sheed and Ward, 1965.

Hunter, J. R. M. *Thinking about Sex and Love.* Toronto: Macmillan, 1980.

Morrison, Eleanor S., and Vera Borosage, eds. *Human Sexuality: Contemporary Perspectives.* 2d ed. Palo Alto, Calif.: Mayfield Publishing Co., Inc., 1977.

Roy, R. *Honest Sex.* New York: New American Library, 1968.

Vannoy, Russell. *Sex Without Love: A Philosophical Exploration.* Buffalo, N.Y.: Prometheus, 1980.

Vetterling-Braggin, Mary, Frederick Elliston, and Jane English, eds. *Feminism and Philosophy.* Totowa, N.J.: Littlefield, Adams and Co., 1977.

Wellman, Carl. *Morals and Ethics.* Glenview, Ill.: Scott, Foresman, and Company, 1975.

Whiteley, C. H., and W. M. Whiteley. *Sex and Morals.* New York: Basic Books, 1967.

People Who Are Close to Us

hat this chapter is about are those *special* obligations that we have to people who are close to us and that are in addition to the obligations that we have to people in general. We have obligations not to steal from our friends or to assault them or to spread slanderous stories about them, but we also obviously have these same obligations to everyone else who is *not* close to us. What is it that is special, from a moral point of view, about being a friend, being a parent or child, being an employee, and so on? These are some of the questions that the present chapter deals with.

Some of the other, and more specific, questions that are dealt with in the present chapter have to do with the legal rights of children. How extensive should such rights be? In recent years children have sometimes sued their parents, arguing that the parents did not provide for their children well enough, for example, in helping them through college. Also in recent years, a lot of attention has been focused on child abuse and neglect. Some laws have been strengthened that give authorities the right to intervene in regard to child-rearing practices that touch upon education, medical treatment, discipline, etc.

Are such laws a good thing, or do they instead threaten the existence of the so-called nuclear family? How important as a social institution is the nuclear family? Is the recent "children's rights movement" a good thing or does it pose a threat to the nuclear family? According to one recent writer, "There is considerable empirical evidence of the ineffectiveness of state intervention into family life."[1] At the same time, the growing evidence for the many different kinds of child abuse and neglect is a great cause for concern.

Two of the reading selections in this chapter have to do with the obligations of parents to children. David J. Rothman and Sheila M. Rothman emphasize children's rights. As they see it, parents and others may have too much power over children unless children's rights are given protection. In contrast, Ferdinand Shoeman emphasizes the value of closeness and intimacy in family relationships. He believes that if too much emphasis is placed on children's rights, then the institution of the family will suffer, since increasing the protection of children's rights will require that the privacy of the family be invaded.

The article by Rothman and Rothman has to do with a 1979 Supreme Court case, *Parham vs. J.L. and J.R.* In this case, the majority of the court in effect ruled against an extension of legal rights to children in regard to the question of whether or not parents should be allowed to choose to have their children committed to a mental hospital. A lower court in the state of Georgia had ruled that such commitments denied the minors due process of law. The Supreme Court overturned this decision. It ruled that due process procedures were not required for the commitment of children. In the paper that is reprinted here, Rothman and Rothman attack the ruling of the Supreme Court in their defense of children's rights.

From one perspective, the issue of children's rights has to do with the *autonomy* of children—that is, the freedom of children to make certain decisions for themselves. The question of how much autonomy a person should be given applies, of course, to adults as well as to children. Everyone agrees that adults should have more autonomy than children. But how much? In the present chapter, some interesting questions regarding the autonomy of adults are raised by Thomas E. Hill, Jr., in the article entitled "Autonomy and Benevolent Lies." A benevolent lie is one that is told with the intention to help someone. Some people believe that a person who is your good friend should be willing to lie to you in certain cases where this is taken to be in your best interest. Also, it is believed that in several other sorts of more or less close relationships, benevolent lies are either morally permitted or are morally required. An example that is mentioned by Hill is the relationship between a doctor and a patient. Hill's own position, which is defended in the paper reprinted here, is that benevolent lying usually is a bad thing because it undermines autonomy.

(It should perhaps be noted that questions about autonomy are discussed elsewhere in this book in connection with quite a number of different issues. For example, Ronald Dworkin, in the article in chapter 8 entitled "Paternalism," discusses the autonomy of the individual versus the paternalistic power of the government to coerce the individual into doing things that are in his or her own best interest. The article in chapter 8 by Robert L. Arrington entitled "Advertising and Behavior Control" deals with possible threats to autonomy from the advertising industry. The issue of autonomy is also relevant to discussions of marriage, abortion and euthanasia, and preferential treatment of minorities and women.)

The general question of the moral nature of friendship is discussed in the paper by Dan Passell included in the present chapter. He argues that there are *no* duties that are peculiar to friendship since, he claims, anything that would be wrong to do to a friend would be wrong to do to anyone else in the same circumstances. If it is wrong to deny help to a friend in need, then it is wrong to deny help to anyone else who has the same need. If the person is a good friend, says Passell, then we will certainly *feel* a stronger obligation to help him or her; but that is all it is, simply a feeling. It is not a moral obligation. If we did not act upon the feeling, then we would not be doing anything morally wrong. The basis for the feeling is the sympathy that friends have for each other, which is an essential part of friendship.

Many philosophers would disagree with Passell's claim that there are no duties that belong to friendship alone. Some of the philosophers who would disagree with Passell would argue that friendship has special duties that are imposed by the *institution* of friendship, and that the institution of friendship is necessary in any society if we are to bring about the greatest good for the greatest number of people. That is, these philosophers would appeal to the Principle of the Common Good: they would say that unless people acknowledge that they have a duty to help their friends in ways that they need not help strangers, friendship will cease to exist or will lose its importance, which would be a bad thing for people generally. Passell, on the other hand, writes as though our duties to help others were in all cases determined by either the Principle of Rights or the Principle of Justice. These principles and the moral obligations that they impose apply to everyone in the same sort of way, regardless of whether the person is a friend or a stranger.

Another possible argument for rejecting Passell's position (in addition to appealing to the Principle of the Common Good) is given by Harry Browne in the selection entitled, "The Unselfishness Trap." Throughout the selection, and indeed throughout the book from which it is taken, Browne appeals to only one moral principle: that of Self-Interest. To Browne, it is obvious that we do have special obligations to our friends since they are in a position to help *us*, which strangers most likely would not be. If someone is a good friend, says Browne, that means that the person has something—help, affection, companionship, and so on—that we want. In turn, we have something that the friend wants. Our friendship is a kind of contract between us for the exchange of values. Therefore, if we don't give special help to our friends, we are letting ourselves down since we are breaking the contract.

The reading selection from Browne has been placed first in the chapter because it is the most general. It raises questions about the basis for *all* moral obligations to people who are close to us.

One of the basic themes of this book is that answering moral questions almost always means finding a balance among the basic and important moral principles. In quite a few of the reading selections you will find that an appeal is being made implicitly or explicitly to one moral principle while other principles are ignored. The reading selection from Browne is a good example of this. In other selections an appeal is being made to two or three principles while the others are ignored. You will need to ask yourself how the proper balance should be achieved. Now, overall in one's moral philosophy of life, no one of the principles should be ignored; but in certain individual situations, it may be correct to place a very strong emphasis on one principle. Is Browne correct to do that in regard to questions about friendship, when he appeals only to the Principle of Self-Interest? Is Passell in his discussion of friendship correct to ignore, as he appears to, the Principle of Self-Interest and the Principle of the Common Good? These are some of the questions that you may find it helpful to consider as you read the selections by Browne and Passell. Similar questions can be posed for the other readings.

Note

1. Natalie Abrams, "Problems in Defining Child Abuse and Neglect," in *Having Children*, ed. Onora O'Neill and William Ruddick (New York: Oxford University Press, 1979), 156.

H A R R Y B R O W N E

The Unselfishness Trap

The Unselfishness Trap is the belief that you must put the happiness of others ahead of your own.

Unselfishness is a very popular ideal, one that's been honored throughout recorded history. Wherever you turn, you find encouragement to put the happiness of others ahead of your own—to do what's best for the world, not for yourself.

If the ideal is sound, there must be something unworthy in seeking to live your life as you want to live it.

So perhaps we should look more closely at the subject—to see if the ideal *is* sound. For if you attempt to be free, we can assume that someone's going to consider that to be selfish.

We saw in chapter 2 that each person always acts in ways he believes will make him feel good or will remove discomfort from his life. Because everyone is different from everyone else, each individual goes about it in his own way.

One man devotes his life to helping the poor. Another one lies and steals. Still another person tries to create better products and services for which he hopes to be paid handsomely. One woman devotes herself to her husband and children. Another one seeks a career as a singer.

In every case, the ultimate motivation has been the same. Each person is doing what *he* believes will assure his happiness. What varies between them is the *means* each has chosen to gain his happiness.

We could divide them into two groups labeled "selfish" and "unselfish," but I don't think that would prove anything. For the thief and the humanitarian each have the same motive—to do what he believes will make him feel good.

In fact, we can't avoid a very significant conclusion: *Everyone is selfish*. Selfishness isn't really an issue, because everyone selfishly seeks his own happiness.

What we need to examine, however, are the means various people choose to achieve their happiness. Unfortunately, some people oversimplify the matter by assuming that there are only two basic means: sacrifice yourself for others or make them sacrifice for you. Happily, there's a third way that can produce better consequences than either of those two.

A Better World?

Let's look first at the ideal of living for the benefit of others. It's often said that it would be a better world if

Harry Browne has written several books on topics concerned with ethics, finance, and investment.

Reprinted with permission of Macmillan Company from *How I Found Freedom in an Unfree World* by Harry Browne. Copyright © 1973 by Harry Browne.

everyone were unselfish. But would it be?

If it were somehow possible for everyone to give up his own happiness, what would be the result? Let's carry it to its logical conclusion and see what we find.

To visualize it, let's imagine that happiness is symbolized by a big red rubber ball. I have the ball in my hands—meaning that I hold the ability to be happy. But since I'm not going to be selfish, I quickly pass the ball to you. I've given up my happiness for you.

What will you do? Since you're not selfish either, you won't keep the ball; you'll quickly pass it on to your next-door neighbor. But he doesn't want to be selfish either, so he passes it to his wife, who likewise gives it to her children.

The children have been taught the virtue of unselfishness, so they pass it to playmates, who pass it to parents, who pass it to neighbors, and on and on and on.

I think we can stop the analogy at this point and ask what's been accomplished by all this effort. Who's better off for these demonstrations of pure unselfishness?

How would it be a better world if everyone acted that way? Whom would we be unselfish for? There would have to be a selfish person who would receive, accept, and enjoy the benefits of our unselfishness for there to be any purpose to it. But that selfish person (the object of our generosity) would be living by lower standards than we do.

For a more practical example, what is achieved by the parent who "sacrifices" himself for his children, who in turn are expected to sacrifice themselves for *their* children, etc.? The unselfishness concept is a merry-go-round that has no ultimate purpose. No one's self-interest is enhanced by the continual relaying of gifts from one person to another to another.

Perhaps most people have never carried the concept of unselfishness to this logical conclusion. If they did, they might reconsider their pleas for an unselfish world.

Negative Choices

But, unfortunately, the pleas continue, and they're a very real part of your life. In seeking your own freedom and happiness, you have to deal with those who tell you that you shouldn't put yourself first. That creates a situation in which you're pressured to act negatively—to put aside your plans and desires in order to avoid the condemnation of others.

As I've said before, one of the characteristics of a free man is that he's usually choosing positively—deciding which of several alternatives would make him the happiest; while the average person, most of the time, is choosing which of two or three alternatives will cause him the least discomfort.

When the reason for your actions is to avoid being called "selfish" you're making a negative decision and thereby restricting the possibilities for your own happiness.

You're in the Unselfishness Trap if you regretfully pay for your aunt's surgery with the money you'd saved for a new car, or if you sadly give up the vacation you'd looked forward to in order to help a sick neighbor.

You're in the trap if you feel you're *required* to give part of your income to the poor, or if you think that your country, community, or family has first claim on your time, energy, or money.

You're in the Unselfishness Trap any time you make negative choices that are designed to avoid being called "selfish."

It isn't that no one else is important. You might have a self-interest in someone's well-being, and giving a gift can be a gratifying expression of the affection you feel for him. But you're in the trap if you do such things in order to appear unselfish.

Helping Others

There *is* an understandable urge to give to those who are important and close to you. However, that leads many people to think that indiscriminate giving is the key to one's own happiness. They say that the way to be happy is to make others happy; get your glow by basking in the glow you've created for someone else.

It's important to identify that as a personal opinion. If someone says that giving is the key to happiness, isn't he saying that's the key to *his* happiness? To assume that his opinions are binding upon you is a common form of the Identity Trap.

I think we can carry the question further, however, and determine how efficient such a policy might be. The suggestion to be a giver presupposes that you're able to judge what will make someone else happy. And experience has taught me to be a bit humble about assuming what makes others happy.

My landlady once brought me a piece of her freshly baked cake because she wanted to do me a favor. Unfortunately, it happened to be a kind of cake that was distasteful to me. I won't try to describe the various ways I tried to get the cake plate back to her without being confronted with a request for my judgment of her cake. It's sufficient to say that her

well-intentioned favor interfered with my own plans.

And now, whenever I'm sure I know what someone else "needs," I remember that incident and back off a little. There's no way that one person can read the mind of another to know all his plans, goals, and tastes.

You may know a great deal about the desires of your intimate friends. But *indiscriminate* gift-giving and favor-doing is usually a waste of resources—or, worse, it can upset the well-laid plans of the receiver.

When you give to someone else, you might provide something he values—but probably not the thing he considers most important. If you expend those resources for *yourself*, you automatically devote them to what you consider to be most important. The time or money you've spent will most likely create more happiness that way.

If your purpose is to make someone happy, you're more apt to succeed if you make yourself the object. You'll never know another person more than a fraction as well as you can know yourself.

Do you want to make someone happy? Go to it—use your talents and your insight and benevolence to bestow riches of happiness upon the one person you understand well enough to do it efficiently—yourself. I guarantee that you'll get more genuine appreciation from yourself than from anyone else.

Give to you.

Support your local self.

Alternatives

As I indicated earlier in this chapter, it's too often assumed that there are only two alternatives: (1) sacrifice your interests for the benefits of others; or (2) make others sacrifice their interests for you. If nothing else were possible, it would indeed be a grim world.

Fortunately, there's more to the world than that. Because desires vary from person to person, it's possible to create exchanges between individuals in which both parties benefit.

For example, if you buy a house, you do so because you'd rather have the house than the money involved. But the seller's desire is different—he'd rather have the money than the house. When the sale is completed, each of you has received something of greater value than what you gave up—otherwise you wouldn't have entered the exchange. Who, then, has had to sacrifice for the other?

In the same way, your daily life is made up of dozens of such exchanges—small and large transactions in which each party gets something he values more than what he gives up. The exchange doesn't have to involve money; you may be spending time, attention, or effort in exchange for something you value.

Mutually beneficial relationships are possible when desires are compatible. Sometimes the desires are the same—like going to a movie together. Sometimes the desires are different—like trading your money for someone's house. In either case, it's the *compatibility* of the desires that makes the exchange possible.

No sacrifice is necessary when desires are compatible. So it makes sense to seek out people with whom you can have mutually beneficial relationships.

Often the "unselfishness" issue arises only because two people with nothing in common are trying to get along together—such as a man who likes bowling and hates opera married to a woman whose tastes are the opposite. If they're to do things

together, one must "sacrifice" his pleasure for the other. So each might try to encourage the other to be "unselfish."

If they were compatible, the issue wouldn't arise because each would be pleasing the other by doing what was in his own self-interest.

An efficiently selfish person *is* sensitive to the needs and desires of others. But he doesn't consider those desires to be demands upon him. Rather, he sees them as *opportunities*—potential exchanges that might be beneficial to him. He identifies desires in others so that he can decide if exchanges with them will help him get what he wants.

He doesn't sacrifice himself for others, nor does he expect others to be sacrificed for him. He takes the third alternative—he finds relationships that are mutually beneficial so that no sacrifice is required.

Please Yourself

Everyone is selfish; everyone is doing what he believes will make himself happier. The recognition of that can take most of the sting out of accusations that you're being "selfish." Why should you feel guilty for seeking your own happiness when that's what everyone else is doing, too?

The demand that you be unselfish can be motivated by any number of reasons: that you'd help create a better world, that you have a moral obligation to be unselfish, that you give up your happiness to the selfishness of someone else, or that the person demanding it has just never thought it out.

Whatever the reason, you're not likely to convince such a person to stop his demands. But it will create much less pressure on you if you realize that it's *his* selfish reason.

And you can eliminate the problem entirely by looking for more compatible companions.

To find constant, profound happiness requires that you be free to seek the gratification of your own desires. It means making positive choices.

If you slip into the Unselfishness Trap, you'll spend a good part of your time making negative choices—trying to avoid the censure of those who tell you not to think of yourself. You won't have time to be free.

If someone finds happiness by doing "good works" for others, let him. That doesn't mean that's the best way for you to find happiness.

And when someone accuses you of being selfish, just remember that he's only upset because you aren't doing what *he* selfishly wants you to do.

C O M M E N T S ▪ Q U E S T I O N S

1. Browne defends psychological egoism, the doctrine that everyone by nature is selfish. Does Browne have, or could he produce, an adequate reply to the arguments against psychological egoism that are discussed in chapter 1?

2. Browne also defends ethical egoism, the doctrine that everyone should put his or her own interests ahead of the inerests of other people. In other words, Browne in effect rejects the claim made in chapter 1 that morality means concern for others as well as respect for oneself. According to Browne, "how your actions affect others is only important insofar as that, in turn, affects you." Does Browne have, or could he produce, an adequate defense of this position?

3. According to Browne, "A universal morality is a code of conduct that is presumed to bring happiness to anyone who uses it. I don't believe there can be such a thing." Is Browne correct? If we assume that Browne *is* correct, what does this tell us about whether or not a "universal morality" should be accepted? Is it necessary for a system of morality to bring happiness or appear likely to bring happiness to a person in order for the system of morality to be acceptable to that person?

Friends

This paper offers a theory of friendship, tests it against some of the facts, and uses it to explain a paradoxical feature of the relation. Briefly, the theory is that the elements are liking, sharing, sympathy, and trust; the facts are that we make comparative judgments about friends; and the paradoxical feature is that there are no special duties to friends. Philosophical interest in the subject comes perhaps from two sources: curiosity about the kind of concept friendship is, and the thought that friendship might have its own special obligations. Prudential interest arises from the conviction that much of the quality of our life lies in the kind of association we establish with other people.

1. Being friends is not merely being acquaintances. Acquaintances know each other. But what more is there to being friends? Siblings grown to adulthood, though long separated, still have memories in common, and from formative years. Fellow countrymen or townsmen have less than this, perhaps only experience of the same objects: having gone to the same school, having watched the same parade, or merely having spoken the same language. Still, something is shared, and enjoyed.

But shared experience doesn't of itself make a friendship. A may trade stories or share memories with B, and enjoy himself, without taking B as his friend. For he may not *like* B all that much. Well, then, is liking each other sufficient? Not by itself. A and B may like each other and not be friends. I like the Dean; let us suppose he likes me. But we are not good friends; we don't share or seek to share experiences with each other. Still, though neither is sufficient, liking and sharing do seem to be necessary conditions of friendship.

Must the liking be mutual? Suppose, for instance, that A likes B, but B doesn't like A in return. That is not friendship; not even if A thinks it is. Of course, if each thinks of the other as his friend, then that is usually enough reason to say that they are friends. But the connection is not a necessary one. For there is at least the logical possibility of two people thinking that they are friends but being mistaken.

Preliminarily then, what we have is that for two people to be friends they must (a) like each other and (b) share experiences together. Are these conditions jointly sufficient? Perhaps. But isn't there something further, a matter

Dan Passell is an associate professor of philosophy at Portland State University. In addition to the article which is reprinted here, he has written papers on questions regarding sense and meaning.

The Journal of Value Inquiry, Vol. 14, No. 1 (1980) pp. 1–6. Reprinted by permission of the publisher.

of warmth or hitting-it-off, a pull toward intimacy that marks the difference between mere acquaintances and friends? Let us consider.

When you seek a companion for an outing or a game, when you desire someone to talk things over with, when you are in trouble, you call upon a friend. He understands you. With him you can be yourself. Moreover, there is a comfort in the feeling that you are important to him; that your well-being makes a difference. And when he fails, there is the corresponding letdown. Suppose, for example, that you have confided in your friend that you are infatuated with a certain woman, and he proceeds to bandy the information about in company at large. That *is* a breach of confidence. You will lose trust in him and have to draw back. Or, suppose that when you call him to help you through an emotional crisis, he promises but doesn't show. There is also the other side to this. Suppose that someone whom you know rather well has become pregnant and the man has taken off. She cannot decide whether to have the baby or get an abortion. When you hear of it, a feeling of sympathy arises in you. You would be disappointed not to be consulted or asked to help.

Indeed, sympathetic feelings are not confined to friends. We are so constituted that we cannot witness suffering, or joy, without being affected. If the sufferer is an animal or a stranger it may take a more extreme or obvious circumstance to affect us very deeply. But where the sufferer is our friend, our sympathy, sometimes even our empathy, arises naturally. We almost do his feeling for him. I submit that sympathy, in both its giving and receiving aspects, is a third element in friendship. Trust, which so often goes along with it, is the fourth.

In sum, to be friends, people must not only like each other and enjoy experiences together, but they must also have feelings of sympathy for, and trust in each other as well. This is our theory.

2. Let us now test and amplify it in the light of a certain kind of fact. We speak of good friends, of one person being a better friend than another, even, sometimes, of a best friend. Of course, some of this is mere idiom: "My good friend," for example, is semi-formal, a part of the rhetoric of public address rather than a phrase referring to a good friend. Furthermore while we apply the adjectives 'good,' 'better,' 'best' to friends, it is possible while having friends to have no best friend, and of two friends not to be able to say which is the better. Often we use the comparative 'better' more comfortably where the difference is obvious; perhaps with most assurance where the difference is hyperbolic, as we might say of A, who is our friend, that he is a better friend than B, whom we can't stand.

But still, we do sometimes make judgments of comparison about friends, and, at least, up to the silliest or grossest of them, the judgments are meaningful. How then do we decide which of two people is our better friend? Consider the following two tales:

1. I come to *think* of A as a better friend than B when A goes out of his way to lend me a hand in some emergency in which B has failed me. I am disappointed by B's behavior and pleased with A's. From the experience I judge that A is the

sort of person I can count on, and B is not. I find that A is a better friend than B.

2. I come to *think* of A as a better friend than B when I find myself drawn to A more than to B. Maybe it is that A sometimes looks right at me instead of over my shoulder; or that his way of telling a story arouses my interest; or that his laugh inspires mine; or that my enthusiasm sparks his. Or maybe there are things in B's behavior that shut me down: his prying, his uncouthness, his talking with spittle in his throat, his being overly competitive, or not competitive enough. At any rate, it is this "hitting if off better" with the one than the other that is the basis of my judging A to be the better friend.

From the first tale the feature of how much I can count on or trust my two friends emerges as the ground of comparison between them. From the second, the feature of how much rapport or camaraderie I establish with each, appears as the ground of comparison. (I take liking, sharing and sympathy to be equivalent to rapport or camaraderie.)

But if this is the case, a contradiction can arise. For, I might trust A more than B, and at the same time have established better rapport with B than A. Then apparently each would be a better friend than the other. And that, surely, is impossible.

Here is the dilemma. Judgments about which person is the better friend imply a ground of comparison. That is, they imply that there must be more of some *one* kind of quantitative entity—liking, sharing, sympathy, trust, or whatever—with respect to

the friend who is better liked than with respect to the other. But, on the other hand, there seems in fact to be not just one but *several* such features associated with friendship.

Two possibilities arise. First, we have missed the key ground by which comparisons of friends are made. Or, second, we have missed the point with our essence-type definition, friendship being perhaps a disjunctive or family resemblance concept about which none or few inferences of a strictly logical sort can be drawn from comparisons.

In fact, I think, the truth is this. Although we do make judgments about which of two people is our better friend, we often are reluctant to do so. In the latter case there is a feeling that such a judgment could not help but be a distortion. I suggest that reluctance arises in those cases where the basis of the one friendship is different from that of the other. In the other cases, in which the comparison judgment is willingly made, there is a common ground. Sometimes the common ground is narrow, as, for example, when I decide one person is a better friend than another by determining that I like him more. But usually the ground is wide. For although it is possible to have sympathy with a person but not to trust him, usually the elements of friendship go along together, and in something like equal measure. He whom I trust, I also have sympathy for. Furthermore, where I have such feelings for and relations with another, he usually has them for and with me. Indeed, it is something of a shock to find otherwise.

So, there is a logic, of a sort, of *comparative* relations of friends. However, it is a logic of probability not of necessity. Thus, if A is a better friend of mine than B, I *probably* like A more, am more sympathetic to him, share more experiences with him than with B, trust him more, and vice versa. Where the facts are appreciably otherwise, they carry away with them the possibility of a judgment as to which is the better friend. This probable nature of comparative judgments about friends is in contrast to the necessary character of assertoric judgments about friends. Thus, if I don't like A, or have never shared experiences or confidences with him, or have never felt sympathy for him nor desired it from him, or don't trust him, I could not properly be said to be his friend.

3. As we have made it out, there are no rules or practices implied in friendship. Friendship is not an institution. From this, non-institutional, character derives the answer to the question, "Are there duties peculiar to friendship?" That answer is that there are none. Those of what are called duties to friends which really are duties, are obligations that we would owe to anyone in the circumstances.

There are apparent counterexamples, however. For example, if my friend lands a job in town, I would appear to have an obligation if he asks me, to lodge and feed him until he gets established. Yet, I have no such obligation toward a stranger. When I take a stranger in, it is more of a gift to him than a duty. Here then it seems, is a duty to a friend which would not be a duty to one who is not a friend.

I shall try to explain away such apparent duties as arising from *feelings* of obligation which are not necessarily connected to real obligations. When you agree to go on a hike with your friend, you expect to enjoy the scenery, the clean air, and each other's company. The latter will require your responding to his remarks and perhaps telling a few stories of your own. But now, see how these involve their 'little obligations.' Suppose, for instance, that though you agree to hike, you feel morose and, once on the trail, become silent. Haven't you let your friend down? Or suppose it is a game of chess. At a critical stage he ponders for a full twenty minutes before he makes his move. You respond with a superficial glance and an impulsive threat which leaves a bishop *en prise*. Such behavior might well ruin an evening.

The point of the examples is that what we feel as obligations to friends take their root in the activities of shared experiences. Whether it be hiking, where you produce nothing much more than 'good vibes'; or chess, where, as opponents, you produce a game; or bridge, where, as partners and against opponents you indulge in a still more complicated social relationship, the activities impose their 'duties.' And, although we may not honor the obligation to play seriously with the label 'obligation,' where both players have been serious and the game has been good, the situation squares in many respects with those that get the title. The excuse "It's just a game" can be quite lame. It would hardly restore your friend's trust in you.

I suppose that the kind of thing that goes on here is this. You know how wrapped up you yourself get when you take a game seriously— what a disappointment it is when your partner lets you down. You find it natural to project your own feelings onto him should the tables be turned. As you don't want him to spoil your fun, you feel, and sometimes you even know, that he wouldn't want you to spoil his. More than this, you might wonder if the incident wouldn't cause him to draw back from you; to find it more difficult to devote himself wholeheartedly to activities with you, much as you might be, should the situation be reversed, with him.

Compare these with the 'recognized' duties of friendship. The latter do show one further characteristic. They are not an intimate aspect of any shared experience. The activities of friendship are things you do *with* your friends; the 'duties' involve things you do *for* them. The two are not entirely the same. For example, it may be my duty to care for a sick friend; or to vouch for him on his loan application. Perhaps it is this separation from the ordinary activities of friendship which prods us to recognize these as obligations.

Whatever the truth here, my claim is that the relatively explicit duties which we feel we owe to friends grow out of sympathetic feelings we have for our friends. For it is because of these sympathetic feelings for our friends, especially unhappiness over their unhappiness, that we can come to *feel* something like obligation toward them.

The fact is, however, that this is only an account of the feeling, while the issue is not the feeling but the thing. And with respect to that, though there are obligations, there are no special obligations to friends.

Consider the possibilities. Could the obligation consist of the feeling? Clearly not. A person may be obligated and not feel it. And he may feel obligated without being obligated. For if the feeling constituted the obligation, what might be obligatory to one person might not necessarily be obligatory to another. And this is just false. Objective circumstances determine obligations. Take some typical, clear cases. You either do or do not owe your parents respect. You either did or did not borrow the money, and therefore, other things being equal, you either are or are not obligated to pay it back. Secondly, if the feelings were definitive, there could be no false feelings. The fact is, however, that there are people overburdened with feelings of obligation who are demented in that respect. But then their feelings are misplaced, an impossibility if the feelings constituted the obligation.

But let me argue the case against duties to friends in a more general way. There seem to be two subcases. First, there is the one in which someone who has been a friend, and to whom you owe a duty, becomes no longer a friend. Second, there is the case in which someone not a friend, to whom you owe no duty, becomes a friend.

Suppose someone who has been your friend presents himself at your doorstep in circumstances of dire need. And, just for the sake of the present argument, assume that you discover that you no longer like him, wish to be with him, or have sympathy for or trust in him; that is, you discover that he no longer is your friend. Now, suppose further that you did have a duty to him as a friend. Would that no longer be a duty, since he no longer is your friend? Hardly.

Let me try to indicate why. Duties can be of two sorts. First, they can be, roughly, contractual. Typically this is within an institution, as in promising (duty—keeping the promise), asserting (duty—telling the truth), incurring debts (duty—repaying). Second, the duties can be noncontractual.

Typically, these belong to no particular institution, unless humanity be an institution. Examples are non-maleficence, relief of distress. But now, friendship is not institutional in character, for it has no essential rules or procedures. And, non-institutional duties are all of them wider in scope than friendship. For instance, it is not only our *friend*'s (severe) distress that we have a duty to relieve (where we can), but anyone's.

The other possibility, the change from non-friend to friend, presents an equally weak case for the thesis that there are special duties to friends. Suppose a situation similar to that described above, except that this time the person on the doorstep is an apparent stranger with a Roman nose and dark glasses. Your observation and his pleading prove his need; but, let us say to make the case, there is no obligation on you to meet that need. Suddenly he removes his disguise of false nose and glasses to reveal himself as your friend. The question is: has he in the process also revealed to you an obligation to meet his need? Hardly.

But perhaps our contention is mistaken because we have chosen the wrong instances. For if there are any special duties to friends they would very likely derive from special features of the friendship relation rather than as ordinary duties do.

Suppose, to try a more promising example, that because you invariably feel dizzy and out of breath after climbing stairs, you arrange a medical examination. At its conclusion the doctor tells you that your fears have a real basis; you have a serious heart condition. Nonplussed by the bad news, you wonder whether to tell your friend. You know that he would want to hear; even that he would be hurt not to be told. At the same time your fear and anguish are too intense for you to bear telling anyone. The question is, do you have an obligation to tell him anyhow. I think that the answer is simply, no. You are free to tell him or not. Your friend has no right to be told if you do not choose to tell him.

The cases, I believe, are conclusive. There are no special duties to friends.

In this paper I have tried to say what friendship is, and to probe possible connections between friendship and moral obligations. I have not tried to examine the role of friendship in life.

C O M M E N T S ■ Q U E S T I O N S

1. According to Passell, *contractual* duties, such as keeping contracts and paying debts, are owed regardless of friendship. However, would it be possible to argue that two people who are good friends have made an *implicit* contract between themselves to help each other in circumstances when they would not be obligated to help strangers? Are there any examples of this?
2. According to Passell, *noncontractual* duties, such as relieving a person's distress, are likewise owed to anyone regardless of whether or not the person is or was a friend.

However, if two people equally need help that we can give to them and only one of them is a friend—but we cannot help both of them—do we not have an obliga-

tion to give our help to the friend and not the other person?

3. Is Passell's description of the basis for friendship complete?

D A V I D   J.   R O T H M A N   A N D   S H E I L A   M.   R O T H M A N

The Conflict over Children's Rights

An Historical Perspective

To historians of the family, the conflict between the Court majority in *Parham* [A Supreme Court case that ruled in effect *against* giving rights to children and in favor of giving power to parents and institutions to make decisions on behalf of children.] and the proponents of children's rights is an open invitation to use history to inform social policy. Over the past two decades, the family has been the subject of exciting and innovative research and some of the knowledge uncovered has direct relevance to the premises that divide the Court from the children's rights movement.

There is no doubt that the Court's perspective on the family was the prevalent view for most of the nineteenth century and well into the twentieth. Through this period, the notion that conflict was intrinsic to family relationships was rejected out of hand.

Yet, if one moves back in time, the assumptions of the children's rights movement become more familiar. Seventeenth- and eighteenth-century commentators on the family and, more important, actual practices within the family reveal a distinct affinity for analysis that has more to do with power than with sentiment. Take the debates on the role of the state between John Locke and his opponents in which analogies to

David J. Rothman is Bernard Schoenberg Professor of Social Medicine at the Columbia College of Physicians and Surgeons and Director of its Center for the Study of Society and Medicine. His books include The Discovery of the Asylum, Doing Good: The Limits of Benevolence, *and* Social History and Social Policy. *Sheila M. Rothman is Senior Research Associate, Center for Policy Research, and the author of* Woman's Proper Place.

From *The Hastings Center Report, June 1980.* © Institute of Society, Ethics and the Life Sciences, 360 Broadway, Hastings-on-Hudson, N.Y. 10706. Reprinted by permission of the author and publisher.

family government figured prominently. If one reviews the arguments not for constitutional principles but for insights into the family, it is apparent that everyone appreciated the prominence that the exercise of power assumed in father-son, husband-wife relations.

Even more to the point, as Philip Grevin has so ably demonstrated in *Four Generations*, a study of colonial Andover, Massachusetts, an acute tension existed between the father who was holding onto his land and the son who was waiting for his inheritance. This tension did not surface in raw fashion, in sons writing letters or diary entries looking to their fathers' rapid demise. But it did emerge in not very subtle form in the composition of family wills. These seventeenth- and eighteenth-century documents set down in exquisite detail the widow's entitlements. The wills carefully instructed the heirs that the mother was to keep her large bed in the master bedroom in the main house; she was not to be denied access through the front door. In stipulation upon stipulation, the son was commanded to accommodate himself to the mother's presence—and the nature of the accommodation was spelled out in such precise terms that it is unmistakable that fathers recognized and acted upon a sense that power, rather than "natural affection," was intrinsic to family life. Fathers did not entrust the best interests of the widow to the good sentiments of the son. In other words, an assumption of identity of interests between parent and child is a far more modern concept than casual observers of the family appreciate.

It is not difficult to date the origins of the more sentimental idea. In the opening decades of the nineteenth century, a "cult of domesticity," or a doctrine of "virtuous womanhood" swept through Jacksonian America. Briefly put, these concepts posited that the mother would predictably act in the best interest of the child—both for reasons of nature (it was her instinct to do so, part of her innate character as a woman), and for reasons of social reality (there was no other competing interest in her life). Prescriptions for proper womanhood instructed women that they belonged at home; and within the home, they were to give primary loyalty to their children, not their husband. There is good reason to believe that these principles were followed in practice, at least among the middle classes. Married women (some immigrants aside) were not employed outside the home; and from what we suspect of sexual practices, married women spent much more time in the nursery than in the bedroom. Contraceptive devices, which might have freed women to enjoy sexual relations without fear of pregnancy, were not only crude but, in the popular mind, were understood to be the prostitute's tools. Abortion was obviously the cardinal sin, the clearest violation of the principles of motherhood. Under such circumstances, a social definition of the mother-child relationship as affectionate, emotive, and without conflict seemed appropriate.

The Women's Movement

Although concepts and practices affecting the mother-child relationship were not static over 150 years, still the belief that mothers had no real interest apart from the child persisted right down to the 1960s. To be sure, in the 1920s women more comfortably assumed the role of wife (with all the sexual implications intended), but greater attention to the husband did not signal a demise in her attention to the child or social concern for the child's welfare. As late as 1963, in *The Feminine Mystique* Betty Friedan assured her readers that women entering the work force would become better mothers and wives. The earliest feminist tracts were by no means adversarial in tone or in content to the child or family.

This posture, however, could not and did not persist. The women's rights movement soon adopted a much more critical position on the family, setting off the rights of women against the demands of husband or child. Once women began proclaiming their independence from the role of mother (and in all sorts of ways—from pursuing careers to limiting the number of children—acting on it too), it became apparent to many observers that the identity of interest between mother and child was no longer operative. In this sense, the children's rights movement gathered added strength as an antidote to the women's rights movement. If women were determined to pursue their own interests, whatever they might be, then who would pursue the best interests of the child?

The rhetoric of the women's rights movement was not explicitly anti-child but its silence was no less revealing than a diatribe. Even the most thoughtful feminist literature generally refused to analyze the implications of the movement for the child, on the altogether understandable grounds that if women were going to pursue their own destinies, why should they, and not men, have sole responsibility for child care? Aside from a few bland and over-general phrases to the effect that child-raising should be shared by father and mother or that the state, through day care, should assume greater responsibility, little attention went to children. Second-rate, pop literature was also silent. Nena and George O'Neill advocated *Open Marriage*, revealing to the husband that his wife of today was unlikely to be his wife of tomorrow. They did not address what open marriage might mean to children. The O'Neills were not prepared, at least openly, to tell children that their mother of today might well not be their mother of tomorrow. By the same token, Gail Sheehy's *Passages* readies readers for their forthcoming divorce. Since the male at forty wants to settle down and his wife wants to climb mountains, divorce is well-nigh inevitable. But Sheehy has nothing to say on what to do with the children when his plateaus and her peaks are not compatible.

The one issue that probably did more to symbolize the passing of the older ideology and the triumph of the new was abortion. Morality and rights aside, the legalization of what was once the mother's cardinal sin could not help but symbolize just how far the post-1960 generation had moved from inherited doctrines. If one could now posit that a woman had rights over a fetus, how maintain the view that mother and child shared a harmony of interests? When the feminist movement so strongly advocated abortion and so many women were prepared to use the procedure, the nineteenth-century sense of a natural link between woman's instincts and a child's best interests disappeared.

It would not be useful to belabor the conflict between children's rights and women's rights because in this post-1960 society adversarial relationships are overdetermined. To see conflict where no one perceived it before has become the trademark of our times. Anyone who now promises to act in the best interest of another would have enormous difficulty in sustaining the position. The list of those whose claims would no longer be accepted includes psychiatrists, wardens, deans, teachers, social workers, husbands, university presidents, and research scientists.

Liberty Rights & Claim Rights

However pervasive the adversarial posture is in American society today, its extension to children and the family creates deep unease, not only for political and social reasons, but for conceptual ones as well. Some contemporary philosophers, such as William Ruddick, writing in *Having Children: Philosophical and Legal Reflections on Parenthood*, have attempted to distinguish between rights of two sorts: liberty rights (the freedom to, a right against the state, a right not to be interfered with), and claim rights (entitlements to, positive obligations that the state must fulfill). This analysis contends that children do not have liberty rights but they possess claim rights—and thus the argument seems to fall within the rights camp, albeit in terms of entitlements rather than freedoms. But there is a certain sleight-of-hand quality to this distinction; to speak of claims as rights muddies the issue.

Historically, the two positions have been quite separate—indeed, the movement for one preceded the movement for the other. It was Progressives who were most determined to satisfy children's claims. Reformers in the period 1900–1920 (whose ideology prevailed through the 1950s) fashioned numerous programs to meet children's needs; they estab-

lished special privileges and protections, from juvenile courts to restrictive child labor laws. On the other hand, reformers in the 1960s and 1970s looked to enhance children's liberties, to give them the prerogatives that normally came with adulthood.

The chronological distinction here, with liberty rights succeeding claim rights as the goal of reform effort, points to something more significant—the conflict between claims and liberties. Philosophers who would lump both categories within a rights framework minimize the tension between the two positions, as though claims and freedoms may co-exist, as though claims can be satisfied without penalty to freedoms. But such a view is altogether misleading, if not conceptually then certainly empirically. Claims have typically been satisfied at the expense of rights. Programs designed to advance the entitlement of children are not neutral on the question of liberties but negative, depriving of liberties. To historians it is apparent that efforts to satisfy the needs of children have led to a stark disregard for their liberties. Even more, when one turns to the fate of programs that advanced claims over liberties, the results turn out to be disastrous.

The juvenile court is the best-known example of a program that attempted to meet claims and so sacrificed rights. Seemingly it would do good for children, fulfilling their entitlements to special treatment. But it would do good, not by giving children all the rights of adults and then adding new measures to satisfy claims. Instead, it stripped children of adult rights and only then attempted to meet claims. The outcome of all of this, to understate the evidence, was disappointing. Juvenile court proceedings generate a mischief of their own. For example, the efforts to implement alternatives to incarceration, such as juvenile probation, created supplements to incarceration. The same number of children went off to grossly inadequate "training schools." The difference was that probation allowed the state to exercise added authority over a greater number of children, those who before would have had their cases dismissed. The relaxed rules of procedure within the juvenile court facilitated decisions. At the least, children treated as adults would have the protections of a jury trial or an attorney.

The Family or the State?

The changing character of family life and the results of past practices designed to meet children's needs substantiates many of the premises of children's rights advocates. A sensitivity to the historical record creates a distinct bias in favor of an analysis of the family that gives precedence to power as against the "natural affection" attitude expressed by the Court in *Parham*. Still, given the difficulties that pervade all efforts to construct a nonmischievous social policy toward children, it is best to frame principles of limited scope and applicability.

We would *begin* an analysis of specific issues in children's rights with an inclination to favor the child's side, to enlarge the autonomy of the child to decide matters of life-choice and style. On the basis of the historical record, we share a preference for expanding the prerogatives of the child. But that point is no sooner made than a series of qualifications must intrude.

First, it does not take very long to raise a series of decisions that ought not to be left to a child. Irreversible surgical procedures, such as steriliza-

tion, represent such a category. Second, one must be aware of the distinction between granting children autonomy to make their own decisions and appointing surrogates for them—and it is by no means obvious that lawyers will make better decisions for children than their parents will. Furthermore, the burden of parenting is already so heavy that one might well be reluctant to invent new forms of discouragement. With a national birth rate that is below the replacement figure, couples ought not have to think of their offspring as potential opponents in a lawsuit. There is more than a touch of truth in the recent *New Yorker* cartoon that had father turning incredulously to son at dinner table to ask: "You mean if I make you drink your milk, you'll sue me?"

The primary consideration that must counterbalance the elevation of children's rights is that enhancing the power of the child against the parent inevitably enhances the power of the state against the family. To draw out the practical implications of children's rights makes evident that the child's autonomy will typically be realized through the intervention of the state, through the judge or the agency moving against the parent. As concerned as we may be about the parent's potential abuse of power, we are even more concerned about the state's potential abuse of power. Any one parent can only do mischief on a small scale. The state can do harm on a large scale. This difficulty does not occur when the right of the child is exercised against the state itself, as in the case of the expression of students' rights. Then, the child, perhaps in alliance with the parent, moves directly against the state, reducing the potential for unintended consequences. But asserting the rights of children over the parent does break down the privacy of the family before the intrusions of the state—which is hardly the purpose of the children's rights movement.

Thus, we come to a competing, really overriding consideration: where a family is intact and functioning, it would be inappropriate to introduce procedures or parties to coerce the parents. As long as the parent is fulfilling his or her responsibilities in lawful fashion (so neglect or abuse is not at issue), the rights of the child ought not to be established through the exercise of state power. Yes, parents may not act consistently in the best interest of the child. Still, it is impossible to locate an actor or identify a process that will do the job better.

However, as soon as parents begin to loosen their responsibility in child care, as soon as the wall around the family shows signs of crumbling, then it becomes vital to expand children's rights, even at the risk of enlarging state authority. At the first evidence of a break in family insularity, one should abandon notions of natural family affection and scrutinize the matter from the perspective of power. So in custody battles or in foster care decisions, children should have at their disposal the full protection of the law, with all due process protections, including the right to independent counsel. Once parents have relaxed their control, the balance in decision-making should shift dramatically to the side of rights.

The *Parham* case demonstrates both the significance and propriety of this principle. In the first instance, it is altogether invalid that the state should enjoy the same rights as parents in commitment. Just as the child, without danger to the integrity of the family, can express rights against schools, so too it ought to be able to express rights against an institution. The Court's decision to allow the state to commit its ward to the institution as a voluntary patient becomes a travesty of principle. So, too, a parent committing a child is clearly loosening control over the child, calling upon the state to assume his or her tasks. In this instance, the expansion of the right of the child against the parent does not present the same difficulties. The state is already deeply involved in the family, and so the child rightfully should enjoy all due process protections, including the right to counsel. And even the most adversarial commitment contest carries little cost. At the worst, the parent has been reminded of just how drastic a step commitment is.

Moreover, allowing the child independent counsel in such a case as *Parham* might well have expanded the rights of the child without undercutting parental authority. The institutional psychiatrists were prepared to discharge both J.L. and J.R. but could find no place other than the hospital's wards for the delivery of treatment. At an adversarial hearing, the focus need not have been the rights of the parent versus the rights of the child, but the right of the child to receive services in a setting that would maximize his options and aid his future development. The child's advocate, arguing the case from this perspective, might well have been able to persuade the court to compel the state of Georgia to set up the services that were essential. The parents in the case of J.L. were either unable or unwilling to fight to gain such community facilities; the state, as the ward of J.R., was not about to protest against itself. The Supreme Court brushed over these matters, not examining in any detail the service delivery system in Georgia; it simply proclaimed that the state had a clear interest in reducing the use of costly mental hospital stays. But either through ignorance or naiveté, the court paid no attention to the reality of funding reimbursements, to the fact that because of federal money and requirements, the state might actually find it more convenient to keep mentally ill persons in large, hospital-like facilities than to create community programs. It is these types of considerations that an advocate for the child might have raised—in this way securing the rights of the child against the state.

Such an orientation to children's rights opens up some interesting questions, and while we will not pursue them here, the questions appear to be the right ones. Should a child about to undergo a life-threatening operation have the right to independent counsel? Reasons of administra-tion alone make it difficult to think of extending the issue to non-life threatening procedures—but what about the case of open heart surgery? If one says, "no," is it because surgeons are more trustworthy than institutional psychiatrists? Similarly, parental decisions on education are well within the proper framework of their authority. But what is the difference between a first-rate private mental hospital and a third-rate military school? Ought the runaway from a military school have some of the rights of the child about to be institutionalized? This may not be a bad idea, yet how far can one pursue this line without fear of excessive state interference?

Questions such as these are significant because they ask how deeply an adversarial framework can be imposed upon parent-child relations. Rather than subverting or distorting the issues, as the Court did in *Parham*, it is time that we tested the outer limits of a power-rights model.

C O M M E N T S ■ Q U E S T I O N S

1. The traditional idea that parents can be fully trusted to act in the best interests of their children is in conflict with the more recent movement to give children rights against their parents, and also against professionals such as psychiatrists who may take on the role of parents. In the article, do the authors achieve a proper balance among the following: the needs of children, the rights of parents, and the well-being of society?

2. At the present time, according to the Rothmans, because of the women's rights movement and other factors, we have clearly lost the "nineteenth-century sense of a natural link between woman's instinct and a child's best interests." Overall, in what ways has the women's rights movement changed the family's relation to children?

3. In applying the Principle of Justice, we must determine who has the greatest need. In your opinion, are

children the most needy group in America at the present time? If they are not, what group is most needy?

4. In applying the Principle of the Common Good, it would be helpful if we could determine which of our institutions is the most important for the well-being of society. Is the traditional nuclear family the most important institution? Why or why not?

5. Do you believe that the following quotation from the article is correct: "To see conflict where no one perceived it before has become the trademark of our times."

F E R D I N A N D   S C H O E M A N

Rights of Children, Rights of Parents, and the Moral Basis of the Family

P hilosophers debate whether children, especially infants, are the kinds of beings who can have moral rights; whether rights talk in general has any point unless the being to whom rights are ascribed is in a position to exercise choice (which infants are not); and whether ascribing some rights to beings commits us to ascribing others (i.e., must one have a whole packet of general rights or none at all, or may one ascribe certain rights to one kind of being and other rights to other kinds of beings?).[1] Not only have

one from undue interference by the state and from the harmful acts of others; and (2) legal rights that permit persons to make choices which have significant long-term consequences—choices which seem to require mature capacities. These latter rights, called 'choice rights,' are not, Hafen argues, appropriately ascribed to children. Consequently, children's rights include the right to be protected from their own immaturity. Arguing to a similar effect, Jeffrey Murphy has distinguished between 'autonomy rights' and 'social contract rights.' While the role of autonomy rights is to mark out the special kind of treatment which is appropriate toward autonomous rational per-

Ferdinand Schoeman is an associate professor of philosophy at the University of South Carolina. He has published widely in the areas of the philosophy of criminal justice, the philosophy of law, social and political philosophy, and ethics.

1. It is perhaps worth mentioning two related conceptual proposals for thinking about rights of children in response to the worries just indicated. First of all, Bruce Hafen has suggested that we distinguish between two kinds of legal rights: (1) legal rights which protect

Ferdinand Schoeman, "Rights of Children, Rights of Parents, and the Moral Basis of the Family," in *Ethics*, vol. 91 (Oct. 1980), 6–13. Copyright © 1980 by the University of Chicago. Reprinted by permission of the author and publisher.

many of these abstract philosophical issues about rights been argued inconclusively, but for the most part we can do without talk about children's rights and can express ourselves instead in terms of the needs and welfare of (small) children and the duties of their parents. I shall regard it as given that parents have a duty to protect their children from abuse and neglect, both physical and emotional, recognizing that what should count as

abuse or neglect for legal purposes is difficult to determine and may even change from context to context.[2] Also I shall assume that, if a parent or guardian fails to promote the child's interest at some threshold level of adequacy, a form of intervention, ranging from counseling to imprisonment of the parent as well as loss of parental rights to the child, may be legitimate.

There is a different and more practical reason for hesitating to stress the rights of infants vis-à-vis their parents. We typically pay attention to the rights of individuals in order to stress their moral independence—the fact that one individual constitutes a limit on what others, whether well intentioned or not, may legitimately do. In other words, the language of rights typically helps us to sharpen our appreciation of the moral boundaries which separate people, emphasizing the appropriateness of seeing other persons as independent and autonomous agents. While such emphasis constitutes an important point when it comes to structuring relationships between older children and their parents, it may obscure the real point of moral criticism intended in the case of parent-infant relationships. When we are tempted to admonish parents for morally failing in their relationship to their young children, it is presumably and usually because we find them not furnishing the love, attention, and

---

sons whose choices are to be respected, the role of social contract rights is to guarantee legally the satisfaction of certain moral claims—ones rational agents under a veil of ignorance would find morally reasonable to insure. The child's right to paternalistic treatment, argues Murphy, loses its sense of paradox when understood as a social contract right (see Bruce Hafen, "Children's Liberation and the New Egalitarianism: Some Reservations about Abandoning Youth to Their 'Rights,'" *Brigham Young University Law Review* 1976 [1976]:605–58, esp. pp. 644–70; 644–70; and Jeffrey Murphy, "Rights and Borderline Cases," *Arizona Law Review* 19[1977]: 228–41). For the debate on the general nature of rights and the grounds for the meaningful ascription of rights, see H. L. A. Hart, "Are There Any Natural Rights?" *Philosophical Review* 64 (1955): 175–91; David Lyons, "Rights, Claimants, and Beneficiaries," *American Philosophical Quarterly* (1969): 173–85; Joel Feinberg, "Duties, Rights, and Claims," *American Philosophical Quarterly* 3 (1966): 137–44, "The Nature and Value of Rights," *Journal of Value Inquiry* 4 (1971): 263–77, and "The Rights of Animals and Unborn Generations," in *Philosophy and Environmental Crisis*, ed. William Blackstone (Athens: University of Georgia Press, 1974); Kurt Baier, "The Right of Life" (paper delivered at Conference on Human Rights and Justice, University of North Carolina at Greensboro, Spring 1978); H. L. A. Hart, "Bentham on Legal Rights," in *Oxford Essays in Jurisprudence: Second Series*, ed. A. W. Simpson (Oxford: Oxford University Press, 1973), pp. 171–201; R. Flathman, *The Practice of Rights* (Cambridge, Mass.: Harvard University Press, 1976); and A. I. Melden, *Rights and Persons* (Berkeley: University of California Press, 1977), pp. 166–224.

---

2. See Michael Wald, "State Intervention on Behalf of 'Neglected' Children: A Search for Realistic Standards," *Stanford Law Review* 27 (1974–75): 985–1040 (reprinted in *Pursuing Justice for the Child*, ed. Margaret K. Rosenheim [Chicago: University of Chicago Press, 1976]; page references are to *Stanford Law Review*); and "Symposium: Juvenile Justice," *Boston University Law Review* 57 (1977): 663–731.

security we think it every parent's duty to provide. We find them short on caring and intimacy and insensitive to the state of dependency and vulnerability into which children are born and remain for several years.

Ideally the relationship between parent and infant involves an awareness of a kind of union between people which is perhaps more suitably described in poetic-spiritual language than in analytic moral terminology. We *share our selves* with those with whom we are intimate and are aware that they do the same with us.[3] Traditional moral boundaries, which give rigid shape to the self, are transparent to this kind of sharing. This makes for nonabstract moral relationships in which talk about rights of others, respect for others, and even welfare of others is to a certain extent irrelevant.[4] It is worth mentioning that the etymology of 'intimate' relates it to a verb meaning 'to bring within,' and that the primary meanings of 'intimate' focus on this character of being innermost for a person. It is also worth mentioning that establishing such relationships tends to be the

primary reason adults in our culture give for wanting and having children.[5]

The danger of talk about rights of children is that it may encourage people to think that the proper relationship between themselves and their children is the abstract one that the language of rights is forged to suit. So, rather than encouraging abusive parents to feel more intimate with their children, it may cause parents in intimate relationships with their infants to reassess the appropriateness of their blurring the boundaries of individual identity and to question their consciousness of a profound sense of identification with, and commitment toward, their families. Emphasis on the rights of children might foster thinking about the relationship between parent and child as quasi-contractual, limited, and directed toward the promotion of an abstract public good. Such emphasis unambiguously suggests that the relationship is a one-way relationship aimed almost solely at promoting the best interest of the child.

There are many circumstances when the independence of children, primarily older ones, ought to be stressed; for these circumstances, stress on children's rights makes sense. But when it is the dependence and vulnerability of the child that we want to emphasize, as we unfortunately must at times do, some different moral strategy would be more appropriate. And when we become conscious of the possibilities that intimacy here, as in other relations, is a two-way sharing of benefits, primary

---

3. See Martin Buber, "Dialogue," in *Between Man and Man*, ed. Martin Buber (London: Routledge & Kegan Paul, 1949); Robert Burt, "The Limits of the Law: Can It Regulate Health Care Decisions?" *Hastings Center Report* 7 (1977): 29–32.

4. See Hegel, *Philosophy of Right*, secs. 158–64. But note that for Hegel, once civil society makes its appearance, the abstract relations which aim at social well-being come to predominate over rights of intimacy and privacy (see secs. 238–341). Aristotle, though generally subordinating family relationships to the goals of the polis (*Politics* 1:13.15 and 7.16–17), does describe children as "another self" of the parents (*Nichomachean Ethics* 8.12) and also says that justice is irrelevant between friends (ibid., 8.1).

---

5. Lois Hoffman, "The Value of Children to Parents—a National Sample Survey" (paper read at the meeting of the American Public Health Association, Los Angeles, October 1978).

emphasis on the rights perspective becomes even more distorting. To avoid misunderstanding, however, I wish to reiterate that in recommending a different moral strategy I am not to be taken as denying that infants have rights, either in relation to their parents or in relation to abstract others. Rather, I am questioning the moral advantages of extolling the rights of infants in our consciousness of their most important relationships.

Let me try now to articulate briefly the principles at which we have arrived and then proceed to describe and execute the objective of this paper. As persons, children ought to be thought of as possessing rights; but as infants in relationship to their parents, they are to be thought of primarily as having needs, the satisfaction of which involves intimate and intense relationships with others. As against society, we might yet think of infants and parents as having rights to conditions which permit or encourage, or at least do not discourage, the social and material conditions conducive to parent-child intimacy—a point we will return to in Section III. What I want to discuss primarily is the moral basis for thinking that biological parents have a presumptive right to keep their children under their care in the setting of privacy, autonomy, and responsibility which is usually accorded the family.

For purposes of this paper, I shall mean by 'family' an intense continuing and intimate organization of at least one adult and child, wherein the child is extensively and profoundly dependent on the adult, in which the adult supplies the child with its emotional and material needs, and in which the parent is dependent on the child for a certain kind of intimacy.

This relationship is to be understood as moral, not biological. Furthermore, the family is to be understood as entitled to certain rights of privacy and autonomy. The right of privacy entitles the adults of the family to exclude others from scrutinizing obtrusions into family occurrences. The right to autonomy entitles the adults of the family to make important decisions about the kinds of influences they want the children to experience and entitles them to wide latitude in remedying what they regard as faults in the children's behavior. Neither the right to privacy nor the right to autonomy associated with the family is absolute. These rights are to be conceived as rights against society at large. In relation to the children, they impose upon parents the duty to employ considered judgments in taking into account each child's needs, and eventually his rights. But in large part, such duties are unenforceable by the state because of the rights of privacy and autonomy already mentioned.

Just how much discretion should be left to the parents—how wide should their latitude be in structuring the environment of their children? For theoretical reasons to be advanced in Section III, I follow Michael Wald and others in setting strict threshold conditions (amounting to a clear-and-present danger criterion) which must be met before coercive state intervention is permitted. Wald argues that coercive intervention should be authorized only if (1) serious physical or emotional harm to the child is imminent and (2) the intervention is likely to be less detrimental than the status quo.[6] Wald cites

---

6. Wald, "State Intervention . . .," pp. 992–93, 1005.

several practical factors in justifying his recommended policy of restraint. (1) Typically, good alternatives to unfortunate family circumstances are not available. (2) It is difficult to predict which circumstances will have harmful long-range effects. (3) There is a lack of consensus about proper methods of child rearing and the ideal end product of child rearing. (4) Our social commitment to diversity of life-styles requires a great deal of tolerance in what should be permitted.

While such factors reflect important desiderata, it is notable that concern for the parent appears to be irrelevant in Wald's article, as in much of the legal literature of recent vintage.[7] Though I find this exclusion of the parents' perspective peculiar, very widespread, and in need of remedy, it is to a certain extent understandable. For the infant, the family as here defined involves an intimate relationship with at least one adult. Since the psychological evidence suggests that children need this type of relationship for their cognitive and emotional well-being,[8] we may conclude that children must be provided with such an arrangement (or, if you prefer, that they have a right to it). But

from the child's perspective it does not matter whether the adult who will become its psychological parent is also its biological parent.

In what follows, I shall focus on the parents' perspective and attempt to address this question: Why should the biological parents be thought to have a right to raise their child in an intimate setting even before it is determined that their child will fare best under their care and guidance (*however* 'faring best' is defined)? Ultimately, what I shall want to emphasize is that the functional, efficiency-oriented approach to the family found in much of the literature defending family autonomy represents neither the only nor the best assessment of the moral basis of the family.

It should, however, be noted that not all social theorists see the family as an institution worth preserving. For not only does it provide a context for abuse and brutality in which the law has traditionally declined to take an interest, it also interferes with what might be called 'equality of opportunity' because it makes children depend on the spiritual and material resources of the family they happen to be born into.[9] Though these points do constitute genuine moral worries which are theoretically inseparable from family institutions, pursuing such worries is not part of my present interest, though they will be

---

7. Amy Gutmann nas trenchantly discussed the paternalistic and nonpaternalistic basis of parental rights within liberal theory in "Children, Paternalism, and Education: A Liberal Argument," photocopied (Princeton, N.J.: Princeton University).

8. Urie Bronfenbrenner, *A Report on Longitudinal Evaluation of Preschool Programs,* vol. 2, *Is Early Intervention Effective?* DHEW Publication no. (OHD), 75-25 (Washington, D.C.: Government Printing Office, 1975); and Joseph Goldstein, Anna Freud, and Albert Solnit, *Beyond the Best Interest of the Child* (New York: Free Press, 1973).

---

9. John Rawls, *A Theory of Justice* (Cambridge, Mass.: Harvard University Press, 1971), p. 511; Charles Fried, *Right and Wrong* (Cambridge, Mass.: Harvard University Press, 1978), pp. 150–55; and Lorenne Clark, "Privacy, Property, Freedom and the Family," in *Philosophical Law*, ed. Richard Bronaugh (London: H. Greenwood & Co., 1978), pp. 167–87.

touched on in the final portion of the paper.

II

Since surprisingly little philosophical attention has been devoted to the moral meaning of intimate relationships such as arise in family settings,[10] it should prove a useful exercise to see just what can be said in behalf of the biological parents' rights to raise their offspring, obvious though it may appear. The right of biological parents (hereinafter referred to as just 'parents') with which I am concerned is not a right to certain services from their children, but a right against all the rest of society to be indulged, within wide limits, to share life with each child and thus inevitably to fashion the child's environment as they see fit, immune from the scrutiny of and direction from others.

It might be impatiently suggested that parents' rights to raise their children stem from an evolutionary phenomenon: parents' natural affections for their offspring and their infants' needs make for something like a preestablished harmony of interests. Since everyone, or almost everyone, benefits from this arrangement, and since provisions can be made for those few biological anomalies in which natural passions and natural needs do not correlate, what better basis could there be for our traditional arrangement? The suggestion might be given added weight by calling to mind the reported deleterious effects of impersonal, institutional efforts at raising children.

Three comments are in order in response. First, it has been observed that parental attachments may be more the result of enculturation than we naively suppose.[11] Second, there is sufficient evidence to suggest that not all alternative modes of distributing children involve impersonal institutions in which children languish emotionally and intellectually.[12] Third, and philosophically most significant, I wish to consider what we would think parents' rights would amount to if means equal or superior to those parents can typically supply could be found for benefiting the child outside the biological parents' domain. Would parents still have a claim on their children, as against society? And if so, what would its basis be? Is the parents' right to their children contingent on the biological family's being the most efficient arrangement for benefiting children? Or is there some less incidental account of parental prerogative? (As indicated above, most recent proponents of family autonomy and state restraint have argued that promoting the child's interest is the primary or sole basis of their advocacy.[13] Though I am in agreement with these policy recommendations, I find that more needs to be said about their justification.)

One not very plausible account for the parents' right, despite the fact that the account can be traced back to Aristotle, involves looking at the child

---

10. Notable exceptions include Francis Schrag, "Justice and the Family," *Inquiry* 19 (1976): 193–208; Melden; and Fried.

---

11. P. Aries, *Centuries of Childhood: A Social History of Family Life* (New York: Alfred A. Knopf, Inc., 1962), pt. 1, chap. 2; and Arlene Skolnick, *The Intimate Environment* (Boston: Little, Brown & Co., 1973), pp. 60–62.

12. Bronfenbrenner, pp. 46–48.

13. Hafen, p. 651; Wald, "State Intervention . . ."; Goldstein et al., pp. 7, 25.

as the property of the parent, analogous to teeth and hair which have fallen out.[14] Since the child is the product of material and labor supplied prenatally by the mother, the child would seem to be the natural possession par excellence but for the fact that this product is a person. (I suppose that those who think that the newborn infant is not yet a person would have an easy time thinking of the parent as entitled to the infant in Aristotelian fashion.)[15]

Another justification for our current arrangements might follow these lines: as long as children are adequately cared for under our present practices, we can take into account parental preferences. True, these preferences as such do not constitute rights, but in our way of allocating benefits, once children's needs are satisfied—a precondition we have set into our scheme—preferences should count in our determination of which claims will be recognized as entitlements.

This account of the basis of parental rights is not contingent solely on the fact of benefiting children but also makes essential reference to parents as persons with preferences which must be considered as long as the child's basic needs are met. But ultimately this justification of parental right is not satisfying, for all that would be necessary to override it would be a showing of some increased benefit to children in nonparental settings. True, the needs of the children and the preferences of the parents go some way toward showing that it is the parents, and not someone else, that should be accorded rights over their children. But if marginally more good resulted for children from alternative setups, this fact could immediately outweigh parental preferences and militate against according parents' rights. I take it as a given that a parent's stake in her relationship to her children is based on something more profound than parental preferences, even when we add to such preferences a realistic skepticism about the state's competence to distribute children in a manner more advantageous to them.

In discussing sources of authority, Elizabeth Anscombe has recently proposed that institutionalized practices which carry out important tasks thereby gain legitimization or authority.[16] Anscombe suggests that the parent's rights to obedience from her child and respect for her exercise of discretion from others outside the family evolve from the manifestly cru-

---

14. Aristotle adopts the view that the child is the parent's possession, actually comparing the child to a tooth and a piece of hair (*Nichomachean Ethics* 8.12). But since Aristotle also thinks that slaves are possessions toward which the master owes nothing, and since vis-à-vis their children Aristotle's view is that parents ought to make their benefit primary (*Politics* 3.6.7), it is not the best of analogies that Aristotle picked to represent his own views of parent-child relationships. For a critical discussion of Locke's treatment of this view, see Robert Nozick, *Anarchy, State, and Utopia* (New York: Basic Books, 1974), pp. 287–91. It may be worth noting that we often use the possessive idiom to indicate a special relationship to something and not legal or moral proprietorship. An architect might say of a building, "That's mine!" or a child might say of a teacher, "That's my teacher," without suggesting ownership.

15. Michael Tooley, "Abortion and Infanticide," *Philosophy and Public Affairs* 2 (1972): 37–65.

16. Elizabeth Anscombe, "On the Source of Authority of the State," *Ratio* 20 (1978): 1–28.

cial functions parental authority performs. So long as families maintain their position of being necessary conditions for the performance of such functions, Anscombe's argument captures common sense and preserves family entitlements. But the emergence of alternative, possibly superior (relative to the child), means of rearing children would deprive the family of its position of being necessary and hence undermine its claim to rightful autonomy, except on a customary basis.

We must note that these last two theories are by no means clearly false or even clearly wanting. Whether they are fully adequate must be judged in light of alternative dimensions we can manage to elaborate.

C O M M E N T S ■ Q U E S T I O N S

1. If we emphasize too much the rights of children, says Schoeman, we may make it difficult for parents to have an intimate relationship in which they share themselves with their children. For the closeness of a family to be possible, the *family* must have certain rights of privacy and autonomy. Is Schoeman correct to emphasize the closeness and sharing of parent/child relationships over and above the rights and autonomy of children?

2. Compare the views of Schoeman to the views presented in the preceding paper by David and Sheila Rothman. Which do you believe makes the stronger case?

3. Schoeman allows that parents sometimes fail to provide an intimate, sharing relationship with their children. But even when this is the case, the government should not intervene unless there is a "clear and present danger" to the child since the government cannot be given the authority to judge which relationships are intimate and which are not. "The state is unequipped to investigate souls." How would David and Sheila Rothman respond to this argument?

4. Examine what Schoeman says in relation to the Principle of Self-Interest. How important to a child's self-interest are close, sharing relationships with parents? How important to a *parent's* self-interest are such relationships to children?

5. "The right of privacy entitles the adults of the family to exclude others from scrutinizing obtrusions into family occurrences." This right should be limited, essentially, only when there is a "clear and present danger" to the child. Is there any reason to believe that a family's "right to privacy" is likely to keep many cases of child abuse hidden from public view?

T H O M A S E. H I L L, J R.

Autonomy and Benevolent Lies

A former teacher related to me the following true story (which I have modified slightly). He had a student who showed in tutorial conversations signs of deep, suicidal depression. The student was later found dead, and the circumstances were such that others could easily have seen his death as accidental. The professor helped to gather up the boy's belongings to return to his mother, and no suicide note was found. But the mother, a devout Roman Catholic, was deeply worried about her son's soul, and she asked the professor point blank whether he had any reason to suspect suicide. The professor, an atheist, wanted to comfort her and so, by a quite deliberate lie, assured her that, as far as he knew, the boy had been in good spirits.

Another true story concerns a doctor who discovered that his mother, a very elderly but happy woman, had extremely advanced arteriosclerosis. Her doctor had apparently chosen to treat the problem as best he could without informing the woman how near death she was. The son had no objection to the medical treatment or her doctor's decision to withhold information. Though he thought his mother psychologically and physically capable of handling the truth, he believed that her last days would be happier if she did not know. The problem arose when she asked her son directly, "Do you think the doctor is telling me everything?" The son lied; but since the question concerned his opinion and he had learned of her condition in ways she did not suspect and without anyone else knowing that he knew, he felt confident that she would never discover his lie. He lied to make her more comfortable, and she was in fact happy until her death.

Consider, lastly, a dilemma which could occur even if it has not. Mary has made a painful break from her ex-lover, John, and though pulled towards him, is on the mend. Her roommate is pleased for her, as she knows that John and Mary were, and will remain, painfully incompatible. She is fearful, though, that John and Mary will get together again, causing both unnecessary misery before the inevitable final separation. Overhearing John talking with a friend, she learns that John is ready to "start over" if only he receives an encouraging sign; and she expects that Mary, ever the optimist, would give the sign. Later Mary asks the roommate, "Do

Thomas E. Hill, Jr., is a professor of philosophy at the University of North Carolina at Chapel Hill. He is well known for his work in the areas of ethics and the philosophy of Kant.

From *The Journal of Value Inquiry*, Vol. 18, No. 4 (1984) pp. 251–254, 262–266. Reprinted by permission of the publisher.

you think he would want to try again if I asked him?" As an act of kindness, the roommate replies, "No, I am sure he knows it would never work."

These examples illustrate the special sort of benevolent lies I want to consider. The lies are benevolent because they are intended to benefit the person deceived, for no ulterior motives, and they actually succeed in giving comfort without causing pain. Despite the benevolent motives, there is no denying that deliberate lies were told. We are not dealing with examples of mere silence, evasion, ambiguous response, and the like. The lies, moreover, are not designed to protect incompetents from truths beyond their capacities to handle sanely and responsibly. In our sample cases a lie will protect someone from avoidable pain, but it is not needed to prevent serious physical or psychological damage, violent outbursts, gross misperception of reality, and so on.

Our examples also fall outside a range of special problem situations. Some lies, for example, are told in a context where the liar has rather little chance of being believed; but in our cases there is sufficient credibility to make the deception effective. Other lies concern matters which are, intuitively, "none of the business" of the questioner: for example, a lie told to a curious student who asked his teacher about his private sex life. But the questions in our examples are clearly not "out of bounds" in this way. What is asked for is information or opinion about what deeply concerns the questioner's own life. Also the lies in our stories cannot be deemed trivial. Unlike "little white lies," they are about matters of the utmost importance to the deceived: heaven or hell, life or death, reunion or separation from a loved one. Further, our examples concern lies between individuals, not lies from public officials or to institutions, and so certain questions of public responsibility are left aside. Finally, let us imagine that the deceived has not forfeited a right to know, for example, by his own repeated lying or by having a plain intent to misuse the truth.

Lies are often wrong at least in part because they are breaches of a promise to be truthful, but, to simplify matters, let us suppose that there were no such promises in our examples. It is easy to imagine that the professor, the dying woman's son, and the roommate never made an *explicit* promise to tell the truth as, for example, one is required to do before testifying in court. The more difficult matter is to remove the suspicion that they made a tacit or implicit promise to be truthful. Ross maintained that we make such an implicit promise every time we make an assertion, and so he viewed all lies as breaches of promise. But this position, surely, is implausible. Suppose, for example, two enemies distrust each other, have no desire to be honest with each other, and both know this. As seems to be common in international relations, they tell the truth to each other only when they expect that lying will not give them an advantage. In this situation when one asserts to the other, say, that he has documents damaging to the other's political ambitions, we cannot reasonably interpret this as a promise. Neither person believes that the speaker intends to put himself under obligation. Given their mutual understanding, the speaker cannot seriously intend to lead the other to believe that he is making it a matter of conscience to convey the truth. Furthermore if every assertion amounted to a promise to say what is true, we would not think, as in fact we do, that a lie preceded by an explicit promise to be truthful is usually worse than a lie not preceded by such a promise. There are, of course, implicit promises but it requires more than mere assertion to make one. Suppose, for example, Mary and her roommate had often discussed how they valued each other's honesty and frankness, and each had on other occasions insisted that the other tell the truth, however painful, and neither gave any hint of reservations about giving and counting on complete truthfulness between them. With this special background we might want to say that they had made implicit promises to tell each other the truth. However, to focus attention away from promises, let us suppose that in our examples there were no such special conditions to create implicit promises to be truthful.

Our examples are also meant to minimize the force of utilitarian considerations that so often tell against lying. Most importantly, the lies in our stories are extremely unlikely to be discovered. It is a moralist's fiction that lies can never remain hidden: perhaps a useful fiction but untrue nonetheless. In each of our examples a person is asked about what he knows or believes, and if he is determined to stand by his response there is no practical way others can find out that he is lying. Even if the student's mother learns that her son committed suicide, she cannot know that the professor lied; the elderly woman can find out that she is seriously ill, but not that her son lied about his opinion; Mary may learn that John is still available, but she has no way of discovering that her roommate knew. There is, of course, always *some*

chance, however remote, that those who lie will give themselves away; for example, they may talk in their sleep. If the discovery of the lie would be an utter disaster, then from a utilitarian point of view even this very small risk might not be warranted. But to simplify, let us suppose that in our cases discovery would not be disastrous. The persons deceived, let us say, have an unusually forgiving and trusting nature. If they realized the special circumstances and benevolent intent, they would forgive the lie; and, though disappointed, they would not become unreasonably suspicious and distrustful. Again, typical lies tend to multiply, one lie calling for another and each lie making successive ones easier; but we can imagine this not to be so in our example. Our professor, doctor/son, and roommate, let us suppose, are of firm character and would lie only in the special circumstances we have defined, and they do not need an entangled web of further deception to hide the first.

Lies of the sort pictured here are no doubt rare; but, by minimizing the usual considerations of utility and promises, they enable us to focus on other relevant considerations, which may be important in more typical cases as well. In particular, we can reflect on how lies can fail to respect persons' autonomy.

[The following somewhat complex discussion of autonomy has been omitted. The conclusion of the discussion is that the concept of autonomy centers around a person's capacity to make rational decisions for himself or herself. Specifically, Hill makes the following points regarding autonomy.]

Let us say that persons have autonomy, or live autonomously, in a final sense if the following is true: (1) They have the psychological capacities for rational decision making which are associated with autonomy; (2) they actually use these capacities when they face important choice situations; (3) they have the right of autonomy discussed previously, i.e. a right to make morally and legally permissible decisions about matters deeply affecting their own lives free from threats and manipulation by others; (4) other people actually respect this right as well as their other rights; (5) they are able and disposed to have distinctly human values; (6) others respect this capacity by not presuming that they value only good experiences for themselves and by not counting their comfort more important than their declared values; and, finally, (7) they have ample opportunities to make use of these conditions in living a life over which they have a high degree of control.

* * * * *

The ideal of developing the psychological capacities associated with autonomy may give some reason to hesitate to tell lies to protect people from painful realities, but not a reason that applies in all cases. Probably, as a rule, having to face unpleasant truths about matters deeply affecting one's life helps one to develop the capacity for mature, reflective decision making. If so, there would be a general presumption against benevolent lies, even if it would not always be persuasive as, for example, when we are dealing with the very elderly whose capacities have presumably already been developed as much as they will be.

If we believe in the *right* of autonomy, however, we have more reason to object to benevolent lies. This is most obvious in our example of the roommate lying to keep her friend from re-uniting with her ex-lover. The roommate manipulates her friend's

decision (to call or not to call her "ex") by actively concealing pertinent information. If we accept the right of autonomy, this could only be justified if the reunion would have been so great a disaster that the right is overridden. In other cases the right of autonomy may be violated but in a less obvious way. The professor and the doctor/son, for example, did not lie in order to control the decisions of the people they deceived; they only wanted to spare them avoidable pain. Nevertheless, there were important, life-altering decisions which the deceived might have made if they had not been deprived of relevant information; and surely the professor and the doctor/son knew this. They knowingly prevented certain options presented by the real situation from ever being faced by the people they deceived: to pray or not, and, if so, how; to continue life as usual or to reorder one's priorities; to face death and tragedy stoically or to be open in a new way with friends.

Someone may object as follows: "Sometimes benevolent lies interfere with life-altering decisions, but not always; often benevolent lies merely keep people from suffering unnecessarily because of something which they can do nothing about. When, for example, a widow demands to know whether her husband suffered when he was killed in the war, there is little she can *do* if she is told truthfully that he died in horrible agony. And similarly, if the suicide's mother had been bedridden and terminally ill, the professor's lie would not have interfered with any important decisions."

The appropriate response, I think, is this: Benevolent lies do not necessarily or always violate the right of autonomy, but we should not be hasty in concluding that a particular lie does not concern any significant decisions. Good novelists and biographers know what philosophers too easily forget, namely, that the most important decisions in life are not always about external behavior, about what to *do* in the public world. How we face death, family tragedy, our own successes and failures, and the way others treat us, is partly a matter of decision, as Sartreans knew but exaggerated. Even *whether* to see a situation as success or failure, tragic or routine, is not simply a matter of perception of fact. We can also interfere with these life-altering decisions, or prevent a person from facing them, by keeping certain truths from him—even if he is immobile for the rest of his life.[1]

Consider next the principles associated with autonomy as a capacity for distinctly human values. Their implications for benevolent lies depend upon what we know about the preferences of the person to be deceived. Suppose, first, that we have no reason to doubt that the questioner wants an honest answer. His question is in effect an expression of a desire to know the truth. To give him less because we want to spare him pain would be to count his comfort more important than what he himself professes to value more and so would be contrary to our principles.

Sometimes, of course, people ask questions wanting to be reassured rather than to learn the truth. What should we do if we have indirect evidence that the questioner does not really want to know? Much depends, I think, on the nature and strength of the evidence. Suppose, for example, the evidence is rather evenly mixed: the person often shrinks from painful realities but, on the other hand, he asked in a serious tone, he never said in advance not to reveal the sort of fact in question, and the truth is not outside the range of answers he could anticipate. Often when we are in doubt whether a person really prefers what he professes, we can remove the uncertainty by asking further questions; but the peculiarity of the dilemma of the would-be benevolent liar is that he cannot resolve the uncertainty this way. To ask, "Would you *really* prefer the truth even though it will hurt?" is in effect to give away the answer. When faced with such mixed evidence and unresolvable uncertainty, one guided by our principles of autonomy would, I believe, again be disposed to tell the truth; for respecting a person's capacity for distinctly human values implies that, other things equal, it is worse to presume that someone prefers comfort to some other declared value than to presume the opposite.[2]

If there were definitive evidence

---

1. Several have suggested to me that opposition to lying in these cases stems from the judgment that knowing the truth, or facing tragic realities, is intrinsically valuable regardless of the pain it causes; but I suspect that theories (such as G. E. Moore's) which make it a duty to promote an objective intrinsic value will repeatedly call for interference with autonomy. Robert Adams suggested that an ideal of autonomy might include "*living* one's own life", e.g. experiencing the tragic realities actually surrounding one, quite aside from opportunities to make *decisions,* rational or otherwise; but I think that autonomy is so closely associated with the idea of "self-*governing*" that his ideal is probably better classified under some other conception.

---

2. This may seem strange if one supposes (mistakenly) that we should give people what they want—truth or comfort, whichever they prefer. But the principle in question was in fact rooted in a different idea, namely, that persons are to be respected for their distinctly human (e.g., non-hedonistic) values. From this point of view, given uncertainty, it is worse to err in supposing that they prefer comfort to truth than to err in the opposite direction.

that the questioner preferred not to learn the painful truth, then autonomy as a capacity for distinctly human values would not be relevant. This would be the case if, for example, the questioner had explicitly requested in advance not to be told the truth in specified circumstances, and then, later, those circumstances arose and ample evidence indicated that he had not changed his mind.

Such cases, however, are probably rare. Normally even if a person has previously asked not to be told the truth, his subsequent question raises legitimate doubts about his current preferences. Suppose the earlier request was not made in anticipation of a period of incompetence—like Ulysses' request to his crew before facing the Sirens ("Don't listen to what I say later"). Then the would-be liar is apparently faced with two conflicting requests: an earlier request for deception, and a later request for truth. Unless there are independent reasons for discounting the latter, or for not treating the later question as a request for truth, then one might argue that respect for autonomy gives precedence to the more recent request. Other things equal, we respect a person's autonomy more by allowing changes of mind, honoring what he *does* profess to value over what he *did* profess to value.

The many-sided *ideal* of autonomous living will usually give further reason for hesitating to tell benevolent lies. Even if benevolent lies do not violate a *right*, they still deprive people of a realistic picture of their situation. Insofar as having such a realistic picture is needed for genuine rational control over one's life, to that extent the benevolent liar fails to promote an ideal end.[3]

It may be objected that this argument supports the desirability of volunteering the truth just as much as it supports the desirability of not actively depriving someone of the truth; and yet, it might be said, it is counter-intuitive to suppose that we have as much reason to volunteer painful truths as to tell them when directly asked. The ideal does give reason to volunteer the truth, I think, but there are also reasons why lying in response to a direct question is worse than merely not volunteering the truth. There is a general presumption that one should not cause avoidable pain to others, but this presumption is at least partially set aside when the person requests the painful treatment for the sake of something he wants: e.g. painful medical tests. Thus, although there is a general presumption against expressing truths which cause pain, this presumption is at least partially set aside when a competent person asks for truth; but the presumption is not set aside when one simply volunteers the truth without being asked. Thus, though the ideal of autonomy gives some reason for volunteering painful information about someone's life, the case for volunteering is not as strong as the case for telling the truth when asked.

Another objection might be this: "Sometimes we need to lie in order to increase the chances that a person will make his own decisions (and so live autonomously). For example, when my son asked me where I wanted him to go to college, I lied,

---

3. It may be argued, rightly, that sometimes benevolent lies may promote the ideal of autonomous living in other respects. This might be so if, for example, coping with a painful truth, about which little could be done, would so preoccupy a person that other important aspects of life would be comparatively neglected. Sometimes, perhaps, too much information can also interfere with rational decision-making.

telling him that I did not care. Actually I wanted very much for him to go where I went; but I figured that he could make up his own mind better if I kept my preference to myself."

The objection points to a practical problem difficult to resolve in real cases, but it does not, I think, show that the ideal of autonomy unequivocally recommends lying even in the example just presented. *One* aspect of ideal, to be sure, was encouraging people to make their important decisions in a rational way free from inner psychological obstacles such as neurotic need for a father's approval. Thus, if the son in our example was so dominated by his father's opinions that he could not make a rational choice once his father expressed his desires, then one aspect of the ideal of autonomy would urge the father to hide his opinion. But let us suppose, as in our previous examples, the person deceived is rationally competent with respect to his choice problem and so is not a slave to his father's wishes. In this case another aspect of the ideal of autonomy would urge the father to express his wishes: he should make clear both that he prefers his son to go to his old college and also that he wants his son to decide on the basis of what he, the son, most wants. This puts the pertinent facts on the table, giving the son an opportunity he would have otherwise lacked, namely, to choose whether to give weight to his father's wishes or not and, if so, which wish to count more important. By lying, the father would have helped the son make a self-interested choice; but, as we have seen, one's autonomous choice is not always self-interested. To "make up one's own mind" is not necessarily to decide without regard for others' wishes but to decide maturely in the

light of the facts about the situation.

So far we have considered ways in which principles and ideals of autonomy help to explain why we view even benevolent lies as to some degree objectionable; but we also have intuitive opinions about which sort of lies (or deceptions) are worse than others. Let us consider, then, whether considerations of autonomy help to explain these intuitions as well.

To consider several factors together, I suppose it is commonly accepted that deceptive responses to questions are worse, other things equal, when (a) the response is a direct lie rather than a merely evasive, misleading, or deceptively ambiguous response, (b) the person deceived trusts the deceiver and was encouraged to do so, and (c) the lie concerns the life of the deceived rather than matters only remotely touching him. The lies of the roommate and the doctor/son described earlier exemplify the first sort. An example of the second, less significant sort of deception might be this: A person asks me, simply from curiosity, "Do you know whether so-and-so is gay?", and, though I know, I answer, "How would I know?"

Now utilitarians will have familiar explanations why the first sort of lie is regarded as more serious than the second; but it is worth nothing that our principles and ideals of autonomy provide an alternative, or additional, explanation. In brief, one's opportunity to live in rational control of one's life is increased when there are people one can unmistakenly identify as prepared to give straight, honest answers to direct pointed questions. If one does not want to know, one can refrain from asking; if the first answer is evasive or ambiguous, suggesting a reluctance on the other's part to reveal the truth, then one can choose to put the question again more pointedly or to back off; and if one does insist ("I want a straight, honest answer!"), then, while allowing for honest errors, one can make important decisions with more confidence that one understands the real situation. To live in a world without people we can rely on in this way would be to live in a world in which we have less control over our lives. Utilitarians often stress the unpleasantness that results when lies which violate trust become discovered, and for this reason our examples were designed to minimize the risk of discovery. But now it emerges that ideals of autonomy not only oppose undiscoverable benevolent lies; they also oppose lies which risk discovery of a breach of trust; for discovery of such lies encourages us to be distrustful and suspicious and so less able to make use of even the honest answers trustworthy persons give us; and this limits our opportunities for rational control over our lives.

IV

These conclusions, of course, are both hypothetical and intuitive; that is, the argument has been that if one accepts certain principles of autonomy, then one has reasons to refrain from benevolent lies. But imagine now an objection from a normative hedonist unwilling to rest the issue on intuitive principles. He argues that, intuitions aside, it is *irrational* to prefer truth to comfort, unless having the truth would maximize one's pleasure in the long run. Thus, he continues, when one aims to be benevolent towards another, it is *irrational* to give him the truth if a lie will contribute more to his total satisfaction.

The objection rests on the common, but mistaken, assumption that, at least when free from moral constraints, a fully rational person would always aim for his most favorable pleasure/pain ratio. But why so? As we have seen, people do in fact have (non-moral) concerns independent of any anticipated good experiences. Some, perhaps, make maximum pleasure their goal; and others do not. What determines whether one is rational is not, by itself, the content of one's aims, but how they are arrived at, how they fit into one's life plan, etc. More plausible than the hedonist's conception of rationality, I think, is that of John Rawls, who defines ideal rationality, roughly, as satisfying certain "counting principles" (means-end efficiency, inclusion, etc.) and then deciding in light of full information about one's desires, circumstances, etc. Given this conception and the falsity of *psychological* hedonism (i.e., that all seek only to maximize their pleasure), then the rational life will be different for different people. For some, maybe, it will be predominantly pursuit of pleasure; but, unless we suppose that all non-hedonistic desires would extinguish when exposed to more information, for many the rational life will include pursuit of other values, such as truth, independently of their pay-off in personal satisfaction.

The principles of autonomy which we have considered, though still un-unified in a general theory, point toward a conception of morality quite different in spirit from familiar forms of utilitarianism, hedonistic and otherwise. The latter start with views about what is intrinsically valuable as an end, and then define morality, in one way or another, as what promotes this end. A theory of autonomy, following, Kant, Rawls, and others, would first define principles for moral institutions and personal interactions, leaving each person, within these constraints, the freedom to choose and pursue whatever ends they will. Such a theory would not oppose benevolent lies on the ground that truth-telling will maximize some intrinsic value other than pleasure (e.g., self-awareness); rather, it would encourage truthfulness as, in general, a way of respecting people as free to choose their own ends.

C O M M E N T S ■ Q U E S T I O N S

1. A benevolent lie is one intended to benefit the person or persons who are lied to. The three examples that Hill discusses—the professor, the son, and the roommate—probably all appear to have some plausibility as examples of benevolent lies that are morally defensible. Can you think of any examples which, at first glance anyway, would appear to be even more plausible?

2. Sometimes lying means breaking an explicit or implicit promise. Keeping promises is usually thought to be one of the most important moral obligations. Do the points that Hill makes give support to the idea that promises ought not to be broken? Is the obligation to keep promises supported strongly by the Principle of the Common Good? By the Principle of Rights? By the Principle of Justice?

3. The major sort of objection to benevolent lies discussed by Hill is an appeal to the concept of *autonomy*. Some of his extended discussion of this concept in the original article has been omitted, but the essential idea is that a person is autonomous when the person has the psychological capacities to make rational decisions for himself or herself and is also supported in doing this by other people. That is, others must respect the individual's right to make decisions and not attempt to manipulate the individual. Out of all the things in life that have value, how important in your opinion is autonomy? Is anything more important than autonomy?

4. "Ideals of autonomy," says Hill, are threatened by both of these types of benevolent lies: (a) those that will never be discovered and (b) those that might be discovered. Is Hill correct in making both of these claims? What is your overall assessment of the moral reservations that Hill expresses regarding benevolent lies? Does his position generally offer good advice to be applied in your relationships to people who are close to you?

R E A D I N G S

Aristotle. *Nichomachean Ethics. Book 9.*

Bernard, Jessie. *The Future of Motherhood.* New York: Penguin, 1975.

Bluestein, Jeffrey. *Parents and Children: The Ethics of the Family.* Oxford: Oxford University Press, 1983.

Bok, Sissela. *Lying: Moral Choice in Public and Private Life.* New York: Random House, 1978.

Clark, Homer H., Jr. *The Law of Domestic Relations.* St. Paul, Minn.: West Publishing Company, 1968.

Emerson, Ralph Waldo. "Friendship." In *Centenary Edition, The Complete Works of Ralph Waldo Emerson.* Boston: Houghton Mifflin Company, 1903–4.

Freud, Anna and Albert Solnit. *Beyond the Best Interests of the Child.* New York: The Free Press, 1973.

Helfer, Ray E. and Henry Kempe, eds. *Child Abuse and Neglect.* Cambridge: Ballinger Publishing Company, 1976.

Olson, Robert G. *The Morality of Self-Interest.* New York: Harcourt, Brace and World, 1965.

O'Neil, Onora and William Ruddick, eds. *Having Children: Philosophical and Legal Reflections on Parenthood.* New York: Oxford University Press, 1979.

Rand, Ayn. *The Virtue of Selfishness.* New York: Signet, 1964.

Twain, Mark. *The Adventures of Huckleberry Finn* (New York: Dodd, Mead, 1979).

People Who Are Not Close To Us

T here are two classes of people who are not close to us: those distant from us in space (people living in foreign countries) and those distant from us in time (people belonging to future generations). Those who are distant from us in space can be identified and we can learn what their problems and needs are. But there is much less that we can know about people who are distant from us in time; indeed, if we project ourselves far enough into the future then we will come to a time about which nothing, or nearly nothing, can be known. We cannot know even that human beings will exist in the truly far-off future. For that matter, we can't be entirely sure that they will exist next year.

It doesn't follow that we are morally justified in forgetting about people who, hopefully, will live in the distant future, let alone those who will live in the immediate future. This is because our actions at the present time will very likely affect their lives significantly. If we take an optimistic view and assume that the human race will continue to exist indefinitely, then unquestionably the quality of human life in the future—if not the existence itself of human life—will depend in some very important ways upon what is done in the world at the present time and in the more or less immediate future. Many of the world's resources are being used up. Civilization is threatened by nuclear war (a discussion of which is to be found in chapter 10). The world's population is increasing at a frightening pace. Technological advances that address one set of problems often create new problems, such as insect damage to crops treated by insecticides and resulting in water pollution. Entirely new technologies, such as genetic engineering, can produce new organisms that will, eventually, very likely require that we find new ways to look at ourselves and other species.

These issues and others present us with a formidable complex of moral problems that the present chapter can touch upon only briefly. The first point that needs to be made is that questions about our moral obligations to people who are distant from us, first in space and second in time, are interrelated for a number of different reasons. One of them is that the extent and type of aid that is given to people in developing third world countries will have a considerable impact on population growth or containment in these countries. If the world in twenty years or fifty years contains a much larger number of people than it does now, then the present scarcities of resources and affordable energy will be even greater.

The question of scarcity is the most pressing of the topics to be dealt with in this chapter. People in the poorer countries of the world suffer very much from a scarcity of almost everything that is needed to live a comfortable or even minimally decent life: food, housing, medical aid, adequate transportation, and so on. At the same time, the rich nations of the world are using up many important resources. If that continues, many of the things that play essential roles in maintaining comfortable lives will not be available for future generations. These points are elaborated upon in the readings for this chapter. The selection from Peter Singer, in particular, elaborates upon the disparities in wealth between rich and poor countries, while the selection from Gus Speth elaborates upon the fact that many of the world's resources—both those that are nonrenewable such as oil and those that are renewable such as trees—are being used up.

Now, the question that needs to be asked is, what are the moral implications of the facts stated by Singer and Speth? As a way of orienting ourselves to some of the diverse answers to this question, it may be helpful to recall that the principles of Rights and Justice in chapter 1 are stated in a completely *impersonal* way. The Principle of Rights enjoins us to try to protect the rights of everyone equally, and the Principle of Justice enjoins us to try in a completely evenhanded way to equalize the good of everyone by helping the most those who most need help, whomever they may be. If these two principles are taken seriously, there will be a *prima facie* reason to suppose that we have a strong moral obligation to help people in distant countries and to look out for the welfare of future generations. Singer's paper argues for the need to help people in third world countries, while Speth's paper argues for the need to be concerned for future generations as well as for people in third world countries. (Speth emphasizes the interrelatedness of the two groups.)

How much help should be given to people in third world countries? How much should we be concerned about future generations? John Arthur, in the paper reprinted here, argues against the position of Singer. It is not that Arthur believes that we should give no help to third world countries, but rather that he believes that Singer is asking that we give more help than we are morally obligated to give. According to Arthur, the moral obligation to help starving people should be balanced against the moral right of people who are relatively well-off to keep what they have earned.

The reading selections by Speth and Richard T. De George are not as strongly in opposition as are the articles by Singer and Arthur. De George intends to minimize our obligations to future generations by doing the following things: distinguishing between *actual rights* and *possible rights*, rejecting any appeal to what we are calling the Principle of the Common Good (which he refers to as the doctrine of utilitarianism), and appealing to his own version of the Principle of Self-Interest (he argues against any need to pursue a purely altruistic good regarding future generations). Speth attempts to demonstrate how broad our obligations to future generations are by appealing to three concepts that he calls *conservation, sustainable development,* and *equity.*

For want of space, this chapter does not contain reading selections addressed specifically to an important dimension of the moral controversy regarding aid to starving people in third world countries. This is the complex question of what *kind* of aid should be given. Singer does touch upon this matter. At the heart of the present-day controversy is the opposition between (a) those who argue, as Singer does, that we have a very strong obligation to feed starving people, and (b) those who argue that feeding starving people in many third world countries will only make situations worse, leading to an even greater disparity in those countries between the size of the population and available resources of food, clothing, medical aid, and so on.

Garrett Hardin, who is a social scientist, has become widely known in recent years for defending what has been called the "tough-love" position, which calls for massive aid to starving people to be withheld in many cases in order to prevent the need in the next generation to give food to even greater numbers of starving people.[1] Simply giving aid, says Hardin, will not teach people in poor countries that they must "mend their ways."

Those who oppose Hardin usually take the position, which Singer has defended, that giving food to starving people in third world countries must in some way be seen as a response to emergencies, not a long-term policy. For long-term solutions, aid must be addressed primarily to education and development.

Notes

1. Garrett Hardin, "The Case Against Helping the Poor," *Psychology Today* (September 1974): 36–43 and 123–126.

PETER SINGER

The Obligation to Help

Consider these facts: by the most cautious estimates, 400 million people lack the calories, protein, vitamins and minerals needed for a normally healthy life. Millions are constantly hungry; others suffer from deficiency diseases and from infections they would be able to resist on a better diet. Children are worst affected.

Peter Singer is a professor of philosophy at Monash University. He is very well known for his books and articles in the areas of ethics and politics.

Peter Singer, "The Obligation to Help," in *Practical Ethics*, Cambridge University Press, 1979. Reprinted by permission of the publisher.

According to one estimate, 15 million children under five die every year from the combined effects of mal-nutrition and infection. In some areas, half the children born can be expected to die before the fifth birthday.

Nor is lack of food the only hard-ship of the poor. To give a broader picture, Robert McNamara, President of the World Bank, has suggested the term 'absolute poverty'. The poverty we are familiar with in industrialized nations is relative poverty—meaning that some citizens are poor, relative to the wealth enjoyed by their neigh-bours. People living in relative pover-ty in Australia might be quite comfort-ably off by comparison with old-age pensioners in Britain, and British old-age pensioners are not poor in com-parison with the poverty that exists in Mali or Ethiopia. Absolute poverty, on the other hand, is poverty by any stan-dard. In McNamara's words:

Poverty at the absolute level . . . is life at the very margin of existence.

The absolute poor are severely de-prived human beings struggling to survive in a set of squalid and degraded circum-stances almost beyond the power of our sophisticated imaginations and privileged circumstances to conceive.

Compared to those fortunate enough to live in developed countries, individuals in the poorest nations have:

An infant mortality rate eight times higher

A life expectancy one-third lower

An adult literacy rate 60% less

A nutritional level, for one out of every two in the population, below acceptable standards; and for millions of infants, less protein than is sufficient to permit opti-mum development of the brain.

And McNamara has summed up abso-lute poverty as:

a condition of life so characterized by malnutrition, illiteracy, disease, squalid surroundings, high infant mortality and low life expectancy as to be beneath any reasonable definition of human decency.

Absolute poverty is, as McNamara has said, responsible for the loss of count-less lives, especially among infants and young children. When absolute poverty does not cause death it still causes misery of a kind not often seen in the affluent nations. Malnutrition in young children stunts both physical and mental development. It has been estimated that the health, growth, and learning capacity of nearly half the young children in developing coun-tries are affected by malnutrition. Mil-lions of people on poor diets suffer from deficiency diseases, like goitre, or blindness caused by a lack of vita-min A. The food value of what the poor eat is further reduced by para-sites such as hookworm and ring-worm, which are endemic in condi-tions of poor sanitation and health education.

Death and disease apart, absolute poverty remains a miserable condi-tion of life, with inadequate food, shelter, clothing, sanitation, health services and education. According to World Bank estimates which define absolute poverty in terms of income levels insufficient to provide adequate nutrition, something like 800 million people—almost 40% of the people of developing countries—live in abso-lute poverty. Absolute poverty is prob-ably the principal cause of human misery today.

This is the background situation, the situation that prevails on our planet all the time. It does not make headlines. People died from malnutri-tion and related diseases yesterday, and more will die tomorrow. The occasional droughts, cyclones, earth-quakes and floods that take the lives of tens of thousands in one place and at one time are more newsworthy. They add greatly to the total amount of human suffering; but it is wrong to assume that when there are no major calamities reported, all is well.

The problem is not that the world cannot produce enough to feed and shelter its people. People in the poor countries consume, on average, 400 lbs of grain a year, while North Americans average more than 2000 lbs. The difference is caused by the fact that in the rich countries we feed most of our grain to animals, converting it into meat, milk and eggs. Because this is an inefficient process, wasting up to 95% of the food value of the animal feed, people in rich countries are responsible for the consumption of far more food than those in poor countries who eat few animal products. If we stopped feeding animals on grains, soybeans and fishmeal the amount of food saved would—if distributed to those who need it—be more than enough to end hunger throughout the world.

These facts about animal food do not mean that we can easily solve the world food problem by cutting down on animal products, but they show that the problem is essentially one of distribution rather than production. The world does produce enough food. Moreover the poorer nations themselves could produce far more if they made more use of improved agricultural techiques.

So why are people hungry? Poor people cannot afford to buy grain grown by American farmers. Poor farmers cannot afford to buy improved seeds, or fertilizers, or the machinery needed for drilling wells and pumping water. Only by transferring some of the wealth of the developed nations to the poor of the undeveloped nations can the situation be changed.

That this wealth exists is clear. Against the picture of absolute pov-erty that McNamara has painted, one might pose a picture of 'absolute affluence'. Those who are absolutely affluent are not necessarily affluent by comparison with their neighbours, but they are affluent by any reasonable definition of human needs. This means that they have more income than they need to provide themselves adequately with all the basic necessities of life. After buying food, shelter, clothing, necessary health services and education, the absolutely affluent are still able to spend money on luxuries. The absolutely affluent choose their food for the pleasures of the palate, not to stop hunger; they buy new clothes to look fashionable, not to keep warm; they move house to be in a better neighbourhood or have a play room for the children, not to keep out the rain; and after all this there is still money to spend on books and records, colour television, and overseas holidays.

At this stage I am making no ethical judgments about absolute affluence, merely pointing out that it exists. Its defining characteristic is a significant amount of income above the level necessary to provide for the basic human needs of oneself and one's dependents. By this standard Western Europe, North America, Japan, Australia, New Zealand and the oil-rich Middle Eastern states are all absolutely affluent, and so are many, if not all, of their citizens. The USSR and Eastern Europe might also be included on this list. To quote McNamara once more:

The average citizen of a developed country enjoys wealth beyond the wildest dreams of the one billion people in countries with per capita incomes under $200. . . .

These, therefore, are the countries—and individuals—who have wealth which they could, without threatening their own basic welfare, transfer to the absolutely poor.

At present, very little is being transferred. Members of the Organization of Petroleum Exporting Countries lead the way, giving an average of 2.1% of their Gross National Product. Apart from them, only Sweden, The Netherlands and Norway have reached the modest UN target of 0.7% of GNP. Britain gives 0.38% of its GNP in official development assistance and a small additional amount in unofficial aid from voluntary organizations. The total comes to less than £1 per month per person, and compares with 5.5% of GNP spent on alcohol, and 3% on tobacco. Other, even wealthier nations, give still less: Germany gives 0.27%, the United States 0.22% and Japan 0.21%.

*   *   *   *   *

The Argument for an Obligation to Assist

The path from the library at my university to the Humanities lecture theatre passes a shallow ornamental pond. Suppose that on my way to give a lecture I notice that a small child has fallen in and is in danger of drowning. Would anyone deny that I ought to wade in and pull the child out? This will mean getting my clothes muddy, and either cancelling my lecture or delaying it until I can find something dry to change into; but compared with the avoidable death of a child this is insignificant.

A plausible principle that would support the judgment that I ought to pull the child out is this: if it is in our power to prevent something very bad happening, without thereby sacrificing anything of comparable moral significance, we ought to do it. This principle seems uncontroversial.

It will obviously win the assent of consequentialists; but non-consequentialists should accept it too, because the injunction to prevent what is bad applies only when nothing comparably significant is at stake. Thus the principle cannot lead to the kinds of actions of which non-consequentialists strongly disapprove—serious violations of individual rights, injustice, broken promises, and so on. If a non-consequentialist regards any of these as comparable in moral significance to the bad thing that is to be prevented, he will automatically regard the principle as not applying in those cases in which the bad thing can only be prevented by violating rights, doing injustice, breaking promises, or whatever else is at stake. Most non-consequentialists hold that we ought to prevent what is bad and promote what is good. Their dispute with consequentialists lies in their insistence that this is not the sole ultimate ethical principle: that it is *an* ethical principle is not denied by any plausible ethical theory.

Nevertheless the uncontroversial appearance of the principle that we ought to prevent what is bad when we can do so without sacrificing anything of comparable moral significance is deceptive. If it were taken seriously and acted upon, our lives and our world would be fundamentally changed. For the principle applies, not just to rare situations in which one can save a child from a pond, but to the everyday situation in which we can assist those living in absolute poverty. In saying this I assume that absolute poverty, with its hunger and malnutrition, lack of shelter, illiteracy, disease, high infant mortality and low life expectancy, is a bad thing. And I assume that it is within the power of the affluent to reduce absolute poverty, without sacrificing anything of comparable moral significance. If these two assumptions and the principle we have been discussing are correct, we have an obligation to help those in absolute poverty which is no less strong than our obligation to rescue a drowning child from a pond. Not to help would be wrong, whether or not it is intrinsically equivalent to killing. Helping is not, as conventionally thought, a charitable act which it is praiseworthy to do, but not wrong to omit; it is something that everyone ought to do.

This is the argument for an obligation to assist. Set out more formally, it would look like this.

- First premise: If we can prevent something bad without sacrificing anything of comparable significance, we ought to do it.
- Second premise: Absolute poverty is bad.
- Third premise: There is some absolute poverty we can prevent without sacrificing anything of comparable moral significance.
- Conclusion: We ought to prevent some absolute poverty.

The first premise is the substantive moral premise on which the argument rests, and I have tried to show that it can be accepted by people who hold a variety of ethical positions.

The second premise is unlikely to be challenged. Absolute poverty is, as McNamara put it, 'beneath any reasonable definition of human decency' and it would be hard to find a plausible ethical view which did not regard it as a bad thing.

The third premise is more controversial, even though it is cautiously framed. It claims only that some absolute poverty can be prevented without the sacrifice of anything of comparable moral significance. It thus avoids the objection that any aid I can give is just 'drops in the ocean' for the point is not whether my personal contribution will make any noticeable impression on world poverty as a whole (of course it won't) but whether it will prevent some poverty. This is all the argument needs to sustain its conclusion, since the second premise says that any absolute poverty is bad, and not merely the total amount of absolute poverty. If without sacrificing anything of comparable moral significance we can provide just one family with the means to raise itself out of absolute poverty, the third premise is vindicated.

I have left the notion of moral significance unexamined in order to show that the argument does not depend on any specific values or ethical principles. I think the third premise is true for most people living in industrialized nations, on any defensible view of what is morally significant. Our affluence means that we have income we can dispose of without giving up the basic necessities of life, and we can use this income to reduce absolute poverty. Just how much we will think ourselves obliged to give up will depend on what we consider to be of comparable moral significance to the poverty we could prevent: colour television, stylish clothes, expensive dinners, a sophisticated stereo system, overseas holidays, a (second?) car, a larger house, private schools for our children . . . For a utilitarian, none of these is likely to be of comparable significance to the reduction of absolute poverty; and those who are not utilitarians surely must, if they subscribe to the principle of universalizability, accept that at least *some* of these things are of far less moral significance than the absolute poverty that could be prevented by the money they cost. So the third premise seems to be true on any plausible ethical view—although the precise amount of absolute poverty that can be prevented before anything of moral significance is sacrificed will vary according to the ethical view one accepts.

Objections to the Argument

Taking care of our own Anyone who has worked to increase overseas aid will have come across the argument that we should look after those near us, our families and then the poor in our own country, before we think about poverty in distant places.

No doubt we do instinctively prefer to help those who are close to us. Few could stand by and watch a child drown; many can ignore a famine in Africa. But the question is not what we usually do, but what we ought to do, and it is difficult to see any sound moral justification for the view that distance, or community membership, makes a crucial difference to our obligations.

Consider, for instance, racial affinities. Should whites help poor whites before helping poor blacks? Most of us would reject such a suggestion out of hand, and our discussion of the principle of equal consideration of interests in Chapter 2 has shown why we should reject it: people's need for food has nothing to do with their race, and if blacks need food more than whites, it would be a violation of the principle of equal consideration to give preference to whites.

The same point applies to citizenship or nationhood. Every affluent nation has some relatively poor citizens, but absolute poverty is limited largely to the poor nations. Those living on the streets of Calcutta, or in a drought-stricken region of the Sahel, are experiencing poverty unknown in the West. Under these circumstances it would be wrong to decide that only those fortunate enough to be citizens of our own community will share our abundance.

We feel obligations of kinship more strongly than those of citizenship. Which parents could give away their last bowl of rice if their own children were starving? To do so would seem unnatural, contrary to our nature as biologically evolved beings—although whether it would be wrong is another question altogether. In any case, we are not faced with that situation, but with one in which our own children are well-fed, well-clothed, well-educated, and would now like new bikes, a stereo set, or their own car. In these circumstances any special obligations we might have to our children have been fulfilled, and the needs of strangers make a stronger claim upon us.

The element of truth in the view that we should first take care of our own, lies in the advantage of a recognized system of responsibilities. When families and local communities look after their own poorer members, ties of affection and personal relationships achieve ends that would otherwise require a large, impersonal bureaucracy. Hence it would be absurd to propose that from now on we all regard ourselves as equally responsible for the welfare of everyone in the world; but the argument for an obligation to assist does not propose that. It applies only when some are in absolute poverty, and others can help without sacrificing anything of comparable moral significance. To allow one's own kin to sink into absolute poverty would be to sacrifice something of comparable significance; and before that point had been reached, the breakdown of the system of family and community responsibility would be a factor to weigh and balance in favour of a small degree of preference for family and community. This small degree of preference is, however, decisively outweighed by existing discrepancies in wealth and property.

Property rights Do people have a right to private property, a right which contradicts the view that they are under an obligation to give some of their wealth away to those in absolute poverty? According to some theories of rights (for instance, Robert Nozick's) provided one has acquired one's property without the use of unjust means like force and fraud, one may be entitled to enormous wealth while others starve. This individualistic conception of rights is in contrast to other views, like the early Christian doctrine to be found in the works of Thomas Aquinas, which holds that since property exists for the satisfaction of human needs, 'whatever a man has in superabundance is owed, of natural right, to the poor for their sustenance'. A socialist would also, of course, see wealth as belonging to the community rather than the individual, while utilitarians, whether socialist or not, would be prepared to override property rights to prevent great evils.

Does the argument for an obligation to assist others therefore presuppose one of these other theories of property rights, and not an individualistic theory like Nozick's? Not necessarily. A theory of property rights can insist on our *right* to retain

wealth without pronouncing on whether the rich *ought* to give to the poor. Nozick, for example, rejects the use of compulsory means like taxation to redistribute income, but suggests that we can achieve the ends we deem morally desirable by voluntary means. So Nozick would reject the claim that rich people have an 'obligation' to give to the poor, in so far as this implies that the poor have a right to our aid, but might accept that giving is something we ought to do and failing to give, though within one's rights, is wrong—for rights is not all there is to ethics.

The argument for an obligation to assist can survive, with only minor modifications, even if we accept an individualistic theory of property rights. In any case, however, I do not think we should accept such a theory. It leaves too much to chance to be an acceptable ethical view. For instance, those whose forefathers happened to inhabit some sandy wastes around the Persian Gulf are now fabulously wealthy, because oil lay under those sands; while those whose forefathers settled on better land south of the Sahara live in absolute poverty, because of drought and bad harvests. Can this distribution be acceptable from an impartial point of view? If we imagine ourselves about to begin life as a citizen of either Kuwait or Chad—but we do not know which— would we accept the principle that citizens of Kuwait are under no obligation to assist people living in Chad?

Population and the ethics of triage Perhaps the most serious objection to the argument that we have an obligation to assist is that since the major cause of absolute poverty is overpopulation, helping those now in poverty will only ensure that yet more people are born to live in poverty in the future.

In its most extreme form, this objection is taken to show that we should adopt a policy of 'triage.' The term comes from medical policies adopted in wartime. With too few doctors to cope with all the casualties, the wounded were divided into three categories: those who would probably survive without medical assistance, those who might survive if they received assistance, but otherwise probably would not, and those who even with medical assistance probably would not survive. Only those in the middle category were given medical assistance. The idea, of course, was to use limited medical resources as effectively as possible. For those in the first category, medical treatment was not strictly necessary; for those in the third category, it was likely to be useless. It has been suggested that we should apply the same policies to countries, according to their prospects of becoming self-sustaining. We would not aid countries which even without our help will soon be able to feed their populations. We would not aid countries which, even with our help, will not be able to limit their population to a level they can feed. We would aid those countries where our help might make the difference between success and failure in bringing food and population into balance.

Advocates of this theory are understandably reluctant to give a complete list of the countries they would place into the 'hopeless' category; but Bangladesh is often cited as an example. Adopting the policy of triage would, then, mean cutting off assistance to Bangladesh and allowing famine, disease and natural disasters to reduce the population of that country (now around 80 million) to the level at which it can provide adequately for all.

In support of this view Garrett Hardin has offered a metaphor: we in the rich nations are like the occupants of a crowded lifeboat adrift in a sea full of drowning people. If we try to save the drowning by bringing them aboard our boat will be overloaded and we shall all drown. Since it is better that some survive than none, we should leave the others to drown. In the world today, according to Hardin, 'lifeboat ethics' apply. The rich should leave the poor to starve, for otherwise the poor will drag the rich down with them.

Against this view, some writers have argued that overpopulation is a myth. The world produces ample food to feed its population, and could, according to some estimates, feed ten times as many. People are hungry not because there are too many but because of inequitable land distribution, the manipulation of Third World economies by the developed nations, wastage of food in the West, and so on.

Putting aside the controversial issue of the extent to which food production might one day be increased, it is true, as we have already seen, that the world now produces enough to feed its inhabitants—the amount lost by being fed to animals itself being enough to meet existing grain shortages. Nevertheless population growth cannot be ignored. Bangladesh could, with land reform and using better techniques, feed its present population of 80 million; but by the year 2000, according to World Bank estimates, its population will be 146 million. The enormous effort that will have to go into feeding an extra 66 million people, all added to the population within a quarter of a century, means that Bangladesh must develop at full speed to stay where she is. Other low income countries are in similar situations. By the end of the century, Ethiopia's population is expected to rise from 29 to 54 million; Somalia's from 3 to 7 million, India's from 620 to 958 million, Zaire's from 25 to 47 million. What will happen then? Population cannot grow indefinitely. It will be checked by a decline in birth rates or a rise in death rates. Those who advocate triage are proposing that we allow the population growth of some countries to be checked by a rise in death rates—that is, by increased malnutrition, and related diseases; by widespread famines; by increased infant mortality; and by epidemics of infectious diseases.

The consequences of triage on this scale are so horrible that we are inclined to reject it without further argument. How could we sit by our television sets, watching millions starve while we do nothing? Would not that (far more than the proposals for legalizing euthanasia discussed in the last chapter) be the end of all notions of human equality and respect for human life? Don't people have a right to our assistance, irrespective of the consequences?

Anyone whose initial reaction to triage was not one of repugnance would be an unpleasant sort of person. Yet initial reactions based on strong feelings are not always reliable guides. Advocates of triage are rightly concerned with the long-term consequences of our actions. They say that helping the poor and starving now merely ensures more poor and starving in the future. When our capacity to help is finally unable to cope—as one day it must be—the suffering will be greater than it would be if we stopped helping now. If this is correct, there is nothing we can do to prevent absolute starvation and poverty, in the long run, and so we

have no obligation to assist. Nor does it seem reasonable to hold that under these circumstances people have a right to our assistance. If we do accept such a right, irrespective of the consequences, we are saying that, in Hardin's metaphor, we would continue to haul the drowning into our lifeboat until the boat sank and we all drowned.

If triage is to be rejected it must be tackled on its own ground, within the framework of consequentialist ethics. Here it is vulnerable. Any consequentialist ethics must take probability of outcome into account. A course of action that will certainly produce some benefit is to be preferred to an alternative course that may lead to a slightly larger benefit, but is equally likely to result in no benefit at all. Only if the greater magnitude of the uncertain benefit outweighs its uncertainty should we choose it. Better one certain unit of benefit than a 10% chance of 5 units; but better a 50% chance of 3 units than a single certain unit. The same principle applies when we are trying to avoid evils.

The policy of triage involves a certain, very great evil: population control by famine and disease. Tens of millions would die slowly. Hundreds of millions would continue to live in absolute poverty, at the very margin of existence. Against this prospect, advocates of the policy place a possible evil which is greater still: the same process of famine and disease, taking place in, say, fifty years time, when the world's population may be three times its present level, and the number who will die from famine, or struggle on in absolute poverty, will be that much greater. The question is: how probable is this forecast that continued assistance now will lead to greater disasters in the future?

Forecasts of population growth are

notoriously fallible, and theories about the factors which affect it remain speculative. One theory, at least as plausible as any other, is that countries pass through a 'demographic transition' as their standard of living rises. When people are very poor and have no access to modern medicine their fertility is high, but population is kept in check by high death rates. The introduction of sanitation, modern medical techniques and other improvements reduces the death rate, but initially has little effect on the birth rate. Then population grows rapidly. Most poor countries are now in this phase. If standards of living continue to rise, however, couples begin to realize that to have the same number of children surviving to maturity as in the past, they do not need to give birth to as many children as their parents did. The need for children to provide economic support in old age diminishes. Improved education and the emancipation and employment of women also reduce the birthrate, and so population growth begins to level off. Most rich nations have reached this stage, and their populations are growing only very slowly.

If this theory is right, there is an alternative to the disasters accepted as inevitable by supporters of triage. We can assist poor countries to raise the living standards of the poorest members of their population. We can encourage the governments of these countries to enact land reform measures, improve education, and liberate women from a purely child-bearing role. We can also help other countries to make contraception and sterilization widely available. There is a fair chance that these measures will hasten the onset of the demographic transition and bring population growth down to a manageable level. Success cannot be guaranteed; but the evidence that improved economic security and education reduce population growth is strong enough to make triage ethically unacceptable. We cannot allow millions to die from starvation and disease when there is a reasonable probability that population can be brought under control without such horrors.

Population growth is therefore not a reason against giving overseas aid, although it should make us think about the kind of aid to give. Instead of food handouts, it may be better to give aid that hastens the demographic transition. This may mean agricultural assistance for the rural poor, or assistance with education, or the provision of contraceptive services. Whatever kind of aid proves most effective in specific circumstances, the obligation to assist is not reduced.

C O M M E N T S ■ Q U E S T I O N S

1. Which of the principles—Rights, Justice, The Common Good, Self-Interest—does Singer's basic argument appeal to? Do you believe that Singer's argument constitutes a balanced appeal to these principles?
2. In the light of what Singer has said, comment on the saying, "charity begins at home."

3. Do you—or does your family—have luxury items such as color TV sets, expensive clothes, or a large house that you believe you can readily do without? Do you accept Singer's argument that it is morally wrong to have such things as long as there are many starving people in the world?

4. Do you accept Singer's claim that we should eat less meat in order to help conserve the world's food resources?

5. Do you accept Singer's round figure of 10 percent of income as an appropriate measure of the minimum amount that people in rich countries should give to poor countries?

J O H N   A R T H U R

Equality, Entitlements and the Distribution of Income

Introduction

My guess is that everyone who reads these words is wealthy by comparison with the poorest millions of people on our planet. Not only do we have plenty of money for food, clothing, housing, and other necessities, but a fair amount is left over for far less important purchases like phonograph records, fancy clothes, trips, intoxicants, movies, and so on. And what's more we don't usually give a thought to whether or not we ought to spend our money on such luxuries rather than to give it to those who need it more; we just assume it's ours to do with as we please.

Peter Singer, "Famine, Affluence, and Morality,"[1] and Richard Watson, "Reason and Morality in a World of Limited Food,"[2] argue that our assumption is wrong, that we should

1. Peter Singer, "Famine, Affluence, and Morality," *Philosophy and Public Affairs*, vol. 1, no. 3 (1972): 229–243.

2. Richard Watson, "Reason and Morality in a World of Limited Food," in *World Hunger and Moral Obligation*, eds. William Aiken and Hugh LaFollette (Englewood Cliffs, N.J.: Prentice-Hall, 1977).

John Arthur is a Professor of Philosophy at Tennessee State University who specializes in social philosophy and the philosophy of law. He is the editor of three books and author of many journal articles.

not buy luxuries when others are in severe need. But are they correct? In the first two sections of this paper my aim is to get into focus just what their arguments are, and to evaluate them. Both Singer and Watson, it seems to me, ignore an important feature of our moral code, namely that it allows people who deserve or have rights to their earnings to keep them.

But the fact that our code encourages a form of behavior is not a complete defense, for it is possible that our current moral attitudes are mistaken. Sections 3 and 4 consider this possibility from two angles: universalizability and the notion of an ideal moral code. Neither of these approaches, I argue, requires that desert and rights be sacrificed in the name of redistribution.

1. Equality and the Duty to Aid

What does our moral code have to say about helping people in need? Watson emphasizes what he calls the "principle of equity." Since "all human life is of equal value," and difference in treatment should be "based on freely chosen actions and not accidents of birth or environment," he thinks that we have "equal rights to the necessities of life." To distribute food unequally assumes that some lives are worth more than others, an assumption which, he says, we do not accept. Watson believes, in fact, that we put such importance on the "equity principle" that it should not be violated even if unequal distribution is the only way for anybody to survive. (Leaving aside for the moment whether or not he is correct about our code, it seems to me that if it really did require us to commit mass suicide rather than allow ine-

quality in wealth, then we would want to abandon it for a more suitable set of rules. But more on that later.)

Is Watson correct in assuming that all life is of equal value? Did Adolph Hitler and Martin Luther King, for example, lead two such lives? Clearly one did far more good and less harm than the other. Nor are moral virtues like courage, kindness, and trustworthiness equally distributed among people. So there are at least two senses in which people are not morally equal.

Yet the phrase "All men are equal" has an almost platitudinous ring, and many of us would not hesitate to say that equality is a cornerstone of our morality. But what does it mean? It seems to me that we might have in mind one of two things. First is an idea that Thomas Jefferson expressed in the *Declaration of Independence*. "All men are created equal" meant, for him, that no man is the moral inferior of another, that, in other words, there are certain rights which all men share equally, including life and liberty. We are entitled to pursue our own lives with a minimum of interference from others, and no person is the natural slave of another. But, as Jefferson also knew, equality in that sense does not require equal distribution of the necessities of life, only that we not interfere with one another, allowing instead every person the liberty to pursue his own affairs, so long as he does not violate the rights of his fellows.

Others, however, have something different in mind when they speak of human equality. I want to develop this second idea by noting briefly the details of Singer's argument in "Famine, Affluence, and Morality." He first argues that two general moral principles are widely accepted, and then that those principles imply an obligation to eliminate starvation.

The first principle is simply that "suffering and death from lack of food, shelter and medical care are bad." Some may be inclined to think that the mere existence of such an evil in itself places an obligation on others, but that is, of course, the problem which Singer addresses. I take it that he is not begging the question in this obvious way and will argue from the existence of evil to the obligation of others to eliminate it. But how, exactly, does he establish this? The second principle, he thinks, shows the connection, but it is here that controversy arises.

This principle, which I will call the greater moral evil rule, is as follows:

If it is in our power to prevent something bad from happening, without thereby sacrificing anything of comparable moral importance, we ought, morally, to do it.[3]

In other words, people are entitled to keep their earnings only if there is no way for them to prevent a greater evil by giving them away. Providing others with food, clothing, and housing would generally be of more importance than buying luxuries, so the greater moral evil rule now requires substantial redistribution of wealth.

Certainly there are few, if any, of us who live by that rule, although that hardly shows we are *justified* in our way of life; we often fail to live up to

our own standards. Why does Singer think our shared morality requires that we follow the greater moral evil rule? What arguments does he give for it?

He begins with an analogy. Suppose you came across a child drowning in a shallow pond. Certainly we feel it would be wrong not to help. Even if saving the child meant we must dirty our clothes, we would emphasize that those clothes are not of comparable significance to the child's life. The greater moral evil rule thus seems a natural way of capturing why we think it would be wrong not to help.

But the argument for the greater moral evil rule is not limited to Singer's claim that it explains our feelings about the drowning child or that it appears "uncontroversial." Moral equality also enters the picture. Besides the Jeffersonian idea that we share certain rights equally, most of us are also attracted to another type of equality, namely that like amounts of suffering (or happiness) are of equal significance, no matter who is experiencing them. I cannot reasonably say that, while my pain is no more severe than yours, I am somehow special and it's more important that mine be alleviated. Objectivity requires us to admit the opposite, that no one has a unique status which warrants such special pleading. So equality demands equal consideration of interests as well as respect for certain rights.

But if we fail to give to famine relief and instead purchase a new car when the old one will do, or buy fancy clothes for a friend when his or her old ones are perfectly good, are we not assuming that the relatively minor enjoyment we or our friends may get is as important as another

---

3. Singer also offers a "weak" version of this principle which, it seems to me, is *too* weak. It requires giving aid only if the gift is of *no* moral significance to the giver. But since even minor embarrassment or small amounts of happiness are not completely without moral importance, this weak principle implies little or no obligation to aid, even to the drowning child.

person's life? And that a form of prejudice; we are acting as if people were not equal in the sense that their interests deserve equal consideration. We are giving special consideration to ourselves or to our group, rather like a racist does. Equal consideration of interests thus leads naturally to the greater moral evil rule.

2. Rights and Desert

Equality, in the sense of giving equal consideration to equally serious needs, is part of our moral code. And so we are led, quite rightly I think, to the conclusion that we should prevent harm to others if in doing so we do not sacrifice anything of comparable moral importance. But there is also another side to the coin, one which Singer and Watson ignore. This can be expressed rather awkwardly by the notion of entitlements. These fall into two broad categories, rights and desert. A few examples will show what I mean.

All of us could help others by giving away or allowing others to use our bodies. While your life may be shortened by the loss of a kidney or less enjoyable if lived with only one eye, those costs are probably not comparable to the loss experienced by a person who will die without any kidney or who is totally blind. We can even imagine persons who will actually be harmed in some way by your not granting sexual favors to them. Perhaps the absence of a sexual partner would cause psychological harm or even rape. Now suppose that you can prevent this evil without sacrificing anything of comparable importance. Obviously such relations may not be pleasant, but according to the greater moral evil rule that is not enough; to be justified in refusing,

you must show that the unpleasantness you would experience is of equal importance to the harm you are preventing. Otherwise, the rule says you must consent.

If anything is clear, however, it is that our code does not *require* such heroism; you are entitled to keep your second eye and kidney and not bestow sexual favors on anyone who may be harmed without them. The reason for this is often expressed in terms of rights; it's your body, you have a right to it, and that weighs against whatever duty you have to help. To sacrifice a kidney for a stranger is to do more than is required, it's heroic.

Moral rights are normally divided into two categories. Negative rights are rights of noninterference. The right to life, for example, is a right not to be killed. Property rights, the right to privacy, and the right to exercise religious freedom are also negative, requiring only that people leave others alone and not interfere.

Positive rights, however, are rights of recipience. By not putting their children up for adoption, parents give them various positive rights, including rights to be fed, clothed, and housed. If I agree to share in a business venture, my promise creates a right of recipience, so that when I back out of the deal, I've violated your right.

Negative rights also differ from positive in that the former are natural; the ones you have depend on what you are. If lower animals lack rights to life or liberty it is because there is a relevant difference between them and us. But the positive rights you may have are not natural; they arise because others have promised, agreed, or contracted to give you something.

Normally, then, a duty to help a stranger in need is not the result of a right he has. Such a right would be positive, and since no contract or promise was made, no such right exists. An exception to this would be a lifeguard who contracts to watch out for someone's children. The parent whose child drowns would in this case be doubly wronged. First, the lifeguard should not have cruelly or thoughtlessly ignored the child's interests, and second, he ought not to have violated the rights of the parents that he help. Here, unlike Singer's case, we can say there are rights at stake. Other bystanders also act wrongly by cruelly ignoring the child, but unlike the lifeguard they do not violate anybody's rights. Moral rights are one factor to be weighed, but we also have other obligations; I am not claiming that rights are all we need to consider. That view, like the greater moral evil rule, trades simplicity for accuracy. In fact, our code expects us to help people in need as well as to respect negative and positive rights. But we are also entitled to invoke our own rights as justification for not giving to distant strangers or when the cost to us is substantial, as when we give up an eye or kidney.

Rights come in a variety of shapes and sizes, and people often disagree about both their shape and size. Can a woman kill an unborn child because of her right to control her body? Does mere inheritance transfer rights to property? Do dolphins have a right to live? While some rights are widely accepted, others are controversial.

One more comment about rights, then we'll look at desert. Watson's position, which I criticized for other reasons earlier, is also mistaken because he ignores important rights. He claims that we must pay no attention to "accidents of birth and environment" and base our treatment of people on "what they freely choose." But think about how you will (or did) select a spouse or lover. Are you not entitled to consider such "accidents of birth and environment" as attractiveness, personality, and intelligence? It is, after all, your future, and it is certainly a part of our shared moral code that you have a right to use those (or whatever) criteria you wish in selecting a mate. It is at best an exaggeration to say we must always "ignore accidents of birth and environment" in our treatment of people.

Desert is a second form of entitlement. Suppose, for example, an industrious farmer manages through hard work to produce a surplus of food for the winter while a lazy neighbor spends his summer fishing. Must our industrious farmer ignore his hard work and give the surplus away because his neighbor or his family will suffer? What again seems clear is that we have more than one factor to weigh. Not only should we compare the consequences of his keeping it with his giving it away; we also should weigh the fact that one farmer deserves the food, he earned it through his hard work. Perhaps his deserving the product of his labor is outweighed by the greater need of his lazy neighbor, or perhaps it isn't, but being outweighed is in any case not the same as weighing nothing!

Desert can be negative, too. The fact that the Nazi war criminal did what he did means he deserves punishment, that we have a reason to send him to jail. Other considerations, for example the fact that nobody will be deterred by his suffering, or that he is old and harmless, may weigh against punishment and so we may let him go; but again that does not mean he doesn't still deserve to be punished.

Our moral code gives weight to both the greater moral evil principle and entitlements. The former emphasizes equality, claiming that from an objective point of view all comparable suffering, whoever its victim, is equally significant. It encourages us to take an impartial look at all the various effects of our actions; it is thus forward-looking. When we consider matters of entitlement, however, our attention is directed to the past. Whether we have rights to money, property, eyes, or whatever, depends on how we came to possess them. If they were acquired by theft rather than from birth or through gift exchange, then the right is suspect. Desert, like rights, is also backward-looking, emphasizing past effort or past transgressions which now warrant reward or punishment.

Our commonly shared morality thus requires that we ignore neither consequences nor entitlements, neither the future results of our action nor relevant events in the past. It encourages people to help others in need, especially when it's a friend or someone we are close to geographically, and when the cost is not significant. But it also gives weight to rights and desert, so that we are not usually obligated to give to strangers.

One path is still open as a defense of the greater moral evil rule, and it deserves comment. I have assumed throughout that Singer wants to emphasize the great disparity in the amount of enjoyment someone may get from, say, a new car, as compared with the misery that could be prevented by using the money to save another's life. The fact that the two are not comparable means that the money should not be spent on the car. It is possible to interpret the rule differently, however. By admitting that having rights and deserving things are also of moral significance Singer could accept what I have said so that the greater moral evil rule would survive intact.

The problem with this response, however, is that the greater moral evil rule has now become an empty platitude, urging nothing more than that we should prevent something bad unless we have adequate moral reason not to do so. Since rights and desert often provide such reasons, the rule would say nothing useful about our obligation to help others, and it certainly would not require us to "reduce ourselves to the level of marginal utility" so that the "consumer society" would "slow down and perhaps disappear" as Singer claims. I will therefore assume he would not accept such an interpretation of his view, that entitlements are not among the sacrifices which could balance off the suffering caused by failing to help people in need.

But unless we are moral relativists, the mere fact that entitlements are an important part of our moral code does not in itself justify such a role. Singer and Watson can perhaps best be seen as moral reformers, advocating the rejection of rules which provide for distribution according to rights and desert. Certainly the fact that in the past our moral code condemned suicide and racial mixing while condoning slavery should not convince us that a more enlightened moral code, one which we would want to support, would take such positions. Rules which define acceptable behavior are continually changing, and we must allow for the replacement of inferior ones.

Why should we not view entitlements as examples of inferior rules we are better off without? What could justify our practice of evaluating actions by looking backward to rights and desert instead of just to their consequences? One answer is that more fundamental values than rights and desert are at stake, namely fairness, justice, and respect. Failure to reward those who earn good grades or promotions is wrong because it's *unfair*; ignoring past guilt shows a lack of regard for *justice*; and failure to respect rights to life, privacy, or religious choice suggests a lack of *respect for other persons*.

Some people may be persuaded by those remarks, feeling that entitlements are now on an acceptably firm foundation. But an advocate of equality may well want to question why fairness, justice, and respect for persons should matter. But since it is no more obvious that preventing suffering matters than that fairness, respect, and justice do, we again seem to have reached an impasse.

* * * * *

The lesson to be learned here is a general one: The moral code it is rational for us to support must be practical; it must actually work. This means, among other things, that it must be able to gain the support of almost everyone.

But the code must be practical in other respects as well. I have emphasized that it is wrong to ignore the possibilities of altruism, but it is also important that a code not assume people are more unselfish than they are. Rules that would work only for angels are not the ones it is rational to support for humans. Second, an ideal code cannot assume we are more objective than we are; we often tend to rationalize when our own

interests are at stake, and a rational person will also keep that in mind when choosing a moral code. Finally, it is not rational to support a code which assumes we have perfect knowledge. We are often mistaken about the consequences of what we do, and a workable code must take that into account as well.

I want now to bring these various considerations together in order to decide whether or not to reject entitlements in favor of the greater moral evil rule. I will assume that the egoist is not a serious obstacle to acceptance of a welfare maximizing code, either because egoists are, like angels, merely imaginary, or because a practical egoist would only support a code which can be expected to gain wide support. We still have to ask whether entitlements would be included in a welfare maximizing code. The initial temptation is to substitute the greater moral evil rule for entitlements, requiring people to prevent something bad whenever the cost to them is less significant than the benefit to another. Surely, we might think, total welfare would be increased by a code requiring people to give up their savings if a greater evil can be prevented.

I think, however, that this is wrong, that an ideal code would provide for rights and would encourage rewarding according to desert. My reasons for thinking this stem from the importance of insuring that a moral code really does, in fact, work. Each of the three practical considerations mentioned above now enter the picture. First, it will be quite difficult to get people to accept a code which requires that they give away their savings, extra organs, or anything else merely because they can avoid a greater evil for a stranger. Many people simply wouldn't do it, they aren't that altruistic. If the code attempts to require it anyway, two results would likely follow. First, because many would not live up to the rules, there would be a tendency to create feelings of guilt in those who keep their savings in spite of having been taught it is wrong, as well as conflict between those who meet their obligations and those who do not. And, second, a more realistic code, one which doesn't expect more than can be accomplished, may actually result in more giving. It's a bit like trying to influence how children spend their money. Often they will buy less candy if rules allow them to do so occasionally but they are praised for spending on other things than if its purchase is prohibited. We cannot assume that making a charitable act a requirement will always encourage such behavior. Impractical rules not only create guilt and social conflict, they often tend to encourage the opposite of the desired result. By giving people the right to use their savings for themselves, yet praising those who do not exercise the right but help others instead, we have struck a good balance; the rules are at once practical yet reasonably effective.

Similar practical considerations would also influence our decision to support rules that allow people to keep what they deserve. For most people, working is not their favorite activity. If we are to prosper, however, goods and services must be produced. Incentives are therefore an important motivation, and one such incentive for work is income. Our code encourages work by allowing people to keep a large part of what they earn, indeed that's much the point of entitlements. "I worked hard

for it, so I can keep it" is an oft-heard expression. If we eliminate this rule from our code and ask people to follow the greater moral evil rule instead, the result would likely be less work done and so less total production. Given a choice between not working and continuing to work knowing the efforts should go to benefit others, many would choose not to work.

Moral rules should be practical in a third sense, too. They cannot assume people are either more unbiased or more knowledgeable than they are. This fact has many implications for the sorts of rules we would want to include in a welfare maximizing code. For example, we may be tempted to avoid slavish conformity to counterproductive rules by allowing people to break promises whenever they think doing so would increase total welfare. But again we must not ignore human nature, in this case our tendency to give special weight to our own welfare and our inability to be always objective in tracing the effects of our actions. While we would not want to teach that promises must never be broken no matter what the consequences, we also would not want to encourage breaking promises any time a person can convince himself the results of doing so would be better than if he kept his word.

Similar considerations apply to the greater moral evil rule. Imagine a situation where someone feels he can prevent an evil befalling himself by taking what he needs from a large store. The idea that he's preventing something bad from happening (to himself) without sacrificing anything of comparable moral significance (the store won't miss the goods) would justify robbery. Although sometimes a particular act of theft really is welfare maximizing, it does not follow that we should support a *rule* which allows theft whenever the robber is preventing a greater evil. Such a rule, to work, would require more objectivity and more knowledge of long-term consequences than we have. Here again, including rights in our moral code serves a useful role, discouraging the tendency to rationalize our behavior by underestimating the harm we may cause to others or exaggerating the benefits that may accrue to ourselves.

The first sections of this paper attempted to show that our moral code is a bit schizophrenic. It seems to pull us in opposite directions, sometimes toward helping people who are in need, other times toward the view that rights and desert justify keeping things we have even if greater evil could be avoided were we to give away our extra eye or our savings account. This apparent inconsistency led us to a further question: Is the emphasis on entitlements really defensible, or should we try to resolve the tension in our own code by adopting the greater moral evil rule and ignoring entitlements? In this section I considered the idea that we might choose between entitlements and the greater moral evil rule by paying attention to the general nature of a moral code, and in particular to the sort of code we might want to support. I argued that all of us, including egoists, have reason to support a code which promotes the welfare of everyone who lives under it. That idea, of an ideal moral code which it is rational for everyone to support, provides a criterion for deciding which rules are sound and which ones we should support.

My conclusion is a conservative one: Concern that our moral code encourages production and not fail because it unrealistically assumes people are more altruistic or objective than they are means that our rules giving people rights to their possessions and encouraging distribution according to desert should be part of an ideal moral code. And since this is so, it is not always wrong to invoke rights or claim that money is deserved as justification for not giving aid, even when something worse could be prevented by offering help. The welfare maximizing moral code would not require us to maximize welfare in each individual case.

I have not yet discussed just how much weight should be given to entitlements, only that they are important and should not be ignored as Singer and Watson suggest. Certainly an ideal moral code would not allow people to overlook those in desperate need by making entitlements absolute, any more than it would ignore entitlements. But where would it draw the line?

It's hard to know, of course, but the following seems to me to be a sensible stab at an answer. Concerns about discouraging production and the general adherence to the code argue strongly against expecting too much; yet on the other hand, to allow extreme wealth in the face of grinding poverty would seem to put too much weight on entitlements. It seems to me, then, that a reasonable code would require people to help when there is no substantial cost to themselves, that is, when what they are sacrificing would not mean *significant* reduction in their own or their families' level of happiness. Since most people's savings accounts and nearly everybody's second kidney are not insignificant, entitlements would in those cases outweigh another's need. But if what is at stake is trivial, as dirtying one's clothes would normally be, then an ideal moral code would not allow rights to override the greater evil that can be prevented. Despite our code's unclear and sometimes schizophrenic pos- ture, it seems to me that these judgments are not that different from our current moral attitudes. We tend to blame people who waste money on trivia when they could help others in need, yet not to expect people to make large sacrifices to distant strangers. An ideal moral code thus might not be a great deal different from our own.

C O M M E N T S ■ Q U E S T I O N S

1. The primary thrust of Arthur's paper is to argue against the sort of position that is defended by Peter Singer in the previous reading selection. Singer appeals primarily to what we are calling the Principle of Justice; Arthur argues that we must also give significant weight to what we are calling the Principle of Rights (Arthur sometimes refers to it as the principle of rights, sometimes as the principle of entitlements). At the very end of the article, Arthur states what he takes to be the way to achieve the correct sort of balance between the two principles. Do you believe that he has, indeed, described the best possible sort of balance? What might Singer say in response to Arthur?

2. Arthur places a lot of emphasis on the practical side of morality: "The moral code it is rational for us to support must be practical; it must actually work." This means, for one thing, that we ought not to assume that people are more unselfish than they actually are. Do you believe that Arthur is correct to place as much emphasis as he does on the practical aspect of morality? Is ethics at all concerned with a possible transformation of human nature?

R I C H A R D   T.   D e G E O R G E

The Environment, Rights, and Future Generations

T he rapid growth of technology has outstripped our moral intuitions, which are consequently unclear and contradictory on many environmental issues. As we try to handle new moral problems we stretch and strain traditional moral concepts and theories. We do not always do so successfully. The difficulties, I believe, become apparent as we attempt to deal with the moral dimension of the depletion of nonrenewable resources.

Consider the use of oil, presently our chief source of energy. The supply of oil is limited. Prudence demands that we not waste it. But who has a right to the oil or to its use? From one point of view the owners of the oil have a right to it. And we each have a right to the amount we are able to buy and use. From another point of view everyone has a right to oil, since it is a natural resource which should be used for the good of all. Americans, as we know, use a great deal more oil than most other people in the world. Is it moral of us to do so? Will our use preclude people in other parts of the world from having it available to them when they will need it for uses we presently take for granted? Will some unborn generations not have the oil they will probably need to live as we presently do?

These questions trouble many people. They have a vague sense of moral uneasiness, but their intuitions concerning the proper answers are not clear. They feel that they should not waste oil or fuel or energy. They feel that they should not keep their houses as cool in summer and as warm in winter as they used to. They feel that they should impose these conditions on their children. Yet they are not, simply on moral grounds, ready to give up too much in the way of comfort. Once forced to do so by economics, they will. But they are somewhat uneasy about their own attitude. Is it morally proper that affluent individuals or nations are able to live in greater comfort and will have to make fewer sacrifices than the less well-to-do, simply because they have more money?

My intuitions on the issue of energy and oil are in no way privileged. I do not know how much oil or energy I have a right to; nor can I say with any certainty how much those in underdeveloped countries presently have a right to, or how much should be saved for them, or how much

---

Richard T. DeGeorge is a professor of philosophy at the University of Kansas. He is widely known for his work in the area of business ethics.

Reprinted with permission from K. E. Goodpaster and K. M. Sayre, eds., *Ethics and Problems of the 21st Century* (Notre Dame: University of Notre Dame Press, 1979) pp. 93–105. Copyright © 1979 by University of Notre Dame Press.

should be saved for generations yet to come. Nor do I know clearly how to weigh the claims to oil of the people in underdeveloped countries vis-à-vis the future claims to oil of generations yet unborn. If all presently existing members of the human race used energy at the rate that the average American does, there would obviously be much less left for future generations. Does this mean that others in the world should not use as much oil as Americans; or that Americans should use less, so that those in other countries will be able to use more; or that people in less developed countries should not use more in order that future generations of Americans will be able to use as much as present-day Americans?

Though our intuitions are not very clear on these issues, there is some consensus that present people have moral obligations vis-à-vis future generations. Yet stating the grounds for even these obligations is not an easy task and it is one that I do not think has been adequately accomplished. The attempt to state them in terms of rights has not been fruitful. And the utilitarian or consequentialist approach has fared no better. Lack of clarity about collective responsibility further magnifies the complexity of the problem.

In this paper I shall not be able to solve the question either of the proper use of oil or of the basis of our obligations to future generations. I shall attempt only to test the ability of some moral theories and language to express them adequately. I shall negatively show why some approaches are not fruitful lines to pursue. And positively I shall argue for some considerations which I think are applicable, though by themselves

they are not adequate to solve the moral problems at issue.

Talk about rights has proliferated in recent years.[1] Moral feelings and concerns have been put in terms of rights in a great many areas. It does not fit in some of them. Thus for instance some people concerned with the environment have come to speak of the rights of nature, or the rights of trees, or the rights of a landscape.[2] The intent of people who use such language is easy enough to grasp. They are concerned about man's abuse of the environment, his wanton cutting of trees, or his despoiling the countryside. But those who wish to attribute rights to nature or trees or landscapes must come up with some way of interpreting the meaning of rights which makes their assertions plausible. The usual ways of unpacking rights in terms of justifiable moral claims, or in terms of interests, or in terms of freedom do not apply to nature or trees.[3] Yet failure to provide an interpretation which both grounds the purported rights of trees and relates them to the rights of humans, while accounting for the obvious differences between them, leads to

---

1. See Rex Martin and James W. Nickel, "A Bibliography on the Nature and Foundations of Rights 1947–1977," *Political Theory* (forthcoming).

2. See, for example, Aldo Leopold, *A Sand County Almanac and Sketches Here and There* (New York: Oxford University Press, 1949); Christopher Stone, *Should Trees Have Standing?: Toward Legal Rights for Natural Objects* (Los Altos, Ca.: Kaufmann, 1974).

3. H. L. A. Hart, "Are There Any Natural Rights?," *Philosophical Review 64* (1955): 175–91 argues that the natural right of men to be free is basic; Joel Feinberg, "Duties, Rights and Claims," *American Philosophical Quarterly* 3 (1966): 137–44; David Lyons, "The Correlativity of Rights and Duties," *Nous* 4 (1970): 45–57.

confusion and precludes arriving at a satisfactory solution to the moral problems posed.

These attempts are nonetheless instructive. For rights can be ascribed and rights-talk can be used with respect to almost anything,[4] even if the claims involved cannot always be adequately defended. When we restrict our use of rights-talk to human beings, therefore, it should be clear that the question of whether people have rights is not a factual one comparable to the question of whether they have brains, or whether they usually have two arms or two legs. The question of whether future generations have rights is similarly not one simply of fact; and the answer is compounded because there is no consensus and little precedent. Thus simply looking at ordinary language, or simply unpacking the concepts of person or rights, will not yield a definitive answer. Since the question is not a factual one, it is to be solved in part by making a decision. It is possible to say that future generations have rights. But I shall argue that we avoid more problems if we maintain that, properly speaking, future generations do not presently have rights, than if we say they do.

Future generations by definition do not now exist. They cannot now, therefore, be the present bearer or subject of anything, including rights. Hence they cannot be said to have rights in the same sense that presently existing entities can be said to have them. This follows from the briefest analysis of the present tense form of the verb 'to have'. To claim that what does not now exist cannot now have rights in any strong sense does not deny that persons who previously existed had rights when they existed, or that persons who will exist can properly be said to have rights when they do exist, or that classes with at least one presently existing member can correctly be said to have rights now. Nor does it deny that presently exiting persons can and sometimes do make rights claims for past or future persons. It emphasizes, however, that in ascribing rights to persons who do not exist it is the existing person who is expressing his interests or concerns.

Those who claim that present existence is not necessary for the proper ascription of present rights sometimes cite the legal treatment of wills as a counterexample. In this instance, they argue, the courts act as if the deceased continued to have rights, despite the fact that he no longer exists. But this is not the only way of construing wills or the actions of courts. If we consider those countries in which inheritance laws were suddenly changed so that all the property of a deceased went to the state rather than to the heirs named in a will, it would be more plausible to argue that the rights of a particular heir were violated rather than the

---

4. H. J. McCloskey, "Rights," *Philosophical Quarterly* 15 (1965): 115–27, raises the question of whether art objects can have rights. A number of philosophers have recently argued for the rights of animals: Andrew Linzey, *Animal Rights* (London: S. C. M. Press, 1976); Peter Singer, *Animal Liberation* (London: Jonathan Cape, 1976); on the other hand, see Joseph Margolis, "Animals Have No Rights and Are Not Equal to Humans," *Philosophic Exchange* 1 (1974): 119–23. See also M. and N. Golding, "Value Issues in Landmark Preservation." *Ethics and Problems of the 21st Century* ed. K. E. Goodpaster aand K. M. Sayre. (Notre Dame: University of Notre Dame Press, 1979), 175–190.

rights of the deceased. Equally plausible construals can, I believe, be made for each of the other standard supposed counterexamples.[5]

Consider next the supposed present rights of some future individual. Before conception potential parents can and should take into account the obligations they will have in connection with caring for the children they might produce. They can and should consider the rights their children will have if they come into being. But since the children do not yet exist, we should properly say they do not now have rights. Among the rights they do not have (since they have none) is the right to come into existence. By not bringing them into existence we do not violate *that* right, and we can obviously prevent their having any other rights. Now if we attempt to speak otherwise, I suggest, we invite confusion. What sense would it make to say that some entity which was not conceived had a right to be conceived? We cannot sensibly or intelligibly answer the question of whose right was infringed when there is no bearer of the right.

A similar difficulty, and therefore a similar reason for not using rights-talk, arises in speaking of the rights of future generations, providing we mean by that term some generation no members of which have presently been conceived and so in no sense presently exist. Such future generations could at least in theory be prevented from coming into existence. If they were never produced it

5. Joel Feinberg, "The Rights of Animals and Unborn Generations," *Philosophy and Environmental Crisis*, ed. William T. Blackstone (Athens: University of Georgia Press, 1974), pp. 43–68, defends the opposite view.

would be odd to say that their rights had been violated. For since they do not now exist they can have no right to exist or to be produced. Now, they have no present rights at all.

Nonetheless, possible future entities can be said to have possible future rights. And future generations when they exist will have rights at that time. But the temptation to consider all rights as temporarily on a par should be resisted. Moreover, the weight which should now be given to the rights claims which future individuals or future generations will have should be proportional to the likelihood that such individuals will exist, and by analogy with the case of parents the obligations should be borne by those individuals (and collectively by those groups) most responsible for bringing the individuals into existence.

Future persons do not, individually or as a class, presently have the right to existing resources. They differ from presently existing persons who in general have the right to the judicious use of the goods necessary for them to continue in existence. And if some of these goods, because of present rational demands, are used up, then it is a mistake to say that future persons or future generations have or will have a right to *those* goods and that we violate their rights by using them up. Future generations or future individuals or groups should correctly be said to have a right only to what is available when they come into existence, and hence when their possible future rights become actual and present.

Many people feel that this is incorrect and that future persons and generations have as much right as presently existing persons to what presently exists, for example, in the way of resources. A few considerations, however, should suffice to show that such a view is mistaken. The first consideration is conceptual. Only once a being exists does *it* have needs or wants or interests. It has a right only to the kind of treatment or to the goods available to it at the time of its conception. It cannot have a reasonable claim to what is not available. Consider this on an individual level. Suppose a couple are so constituted that if they have a child, the child will have some disease, for example, sickle-cell anemia. Suppose the woman conceives. Does the fetus or baby have a right not to have sickle-cell anemia? Before it was conceived there was no entity to have any rights. Once it is conceived, its genetic make-up is such as it is. It makes no sense to speak of *its* having the right not to have the genetic make-up it has, since the alternative is its not being. This does not mean that it does not have the right to treatment, that if genetic engineering is able to remedy its defect it does not have the right to such remedy, and so on. But it does mean that there is no *it* to have rights before conception, and that once conceived it is the way it is. There is therefore no sense in speaking of the antecedent right for it not to be the way it is, though it may have a subsequent right to treatment. Similarly, prehistoric cave men had no right to electric lights or artificial lungs since they were not available in their times, and we have no right to enjoy the sight of extinct animals. To claim a right to what is not available and cannot be made available is to speak vacuously. Some future people, therefore, will have no right to the use of gas, or oil, or coal, if, when they come into existence, such goods

no longer exist. If the goods in question are not available, *they* could not be produced with a right to them.

Second, suppose we attempt to speak otherwise. Suppose we assume that all future generations have the same right to oil as we do; and suppose that since it is a nonrenewable resource, it is used up—as it is likely to be—by some future generation. What of the next generation that follows it? Should we say that since that generation cannot be produced without violating its right to oil it has a right not to be produced? Surely not. Or should we say that if it is produced one of its rights is necessarily infringed, and that the right of all succeeding generations will similarly necessarily be infringed? It is possible to speak that way; but to do so is at least confusing and at worst undermines the whole concept of rights by making rights claims vacuous.

The third reason for not speaking of the rights of future generations as if their rights were present rights is that it leads to impossible demands on us. Suppose we consider oil once again. It is a nonrenewable resource and is limited in quantity. How many generations in the future are we to allow to have present claim to it? Obviously if we push the generations into the unlimited future and divide the oil deposits by the number of people, we each end up with the right to a gallon or a quart or a teaspoon or a thimble full. So we must reconstrue the claim to refer to the practical use of oil. But this means that we inevitably preclude some future generation from having oil. And if all future generations have equal claim, then we necessarily violate the rights of some future generations. It is clear, then, that we do not wish to let unending future claims have equal weight with present claims. The alternative, if we do not consistently treat future rights differently from the rights of presently existing persons, is arbitrarily to treat some rights, those of sufficiently distant generations, as less deserving of consideration than the same claims of generations closer to us. What I have been arguing is that our approach turns out to be less arbitrary and more consistent if we refuse to take even the first step in considering future rights as anything other than future, and if we do not confuse them or equate them with the rights of presently existing people.

To ascribe present rights to future generations is to fall into the trap of being improperly motivated to sacrifice the present to the future, on the grounds that there will possibly (or probably) be so innumerably many future generations, each of which has a presently equal right to what is now available, as to dwarf the rights of present people to existing goods. The trap can be avoided by maintaining that present existence is a necessary condition for the possession of a present right. To the extent that rights-talk tends to be nontemporal and future generations are considered to have present rights, such talk tends to confuse rather than clarify our obligations for the future, and the ground for such obligations. For this and similar reasons future generations should not be said to have present rights.

If the argument so far is correct, however, we have not solved a problem, but merely seen how not to approach it if we want a solution. That future generations do not have present rights does not mean that present people, individually and collectively,

have no obligations to try to provide certain kinds of environment and to leave open as many possibilities as feasible for those who will probably come after them, consistent with satisfying their own rational needs and wants. How are we to describe this felt moral imperative?

If the language of rights will not do, a theory such as utilitarianism does not fare much better. Consider once again the problem of how much oil we can legitimately use and how much we are morally obliged to save for future generations. Let every person count for one and let us decide on the basis of what produces the greatest good for the greatest number of people. The task is difficult enough in dealing with micro-moral problems, though we have the history of human experience to help us solve with at least a certain amount of assurance many ordinary moral questions. We can be fairly sure that lying in general is wrong, as is murder, and theft, and perjury, and so on.

When we try to carry out the analysis with respect to nonrenewable resources, the question of how many future generations we are to count is one problem. We have already seen the difficulties it leads to. Second, we cannot know how long people will actually need oil. We cannot know when a substitute will be found. We therefore do not know how many generations to count and how many to discount. Third, generations of people lived long before oil was discovered and put to its present uses. As oil becomes less available, if no substitute is found people may have to go back to doing things the way they did before the discovery of oil. Will such a world be morally poorer than ours? On a utilitarian calculation the answer may well be negative. But we can plausibly argue that good is not maximized if we waste our resources, and that more good will probably be done for more people if we stretch out our resources while providing for our own rational needs. The difficulty of course, consists in specifying our rational and justifiable needs. Utilitarianism does not help us do this, nor does it help us decide between the somewhat greater good (however defined) of presently existing people versus the lesser good of more people in the future when the totals are equal. Therefore this approach, too, does not provide the key for determining the proper use of our non-renewable resources.

There is another dimension to the problem, however, which I have ignored thus far and which it would be well to consider at least briefly. With respect to the use of oil and future generations I have spoken of "we" and "they" and have traded on our common understanding of the terms. Moral obligation and responsibility, however, have for the most part been discussed in individual terms. The notion of collective responsibility and collective obligation and other collectively applied moral terms are in need of clarification. The concept of collective responsibility, for instance, despite some of the work that has been done on it,[6] remains in many cases obscure.

_____

6. See Peter A. French, ed., *Individual and Collective Responsibility: Massacre at My Lai* (Cambridge, Mass.: Schenkman 1972); Joel Feinberg, "Collective Responsibility," *Journal of Philosophy* 45 (1968): 674–87; W. H. Walsh, "Pride, Shame and Responsibility," *The Philosophical Quarterly* 20 (1970): 1–13; D. E. Cooper, "Collective Responsibility," *Philosophy* 43 (1968): 258–68.

One difficulty arises in attempting to allocate individual responsibility under conditions in which individual effort has no real effect by itself. Who is responsible for preserving the environment for our children and grandchildren? The answer may be all of us. But what is required of each of us individually is far from clear. How responsible for strip mining is a carpenter in New York City? How responsible for oil depletion is someone who drives to work in a car? Is he morally obliged to drive less or not at all or to buy and use a smaller car? What if smaller cars are not available or if he cannot afford to buy one or if none of his neighbors drive less or buy smaller cars? Is the collective responsibility to fall primarily on collective agencies—on corporations and government? But this collective responsibility must also be allocated to individuals. Does each person have a responsibility to preserve resources no matter what others do? Or is it a prima facie obligation which becomes a real obligation only when our action and the action of others will effect the results desired? Are we therefore individually freed of our responsibility when others do not do their share? Does collective failure to fulfill a collective moral obligation absolve an individual of his individual obligation to do what he should under the collective obligation on the grounds that his sacrifice without that of the others is inefficacious? My claim is not that these questions do not have answers but that they have not been sufficiently discussed and that until we get clear about the answers we are unlikely to feel the pressure of the moral obligations we may have or to be able to weigh them against the individual moral pressures we feel with respect, for instance, to supplying our children or our fellow citizens with as high a quality of life as we can.

Consider further the questions of resources in the light of populations. If the population of one country grows unchecked to the detriment of the people of that country and to the exhaustion of that country's resources, do the people of other countries have the obligation to keep alive the individuals produced by parents who had no regard for whether the children could be supported? Who is the "we" who should preserve resources, and for whom should they be preserved? If the people of one nation sacrifice, should it be the heirs of that nation's people who reap the rewards of such sacrifice, or should it be all people wherever they might be and whoever they are? On the one hand our intuitions tell us that no country can do everything for the whole world, that people have to help themselves, and that each country's primary responsibility is to its own people and their descendants. On the other hand we have the unrelieved plight of human misery and death, some of which could be alleviated if some people would share more of what they have. By what right do some use many times more in the way of natural resources than others, especially when it is not by merit but partially by luck that they have natural riches available to them that are not available in their own countries to other people?

I mentioned earlier that our moral intuitions were still adequate to some of the moral problems which seem to be looming before us. Part of the reason is that we have no precedent on which to build. Another is that we have no adequate institutions and practices on a global scale with which to relate global moral problems. Morality is a social institution and moral obligations are often closely tied to particular social practices. The moral obligations of parents with respect to their children, for instance, are different in a society with a nuclear family in which parents have almost exclusive responsibility for the support and care of their children, and in a society in which all children are raised by the state, cared for in communal nurseries, state schools, and so on. Moral problems about the use of resources and the preservation of the environment transcend national boundaries. Yet we have no world institutions or practices adequate to help ground pertinent moral judgments.

National sovereignty may be an anachronism in an age of such interdependence. But while it remains it sets a real limit to certain kinds of moral obligations richer nations have to poorer ones. Within the boundaries of a given country transfer payments can be effected in a variety of ways and are justified within the system because they achieve their goals. Within the system one practice fits together with others. But on the global scale there is no system, there is little in the way of enforceable law, there is great diversity of political systems, and there is disagreement about moral claims. Transfer payments from rich to poor within a nation can be handled, as in the United States, through taxes agreed to by the legislature representing the people. Internationally there is no such system. The extrapolation from individual moral cases to parallel national or collective cases consequently frequently falters.

If my analysis so far is correct the new large moral questions which are impinging upon us cannot be solved all at once. It may be that the most we can do individually—and where possible collectively—is to work on clarifying the problems, to suggest solutions, to impel others to work toward them, to be willing to cooperate in transcending national boundaries, to give up national sovereignty, and so on.

I have been arguing that environmental problems have developed faster than our intuitions, theories, practices, and institutions, and that some attempts to stretch our theories to fit our vague intuitions have not been successful. Yet I do not wish to imply that we are at a total loss from a moral point of view with respect to environmental problems or that they are ultimately unsolvable. I shall briefly argue three points, the first of which, I believe, is relatively uncontroversial and requires little defense.

Consider a couple planning to have a baby. Before they conceive him they have an obligation to be reasonably sure that they can raise him properly, that he will have enough to eat, and that he will under ordinary circumstances have the opportunity to grow and develop. Parents who knowingly and willingly have children whom they know they and their society cannot care for, who they know will soon die of starvation or disease, do not, if my earlier analysis is correct, violate any purported antecedent rights of the child. But they certainly seem to produce suffering and misery which they could have avoided producing. We can plausibly argue that we individually have an obligation to provide the minimum goods of life necessary for those for whom we have a rather close responsibility. And collectively we have a similar responsibility for

preserving the environment in such a way that it can provide the goods necessary for those who come after us—or for roughly fifty or a hundred years. To be uncontroversial, however, the claim must be restricted to those for whom we have a rather close responsibility. For the obligation of care is tied to the causal chain of reproduction. If the population of one country goes unchecked to the detriment of the people of that country, it is not clear that other countries have the obligation to keep alive the individuals so produced. It may be that richer countries have some obligations in this regard. But it is clear that the obligation of the members of a society to care for their own people is greater than the obligation to care for people of other societies.

My two other claims are more controversial and may seem to some mistaken; hence they deserve more comment. The first is that we do not owe to others, either outside our society or to those who will come after us, what we need to maintain a reasonable quality of life and dignity for the present members of our society; the second is that we do not owe others, either in other societies or those who will come after us, a better life than we ourselves are able to attain and enjoy. Present sacrifice for a better future for others may be a noble, altruistic goal. But it is not morally demanded and cannot be legitimately forced on those who do not wish to be noble, altruistic, or heroic.

Moral theorists have long argued that each human being, if the resources are available, deserves enough of the goods of life so that he can enjoy at least a minimal standard of living required for human dignity. My claim is consistent with that view.

It allows room for the moral obligation of those who are well off to help bring those below the minimal standard of dignity up to that standard. How that is to be done within our own society is easier to determine than how that is to be effectively achieved on a global scale. But my claim denies that any generation or people have to fall below that level in order to help others rise above it. The argument for that is fairly straightforward.

Starting from the equality of all persons qua persons my good for me is as valuable as your good for you. Other things being equal your good is not better or more important than mine. Hence, again other things being equal, there is no reason why, given a choice, I should be morally obliged to choose your good over mine. Otherwise, by like reasoning you would have to choose my good over yours. Secondly, my claim is that other things being equal those who, where it is possible to avoid it, bring misery on themselves or on those close to them, are the ones who should bear the brunt of consequences of their actions. This is part of what it means to accept the moral responsibility for one's actions. Hence there are limits to the sacrifice which can be morally required of one people to help those less well off than they. One limit is that equality is not required; what is required is simply helping those below the minimal standard to rise up to it. Another limit is that those who are aided can legitimately be expected, as a condition of such aid, to take the means available to them to help themselves.

My second more controversial claim was that there is no moral imperative that requires each generation to sacrifice so that the next generation may be better off than it is. Parents do not owe their children better lives than they had. They may wish their children to have better lives; but they do not owe it to them. If there is to be a peak followed by a decline in the standard of living, and if such a peak is tied to the use of natural resources, then providing there is no profligate waste, there is no reason why the present rather than a future generation should enjoy that peak. For no greater good is served by any future group enjoying the peak, since when its turn comes, if enjoying the peak is improper for us, it will be improper for them also.

We do not owe future generations a better life than we enjoy nor do we owe them resources we need for ourselves. When dealing with renewable resources, other things being equal, they should not be used up faster than they can be replaced. When they are needed at a greater rate than they can be replaced, they raise the same problem raised by nonrenewable resources. We should use what we *need*, but we should keep our needs rational, avoid waste, and preserve the environment as best we can. How this is to be translated into the specific allocation of goods and resources is not to be determined a priori or by the fiat of government but by as many members of the society at large who are interested and aware and informed enough to help in the decision-making process. Part of that process must involve clarifying the moral dimensions of the use of resources and developing the moral theory to help us state consistently and evaluate our moral intuitions.

Up until relatively recent times it may have seemed that each generation was better off than the previous one, and that just as each successive generation had received a better lot than its predecessor, it had an obligation to continue the process. But we are now at the stage where our own efforts are frequently counterproductive. Our progress in transportation has led to pollution; our progress in pest control has led to new strains of insects resistant to our chemicals or has resulted in pollution of our food; our expansion of industry has taken its toll in our rivers and in the ocean; and so on. We are now faced with shortages of the type we used to experience only during war times. So we can argue that in some ways we are already over the peak and will all be forced to cut down on certain kinds of consumption. That our children have to bear our fate is no reason for reproach. What would be reprehensible on the individual level is if we lived in luxury and allowed our children to exist at a subsistence level. It is appropriate that we help them to live as well as we, where that is possible. But we have no responsibility for helping them live better at great expense to ourselves. Nor does it make much sense to speak in those terms where overlapping generations are concerned.

What I have been maintaining is that we should be careful not to assume the burden of the future on some mistaken notion of the need to sacrifice the present to the future. The past appeal of the call to sacrifice the present to the future depended on the foreseeable future being increasingly better, and each generation both being better off than the previous one and worse off than the following in an unending chain. The realization that the goods of the earth are limited should mitigate somewhat that appeal. The earth will not in the foreseeable future be able to support limitless numbers of human beings at a high standard of living.

There is one last caveat that I should like to add, however. I have been arguing that we do not owe the future more than we have in the way of goods of the earth or in terms of standard of living. This does not mean that we do not owe them the benefit of what we have learned, that we should not preserve and pass on culture, knowledge, moral values—all increased to the extent possible. For standard of living is not the only good in life and quality of life should not be confused with quantity of goods. In fact, if we do soon suffer a decline in our standard of living either voluntarily by freely sacrificing for others or simply because we use up our resources before we find adequate substitutes, then what we should pass on to our children are the qualities of mind and spirit which will help them to cope with what they have, to live as fully as possible with what is available, and to value the quality of life rather than the quantity of goods they have.

My three claims are not a solution to the problems of limited resources or a full analysis of what we owe to future generations. They are a start which needs a fuller theory to ground it and a set of institutions to work within. But they do not constitute a call to selfishness. Enlightened self-interest may well benefit mankind as a whole more than unenlightened self-sacrifice, even if the latter could be sold to large segments of the world's population. For we have come to a point where, if we limit our use and abuse of the environment, it is in our self-interest to do so. The needs of the present and of already existing generations should take precedence over consideration of the needs of those who may exist at some far distant time. Perhaps all we can expect is that each generation look that far ahead.

The moral issues raised by environmental questions are in some ways truly new and test both our moral intuitions and concepts. Not all our moral values and intuitions are inapplicable. But we have much analytic work to do before we can fully and clearly state—much less solve—some of the problems which face us.

C   O   M   M   E   N   T   S   ■   Q   U   E   S   T   I   O   N   S

1. Future persons do not have rights to resources that exist at the present, but will have rights only to resources that will exist when *they* exist. In support of this claim, De George argues that if all future persons had the same rights to oil as present persons have, then the amount of oil that each person would have a right to would be miniscule. Is the argument sound? Could it be extended to other resources besides oil?

2. We do not owe to future generations a better life than we ourselves have, nor do we owe to future generations "what we need to maintain a reasonable quality of life and dignity for the present members of society." Our obligation is only to help "those below the minimal standard to rise up to it." Do you agree?

3. De George rejects a utilitarian solution to problems about future generations. What arguments does he give? Are they good arguments?

GUS SPETH

Perspectives from the Global 2000 Report

Throughout the past decade, a wide variety of disturbing studies and reports have been issued by the United Nations, the Worldwatch Institute, the World Bank, the International Union for the Conservation of Nature and Natural Resources, and other organizations. These reports have sounded a persistent warning: our international efforts to stem the spread of human poverty, hunger and misery are not achieving their goals; the staggering growth of human population, coupled with ever-increasing human demands, are beginning to cause permanent damage to the planet's resource base.

The most recent such warning—and the one with which I am most familiar—was issued in July of 1980 by the Council of Environmental Quality and the U.S. State Department. Called *Global 2000 Report to the President*, it is the result of a three-year effort by more than a dozen agencies of the U.S. Government to make long-term projections across the range of population, resource and environmental concerns. Given the obvious limitations of such projections, the *Global 2000 Report* can best be seen as a reconnaissance of the future. And the results of that reconnaissance are disturbing.

I feel very strongly that the *Global 2000 Report*'s findings confront the United States and other nations with one of the most difficult challenges facing our planet during the next two decades—rivaling the global arms race in importance.

The report's projections point to continued rapid population growth, with world population increasing from 4.5 billion today to more than 6 billion by 2000. More people will be added to the world's population each day in the year 2000 than were born today—about 100 million a year as compared with 75 million in 1980. Most of these additional people will live in the poorest countries, which will contain about four-fifths of the human race by the end of the century.

Unless other factors intervene, this planetary majority will see themselves growing worse off compared with those living in affluent nations. The income gap between rich and poor nations will widen, and the per capita gross national product of the less-developed countries will remain at generally low levels. In some areas—

Gus Speth has been a Law Professor at Georgetown University, and—as chairman of the Council on Environmental Quality in the Executive Office of the President—an advisor to President Carter. He is now President of the World Resources Institute, a center for policy research on global resource and environmental issues.

From "Resources and Security: Perspectives from the *Global 2000 Report*," *World Future Society Bulletin* (1981). Reprinted by permission of the author.

especially in parts of Latin America and East Asia—income per capita is expected to rise substantially. But gross national product in the great populous nations of South Asia—India, Bangladesh and Pakistan—will be less than $200 per capita (in 1975 dollars) by 2000. Today, some 800 million people live in conditions of absolute poverty, their lives dominated by hunger, ill health, and the absence of hope. By 2000, if current policies remain unchanged, their number could grow by 50 percent.

While the report projects a 90 percent increase in overall world food production in the 30 years from 1970 to 2000, a global per capita increase of less than 15 percent is projected even for the countries that are already comparatively well-fed. In South Asia, the Middle East, and the poorer countries of Africa, per capita food consumption will increase marginally at best, and in some areas may actually decline below present inadequate levels. Real prices of food are expected to double during the same 30-year period.

The pressures of population and growing human needs and expectations will place increasing strains on the Earth's natural systems and resources. The spread of desert-like conditions due to human activities now claims an area about the size of Maine each year. Croplands are lost to production as soils deteriorate because of erosion, compaction, and water-logging and salinization, and as rural land is converted to other uses.

The increases in world food production projected by the report are based on improvements in crop yields per acre continuing at the same rate as the record-breaking increases of the post-World War II period. These improvements depended heavily on energy-intensive technologies like fertilizer, pesticides, fuel for tractors and power for irrigation. But the report's projections show no relief from the world's tight energy situation. World oil production is expected to level off by the 1990s. And for the one-quarter of humanity who depend on wood for fuel, the outlook is bleak. Projected needs for wood will exceed available supplies by about 25 percent before the turn of the century.

The conversion of forested land to agricultural use and the demand for fuelwood and forest products are projected to continue to deplete the world's forests. The report estimates that these forests are now disappearing at rates as high as 18 to 20 million hectares—an area half the size of California—each year. As much as 40 percent of the remaining forests in poor countries may be gone by 2000. Most of the loss will occur in tropical and subtropical areas.

The loss of tropical forests, along with the impact of pollution and other pressures on habitats, could cause massive destruction of the planet's genetic resource base. Between 500,000 and two million plant and animal species—15 to 20 percent of all species on Earth—could become extinct by the year 2000. One-half to two-thirds of the extinctions will result from the clearing or deterioration of tropical forests. This would be a massive loss of potentially valuable sources of food, pharmaceutical chemicals, building materials, fuel sources and other irreplaceable resources.

Deforestation and other factors will worsen severe regional water shortages and contribute to the deterioration of water quality. Population growth alone will cause demands for water to at least double from 1971 levels in nearly half of the world.

Industrial growth is likely to worsen air quality. Air pollution in some cities in less-developed countries is already far above levels considered safe by the World Health Organization. Increased burning of fossil fuels, especially coal, may contribute to acid rain damage to lakes, plantlife, and the exteriors of buildings. It also contributes to the increasing concentration of carbon dioxide in the Earth's atmosphere, which could possibly lead to climatic changes with highly disruptive effects on world agriculture. Depletion of the stratospheric ozone layer, attributed partly to chlorofluorocarbon emissions from aerosol cans and refrigeration equipment, could also have an adverse effect on food crops and human health.

Disturbing as these findings are, it is important to stress that the *Global 2000 Report*'s conclusions represent not predictions of what will occur, but projections of what could occur if we do not respond. If there was any doubt before, there should be little doubt now—the nations of the world, industrialized and less developed alike, must act urgently and in concert to alter these dangerous trends before the projections of the *Global 2000 Report* become realities.

The warnings, then, are clear. Will we heed them, and will we heed them in time? For if our response is delayed, the costs could be great.

On these matters, I am cautiously optimistic. I like to think that the human race is *not* self-destructive—that it *is* paying, or can be made to pay, attention—that as people throughout the world come to realize the full dimensions of the challenge

before us, we will take the actions needed to meet it.

Our efforts to secure the future must begin with a new appreciation for, and then an application of, three fundamental concepts. They are *conservation, sustainable development*, and *equity*. I am convinced that each of them is essential to the development of the kind of long-term global resource strategy we need to deal with the problems I have been discussing.

Conservation

The first thing we must do is to get serious about the conservation of resources—renewable and non-renewable alike. We can no longer take for granted the renewability of renewable resources. The natural systems—the air and water, the forests, the land—that yield food, shelter and the other necessities of life are susceptible to disruption, contamination and destruction.

Indeed, one of the most troubling of the findings of the *Global 2000 Report* is the effect that rapid population growth and poverty are already having on the productivity of renewable natural resource systems. In some areas, particularly in the less developed countries, the ability of biological systems to support human populations is already being seriously damaged by efforts of present populations to meet desperate immediate needs, such as the needs for grazing land, firewood and building materials.

And these stresses, while most acute in the developing countries, are not confined to them. In recent years, the United States has been losing annually about 3 million acres of rural land—a third of it prime agricultural land—due to the spread of housing developments, highways, shopping malls and the like. We are also losing annually the rough equivalent—in terms of production capability—of another 3 million acres due to soil degradation—erosion and salinization. Other serious resource threats in the United States include those posed by toxic chemicals and other pollutants to groundwater supplies, which provide drinking water for half of the American public, and directly affect both commercial and sport fishing.

Achieving the necessary restraint in the use of renewable resources will require new ways of thinking by the peoples and governments of the world. It will require the widespread adoption of a "Conserver Society" ethic—an approach to resources and environment that, while attuned to the needs of each society, recognizes not only the importance of resources and environment to our own sustenance, well-being and security, but also our obligation to pass this vital legacy along to future generations. Perhaps the most arrogant attitude of which the human spirit is capable is the notion that the riches of the Earth are ours to plunder or carelessly destroy . . . that the needs and the lives of those who will follow us on this tiny and fragile planet are of no concern to us. "Future generations," someone once said, "What have they done for us?"

Fortunately, we are beginning to see signs that people in the United States and in other nations *are* becoming aware of the limits to our resources and the importance of conserving them. Energy problems, for example, are pointing the way to a future in which conservation is the password. As energy supplies go down and prices go up, we are learning that conserving—getting more and more out of each barrel of oil or ton of coal—is the cheapest and safest approach. Learning to conserve nonrenewable resources like oil and coal is the first step toward building a Conserver Society that values, nurtures, and protects all of its resources. Such a society appreciates economy in design and avoidance of waste. It realizes the limits to low-cost resources and to the environment's carrying capacity. It insists that market prices reflect all costs, social as well as private, so that consumers are fully aware in the most direct way of the real costs of consumption.

The Conserver Society prizes recycling over pollution, durability over obsolescence, quality over quantity, diversity over uniformity. It knows that beauty—whether natural or man-made—is too precious to be destroyed and that the Earth's wild creatures demand our conserving restraint not simply for utilitarian reasons but because, as part of the community of life that has evolved here with us, they too call this place home.

In this, the United States must take the lead. We cannot expect the rest of the world to adopt a Conserver Society ethic if we ourselves do not set a strong, successful example.

Sustainable Development

But the Conserver Society ethic, by itself, is not enough. It is unrealistic to expect people living at the margin of existence—people fighting desperately for their own survival—to think about the long-term survival of the planet. When people need to burn wood to keep from freezing, they will cut down trees.

We must find a way to break the cycle of poverty, population growth and environmental deterioration. We must find ways to improve the social and economic conditions of the poor nations and poor people of the world—their incomes, their access to productive land, their educational and employment opportunities. It is only through sustainable economic development that real progress can be made in alleviating hunger and poverty and in erasing the conditions that contribute so dangerously to the destruction of our planet's carrying capacity.

One of the most important lessons of the *Global 2000 Report* is that the conflict between development and environmental protection is, in significant part, a myth. Only a concerted attack on the roots of extreme poverty—one that provides people with the opportunity to earn a decent livelihood in a nondestructive manner—will enable us to protect the world's natural systems. It is also clear that development and economic reforms will have no lasting success unless they are suffused with concern for ecological stability and wise management of resources. The key concept here, of course, is *sustainable* development. Economic development, if it is to be successful over the long term, must proceed in a way that enhances the natural resource base of all the developing nations, instead of exploiting those resources for short-term economic or political gain.

Unfortunately, the realities of the current North-South dialogue between the developed and the developing nations suggest that achieving steady, sustainable development will be a difficult process—one that will require great patience and understanding on all sides. For our part here in the United States, we must resist the strong temptation to turn inward—to tune out the rest of the world's problems and to focus exclusively on our own economic difficulties. We must remember that, relatively speaking, we Americans luxuriate in the Earth's abundance, while other nations can barely feed and clothe their people. Unless we act, this disparity between rich and poor will tend to grow, increasing the possibilities for anger and resentment from those on the short end of the wealth equation—the great majority of mankind. One does not have to be particularly farsighted to see that the trends discussed in *Global 2000* heighten the chances for global instability—for exploitation of fears, resentments, and frustrations; for incitement to violence; for conflicts based on resources.

The *Global 2000 Report* itself discusses some of the destabilizing prospects that may be in store for us if we do not act decisively:

"The world will be more vulnerable both to natural disaster and to disruptions from human causes . . .Most nations are likely to be still more dependent on foreign sources of energy in 2000 than they are today. Food production will be more vulnerable to disruptions of fossil fuel energy supplies and to weather fluctuations as cultivation expands to more marginal areas. The loss of diverse germ plasm in local strains and wild progenitors of food crops, together with the increase of monoculture, could lead to greater risks of massive crop failures. Larger numbers of people will be vulnerable to higher food prices or even famine when adverse weather occurs. The world will be more vulnerable to the disruptive effects of war. The tensions that could lead to war will have multiplied. The potential for conflict over fresh water alone is underscored by the fact that out of 200 of the world's major river basins, 148 are shared by two countries and 52 are shared by three to ten countries."

The 1980 Report of the Brandt Commission on International Development Issues is eloquent in its plea for action: "War is often thought of in terms of military conflict, or even annihilation. But there is a growing awareness that an equal danger might be chaos—as a result of mass hunger, economic disaster, environmental catastrophes, and terrorism, so we should not think only of reducing the traditional threats to peace, but also of the need for change from chaos to order."

Equity

The late Barbara Ward, eminent British scholar, argued that the nations of the world can learn a valuable lesson from the experience of 19th-Century England, where the industrial revolution produced an appalling disparity in the distribution of wealth. It was a time when property owners and industrial managers reaped enormous profits while the laborers and mechanics—and their children—worked themselves into early graves.

Today, Ward observes: "The skew in world income is as great. The already developed peoples—North America, Europe, the Soviet Union, Japan—are the latter-day dukes, commanding over 70 percent of the planet's wealth for less than a quarter of the population. And in all too many developing countries the economic growth of the last two decades has been almost entirely appropriated by

the wealthiest ten percent of the people. The comparisons in health, length of life, diet, literacy all work out on the old Victorian patterns of unbelievable injustice."

Ward recommends—and I heartily agree—that the developed nations of today follow the lead of men like Disraeli, who recognized the need to narrow the gap between rich and poor in 19th-Century England and to create a new social order which allowed every citizen a share of the nation's wealth. Without perceptive leaders like Disraeli and other men of conscience who saw the need for reform, Ward argues that the growing pressure for equality and social justice would have torn British society apart. The result would have been similar to that in other nations where far-thinking leadership and compassion were lacking: "social convulsion, violent revolution and an impetus to merciless worldwide war and conquest."

The situation we face in the world today is all too similar. While the humanitarian reasons for acting generously to alleviate global poverty and injustice are compelling enough in themselves, we must also recognize the extent to which global poverty and resource problems can contribute to regional and worldwide political instability—an instability that can threaten the security of nations throughout the world.

Thus, along with conservation and sustainable development, the development of global resource strategy will require a much greater emphasis on *equity*—on a fair sharing of the means to development and the products of growth—not only among nations, but within nations as well.

C O M M E N T S ■ Q U E S T I O N S

1. A policy that emphasizes conservation of present resources for the sake of the future can be contrasted with a policy that emphasizes a reliance upon future new discoveries and new technologies to replace the resources that are presently being used up. Why does Speth place considerable emphasis upon the first of these alternatives, that is, upon conservation? Does he place too much emphasis on conservation?

2. How would Speth respond to the following claim that is made by De George: "We should be careful not to assume the burden of the future on some mistaken notion of the need to sacrifice the present to the future."

R E A D I N G S

Aiken, William, and Hugh Lafollette. *World Hunger and Moral Obligation.* Englewood Cliffs, N.J.: Prentice-Hall, 1977.

Blackstone, William E., ed. *Philosophy and Environmental Crisis.* Athens: University of Georgia Press, 1974.

Brown, Peter G., and Henry Shue, eds. *Food Policy.* New York: Free Press, 1977.

Commoner, Barry. *The Closing Circle.* New York: Alfred A. Knopf, 1971.

George, Susan. *How the Other Half Dies.* Rev. ed. New York: Penguin Books, 1977.

Gussow, Joan Dye. *The Feeding Web: Issues in Nutritional Ecology.* Palo Alto, Calif.: Bull Publishing Co., 1978.

Hardin, Garrett. *Stalking the Wild Taboo.* Los Altos, Calif.: William Kauffman, 1978.

Lappé, Frances Moore, and Joseph Collins. *Food First: Beyond the Myth of Scarcity.* Rev. ed. New York: Ballantine Books, 1978.

Schumaker, E. F. *Small Is Beautiful.* New York: Harper and Row, 1973.

Abortion and Euthanasia

his chapter contains two historical surveys that might be helpful to read first. One is on attitudes toward abortion and is to be found in the first part of the selection from John T. Noonan, while the other is on attitudes toward euthanasia and suicide and is to be found in the first part of the selection from Joseph Fletcher.

It is appropriate to consider the moral issues of abortion and euthanasia together in the same chapter because they are closely related. Abortion is ending the life of a human fetus, for whatever reason; euthanasia is ending the life of a human organism any time after birth for reasons that can broadly be called "mercy killing." Sometimes abortions also are performed for reasons of mercy killing, when a seriously defective fetus is suspected, but abortions most often are performed for reasons that have nothing to do with the health of the fetus but rather with the mother's circumstances. In contrast, euthanasia is carried out only when strong consideration is given to the potential suffering of the person who dies.

The major questions that are raised by the controversy over euthanasia are the following: Can suicide ever be morally acceptable? Is it ever morally right to bring to an end an innocent life? Is it possible for us to make correct judgments as to whether or not someone else's life is meaningful, valuable, or worthwhile for that person? Can we make such judgments for ourselves? What is the purpose or value of human life itself? Except for the question about suicide, these questions all clearly are relevant to the abortion controversy as well as to the discussion of euthanasia.

When abortion is considered by itself, insofar as that is possible, then the major questions are the following: Is a fetus a person? Does a fetus have a right to life and, if so, what is the status or strength of that right? The abortion controversy is a complex matter, in part because each of these two questions can be answered in a number of different ways. To most of the philosophers who have written about abortion it has seemed that no easy yes or no answers to either question can be found. All four of the present chapter's reading selections on abortion contain answers, either explicitly or implicitly, to both of the above questions. Without oversimplifying these answers in an unfair way, it would not be possible even to state all of them in this introductory essay. But the following points can be made, which hopefully will be of some help.

First, it is important to keep in mind that two quite distinct types of argument are found that are intended as a defense for abortion. One of them rests upon the claim that a fetus is not a person, or is not a person in the "full sense." Two different versions of this argument are given in the readings, one in the selection from Henry Ruf and one in the selection from Mary Anne Warren. Both Ruf and Warren offer restricted and limited defenses of abortion. The selection from Noonan contains arguments *against* any defense of abortion that rests upon the claim that a fetus is not a person or is not a person in the "full sense." Some of these arguments are addressed specifically to the claims discussed by Ruf and Warren. Others are made in the context of certain beliefs from a more strictly theological context, such as the belief that human souls are first joined to the human organism at the time of conception.

The other one of the two major types of argument made in defense of abortion rests upon the following claim: even if it is supposed that a fetus *is* a person— either in a strong or weak sense—a mother's right to autonomy is still a more important consideration than is the fetus's (strong or not so strong) right to its own life. This argument is discussed in all four of the reading selections on the abortion question. In the selection from Warren a particularly strong version of this argument is first stated in some detail and then rejected. The selection from Ruf contains a defense of a much weaker version of this argument. The selection from U.S. Supreme Court Justice Byron White contains a rejection of a somewhat stronger version of the same argument.

The question of whether or not a fetus is a person arises, first and most obviously, because a healthy fetus has the potential for becoming a human being exactly like the rest of us. It arises, second, because of the fact that at successive stages in its development the fetus comes more and more to resemble a mature human being. (In its strictest sense, the term "fetus" should be applied to the developing prenatal organism only after the end of the second month of development. During the first two weeks, the term "zygote" should be applied and after this time the term "embryo" should be applied up to the end of the second month.)

Some of the significant stages of prenatal development are the following:

- End of the second or third week—The heart is pumping.

- End of the sixth week—All of the organs are present.

- End of eighth week—There is readable electrical activity in the brain.

- End of tenth week—There is spontaneous movement.

- End of twelfth to sixteenth week—Movement will be felt by the mother.

- End of sixteenth to twentieth week—Heart beats can be heard.

- End of twentieth week—The earliest time for *any* fetus to survive on its own (approximately 10% could survive)

- End of twenty-eighth week—The typical fetus can be called "viable," that is, able to survive on its own.

Some of the developmental stages of the fetus have special legal significance. The most important Supreme Court decision bearing upon abortion, *Roe vs. Wade* in 1973, makes reference, first, to the end of the third month and, second, to the end of the seventh month. *Roe vs. Wade* is the Supreme Court decision which, in effect, "legalized" abortion across the country. As such, it governs all state laws regarding abortion at the present time, but it governs them differently depending upon the time during a pregnancy at which an abortion may be considered:

a. For the stage prior to approximately the end of the first trimester, the abortion decision and its effectuation must be left to the medical judgment of the pregnant woman's attending physician.
b. For the stage subsequent to approximately the end of the first trimester, the State, in promoting its interest in the health of the mother, may, if it chooses, regulate the abortion procedure in ways that are reasonably related to maternal health.
c. For the stage subsequent to viability the State, in promoting its interest in the potentiality of human life, may, if it chooses, regulate, and even proscribe, abortion except where it is necessary, in appropriate medical judgment, for the preservation of the life or health of the mother. (from *Roe vs. Wade* 1, 410, U.S. 113. 93 S. Ct. 705 (1973)).

The majority of the Court in *Roe vs. Wade* accepted the view that, up until the end of the third month (the end of the first trimester), abortions performed according to current medical practices pose no health hazard for the mother and therefore should not be subject to legal restriction by state laws. After the end of the first trimester, according to the Court, states may pass laws regulating abortion, but only for the purpose of protecting the mother's health:

> Examples of permissible state regulation in this area are requirements as to the qualifications of the person who is to perform the abortion; as to the licensure of that person; as to the facility in which the procedure is to be performed, that is, whether it must be a hospital or may be a clinic or some other place of less-than-hospital status; as to the licensing of the facility; and the like. (from *Roe vs. Wade*)

The Court understood viability to occur at the end of the seventh month, but possibly as early as the end of the sixth month. The Court ruled that states may pass laws that prohibit abortion in the interests of protecting the life of the fetus only after the point when viability has been achieved.

The discussion of abortion in this chapter can readily be understood in terms of conflicts among the moral principles stated in chapter 1. Especially, it can be understood in terms of a conflict between a mother's self-interest and the fetus's right to life, however this may be construed. It can also be seen in terms of a conflict between the Principle of Justice, which would seem to dictate that the fetus not be harmed (since, of all living things, a fetus would appear to be most helpless and most in need), and the Principle of the Common Good, insofar as it may be argued, as Ruf for example does, that a very important social good—namely respect for persons—is best served when abortions are allowed in selected cases.

The discussion of euthanasia in this chapter is not so readily understood in terms of conflicts among the moral principles stated in chapter 1. In the first place, this is because Richard B. Brandt claims that it is not particularly fruitful to discuss the termination of defective newborns in the context of a discussion of the rights, or alleged rights, of newborns. Brandt's treatment of the subject proceeds as though newborns had no rights. (In contrast, if Ruf's arguments regarding abortion are extended to cover euthanasia, as they are in the book from which the selection in this chapter is taken, then defective newborns *may* be assigned rights whose moral value could be weighed against other moral values.)

Some of the traditional arguments against euthanasia as applied to adults are such that it is difficult to relate them directly to the moral principles from chapter 1. To take the major example, the general prohibition of suicide has traditionally not been an appeal to individual rights, justice, the common good, or even self-interest. It has been a different sort of argument—most commonly stated as an appeal to God's will, to the claim that God simply has commanded us not to take our own lives.

Brandt argues that it is best sometimes to end the lives of severely defective newborns *both* for their own good and because keeping them alive may place too great a burden on their parents or on society. Brandt does not argue that euthanasia could ever be justified solely on the grounds that it would decrease the burdens on others, but argues instead that decreasing the burdens on others is an additional reason in some cases for doing what will at the same time eliminate the suffering of the severely defective newborn.

The paper by Brandt is restricted to a discussion of reasons in defense of euthanasia for newborns who are severely defective. The paper by John A. Robertson, which follows the one by Brandt, contains arguments against euthanasia for defective newborns. The selection from Joseph Fletcher contains, in addition to the historical survey referred to above, a survey of arguments for and against euthanasia as applied to adults who are suffering from incurable diseases. Fletcher's intention, overall, is to defend euthanasia by first stating each of the major arguments in opposition to euthanasia, and second, by giving responses to each of the arguments.

There is a controversial distinction that has been much written about in recent years, but which, for want of space, is not given an extended treatment in the present chapter. I am referring to the distinction between "active euthanasia" and "passive euthanasia," which is captured by the phrases "killing" versus "letting die." Both Brandt and Fletcher make reference to this distinction, but neither develops his argument in terms of it. In contrast, some writers, such as Arthur J. Dyck,[1] argue that euthanasia is defensible only when it is passive. Thus, Dyck argues that giving a suffering person a lethal injection is always wrong but that withholding life-prolonging treatment in certain cases is not wrong. The position of Dyck has been argued against by James Rachels,[2] who maintains that passive euthanasia, because it may prolong the life of a suffering person, may be more cruel than active euthanasia. He argues that the real issue is whether or not euthanasia is to be carried out, not the means by which it is to be carried out.

Notes

1. See "An Alternative to the Ethic of Euthanasia" in *To Live and To Let Die*, ed. R. H. Williams (New York: Springer-Verlag 1973).

2. "Active and Passive Euthanasia," *The New England Journal of Medicine*, vol. 292, no. 2, (1975): 78–80.

J O H N T. N O O N A N

An Almost Absolute Value in History

T he Old Testament has nothing to say on abortion, but the Hellenic Jews of the diaspora developed an opinion The Septuagint translation of Exod. 21:22 provided an opportunity. Where the Hebrew had said that when a man accidentally causes an abortion "life is given for life" only if the mother dies, the Greek read "life is given for life" if the embryo is "formed," so that an express penalty was provided for the abortion. In his first-century commentary Philo noted that by implication intentional as well as accidental abortion was thereby condemned. Philo himself associated abortion with infanticide and the abandonment of children, practices of inhumanity which he now found regarded "with complacence" by many nations.[9]

Abortion, indeed, according to contemporary observers, was practiced very generally in the Greco-Roman world. The divided opinions of a few sages scarcely checked the powerful personal motives which made it attractive. The law of the empire punished abortion committed without the father's consent.[10] It also punished the giving of drugs for abortion,[11] but it is unlikely that the law was enforced unless the recipient died. The object of the law was not to protect the embryo as a human person, for it was regarded as part of the mother.[12] The purpose was to restrain "bad example," that is, the bad example of giving magical potions which could cause death to the recipient.[13] As pagan observations and Christian complaints indicated, parents' freedom to dispose of their young offspring was taken for granted by the empire.[14] That the Jews should have

for *"pharmakeia"* toward the children. Plutarch, *Romulus* 22. Probably the use of contraceptive or abortifacient drugs to prevent children is meant.

11. *Digest* 48.19.38.5; cf. *Digest* 48.8.8.

12. *Id.* at 24.4.1.1; 35.2.9.1.

13. The "bad example" rationale for the law is given by the jurist Paul, *Digest* 48.19.38.5, without explanation. As it also applies to the giving of aphrodisiac potions, I take it that the bad example relates to the character of the potion, not to the effect on the birth rate.

14. On the acceptance of abandonment of children by their parents, see SUETONIUS, *Gaius Caligula* 5; on the acceptance of infanticide,

9. *The Special Laws* 3.20.110.

10. *Digest*, ed. Theodore Mommsen, 1 *Corpus juris civilis* (Berlin, 1893) 47.11.4. According to Plutarch, Romulus in his original laws for Rome permitted a husband to divorce his wife

John T. Noonan, Jr. is a professor of law at the University of California at Berkeley. He has written widely on legal, philosophical, and theological issues.

Reprinted by permission of the publishers from *The Morality of Abortion: Legal and Historical Perspectives*, edited by John T. Noonan, Jr., Cambridge, Mass.: Harvard University Press, Copyright © 1970 by the President and Fellows of Harvard College.

children born after their fathers' wills had been made, when heirs were no longer desired by the parents, was a cause for wonder to Tacitus.[15] The Roman upper classes diminished during the empire; the decline was probably due, in good part, to the practice of contraception and abortion.[16]

It was in this culture generally distinguished by its indifference to fetal and early life that the Christian teaching developed; it was in opposition and conflict with the values reflected in popular behavior that the Christian word was enunciated. Where some wise men had raised voices in defense of early life so that the question was in the air and yet not authoritatively decided, where even the wisest presented hesitant and divided counsel, where other authorities defended abortion, the Christians proposed a rule which was certain, comprehensive, and absolute.

The New Testament and the Early Community

The specific Christian teaching on abortion developed in a theological context in which the commands of

---

See SENECA, *De ira 1.15; cf. his praise of his own mother for not having had an abortion, unlike so many, Ad Helviam* 16.1. For references where abortion is taken for granted by contemporary pagans, see PLAUTUS, *Truculentus* 1.2.99; OVID, *De amoribus* 1.2.13; JUVENAL, *Satira* 2.6; AULUS GELLIUS, *Noctes atticae* 12.1. For Christian criticisms of the prevalence of abortion see the texts cited at notes *infra*, 20–36. On the frequency of abortion see also J. H. Waszink, "Abtreibung," in *Reallexicon für Antike und Christentum* 57, ed. Theodore Klauser (Stuttgart, 1950).

15. *Historiae* 5.5.

16. JOHN T. NOONAN, JR. *Contraception: A History of Its Treatment by the Catholic Theologians and Canonists* 18–29 (Cambridge, Mass., 1965).

the Old Testament to love God with all your heart (Deut. 6:5) and to love your neighbor as yourself (Lev. 19:18) were singled out as the two great commandments on which depended "the whole law and the prophets" (Matt. 22:40). The standard for fulfillment of these commandments was set in terms of the sacrifice of man's life for another (John 15:13) and embodied in the self-sacrifice of Jesus. Jesus told the disciples, "This is my commandment, that you love one another as I have loved you"(John 15:32). In terms of his example, the commandment was "a new commandment" (John 13:34). The Christian valuation of life was made in view of this commandment of love.

The place of children in the Christian community was broadly established in the words of the Lord, "Suffer little children [*paidia*] and do not prevent them from coming to me" (Matt. 19:14; Mark 10:14; Luke 18:16). In Luke 18:15, the children the Lord welcomed were expressly described as "newborn babies"(*brephe*). The ethos of the infancy narratives reflected a high interest in infant and fetal life. The infanticide practiced by Herod and its violent threat to the life of Jesus formed the introduction to the life of the Messiah (Matt. 2:1–18). Mary was described as having in her womb what was "from the Holy Spirit" (Matt. 1:18). In Luke she was greeted in pregnancy by Elizabeth "as the mother of my Lord," and the "fruit" of her womb was then described as "blessed" (Luke 1:42). The infant (*brephos*) in Elizabeth's womb "leaps" when Elizabeth is greeted by Mary (Luke 1:40). The interest in the behavior of this holy but not miraculous child of Elizabeth and the interest in the life in Mary's womb reflected the valuations of a community sensitive to the living character of the embryo, and the Gospel accounts must in turn have enhanced that sensitivity. What was unspoken was in its way as important as what was said in reflecting community valuations, attitudes, expectations. It was not necessary in this community to say that a man who protected the state by killing infants was not a good man. It was necessary to say that the first reaction of Joseph to Mary's unexplained pregnancy was "to put her away" (Matt. 2:19); it was not necessary to say that his first thought was not to procure an abortion.

At the level of specific moral rule, the Apostle Paul denounced the foolish carnality of the Christian community in Galatia (Gal. 3:1–6), reminded them that there was a law which was fulfilled in one word, "Love your neighbor as yourself" (5:14), and set out specific types of behavior which violated this law of love (5:19–21). The works of the flesh included not only "lecheries" and "wraths" but *pharmakeia* (5:20). *Pharmakeia* is a term best translated as "medicine" in the sense in which a North American Indian medicine man makes medicine.[17] It is the employment of drugs with occult properties for a variety of purposes, including, in particular, contraception or abortion.[18] Paul's usage here cannot be restricted to abortion, but the term he chose is comprehensive enough to include the use of abortifacient drugs. The asso-

ciation of these drugs with sins of lechery and wrath was indeed a constant aspect of the Christian approach to *pharmakeia* (the practice of "medicine") and *pharmaka* (the drugs employed).

* * * * *

In the period from 450 to 1100, when monks and bishops were the chief transmitters of Christian moral ideas, the teaching on abortion was reiterated. It was conveyed by enactments against abortion by local synods.[48] It was conveyed by collections which contained the canons of Elvira or the canons of the more prestigious council of Ancyra. By the eighth century Ancyra was the law of the Frankish kingdom of Charlemagne.[49] It was conveyed by collections which contained St. Jerome on homocide by abortifacients.[50] The penitentials developed by the monks for use in hearing confession regularly prescribed specific penances for abortion, ranging from one to ten years for the killing of an embryo.[51] When interrogatories for use in questioning penitents were devised in the tenth century, questions on abortion were included.[52] The early Christian and patristic attitudes were faithfully

---

17. See CLYDE PHARR, "The Interdiction of Magic in Roman Law," 63 *Transactions and Proceedings of the American Philological Association* 272–73 (1932). The word is regularly mistranslated as "sorcery" or "witchcraft" in English Bibles.

18. Plutarck, *Romulus* 22, in *Parallel Lives,* trans. B. Perren (New York, 1914–1926).

48. See ROGER JOHN HUSER, *The Crime of Abortion in Canon Law 33–39* (Washington, 1942).

49. *Id.* at 21.

50. E.g., in the eighth century, "Simulated Virgins and Their Morals," in *Womanly Questions, Die irische Kanonsammlung,* ed. F. W. H. Wasserscheben (Leipzig, 1885).

51. See NOONAN, *Contraception supra* n. 16, at 164. Some penitentials have lesser penalties for the destruction of what is less than an embryo—apparently a reflection of the old distinction between the formed and the unformed.

52. BURCHARD OF WORMS, "Interrogatory," *Decretum* 19.4, PL 140.972.

preserved in the various channels communicating the teaching of past authority and instilling its observance. . . .

* * * * *

The work of St. Antoninus of Florence may be taken to mark the beginning of a new era of thought on abortion, for he brought into the main line of moral theology an opinion of an obscure thirteenth-century theologian in favor of abortion to save the mother. His author is another Dominican from Thomas' country, John of Naples, in 1315 teacher at Paris, later holder of a chair of theology at Naples.[88] John based his position on the distinction between the ensouled and unensouled fetus in addressing himself to the duty of the physician. A doctor sinned in giving medicine to cause an abortion "to preserve a pregnant woman" when the fetus was ensouled, for, when "one cannot help one without hurting the other, it is more appropriate to help neither." But if the fetus was not ensouled, then the physician "ought to give such medicine," because "although he impedes the ensoulment of a future fetus, he will not be the cause of death of any man."[89]

* * * * *

In the course of the next two centuries [1750–1950], the teaching of the Church developed to an almost absolute prohibition of abortion. This development represented a substantial return to the patristic prohibition without the glosses and exceptions written in by casuistry; but it was not a naïve invocation of the past; it was a conscious rejection of some solutions which had once been appealing. Hence, it was development—a testing of principles by human experience in the light of the Gospel and a reformulation of doctrine after this testing. Like other developed Christian teaching on slavery, on the rights of labor, on war, it embodied a sensitivity to certain values affirmed in the Gospel but not made effective in Roman, medieval, or post-Reformation culture.

In the formation of teaching, the pastoral interest of the papacy played a strong part; and it was the central authority of the Church, far more prestigious in moral matters in the period 1880–1950 than ever before in its history, which dominated the development. The moral theologians and canonists bent to the papal leadership which, while reflecting the view of moral theologians, incorporated a broader sense of situation and likely trends and dangers. In 1588 Sixtus V, the most energetic of popes, could do nothing to change the views of the dominant moralists; beginning with the papacy of Leo XIII the moralists, in this area of thought, followed the papal lead.

The slowly changing attitude can be seen in the standard works. The most popular manual for seminary instruction in the nineteenth century was the *Compendium of Moral Theology* of the French Jesuit Jean Gury. The book was largely a succinct presentation of St. Alfonso de' Liguori, and in mid-nineteenth century Gury said, "The fetus, although not ensouled, is directed to the forming of man; therefore its ejection is anticipated homicide."[131] In 1869, in the constitution *Apostolicae sedis*, Pius

---

88. H. HURTER, *Nomenclator literarius theologiae catholicae* (Innsbruck, 1906) 2.537.

89. JOHN OF NAPLES, *Quodlibeta*, as quoted in SILVESTER DA PRIERAS, *Summa summarum quae sylvestrina dicitur* (1518) at "Medicus," 4.

---

131. *Compendium theologia moralis* (1864 ed.), "De praeceptis decalogi," n. 402.

IX dropped the reference to the "ensouled fetus" in the excommunication for abortion, so that the excommunication now seemed to include the abortion of any embryo. An implicit acceptance of immediate ensoulment was found in the action: "otherwise it would be making an old law more onerous, which is contrary to the intent of the constitution."[132] Thereafter, Thomas Gousset in his work for the practical instruction of confessors treated immediate ensoulment as the opinion to be followed, so that all abortions were homicides.[133] Augustine Lehmkuhl, the German Jesuit who was perhaps the ablest of the nineteenth-century moralists, taught that abortion is "true homicide," "as follows from what is today the more common opinion that teaches that every fetus is ensouled with a rational soul."[134]

* * * * *

In the allocution, addressed to the Italian Catholic Society of Midwives on October 29, 1951, Pius XII taught: "The baby in the maternal breast has the right to life immediately from God.—Hence there is no man, no human authority, no science, no medical, eugenic, social, economic or moral 'indication' which can establish or grant a valid juridical ground for a direct deliberate disposition of an innocent human life, that is a disposition which looks to its destruction either as an end or as a means to another end perhaps in itself not illicit.—The baby, still not born, is a

man in the same degree and for the same reason as the mother."[155] A more succinct and complete assertion of the rights of the embryo had not been made.

* * * * *

Conclusion

The most fundamental question involved in the long history of thought on abortion is: How do you determine the humanity of a being? To phrase the question that way is to put in comprehensive humanistic terms what the theologians either dealt with as an explicitly theological question under the heading of "ensoulment" or dealt with implicitly in their treatment of abortion. The Christian position as it originated did not depend on a narrow theological or philosophical concept. It had no relation to theories of infant baptism.[173] It

---

132. "De animatione foetus" *supra* n. 116, at 186. A commentary on *Apostolicae Sedis* in the same magazine (p. 331), however, contended that the old distinction stood.

133. *Théologie morale à des curés et des confesseurs* n. 621 (Paris, 1874 ed.).

134. 1 *Theologia moralis* n. 840 (Freiburg i. Br., 5th ed. 1888).

155. Pius XII, *Address to the Italian Catholic Society of Midwives, Ata apostolicae sedis* 43:838–39 (1951). The draftsmen of this statement were the German Jesuits Franz Hürth and Robert Leiber, according to an interview I have had with Father Leiber.

The most recent condemnation of even therapeutic abortion is Paul VI, *Humanae vitae, Acta apostolicae sedis* 60:481–503 (1968), an encyclical whose concern to protect human life led to comprehensive rule-making against a variety of means interrupting the process of generation.

173. According to Glanville Williams (*The Sanctity of Human Life supra* n. 169, at 193), "The historical reason for the Catholic objection to abortion is the same as for the Christian Church's historical opposition to infanticide: the horror of bringing about the death of an unbaptized child." This statement is made without any citation of evidence. As has been seen, desire to administer baptism could, in the Middle Ages, even be urged as a reason for procuring an abortion. It is highly regrettable that the American Law Institute was apparently misled by Williams' account and repeated after him the same baseless statement. See American Law Institute, *Model Penal Code: Tentative Draft No. 9* (1959), p. 148, n. 12.

appealed to no special theory of instantaneous ensoulment. It took the world's view on ensoulment as that view changed from Aristotle to Zacchia. There was, indeed, theological influence affecting the theory of ensoulment finally adopted, and, of course, ensoulment itself was a theological concept, so that the position was always explained in theological terms. But the theological notion of ensoulment could easily be translated into humanistic language by substituting "human" for "rational soul"; the problem of knowing when a man is a man is common to theology and humanism.

If one steps outside the specific categories used by the theologians, the answer they gave can be analyzed as a refusal to discriminate among human beings on the basis of their varying potentialities. Once conceived, the being was recognized as man because he had man's potential. The criterion for humanity, thus, was simple and all-embracing: if you are conceived by human parents, you are human.

The strength of this position may be tested by a review of some of the other distinctions offered in the contemporary controversy over legalizing abortion. Perhaps the most popular distinction is in terms of viability. Before an age of so many months, the fetus is not viable, that is, it cannot be removed from the mother's womb and live apart from her. To that extent, the life of the fetus is absolutely dependent on the life of the mother. This dependence is made the basis of denying recognition to its humanity.

There are difficulties with this distinction. One is that the perfection of artificial incubation may make the fetus viable at any time: it may be removed and artificially sustained. Ex-

periments with animals already show that such a procedure is possible.[174] This hypothetical extreme case relates to an actual difficulty: there is considerable elasticity to the idea of viability. Mere length of life is not an exact measure. The viability of the fetus depends on the extent of its anatomical and functional development.[175] The weight and length of the fetus are better guides to the state of its development than age, but weight and length vary.[176] Moreover, different racial groups have different ages at which their fetuses are viable. Some evidence, for example, suggests that Negro fetuses mature more quickly than white fetuses.[177] If viability is the norm, the standard would vary with race and with many individual circumstances.

The most important objection to this approach is that dependence is not ended by viability. The fetus is still absolutely dependent on someone's care in order to continue existence; indeed a child of one or three or even five years of age is absolutely dependent on another's care for existence; uncared for, the older fetus or the younger child will die as surely as the early fetus detached from the mother. The unsubstantial lessening in dependence at viability does not seem to signify any special acquisition of humanity.

A second distinction has been

---

174. E.g., R. L. BRINSTER and J. L. THOMSON, "Development of Eight-Cell Mouse Embryos in Vitro," 42 Experimental Cell Research 308 (1966).

175. J. EDGAR MORISON, *Fetal and Neonatal Pathology* 99–100 (1963).

176. PETER GRUENWALD, "Growth of the Human Fetus," 94 *American Journal of Obstetrics and Gynecology* 1112 (1966).

177. MORISON, *Fetal and Neonatal Pathology supra* n. 175, at 101.

attempted in terms of experience. A being who has had experience, has lived and suffered, who possesses memories, is more human than one who has not. Humanity depends on formation by experience. The fetus is thus "unformed" in the most basic human sense.[178]

This distinction is not serviceable for the embryo which is already experiencing and reacting. The embryo is responsive to touch after eight weeks[179] and at least at that point is experiencing. At an earlier stage the zygote is certainly alive and responding to its environment.[180] The distinction may also be challenged by the rare case where aphasia has erased adult memory: has it erased humanity? More fundamentally, this distinction leaves even the older fetus or the younger child to be treated as an unformed inhuman thing. Finally, it is not clear why experience as such confers humanity. It could be argued that certain central experiences such as loving or learning are necessary to make a man human. But then human beings who have failed to love or to learn might be excluded from the class called man.

A third distinction is made by appeal to the sentiments of adults. If a fetus dies, the grief of the parents is not the grief they would have for a living child. The fetus is an unnamed "it" till birth, and is not perceived as personality until at least the fourth month of existence when movements in the womb manifest a vigorous presence demanding joyful recognition by the parents.

Yet feeling is notoriously an unsure guide to the humanity of others. Many groups of humans have had difficulty in feeling that persons of another tongue, color, religion, sex, are as human as they. Apart from reactions to alien groups, we mourn the loss of a ten-year-old boy more than the loss of his one-day-old brother or his 90-year-old grandfather. The difference felt and the grief expressed vary with the potentialities extinguished, or the experience wiped out; they do not seem to point to any substantial difference in the humanity of baby, boy, or grandfather.

Distinctions are also made in terms of sensation by the parents. The embryo is felt within the womb only after about the fourth month.[181] The embryo is seen only at birth. What can be neither seen nor felt is different from what is tangible. If the fetus cannot be seen or touched at all, it cannot be perceived as man.

Yet experience shows that sight is even more untrustworthy than feeling in determining humanity. By sight, color became an appropriate index for saying who was a man, and the evil of racial discrimination was given foundation. Nor can touch provide the test; a being confined by sickness, "out of touch" with others, does not thereby seem to lose his humanity. To the extent that touch still has appeal as a criterion, it appears to be a survival of the old English idea of "quickening"—a possible mistransla-

---

178. This line of thought was advanced by some participants at the International Conference on Abortion sponsored by the Harvard Divinity School in cooperation with the Joseph P. Kennedy, Jr., Foundation in Washington, D.C., Sept. 8–10, 1967.

179. FRANK D. ALLAN, *Essentials of Human Embryology* 165 (1960).

180. FREDERICK J. GOTTLIEB, *Developmental Genetics* 28 (1966).

---

181. ALLAN, *Essentials of Human Embryology supra* n. 179, at 165.

tion of the Latin *animatus* used in the canon law.[182] To that extent touch as a criterion seems to be dependent on the Aristotelian notion of ensoulment, and to fall when this notion is discarded.

Finally, a distinction is sought in social visibility. The fetus is not socially perceived as human. It cannot communicate with others. Thus, both subjectively and objectively, it is not a member of society. As moral rules are rules for the behavior of members of society to each other, they cannot be made for behavior toward what is not yet a member. Excluded from the society of men, the fetus is excluded from the humanity of men.[183]

By force of the argument from the consequences, this distinction is to be rejected. It is more subtle than that founded on an appeal to physical sensation, but it is equally dangerous in its implications. If humanity depends on social recognition, individuals or whole groups may be dehumanized by being denied any status in their society. Such a fate is fictionally portrayed in *1984* and has actually been the lot of many men in many societies. In the Roman empire, for example, condemnation to slavery meant the practical denial of most human rights; in the Chinese Communist world, landlords have been classified as enemies of the people and so treated as nonpersons by the state. Humanity does not depend on social recognition, though often the failure of society to recognize the prisoner, the alien, the heterodox as human has led to the destruction of human beings. Anyone conceived by a man and a woman is human. Recognition of this condition by society follows a real event in the objective order, however imperfect and halting the recognition. Any attempt to limit humanity to exclude some group runs the risk of furnishing authority and precedent for excluding other groups in the name of the consciousness or perception of the controlling group in the society.

A philosopher may reject the appeal to the humanity of the fetus because he views "humanity" as a secular view of the soul and because he doubts the existence of anything real and objective which can be identified as humanity.[184] One answer to such a philosopher is to ask how he reasons about moral questions without supposing that there is a sense in which he and the others of whom he speaks are human. Whatever group is taken as the society which determines who may be killed is thereby taken as human. A second answer is to ask if he does not believe that there is a right and wrong way of deciding moral questions. If there is such a difference, experience may be appealed to: to decide who is human on the basis of the sentiment of a given society has led to consequences which rational men would characterize as monstrous.[185]

* * * * *

---

182. See David W. Louisell and John T. Noonan, Jr., "Constitutional Balance," *infra*.

183. Another line of thought advanced at the Conference mentioned in n. 178. Thomas Aquinas gave an analogous reason against baptizing a fetus in the womb: "As long as it exists in the womb of the mother, it cannot be subject to the operation of the ministers of the Church as it is not known to men" (*In sententias Petri Lombardi* 4.6 1.1.2).

184. Compare John O'Connor, "Humanity and Abortion," 12 *Natural Law Forum* 128–130 (1968), with John T. Noonan, Jr. "Deciding Who Is Human," 12 *Natural Law Forum* 134–138.

185. A famous passage of Montesquieu reads:

"Ceux dont il s'agit sont noirs depuis les pieds jusqu'à la tête; et ils ont le nez si écrasé qu'il est presque impossible de les plaindre.

Even with the fetus weighed as human, one interest could be weighed as equal or superior: that of the mother in her own life. The casuists between 1450 and 1895 were willing to weigh this interest as superior. Since 1895, that interest was given decisive weight only in the two special cases of the cancerous uterus and the ectopic pregnancy. In both of these cases the fetus itself had little chance of survival even if the abortion were not performed. As the balance was once struck in favor of the mother whenever her life was endangered, it could be so struck again. The balance reached between 1895 and 1930 attempted prudentially and pastorally to forestall a multitude of exceptions for interests less than life.

The perception of the humanity of the fetus and the weighing of fetal rights against other human rights constituted the work of the moral analysts. But what spirit animated their abstract judgments? For the Christian community it was the injunction of Scripture to love your neighbor as yourself. The fetus as human was a neighbor; his life had parity with one's own. The commandment gave life to what otherwise would have been only rational calculation.

The commandment could be put in humanistic as well as theological terms: Do not injure your fellow man without reason. In these terms, once the humanity of the fetus is perceived, abortion is never right except in self-defense. When life must be taken to save life, reason alone cannot say that a mother must prefer a child's life to her own. With this exception, now of great rarity, abortion violates the rational humanist tenet of the equality of human lives.

For Christians the commandment to love had received a special imprint in that the exemplar proposed of love was the love of the Lord for his disciples. In the light given by this example, self-sacrifice carried to the point of death seemed in the extreme situations not without meaning. In the less extreme cases, preference for one's own interests to the life of another seemed to express cruelty or selfishness irreconcilable with the demands of love.

"On ne peut se mettre dans l'esprit que Dieu qui est un être très-sage, ait mis une âme, surtout une âme bonne, dans un corps tout noir.

"Il est si naturel de penser que c'est la couleur qui constitue l'essence de l'humanité, que les peuples d'Asie, qui font des eunuques, privent toujours les noirs du rapport qu'ils ont avec nous d'une façon plus marquée." *Montesquieu, De l'esprit des lois*, in *Oeuvres Complètes* book 15, chap. 5 (Paris, 1843).

C   O   M   M   E   N   T   S   ■   Q   U   E   S   T   I   O   N   S

---

1. What relevance does the history of Christian and Catholic thought regarding abortion have to the abortion controversy as it exists at the present time? Are other historical traditions, such as those of non-Christians also relevant? If so, in what ways?

2. Regarding questions about abortion, how important is it for us to

come to terms with the question of "ensoulment"?

3. Do you believe a person's religious beliefs should be the primary basis for determining his or her views on abortion?

JUSTICE BYRON WHITE

Dissenting Opinion in Roe v. Wade

At the heart of the controversy in these cases are those recurring pregnancies that pose no danger whatsoever to the life or health of the mother but are nevertheless unwanted for any one or more of a variety of reasons— convenience, family planning, economics, dislike of children, the embarrassment of illegitimacy, etc. The common claim before us is that for any one of such reasons, or for no reason at all, and without asserting or claiming any threat to life or health, any woman is entitled to an abortion at her request if she is able to find a medical advisor willing to undertake the procedure.

The Court for the most part sustains this position: During the period prior to the time the fetus becomes viable, the Constitution of the United States values the convenience, whim or caprice of the putative mother more than the life or potential life of the fetus; the Constitution, therefore, guarantees the right to an abortion as against any state law or policy seeking to protect the fetus from an abortion not prompted by more compelling reasons of the mother.

With all due respect, I dissent. I find nothing in the language or history of the Constitution to support the Court's judgment. The Court simply fashions and announces a new constitutional right for pregnant mothers and, with scarcely any reason or authority for its action, invests that right with sufficient substance to override most existing state abortion statutes. The upshot is that the people and the legislatures of the 50 States are constitutionally disentitled to weigh the relative importance of the continued existence and development of the fetus on the one hand against a spectrum of possible impacts on the mother on the other hand. As an exercise of raw judicial power, the Court perhaps has authority to do what it does today; but in my view its judgment is an improvident and ex-

---

Byron R. White has been an associate justice of the U.S. Supreme Court since 1962.

---

410 U.S. 219; 93 S. Ct. 762 (1976) Legal references have been omitted.

travagant exercise of the power of judicial review which the Constitution extends to this Court.

The Court apparently values the convenience of the pregnant mother more than the continued existence and development of the life or potential life which she carries. Whether or not I might agree with that marshalling of values, I can in no event join the Court's judgment because I find no constitutional warrant for imposing such an order of priorities on the people and legislatures of the States. In a sensitive area such as this, involving as it does issues over which reasonable men may easily and heat-

edly differ, I cannot accept the Court's exercise of its clear power of choice by interposing a constitutional barrier to state efforts to protect human life and by investing mothers and doctors with the constitutionally protected right to exterminate it. This issue, for the most part, should be left with the people and to the political processes the people have devised to govern their affairs.

It is my view, therefore, that the Texas statute is not constitutionally infirm because it denies abortions to those who seek to serve only their convenience rather than to protect their life or health. . . .

C O M M E N T S ■ Q U E S T I O N S

1. "The court apparently values the convenience of the pregnant mother more than the continued existence and development of the life or potential life which she carries." In this way, Justice White characterizes the "legalization" of abortion by the court majority in *Roe vs. Wade*. What would Mary Anne Warren say about this view of the legal right to have an abortion? What would Henry Ruf say?

2. Justice White describes the state laws prohibiting abortion that were struck down by *Roe vs. Wade* as "efforts to protect human life." In your opinion, is he correct to describe them in this way? Should we say that "human life" is equivalent to "the life of a person"?

MARY ANNE WARREN

On the Moral and Legal Status of Abortion

* * * * *

We turn now to Professor Thomson's case for the claim that even if a fetus has full moral rights, abortion is still morally permissible, at least sometimes, and for some reasons other than to save the woman's life.[7] Her argument is based upon a clever, but I think faulty, analogy. She asks us to picture ourselves waking up one day, in bed with a famous violinist. Imagine that you have been kidnapped, and your bloodstream hooked up to that of the violinist, who happens to have an ailment which will certainly kill him unless he is permitted to share your kidneys for a period of nine months. No one else can save him, since you alone have the right type of blood. He will be unconscious all that time, and you will have to stay in bed with him, but after the nine months are over he may be unplugged, completely cured, that is provided that you have cooperated.

Now then, she continues, what are your obligations in this situation? The antiabortionist, if he is consistent, will have to say that you are obligated to stay in bed with the violinist: for all people have a right to life, and violinists are people, and therefore it would be murder for you to discon-

nect yourself from him and let him die (p. 49). But this is outrageous, and so there must be something wrong with the same argument when it is applied to abortion. It would certainly be commendable of you to agree to save the violinist, but it is absurd to suggest that your refusal to do so would be murder. His right to life does not obligate you to do whatever is required to keep him alive; nor does it justify anyone else in forcing you to do so. A law which required you to stay in bed with the violinist would clearly be an unjust law, since it is no proper function of the law to force unwilling people to make huge sacrifices for the sake of other people toward whom they have no such prior obligation.

Thomson concludes that, if this analogy is an apt one, then we can grant the antiabortionist his claim that a fetus is a human being, and still hold that it is at least sometimes the case that a pregnant woman has the right to refuse to be a Good Samaritan towards the fetus, i.e., to obtain an abortion. For there is a great gap between the claim that x has a right to life, and the claim that y is obligated to do whatever is necessary to keep x alive, let alone that he ought

---

7. Judith Jarvis Thomson, "A Defense of Abortion," *Philosophy and Public Affairs*, Vol. 1 (1971), 47–66.

Mary Anne Warren teaches philosophy at San Francisco State University. She has written articles in the areas of ethics and feminism.

---

to be forced to do so. It is y's duty to keep x alive only if he has somehow contracted a *special* obligation to do so; and a woman who is unwillingly pregnant, e.g., who was raped, has done nothing which obligates her to make the enormous sacrifice which is necessary to preserve the conceptus.

This argument is initially quite plausible, and in the extreme case of pregnancy due to rape it is probably conclusive. Difficulties arise, however, when we try to specify more exactly the range of cases in which abortion is clearly justifiable even on the assumption that the fetus is human. Professor Thomson considers it a virtue of her argument that it does not enable us to conclude that abortion is *always* permissible. It would, she says, be "indecent" for a woman in her seventh month to obtain an abortion just to avoid having to postpone a trip to Europe. On the other hand, her argument enables us to see that "a sick and desperately frightened schoolgirl pregnant due to rape may *of course* choose abortion, and that any law which rules this out is an insane law" (p. 65). So far, so good; but what are we to say about the woman who becomes pregnant not through rape but as a result of her own carelessness, or because of contraceptive failure, or who gets pregnant intentionally and then changes her mind about wanting a child? With respect to such cases, the violinist analogy is of much less use to the defender of the woman's right to obtain an abortion.

Indeed, the choice of a pregnancy due to rape, as an example of a case in which abortion is permissible even if a fetus is considered a human being, is extremely significant; for it is only in the case of pregnancy due to rape that the woman's situation is adequately analogous to the violinist case for our intuitions about the latter to transfer convincingly. The crucial difference between a pregnancy due to rape and the *normal* case of an unwanted pregnancy is that in the normal case we cannot claim that the woman is in no way responsible for her predicament; she could have remained chaste, or taken her pills more faithfully, or abstained on dangerous days, and so on. If, on the other hand, you are kidnapped by strangers, and hooked up to a strange violinist, then you are free of any shred of responsibility for the situation, on the basis of which it could be argued that you are obligated to keep the violinist alive. Only when her pregnancy is due to rape is a woman clearly just as nonresponsible.[8]

Consequently, there is room for the antiabortionist to argue that in the normal case of unwanted pregnancy a woman has, by her own actions, assumed responsibility for the fetus. For if x behaves in a way which he could have avoided, and which he knows involves, let us say, a one percent chance of bringing into existence a human being, with a right to life, and does so knowing that if this should happen then that human being will perish unless x does certain things to keep him alive, then it is by no means clear that when it does happen x is free of any obligation to what he knew in advance would be required to keep that human being alive.

---

8. We may safely ignore the fact that she might have avoided getting raped, e.g., by carrying a gun, since by similar means you might likewise have avoided getting kidnapped, and in neither case does the victim's failure to take all possible precautions against a highly unlikely event (as opposed to reasonable precautions against a rather likely event) mean that he is morally responsible for what happens. .

The plausibility of such an argument is enough to show that the Thomson analogy can provide a clear and persuasive defense of a woman's right to obtain an abortion only with respect to those cases in which the woman is in no way responsible for her pregnancy, e.g., where it is due to rape. In all other cases, we would almost certainly conclude that it was necessary to look carefully at the particular circumstances in order to determine the extent of the woman's responsibility, and hence the extent of her obligation. This is an extremely unsatisfactory outcome, from the viewpoint of the opponents of restrictive abortion laws, most of whom are convinced that a woman has a right to obtain an abortion regardless of how and why she got pregnant.

Of course a supporter of the violinist analogy might point out that it is absurd to suggest that forgetting her pill one day might be sufficient to obligate a woman to complete an unwanted pregnancy. And indeed it *is* absurd to suggest this. As we will see, the moral right to obtain an abortion is not in the least dependent upon the extent to which the woman is responsible for her pregnancy. But unfortunately, once we allow the assumption that a fetus has full moral rights, we cannot avoid taking this absurd suggestion seriously. Perhaps we can make this point more clear by altering the violinist story just enough to make it more analogous to a normal unwanted pregnancy and less to a pregnancy due to rape, and then seeing whether it is still obvious that you are not obligated to stay in bed with the fellow.

Suppose, then, that violinists are peculiarly prone to the sort of illness the only cure for which is the use of someone else's bloodstream for nine months, and that because of this there has been formed a society of music lovers who agree that whenever a violinist is stricken they will draw lots and the loser will, by some means, be made the one and only person capable of saving him. Now then, would you be obligated to cooperate in curing the violinist if you had voluntarily joined this society, knowing the possible consequences, and then your name had been drawn and you had been kidnapped? Admittedly, you did not promise ahead of time that you would, but you did deliberately place yourself in a position in which it might happen that a human life would be lost if you did not. Surely this is at least a prima facie reason for supposing that you have an obligation to stay in bed with the violinist. Suppose that you had gotten your name drawn deliberately; surely *that* would be quite a strong reason for thinking that you had such an obligation.

It might be suggested that there is one important disanalogy between the modified violinist case and the case of an unwanted pregnancy, which makes the woman's responsibility significantly less, namely, the fact that the fetus *comes into existence* as the result of the woman's actions. This fact might give her a right to refuse to keep it alive, whereas she would not have had this right had it existed previously, independently, and then as a result of her actions become dependent upon her for its survival.

My own intuition, however, is that x has no more right to bring into existence, either deliberately or as a foreseeable result of actions he could have avoided, a being with full moral rights (y), and then refuse to do what he knew beforehand would be required to keep that being alive, than he has to enter into an agreement with an existing person, whereby he may be called upon to save that person's life, and then refuse to do so when so called upon. Thus, *x*'s responsibility for *y*'s existence does not seem to lessen his obligation to keep *y* alive, if he is also responsible for *y*'s being in a situation in which only he can save him.

Whether or not this intuition is entirely correct, it brings us back once again to the conclusion that once we allow the assumption that a fetus has full moral rights it becomes an extremely complex and difficult question whether and when abortion is justifiable. Thus the Thomson analogy cannot help us produce a clear and persuasive proof of the moral permissibility of abortion. Nor will the opponents of the restrictive laws thank us for anything less; for their conviction (for the most part) is that abortion is obviously *not* a morally serious and extremely unfortunate, even though sometimes justified act, comparable to killing in self-defense or to letting the violinist die, but rather is closer to being a morally neutral act, like cutting one's hair.

The basis of this conviction, I believe, is the realization that a fetus is not a person, and thus does not have a full-fledged right to life. Perhaps the reason why this claim has been so inadequately defended is that it seems self-evident to those who accept it. And so it is, insofar as it follows from what I take to be perfectly obvious claims about the nature of personhood, and about the proper grounds for ascribing moral rights, claims which ought, indeed, to be obvious to both the friends and foes of abortion. Nevertheless, it is worth examining these claims, and showing how they demonstrate the moral innocuousness of abortion, since this apparently has not been adequately done before.

II

The question which we must answer in order to produce a satisfactory solution to the problem of the moral status of abortion is this: How are we to define the moral community, the set of beings with full and equal moral rights, such that we can decide whether a human fetus is a member of this community or not? What sort of entity, exactly, has the inalienable rights to life, liberty, and the pursuit of happiness? Jefferson attributed these rights to all *men*, and it may or may not be fair to suggest that he intended to attribute them *only* to men. Perhaps he ought to have attributed them to all human beings. If so, then we arrive, first, at Noonan's problem of defining what makes a being human, and, second, at the equally vital question which Noonan does not consider, namely, What reason is there for identifying the moral community with the set of all human beings, in whatever way we have chosen to define that term?

1. On the Definition of 'Human'

One reason why this vital second question is so frequently overlooked in the debate over the moral status of abortion is that the term 'human' has two distinct, but not often distinguished, senses. This fact results in a slide of meaning, which serves to conceal the fallaciousness of the traditional argument that since (1) it is wrong to kill innocent human beings, and (2) fetuses are innocent human beings, then (3) it is wrong to kill fetuses. For if 'human' is used in the same sense in both (1) and (2) then, whichever of the two senses is meant, one of these premises is question-begging. And if it is used in two different senses then of course the conclusion doesn't follow.

Thus, (1) is a self-evident moral truth,[9] and avoids begging the question about abortion, only if 'human being' is used to mean something like "a full-fledged member of the moral community." (It may or may not also be meant to refer exclusively to members of the species *Homo sapiens.*) We may call this the *moral* sense of 'human'. It is not to be confused with what we will call the *genetic* sense, i.e., the sense in which *any* member of the species is a human being, and no member of any other species could be. If (1) is acceptable only if the moral sense is intended, (2) is non-question-begging only if what is intended is the genetic sense.

In "Deciding Who is Human,"[8a] Noonan argues for the classification of fetuses with human beings by pointing to the presence of the full genetic code, and the potential capacity for rational thought (p. 135). It is clear that what he needs to show, for his version of the traditional argument to be valid, is that fetuses are human in the moral sense, the sense in which it is analytically true that all human beings have full moral rights. But, in the absence of any argument showing that whatever is genetically human is also morally human, and he

gives none, nothing more than genetic humanity can be demonstrated by the presence of the human genetic code. And, as we will see, the *potential* capacity for rational thought can at most show that an entity has the potential for *becoming* human in the moral sense.

2. Defining the Moral Community

Can it be established that genetic humanity is sufficient for moral humanity? I think that there are very good reasons for not defining the moral community in this way. I would like to suggest an alternative way of defining the moral community, which I will argue for only to the extent of explaining why it is, or should be, self-evident. The suggestion is simply that the moral community consists of all and only *people*, rather than all and only human beings;[10] and probably the best way of demonstrating its self-evidence is by considering the concept of personhood, to see what sorts of entity are and are not persons, and what the decision that a being is or is not a person implies about its moral rights.

What characteristics entitle an entity to be considered a person? This is obviously not the place to attempt a complete analysis of the concept of personhood, but we do not need such a fully adequate analysis just to determine whether and why a fetus is or isn't a person. All we need is a rough and approximate list of the most basic criteria of personhood,

---

8a. *Natural Law Forum*, 13 (1968).

9. Of course, the principle that it is (always) wrong to kill innocent human beings is in need of many other modifications, e.g., that it may be permissible to do so to save a greater number of other innocent human beings, but we may safely ignore these complications here.

---

10. From here on, we will use "human" to mean genetically human, since the moral sense seems closely connected to, and perhaps derived from, the assumption that genetic humanity is sufficient for membership in the moral community.

and some idea of which, or how many, of these an entity must satisfy in order to properly be considered a person.

In searching for such criteria, it is useful to look beyond the set of people with whom we are acquainted, and ask how we would decide whether a totally alien being was a person or not. (For we have no right to assume that genetic humanity is necessary for personhood.) Imagine a space traveler who lands on an unknown planet and encounters a race of beings utterly unlike any he has ever seen or heard of. If he wants to be sure of behaving morally toward these beings, he has to somehow decide whether they are people, and hence have full moral rights, or whether they are the sort of thing which he need not feel guilty about treating as, for example, a source of food.

How should he go about making this decision? If he has some anthropological background, he might look for such things as religion, art, and the manufacturing of tools, weapons, or shelters, since these factors have been used to distinguish our human from our prehuman ancestors, in what seems to be closer to the moral than the genetic sense of 'human'. And no doubt he would be right to consider the presence of such factors as good evidence that the alien beings were people, and morally human. It would, however, be overly anthropocentric of him to take the absence of these things as adequate evidence that they were not, since we can imagine people who have progressed beyond, or evolved without ever developing, these cultural characteristics.

I suggest that the traits which are most central to the concept of per-

sonhood, or humanity in the moral sense, are, very roughly, the following:

(1) consciousness (of objects and events external and/or internal to the being), and in particular the capacity to feel pain;

(2) reasoning (the *developed* capacity to solve new and relatively complex problems);

(3) self-motivated activity (activity which is relatively independent of either genetic or direct external control);

(4) the capacity to communicate, by whatever means, messages of an indefinite variety of types, that is, not just with an indefinite number of possible contents, but on indefinitely many possible topics;

(5) the presence of self-concepts, and self-awareness, either individual or racial, or both.

Admittedly, there are apt to be a great many problems involved in formulating precise definitions of these criteria, let alone in developing universally valid behavioral criteria for deciding when they apply. But I will assume that both we and our explorer know approximately what (1)–(5) mean, and that he is also able to determine whether or not they apply. How, then, should he use his findings to decide whether or not the alien beings are people? We needn't suppose that an entity must have *all* of these attributes to be properly considered a person; (1) and (2) alone may well be sufficient for personhood, and quite probably (1)–(3) are sufficient. Neither do we need to insist that any one of these criteria is *necessary* for personhood, although once again (1) and (2) look like fairly good candidates for necessary conditions, as does (3), if 'activity' is construed so as to include the activity of reasoning.

All we need to claim, to demonstrate that a fetus is not a person, is that any being which satisfies *none* of (1)–(5) is certainly not a person. I consider this claim to be so obvious that I think anyone who denied it, and claimed that a being which satisfied none of (1)–(5) was a person all the same, would thereby demonstrate that he had no notion at all of what a person is—perhaps because he had confused the concept of a person with that of genetic humanity. If the opponents of abortion were to deny the appropriateness of these five criteria, I do not know what further arguments would convince them. We would probably have to admit that our conceptual schemes were indeed irreconcilably different, and that our dispute could not be settled objectively.

I do not expect this to happen, however, since I think that the concept of a person is one which is very nearly universal (to people), and that it is common to both proabortionists and antiabortionists, even though neither group has fully realized the relevance of this concept to the resolution of their dispute. Furthermore, I think that on reflection even the antiabortionists ought to agree not only that (1)–(5) are central to the concept of personhood, but also that it is a part of this concept that all and only people have full moral rights. The concept of a person is in part a moral concept; once we have admitted that x is a person we have recognized, even if we have not agreed to respect, x's right to be treated as a member of the moral community. It is true that the claim

that x is a *human being* is more commonly voiced as part of an appeal to treat x decently than is the claim that x is a person, but this is either because 'human being' is here used in the sense which implies personhood, or because the genetic and moral senses of 'human' have been confused.

Now if (1)–(5) are indeed the primary criteria of personhood, then it is clear that genetic humanity is neither necessary nor sufficient for establishing that an entity is a person. Some human beings are not people, and there may well be people who are not human beings. A man or woman whose consciousness has been permanently obliterated but who remains alive is a human being which is no longer a person; defective human beings, with no appreciable mental capacity, are not and presumably never will be people; and a fetus is a human being which is not yet a person, and which therefore cannot coherently be said to have full moral rights. Citizens of the next century should be prepared to recognize highly advanced, self-aware robots or computers, should such be developed, and intelligent inhabitants of other worlds, should such be found, as people in the fullest sense, and to respect their moral rights. But to ascribe full moral rights to an entity which is not a person is as absurd as to ascribe moral obligations and responsibilities to such an entity.

3. Fetal Development and the Right to Life

Two problems arise in the application of these suggestions for the definition of the moral community to the determination of the precise moral status of a human fetus. Given that the paradigm example of a person is a normal adult human being, then (1) How like this paradigm, in particular how far advanced since conception, does a human being need to be before it begins to have a right to life by virtue, not of being fully a person as of yet, but of being *like* a person? and (2) To what extent, if any, does the fact that a fetus has the *potential* for becoming a person endow it with some of the same rights? Each of these questions requires some comment.

In answering the first question, we need not attempt a detailed consideration of the moral rights of organisms which are not developed enough, aware enough, intelligent enough, etc., to be considered people, but which resemble people in some respects. It does seem reasonable to suggest that the more like a person, in the relevant respects, a being is, the stronger is the case for regarding it as having a right to life, and indeed the stronger its right to life is. Thus we ought to take seriously the suggestion that, insofar as "the human individual develops biologically in a continuous fashion . . . the rights of a human person might develop in the same way."[11] But we must keep in mind that the attributes which are relevant in determining whether or not an entity is enough like a person to be regarded as having some of the same moral rights are no different from those which are relevant to determining

whether or not it is fully a person— i.e., are no different from (1)–(5)— and that being genetically human, or having recognizably human facial and other physical features, or detectable brain activity, or the capacity to survive outside the uterus, are simply not among these relevant attributes.

Thus it is clear that even though a seven- or eight-month fetus has features which make it apt to arouse in us almost the same powerful protective instinct as is commonly aroused by a small infant, nevertheless it is not significantly more personlike than is a very small embryo. It is *somewhat* more personlike; it can apparently feel and respond to pain, and it may even have a rudimentary form of consciousness, insofar as its brain is quite active. Nevertheless, it seems safe to say that it is not fully conscious, in the way that an infant of a few months is, and that it cannot reason, or communicate messages of indefinitely many sorts, does not engage in self-motivated activity, and has no self-awareness. Thus, in the *relevant* respects, a fetus, even a fully developed one, is considerably less personlike than is the average mature mammal, indeed the average fish. And I think that a rational person must conclude that if the right to life of a fetus is to be based upon its resemblance to a person, then it cannot be said to have any more right to life than, let us say, a newborn guppy (which also seems to be capable of feeling pain), and that a right of that magnitude could never override a woman's right to obtain an abortion, at any stage of her pregnancy.

There may, of course, be other arguments in favor of placing legal limits upon the stage of pregnancy in which an abortion may be performed.

11. Thomas L. Hayes, "A Biological View," *Commonweal*, 85 (March 17, 1967), 677–78; quoted by Daniel Callahan, in *Abortion, Law, Choice, and Morality* (London: Macmillan & Co., 1970).

Given the relative safety of the new techniques of artificially inducing labor during the third trimester, the danger to the woman's life or health is no longer such an argument. Neither is the fact that people tend to respond to the thought of abortion in the later stages of pregnancy with emotional repulsion, since mere emotional responses cannot take the place of moral reasoning in determining what ought to be permitted. Nor, finally, is the frequently heard argument that legalizing abortion, especially late in the pregnancy, may erode the level of respect for human life, leading, perhaps, to an increase in unjustified euthanasia and other crimes. For this threat, if it is a threat, can be better met by educating people to the kinds of moral distinctions which we are making here than by limiting access to abortion (which limitation may, in its disregard for the rights of women, be just as damaging to the level of respect for human rights).

Thus, since the fact that even a fully developed fetus is not person-like enough to have any significant right to life on the basis of its personlikeness shows that no legal restrictions upon the stage of pregnancy in which an abortion may be performed can be justified on the grounds that we should protect the rights of the older fetus; and since there is no other apparent justification for such restrictions, we may conclude that they are entirely unjustified. Whether or not it would be *indecent* (whatever that means) for a woman in her seventh month to obtain an abortion just to avoid having to postpone a trip to Europe, it would not, in itself, be *immoral*, and therefore it ought to be permitted.

4. Potential Personhood and the Right to Life

We have seen that a fetus does not resemble a person in any way which can support the claim that it has even some of the same rights. But what about its *potential*, the fact that if nurtured and allowed to develop naturally it will very probably become a person? Doesn't that alone give it at least some right to life? It is hard to deny that the fact that an entity is a potential person is a strong prima facie reason for not destroying it; but we need not conclude from this that a potential person has a right to life, by virtue of that potential. It may be that our feeling that it is better, other things being equal, not to destroy a potential person is better explained by the fact that potential people are still (felt to be) an invaluable resource, not to be lightly squandered. Surely, if every speck of dust were a potential person, we would be much less apt to conclude that every potential person has a right to become actual.

Still, we do not need to insist that a potential person has no right to life whatever. There may well be something immoral, and not just imprudent, about wantonly destroying potential people, when doing so isn't necessary to protect anyone's rights. But even if a potential person does have some prima facie right to life, such a right could not possibly outweigh the right of a woman to obtain an abortion, since the rights of any actual person invariably outweigh those of any potential person, whenever the two conflict. Since this may not be immediately obvious in the case of a human fetus, let us look at another case.

Suppose that our space explorer falls into the hands of an alien culture, whose scientists decide to create a few hundred thousand or more human beings, by breaking his body into its component cells, and using these to create fully developed human beings, with, of course, his genetic code. We may imagine that each of these newly-created men will have all of the original man's abilities, skills, knowledge, and so on, and also have an individual self-concept, in short that each of them will be a bona fide (though hardly unique) person. Imagine that the whole project will take only seconds, and that its chances of success are extremely high, and that our explorer knows all of this, and also knows that these people will be treated fairly. I maintain that in such a situation he would have every right to escape if he could, and thus to deprive all of these potential people of their potential lives; for his right to life outweighs all of theirs together, in spite of the fact that they are all genetically human, all innocent, and all have a very high probability of becoming people very soon, if only he refrains from acting.

Indeed, I think he would have a right to escape even if it were not his life which the alien scientists planned to take, but only a year of his freedom, or indeed, only a day. Nor would he be obligated to stay if he had gotten captured (thus bringing all these people-potentials into existence) because of his own carelessness, or even if he had done so deliberately, knowing the consequences. Regardless of how he got captured, he is not morally obligated to remain in captivity for *any* period of time for the sake of permitting any number of potential people to come into actuality, so great is the margin by which one actual person's right to liberty outweighs whatever right to life even a hundred thousand potential people have. And it seems reasonable to conclude that the rights of a woman will outweigh by a similar margin whatever right to life a fetus may have by virtue of its potential personhood.

Thus, neither a fetus's resemblance to a person, nor its potential for becoming a person provides any basis whatever for the claim that it has any significant right to life. Consequently, a woman's right to protect her health, happiness, freedom, and even her life,[12] by terminating an unwanted pregnancy, will always override whatever right to life it may be appropriate to ascribe to a fetus, even a fully developed one. And thus, in the absence of any overwhelming social need for every possible child, the laws which restrict the right to obtain an abortion, or limit the period of pregnancy during which an abortion may be performed, are a wholly unjustified violation of a woman's most basic moral and constitutional rights.[13]

---

12. That is, insofar as the death rate, for the woman, is higher for childbirth than for early abortion.

13. My thanks to the following people, who were kind enough to read and criticize an earlier version of this paper: Herbert Gold, Gene Glass, Anne Lauterbach, Judith Thomson, Mary Mothersill, and Timothy Binkley.

C O M M E N T S ■ Q U E S T I O N S

1. Among all of the philosophers who have recently written on the abortion question, says Warren, only one of them—Judith Thomson—has questioned the assumption that *if* a fetus is judged to be a human being, *then* abortion is wrong. B. A. Brody, for example, has argued that abortion should be made illegal because it is the taking of innocent human life. John Noonan, likewise, argues that it is wrong to kill humans and that since a fetus is a human being, abortion is wrong.

   Warren does not support Thomson's conclusion—which is that abortion is permissible even on the assumption that a fetus is a human being with a full-fledged right to life. Warren does, however, believe that Thomson's article is important because it recognizes that the rights of a pregnant woman count for a great deal. In your opinion, has Warren given a correct evaluation of Thomson's position? Is Thomson's position perhaps stronger than Warren makes it out to be? Is it weaker?

2. Warren herself wishes to argue that a fetus is not "a member of the moral community, the set of beings with full and equal moral rights, for the simple reason that it is not a person." Do you agree with this position?

3. Warren distinguishes between the "moral sense" of being human (being a "full-fledged member of the moral community") and the "genetic sense" of being human (being a member of the species *Homo sapiens*). Do you accept this distinction? Do you accept Warren's list of the five traits that she says are most central to the moral concept of being human? If the list is incomplete, what should be added to it? If the list is too extensive, what should be subtracted from it?

H E N R Y   R U F

The Boundaries of Personhood

I f one is going to treat persons as persons, dealing with them fairly, justly and impartially, and granting them all the rights to which all persons are entitled, then one is going to have to know how to identify an individual as a person. Usually there is no difficulty in doing so because usually we are dealing with perfectly clear cases. You are a person, I am a person and so are all the human beings we deal with every day. Surely, all individuals who can indict others and who can demand rights for themselves are persons in the morally relevant sense of the word. Likewise, all individuals who can be held accountable for their behavior and who thereby have duties and obligations are persons who also have these rights. The problem cases arise when we move away from the clear cases and begin to consider the boundary cases. What about the newborn child, the unborn fetus, the senile and the incurably insane, the radically retarded and the living human being in a coma from which death will be the only release? They can't ask for rights. They have no duties. Do they have personal rights? The current moral problems of abortion, genetic experimentation, treatment of seriously retarded children, children suffering from mongolism and the incurably insane, the problems of euthanasia and suicide all deal with the issue of where we should draw the line separating persons, who have a right to be treated as persons, from other individuals who do not have such a right. It is by no means obvious what is involved in drawing such boundaries or what determines whether or not one has drawn them correctly. By examining these problems, which are among the most controversial of current moral problems, let's see if we can get a little clearer about what is involved in correctly settling the boundaries of personhood.

Abortion

Prior to 1973 when the Supreme Court in the United States ruled in *Roe vs. Wade* that states could not pass laws prohibiting abortions in the first six months of pregnancy,[1] the proponents in this country of a woman's right to secure an abortion primarily argued that it was necessary

---

1. For excerpts of the relevant sections of the case and majority and minority opinions, see "Roe vs. Wade" in *Today's Moral Problems*, Richard Wasserstrom (ed.), pp. 65–83.

Henry L. Ruf is professor of philosophy at West Virginia University and has written on ethics and cross-cultural understanding.

From Henry L. Ruf, *Moral Investigations*, University Press of America, 1978. Reprinted by permission of the author.

to grant such a right in order to protect women from being brutally butchered in unsanitary back rooms by the illegal abortionists to whom they had been going in large numbers for years. As a secondary argument, some supporters of the woman's right to secure an abortion argued that it is unfair to a child to bring it into the world unwanted and, since no birth control methods are foolproof and not all women at all times (especially teenagers caught up in a romantic situation) will use such methods, the woman's right to abort a pregnancy must be kept as a birth control measure of the last resort.

Since the time of the Supreme Court decision, the initiative in the debate has shifted over to the side of the opponents of abortion who argue that it is wrong to deliberately murder an unborn child simply because it is inconvenient, or because it might possibly prove dangerous for the mother to carry the pregnancy to completion or because some women will continue to risk their health and lives by seeking illegal abortions. Also, these opponents of abortion have argued that since unwanted children can be handled by adoption agencies, the fear of there being unwanted children constitutes no justification for such murders.

If the issue over abortion were simply a matter of determining whether murder is justified in order to avoid inconvenience or embarrassment or the possible dangers inherent in any pregnancy, then there would be little difficulty in discovering the correct solution to this problem. Such murders would all be horribly unjustified. Murder is far worse than inconvenience and embarrassment. This, of course, is not the issue being debated. No person who claims that a woman has a right to control her own body means to say that this right is so absolute that a woman may do anything with her body even if it means the murder of innocent people. If I use my body to push you over a cliff, that is murder. If I am carrying a dangerous, contagious disease in my body, I can't take it anywhere I want to and thus threaten the lives of others. When the proponents of the right to abortion argue for a woman's right to control her own body, they usually are claiming that no woman should be forced to have her body used against her will in bringing into existence a new person. The assumption made by the proponents of the right to abortion is that a three-month-old fetus is not yet to be treated as a person. They claim that no murder of any person is involved in any way. Therefore, the issue of the appropriateness of abortion hinges on determining when we ought to say that an individual is a person who has a right to be treated as a person and not as a mere thing which could be discarded when unwanted, inconvenient, embarrassing or dangerous.

Many proponents and opponents of abortion take this question about the proper boundaries of personhood to be a factual question which can be resolved by biological considerations. Right to life advocates do not claim that every living thing has an absolute right to live. They really are only talking about the right of all human beings to life. They are not talking about vegetables and non-human animals. They eat salads and hamburgers like everyone else. Neither are they talking about the life of any and all human cells. They are not opposed to operations which kill human cells nor are they opposed to allowing unfertilized human female eggs and male sperm cells to die. They are arguing about the proper boundaries of personhood. They claim that the only clear point at which we can say that a human being with personal rights has begun to live is at the moment of conception. They assume that all human beings have a right to life and, therefore, conclude that killing any living fetus through abortion is murder.

On the other hand, again trying to keep the issue at the level of biology, some proponents of the right to abortion argue that it is not correct to picture a fetus as a human being until the fetus is capable of life independent of the mother or until its brain is so developed that it is capable of consciousness. They claim that the only clear point at which we can say that we have a new human being is after birth. Also, speaking for the majority on the Supreme Court, Justice Blackmun pointed out that whenever the U.S. Constitution speaks of persons it always does so in language which could not be applied to the unborn because it implies that these persons have characteristics not possessed by the unborn (as when it lists the qualifications a person must have to be president or a senator). Also, he pointed out that the law traditionally has viewed life as beginning at birth and has granted legal rights to the unborn only on the assumption that they would be born. Furthermore, Blackmun argued, it is appropriate to settle this abortion issue by appealing to constitutional and legal precedents because the authorities in medicine, philosophy and theology have not been able to reach agreement about who is a

person or when human life does begin. He thereby again implies that we have here a non-moral factual matter, an unresolved factual dispute.

Abortion opponents are quick to reply that even after birth babies are very dependent upon others for their life and that from the moment of the conception of the fetus it has the full potential to become an adult person if given the proper care and assistance. Therefore, if independence is the criterion for being a human being, even babies fail to pass the test. If capacity for consciousness is the test, then the fetus at any age has this potentiality. Consciousness won't fully be realized until some time after birth.

It also has been argued that if it is a matter of not knowing whether a fetus is or is not a person, then we ought not permit abortions for we may very well be killing a person for all we know. To be willing to kill what may be a person morally is just as bad as being willing to kill a person.[2] This argument assumes that the kind of ignorance involved here is something like the ignorance of the deer hunter who shoots into the moving brush knowing that what is there might not be a deer but might be one's hunting partner.

No such ignorance seems to be present, however, in the case of abortion. In the abortion case, it isn't a matter of looking behind the brush or into the shadows to see if a person is present. Biologically, we have extremely precise knowledge of what is present.

2. This argument against abortion is defended by Germain Grise in "Abortion: Ethical Arguments," in *Today's Moral Problems*, pp. 89–90.

The defenders of the right to abortion also retort that the issue can't be resolved by simply appealing to the potential of the fetus because every female egg and male sperm cell has the capacity to become an adult human being if given the right assistance and care. If cloning becomes possible in the case of humans, then every human cell will have this potentiality. Surely, not even the most extreme of anti-abortionists would want to claim that every living thing with the potentiality for becoming an adult being ought to be aided to realize that potentiality. This cannot function as a criterion for separating persons from things which are not persons with personal rights. Besides, it is not obvious that potential persons have the same rights as persons have. After all, potential presidents do not have the rights of the actual commander-in-chief.[3]

This debate on the level of biology between the proponents and opponents of the right to abortion seems to get nowhere. Whenever this happens, it is a good idea to suspect that all parties to the debate may be operating on the basis of questionable assumptions. In this case there seem to be four such questionable assumptions.

(1) Too often it is assumed that a clear line can be drawn between human beings and non-human beings. In fact, here, as with many empirical descriptions, we may be dealing with boundary cases which can be called "human" or "non-human" only through additional stipulations about what it means to call something "human."

In our ordinary use of words we repeatedly encounter borderline cases where the present rules and customs governing our application of the ordinary names of things don't tell us what the borderline cases should be called. Is this color red or orange? It is no more correct to say that it is one than the other. Is this a chair, a stool or a couch? Call it what you will. It is a little bit of each. Is this taxable income? A tax court will decide whether it should be so labeled, not using presently existing criteria governing the linguistic use of the expression "taxable income", but creating new criteria to cover this new case on the basis of the general intent of the tax laws and general principles of fairness and justice. Things often get called by a single name not because they all share some essential characteristic but because they bear family resemblances to each other. At the center of the class are clear and paradigmatic cases, the ones we use when teaching people how to use the word. The word's use then gets extended to cases only relatively similar to the core cases. This continues until we get a whole string of cases, all called by the same name, all arrangeable in such an order that each is very similar to the ones next to it, but also so that those on the ends of the ordered line share almost nothing in common with each other. Think of all the different things we call "games." Is there anything other than a mere family resemblance among them? When new borderline cases arise, it is up to the language

3. This argument against assuming that a potential A has the same rights as does A is presented by Stanley Benn in his "Abortion, Infanticide, and Respect for Persons," in *The Problem of Abortion*, Joel Feinberg (ed.), (Belmont, California, Wadsworth Pub. Co., 1973), pp. 92–104.

community to decide whether they will or will not be called by the same name. If there is a good reason for doing so, then that is the thing to do.[4]

Only a complete failure to see how words get their meaning from customary usage would lead one to think that we have a clear test for separating the human from the non-human. There are no clear breaks in nature and the use of these words were not set up with any consideration of a need to stipulate even relatively sharp breaks. There is no one moment when birth takes place. It takes time. There is no one absolute moment when conception takes place. Fertilization is a process which takes time and which can be broken down into successive moments even as gestation and maturation are such processes. There is no exact moment before which we have a mere part of one human's body and after which we have a new human being. There is no absolute line which can be drawn between being merely a woman, being a pregnant woman and being a mother and a child. The search for such a line seems to be a hopeless search and thus it is not surprising that the debate about where it lies has been so fruitless.

(2) Sometimes in these debates it is assumed that nothing significant is lost by calling everything which is human a "human being." However, by doing so we make it too easy to ignore the differences existing between human zygotes, embryos, fetuses, children and adults. Should

we also call every living human cell a human being? The differences between these various kinds of human things may be more important morally than the similarities. After all, the embryos of humans and chimps in many ways are more similar to each other than they are to adult humans and chimps. Morally, that they are embryos may be more important than that they are members of a certain species. This is what is lost sight of if we lump all these different things together and simply call them "human beings." Besides, since the expression "human being" is taught to us using children and adults and not fetuses as examples, and since it sometimes is used to mean "human person," we have to extend its meaning if we want to use it to cover non-paradigmatic cases like fetuses and embryos. Once the use is extended in this way, we may tend to forget the differences between the original cases and the extended cases and we may tend to transfer associations that held with the original cases but do not hold for the extended cases. Thus, more confusion sets in. Adult human beings make choices and judgments; we have no reason for believing that three-month-old fetuses do this. Be that as it may, the important thing to note is that one cannot settle the debate about whether human fetuses have personal rights simply by pointing out that they are human. One must show that being human in this way is sufficient to warrant the claim that they have personal rights.

(3) It is often assumed that calling something a person and calling it a human being are one and the same thing. It is assumed that all human beings should be called "persons." It

4. The notion of family resemblances was introduced into this area of discussion primarily by Ludwig Wittgenstein in his *Philosophical Investigations* (New York, Macmillan and Co., 1953). In particular, see sections 66–76.

is often assumed that "human being" and "person" are expressions which are equivalent in meaning and that one expression can always be used as a replacement for the other.

However, it does not follow by definition that all persons are human beings. We can conceive of non-human persons (Mickey Mouse, Zeus, Mr. Spock, God). Assuming that "human being" and "person" are equivalent in meaning prevents one from seeing that "human being" has two quite distinct and separate meanings. Some anti-abortionists, for example, equivocate in their use of the term "human being," using it biologically to mean Homo sapiens when claiming that a human embryo is a human being and using it morally to mean human person when claiming that it has a right to life. What needs to be defended, however, is the unexpressed premise that all Homo sapiens, even embryonic ones, should be treated as persons with rights, including the right to life. This is not true by definition. Unless one keeps clear one's use of the expression "human being," this debate about the morality of abortion will go nowhere.

(4) It is often assumed, even by some of the best philosophers, that the word "person" has only a single meaning. In fact, however, in addition to sometimes meaning simply Homo sapiens, it also has a metaphysical and a moral meaning. Not all Homo sapiens are metaphysical persons and some individuals may be moral persons without being metaphysical persons. These different meanings of the word "person" must be kept separate. Being a person in the metaphysical sense means being an individual who is capable of using correctly personal pronouns, who is capable of asking

the question, "Who am I?", who is capable of conception, perception, propositional thought and self-knowledge.[5] Being a person in the moral sense, however, means being an individual with all the moral rights of personhood.

Claiming that all metaphysical persons are moral persons probably will not lead to any trouble because of reasons we shall see in a moment. However, if we claim that only metaphysical persons are moral persons, then we seem to get caught in the undesirable position of saying that newly born infants do not have the right to be treated as persons because they are not yet metaphysical persons.[6] One only gradually becomes a metaphysical person after birth through a process of socialization and personalization. Were we to hold that only metaphysical persons have personal rights, then infanticide and the killing off of the permanently com-

5. For an excellent discussion of this sense of person, see Sidney Shoemaker, *Self Knowledge and Self Identity*; and Peter Strawson, "Persons" in *The Philosophy of Mind*, V. C. Chappell (ed.), (Englewood Cliffs, N.J., Prentice Hall, Inc., 1902), pp. 127–146.

6. For a defense of the claim that newly born infants are not persons with personal rights, see Michael Tooley, "A Defense of Abortion and Infanticide" in *The Problem of Abortion*, pp. 51–91. Tooley's position, it seems to me is the necessary result of claiming that being a metaphysical person is a necessary condition for being a moral person. For attempts to defend this claim see Mary Ann Warren, "On the Moral and Legal Status of Abortion," in *Social Ethics*, Thomas A. Mappes and Jane S. Zembaty (eds.), (New York, McGraw Hill Book Co., 1977), pp. 17–23; and Daniel Dennett, "Conditions of Personhood," in *The Identities of Persons*, Amelie O. Rorty (ed.), (Berkeley, California, University of California Press, 1976), pp. 175–196.

atose morally would be no different from killing off newly born kittens which are not wanted. Kittens cannot wonder who they are or ask for their rights. Neither can infants or the comatose.

Any moral agent who can demand his own rights and who can be held accountable for his behavior surely has the conceptual capacities necessary for being counted as a metaphysical person. Likewise, it seems that anyone who has the capacities necessary for being counted as a metaphysical person has the capacities needed in order to be held accountable for his behavior and for demanding his rights. The metaphysical person is the clear and paradigmatic example of the moral person, the person who participates in the moral form of life, indicting and justifying, claiming rights and having duties and obligations. In the case of such clear and paradigmatic examples, it probably does make sense to say that one has a right only if one can waive the right or demand it, only if the one having the right can conceive of the right being violated. However, it does not follow from this that the concept of moral personhood cannot be extended so that the protection of the umbrella of personal rights can be granted also to some individuals who are not yet able or not able any longer to claim their own rights or to be held responsible for their behavior. There might be very good, morally compelling reasons for adopting such a social policy of extending outward the boundaries of personhood to cover classes of individuals who have no duties and who are incapable of claiming their own rights. Protection of persons in the clear and paradigmatic cases might require that we push the boundaries of personhood out as far as we can, stopping only when the effect becomes counterproductive.

As a matter of fact, the concept of moral personhood already has been expanded in this way because we can and do speak meaningfully of the personal rights of infants, the unconscious, the insane and the comatose. They are not examples of the obviously clear cases of persons in either the metaphysical or moral sense. They do not have the necessary conceptual capacities for metaphysical personhood and they have no duties, but it seems to make perfectly good sense to say that they have personal rights. If we had good reason to do so, we could also say that human embryos and fetuses have personal rights. It is true that if we choose to do so, then we will have to justify this expansion of the boundaries of personhood whenever the rights of such persons place obligations upon other persons. Making such an expansion of the domain of moral personhood, however, is not something which it is logically impossible to do. Only by failing to distinguish the moral sense of personhood from the metaphysical sense does it seem as though this is impossible. Therefore, we must keep separate these various senses of being a person.

If we remove these four questionable assumptions, what is it that does emerge as the real issue which needs to be settled in order to know whether abortion is immoral or not? I would suggest that the real question which needs to be answered is the following question, "Should all the rights and protections morally due to clear cases of persons be granted to all human embryos and fetuses?" Put in another way, the question comes down to asking whether there are morally compelling reasons for adopting a social policy of throwing the mantle of personhood over all human embryos and fetuses, of extending the boundaries of personhood to individuals who are this early in the process of human development and who, therefore, have no duties and who are unable to claim for themselves any rights.

The debate about the appropriateness of adopting such a social policy is carried on by persons who can make claims and counterclaims about how to view other individuals who are incapable of making such claims. Therefore, except for considering the general injunction not to ever cause needless pain and suffering to any sentient being, this debate about whether personal rights should be granted by us to fetuses is carried on by us in terms of what best defends the freedom, rights and dignity of those of us who unquestionably are persons in the full sense of the word because we can legitimately demand our rights. This in fact is how the debate over abortion often has proceeded. Opponents of abortion often argue that we are endangering the rights of all persons if we permit abortions. Defenders of the right of abortion deny that any serious damage to our status as persons is created by allowing abortions and that it costs too much in terms of the pregnant woman's right to exist as a free person to grant such a moral status to the fetus.

It is important to remember that if we take this approach, then we are talking about rights being granted and not about individuals naturally having such rights. Studying the biological characteristics of the embryos of Homo sapiens is relevant in this debate only to the extent that it helps us to understand what would happen to us if we did or did not decide to grant full personal rights to individuals with such characteristics. If human embryos and fetuses were separated from their mothers and then died, would this increase the likelihood that other individuals with personal rights would not be treated as persons? This is where biological evidence takes on relevance. The relevance it has, of course, will depend upon the effect which the death of embryos and fetuses at different ages have upon the attitudes of the people in a particular community.

This suggests the possibility that abortion prohibitions ought to be only local rules, if at all, because what is needed in one community to protect clear cases of persons may not be needed in another community. The cost for such protection in one community may be little but in another community it might be too high. Most Japanese find it almost impossible to comprehend what the debate about abortion in the United States and Western Europe is all about. They find that allowing their women to have the right to abort pregnancies in no way threatens the respect given to other people from the cradle to extremely old age. It seems possible to have very different attitudes towards embryos and fetuses while still greatly respecting the rights of newly born infants, typical adults and senior citizens. Some defenders of the right of abortion claim that mankind's general respect for persons actually will increase if this right is granted. Increased respect for women as persons, increased respect for the wanted children born and the absence of disrespect for unwanted babies will produce this effect, they claim.

We have stated repeatedly that persons are not born; they gradually are made in an interpersonal context of socialization. People teach children how to do things for reasons. We are socially nurtured into becoming persons with rights and duties. Here, of course, we are talking about individuals becoming persons in the full sense of the word. Young children have few if any obligations, but to them has been given a whole battery of rights. In some societies in earlier eras some newly born infants were not given such rights and in such societies infanticide was not considered murder. Almost everyone now agrees that the full rights of personhood should be granted to all newly born, normal children. Birth is such a clear and sharp point of origin. No point after birth could serve as a better place at which to begin giving personal rights. Besides, children begin to get personalized very quickly after birth. Very quickly they become very much like us. Most parents quickly treat them as persons. In the case of wanted pregnancies, parents see the unborn infant as their child long before birth and treat it as a person. Gross disrespect for the parents involved would be shown if the full rights of personhood were not granted to all such fetuses, if persons were forced to have abortions. It is hard to see how anyone can be respected as a person, if newly born infants and the cherished unborn are not so respected. There seems to be no way to guarantee respect for all persons without guaranteeing personal rights to humans from the

moment of birth on. Societies like Sparta which have permitted infanticide seem to have been quite unable to maintain the recognition of the personal rights of adults.

One of the major reasons that abortion exists as such a moral problem in Western nations today is because some Christians (due to their doctrine that an immortal soul comes into existence at the moment of conception) have demanded that we push the boundaries of personhood back to the moment of conception. Many modern Western women have protested, however, that doing this does not protect their status as persons but instead consists in treating them as mere things—procreators of children. Since this religious claim about souls does not seem to be publicly verifiable, it really cannot enter the moral debate and it cannot be used to justify denying women the moral freedom to have an abortion.

The question of where the boundary of personhood should be drawn at the beginning of human life seems to hinge simply on the question of where drawing the line will best further respect for persons in general. As a general principle, it seems to me that we should push outward the boundaries of personhood as far as we can and that we should stop this outward expansion only when respect for persons is violated or threatened more by continued expansion than by restricting expansion. The only restriction on expanding these boundaries should be injuries or threats to respect for persons and not simply because of injuries or threats to the good life of those around us. Without this restriction, there would be nothing wrong with killing off anyone who cannot demand one's rights, if it were done at times and in ways which did not cause suffering to the remaining persons. Such a utilitarian policy does not grant as much protection as is possible or desirable.

Therefore, it seems to me that in the case of abortion, if we draw the line too close to birth, we start threatening all persons because it becomes very difficult to keep separate in our minds, attitudes and emotions the killing of such fetuses and the killing of individuals who unquestionably are persons. On the other hand, if we draw the line too close to conception, respect for women as persons seems to be threatened. We now start seeing them primarily as procreators of children. Respect for the autonomy of women as persons is greatly threatened unless the issue of becoming a mother remains the woman's own private affair. Forcing women to have children they do not want does not seem to enhance the personal dignity and respect of the women involved, the unwanted child or the rest of us. Permitting abortions will decrease the number of infants who will not be respected as persons when born but who end up being abused or stuffed in garbage cans. Human life will become even more precious when its creation is fully up to us and is not something which just happens to us.

C O M M E N T S ▪ Q U E S T I O N S

1. Ruf's basic approach to the abortion question is a flexible one that allows for setting the boundaries of moral personhood at somewhat different places for different societies and different times. Do you believe that this is the correct approach?

2. Ruf's position falls between more extreme positions. Do you believe that a compromise position such as Ruf's is most defensible?

3. Has Ruf given sufficient weight to the mother's rights? To the fetus's rights?

4. To what extent can Ruf's position be seen as an appeal to the Principle of the Common Good?

5. Compare and contrast what Warren, Ruf, and Noonan say on the question of whether or not the fetus is a human being. Which position is most defensible?

R I C H A R D   B.   B R A N D T

Defective Newborns and the Morality of Termination

* * * * *

Suppose that killing a defective newborn, or allowing it to die, would not be an *injury*, but would rather be doing the infant a favor. In that case we should feel intuitively less opposed to termination of newborns, and presumably rational persons would be less inclined to support a moral code with a prohibition against such action. In that case we would feel rather as we do about a person's preventing a suicide attempt from being successful, in order that the person be elaborately tortured to death at a later stage. It is no favor to the prospective suicide to save his life; similarly, if the prospective life of defective newborns is bad we are doing them a favor to let them die.

It may be said that we have no way of knowing what the conscious experiences of defective children are like, and that we have no competence in any case to decide when or what kind of life is bad or not worth living. Further, it may be said that predictions about a defective newborn's prospects for the future are precarious, in view of possible further advances of medicine. It does seem, however, that here, as everywhere, the rational person will follow the evidence about the present or future facts. But there is a question how to decide whether a life is bad or not worth living.

In the case of *some* defective newborns, it seems clear that their prospective life is bad. Suppose, as sometimes happens, a child is hydrocephalic with an extremely low I.Q., is blind and deaf, has no control over its body, can only lie on its back all day and have all its needs taken care of by others, and even cries out with pain when it is touched or lifted. Infants born with spina bifida—and these number over two per one thousand births—are normally not quite so badly off, but are often nearly so.

But what criterion are we using if we say that such a life is bad? One criterion might be called a "happiness" criterion. If a person *likes* a moment of experience while he is having it, his life is so far good; if a person *dislikes* a moment of experience while he is having it, his life is so far bad. Based on such reactions, we might construct a "happiness

Richard B. Brandt, who is a professor of philosophy at the University of Michigan, has written very widely in the area of ethics. Among his books are Ethical Theory *and* A Theory of the Good and the Right.

From *Infanticide and the Value of Life*, ed. by Marvin Kohl, © 1978 by Prometheus Books, Buffalo, New York. Reprinted by permission.

curve" for a person, going up above the indifference axis when a moment of experience is liked—and how far above depending on how strongly it is liked—and dipping down below the line when a moment is disliked. Then this criterion would say that a life is worth living if there is a net balance of positive area under the curve over a lifetime, and that it is bad if there is a net balance of negative area. One might adopt some different criterion: for instance, one might say that a life is worth living if a person would *want* to live it over again given that, at the end, he could remember the whole of it with perfect vividness in some kind of grand intuitive awareness. Such a response to this hypothetical holistic intuition, however, would likely be affected by the state of the person's drives or moods at the time, and the conception strikes me as unconvincing, compared with the moment-by-moment reaction to what is going on. Let us, for the sake of the argument, adopt the happiness criterion.[2]

Is the prospective life of the seriously defective newborn, like the one described above, bad or good according to this criterion? One thing seems clear: that it is *less* good than is the prospective life of a normal infant. But is it bad?

We have to do some extrapolating from what we know. For instance, such a child will presumably suffer from severe sensory deprivation; he is simply not getting interesting stimuli. On the basis of laboratory data, it is plausible to think the child's experience is at best boring or uncomfortable. If the child's experience is painful, of course, its moments are, so far, on the negative side. One must suppose that such a child hardly suffers from disappointment, since it will not learn to expect anything exciting, beyond being fed and fondled, and these events will be regularly forthcoming. One might expect such a child to suffer from isolation and loneliness, but insofar as this is true, the object of dislike probably should be classified as just sensory deprivation; dislike of loneliness seems to depend on the deprivation of past pleasures of human company. There are also some positive enjoyments: of eating, drinking, elimination, seeing the nurse coming with food, and so on. But the brief enjoyments can hardly balance the long stretches of boredom, discomfort, or

---

2. Professor P. Foot has made interesting remarks on when a life is worth living. See her "Euthanasia," *Philosophy and Public Affairs* 6 (1977): 85–112, especially pp. 95–96. She suggests that a good life must "contain a minimum of basic goods," although not necessarily a favorable balance of good over evil elements. When does she think this minimum fails? For one thing, in extreme senility or severe brain damage. She also cites as examples of conditions for minimal goods that "a man is not driven to work far beyond his capacity; that he has the support of a family or community; that he can more or less satisfy his hunger; that he has hopes for the future; that he can lie down to rest at night." Overwhelming pain or nausea, or crippling depression, she says, also can make life not worth living. All of these, of course, except for cases of senility and brain damage, are factors fixing whether stretches of living are highly unpleasant.

If a person thinks that life is not good unless it realizes certain human potentialities, he will think life can be bad even if liked—and so far sets a higher standard than the happiness criterion. But Foot and such writers may say that even when life is not pleasant on balance, it can still be good if human potentialities are being realized or these basic minimal conditons are met; and in that sense they set a lower standard.

even pain. On the whole, the lives of such children are bad according to the happiness criterion.

Naturally we cannot generalize about the cases of all "defective" newborns; there are all sorts of defects, and the cases I have described are about the worst. A child with spina bifida may, if he survives the numerous operations, I suppose, adjust to the frustrations of immobility; he may become accustomed to the embarrassments of no bladder or bowel control; he may have some intellectual enjoyments like playing chess; he will suffer from observing what others have but he cannot, such as sexual satisfactions, in addition to the pain of repeated surgery. How does it all balance out? Surely not as very good, but perhaps above the indifference level.

It may fairly be said, I think, that the lives of some defective newborns are destined to be bad on the whole, and it would be a favor to them if their lives were terminated. Contrariwise, the prospective lives of many defective newborns are modestly pleasant, and it would be some injury to them to be terminated, albeit the lives they will live are ones some of us would prefer not to live at all.

Consent. Let us now make a second suggestion, not this time that termination of a defective newborn would be doing him a favor, but this time that he *consents* to termination, in the sense of expressing a rational deliberated preference for this. In that case I suggest that intuitively we would be *more* favorably inclined to judge that it is right to let the defective die, and I suggest also that for that case rational persons would be more ready to support a moral code permitting termination. Notice that we think that if an ill person has sig-

nified what we think a rational and deliberated desire to die, we are morally better justified in withdrawing life-supporting measures than we otherwise would be.

The newborn, however, is incapable of expressing his preference (giving consent) at all, much less expressing a rational deliberated preference. There could in theory be court-appointed guardians or proxies, presumably disinterested parties, authorizerd to give such consent on his behalf; but even so this would not be *his* consent.

Nevertheless, there is fact about the mental life of the newborn (defective or not) such that, if he could understand the fact, it seems he would not object—even rationally or after deliberation, if that were possible—to his life being terminated, or to his parents substituting another child in his place. This suggestion may seem absurd, but let us see. The explanation runs along the lines of an argument I once used to support the morality of abortion. I quote the paragraph in which this argument was introduced.[3]

Suppose I were seriously ill, and were told that, for a sizeable fee, an operation to save "my life" could be performed, of the following sort: my brain would be removed to another body which could provide a normal life, but the unfortunate result of the operation would be that my memory and learned abilities would be wholly erased, and that the forming of memory brain traces must begin again from scratch, as in a newborn baby. Now,

_____

3. Richard B. Brandt, "The Morality of Abortion," in an earlier form in *The Monist* 56 (1972): 504–526, and in revised form in R. L. Perkins, ed., *Abortion: Pro and Con* (Cambridge, Mass.: Schenkman Publishing Co., 1974).

how large a fee would I be willing to pay for this operation, when the alternative is my peaceful demise? My own answer would be: None at all. I would take no interest in the continued existence of "myself" in that sense, and I would rather add the sizeable fee to the inheritance of my children. . . . I cannot see the point of forfeiting my children's inheritance in order to start off a person who is brand new except that he happens to enjoy the benefit of having my present brain, without the memory traces. It appears that some continuity of memory is a necessary condition for personal identity *in an important sense.*

My argument was that the position of a fetus, at the end of the first trimester, is essentially the same as that of the person contemplating this operation: he will consider that the baby born after six more months will not be *he* in any *important* and *motivating* sense (there will be no continuity of memory, and, indeed, maybe nothing to have been remembered), and the later existence of this baby, in a sense bodily continuous with his present body, would be a matter of indifference to him. So, I argued, nothing is being done to the fetus that he would object to having done if he understood the situation.

What do I think is necessary in order for the continuation of my body with its conscious experiences to be worthwhile? One thing is that it is able to remember the events I can now remember; another is that it takes some interest in the projects I am now planning and remembers them as my projects; another is that it recognizes my friends and has warm feelings for them, and so on. Reflection on these states of a future continuation of my body with its experiences is what makes the idea motivating. But such motivating

reflection for a newborn is impossible: he has no memories that he wants recalled later; he has no plans to execute; he has no warm feelings for other persons. He has simply not had the length of life necessary for these to come about. Not only that: the conception of these things cannot be motivating because the concept of some state of affairs being motivating requires roughly a past experience in which similar states of affairs were satisfying, and he has not lived long enough for the requisite conditioning to have taken place. (The most one could say is that the image of warm milk in his mouth is attractive; he might answer affirmatively if it could be put to him whether he would be aversive to the idea of no more warm milk.) So we can say, not merely that the newborn does not want the continuation of himself as a subject of experiences (he has not the conceptual framework for this); he does not want *anything* that his own survival would promote. It is like the case of the operation: there is nothing I want that the survival of my brain with no memory would promote. Give the newborn as much *conceptual* framework as you like; the *wants* are not there, which could give significance to the continuance of his life.

The newborn, then, is bound to be *indifferent* to the idea of a continuation of the stream of his experiences, even if he clearly has the idea of that. It seems we can *know* this about him.

The truth of all this is still not for it to be the case that the newborn, defective or not, gives *consent* to, or expresses a preference for, the termination of his life. *Consent* is a performance, normally linguistic, but always requiring some conventional *sign*. A newborn, who has not yet learned how to signalize consent, cannot give consent. And it may be thought that this difference makes all the difference.

In order to see what difference it does make in this case, we should ask what makes adult consent morally important. Why is it that we think euthanasia can be practiced on an adult only if he gives his consent, at least his implied consent (e.g., by previous statements)? There seem to be two reasons. The first is that a person is more likely to be concerned with his own welfare, and to take steps to secure it, than are others, even his good friends. Giving an individual control over his own life, and not permitting others to take control except when he consents, is normally to promote his welfare. An individual may, of course, behave stupidly or shortsightedly, but we think that on the whole a person's welfare is best secured if decisions about it are in his hands; and it is best for society in the normal case (not for criminals, etc.) if persons' own lives are well-served. The second reason is the feeling of security a person can have, if he knows the major decisions about himself are in his own hands. When they are not, a person can easily, and in some cases very reasonably, suppose that other persons may well be able to do something to him that he would very much like them not to do. He does not have to worry about that if he knows they cannot do it without his consent.

Are things different with the newborn? At least he, like the fetus, is not yet able to suffer from insecurity; he cannot worry about what others may do to him. So the second reason for requiring consent cannot have any importance in his case. His situation is thus very unlike that of the senile adult, for an adult can worry about what others may do to him if they judge him senile. And this worry can well cast a shadow over a lot of life. But how about the first reason? Here matters are more complex. In the case of children, we think their own lives are better cared for if certain decisions are in the hands of others: the child may not want to visit the dentist, but the parents know that his best interests are served by going, and they make him go. The same for compulsory school attendance. And the same for the newborn. But there is another point: that society has an interest, at certain crucial points, that may not be served by doing just exactly what is for the lifelong interest of the newborn. There are huge costs that are relevant, in the case of the defective newborn. I shall go into that problem in a moment. It seems, then, that in the case of the newborn, *consent* cannot have the moral importance that it has in the case of adults.

On the other hand, then, the newborn will not *care* whether his life is terminated, even if he understands his situation perfectly; and, on the other hand, consent does not have the moral importance in his case that it has for adults. So, while it seems true that we would feel better about permitting termination of defective newborns if only they could give rational and deliberated consent and gave it, nevertheless when we bear the foregoing two points in mind, the absence of consent does not seem morally crucial in their case. We can understand why rational persons deciding which moral code to support for their society would not make the giving of consent a necessary condition for feeling free to terminate an infant's life when such action was morally indicated by the other features of the situation.

Replacement in Order to Get a Better Life

Let us now think of an example owing to Derek Parfit. Suppose a woman wants a child, but is told that if she conceives a child now it will be defective, whereas if she waits three months she will produce a normal child. Obviously we think it would be wrong for the mother not to delay. (If she delays, the child she will have is not the *same* child as the one she would have had if she had not delayed, but it will have a better life). This is the sole reason why we think she should delay and have the later-born child.

Suppose, however, a woman conceives but discovers only three months later that the fetus will become a defective child, but that she can have a normal child if she has an abortion and tries again. Now this time there is still the same reason for having the abortion that there formerly was for the delay: that she will produce a child with a better life. Ought she not then to have the abortion? If the child's life is bad, he could well complain that he had been injured by deliberately being brought to term. Would he complain if he were aborted, in favor of the later normal child? Not if the argument of the preceding section is correct.

But now suppose the woman does not discover until after she gives birth, that the child is seriously defective, but that she could conceive again and have a normal child. Are things really different, in the first few days?

One might think that a benevolent person would want, in each of these cases, the substitution of a normal child for the defective one, of the better life for the worse one.

The Cost and Its Relevance

It is agreed that the burden of care for a defective infant, say one born with spina bifida, is huge. The cost of surgery alone for an infant with spina bifida has been estimated to be around $275,000.[4] In many places this cost must be met by the family of the child, and there is the additional cost of care in an institution, if the child's condition does not permit care at home—and a very modest estimate of the monthly cost at present is $1,100. To meet even the surgical costs, not to mention monthly payments for continuing care, the lives of members of the family must be at a most spartan level for many years. The psychological effects of this, and equally, if not more so, of care provided at home, are far-reaching; they are apt to destroy the marriage and to cause psychological problems for the siblings. There is the on-going anxiety, the regular visits, the continuing presence of a caretaker if the child is in the home. In one way or another the continued existence of the child is apt to reduce dramatically the quality of life of the family as a whole.

It can be and has been argued that such costs, while real, are irrelevant to the moral problem of what should

---

4. See A. M. Shaw and I. A. Shaw, in S. Gorovitz, et al., *Moral Problems in Medicine* (Englewood Cliffs, N.J.: Prentice-Hall, Inc., 1976), pp. 335–341.

be done.[5] It is obvious, however, that rational persons, when deciding which moral code to support, would take these human costs into account. As indeed they should: the parents and siblings are also human beings with lives to live, and any sacrifices a given law or moral system might call on them to make must be taken into account in deciding between laws and moral codes. Everyone will feel sympathy for a helpless newborn; but everyone should also think, equally vividly, of all the others who will suffer and just how they will suffer— and, of course, as indicated above, of just what kind of life the defective newborn will have in any case. There is a choice here between allowing a newborn to die (possibly a favor to it, and in any case not a serious loss), and imposing a very heavy burden on the family for many years to come.

Philosophers who think the cost to others is irrelevant to what should be done should reflect that we do not accept the general principle that lives should be saved at no matter what cost. For instance, ships are deliberately built with only a certain margin of safety; they could be built so that they would hardly sink in any storm, but to do so would be economically unfeasible. We do not think we should require a standard of safety for automobiles that goes beyond a certain point of expense and inconvenience; we are prepared to risk a few extra deaths. And how about the lives we are willing to lose in war, in order to assure a certain kind of economic order or democracy or free speech? Surely there is a point at which the loss of a life (or the abbreviation of a life) and the cost to others become comparable. Is it obvious that the continuation of a marginal kind of life for a child takes moral precedence over providing a college education for one or more of his siblings? Some comparisons will be hard to make, but continuing even a marginally pleasant life hardly has absolute priority.

Drawing Lines

There are two questions which must be answered in any complete account of what is the morally right thing to do about defective newborns.

The first is: If a decision to terminate is made, how soon must it be made? Obviously it could not be postponed to the age of five, or of three, or even a year and a half. At those ages, all the reasons for insisting on consent are already cogent. And at those ages, the child will already care what happens to him. But ten days is tolerable. Doubtless advances in medicine will permit detection of serious prospective defects early in pregnancy, and this issue of how many days will not arise.

Second, the argument from the quality of the prospective life of the defective newborn requires that we

---

5. See, for instance, Philippa Foot, "Euthanasia," especially pp. 109–111. She writes: "So it is not for their sake but to avoid trouble to others that they are allowed to die. When brought out into the open this seems unacceptable; at least we do not easily accept the principle that adults who need special care should be counted too burdensome to be kept alive." I would think that "to avoid trouble to others" is hardly the terminology to describe the havoc that is apt to be produced. I agree that adults should not be allowed to die, or actively killed, without their consent, possibly except when they cannot give consent but are in great pain; but the reasons that justify different behavior in the two situations have appeared in the section, "Consent."

decide which defects are so serious that the kind of life the defective child can have gives it no serious claim as compared with the social costs. This issue must be thought through, and some guidelines established, but I shall not attempt this here.

One might argue that, if the newborn cannot rationally care whether its life ends or not, the parents are free to dispose of a child irrespective of whether he is defective, if they simply do not want it. To this there are two replies. First, in practice there are others who want a child if the parents do not, and they can put it up for adoption. But second, the parents are *injuring* a child if they prevent it from having the good life it could have had. We do not in general accept the argument that a person is free to injure another, for no reason, even if he has that person's consent. In view of these facts, we may expect that rational, benevolent persons deciding which moral code to support would select one that required respect for the life of a normal child, but would permit the termination of the life of a seriously defective child.

Active and Passive Procedures

There is a final question: that of a choice between withdrawal of life-supporting measures (such as feeding), and the active, painless taking of life. It seems obvious, however, that once the basic decision is made that an infant is not to receive the treatment necessary to sustain life beyond a few days, it is mere stupid cruelty to allow it to waste away gradually in a hospital bed—for the child to suffer, and for everyone involved also to suffer in watching the child suffer. If death is the outcome decided upon, it is far kinder for it to come quickly and painlessly.

C O M M E N T S ■ Q U E S T I O N S

---

1. Evaluate each of the following arguments:
   a. In the case of some severely defective newborns, it would be a favor to them if they were killed or allowed to die since—as best we can judge—the prospective quality of their lives is more bad than good (the quality of life argument).
   b. The newborn infant has as yet no significant memory traces and consequently does not as yet have the sort of personal identity whose loss would be something that the infant could perceive as a significantly bad thing. Put another way, "we can say, not merely that the newborn does not *want the continuation of himself as a subject of experiences* (he has not the conceptual framework for this); he does not want *anything* which his own survival would promote" (the consent argument).
   c. If a mother did not need to raise a severely defective newborn, then she could replace it with a normal infant (through another pregnancy or adoption)

and raise it in the place of the defective infant (the replacement argument).

   d. Both the psychological and the monetary costs of raising a severely defective newborn can be extremely high. In some cases they will be too great a burden for the parents to bear, and it is not clear that they can be widely borne by society either (the costs argument).

2. Is Brandt correct not to raise questions about the right to life of a newborn infant?

3. For Brandt, the question of termination is not a question of balancing the rights of newborns against other values. Is Brandt's approach the correct one to take?

4. Brandt's position can instructively be compared to Thomson's position on the abortion question. When taken together, do the two positions strengthen each other? Weaken each other?

5. Brandt's costs argument is in part an appeal to the Principle of the Common Good. Since medical advances are being made all the time that will allow for more costly treatments of defective newborns with multiple crippling conditions, how important is a purely monetary appeal (Brandt's is more than this of course) to the Principle of the Common Good?

J O H N A. R O B E R T S O N

Involuntary Euthanasia of Defective Newborns

A. The Quality of the Defective Infant's Life

C omparisons of relative worth among persons, or between persons and other interests, raise moral and methodological issues that make any argument that relies on such comparisons extremely vulnerable. Thus the strongest claim for not treating the defective newborn is that treatment seriously harms the infant's own in-terests, whatever may be the effects on others. When maintaining his life involves great physical and psychological suffering for the patient, a reasonable person might conclude that such a life is not worth living. Presumably

---

John A. Robertson is Mars McLean Professor of Law at the University of Texas. He has written widely in the areas of constitutional law, criminal law, and law and medicine.

From the *Stanford Law Review*, Vol. 27, pp. 251–261. Copyright 1975 by the Board of Trustees of the Leland Stanford Junior University. Used by permission of the author and the *Stanford Law Review*.

the patient, if fully informed and able to communicate, would agree. One then would be morally justified in withholding lifesaving treatment if such action served to advance the best interests of the patient.

Congenital malformations impair development in several ways that lead to the judgment that deformed retarded infants are "a burden to themselves."[9] One is the severe physical pain, much of it resulting from repeated surgery that defective infants will suffer. Defective children also are likely to develop other pathological features, leading to repeated fractures, dislocations, surgery, malfunctions, and other sources of pain. The shunt, for example, inserted to relieve hydrocephalus, a common problem in defective children, often becomes clogged, necessitating frequent surgical interventions.

Pain, however, may be intermittent and manageable with analgesics. Since many infants and adults experience great pain, and many defective infants do not, pain alone, if not totally unmanageable, does not sufficiently show that a life is so worthless that death is preferable. More important are the psychosocial deficits resulting from the child's handicaps. Many defective children never can walk even with prosthesis, never interact with normal children, never appreciate growth, adolesence, or the fulfillment of education and employment, and seldom are even able to care for themselves. In cases of severe retardation, they may be left with a vegetative existence in a crib, incapable of choice or the most minimal

response to stimuli. Parents or others may reject them, and much of their time will be spent in hospitals, in surgery, or fighting the many illnesses that beset them. Can it be said that such a life is worth living?

There are two possible responses to the quality-of-life argument. One is to accept its premises but to question the degree of suffering in particular cases, and thus restrict the justification for death to the most extreme cases. The absence of opportunities for schooling, career, and interaction may be the fault of social attitudes and the failings of healthy persons, rather than a necessary result of congenital malformations. Psychosocial suffering occurs because healthy, normal persons reject or refuse to relate to the defective, or hurry them to poorly funded institutions. Most nonambulatory, mentally retarded persons can be trained for satisfying roles. One cannot assume that a nonproductive existence is necessarily unhappy: even social rejection and nonacceptance can be mitigated. Moreover, the psychosocial ills of the handicapped often do not differ in kind from those experienced by many persons. With training and care, growth, development, and a full range of experiences are possible for most people with physical and mental handicaps. Thus, the claim that death is a far better fate than life cannot in most cases be sustained.

This response, however, avoids meeting the quality-of-life argument on its strongest grounds. Even if many defective infants can experience growth, interaction, and most human satisfactions if nurtured, treated, and trained, some infants are so severely retarded or grossly deformed that their response to love and care, in fact their capacity to be conscious, is

---

9. Smith & Smith, *Selection for Treatment in Spina Bifida Cystica*, 4 Brit. Med. J. 189, 195 (1973).

always minimal. Although mongoloid and nonambulatory spina bifida children may experience an existence we would hesitate to adjudge worse than death, the profoundly retarded, nonambulatory, blind, deaf infant who will spend his few years in the backward cribs of a state institution is clearly a different matter.

To repudiate the quality-of-life argument, therefore, requires a defense of treatment in even these extreme cases. Such a defense would question the validity of any surrogate or proxy judgments of the worth or quality of life when the wishes of the person in question cannot be ascertained. The essence of the quality-of-life argument is a proxy's judgment that no reasonable person can prefer the pain, suffering, and loneliness of, for example, life in a crib at an IQ level of 20, to an immediate, painless death.

But in what sense can the proxy validly conclude that a person with different wants, needs, and interests, if able to speak, would agree that such a life were worse than death? At the start one must be skeptical of the proxy's claim to objective disinterestedness. If the proxy is also the parent or physician, as has been the case in pediatric euthanasia, the impact of treatment on the proxy's interests, rather than solely on those of the child, may influence his assessment. But even if the proxy were truly neutral and committed only to caring for the child, the problem of egocentricity and knowing another's mind remains. Compared with the situation and life prospects of a "reasonable man," the child's potential quality of life indeed appears dim. Yet a standard based on healthy, ordinary development may be entirely inappropriate to this situation.

One who has never known the pleasures of mental operation, ambulation, and social interaction surely does not suffer from their loss as much as one who has. While one who has known these capacities may prefer death to a life without them, we have no assurance that the handicapped person, with no point of comparison, would agree. Life, and life alone, whatever its limitations, might be of sufficient worth to him.

One should also be hesitant to accept proxy assessments of quality-of-life because the margin of error in such predictions may be very great. For instance, while one expert argues that by a purely clinical assessment he can accurately forecast the minimum degree of future handicap an individual will experience, such forecasting is not infallible, and risks denying care to infants whose disability might otherwise permit a reasonably acceptable quality-of-life. Thus given the problems in ascertaining another's wishes, the proxy's bias to personal or culturally relative interests, and the unreliability of predictive criteria, the quality-of-life argument is open to serious question. Its strongest appeal arises in the case of a grossly deformed, retarded, institutionalized child, or one with incessant unmanageable pain, where continued life is itself torture. But these cases are few, and cast doubt on the utility of any such judgment. Even if the judgment occasionally may be defensible, the potential danger of quality-of-life assessments may be a compelling reason for rejecting this rationale for withholding treatment.

B. The Suffering of Others

In addition to the infant's own suffering, one who argues that the harm of treatment justifies violation of the defective infant's right to life usually relies on the psychological, social, and economic costs of maintaining his existence to family and society. In their view the minimal benefit of treatment to persons incapable of full social and physical development does not justify the burdens that care of the defective infant imposes on parents, siblings, health professionals, and other patients. Matson, a noted pediatric neurosurgeon, states:

[I]t is the doctor's and the community's responsibility to provide [custodial] care and to minimize suffering; but, at the same time, it is also their responsibility not to prolong such individual, familial, and community suffering unnecessarily, and not to carry out multiple procedures and prolonged, expensive, acute hospitalization in an infant whose chance for acceptable growth and development is negligible.[10]

Such a frankly utilitarian argument raises problems. It assumes that because of the greatly curtailed orbit of his existence, the costs or suffering of others is greater than the benefit of life to the child. This judgment, however, requires a coherent way of measuring and comparing interpersonal utilities, a logical-practical problem that utilitarianism has never surmounted. But even if such comparisons could reliably show a net loss from treatment, the fact remains that the child must sacrifice his life to benefit others. If the life of one individual, however useless, may be sacrificed for the benefit of any person, however useful, or for the

benefit of any number of persons, then we have acknowledged the principle that rational utility may justify any outcome. As many philosophers have demonstrated, utilitarianism can always permit the sacrifice of one life for other interests, given the appropriate arrangement of utilities on the balance sheet. In the absence of principled grounds for such a decision, the social equation involved in mandating direct, involuntary euthanasia becomes a difference of degree, not kind, and we reach the point where protection of life depends solely on social judgments of utility.

These objections may well be determinative. But if we temporarily bracket them and examine the extent to which care of the defective infant subjects others to suffering, the claim that inordinate suffering outweighs the infant's interest in life is rarely plausible. In this regard we must examine the impact of caring for defective infants on the family, health professions, and society at large.

The Family

The psychological impact and crisis created by birth of a defective infant is devastating. Not only is the mother denied the normal tension release from the stresses of pregnancy, but both parents feel a crushing blow to their dignity, self-esteem and self-confidence. In a very short time, they feel grief for the loss of the normal expected child, anger at fate, numbness, disgust, waves of helplessness, and disbelief. Most feel personal blame for the defect, or blame their spouse. Adding to the shock is fear that social position and mobility are permanently endangered. The transformation of a "joyously awaited experience into one of catastrophe and

---

10. Matson, *Surgical Treatment of Myelomeningocele*, 42 PEDIATRICS 225, 226 (1968).

profound psychological threat"[11] often will reactivate unresolved maturational conflicts. The chances for social pathology—divorce, somatic complaints, nervous and mental disorders—increase and hard-won adjustment patterns may be permanently damaged.

The initial reactions of guilt, grief, anger, and loss, however, cannot be the true measure of family suffering caused by care of a defective infant, because these costs are present whether or not the parents choose treatment. Rather, the question is to what degree treatment imposes psychic and other costs greater than would occur if the child were not treated. The claim that care is more costly rests largely on the view that parents and family suffer inordinately from nurturing such a child.

Indeed, if the child is treated and accepted at home, difficult and demanding adjustments must be made. Parents must learn how to care for a disabled child, confront financial and psychological uncertainty, meet the needs of other siblings, and work through their own conflicting feelings. Mothering demands are greater than with a normal child, particularly if medical care and hospitalization are frequently required. Counseling or professional support may be nonexistent or difficult to obtain. Younger siblings may react with hostility and guilt, older with shame and anger. Often the normal feedback of child growth that renders the turmoil of childrearing worthwhile develops more slowly or not at all. Family

resources can be depleted (especially if medical care is needed), consumption patterns altered, or standards of living modified. Housing may have to be found closer to a hospital, and plans for further children changed. Finally, the anxieties, guilt, and grief present at birth may threaten to recur or become chronic.

Yet, although we must recognize the burdens and frustrations of raising a defective infant, it does not necessarily follow that these costs require nontreatment, or even institutionalization. Individual and group counseling can substantially alleviate anxiety, guilt, and frustration, and enable parents to cope with underlying conflicts triggered by the birth and the adaptations required. Counseling also can reduce psychological pressures on siblings, who can be taught to recognize and accept their own possibly hostile feelings and the difficult position of their parents. They may even be taught to help their parents care for the child.

The impact of increased financial costs also may vary. In families with high income or adequate health insurance, the financial costs are manageable. In others, state assistance may be available. If severe financial problems arise or pathological adjustments are likely, institutionalization, although undesirable for the child, remains an option. Finally, in many cases, the experience of living through a crisis is a deepening and enriching one, accelerating personality maturation, and giving one a new sensitivity to the needs of spouse, siblings, and others. As one parent of a defective child states: "In the last months I have come closer to people and can understand them more. I have met them more deeply. I did not

---

11. Goodman, *Continuing Treatment of Parents with Congenitally Defective Infants*, SOCIAL WORK, Vol. 9, No. I, at 92 (1964).

know there were so many people with troubles in the world." [12]

Thus, while social attitudes regard the handicapped child as an unmitigated disaster, in reality the problem may not be insurmountable, and often may not differ from life's other vicissitudes. Suffering there is, but seldom is it so overwhelming or so imminent that the only alternative is death of the child.

Health Professionals

Physicians and nurses also suffer when parents give birth to a defective child, although, of course, not to the degree of the parents. To the obstetrician or general practitioner the defective birth may be a blow to his professional identity. He has the difficult task of informing the parents of the defects, explaining their causes, and dealing with the parents' resulting emotional shock. Often he feels guilty for failing to produce a normal baby. In addition, the parents may project anger or hostility on the physician, questioning his professional competence or seeking the services of other doctors. The physician also may feel that his expertise and training are misused when employed to maintain the life of an infant whose chances for a productive existence are so diminished. By neglecting other patients, he may feel that he is prolonging rather than alleviating suffering.

Nurses, too, suffer role strain from care of the defective newborn. Intensive-care-unit nurses may work with only one or two babies at a time.

---

12. Quoted in Johns, *Family Reactions to the Birth of a Child with a Congenital Abnormality* 26 OBSTAT. & GYNECOL. SURVEY 635, 637 (1971).

They face the daily ordeals of care—the progress and relapses—and often must deal with anxious parents who are themselves grieving or ambivalent toward the child. The situation may trigger a nurse's own ambivalence about death and mothering, in a context in which she is actively working to keep alive a child whose life prospects seem minimal.

Thus, the effects of care on physicians and nurses are not trivial, and must be intelligently confronted in medical education or in management of a pediatric unit. Yet to state them is to make clear that they can but weigh lightly in the decision of whether to treat a defective newborn. Compared with the situation of the parents, these burdens seem insignificant, are short term, and most likely do not evoke such profound emotions. In any case, these difficulties are hazards of the profession—caring for the sick and dying will always produce strain. Hence, on these grounds alone it is difficult to argue that a defective person may be denied the right to life.

Society

Care of the defective newborn also imposes societal costs, the utility of which is questioned when the infant's expected quality-of-life is so poor. Medical resources that can be used by infants with a better prognosis, or throughout the health-care system generally, are consumed in providing expensive surgical and intensive-care services to infants who may be severely retarded, never lead active lives, and die in a few months or years. Institutionalization imposes costs on taxpayers and reduces the resources available for those who might better benefit from it, while reducing further the quality of life experienced by the institutionalized defective.

One answer to these concerns is to question the impact of the costs of caring for defective newborns. Precise data showing the costs to taxpayers or the trade-offs with health and other expenditures do not exist. Nor would ceasing to care for the defective necessarily lead to a reallocation within the health budget that would produce net savings in suffering or life; in fact, the released resources might not be reallocated for health at all. In any case, the trade-offs within the health budget may well be small. With advances in prenatal diagnosis of genetic disorders many deformed infants who would formerly require care will be aborted beforehand. Then, too, it is not clear that the most technical and expensive procedures always constitute the best treatment for certain malformations. When com-

pared with the almost seven percent of the GNP now spent on health, the money in the defense budget, or tax revenues generally, the public resources required to keep defective newborns alive seem marginal, and arguably worth the commitment to life that such expenditures reinforce. Moreover, as the Supreme Court recently recognized,[13] conservation of the taxpayer's purse does not justify serious infringement of fundamental rights. Given legal and ethical norms against sacrificing the lives of nonconsenting others, and the imprecisions in diagnosis and prediction concerning the eventual outcomes of medical care, the social cost argument does not compel nontreatment of defective newborns. . . .

---

13. *Memorial Hosp. v. Maricopa County*, 415 U.S. 250 (1974).

C O M M E N T S ■ Q U E S T I O N S

1. "The strongest claim for not treating the defective newborn is that treatment seriously harms the infant's own interests" (the quality-of-life argument). Robertson rejects this argument by discussing various courses of action open to doctors, parents, and society in their responses to defective newborns. Is he justified in concluding that "the claim that death is a far better fate than life cannot in most cases be sustained"? Notice that he shifts the burden of proof to those who argue, as does for example Richard B. Brandt in another of this chapter's reading selections, that the defective newborn's life is *not* worth living. What arguments would Brandt give in response to Robertson's conclusion?

2. "One who has never known the pleasures of mental operation, ambulation, and social interaction surely does not suffer from their loss as much as one who has." Robertson wants to know how *we* can be justified (by proxy, as he says) in judging the quality of life of the defective newborn. Do you

share Robertson's point of view on this matter?

3. Has Robertson given an accurate assessment of the degree of suffering that a defective newborn's subsequent life would bring to others (family, health professionals, society)? Has he supported his conclusion that "the social cost argument does not compel nontreatment of defective newborns"?

4. Robertson objects to the utilitarian nature of the social costs argument. That is, he objects to the fact that it is usually presented as an appeal *solely* to what we are calling the Principle of the Common Good. Do you suppose that Robertson would welcome the approach to moral decision making given in chapter 1 of this book, according to which other moral principles, such as Rights, always need to be weighed against the Common Good?

J O S E P H   F L E T C H E R

Euthanasia: Our Right to Die

Where Is the Sting of Death?

Euthanasia, the deliberate easing into death of a patient suffering from a painful and fatal disease, has long been a troubling problem of conscience in medical care. For us in the Western world the problem arises, *pro forma*, out of a logical contradiction at the heart of the Hippocratic Oath. Our physicians all subscribe to that oath as the standard of their professional ethics. The contradiction is there because the oath promises two things: first, to relieve suffering, and second, to prolong and protect life. When the patient is in the grip of an agonizing and fatal disease, these two promises are incompatible. Two duties come into conflict. To prolong life is to violate the promise to relieve pain. To relieve the pain is to violate the promise to prolong and protect life.

Ordinarily an attempt is made to

Joseph Fletcher is Robert Treat Paine Professor of Social Ethics, Emeritus, at the Episcopal Theological School in Cambridge, Mass. He is very well known for his extensive writing in the area of ethics, and especially for his widely read book Situation Ethics.

escape the dilemma by relieving the pain with an analgesic that does not induce death. But this attempt to evade the issue fails in many cases for the simple reason that the law of diminishing returns operates in narcosis. Patients grow semi-immune to its effects, for example in some forms of osteomyelitis, and a dose which first produces four hours of relief soon gives only three, then two, then almost none. The dilemma still stands: the choice between euthanasia or suffering. Euthanasia may be described, in its broadest terms, as a "theory that in certain circumstances, when owing to disease, senility or the like, a person's life has permanently ceased to be either agreeable or useful, the sufferer should be painlessly killed, either by himself or by another."[1] More simply, we may call euthanasia merciful release from incurable suffering.

Our task in this book is to put the practice under examination in its strictly medical form, carefully limiting ourselves to cases in which the patient himself chooses euthanasia and the physician advises against any reasonable hope of recovery or of relief by other means. Yet even in so narrowly defined an application as this, there are conscientious objections, of the sort applied to broader concepts or usages. In the first place it is claimed that the practice of euthanasia might be taken as an encouragement of suicide or of the wholesale murder of the aged and infirm. Again, weak or unbalanced people may more easily throw away their lives if medical euthanasia has approval. Still another objection

raised is that the practice would raise grave problems for the public authority. Government would have to overcome the resistance of time-honored religious beliefs, the universal feeling that human life is too sacred to be tampered with, and the problem of giving euthanasia legal endorsement as another form of justifiable homicide. All of this could lead to an appalling increase of crimes such as infanticide and geronticide. In short, in this problem as in others which we have been analyzing there is a common tendency to cry abuse and to ignore *abusus non tollit usum*.

Prudential and expedient objections to euthanasia quickly jump to mind among many people confronted with the issue. There are few, presumably, who would not be moved by such protests as this one from the *Linacre Quarterly*: "Legalized euthanasia would be a confession of despair in the medical profession; it would be the denial of hope for further progress against presently incurable maladies. It would destroy all confidence in physicians, and introduce a reign of terror.... [Patients] would turn in dread from the man on whose wall the Hippocratic Oath proclaims, 'If any shall ask of me a drug to produce death I will not give it, nor will I suggest such counsel.' "[2]

However, it is the objection that euthanasia is inherently wrong, that the disposition of life is too sacred to be entrusted to human control, which calls for our closest analysis. As in preceding chapters, here too we shall be dealing with the *personal* dimensions of morality in medical care. The social ethics of medical care, as it is

---

1. H. J. Rose, "Euthanasia," *Encyc. of Rel. and Ethics*, v, 598–601.

2. Hilary R. Werts, S. J., in April, 1947, 19.2, p. 33.

posed to conscience by proposals to use euthanasia for eugenic reasons, population control, and the like, have to be left for another time and place.

Not infrequently the newspapers carry stories of the crime of a spouse, or a member of the family or a friend, of a hopelessly stricken and relentlessly tortured victim of, let us say, advanced cancer. Desperate people will sometimes take the law into their own hands and administer some lethal dose to end it all. Sometimes the euthanasiast then commits suicide, thus making two deaths instead of one. Sometimes he is tried for murder in a court of law, amid great scandal and notoriety. But even if he is caught and indicted, the judgment never ends in conviction, perhaps because the legalism of the charge can never stand up in the tested conscience of a sympathetic jury.

For the sake of avoiding offense to any contemporaries, we might turn to literary history for a typical example of our problem. Jonathan Swift, the satirist and Irish clergyman, after a life of highly creative letters ended it all in a horrible and degrading death. It was a death degrading to himself and to those close to him. His mind crumbled to pieces. It took him eight years to die while his brain rotted. He read the third chapter of Job on his birthday as long as he could see. "And Job spake, and said, Let the day perish when I was born, and the night in which it was said, There is a man child conceived." The pain in Swift's eye was so acute that it took five men to hold him down, to keep him from tearing out his eye with his own hands. For the last three years he sat and drooled. Knives had to be kept entirely out of his reach. When the end came, finally, his fits of convul-

sion lasted thirty-six hours.[3] Now, whatever may be the theological meaning of St. Paul's question, "O death, where is thy sting?"[4] the moral meaning—in a word, the evil—of a death like that is only too plain.

We can imagine the almost daily scene preceding Swift's death. (Some will say we should not imagine such things, that it not fair to appeal to emotion. Many good people cannot willingly accept the horrendous aspects of reality as a factor of reasoning, especially when reality cuts across their customs and commitments. The relative success with which we have repressed the reality of atomic warfare and its dreadful prospects is an example on a wider scale.) We can easily conceive of Dean Swift grabbing wildly, madly, for a knife or a deadly drug. He was *demoralized*, without a vestige of true self-possession left in him. He wanted to commit what the law calls suicide and what vitalistic ethics calls sin. Standing by was some good doctor of physick, trembling with sympathy and frustration. Secretly, perhaps, he wanted to commit what the law calls murder. Both had full knowledge of the way out, which is half the foundation of moral integrity, but unlike his patient the physician felt he had no freedom to act, which is the other half of moral integrity. And so, meanwhile, necessity, blind and unmoral, irrational physiology and pathology, made the decision. It was in reality no decision at all, no moral behavior in the least, unless submission to physical ruin and spiritual disorganization can be called a decision and a moral

3. Virginia Moore, *Ho for Heaven*, New York, 1946, pp. 180–182.
4. I Cor. 15:55.

choice. For let us not forget that in such tragic affairs there is a moral destruction, a spiritual disorder, as well as a physical degeneration. As Swift himself wrote to his niece fully five years before the end: "I am so stupid and confounded that I cannot express the mortification I am under both of body and soul."[5]

The story of this man's death points us directly to the broad problem of suicide, as well as to the more particular problem of euthanasia. We get a glimpse of this paradox in our present customary morality, that it sometimes condemns us to live or, to put it another way, destroys our moral being for the sake of just *being*. This aspect of suicide makes it important for us to distinguish from the outset between voluntary and involuntary euthanasia. They are by no means the same, either in policy or ethical meaning. Those who condemn euthanasia of both kinds would call the involuntary form murder and the voluntary form a compounded crime of murder and suicide if administered by the physician, and suicide alone if administered by the patient himself. As far as voluntary euthanasia goes, it is impossible to separate it from suicide as a moral category; it is, indeed, a form of suicide. In a very proper sense, the case for medical euthanasia depends upon the case for the righteousness of suicide, given the necessary circumstances. And the justification of its administration by an attending physician is therefore dependent upon it too, under the time-honored rule that what one may lawfully do another may help him to do.

5. Quoted by Richard Garnett, "Jonathan Swift" in *Encyc. Brit.*, 11th ed.

"Untouchability"

Felo de se—literally, being a criminal toward oneself, but in common usage meaning to take one's own life—is, of course, as old as mankind and human pain. This is true in spite of the valid generalization that the wish to live is among the strongest instinctual drives in the higher animals, including men. It is true regardless of the reasons we may offer, psychological or otherwise, to explain the frequent occurrence of exceptions to the rule. Some savage tribes laugh at suicide; some practice it freely. Others believe it earns a terrible punishment in the next world, and, like some Christian churches, deny all suicides a religious burial. Many of the Eastern religions allow it without censure, and even encourage it ceremonially. We find this to be true in the ancient Aztec and Inca cultures, but also more recently in the traditional Hindu practice of *suttee*, in which a widow throws herself onto the funeral pyre alongside her husband's body. The Japanese, of Buddhist and Shinto belief, have committed *hari-kiri* after losing face or suffering loss of prestige, or as a remarkably unaggressive reply to insult, as compared, for example, to the dueling code in Western manners. The Greeks and Romans were divided in their opinions about suicide, and therefore about euthanasia. If there were those among them who condemned it rigidly and absolutely, they were few and not given to publishing their views. Some moralists repudiated it as a general practice. For example, Pythagoras, Plato, and Aristotle held that suicide was a crime against the community because it robbed society of a resource, and Plato added that it was a like crime against God. But all of these were willing to justify suicide in cases calling for a merciful death.[6] Stoics usually, but not always, approved of suicide. Cicero, for example, condemned it, whereas Seneca praised it. Epictetus sided with Seneca. But they *all* favored euthanasia. Valerius Maximus said that magistrates at Marseilles kept a supply of poison on hand for those who could convince them that there was good reason for them to die.

The Semitic religions, Judaism and Mohammedanism, were opposed consistently to suicide. Being more Oriental than the Hellenic doctrines, they tended to regard physiological life as sacrosanct and untouchable, and they also tended to be more materialistic in their conception of the vital principle, so that the Jews located life in the blood—and thus their rules about kosher meat. The Christians, as a Jewish sect, went even further with a belief in physical or bodily resurrection to eternal life. Nevertheless, neither the Bible nor the Koran actually set forth an explicit condemnation of suicide, in any form, even though Jewish and Moslem commentators generally were against it. There is a tradition that Mohammed himself refused to bury a suicide. Certainly under the Hebrew influence, which put a heavier stamp of approval and meaning upon historical existence, being this-worldly rather than other-worldly, there was little philosophical ground in the West for the *tedium vitae* of Hinduism. A practice such as *suttee* was simply not within its ideological orbit.

The early Christians, like Chrysos-tom, followed the rabbis for the most part. A great many of the patristic writers allowed for suicide in certain forms, however, usually to achieve martyrdom, to avoid apostasy, or to retain the crown of virginity. Thus Lactantius declared that it is wicked to bring death upon oneself voluntarily, unless one was "expecting all torture and death" at the hands of the pagan persecutors.[7] Unfortunately for the precedent moralists he never bothered to apply his logic about torture and death to incurable diseases.

But once Christianity and the Roman government joined forces, the authority permitting suicide in persecution was withdrawn. We find St. Jerome allowing it only as a defense of chastity.[8] And then St. Augustine swept away even that exception by announcing that chastity, after all, is a virtue of the soul rather than of the body, so that physical violation did not touch it. St. Augustine cast aside the observation that the Scriptures nowhere condemned suicide, and that they even reported without comment or condemnation the suicides of Ahithophel by hanging, Zimri by fire, Abimelech by sword, Samson by crushing, and Saul by sword. He said with fine simplicity that the Scriptures nowhere *authorized* us to eliminate ourselves.[9] This became the conventional Christian position, and St. Thomas Aquinas gave it its classical form in the saying, "Suicide is the most fatal of sins, because it cannot be repented of."[10] We find that Christian burial was

---

6. Plato, *Laws*, IX, 873 C; Aristotle, *Politics*, 1335 b, 19ff.; for Pythagoras, cf. Cicero, *Cato Major* 20 (72 sq.) and *De Officiis*, i.31 (112).

---

7. *Divinae institutiones,* vi.17.
8. *Commentarii in Jonam,* i.12.
9. *De civitate dei,* i.16 sq.
10. *Summa Theologica,* ii.–ii 64.5.3.

denied to suicides as early as A.D. 563.[11] The Roman Church to this day, by canonical prohibition, refuses to bury a suicide.

Unlike Judaism and Catholicism, Protestantism does not unanimously outlaw suicide, although various bodies will from time to time condemn euthanasia, or call it into question. As recently as 1951 the General Assembly of the Presbyterian Church in the U.S.A. resolved that suicide is contrary to the Sixth Commandment. In the Renaissance the reverence of West Europeans for the Greeks and Romans led to some easing of the old prohibition of suicide, especially in favor of euthanasia, but this was in tension with the Semitic attitude in Christianity. Here and there, occasionally, but almost always outside the Roman jurisdiction, there were testimonies to a new attitude. Thomas More, whose Utopia included euthanasia, was reflecting a new evaluation of human worth and integrity.[12] Lord Francis Bacon in his *New Atlantis* said, "I esteem it the office of a physician not only to restore the health, but to mitigate pains and dolors; and not only when such mitigation may conduce to recovery, but when it may serve to make a fair and easy passage." It was more commonly the Protestant and humanist moralists who relaxed the old prohibition. A typical effort was made in a little book called *Biathanatos* by John Donne, the Anglican priest and poet, dean of St. Paul's, a book which he described on the title page as a "Declaration of that paradoxe, or

thesis, that self-homicide is not so naturally sin, that it may never be otherwise."[13] John Donne was a man who knew what death could be, because he lived for so long in its shadow and marked its many turns. His lines will always live, "Send not to ask for whom the bell tolls; it tolls for thee."[14] It is possible, but not certain, that Jeremy Taylor's *Holy Dying* favored merciful release in somewhat equivocal terms. At any rate, even theologians were beginning to doubt that Hamlet was altogether correct in supposing that "the everlasting" had "fixed his canon 'gainst self-slaughter."

The common civil law has always followed the line of the moral theologians. For centuries suicides were refused last rites by the church and their property impounded by the state. The English law about staking out a suicide's body at the cross roads—a law due partly to Christian theory and partly to fear of ghosts—was not abolished until the reign of George IV. The first really sharp break came with the French Revolution, when France abolished her old laws about suicide, especially the more grotesque priestly features. Then other continental countries began to follow suit. The churches had held to their absolute prohibition, except for sporadic practices like that of the seventeenth-century people of Brittany, who allowed an incurable sufferer to appeal to the parish priest for the Holy Stone. The family gathered, the patient received the viaticum and last rites, and the oldest living relative raised the heavy stone above the patient's head and let it fall.

*   *   *   *   *

11. Westermarck, *Christianity and Morals,* op. cit., p. 254.

12. *Utopia*, II, viii, "Of bondemen, sicke persons etc."

13. London, 1648.

14. *Sermon on the Bells.*

I. It is objected that euthanasia, when voluntary, is really suicide. If this is true, and it would seem to be obviously true, then the proper question is: have we ever a right to commit suicide? Among Catholic moralists the most common ruling is that "it is never permitted to kill oneself intentionally, without explicit divine inspiration to do."[31] Humility requires us to assume that divine inspiration cannot reasonably be expected to occur either often or explicitly enough to meet the requirements of medical euthanasia. A plea for legal recognition of "man's inalienable right to die" is placed at the head of the physicians' petition to the New York State Assembly. Now, has man any such right, however limited and imperfect it may be? Surely he has, for otherwise the hero or martyr and all those who deliberately give their lives are morally at fault. It might be replied that there is a difference between the suicide, who is directly seeking to-end his life, and the hero or martyr, who is seeking directly some other end entirely, death being only an undesired by-product. But to make this point is only to raise a question as to what purposes are sufficient to justify the loss of one's life. If altruistic values, such as defense of the innocent, are enough to justify the loss of one's life (and we will all agree that they are), then it may be argued that personal integrity is a value worth the loss of life, especially since, by definition, there is no hope of relief from the demoralizing pain and no further possibility of serving others. To call euthanasia egoistic or self-regarding makes no sense, since in the nature of the case the patient is not choosing his own good rather than the good of others.

Furthermore, it is important to recognize that there is no ground, in a rational or Christian outlook, for regarding life itself as the *summum bonum*. As a ministers' petition to buttress the New York bill puts it, "We believe in the sacredness of *personality*, but not in the worth of mere existence or 'length of days.' . . . We believe that such a sufferer has the right to die, and that society should grant this right, showing the same mercy to human beings as to the sub-human animal kingdom." (The point might be made validly in criticism of this statement that society can only recognize an "inalienable right," it cannot confer it. Persons are not mere creatures of the community, even though it is ultimately meaningless to claim integrity for them unless their lives are integrated into the community.) In the personalistic view of man and morals, asserted throughout these pages, personality is supreme over mere life. To prolong life uselessly, while the personal qualities of freedom, knowledge, self-possession and control, and responsibility are sacrificed is to attack the moral status of a person. It actually denies morality in order to submit to fatality. And in addition, to insist upon mere "life" invades religious interests as well as moral values. For to use analgesic agents to the point of depriving sufferers of consciousness is, by all apparent logic, inconsistent even with the practices of sacramentalist Christians. The point of death for a human person *in extremis* is surely by their own account a time when the use of reason and conscious self-commitment is most meritorious; it is the time when a responsible

---

31. Davis, *op. cit.*, 11, 142. This author explains that Jerome and Lessius excused suicide in defense of chastity, but that Aquinas opposed even this exception to the prohibition.

competence in receiving such rites as the viaticum and extreme unction would be most necessary and its consequences most invested with finality.

2. It is objected that euthanasia, when involuntary, is murder. This is really an objection directed against the physician's role in medical euthanasia, assuming it is administered by him rather than by the patient on his own behalf. We might add to what has been said above about the word "murder" in law and legal definition by explaining that people with a moral rather than a legal interest— doctors, pastors, patients, and their friends—will never concede that malice means only premeditation, entirely divorced from the motive and the end sought. These factors are entirely different in euthanasia from the motive and the end in murder, even though the means—taking life—happens to be the same. If we can make no moral distinction between acts involving the same means, then the thrifty parent who saves in order to educate his children is no higher in the scale of merit than the miser who saves for the sake of hoarding. But, as far as medical care is concerned, there is an even more striking example of the contradictions which arise from refusing to allow for anything but the consequences of a human act. There is a dilemma in medication for terminal diseases which is just as real as the dilemma posed by the doctor's oath to relieve pain while he also promises to prolong life. As medical experts frequently point out, morphine, which is commonly used to ease pain, also shortens life, i.e., it induces death. Here we see that the two promises of the Hippocratic Oath actually conflict at the level of means as well as at the level of motive and intention.

3. What of the common religious opinion that God reserves for himself the right to decide at what moment a life shall cease? Koch-Preuss says euthanasia is the destruction of "the temple of God and a violation of the property rights of Jesus Christ."[32] As to this doctrine, it seems more than enough just to answer that if such a divine-monopoly theory is valid, then it follows with equal force that it is immoral to lengthen life. Is medical care, after all, only a form of human self-assertion or a demonic pretension, by which men, especially physicians, try to put themselves in God's place? Prolonging life, on this divine-monopoly view, when a life appears to be ending through natural or physical causes, is just as much an interference with natural determinism as mercifully ending a life before physiology does it in its own amoral way.

This argument that we must not tamper with life also assumes that physiological life is sacrosanct. But as we have pointed out repeatedly, this doctrine is a form of vitalism or naturalistic determinism. Dean Sperry of the Harvard Divinity School, who is usually a little more sensitive to the scent of anti-humane attitudes, wrote recently in the *New England Journal of Medicine* that Albert Schweitzer's doctrine of "reverence for life," which is often thought to entail an absolute prohibition against taking life, has strong claims upon men of conscience.[33] Perhaps so, but men of conscience will surely reject the doctrine if it is left unqualified and absolute. In actual fact, even Schweitzer has suggested that the principle is

---

32. *Op. cit.*, 11, 76. He cites texts such as 1 Cor. 3:16–17.

33. Dec. 23, 1948. Incorporated in *The Ethical Basis of Medical Care, op. cit.*, p. 160 sq.

subject to qualification. He has, with apparent approval, explained that Gandhi "took it upon himself to go beyond the letter of the law against killing. . . . He ended the sufferings of a calf in its prolonged death-agony by giving it poison."[34] It seems unimaginable that either Schweitzer or Gandhi would deny to a human being what they would render, with however heavy a heart, to a calf. Gandhi did what he did in spite of the special sanctity of kine in Hindu discipline. In any case Dr. Schweitzer in his African hospital at Lambaréné is even now at work administering death-inducing-because-pain-relieving drugs. As William Temple once pointed out, "The notion that life is absolutely sacred is Hindu or Buddhist, not Christian." He neglected to remark that even those Oriental religionists forget their doctrine when it comes to *suttee* and *hara-kiri*. He said further that the argument that it cannot ever be right to kill a fellow human being will not stand up because "such a plea can only rest upon a belief that life, physiological life, is sacrosanct. This is not a Christian idea at all; for, if it were, the martyrs would be wrong. If the sanctity is *in* life, it must be wrong to give your life for a noble cause as well as to take another's. But the Christian must be ready to give life gladly for his faith, as for a noble cause. Of course, this implies that, *as compared with some things*, the loss of life is a small evil; and if so, then, *as compared with some other things*, the taking of life is a small injury."[35]

Parenthetically we should explain, if it is not evident in these quotations

themselves, that Dr. Temple's purpose was to justify military service. Unfortunately for his aim, he failed to take account of the ethical factor of free choice as a right of the person who thus loses his life at the hands of the warrior. We cannot put upon the same ethical footing the ethical right to take our own lives, in which case our freedom is not invaded, and taking the lives of others in those cases in which the act is done against the victim's will and choice. The true parallel is between self-sacrifice and a merciful death provided at the person's request; there is none between self-sacrifice and violent or coercive killing. But the relevance of what Dr. Temple has to say and its importance for euthanasia is perfectly clear. The non-theological statement of the case agrees with Temple: "Are we not allowing ourselves to be deceived by our self-preservative tendency to rationalize a merely instinctive urge and to attribute spiritual and ethical significance to phenomena appertaining to the realm of crude, biological utility?"[36]

4. It is also objected by religious moralists that euthanasia violates the Biblical command, "Thou shalt not kill." It is doubtful whether this kind of Biblicism is any more valid than the vitalism we reject. Indeed, it is a form of fundamentalism, common to both Catholics and reactionary Protestants. An outspoken religious opponent of euthanasia is a former chancellor to Cardinal Spellman as military vicar to the armed forces, Monsignor Robert McCormick. As presiding judge of the Archdiocesan Ecclesiastical Tribunal of New York,

---

34. *Indian Thought and Its Development*, London, 1930, pp. 225–238.

35. *Thoughts in War Time*, London, 1940, pp. 31–32. Italics in original.

---

36. H. Roberts, "Two Essays on Medicine," in *Living Age*, Oct. 1934, 347.159–162.

he warned the General Assembly of that state in 1947 not to "set aside the commandment 'Thou shalt not kill.' "[37] In the same vein, the general secretary of the American Council of Christian Churches, an organization of fundamentalist Protestants, denounced the fifty-four clergymen who supported the euthanasia bill, claiming that their action was "an evidence that the modernistic clergy have made further departure from the eternal moral law."[38]

Certainly those who justify war and capital punishment, as most Christians do, cannot condemn euthanasia on this ground. We might point out to the fundamentalists in the two major divisions of Western Christianity that the beatitude "Blessed are the merciful" has the force of a commandment too! The medical profession lives by it, has its whole *ethos* in it. But the simplest way to deal with this Christian text-proof objection might be to point out that the translation "Thou shalt not kill" is incorrect. It should be rendered, as in the responsive decalogue of the *Book of Common Prayer*, "Thou shalt do no murder," i.e., unlawful killing. It is sufficient just to remember that the ancient Jews fully allowed warfare and capital punishment. Lawful killing was also for hunger-satisfaction and sacrifice. Hence, a variety of Hebrew terms such as *shachat, harag, tabach*, but *ratsach* in the Decalogue (both Exodus 20:13 and Deut. 5:17), clearly means *unlawful* killing, treacherously, for private vendetta or gain. Thus it is laid down in Leviticus 24:17 that "he who kills a man shall be put to death," showing that the lawful forms of killing may even be used to punish the unlawful! In the New Testament references to the prohibition against killing (e.g., Matt. 5:21, Luke 18:20, Rom. 13:9) are an endorsement of the commandments in the Jewish law. Each time, the verb *phoneuo* is used and the connotation is *unlawful* killing, as in the Decalogue. Other verbs connote simply the fact of killing, as *apokteino* (Luke 12:4, "Be not afraid of them that kill the body") and *thuo* which is used interchangeably for slaughter of animals for food and for sacrifice. We might also remind the Bible-bound moralists that there was no condemnation either of Abimelech, who chose to die, or of his faithful swordbearer who carried out his wish for him.[39]

5. Another common objection in religious quarters is that suffering is a part of the divine plan for the good of man's soul, and must therefore be accepted. Does this mean that the physicians' Hippocratic Oath is opposed to Christian virtue and doctrine? If this simple and naive idea of suffering were a valid one, then we should not be able to give our moral approval to anesthetics or to provide any medical relief of human suffering. Such has been the objection of many religionists at every stage of medical conquest, as we pointed out in the first chapter in the case of anesthetics at childbirth. Here is still another anomaly in our mores of life and death, that we are, after much struggle, now fairly secure in the righteousness of easing suffering at birth but we still feel it is wrong to ease suffering at death! Life may be begun

---

37. Quoted H. N. Oliphant, *Redbook Magazine*, Sep. 1948.
38. *Ibid.*

---

39. Judges 9:54.

without suffering, but it may not be ended without it, if it happens that nature combines death and suffering.

Those who have some acquaintance with the theological habit of mind can understand how even the question of euthanasia may be colored by the vision of the Cross as a symbol of redemptive suffering in Christian doctrine. As Emil Brunner has said of the crucifix, "it is not without its significance that the picture of a dying man is the sacred sign of Christendom."[40] But when it is applied to suffering in general it becomes, of course, a rather uncritical exemplarism which ignores the unique theological claims of the doctrine of the Atonement and the saving power of the Cross as a singular event. It is, at least, difficult to see how any theological basis for the suffering argument against medical euthanasia would be any different or any more compelling for keeping childbirth natural and "as God hath provided it."

It is much more realistic and hum-

_____

40. *Man in Revolt*, New York, 1939, pp. 388–389.

ble to take as our regulative principle the rule that "Blessed are the merciful, for they shall see mercy," since this moral standard gives more recognition in actual fact to the motive of compassion, which, according to the theology of Atonement, lies behind the crucifixion of Jesus and gave it its power and its *ethos*. "All things whatsoever you would that men should do unto you, do you even so unto them." Mercy to the suffering is certainly the point of Psalm 102, vs. 12: "As a father hath compassion on his children, so hath the Lord compassion on them that fear him: for he knoweth our frame." Let the Biblicist take his position on the story of Job! Job explored the problem of human suffering and left it a mystery for the man of faith. Some have tried to find a recommendation of suicide in Job's wife's advice, but it is hardly more than a warning that he must not curse God.[41] In Job 7:15 there may be a thought of suicide, but nothing more than that. Our point here is that even Job never hinted that euthanasia was wrong; he only wondered, as we all do sometimes, why such a thing is ever needed or desired.

C O M M E N T S ■ Q U E S T I O N S

1. Fletcher goes to some length to make the following point: where euthanasia is not permitted, as in the case of Jonathan Swift, there may not only be great pain resulting from an incurable disease, but also psychological degradation as well. Is there any reason to believe

that preventing psychological degradation is even more important than relieving physical pain?

2. Is there reason to believe that what Fletcher advocates is merely an easy way out for people whose suffering may have a purpose that they do not understand? Some-

times it is argued that euthanasia is wrong because suffering is a part of the divine plan for the good of man's soul. But if this view were then accepted, says Fletcher, it would appear to follow that anything that human beings did to relieve suffering was wrong. Even the use of anesthetics in medicine would be wrong. But could arguments not be made to show that there is a very important difference between euthanasia and the use of anesthetics?

3. The Principle of Self-Interest needs to be balanced against the other moral principles. Of course, it cannot be given a great deal of weight in every circumstance, but it does need to be given significant weight in some circumstances. Is a person's decision to choose death over prolonged suffering one of the special cases where the Principle of Self-Interest should be given a particularly strong emphasis?

4. We must, says Fletcher, grant that there is a right to die since otherwise all the heroes and martyrs who have given their lives for a cause would be morally at fault. Is this a good argument?

5. "To prolong life uselessly, while the personal qualities of freedom, knowledge, self-possession and control, and responsibility are sacrificed is to attack the moral status of a person." Is the point that Fletcher makes in this quotation relevant to the assertion in chapter 1 that morality requires a concern for others *as persons*?

R E A D I N G S

Abernathy, Virginia, ed. *Frontiers in Medical Ethics.* Cambridge, Mass.: Ballinger, 1980.

Beauchamp, Tom L. "Suicide and the Value of Life." In *Matters of Life and Death*, edited by Tom Regan. New York: Random House, 1980.

Beauchamp, Tom L., and Seymour Perlin, eds. *Ethical Issues in Death and Dying.* Englewood Cliffs, N.J.: Prentice-Hall, 1978.

Beck, Robert N., and John B. Orr. *Ethical Choice: A Case Study Approach.* New York: Free Press, 1970.

Brandt, Richard B. "The Morality and Rationality of Suicide." In *A Handbook of the Study of Suicide*, edited by Seymour Perlin. Oxford: Oxford University Press, Inc., 1975.

Burtcheall, James T., ed. *Abortion Parley.* Kansas City: Andrew & McMeel, 1980.

Callahan, Daniel. *Abortion: Law, Choice and Morality.* New York: Macmillan, 1970.

Downing, A. B., ed. *Euthanasia and the Right to Death: The Case for Voluntary Euthanasia.* New York: Humanities Press, 1969.

Etziony, M. B., ed. *The Physician's Creed.* Springfield, Ill.: Charles C. Thomas, 1973.

Grisez, Germain. *Abortion: The Myths, The Realities, and the Arguments.* New York: Corpus Books, 1970.

Kohl, Marvin, ed. *Beneficent Euthanasia.* Buffalo, N.Y.: Prometheus, 1975.

McMullin, Ernan, ed. *Death and Discussion.* AAAS Selected Symposia

Series. Boulder, Colo.: Westview Press, 1978.

Perkins, Robert L., ed. *Abortion: Pro and Con.* Cambridge, Mass.: Schenkman, 1974.

Ramsey, Paul. *The Patient as Person.* New Haven: Yale University Press, 1970.

Reiser, Stanely Joel, Arthur J. Dyck, and William J. Curran. *Ethics in Medicine: Historical Perspectives and Contemporary Concerns.* Cambridge, Mass.: Massachusetts Institute of Technology, 1977.

Veatch, Robert M. *Death, Dying, and the Biological Revolution: Our Last Quest for Responsibility.* New Haven, Conn.: Yale University Press, 1976.

Preferential Treatment of Minorities and Women

he basic question for this chapter can be stated in a deceptively simple fashion: Should women and minorities be treated in any way that is special when they are being considered for employment or admission to professional schools? Answering this question is a very complex task for two reasons. First, "treating minorities and women in a special way" can mean several different things:

1. It can mean hiring (or admitting to a professional school) a woman or member of a minority group who is *less* well qualified than a white male candidate.

2. It can, instead, mean giving preference to a woman or minority group member who is *equally* well qualified with other candidates.

3. It can also mean hiring the candidate who is best qualified, whoever that may be, but only after a greater effort has been made to seek out candidates who are women or minority group members than has been made to seek out other candidates. (Doing this is what the U.S. Department of Health, Education, and Welfare (HEW) calls making a "good faith" effort to hire women and minority group members. This and other HEW directives are discussed by Gertrude Ezorsky in her article that is reprinted in this chapter.)

4. "Treating minorities and women in a special way" can, lastly, mean setting numerical goals in hiring or admissions policies. For example, it can mean that a university department will establish the goal of hiring additional women faculty members until, say, one-fourth of the faculty in the department are women. (Numerical hiring goals such as this are discussed by Ezorsky.)

The second reason for the complexity of this chapter is that many different arguments can be made, both for and against policies that reflect *each one* of the four different meanings for "treating minorities and women in a special way" that are stated above. What we end up with, therefore, could be called complexity multiplied by complexity! Because of limitations of space in the present chapter, the complexity of arguments regarding preferential treatment has been reduced somewhat. But most of the complexity needs to remain since it is essential for an adequate examination of preferential treatment.

Among the philosophers included in this chapter, George Sher is the one who does the most to distinguish among the various arguments made regarding preferential treatment. (It should be pointed out that he refers to preferential treatment as "reverse discrimination.") Sher first distinguishes between "backward-looking" arguments and "forward-looking" arguments. In backward-looking defenses for preferential treatment, the basic claim is that since *in the past* women and minority group members were unfairly discriminated against, society now and in the future should do things to compensate for past injustices. In forward-looking defenses, the basic claim is that preferential treatment at the present time will help to reduce discrimination in the future. In contrast to backward-looking arguments, forward-looking arguments make no reference to the idea of compensation for past wrongs.

Some of the major objections to backward-looking defenses for affirmative action, which Sher elaborates upon, are the following:

1. How can preferential treatment at the present time benefit individuals who ten, twenty, fifty, one hundred years ago, and so on, were discriminated against? Most have died and many of those who are living are too old to be trained for the jobs that they once could have become qualified to hold. It would seem too late for them.
2. Not all individual women or minority group members at the present time have suffered excessively from discrimination. Why should *they* be given special treatment?
3. It would seem that rights belong to individuals, not to groups. But backward-looking defenses for affirmative action seem to presuppose that rights *can* be assigned to groups.

Anne C. Minas defends a version of the backward-looking defense for preferential treatment that may appear to escape from the objections raised by Sher. Her argument is addressed to preferential treatment of women, but her points apply equally well to preferential treatment of blacks and other minority group members. She argues that when some women are given preference in hiring (regardless of whether or not they as individuals are especially deserving of compensation), due compensation is made to the entire class of women by restoring to them something that past discrimination took from them: namely, a correct view of their own worth. Because of discrimination, she argues, women—and also of course their prospective employers—have come to believe that women are not as good as men at various sorts of jobs. Women and their prospective employers believe this because they see few women in these jobs. As a consequence, few women train for certain jobs, the paucity of women in them is perpetuated, and the class of all women continues to be treated unfairly.

Minas argues that no individual women have any special rights over men to particular jobs. She also argues that preferential treatment should not give jobs to women who are *less* qualified than men; but a woman should be favored over a man when both are fully qualified for the job. Minas also favors policies that stipulate that special efforts be made to seek out qualified female candidates.

Backward-looking defenses of preferential treatment are different, we said, from forward-looking defenses. The purpose of the latter type of argument is to claim that preferential treatment is a good thing, not because it will in any way make up for past injustices, but because it will improve society in the future. Sher discusses two major versions of this type of argument. The first is an appeal to what we are calling the Principle of the Common Good, which Sher refers to as the "principle of utility." The greatest good for the greatest number will occur, according to this argument, if discrimination against women and minority group members is ended, and preferential treatment is needed to end it. The major objection to this argument, says Sher, is the following: If it is acceptable to impose *reverse* discrimination in order to bring about the common good, then why shouldn't it also be acceptable to impose straightforward discrimination if it should happen that doing so would bring about the common good? Sher's treatment of this issue, pro and con, is too complex to be summarized here.

The same is true for Sher's discussion of the second type of forward-looking defense of preferential treatment, which is an appeal to what Sher calls the "principle of equality." (This principle has much in common with what in this book we are calling the Principle of Justice.) The basic claim here is that preferential treatment will in the future make society more egalitarian and that this is a very desirable social goal. Sher discusses the major problems with this argument.

The most important recent decision of the U.S. Supreme Court bearing upon preferential treatment is in the case of Allan Bakke, who was denied admission to the medical school at the University of California at Davis. Bakke, a white male, claimed that he was denied admission as a consequence of the school's preferential treatment policies. Bakke sued the school, arguing that the University of California had violated the Equal Protection Clause of the Fourteenth Amendment to the U.S. Constitution. The California Supreme Court decided in Bakke's favor and decreed that the medical school at the University of California at Davis should admit him since he was somewhat better qualified than some of the minority group members who had been admitted at the time when Bakke was denied admission.

In an effort to defend its affirmative action programs, the University of California appealed the case to the U.S. Supreme Court, which in 1978 in part upheld and in part reversed the decision of the California Supreme Court. According to the Court in a majority opinion, the University of California at Davis *had* violated the Equal Protection Clause in having admission quotas—reserving sixteen out of one hundred openings for qualified minority group members. At the same time, the Court ruled that it was constitutionally acceptable for the University of California at Davis's Medical School to make use of race or ethnic origin as a "factor" in deciding who would be admitted. Justices who dissented from this opinion argued that the distinction between the "quota" use of race and the "factor" use of race was not clear. This issue was resolved in *Weber vs. United States* (1979) when the majority of the Court ruled that quotas could be used in affirmative action programs.

Regents of the University of California vs. Allan Bakke has become the most important Supreme Court case bearing upon racial equality since *Brown vs. Board of Education* (1954) ruled that "separate but equal" schools and other public facilities were unconstitutional. The main force of the Bakke case was the Court ruling that preferential treatment programs could have racial criteria:

> Government may take race into account when it acts not to demean or insult any racial group, but to remedy disadvantages cast on minorities by past racial prejudice, at least when appropriate findings have been made by judicial, legislative, or administrative bodies with competence to act in this area. . . . Claims that law must be "colorblind" or that the datum of race is no longer relevant to public policy must be seen as aspiration rather than as description of reality. This is not to denigrate aspiration; for reality rebukes us that race has too often been used by those who would stigmatize and oppress minorities. Yet we cannot—and as we shall demonstrate, need not under our Constitution or Title VI, [of the Civil Rights Act of 1964] which merely extends the constraints of the Fourteenth Amendment to private parties who receive federal funds—let color blindness become myopia which marks the reality that many "created equal" have been treated within our lifetimes as inferior both by law and by their fellow citizens. (From the concurring judgment of Justices Brennan, White, Marshall, and Blackmun in *Regents of the University of California v. Allan Bakke*, 438 U.S. 265, 98 S. Ct. 2733 (1978).)

The paper by Sidney Hook opposes preferential treatment, and in particular the policies of the U.S. Department of Health, Education, and Welfare (HEW) that are defended by Ezorsky. Hook's major argument is that preferential treatment has compelled universities—and by extension other employers—to hire blacks and women who are not qualified for their jobs.

The reading selections for this chapter contain many more arguments and positions than those that have been mentioned in this introductory essay. Special efforts will be needed to sort them all out. In doing so, you will need to consider two important points. The first is factual correctness or accuracy. Do the various writers present a correct picture of the effects of racial and sexual discrimination in the past and present, and do they accurately describe what is likely to happen in the future as a consequence of whichever policy or policies they are defending or attacking? Second is the matter of moral principles. Do the various writers take a sufficiently broad view of the moral principles relevant to their discussions? Are questions of the common good perhaps defended at too great an expense over rights? Or vice versa? Or is justice perhaps emphasized too much over other values?

The final selection in this chapter, by Joyce Treblicot, is on a topic that is closely related to affirmative action programs for women: namely, the question of whether or not social policies should encourage or discourage distinct sexual roles for women and men.

GEORGE SHER

Reverse Discrimination, the Future, and the Past

T here exist in our society some groups whose members, in the past, were discriminatorily denied jobs, admission to educational institutions, and other goods; and many people believe that members of these groups should be given special preference in these areas now. Although the groups most often mentioned in this connection are blacks and women, the current affirmative action guidelines list also American Indians and Alaskan natives, certain Asians and Pacific Islanders, and persons of Hispanic background; and I suspect that most proponents of a policy of reverse discrimination which follows group lines would want it to apply to these groups as well. For simplicity, I will use the term "minority" to designate all the groups except women for which preference is advocated. Because the areas in which preference is urged are so closely related to those in which the initial discrimination took place, it is natural to view the proponents of reverse discrimination as arguing not merely that it will improve the lot of the current group members, but rather that in doing so it will compensate for the earlier discrimination. To the extent that the argument for reverse discrimination is a compensatory one, that argument will involve an essential reference to the unjust actions of the past, and so will be fundamentally backward-looking.

Although explicitly backward-looking justifications of reverse discrimination are common enough, they have tended to call forth an equally common objection. Put simply, the objection is that the current beneficiaries of reverse discrimination are not often the same persons as those who were harmed by the original discrimination, and those who now bear the burden of reverse discrimination are seldom the same persons as those who practiced the original discrimination. Because of this, reverse discrimination is said to be both irrelevant to the aim of compensating for past injustices and unfair to those whose superior qualifications are bypassed. To meet this objection, the backward-looking defender of reverse discrimination may elaborate his position in one of three ways. He may hold either that (1) every woman and minority group member has suffered and every non-minority male has benefited at least indirectly from the effects of past

George Sher is a professor of philosophy at the University of Vermont. He has written in the areas of ethics and social and political philosophy.

From *Ethics*, Vol. 90 (1979), pp. 81–87. Copyright © 1979 by the University of Chicago. Reprinted by permission of the author and publisher.

discrimination;[1] or that (2) the entities to be compensated are not individuals at all but rather the groups to which the initial victims belonged;[2] or that (3) we should extend preference not to every woman and minority group member but rather only to those group members who have actually suffered from past discrimination.[3] However, (1) and (2) raise obvious and well-known difficulties in their turn,[4] and (3) represents what many regard as an intolerable weakening of the original thesis.

In light of these difficulties, some defenders of reverse discrimination have attempted to justify that practice in what appears to be a different way altogether. On the alternative justification they propose, the aim of reverse discrimination is not to compensate anyone for any harm caused by past wrongdoing, but rather simply to promote certain highly desirable forms of social change. Although the details of this account have tended to vary, its fundamental thrust is that reverse discrimination is a necessary tool for improving the socioeconomic position of minorities and for providing role-models for both members of minority groups and women, and that these results are in turn essential steps toward bringing the present and future members of these groups into society's mainstream. The fundamental point is that reverse discrimination should be seen not primarily as redressing past wrongs, but rather simply as breaking what would otherwise be an endlessly continuing cycle of poverty and subservience. Since the latter aim seems compelling independently of any historical considerations, a strong policy of preferential treatment for all members of the affected groups is said to be justified in a purely forward-looking way.[5]

It must be conceded that a genuinely forward-looking justification of reverse discrimination would avoid the need to establish what must be the extremely complicated causal connections between past wrongs and the current positions of particular individuals. However, the advantage gained here may be more apparent than real; for in place of this task, the forward-looking justification will face the equally difficult challenge of marshalling enough detailed social scientific evidence to show that reverse discrimination would indeed disrupt

1. Judith Jarvis Thomson, "Preferential Hiring," *Philosophy and Public Affairs* 2 (1973): 381; and Allison Jaggar, "Relaxing the Limits on Preferential Hiring," *Social Theory and Practice* 4 (1977): 231.

2. Paul W. Taylor, "Reverse Discrimination and Compensatory Justice," *Analysis* 33 (1973): 177–82; and Michael D. Bayles, "Reparations to Wronged Groups," ibid., pp. 182–84.

3. George Sher, "Justifying Reverse Discrimination in Employment," *Philosophy and Public Affairs* 4 (1975): 159–70; and Alan H. Goldman, "Limits to the Justification of Reverse Discrimination," *Social Theory and Practice* 3 (1975): 289–306.

4. For discussion of these difficulties, see George Sher, "Groups and Justice," *Ethics* 87 (1977): 174–81; and Robert Simon, "Preferential Hiring: A Reply to Judith Jarvis Thomson," *Philosophy and Public Affairs* 3 (1974): 312–20.

5. For versions of the forward-looking approach, see Ronald Dworkin, *Taking Rights Seriously* (Cambridge, Mass.: Harvard University Press, 1977), pp. 223–39; Thomas Nagel, "Equal Treatment and Compensatory Discrimination," *Philosophy and Public Affairs* 2 (1973): 348–63; Irving Thalberg, "Reverse Discrimination and the Future," *Philosophical Forum* 5 (1973–74): 294–308; and Richard Wasserstrom, "The University and the Case for Preferential Treatment," *American Philosophical Quarterly* 13 (1976): 165–70. For additional discussion, see Richard Wasserstrom, "Racism, Sexism, and Preferential Treatment: An Approach to the Topics," *UCLA Law Review* 24 (1977): 581–622.

the relevant cycles of disadvantage, and that no other, fairer way of doing so would be as effective. Moreover, even if such empirical evidence could be mustered, a deeper difficulty with the forward-looking approach to reverse discrimination would remain. If that approach is to be genuinely acceptable, then the disruption of the relevant cycles of disadvantage will itself have to be called for by some independently grounded and forward-looking moral principle. However, although the principles of utility and equality have both been invoked in this connection, I shall argue in what follows that neither of them could plausibly be said to justify a policy with just the effects that reverse discrimination is claimed to have. If this contention is correct, then the forward-looking approach to reverse discrimination will be considerably more problematic than it first appears to be.

Let us begin by examining the appeal to utility. In its most basic form, a utilitarian defense of reverse discrimination will consist simply of the claim that interrupting the ongoing cycles of disadvantage would bring more overall benefit than allowing those cycles to continue; while a more sophisticated version will supplement this utility claim with a further argument that qualifications of the traditional sort do not themselves confer any right to a contested good.[6] Assuming that the relevant factual claims are correct, such utilitarian arguments may appear to offer a quick and decisive justification for a sustained policy of reverse discrimination. However, a closer look reveals that on either formulation, the utilitarian defense is vulnerable to a simple but serious objection. Put briefly, the objection is that if it is acceptable to discriminate in *favor* of minorities and women when doing so maximizes utility, then it is hard to see why it should not also be acceptable to discriminate *against* minorities and women when *that* policy maximizes utility. However, the possibility that racial, ethnic, or sexual discrimination might be legitimate is surely not one that any defender of reverse discrimination could accept.

The force of this objection has not been lost on the utilitarian defenders of reverse discrimination. One of these defenders, Thomas Nagel, has attempted to rebut the objection by contending that racial and sexual discrimination, unlike reverse discrimination, "has no social advantages . . . and attaches a sense of reduced worth to a feature with which people are born."[7] Moreover, another utilitarian defender, Ronald Dworkin, has attempted to bolster the utilitarian defense by distinguishing between two sorts of preferences. According to Dworkin: "The preferences of an individual for the consequences of a particular policy may be seen to reflect, on further analysis, either a *personal* preference for his own enjoyment of some goods or opportunities, or an *external* preference for the assignment of goods and opportunities to others, or both."[8] To whatever extent a utility claim rests on external preferences, it will tie someone's chances of satisfaction to "the respect or affection [others] have for him or for his way of life,"[9] and so will not be

---

6. See Wasserstrom, "The University and the Case for Preferential Treatment," and Dworkin.

7. Nagel, p. 360.
8. Dworkin, p. 234.
9. Ibid., p. 235.

legitimate. Thus, since utilitarian arguments for racial (and, we may add, ethnic and sexual) discrimination are evidently based on just such external preferences while utilitarian arguments for reverse discrimination are not, Dworkin concludes that we may safely accept the latter arguments without being forced to accept the former also.

Nagel and Dworkin have both attempted to show how the utilitarian can avoid the charge that his principle cuts two ways. However, even if we accept both Nagel's empirical claim and Dworkin's distinction between personal and external preferences, it will remain doubtful whether either has successfully answered the difficulty. What Nagel and Dworkin have shown is that no legitimate utilitarian argument can justify a policy of racial, ethnic, or sexual discrimination under the conditions which now prevail. However, it is one thing to show this, and quite another to show that no legitimate utilitarian argument could justify such discrimination under *any circumstances at all.* As far as I can see, Nagel has offered us no reason to believe that there could never be alternative circumstances in which racial, ethnic, or sexual discrimination had social advantages which *did* outweigh the sense of reduced worth it produced; and neither, despite his bare assertion to the contrary, has Dworkin produced any reason to suppose that such discrimination could never maximize the satisfaction of purely personal preferences. Because these possibilities still remain open, the utilitarian will still have to regard the wrongness of racial, ethnic, and sexual discrimination as fundamentally an empirical accident. However, this claim is precisely the one which the propo-

nent of reverse discrimination will presumably be unwilling to accept. Because this is so, a viable forward-looking defense of reverse discrimination will evidently have to appeal to some principle other than that of mere utility.

The other main consequentialist principle that has been invoked to support reverse discrimination is the principle of equality. By breaking the existing cycles of disadvantage, reverse discrimination is said to be a way of eliminating the gaps which now separate the different races, sexes, and ethnocultural groups, and so of promoting greater social equality.[10] By thus appealing to the aim of equality, the defender of reverse discrimination can avoid the failure of generalization which vitiates the utilitarian approach. However, by making such an appeal, he will raise a further problem in its turn. This further problem stems from the fact that even if he is committed to the ideal of equality among races, sexes, and other groups, the proponent of reverse discrimination must *ex hypothesi* continue to accept a framework of *inequality* among individuals. This acceptance of inequality follows directly from the nature of reverse discrimination itself. To practice reverse discrimination is just to award certain contested goods to women and minority group members in preference to other, more traditionally qualified claimants; and to award goods in this way is not to abolish, but merely to rearrange, the inequalities of distribution that now prevail. Moreover, since the goods to be awarded preferentially are them-

---

10. For such an approach, see Thalberg and Dworkin.

selves instrumental to the procuring of further goods, it is clear that any inequalities which are perpetuated by reverse discrimination must result in yet further inequalities in the future. Because this is so, and because many other egalitarian strategies (for example, the direct redistribution of wealth) are likely not to have this consequence to the same degree, any egalitarian who argues for reverse discrimination will have to explain why we should stop at just the amount of equality which that practice would produce. If he cannot answer this question, then the egalitarian's refusal to tolerate racial, ethnic, and sexual inequalities will be flatly inconsistent with his willingness to tolerate the other inequalities which reverse discrimination perpetuates.

One possible way for the egalitarian proponent of reverse discrimination to defend his stopping point would be for him to maintain that more equality would indeed be desirable, but that no alternative strategy for achieving it is politically and economically feasible. If this claim were correct, then the egalitarian's willingness to settle for the amount of equality which can be achieved through reverse discrimination could be defended on pragmatic grounds. However, anyone who pursued this line would have to assume that reverse discrimination is in fact the most effective egalitarian strategy now available; and in light of the many possible alternative strategies and the open-ended time period which reverse discrimination is said to require to work its effects, this unproven factual assumption is even more problematical than the others already encountered. Perhaps because of this, few egalitarians have tried to defend

reverse discrimination in this way.[11] Instead, the prevailing egalitarian view appears to be that racial, ethnic, and sexual inequalities are somehow especially wrong, and so are especially deserving of eradication. But how, exactly, is this further claim to be supported in its turn?

One way of showing that continuing racial, ethnic, and sexual inequalities are worse than others would be to argue that the former inequalities deprive groups as well as individuals of equal shares of goods, and so violate the principle of equality twice over. However, to make this argument, one would have to presuppose that the relevant groups are themselves proper candidates for equal treatment; and this supposition seems no more supportable in a forward-looking context than it is in a backward-looking one. Moreover, neither could it be argued that at least racial and sexual inequalities are especially wrong because they are based on morally arbitrary or unchangeable characteristics; for if these inequalities are genuinely self-perpetuating, then they will persist independently of any future discriminatory acts, and so will not be based on any personal characteristics at all. In light of these facts, the only remotely plausible forward-looking way of showing that racial, ethnic, and sexual inequalities are especially wrong is to reinvoke Nagel's observation that these inequalities, unlike others, are apt to lead to further inequalities of self-respect. A white who is poor and uneducated is not likely to despise himself for belonging to an inferior group, while even an affluent and well-educated black

---

11. However, see Thalberg, pp. 306–7.

may think badly of himself because so many other blacks have occupied inferior positions; and something similar may hold, *mutatis mutandis*, for members of other minorities and women as well. We saw above that such observations do not rescue the utilitarian from the charge that his principle might sometimes justify racial, ethnic, or sexual discrimination. However, they may appear far more effective when they are marshalled to show that racial, ethnic, and sexual inequalities are decisively worse than others.

It must be acknowledged that any distributional inequality which leads to a further inequality in self-respect is *ceteris paribus* worse than one which does not. However, properly understood, this fact offers little comfort to the egalitarian defender of reverse discrimination. What that defender needs to show is that it is consistent to denounce whichever inequalities follow racial, ethnic, or sexual lines, while at the same time *not* denouncing those other inequalities which reverse discrimination inevitably perpetuates. However, the fact that racial, ethnic, and sexual inequalities are accompanied by further psychological inequalities while others are not simply does not yield this conclusion. At best, it shows only that the former inequalities would have first claim on our attention if we were forced to choose among inequalities—which, as we have seen, there is not good reason to think we are. It does not show, and no further argument *could* show, that any consistent egalitarian could ignore the import of the other inequalities altogether. Because this is so, the appeal to equality is in the end just as dubious as the previous appeal to utility.

We have now examined the two most common forward-looking defenses of reverse discrimination. Although there is plainly more to be said about each, we have seen enough to show that both are vulnerable to what is at bottom the same objection. To the utilitarian defense, the objection is that it is merely a logical accident that the principle of utility now dictates practices which favor women and minority group members instead of nonminority males; while for the egalitarian defense, the difficulty is to explain why we should adopt a policy which equalizes only the positions of women and the specified minorities. Because neither forward-looking principle tells us why we should restrict our attention to the members of these groups, it is reasonable to seek the justification for this restriction in some further premise which has hitherto been suppressed. Moreover, given the context in which the whole discussion has taken place, the relevant suppressed premise is not difficult to find. Because the most salient fact about blacks, women, American Indians, Hispanics, etc., is just that they *were* so often discriminated against in the past, the suppressed reason for focusing attention on them now can hardly fail to be that they, unlike the others, are now deserving of compensation.

If this suggestion is correct, of course, then even those defenses of reverse discrimination which at first appear to be entirely forward-looking will in the end not be purely forward-looking at all. They will indeed be forward-looking to the extent that they attempt to justify reverse discrimination by claiming that it will maximize future utility or equality for women and members of the specified minorities; but their concentration on women and members of these minorities will itself be warranted by the fact that these persons' lack of goods or unequal status is likely to call for compensation if it does occur. They will indeed shift the emphasis from the amelioration of harms already done to prophylaxis to avoid future harms; but the future harms which they aim at avoiding will themselves be singled out by their immoral causal antecedents. Because the scope of the proposed arguments will thus be determined by the demands created by past wrongs, the arguments in question will reach no further than those future persons who are genuinely in danger of suffering compensable harms. These persons will undoubtedly include many blacks and members of the other official minorities; but there is little reason to believe that they will include all the members of these groups. Moreover, to be consistent, we should also expect them to include a good many Italians, Jews, Slavs, and members of the various other groups which have suffered past discrimination, but which are not included in the official list. Because so many groups have been subjected to active discrimination, any attempt to single out the endangered future members of some few of them is likely to be quite arbitrary. All in all, therefore, the proposed arguments do not avoid, but rather actually extend, the crucial question of which individuals deserve compensation for past discrimination.[12]

---

12. I am indebted to Alan Wertheimer for his helpful criticisms and suggestions.

Preferential Treatment of Minorities and Women

C O M M E N T S ■ Q U E S T I O N S

---

1. Sher appeals to what he calls the principle of utility and the principle of equality. Do you believe that he places adequate stress upon these principles? Are there other principles, such as the Principle of Rights, that also should be appealed to in a discussion of the arguments in this section?

2. Does Sher respond adequately to backward-looking defenses for preferential treatment? (The article by Anne Minas, which follows the one by Sher, presents such a defense.)

3. Many different groups of people, including Italians, Jews, and Slavs, in addition to the "official" list of groups, have been discriminated against. Therefore, "Any attempt to single out the endangered future members of some few of them is likely to be quite arbitrary." In making this argument, has Sher failed to recognize that discrimination against blacks and women has been more serious than discrimination against Italians, Jews, etc? Or is Sher entirely correct in what he says in this regard?

4. Do you agree with the following arguments which are made by Sher? (a) Forward-looking defenses of reverse discrimination,

which appeal to the principle of utility, will have difficulty showing why making society better overall through reverse discrimination is acceptable when it would never be acceptable to make society better overall through racist and sexist policies. (b) Forward-looking defenses of reverse discrimination that appeal to the principle of equality will have difficulty showing that inequalities between races or between sexes need to be eliminated, while great inequalities among individuals may remain, or in some cases be caused by reverse discrimination.

A N N E C. M I N A S

How Reverse Discrimination Compensates Women

Hiring is discriminatory if the reasons a candidate is hired extend beyond what are believed to be the qualifications for performing the functions of the position. Thus, for instance, if a candidate is hired because of, or partly because of, being a male or a WASP and these characteristics are not believed to qualify the candidate to perform in the position, there has been discrimination in the hiring. Discrimination involves a deliberate intention to consider as relevant characteristics not believed to be related to job performance. This intention may be imbedded in rules and procedures in hiring or may function more informally as considerations in the minds of those making the decisions.

'Discrimination' has connotations of injustice and prejudice. But as I have just defined the term, sometimes discrimination is required by considerations of justice. A person's unusual need for a position, or his being owed a debt of gratitude for services rendered, or fulfillment of some past agreement by an institution are all factors not related to job performance, but which, on occasion, ought to be considered relevant in hiring decisions. I will argue that, as a matter of justice, women are owed compensation for past discrimination against them in hiring, and that the form this compensation should take is

Anne C. Minas is an associate professor of philosophy at the University of Waterloo in Ontario, Canada. She has written on topics in social philosophy and feminism.

From *Ethics*, Vol. 88 (1977), pp. 74–79. Copyright © 1977 by the University of Chicago. Reprinted by permission of the author and publisher.

"reverse discrimination" favoring them.

I

It is generally agreed that in the past, and probably also in the present, women candidates have been discriminated against by procedures which have been structured so that a woman is less likely to get a position than a man, all other things being equal. This has been especially true in the case of the most prestigious jobs. There is also, I believe, some general feeling that the situation ought to be corrected. What is more controversial is whether justice requires anything further as compensation. Correcting the situation means not discriminating either in favor of men or in favor of women, but compensating women by reverse discrimination would be favoring women. The objections to the latter are well known.[1] Such compensatory favoring will not compensate fairly. Those deprived of jobs through discrimination will not have them restored, since the compensatory measures will apply mainly to the new crop of candidates who are currently looking for jobs but have not sought them in the past. Moreover, only the most "marketable" candidates will actually get the jobs, and there is no reason to believe that a candidate's marketability bears much proportion to past injustices suffered.

The mistake in being guided by such objections lies in identifying jobs as the good which compensatory measures aim to restore. What I wish to argue is that it is not, primarily,

jobs which have unjustly been taken from women in the past and which, as a matter of justice should now be restored to them. Rather, past discriminatory measures in hiring, especially for the more prestigious positions, have deprived women of the more personal goods of self-esteem, esteem by others, an enriched view of themselves, and maximal inclusion in the community. It is these goods which can and ought to be restored to women by compensatory discrimination.

II

Where men are systematically favored for positions requiring a high level of competence, the qualifications of a woman for these positions will not be as well noticed by those doing the hiring, by the woman herself, or by anyone else. This I will label the "O-phenomenon" ('O' for 'opportunity'). An individual's qualifications to perform in a certain way will become prominent in the eyes of others and to the individual himself or herself to the degree to which this individual has an opportunity to exercise his or her qualifications. We tend to regard others and ourselves according to what we are doing or have the "potential" to do, where "potential" includes opportunities which are socially determined.

A limiting case of the O-phenomenon as a focus on qualifications is where the individual occupies a position which requires these qualifications for performance of the activities of the position. If an individual is a doctor, lawyer, or landscape artist, his qualifications for medicine, law, etc., will then be among his most prominent features. But those appearing to be on the way to these posi-

---

1. And well argued in Robert Simon's "Preferential Hiring: A Reply to Judith Jarvis Thompson," in *Philosophy and Public Affairs* 3, no. 3 (Spring 1974): 312–20.

tions, having a good chance at getting them, also tend to have their qualifications for them in the foreground of the point of view from which they are seen. Qualified students are usually seen as having good potential for P where P is the profession they are studying for. A man looks at his four-year-old son and sees him as a lawyer, not because of his adeptness at legalistic argument, but because he sees him as having opportunities he never had. Daughters, or so the feminists tell us, are more likely to be seen as future wives and mothers, because this is the path most open to them.

Conversely, when an individual is denied opportunity to make use of his qualifications, the latter will be neglected in how he sees himself and how others see him. This impoverished concept of self is artificially induced by legal, economic, and social measures reducing his opportunities. And such measures are unjust when they deprive without justification, because something is being taken away from an individual which is rightfully his. Everyone, I believe, has a presumptive right to as rich a conception of himself as is compatible with the truth, to the most adequate view of his own potential and qualification as is possible for him to obtain. This right may, on occasion, be overridden for reasons of social utility or other considerations of justice. But in the case of discrimination against women in hiring there have not usually been any such reasons; therefore their deprivation of self-esteem has been unjust. They have been deprived of an adequate perception of themselves that was rightfully theirs.

The O-phenomenon is a function not only of the magnitude of the opportunities (or lack of them), but also of their structure, that is, the reasons why the opportunities are of the magnitude that they are. These reasons have to do with social attitudes, values, preferences, etc., as worked out in selection practices which focus, or fail to focus, on certain characteristics. Thus a candidate who is pessimistic about being selected because of feared neglect of his qualifications will feel this negative impact on his view of these qualifications much more than a candidate who knows he has a small chance of being selected because selection is carried out by rolling dice and he has never been lucky at dice. Sexual discrimination is especially vicious for this reason. Sex being for most of us right at the core of our identity, any discrimination on this basis is much more deeply felt than, say, discrimination occurring on the basis of accent, life-style, company kept, or other matters about an individual which he feels could be changed without losing himself in the process.

The most visible victims of sexual discrimination are those women who start a career and then abandon it from a reduced sense of self-worth, loss of motivation and identification with their work, frustration, and a sense of pessimism. But even women who have found positions suited to their best interests, whether they are successful professionals or that bane of some feminist thinking, happy housewives, also suffer losses through reduced opportunities for prestigious positions in which they have no interest. Knowledge that she can never be a doctor, successful artist, conductor, or editor because of lack of opportunity will lead an individual not to notice in herself, and not to develop, the qualities associated with these positions.

III

I have been arguing that it is a woman's right to a fair and adequate perception of herself, and not rights to jobs, that has been violated by discrimination. A little reflection will show, I believe, there there is no such thing as a right to a job, and especially, there are no rights to the more prestigious jobs which are the focus of this paper. Society should guarantee everyone political rights and also perhaps such essentials as food, medical care, and shelter. But surely society has no special obligation to provide professorships, positions in the medical professions, judgeships, to anyone who wants them and is qualified for them. This would be asking the rest of society to make sacrifices to create positions for a privileged few who have the natural endowment and training necessary for such positions.

Do the best qualified have a right to such jobs as are in fact available? Only if the fairest hiring procedures are aimed, mainly or exclusively, at selecting the best qualified for the job. Everyone does have a right to *fair opportunity*; this is a right to be considered by fair hiring procedures for any job for which the individual wishes to be considered. Fair opportunity is not "equal opportunity" if this means giving everyone an equal chance at getting the job, for equal chances for everyone would be selection by lottery or some such bizarre procedure. Rather, fair opportunity involves giving the right amount of weight to the right characteristics of the candidates. Qualification for performing the job well is quite clearly a

pertinent characteristic most of the time, but so are others, sometimes, like the considerations of justice I mentioned at the beginning of the paper; need, commitment, desert on the basis of past service. But if qualification is the only characteristic that should be considered by a fair procedure, such a procedure will result in the best qualified being hired for the job. In this derivative sense the best qualified have rights to jobs; they, along with everyone else, have a right to be considered by fair procedures, and the procedure hasn't really been followed unless the result is adhered to. So if the result is an offer of the positions to the best qualified, these individuals have a right to be made such offers. If, on the other hand, the fair procedure yields some other result, they have no such right.

IV

Women have not been given "equal opportunity" in hiring procedures in another sense of the expression; sex has been considered a relevant characteristic (i.e., women have been discriminated against) unjustly. So justice at least requires restoration of women's rights to be considered by fair hiring procedures, which in most cases means no more discrimination against them. But why compensate by discriminating in their favor? Let us look again at the goods they lost through unjust favoring of men. These were the goods of self-esteem, esteem by others, an adequate view of themselves, and a sense of maximal inclusion in the community. Since they were deprived of these goods unjustly, justice requires their restoration, and the question is, will simply eliminating sex discrimination restore these goods?

That it will not is amply evidenced by the fact that, even when discrimination against them is eliminated, women hang back from competing for prestigious positions for fear of not being well enough qualified. In contrast, when discrimination against religious groups and geographical areas is corrected, the individuals concerned only too gladly rush in to seize the opportunities that are at last being offered them. Women may have the good of inclusion in the community restored to them once they know they are being considered equally with men for all positions; however, more seems to be required to restore their sense of their own worth, as this relates to qualification for positions.

My idea of the O-phenomenon was that an individual tends to gain awareness of his or her potential according to the degree of opportunity open to him or her to exercise this potential. Thus women's awareness of their qualifications will be increased the more the opportunities are adjusted in their favor. This is the justification for "reverse discrimination." Discrimination is reversed so that the group previously discriminated against is now favored. The point is compensatory: to restore goods lost through injustice.

An obvious effect of such reversals will be more women getting more positions. But the point of the measures is not only to benefit the few who happen to get positions under these measures and who wouldn't have obtained them otherwise. Rather, everyone in the group having been discriminated against is benefited (these individuals being all those who possess the characteristic on the basis of which the discrimination took place, all women). The benefit is the new focus on the potentialities, qualifications, activities of these individuals, which greater opportunities for them bring.

The strongest objection to the kind of program I am proposing is that it would be self-defeating. To favor women in hiring practices is discrimination, as I have defined the term, meaning that a characteristic not related to job performance carries some weight in how hiring decisions are made. Now making the criterion used in such decisions predominantly sexual would, by the O-phenomenon, make the *sexual* characteristics of the candidates too prominent in their own eyes and the eyes of others; the magnitude of opportunities for women would have increased, but their nature and structure would be sexual. While this situation still might increase women's sense of their qualifications (after all, weighting opportunities in favor of men seems to have had this impact on men), this would be mitigated by everyone's awareness that sex had played an important role in hiring.[2]

Therefore the association between qualification and position must be maintained if women are to get an increased sense of their own qualifications by being favored. How can this be done?

---

2. So Thomas Nagel notes, "such a practice [which favors sex over qualification] cannot do much for the self-esteem of those who know they have benefited from it, and it may threaten the self-esteem of those in the favored group who would in fact have gained their positions even in the absence of the discriminatory policy, but who cannot be sure that they are not among its beneficiaries" (p.362) in "Equal Treatment and Compensatory Discrimination," *Philosophy and Public Affairs* 2, no. 4 (Summer 1973): 348–63.

Good hiring practices, especially those connected with prestigious positions, have made qualification to perform in the position the most important consideration. But qualification has often functioned only up to the point where differences in qualification among the candidates are (*a*) discernible, and (*b*) seen to be important. At this point there may still be a field of several candidates, so other considerations are used to make a selection of one candidate from the field. At the beginning of this paper I mentioned some such considerations which appear to be matters of justice. And there are other matters, like geographical area and citizenship of the candidate, his or her institution of matriculation, appearance, level of congeniality, personal ties with those already holding positions, and, of course, the traditional favoring of men. These considerations are supposedly all secondary to qualification, in that they are used only when qualification gives out as a method for winnowing the field. But use of them still fits my definition of 'discrimination,' since characteristics are being considered as relevant which are unrelated to job performance.

Discriminations which are matters of justice should be given precedence over those which are not, once qualification gives out as a method. According to the argument of this paper, reverse discrimination in favor of women is a matter of justice, compensatory justice. Thus, my suggestion for favoring women while maintaining the connection of qualification with position is to favor women *after* qualification is of no more use.

Questions arise immediately in this connection of how favoring of women should figure among other considerations of justice; some of these may involve reverse discrimination for other individuals that have been deprived of the same goods women have. (I remarked earlier that persons discriminated against on geographical or religious grounds do not appear to have been so deprived; but racial discrimination seems to have had the same pernicious impact as sexual discrimination.) Certainly, a necessary condition for favoring women at all is that they continue to be unjustly deprived of self-esteem through past or present discrimination against them. I cannot see how this condition could continue for more than a few years after discrimination against them had been eliminated. But I have no general suggestions about how important this consideration of justice is as opposed to others. Its relative importance will vary from situation to situation. In the academic world there appears to have been a good deal of discrimination against women in the recent past and relatively little against racial, religious, and national groups. Therefore, prima facie, women have a stronger claim in this area than, say, Negroes or Catholics. However this paper is not addressed to the subject of how much discrimination there has actually been against women in this area or any others. The argument is merely that *if* discrimination of the kind described in this paper has taken place, there has been an injustice, and that reverse discrimination in the form described in the paragraph above is an appropriate method of compensation.

C O M M E N T S ■ Q U E S T I O N S

1. "Discrimination involves a deliberate intention to consider as relevant characteristics not believed to be related to job performance. . . . 'Discrimination' has connotations of injustice and prejudice. But as I have just defined the term, sometimes discrimination is required by considerations of justice." In making these points, is Minas being consistent? Is her view defensible?

2. According to Minas, the following arguments against reverse discrimination can safely be *ignored*:
   a. Those who actually were deprived of jobs in the past will usually not be the ones who benefit in the present from reverse discrimination.
   b. Only the most 'marketable' candidates will actually get the jobs; but there is no reason to believe that these are the candidates who have suffered the most from injustice.

   The above arguments can safely be ignored since they mistakenly view jobs as the good that reverse discrimination will restore. But the primary goal of reverse discrimination should be to restore to women *other goods*: "self-esteem, esteem by others, an enriched view of themselves, and maximal inclusion in the community." Do you agree?

3. There is no such thing as a right to a job; but there is, says Minas, a right to fair opportunity, the implementation of which can be enhanced by reverse discrimination insofar as it helps to restore women's sense of self-worth. The purpose of reverse discrimination is more to help the *class* of women than it is to help the few women who get better jobs as a consequence of it. What should be said about the question of unfairness to individual *men* who do *not* get jobs as a consequence of reverse discrimination?

4. According to Minas, women should not be favored in hiring at the expense of qualifications since this will hurt their self-esteem. They should be favored only from among a pool of candidates all of whom are *fully qualified* for the job. Is this way of characterizing affirmative action realistic?

5. Minas's defense of reverse discrimination appears to fall primarily under the Principle of Justice. Can her position be defended further by an appeal to any other basic moral principles? Are there any ways that Minas's position can be argued against by appealing to basic moral principles such as the Principle of Rights? On balance, and considering all relevant moral principles, is Minas's position defensible?

6. Is Minas correct in what she says about the "O-phenomenon," which links together a person's level of awareness of his or her potential and the degree of opportunity open to the person?

S I D N E Y   H O O K

Discrimination, Color Blindness, and the Quota System

E very humane and fair-minded person must approve of the presidential executive order of 1965, which forbade discrimination with respect to race, religion, national origin or sex by any organization or group that receives financial support from the government in the course of fulfilling its contractual obligations with it. The difficulties in enforcing this order flow not from its ethical motivation and intent, but in establishing the criteria of evidence that discrimination has been practiced. Very rarely are the inequities explicitly expressed in the provisions guiding or regulating employment. They must be inferred. But they cannot be correctly inferred from the actual figures of employment independently of the *availability* of different minority groups, their *willingness* to accept employment, and the objective *qualifications* of those able and willing to apply. To be sure, the bigoted and prejudiced can distort these considerations in order to cover up flagrant discriminatory practices. But only the foolish and unperceptive will dismiss these considerations as irrelevant and assume that reference to them is an obvious sign of prejudice.

There is, unfortunately, evidence that some foolish and unperceptive persons in the Office of Civil Rights of the Department of Health, Education, and Welfare are disregarding these considerations and mechanically inferring from the actual figures of academic employment in institutions of higher learning the existence of discriminatory practices. What is worse, they are threatening to cancel federal financial support, without which many universities cannot survive, unless, within a certain period of time, the proportion of members of minorities on the teaching and research staff of universities approximate their proportion in the general population. Further, with respect to women, since it is manifestly absurd to expect that universities be staffed in an equal sexual ratio in all departments, the presence of discrimination against them is to be inferred if the composition of the teaching and research staffs does not correspond to the proportion of *applicants*—independently of the qualifications of the applicants.

In the light of this evidence, a persuasive case can be made that those who have issued these guidelines and ultimata to universities, whether they are male or female, black or white, Catholic, Jewish, or Protestant are unqualified for the

---

Sidney Hook is an emeritus professor of philosophy at New York University. He has published very widely, particularly on social, political, and legal issues.

From *Measure*, No. 30 (Summer, 1974). Reprinted by permission of the author.

offices they hold and therefore unable to properly enforce the presidential executive order. For they are guilty of fostering the very racialism and discrimination an executive order was issued to correct and forestall.

It is not hard to demonstrate the utter absurdity of the directives issued by the Office of Civil Rights of the Department of Health, Education, and Welfare. I shall use two simple instances. A few years ago, it was established that more than 80 percent of the captains of tugboats in the New York Harbor were Swedish. None were black. None were Jewish. And this in a community in which blacks and Jews outnumbered Swedes by more than a hundred to one. If one were to construe these figures along the lines laid down by the office of Civil Rights of HEW, this would be presumptive proof of crass discrimination against Negroes and Jews. But it is nothing of the sort. Negroes and Jews, for complex reasons we need not here explore, have never been interested in navigating tugboats. They have not applied for the positions. They have therefore never been rejected.

The faculties of many Negro colleges are overwhelmingly black out of all proportion to their numbers in the country, state, or even local community. It would be a grim jest therefore to tax them with discriminatory practices. Until recently, they have been pathetically eager to employ qualified white teachers, but they have been unable to attract them.

The fact that HEW makes a distinction between women and minorities, judging sexual discrimination not by simple proportion of women teachers and researchers in universities to their proportion in the general population, but only to their propor-

tion among *applicants*, shows that it has a dim understanding of the relevant issue. There are obviously various occupational fields—military, mining, aeronautical, and so forth, for which women have, until now, shown little inclination. Neither the school nor the department can be faulted for the scarcity of female applications. But the main point is this: no matter how many applicants there are for a post, whether they are male or female, the only relevant criterion is whether or not they are qualified. Only when there is antecedent determination that the applicants, with respect to the job or post specifications are equally or even roughly equally qualified, and there is a marked and continued disparity in the relative numbers employed, is there legitimate ground for suspicion and inquiry.

The effect of the ultimata to universities to hire blacks and women under threat of losing crucial financial support is to compel them to hire *unqualified* Negroes and women, and to discriminate *against* qualified nonblacks and men. This is just as much a manifestation of racism, even if originally unintended, as the racism the original presidential directive was designed to correct. Intelligent, self-respecting Negroes and women would scorn such preferential treatment. The consequences of imposing any criterion other than that of qualified talent on our educational establishments are sure to be disastrous on the quest for new knowledge and truth as well as subversive of the democratic ethos. Its logic points to the introduction of a quota system, of the notorious *numerus clausus* of repressive regimes of the past. If blacks are to be hired merely on the basis of their color and women merely on the basis of their sex, because they are *under*represented in the faculties of our universities, before long the demand will be made that Jews or men should be fired or dismissed or not hired as Jews or men, no matter how well qualified, because they are *over*represented in our faculties.

The universities should not yield to the illiberal ultimata of the Office of Civil Rights of HEW. There is sufficient work for it to do in enforcing the presidential directive in areas where minorities are obviously qualified and are obviously suffering from unfair discrimination. It undoubtedly is true, as some members of UCRA who have long been active in the field of civil rights have long pointed out,

that some educational institutions or their departments have been guilty of obvious religious and racial discrimination. The evidence of this was flagrant and open and required no elaborate questionnaires to establish. The Office of Civil Rights could cooperate with the Department of Justice here. Currently, its activities in the field of higher education are not only wasting time, effort, and the taxpayer's money but debasing educational standards as well. It is bringing confusion and conflict into an area where, prior to its intervention, the issues were well understood and where voluntary efforts to hire qualified women and members of minorities were being made with increasing success.

C O M M E N T S ■ Q U E S T I O N S

1. Hook has ignored the arguments for reverse discrimination made by Anne Minas. Do you believe that Hook is correct in doing this?

2. Which of the basic moral principles can be appealed to in defending Hook's position? The Principle of Rights or the Principle of the Common Good? On balance, considering all of the principles, is Hook's position defensible?

3. Evaluate the following:
   "The effect of the ultimata to universities to hire blacks and women under threat of losing crucial financial support is to compel them to hire *unqualified* Negroes and women, and to discriminate *against* qualified nonblacks and men. This is just as much a manifestation of racism, even if origi-

nally unintended, as the racism the original presidential directive was designed to correct."

4. According to Hook the only criterion that should ever be relevant in hiring practices is the candidate's qualification for the job. But according to the "role models" argument, a person's race or sex may be a relevant factor in judging a person's qualifications for certain sorts of jobs, such as teaching. What do you suppose Hook's response to this claim would be? (According to one version of the role models argument, it is good to have women or minority members on university faculties since they are able to serve as role models for

women or minority members who are choosing careers.) Judging from your experience as a student, how important would you say are teachers who serve as role models?

GERTRUDE EZORSKY

Hiring Women Faculty

"Sex discrimination is rampant in academe." So stated a team of sociologists after sifting data provided by the extensive 1969 Carnegie survey. Controlling for practically all relevant items that affect academic reward (for example, number of publications), the team independently confirmed the mounting evidence of sex bias in university hiring, salary, and rank.[1]

How can such rampant discrimination be remedied? The government's answer—"affirmative action"—requires, first, "good faith" efforts to ensure that women candidates are visible at hiring time. All departments should advertise jobs, inform professional organizations, and invite women to apply.

Such measures may ensure that women will be *seen* as candidates. But that's not good enough. Women candidates were not invisible in the major universities which granted them doctorates but denied them faculty appointments. Where the concepts are biased, the percepts are blind.

Hence, departments whose records show that they have "overlooked" qualified women are correctly required by affirmative action to do more than collect women's dossiers. Such departments are obligated to set

Earlier versions of this paper were given at the Center for the Study of Law and Society at the University of California, Berkeley, and a Bicentennial Symposium of Philosophy, sponsored by The City University of New York Graduate School. An excerpt was adapted as a *New York Times* Op. Editorial, 11 October 1976.

1. Helen S. Astin and Alan E. Bayer, "Sex Discrimination in Academe," *Educational Record* (Spring 1972), p. 115.

Gertrude Ezorsky is a professor of philosophy at the City University of New York (both at Brooklyn College and at the Graduate School and University Center). She has written in the areas of ethics, philosophy of law, and social philosophy.

numerical goals for women faculty.[2]

How are hiring goals devised? It is important, as we shall see, to distinguish between two types of goals, impartial and preferential.

Suppose that, although one out of every four doctorates in psychology granted in the United States is held by a woman, the psychology department in a major university is composed (from the rank of instructor and up) of 41 men and no women.[3] (Such an enormous disparity between the number of women holding doctorates and the number holding faculty appointments is not uncommon in major universities.) The number of women on the faculty of the psychology department of this university is thus lower than could "reasonably" be expected given the ratio of women to the total number of people having the "requisite skills" (hereafter the *availability* ratio).[4] Since this "underutilization" of women occurs in a general context of proven sex bias, it is reasonable to infer that such departments have failed in their duty to be impartial in appointing faculty members.

Impartial goals require that the ratio of women to the total number hired be equal to the availability ratio. Since one out of every four doctorates in psychology is held by a woman, an impartial goal for our hypothetical psychology department is one woman among the next four persons hired. Such goals increase the probability that hiring by a department that has underutilized women will approximate impartial selection.

Preferential goals remedy underutilization more rapidly than impartial goals. Thus preferential goals for women faculty exceed the availability ratio. Hence, although only one out of every four doctorates in psychology is held by a woman, a preferential goal for the psychology department we have been considering would require that more than one of the next four persons hired be women.

The Policy of HEW

While all departments are supposed to make good-faith efforts to find women candidates, only departments that have underutilized women are required to set hiring goals. When the ratio of women to the total faculty (hereafter the *faculty* ratio) is equal to the availability ratio, the department's "ultimate" goal is reached. Assuming that a stable 25 percent of people holding doctorates in psychology are women, our hypothetical psychology department's "ultimate" goal is to have 25 percent of its faculty be women.

But such ultimate goals are to be achieved by a series of three-year "interim" goals that are acceptable to HEW if they are set impartially

2. U.S. Department of Health, Education, and Welfare, "Revised Order No. 4." *Higher Education Guidelines, Executive Order 11246.* The Executive Order—amended in 1968 to cover sex discrimination—prohibits sex discrimination by employers holding government contracts. Employers are required to draw up "affirmative action" plans identifying their discriminatory practices and outlining remedial measures, including hiring goals and timetables.

3. Scientific Manpower Commission, "Number and Percent of Doctoral Degrees Granted to Women by Field and Decade, 1920–1974," *Professional Women and Minorities, A Manpower Data Resource Service* (1975), p. 51.

4. *Federal Register* 36, no. 234 (4 December 1971), U.S. Department of Labor, Office of Federal Contract Compliance, "Revised Order No. 4," Subpart No. 60-2.11.

according to the availability ratio.[5] Thus, in 1973 Harvard set impartial goals for women faculty at 15 to 16 percent, determined approximately by the projected availability ratio.[6] According to Columbia's 1972 plan, departments that have underutilized women would give new appointments to women at their "national pool rate" (as determined by the availability ratio).[7] Universities that fail to meet their goal are not penalized if they can demonstrate good faith efforts to find women candidates.

Given a slow rate of hiring, decades will pass before departments that have seriously underutilized women could, by impartial goals, reach the ultimate goal of equality between the faculty ratio and the availability ratio.

Are HEW's impartial hiring goals fair to academic women? The rationale for impartial goals is equal employment opportunity. Hence, such goals are intended to approximate impartial selection. But preferential goals would give women more than equal opportunity requires. As a consequence, some males who had recently received doctorates would be denied instructorships they merit and would thus be excluded from academic employment.

It does seem true that academic women, newly arrived in the workplace, are not entitled to more than the impartial goals which now give them equal opportunity with their male competitors. But women not so recently arrived could claim that acceptance of equal opportunity *now*, as all they are owed, would require a bath in the waters of forgetfulness. They might remind HEW that in yesterday's competition they were denied impartial consideration according to their merits. Why does our hypothetical psychology department (and too many others like it) have no senior women? Because for decades such academic departments have unfairly excluded women. Instructorships which women deserved by virtue of their work and ability were given to less deserving men. Restitution for the injury done these women might now be made in some measure if such departments gave preference to women in appointing senior professors. In that case, some women would obtain the kind of positions they deserve and would already have if in the past universities had—on their own and without government interference—really lived up to merit standards in hiring faculty.

Note that offers of senior positions are usually made to those already employed by other universities. Hence preference given to women for senior openings, unlike that for junior positions, would not deprive men of academic employment.

Hiring goals—preferential in the upper ranks, impartial in the lower— would yield deserved compensation

5. U.S. Department of Health, Education, and Welfare, *Format for Development of an Affirmative Action Plan by Institutions of Higher Education* (1975), p. 15. "For each faculty and other instructional staff job group in which underutilization exists, the university must project rates of hiring and/or promoting minorities and women until underutilization is eliminated . . . these rates may be established for three year periods . . . and must not be lower than the percentage rates set as representing the percentage availability of women and minorities in the applicable job market."

6. See *Harvard University Affirmative Action Program*, 31 July 1973; and Scientific Manpower Commission, "Research Doctorates Awarded by U.S. Universities, Selected Years, 1920–1974," *Professional Women and Minorities*, p. 52.

7. *Columbia University Affirmative Action Program* (condensed version), December 1972 p. 6.

for injustice past as well as equal opportunity in the present. It is true that the position of senior women is somewhat improved by HEW's impartial goals. But it should not be supposed that our government has gone as far as it should in requiring fairness to academic women.

Nonetheless, even HEW's modest start has set off enormous opposition. Critics insist that HEW's hiring goals are disguised quotas which yield reverse discrimination. Some grant that good faith efforts, such as advertising of jobs, are required to straighten out recruitment procedures. But, critics claim, such efforts should suffice to create equal opportunity.

Quotas

In 1974 over sixty academics signed a letter to President Ford, characterizing hiring goals as "unjust and discriminatory *quota* programs."[8] Why do political opponents of HEW's hiring goals insist on describing them as "quotas"?

Historically, so called quota systems were used to prevent fair selection and enforce prejudice. (How many Jews can we tolerate in our university?) Critics who insist that today's goals be called "quotas" are suggesting that HEW's goals, like yesterday's quotas, work against impartiality. But that suggestion is false. As we have seen, HEW's hiring goals for women instructors raise the probability that the hiring outcome will approximate impartial selection. Hence, while yesterday's quotas served bias, today's goals are designed to prevent bias. No amount of "quota"-baiting can destroy that radical difference of moral intent.

It is true that both numerical goals and quotas are semantically equivalent to numerical objectives. Alan Goldman is therefore perfectly correct in denying any "semantic distinction" between numerical goals and quotas.[9] He fails to note, however, that the expression "quota," as distinguished from the expression "numerical goal," is associated with a past policy of university discrimination. Hence HEW's political opponents can use the expression "quota" for the propagandistic purpose of suggesting (falsely) that HEW imposes a policy of discrimination on universities.

Reverse Discrimination

Critics claim that goals in hiring tend to create reverse discrimination, which denies men the kind of appointments they merit. Alan Goldman claims that this tendency is encouraged by the sort of goals that HEW requires and by the response of administrators to such regulations.

According to Goldman, "affirmative action goals are . . . meant simply to compensate past injustice" (p. 183). He suggests that goals in a university (as in a factory) are expected to "*rapidly* result in statistical balance" (p. 186, emphasis added). Although the overall target is equal opportunity, "the purpose of these goals" is really "to increase the percentage of minority employment" (p. 180).

Evidently Goldman believes, incorrectly, that HEW imposes preferential

8. *New York Times*, 9 December 1974 (emphasis added).

9. Alan H. Goldman, "Affirmative Action," *Philosophy & Public Affairs* 5, no. 2 (Winter 1976): 182. All page references in text are to this article.

goals designed to "rapidly" balance faculty and availability ratios. However, he is simply unfamiliar with HEW practice.

Harvard's hiring goals of 1973 to 1976 allotted women only an impartial 15 to 16 percent of projected vacancies. But to end underutilization a highly preferential goal, hiring women for 70 percent of faculty openings, would have been required.[10]

Berkeley's 1974 affirmative action plan indicates just how rapidly underutilization of women is expected to disappear: "The range for achievement of parity at all ladder rank levels ranges from 23 to not less than 30 years."[11]

It is irrational, Goldman argues, to expect an institution "to mirror the overall [availability] ratio by a *specific* date after fair competition begins" (p. 186, emphasis added). Why is it irrational to expect that Berkeley end underutilization of women in three decades?

Goldman claims that "there can be little doubt that, in practice, the *natural* response of administrators is to interpret goals as pressure for reverse discrimination" (p. 184, emphasis added). It would be *natural*, even correct, to regard preferential goals designed to end underutilization rapidly as pressure for reverse discrimination. But such goals are not being imposed by HEW.

According to Goldman, it is easier for chairpersons "faced with pres-

sure" from university authorities to meet the stated goal than to demonstrate to HEW that they have made good faith efforts to seek women candidates (p. 184). Hence, administrators are inclined to practice reverse discrimination.

Suppose, as Goldman claims, that departments which have underutilized women in the past, now tend to fill their goals. In that case, the all-male psychology department we have discussed will probably hire its first woman to fill one of the next four openings. Would such hiring tend to deprive superior male candidates of appointments they would otherwise receive? Such deprivation is predictable only on the (false) assumption that women candidates are probably inferior because of their sex.

Goldman offers a final "empirical" consideration: "The fact that the 'quotas' charge continues to be heard despite official denials is evidence" of reverse discrimination (p. 184).

Yes, sometimes where there's smoke there's fire. Hence when a charge "continues to be heard," one might plausibly investigate. But Goldman should be showing that the reverse discrimination claim is true, not merely that charges might be looked into. Moreover, charges of reverse discrimination, even if entirely false, might still be made by some young male academics (to their shame) who, in competing for scarce faculty appointments, have lost out to *women*, or by some biased employers who resent interference from outsiders such as civil rights investigators.

Is there now a general tendency to favor women in hiring? Some may infer such favoritism from the relative increase of women in junior posi-

---

10. *Harvard University Affirmative Action Program.*

11. "Revisions to the Affirmative Action Personnel Program," University of California, Berkeley, *Affirmative Action Program and Related Documents,* vol. 1, (30 September 1974), p. 50.

tions. But that inference is invalid. In the last decade, the increase in the percentage of women holding assistant professorships did not keep pace with the increase in the percentage available as candidates.[12]

Moreover, studies indicate that women who have recently received doctorates are having a harder time finding appointments than their male counterparts. Among 1974 and 1975 Ph.D. recipients seeking appointments 20 percent of the women, but only 15 percent of the men, had no definite prospects in the year their degrees were granted.[13] Such relevant evidence suggests no general tendency to favor women in academic employment. Where has evidence showing such favoritism been displayed for inspection?

Alternatives to Goals

Some critics of goals do say that sex discrimination ought to stop. Goldman, for example, grants that "widespread discrimination has occurred . . . especially against women in university hiring and promotion" (p. 181). Yet he later claims, inconsistently, that universities use a "merit system of hiring," (p. 186).

In Goldman's opinion, good faith efforts "seem enough to guarantee equal treatment. . . . Even without goals, employers would be susceptible to intense official pressure to be fair. . . . The current HEW policies may presuppose deeper and more intractable attitudes on the part of employers than is in fact the case—I *suspect* most simply go along with the current hiring practices" (p. 185, emphasis added).

How would Goldman's proposal to require only good faith efforts work in practice? The point of these efforts is to make employers aware of women as candidates. But consider those administrators who have never once offered a woman an appointment. According to Goldman, they should be required merely to show that they really and truly did try to make themselves aware that woman candidates exist. But, as I have noted, administrators in the institutions that underutilized women most seriously—the major universities—surely knew their women graduate students. Yet, even when they hired their own graduates, outstanding women students were usually passed over in favor of less deserving men.

The essence of good faith efforts lies in sending letters—to publications, placing job advertisements; to professional agencies, requesting the names of women candidates; to women, asking for their dossiers. But once a bundle of dossiers is locked in the file, good faith efforts are done with.

An administrator intractably opposed to women can easily learn to play—and win—this game of mail. Those not so intractable, once affirmative action is completed *on paper*,

---

12. The percentage of women assistant professors rose from 19.4 percent in 1965–1966 to 26.3 percent in 1974–1975. However, the percentage of women receiving doctoral degrees rose from 10.9 percent in 1964 to 19.4 percent in 1974. See "Research Doctorates Awarded by U.S. Universities, Selected Years 1920–1974," p. 152, and "Women as a Percentage of Faculty Members in Four Year Colleges and Universities," p. 142, in *Professional Women and Minorities*.

13. Data available from Board on Human Resource Data and Analyses, Commission on Human Resources, National Research Council, National Academy of Sciences, Washington, D.C., publishers of 1974 and 1975 *Summary Reports, Doctorate Recipients from U.S. Universities*.

can settle back into old habits and hire the *man* they really want for the job.

Goldman's confidence in good faith, supported only by what he "suspects" to be true, is called into question by recent reports from affirmative action specialists that many good faith measures are performed as charades. "Privately" selecting the candidate to be hired, then advertising the job is not uncommon.[14] An administrator is reported to have explained good faith efforts to his faculty in this way: "It was not necessary for the University to be an equal opportunity employer—it was only necessary to *say* in advertisements that it was" (emphasis added).[15] A Harvard affirmative action officer stated, "*The whole process becomes a sham.*"[16] Thus, it seems fair to say that it is not the hiring goals but the good faith efforts that need critical scrutiny.

Another alternative to goals has been offered by Sidney Hook: "Why not drop all . . . sex . . . bars in honest quest for the best qualified" candidate?[17] Such advice has all the practical value of suggesting that sin go away. Where the best candidate competing for a faculty appointment is a woman, she has two handicaps. First, there is the fact, by now overwhelmingly confirmed, of prejudice against women's intellect. Studies have shown that the same professional record or performance is rated lower when attributed to a woman.[18] Second, academics can cover up individual cases of sex discrimination more easily than other employers. Who is the best pitcher for a professional baseball team? Simple arithmetic tells a large part of that story. Hence, prejudice is more easily discernible. Who is the best candidate for a philosophy instructorship? Not so easy. Judgments about the quality of a person's scholarship may differ widely and no mechanical resolution is possible. Where purely objective rules of selection are absent, a sex-biased choice is more easily rationalized.

It is significant that since the ad-

14. Janet W. Brown, Director of Office of Opportunities in Science, AAAS, *Hearings before the Special Subcommittee on Education of the Committee on Education and Labor, House of Representatives* (Government Printing Office, 1974), pp. 178–179. Hereafter cited as *Hearings*). See also, statement of Betty Vetter, Executive Director of the Scientific Manpower Commission, *Hearings;* James C. Goodwin, Assistant to the Vice-President for University Relations of the University of California System, "Playing Games with Affirmative Action," *The Chronicle of Higher Education*, 28 April 1975; Walter J. Leonard, Special Assistant to the President, Harvard University, "To the Harvard Community," *Harvard University Gazette*, 14 March 1975; Statement of Mary Gray for Committee W, on the Status of Women in the Academic Profession, of the American Association of University Professors, made at the Department of Labor, Office of Federal Contract Compliance, Fact-Finding *Hearings,* 1 October 1975.

15. Statement of Mary Gray.

16. Leonard, "To the Harvard Community."

17. *New York Times*, 14 November 1974.

18. See L. S. Videll, "Empirical Verification of Sex Discrimination in Hiring Practices in Psychology," *American Psychologist* 25 (1970); Philip Goldberg, "Are Women Prejudiced Against Women," *Transaction* (April 1968); Sandra L. and Daryl J. B. Bem, "Training the Woman to Know her Place: The Power of a Nonconscious Ideology," in *Women's Role in Contemporary Society, The Report of the New York City Commission on Human Rights* (New York, 1970); S. L. Labovitz, "Some Evidence of Canadian Ethnic, Racial and Sexual Antagonism," *The Canadian Review of Sociology and Anthropology* (August 1974).

vent of antibias regulations, sex discrimination has disappeared in an area where it is not easily hidden: salary inequities between men and women instructors at the *beginning* of their academic careers have now been eliminated.[19] While extra paperwork imposed by government bureaucrats does not enhance the quality of life, academic women may

be justified in feeling that more paperwork is a small price to pay for decades of injustice.

Most of us prefer to think that, left on our own, we make objective choices. But what is the likelihood that any of us could have been so lucky, morally speaking, as to escape the mark of social prejudice? Hiring goals serve as a check on the workings of such prejudice; by voluntarily acceding to that check, we free ourselves from culpability.

19. Helen S. Astin and Alan E. Bayer, "Sex Differentials in the Academic Reward System," *Science* 188 (23 May 1975).

C O M M E N T S ■ Q U E S T I O N S

1. Women are *underutilized* in college and university faculties if the proportion of women on these faculties is less than the proportion of women having the requisite skills for faculty positions. The U.S. Department of Health, Education, and Welfare (HEW) requires that academic departments that have underutilized women set hiring goals to achieve equality between the proportion of women faculty and the proportion of women having requisite skills. There are two ways that such goals might be achieved: (a) by impartial hiring goals; that is, hiring women in the same proportion as the proportion of women, out of all qualified persons, having the requisite skills, or (b) through preferential hiring goals; that is, hiring women in a greater proportion. Health, Education, and Welfare requires only impartial hiring goals. Do HEW policies go far enough? Are stronger measures—such as the preferential hiring defended by Ezorsky for senior academic positions—needed in order to eliminate discrimination against women? Do HEW policies go too far?

2. Has Ezorsky adequately responded to the arguments made by Sidney Hook in "Discrimination, Color Blindness, and the Quota System"?

3. Is it reasonable to believe, as Ezorsky does, that there is evidence of discriminatory hiring if a university department such as psychology (to use her example) has a lower percentage of women than the percentage of those having Ph.D.'s in psychology who are women? Could this be accounted for in any reasonable way that would not imply discrimination?

J O Y C E   T R E B I L C O T

Two Forms of Androgynism

Traditional concepts of women and men, of what we are and should be as females and males, of the implications of sex for our relationships to one another and for our places in society, are not acceptable. But what models, if any, should we adopt to replace them? In this paper I consider just two of the alternatives discussed in recent literature—two versions of androgynism.

In discussing these two views I follow the convention of distinguishing between sex (female and male) and gender (feminine and masculine). Sex is biological, whereas gender is psychosocial. Thus, for example, a person who is biologically female may be—in terms of psychological characteristics or social roles—feminine or masculine, or both.

Although what counts as feminine and masculine varies among societies and over time, I use these terms here to refer to the gender concepts traditionally dominant in our own society. Femininity, on this traditional view, has nurturing as its core: it centers on the image of woman as mother, as provider of food, warmth, and emotional sustenance. Masculinity focuses on mastery: it comprises the notion of man struggling to overcome obstacles, to control nature, and also the notion of man as patriarch or leader in society and the family.

The first form of androgynism to be discussed here takes the word "androgyny" literally, so to speak. In this word the Greek roots for man (*andros*) and woman (*gynē*) exist side by side. According to the first form of androgynism, both feminine and masculine characteristics should exist "side by side" in every individual: each woman and man should develop personality traits and engage in activities traditionally assigned to only one sex. Because this view postulates a single ideal for everyone, I call it monoandrogynism, or, for brevity, *M*.

Monoandrogynism, insofar as it advocates shared roles, is now official policy in a number of countries. For example, the Swedish government presented a report to the United Nations in 1968 specifying that in Sweden, "every individual, regardless of sex, shall have the same practical opportunities not only for education and employment but also fundamentally the same responsibility for his or her own financial support as

---

Joyce Trebilcot is coordinator of women's studies and associate professor of philosophy at Washington University in St. Louis. Her work is in the area of feminist philosophy and includes Taking Responsibility for Sexuality *and* Mothering: Essays in Feminist Theory.

Joyce Trebilcot, "Two Forms of Androgynism," *Journal of Social Philosophy*, vol. 8 (1977). Reprinted by permission.

well as shared responsibility for child upbringing and housework."[1]

Closer to home, Jessie Bernard, in her discussion of women's roles, distinguishes the one-role view, according to which woman's place is in the home; the two-role pattern, which prescribes a combination of the traditional housewife-mother functions and work outside the home; and what she calls the "shared-role ideology" which holds "that children should have the care of both parents, that all who benefit from the services supplied in the household should contribute to them, and that both partners should share in supporting the household."[2]

Caroline Bird in her chapter "The Androgynous Life" writes with approval of role-sharing. She also suggests that the ideal person "combines characteristics usually attributed to men with characteristics usually attributed to women."[3]

The psychological dimension of M is stressed by Judith M. Bardwick. In her essay "Androgyny and Humanistic Goals, or Goodbye, Cardboard People," she discusses a view according to which the ideal or "healthy" person would have traits of both genders. "We would then expect," she says, "both nurturance and competence, openness and objectivity, compassion and competitiveness from both women and men, as individuals, according to what they were doing."[4]

The work of these and other writers provides the basis for a normative theory, M, which prescribes a single ideal for everyone: the person who is, in both psychological characteristics and social roles, both feminine and masculine.

The second form of androgynism shares with the first the principle that biological sex should not be a basis for judgments about the appropriateness of gender characteristics. It differs from the first, however, in that it advocates not a single ideal but rather a variety of options including "pure" femininity and masculinity as well as any combination of the two. According to this view, all alternatives with respect to gender should be equally available to and equally approved for everyone, regardless of sex. Thus, for example, a female might acceptably develop as a completely feminine sort of person, as both feminine and masculine in any proportion, or as wholly masculine. Because this view prescribes a variety of acceptable models, I call it polyandrogynism, or P.[5]

1. Official Report to the United Nations on the Status of Women in Sweden, 1968. Quoted in Rita Liljeström, "The Swedish Model," in *Sex Roles in Changing Society*, ed. Georgene H. Seward and Robert C. Williamson (New York: Random House, 1970), p. 200.

2. Jessie Bernard, *Women and the Public Interest* (Chicago: Aldine, 1971); and idem, *The Future of Marriage* (New York: Bantam Books, 1972). The quotation is from the latter book, p. 279.

3. Caroline Bird, *Born Female* (New York: Pocket Books, 1968), p. xi.

4. Judith M. Bardwick, "Androgyny and Humanistic Goals, or Goodbye, Cardboard People," in *The American Woman: Who Will She Be?* ed. Mary Louise McBee and Kathryn A. Blake (Beverly Hills, Calif.: Glencoe Press, 1974), p. 61.

5. "Monoandrogynism" and "polyandrogynism" are perhaps not very happy terms, but I have been unable to find alternatives which are both descriptive and non-question-begging. In an earlier version of this paper I used "A_1" and "A_2," but these labels are not as perspicuous as "M" and "P." Mary Anne Warren, in "The Ideal of Androgyny" (unpublished) refers to "the strong thesis" and "the weak thesis," but this terminology tends to prejudice judgment as to which view is preferable. Hence, I use "M" and "P."

Constantina Safilios-Rothschild supports *P* in her recent book *Women and Social Policy*. In this work she makes a variety of policy recommendations aimed at bringing about the liberation of both sexes. Liberation requires, she says, that individuals live "according to their wishes, inclinations, potentials, abilities, and needs rather than according to the prevailing stereotypes about sex roles and sex-appropriate modes of thought and behavior." Some persons, she adds, "might *choose* to behave according to their sex's stereotypic . . . patterns. But some women and some men may *choose*, if they are so inclined, to take options in some or all of the life sectors now limited to the opposite sex."[6]

Carolyn Heilbrun's work also suggests *P*. In *Toward a Recognition of Androgyny* she writes, "The ideal toward which I believe we should move is best described by the term 'androgyny.' This ancient Greek word. . . defines a condition under which the characteristics of the sexes, and the human impulses expressed by men and women, are not rigidly assigned. Androgyny seeks to liberate the individual from the confines of the appropriate." Androgyny suggests, Heilbrun says, "a full range of experience open to individuals who may, as women, be aggressive, as men, tender; it suggests a spectrum upon which human beings choose their places without regard to propriety or custom."[7]

This second form of androgynism focuses on a variety of options rather than on the single model of the part-woman/part-man (that is, of the androgyne in the classic sense). It is appropriate, however, to extend the term "androgynism" to apply to it; for, like *M*, it seeks to break the connection between sex and gender.

For both forms of androgynism, the postulated ideals are best construed so as to exclude aspects of traditional gender concepts which are morally objectionable. Femininity should not be taken to include, for example, weakness, foolishness, or incompetence. Similarly, tendencies such as those to authoritarianism and violence should be eliminated from the concept of masculinity. Most importantly, aspects of the gender concepts which prescribe female submissiveness and male domination (over women and over other men) must, on moral grounds, be excluded from both the single ideal advocated by *M* and the range of options recommended by *P*.

Either form of androgyny may, in the long run, lead to major changes in human attributes. It is often suggested that the androgyne is a person who is feminine part of the time and masculine part of the time. But such compartmentalization might be expected to break down, so that the feminine and masculine qualities would influence one another and be modified. Imagine a person who is at the same time and in the same respect both nurturant and mastery-oriented, emotional and rational, cooperative and competitive, and so on. I shall not undertake here to speculate on whether this is possible, or, if it is, on how such qualities might combine. The point is just that androgyny in the long run may lead to an integrating of femininity and masculinity that will

6. Constantina Safilios-Rothschild, *Women and Social Policy* (Englewood Cliffs, N.J.: Prentice-Hall, 1974), p. 7; emphasis hers.

7. Carolyn Heilbrun, *Toward a Recognition of Androgyny* (New York: Harper & Row, 1973), pp. 7–8.

yield new attributes, new kinds of personalities. The androgyne at this extreme would perhaps be not part feminine and part masculine, but neither feminine nor masculine, a person in whom the genders disappear.

I turn now to the question of which of these two forms of androgynism is more acceptable. I am not concerned here to evaluate these positions in relation to other alternatives (for example, to the traditional sexual constitution of society or to matriarchy).[8] For the sake of this discussion, I assume that either M or P is preferable to any alternative, and that the problem is only to decide between them. Let us first consider this problem not as abstract speculation, and not as a problem for some distant society, but rather as an immediate issue for our own society. The question is then: Which form of androgynism is preferable as a guide to action for us here and now?

Suppose we adopt M. Our task then is to provide opportunities, encouragement, and perhaps even incentives for those who are now feminine to be also masculine, and conversely. Suppose, on the other hand, that we adopt P. Our task is to create an environment in which, without reference to sex, people choose among all (moral) gender alternatives. How can this best be accomplished? What is required, clearly, is

that the deeply-entrenched normative connection between sex and gender be severed. Virtually everyone now, in formulating preferences for the self and in judging the appropriateness of gender characteristics for others, at least on some occasions takes it, consciously or otherwise, that the sex of the individual in question is a relevant consideration: that one is female tends to count in favor of a feminine trait and against a masculine one, and conversely. In order to break this connection, it must be shown that masculinity is acceptable for females and femininity for males. There must, then, be opportunities, encouragement, and perhaps even incentives for gender-crossing. But this is what is required by M. Hence, under present conditions, the two forms of androgynism prescribe the same course of action—that is, the promotion of gender-crossing.

The question "Which form of androgynism is preferable here and now?" then, is misconstrued. If one is an androgynist of either sort, what one must do now is seek to break the normative connection between sex and gender by bringing about gender-crossing. However, once the habit of taking sex as a reason for gender evaluation is overcome, or is at least much weaker and less widespread than it is today, then the two forms of androgynism do prescribe different courses of action. In particular, on M "pure" gender is condemned, but on P it is accepted. Let us consider, then, which version of androgynism is preferable for a hypothetical future society in which femininity and masculinity are no longer normatively associated with sex.

The major argument in favor of P is, of course, that because it stipulates a variety of acceptable gender alterna-

8. My current view is that we should work for the universal realization of women's values; but that is another paper. (For some arguments against the use of the term "androgyny" in feminist theory, see, for example, Mary Daly, "The Qualitative Leap beyond Patriarchal Religion," *Quest: A Feminist Quarterly*, vol. 1, no. 4 [Spring 1975], pp. 29ff.; and Janice Raymond, "The Illusion of Androgyny," *Quest*, vol. 2, no. 1 [Summer 1975].)

tives it provides greater gender freedom than *M*. Now, freedom is a very
high priority value, so arguments for
M must be strong indeed. Let us
consider, then, two arguments used to
support *M* over *P*—one psychological, one ethical.

The psychological argument holds
that in a society which is open with
respect to gender, many people are
likely to experience anxiety when
faced with the need, or opportunity,
to choose among different but equally
acceptable gender models. Consider
the words of Judith M. Bardwick:

People need guidelines, directions that
are agreed upon because they help each
individual to know where one ought to
go, how one can get there, and how far
one is from one's goal. It is easier to
sustain frustration that comes from knowing how far you are from your objective
or what barriers are in your way than it is
to sustain the anxiety that comes from not
being sure about what you want to do or
what others want you to do. It will be
necessary, then, to develop new formu-
lations by which people will guide
their lives.[9]

Bardwick says that anxiety "comes
from not being sure about what you
want to do or what others want you to
do." But in a society of the sort
proposed by *P*, the notion that one
should seek to please others in deciding among gender models would be
rejected; ideally "what others want
you to do" in such a society is to
make your own decisions. Of course
there is still the problem of not being
sure about what *you* want to do.
Presumably, under *P*, people would
provide one another with help and
support in finding suitable life
styles. Nevertheless, it could be that

for some, choosing among alternatives would be anxiety-producing. On
the other hand, under *M*, the lack of
approved alternatives could produce
frustration. Hence, the argument from
anxiety should be paired with an
argument from frustration. In *M*,
socialization is designed to make
everyone androgynous (in ways similar, perhaps, to those which have
traditionally produced exclusive femininity and masculinity in our own
society), and frustration is part of the
cost. In *P*, socialization is directed
toward enabling people to perceive,
evaluate, and choose among alternatives, and there is a risk of anxiety. We
are not now in a position to decide
whether the frustration or the anxiety
is worse, for there are no data on the
numbers of people likely to suffer
these emotions nor on the extent of
the harm that they are likely to do.
Hence, neither the argument from
anxiety nor the argument from frustration is of any help in deciding between the two forms of
androgynism.

I turn now to a more persuasive
argument for *M*, one which claims
that androgyny has universal value.
This argument supports *M* not, as the
argument from anxiety does, because
M prescribes some norm or other,
but rather because of the content of
the norm. The argument holds that
both traditional genders include qualities that have value, qualities that it
would be good for everyone to have.
Among the elements of femininity,
candidates for universal value are
openness and responsiveness to
needs and feelings, and being gentle,
tender, intuitive, sensitive, expressive,
considerate, cooperative, compassionate. Masculine qualities appealed to in
this connection include being logical,
rational, objective, efficient, responsi-

9. Bardwick, op. cit., p. 50.

ble, independent, courageous. It is claimed, then, that there are some aspects of both genders (not necessarily all or only the ones I have mentioned) which are desirable for everyone, which we should value both in ourselves and in one another. But if there are aspects of femininity and masculinity which are valuable in this way—which are, as we might call them, virtues—they are *human* virtues, and are desirable for everyone. If Smith is a better person for being compassionate or courageous, then so is Jones, and never mind the sex of Smith or Jones. Hence, the argument concludes, the world envisioned by *M*, in which everyone or nearly everyone is both feminine and masculine, is one in which life for everyone is more rewarding than the world advocated by *P*, in which some people are of only one gender; therefore we should undertake to bring about *M*.

The argument claims, then, that both genders embody traits that it would be valuable for everyone to have. But how is this claim to be tested? Let us adopt the view that to say that something is valuable for everyone is, roughly, to say that if everyone were unbiased, well-informed, and thinking and feeling clearly, everyone would, in fact, value it. As things are now, it is difficult or impossible to predict what everyone would value under such conditions. But there is an alternative. We can seek to establish conditions in which people do make unbiased, informed, etc., choices, and see whether they then value both feminine and masculine traits.

But this reminds us, of course, of the program of *P*. *P* does not guarantee clear thought and emotional sensitivity, but it does propose an environment in which people are informed about all gender options and are unbiased with respect to them. If, in this context, all or most people, when they are thinking clearly, etc., tend to prefer, for themselves and others, both feminine and masculine virtues, we will have evidence to support the claim that androgyny has universal value. (In this case, *P* is likely to change into *M*). On the other hand, if "pure" gender is preferred by many, we should be skeptical of the claim that androgyny has universal value. (In this case we should probably seek to preserve *P*.) It appears, then, that in order to discover whether *M* is preferable to *P*, we should seek to bring about *P*.

In summary, we have noted the argument from freedom, which supports *P*; arguments from anxiety and frustration, which are indecisive; and the argument from universal value, whose analysis suggests the provisional adoption of *P*. As far as I know, there are no additional major arguments which can plausibly be presented now for either side of the issue. Given, then, the problem of deciding between *M* and *P* without reference to other alternatives, my tentative conclusion is that because of the great value of freedom, and because in an atmosphere of gender-freedom we will be in a good position to evaluate the major argument for *M* (that is, the argument from the universal value of androgyny), *P* is preferable to *M*.

Of course all we have assumed about the specific nature of the hypothetical society for which we are making this judgment is that the connection between sex and gender would be absent, as would be the unacceptable components of traditional gender concepts, particularly dominance and submission. It might be, then, that particular social conditions would constitute grounds for supporting *M* rather than *P*. For example, if the society in question were hierarchical with leadership roles tightly held by the predominantly masculine individuals, and if leaders with feminine characteristics were more likely to bring about changes of significant value (for example, eliminating war or oppression), it could reasonably be argued that *M*, in which everyone, including leaders, has both feminine and masculine characteristics, would be preferable to *P*. But such considerations are only speculative now.

C O M M E N T S ■ Q U E S T I O N S

1. Trebilcot's intention is to discuss alternatives to traditional views of gender, or sexual roles. Some people might argue that her description of traditional sexual roles is inaccurate, or at the best that it is misleading:

   Femininity, on this traditional view, has nurturing as its core: it centers on the image of woman as mother, as provider of food, warmth, and emotional sustenance. Masculinity focuses on mastery: it comprises the notion of man struggling to overcome obstacles, to control nature, and also the notion of man as patriarch or leader in society and the family (from "Two Forms of Androgynism").

   Some people might argue that the above description ignores certain "crossovers" between the sexes that have always been recognized—such as a father's concern and compassion for his children. In short, some people might argue that a certain degree of androgynism has always been accepted and even welcome. Is there any truth to such a view? To what extent would you say that the ideal of androgynism—in either of the forms discussed by Trebilcot—is a new concept in society?

2. Are there any important dangers, either to individuals or to society, in the advocacy of androgynism that are not discussed by Trebilcot? Is there any reason to believe that androgynism would threaten romantic attractions between men and women? Would it be likely to strengthen such attractions?

3. Does the Principle of Rights provide any significant support for what Trebilcot calls polyandrogynism, or *P*?

R E A D I N G S

Beauvoir, Simone de. *The Second Sex*. Translated by H. M. Parshley. New York: Knopf, 1953.

Bishop, Sharon and Majorie Weinzweig, eds. *Philosophy and Women*. Belmont, Calif.: Wadsworth, 1979.

Blackstone, William T., and Robert D. Heslep, eds. *Social Justice and Preferential Treatment*. Athens, Ga.: The University of Georgia Press, 1977.

Cohen, Marshall, Thomas Nagel, and Thomas Scanlon, eds. *Equality and Preferential Treatment*. Princeton, N.J.: Princeton University Press, 1976.

English, Jane, ed. *Sex Equality*. Englewood Cliffs, N.J.: Prentice-Hall, Inc., 1977.

Fullinwider, Robert K. *The Reverse Discrimination Controversy*. Totowa, N.J.: Rowman & Littlefield, 1980.

Goldman, Alan H. *Justice and Reverse Discrimination*. Princeton, N.J.: Princeton University Press, 1979.

Gross, Barry, ed. *Reverse Discrimination*. Buffalo, N.Y.: Prometheus Press, 1977.

Jagger, Alison M., and Paula Rotherberg Struhl, eds. *Feminist Frameworks*. New York: McGraw-Hill Book Company, 1978.

Vetterling-Braggin, Mary, Frederick A. Elliston, and Jane English, eds. *Feminism and Philosophy*. Totowa, N.J.: Littlefield, Adams & Co., 1977.

The Scope and Nature of Government

How much control should government have over our lives? Answers to this question can be given from many different perspectives that, needless to say, cannot all be canvassed in the present chapter. Our attention will be given primarily to answering the following question: To what extent should government control economic matters in a country? The economic perspective is the single most important one since matters of economics affect all other aspects of life in important ways. "Money talks," as the saying goes. The first three reading selections in this chapter address the economic perspective of government control. The fourth selection is on the issue of paternalism and is not addressed to the economic perspective.

How much control over economic matters should government have? It will be convenient to think of all the major answers to this question as falling on a continuum. The two most basic answers lie at each end of the continuum with all other possible answers somewhere in between these two extremes. At the one extreme is the negative answer that government should not control economic matters at all. Government control should be absolutely minimal, having as its proper functions only those of police, law, courts and military. This view of government is proposed in the reading selection by Ayn Rand, who is a defender of what is most often referred to as *laissez-faire capitalism*, or complete free enterprise.

Under laissez-faire capitalism the government does not own or run any businesses (with the possible exception of some that are needed for national defense); it does not control trade within a country or among countries; it does not run schools, libraries, or hospitals; it does not provide any welfare programs or any old-age pensions; it makes no attempts at all to redistribute income through a progressive income tax; and so on. What government does is to protect people's lives, liberties, and property (*if* they have any property). Everything else is left in the hands of private individuals, who—once the police, law courts, and military are paid for through taxes—are free to keep all the money that they make. They are free to buy insurance against unemployment, sickness, and old age; and they are free, if they choose, to give money to anyone whom they believe deserves it or needs it. Rand does not oppose charity as long as it is completely voluntary. She has said elsewhere that what she is defending is a separation of economic matters and government that is as complete as our present separation of church and state.

At the opposite extreme from laissez-faire capitalism is *socialism*, according to which government should control all or most economic matters. The government should own all or most businesses and it should control all trade, prices, wages, employment, production, welfare, education, hospitals, and so on. Under socialism, or complete socialism, no significant economic decisions are made by private individuals, but are all made as a consequence of government policies and government planning.

Now, it may seem that no one would want socialism since no one would want to give such nearly complete power to government. It may seem that socialism must inevitably produce a totalitarian government. However, in order to understand why it is that socialism is seriously defended by some writers, such as Michael Harrington in a reading selection for this chapter, it is necessary to distinguish between two versions of it: totalitarian socialism and what is usually called "democratic socialism," which is what Harrington defends. Harrington rejects the kind of totalitarian socialism that is to be found in most present-day communist countries such as the Soviet Union and the People's Republic of China. He defends in its place a system of government whereby all, or most, economic decisions are made by the government, but since the government is completely democratic, those decisions represent what the majority of the people want. In defending his version of socialism, Harrington is not defending the idea that the federal government in the United States should run major corporations. What Harrington wants is for the public to elect the directors of large corporations. In general, what Harrington wants is for people to have much more input into the decisions of business that affect them.

The views of Rand and Harrington are the two extreme positions that are being seriously defended by present-day writers. In between the positions of Rand and Harrington are a great number of compromise positions that are usually lumped together under the heading of *mixed economies*; that is, mixtures of some of the aspects of both laissez-faire capitalism and socialism. One such position is defended by Bertrand Russell, who believes that government should own and run some businesses, but by no means all businesses. Needless to say, at the present time in the United States we live under a type of mixed economy. The extent of government control in the United States currently is less than what Russell defends; that is, it is closer to the laissez-faire capitalist end of the continuum than is the position of Russell. Russell's position is modeled on the post-war British system, which is much more socialistic than is the present system in the United States.

Thus far we have said nothing about the sorts of arguments that are made in defense of laissez-faire capitalism, socialism, or mixed economies. Possible grounds for defending the various positions can be stated in terms of the principles discussed in chapter 1. Traditionally, laissez-faire capitalism has been defended by an appeal to the principles of Rights and the Common Good, socialism has been defended by an appeal to the principles of Justice and the Common Good, and mixed economies by an appeal to all three of these principles.

Defenders of laissez-faire capitalism have very plausibly argued that it is the only type of governmental system that contains absolute guarantees of the rights to life, liberty, and the ownership of property. They have argued that under socialism or a mixed economy the government can always take part or all of a person's property in order to serve the general welfare, and that this infringes upon the right to own the property that a person has acquired through his or her own industry or good fortune. Furthermore, they have argued that personal liberty is infringed upon whenever the right to own property is infringed upon, since freedom is meaningless unless it is the freedom to do things and to control one's own property.

Beyond appealing to the Principle of Rights, defenders of laissez-faire capitalism have usually also argued that under capitalism a country has the best chance of becoming rich and that the *overall* level of wealth in a country will ensure the greatest good for the greatest number. People who are rich will be better off, but so also will almost everyone else, benefiting from the "trickle down" effect. This view was defended as early as the eighteenth century when Adam Smith in *The Wealth of Nations* said that an "Unseen Hand" guides a free enterprise society toward maximizing the common good of all.

On the other hand, defenders of socialism have very plausibly argued that it is the only type of government that contains an absolute guarantee that there will be distributive justice. They have argued that laissez-faire capitalism will inevitably produce very great inequalities in wealth since it is a system expressly designed to give the greatest monetary rewards to those with ability or good fortune.

Socialism, not capitalism, they argue, is a system designed to help the most those who most need help. In addition, defenders of socialism argue that it will produce the greatest good for the greatest number, not necessarily by producing the most wealth, but instead by providing for the most healthy psychological atmosphere in a country. Capitalism, they say, because it is geared toward competition, will produce alienation and exploitation of workers, while socialism, because it is geared toward meeting people's needs, will make them feel that they belong to a community.

The defense of various types of mixed economies will appeal to all three of the principles of Rights, Justice, and the Common Good. Those who defend a mixed economy want to achieve some type of balance among these principles where some recognition can be given to each of them and where, in regard to the Principle of the Common Good, some recognition can be given to all of the factors important to achieving the common good.

The final reading selection in the chapter is a discussion of paternalism, the view that government should in some sense be a parent to its citizens. That is, government should not simply leave people alone to do whatever *they* believe is best for themselves, but instead should give some more positive direction to their lives. Dworkin's discussion of paternalism is within the context of the presently existing mixed economy in the United States.

Corporate Collectivism: A System of Social Injustice

I do not believe the United States is a free enterprise society. I think the people who want us to use this term wish to rationalize and defend rather than describe the society. There may have been a free enterprise society for five minutes in Great Britain in the nineteenth century, although personally I doubt it. It certainly has never existed in the United States. Among other things, we fought a war, the Civil War, in which one of the issues was free trade versus protectionism. Protectionism won. The infrastructure of our society, the railroad, was built by federal donations. The United States today does not have a free enterprise society in any kind of Adam Smithian sense of the term. Rather, we have gigantic oligopolies administering prices, shaping tastes, working together with an all-pervasive government which follows corporate priorities. Therefore, I suggest that rather than using the term "free enterprise" to describe our system we get closer to reality and call it "corporate collectivism."

I maintain that corporate collectivism, in its historical thrust and tendency, is not compatible with social justice. Moreover, I am absolutely certain that capitalism—corporate collectivism in its latest phase— is coming to an end. As a socialist, I am not necessarily filled with joy at this prospect because there is more than one end possible to this society. The question before us is not *whether* there is going to be a collectivist society in the future, because that is already decided. The real question is, what kind of collectivist society will there be? When we play around with terms like "free enterprise," we ask the wrong questions and cannot possibly come up with the right answers.

I will approach these issues from three angles. First of all, I shall look at capitalist society in its classic and heroic phase, and give a very procapitalist analysis, because that has always been part of the socialist case. I want to do so not simply to praise capitalism, but to understand its origins as they impinge on the second point, contemporary capitalism. That will allow me to proceed to the third point, the alternatives to contemporary capitalism. In short, I shall touch on the past, the present, and the future of capitalist society in the United States, or, for that matter, in the world.

Michael Harrington, a professor of political science at the City University of New York, is well known for his many books and articles on topics regarding socialism, capitalism, and labor.

I Capitalism:

An Historical Perspective

First of all, the capitalist past. Capitalist society is the greatest human society that has ever existed. It started in the West, of course, and brought to the world a number of enormous benefits. I state this without any hint or trace of irony. The capitalist revolution saw the spread of science and rationality. It gave democracy to the world. It gave the world a concept of individual worth that did not exist on anything like a mass basis in any precapitalist society.

Nonetheless, my enthusiasm should not be taken as too procapitalist. One of my criticisms of the *Communist Manifesto* is that Marx is excessively procapitalist, that he gives the capitalism of his age credit for prodigious things which it was not to accomplish for another fifty years. In talking about the accomplishments of capitalism, I also want to recognize its Hobbesian reality, which is so marvelously described in the *Leviathan* and its Darwinian struggle of each against all. The capitalist revolution was not pretty; yet on balance, it was one of the most magnificent advances that humankind has ever made.

Now, I want to understand that advance. What was the principle of precapitalist society? What was the big gulf between capitalist society and previous societies? In all that went before capitalism, the political, the economic, and the social were one. The individual's economic position in society was not independent of his political and social position. If you were a duke, a slave owner, or a member of a mandarin bureaucracy, there was a seamless whole which defined you politically, economically, and socially. In the Middle Ages, a

young serf did not decide to try to become a duke. There was only one institution in the Middle Ages which made that possible—the Catholic Church. But, by and large, it was a society where one's economic, political, and social position was fixed at birth and was part of this whole.

As a result, in these precapitalist societies (what Marx called Oriental despotism, and slave society, as well as feudal society), the ruling class had a very specific way of extracting an economic surplus from the direct producers. Feudal society achieved the surplus through force sanctioned by religion. That is to say, the serf labored free for the lord or gave him rent in kind, or later gave him money, because the lord was his military protector, sanctioned by God, in an order which was accepted from the very start.

Capitalism did a number of absolutely magnificent things in terms of those precapitalist societies. First it separated, or as a system had a tendency to separate, the political, economic, and social orders. Properly speaking, social classes are an invention of capitalism. Before capitalism, there were "estates," caste systems, hereditary systems. Only with the advent of capitalism and its separation of the political, economic, and social systems was there a society that offered individual choice, the possibility of mobility, and an opportunity to rise above the status of one's birth.

Second, capitalism normally did not extract a surplus by naked force. That was a great advance. Capitalism is the system which uses economic means to get the surplus out of the direct producer. That is to say, it is based on a contract. It is absolutely true that the contract is utterly unfair, but it is nevertheless a contract, and that means a rise, so to speak, in civil liberties—a rise in the ethical and personal level of the society. The contract is unfair because, in the capitalist mythology, a free worker with nothing to sell but his labor freely contracts with someone who has enormous wealth and who is able to gain a surplus through that contract. It is an unfair contract, but it is a system that works on the basis of contract and law rather than force. It is a system which prefers to organize itself democratically. There are times when this system will leave democracy—the Germany of Adolf Hitler is one of the most monstrous and horrible examples—in a period of crisis. But normally, capitalist society prefers to function democratically with certain civil liberties. That is the second enormous contribution to society.

Third, capitalism discovered the social power of people working together. That, I submit, was its economic invention. Capitalism did not begin with a technological revolution. Indeed, capitalist technology—the technology of the sixteenth and seventeenth centuries during the origins of capitalism—was, on the whole, conservative and was borrowed from other cultures. We borrowed the compass, gunpowder, and the printing press. We borrowed something of enormous importance, Arabic numerals, from the Arabs, who had taken them from the Chinese. A modern society cannot be built on the basis of Roman numerals; it needs the zero concept and positional notation. We were technologically, perhaps, somewhat behind Chinese and Byzantine societies of the fifteenth century. What capitalism discovered was not technology; it discovered that allowing people to work together enormously increased their productivity. That was social invention. The discovery of the social nature of work, of people working together rather than in isolation, was the decisive moment in the rise of capitalism and again, an enormous contribution to humankind.

This brings me to the final point of this brief history: the capitalist system bases itself on a contradiction. It is a system which is increasingly and progressively social capitalism. Capitalism is a socializing system. It first socializes work, with entrepreneurs getting artisans together under a single roof, achieving certain economies of scale. Larger entrepreneurs socialize smaller entrepreneurs. There is a tendency toward concentration, toward monopoly, toward oligopoly, cartels, trusts—larger and larger units. Capitalism develops a revolutionary technology, with social consequences permeating the entire society. Henry Ford obviously is one of the great radicals, one of the great revolutionaries of modern life.

Capitalism is from the very first moment a world system. It reaches all over the world, destroys ancient cultures, and upsets the international balance. It tries to bring the entire world, every last person, into the same integrated unit. Capitalism is profoundly social and profoundly revolutionary. But at the same time that capitalism becomes more social, at the same time that the technological decisions today of a U. S. Steel or an IBM have more social consequences than most of the decisions of state legislatures, the system remains private in its decision making and its allocation of resources and benefits. And there, I suggest, is the genius of capitalism and the contradiction that will destroy it. Here I am using a paradox defined by Joseph Schumpeter, one of the great conservatives of the modern age, but I think it very much in the spirit of my good friend, Karl Marx, viz., that capitalism is destroyed by its success, not its failure. Capitalism so successfully socializes that the socialized world which it creates becomes incompatible with the institutional decision-making process in private hands.

Finally, I am perfectly aware that capitalism today is no longer run by individual entrepreneurs making personal decisions. I am perfectly aware that there are huge corporate bureaucracies, technostructures if you want. Of course, corporate bureaucracies tend to view profit maximizing on a much longer time span than a nineteenth century robber baron. But what I am saying is, for example, that the American automobile industry still considers the problem of pollution or the problem of automobile safety from the point of view of making as much money in a sophisticated way as it possibly can. This is in contradiction with the extremely social system which capitalism creates.

So my first point is this. Capitalism is a magnificent, revolutionary, and liberating system which, by its own success, becomes conservative and reactionary. It will bring about its own demise.

II Contemporary Capitalism

What about contemporary capitalism? I now move from general theorizing about the nature of capitalism to some current facts. I call our present system corporate collectivism. Its origins are to be found in three historical periods and the events associated with them. The first period was from about 1880 to 1900, when European and American capitalism went

through a crisis which it solved by monopolies, trusts, and by the intervention of the state, the beginning of the state's entrance into the economy.[1] The first move toward corporate collectivism is the end of the entrepreneurial capitalism at the end of the last century.

The second period was World War I, a tremendous watershed. Here I use the rather classical, conservative, contemporary economist Hicks as my source.[2] Hicks points out that during World War I, the government had to mobilize the war effort. This brought about the discovery of military socialism, the capacity of the state to administer the economy. There had been government intervention into the economy before World War I, particularly social welfare intervention under Bismarck in Germany and Lloyd George in Britain. But in World War I, government actually operated industries. For example, the railroads were run by the United States government. That was, Hicks says, the beginning of an administrative revolution in which the state learned its capacity for economic intervention.

The third period was during the Great Depression of the 1930's, when Keynesianism triumphed in its most conservative variant. In the 1930's, some nations began to understand that the government had to be responsible for the economic management of the macro-economy. A new

1. In this area, I would recommend to you a marvelous book. Though I think it is one of the greatest books of the twentieth century, it has not gotten all the attention it deserves: Rudolf Hilferding's *Finance Capital*. It is a book which an obscure Russian by the name of V. I. Lenin also found interesting.

2. John Hicks, *A Theory of Economic History*, Oxford University Press, 1969, p. 162.

role for government was defined in the 1930's, by two countries in particular. One was Nazi Germany, which solved the crisis of the Great Depression by a kind of military Keynesianism, by a fascist planned economy that eliminated unemployment but cost the world the horrors of genocide and World War II. The other practical demonstration of the power of the government to manage an economy was, of course, made by the Swedes, who were the first democratic people to think their way through the problems of capitalism and to solve the Depression of the 1930's. The Swedish people repaid the Swedish Socialist Party for that accomplishment by keeping it in office for forty-four years.

This Keynesian revolution in its democratic variant, particularly in its American variant, was conservative. Many in the United States, including conservatives, think that Keynes was some kind of radical. I suggest they read his life. Keynes was not only a theorist, he was a man who made money for himself and various charitable causes for which he worked as an investment advisor. Keynes was an upper-class aristocratic snob who regarded the workers as a bunch of boobs and who said that he was a Keynesian precisely because he was not a socialist.

Now there are Keynesians who, in my opinion, are much better than Keynes. But American conservatives will have to learn one of these days that the ideology of conservatism in the late twentieth century is Keynesianism or at least conservative Keynesianism. The point of Keynesianism was that the corporate infrastructure was fundamentally sound and that all the government did, merely by fiscal and monetary policy, was to match the macro-aggregates of supply and demand through public and private investment at a full employment level. But the assumption behind Keynes's policy, and particularly behind the Roosevelt New Deal version of Keynesianism, was that the basic investment decisions are made by corporations and that the government simply creates an environment in which they will be able to carry out that function.

So Keynesianism, I suggest, has this profoundly conservative aspect. It has another aspect—an aspect which makes any government, including a liberal government, a hostage to the corporations. I take a very wise sentence from a contemporary German sociologist, Klaus Hoffa: "The capitalist state is not itself a capitalist." That is to say, the capitalist state is dependent for the success of its policies on the private sector. In this society of supposed equals, some people are more equal than others. When a John Kennedy is elected in 1960 or a Jimmy Carter in 1976, they must assure themselves of the cooperation of the corporate community because that community makes investment decisions, and private investment decisions are the key to full employment.

I therefore suggest that the concept of "trickle down," the concept of the government rewarding the corporate rich more than anyone else, is not a policy of American society. It is *the* policy of American society. The policy is imposed upon this society by the fact that corporations are in charge of the investment process. Therefore, if one considers the Kennedy/Johnson tax cuts, as has Leon Keyserling, who was chairman of the Council of Economic Advisors under Truman, one finds that the rich received much more than anyone else. Indeed, I would suggest to you that the welfare state does much more for the corporate rich than for anybody else.

For now, I just want to focus on the fact that macroeconomic policy has to be pro-corporate. If we elected a government in the United States composed solely of left-wing trade union leaders, militant civil rights advocates, feminists and reformers, but kept corporations in charge of investment, that government would be nicer to corporations than to workers or minorities or women or to the people in general—not because it sold out but because that is the reality of government in our society. What I am saying is: the political freedom of society is profoundly restricted by the economic and social institutions. So it is that today in Great Britain a Socialist Chancellor of the Exchequer, a former member of the Young Communist League, is presiding over increasing unemployment and holding wages down as a socialist policy. Under the circumstances in Britain, corporate people are more important than working people; people in board rooms are more important than unemployed people. That is built in, I suggest, to this kind of society.

This leads me to a proposition about the kinds of decisions that are made in our society. I am not suggesting that there is a capitalist conspiracy, that there are a bunch of bloated plutocrats in top hats who sit around the table in the morning and say, "Let us now go and see how we can do harm to the weak and the poor in this society." What I am saying is that there is a structure of power that dictates pro-corporate outcomes to democratically elected representatives.

The transportation industry is an

example. Think of what we have done about transportation in this society in recent years. We started a federal highway program under Dwight Eisenhower in the late 1950's. I believe that it is probably, with the possible exception of Medicare, the most important social program of the United States since the New Deal. This program helped the middle class get out of the cities, isolated the cities, helped destroy the railroads, helped destroy mass transportation within the cities, isolated the poor, isolated the minorities, and was a profound contributor to the crisis which is now taking place in New York City. We are seeing the greatest city in the United States deteriorating and dying—in considerable measure because of the unintended and unplanned consequences of federal social investments in transportation, in housing, and in agriculture. We paid billions upon billions of dollars for the crisis in the United States that we are suffering today.

I could take that point and apply it to practically every department of government. But it is not because Eisenhower was an evil man, or because the Congress of the United States that went along with him was composed of evil men and women. We have a society in which one out of six workers is in some way involved in the automobile industry and in which three or four of the top ten major corporations are oil corporations. In such a society, it is just plain common sense to maximize the priorities of auto corporations and petroleum corporations rather than of working people, cities, minorities, women, and so on. This is built into the society; it is not conspiratorial.

Nonetheless, of course, there are conspiracies. The *Wall Street Journal*, which has a penchant for the idealization of greed and nastiness that never ceases to surprise me, came out with the following program for President Jimmy Carter: Cut down on social spending and increase tax exemptions for the corporate rich. The reason is that there is a capital shortage which the corporate rich discovered about two years ago. Nobody else has seen it, but Secretary Simon, President Ford, and the *Wall Street Journal* have been motivating programs for about two years on the basis of a nonexistent capital shortage. We are absolutely awash in liquidity in this country and the government is being asked to create more liquidity by giving privileges to the rich. There is that kind of conscious attempt to manipulate the system on behalf of the rich. But I will say that the *Wall Street Journal* probably believes that this policy would create the greatest happiness for the greatest number of people.

In conclusion, the issue before American society is not whether there will be national economic planning. We already have it. Our problem is that the plan on which we operate today proceeds according to the priorities of a hidden agenda. That hidden agenda, which has a remarkable consistency, is that government shall on all major decisions maximize corporate priorities. I suggest therefore that the issue is whether the plan will become democratic with a small "d," transparent and open, or whether it will remain bureaucratic and secret.

And, in terms of that point, one last unkind word for the American corporation. I believe the American corporation is now becoming decadent. The typical corporate executive, after reading the *Wall Street Journal* editorial in the morning about the glories of free enterprise and the free market system, immediately tries to figure how to get another subsidy from the government. There is a sense—and please understand me clearly, because there are enormous differences between the United States and the Soviet Union—but there is a sense in which executives in the United States are increasingly playing the role that commissars play in the Soviet Union. They act as a bureaucratic elite with a government at their disposal, taking money from the people to fulfill their priorities and their interests and to make their decisions.

My second point, then, is that capitalism, which was such a magnificent and revolutionary system, has by its very socialization now created a corporate collectivist society in which government and the corporations cooperate with the public's money on the basis of corporate priorities.

III. The Alternatives to Capitalism

What are the alternatives? What would be a perspective for freedom and social justice in the modern world? Now let me state at the outset that I am a socialist, a democratic socialist. That is, I do not regard any of the totalitarian societies which claim to be socialist as being socialist. I think they are bureaucratic collectivisms, not democratic and free collectivisms. But much of what I am going to say does not require that you be a socialist to agree with me. I hope everybody becomes a socialist. However, I would like to illuminate the minds of those who perversely will not go the whole way but are only willing to accept this or that reform. Many of the things that I am about to say are acceptable to any intelligent, humane liberal who does not want to transform the basic system but to make it better.

The principle of the alternative to corporate collectivism, it seems to me, is the democratization of economic and social decision making. This is the fundamental principle that one then wants to follow in absolutely every aspect of the society. Under capitalism, by an (I hope) imperishable conquest of the human spirit, the idea of political freedom came into being, and we are eternally in the debt of the capitalist society for that. But now the concept of freedom and democracy must be applied to areas in which capitalism never applied it. Unless we democratize our increasingly collectivist state, which acts on the basis of a hidden agenda, we will lose freedom. Therefore, I believe that the democratization of economic and social power is the fundamental principle.

Now let me suggest some very specific ways that this can be done. First, there is a very moderate bill to which the Democratic Party platform was formally committed in 1976 and which a good many Democrats are busily running away from as fast as they possibly can. The bill is the Hawkins-Humphrey Full Employment Bill. It is a bill for the most conservative modicum of liberal capitalist planning. It says that the President of the United States[3] every year will make an analysis of all the investment decisions, public and private, that can

be anticipated for that year, add up those investment decisions, and discover what level of unemployment will result, given the population, technology, and so on. If adult unemployment exceeds 3 percent, which in plainer English is about 4 percent total unemployment, then the President is required by law to present to the Congress in an annual message those programs which will make up the shortfall and reduce unemployment to 4 percent or 3 percent adult unemployment. It is a very modest bill. It is viewed in some quarters as being practically the equivalent of Bolshevism. But it would begin to attack the most outrageous and abiding evil in this society today, its high level of unemployment, which is not randomly distributed but particularly discriminates against minorities, youth, and women.

This would commit us to reduce unemployment to 4 percent over the next four years. Sweden last year had 1.4 percent unemployment. We have not had anything that good since World War II. The problem is that many people are now saying we cannot do that, and some of them are liberals. Charles Schultze of the Brookings Institution says, in effect, that American society requires 5 percent unemployment in order to function. He maintains that as soon as we get to 5.5 percent unemployment, the inflationary tendencies become so strong that we must give up our campaign against unemployment in order to fight inflation. This implies that the people composing that reserve army of the unemployed, as Marx would describe it—this reserve army which is disproportionately black, Hispanic, female, and young— will pay for the struggle against inflation.

---

3. It has one interesting syntactic feature: "The President of the United States, he or she." It is the first bill that I know of that makes the grammatical admission that it is possible for a woman to become President of the United States.

Now Schultze is absolutely right. If we accept American society today as an eternal given, we cannot achieve full employment without ruinous inflation. But the society is not an eternal given. One could, through the tax laws, redistribute wealth and have the corporate rich pay rather than the minorities, the females, and the young. One could have a redistribution income policy in the United States to deal with these problems. But this is the kind of issue that is not on the agenda. Here is a planning issue, a modest planning issue. A first tentative step is to have democratic decision making in the area of the economy. The achievement of this goal is going to take a tremendous struggle in this society, a struggle that is going to pit some of us against people who are Keynesian liberals but who say we need high unemployment to avoid inflation.

I view this Humphrey-Hawkins Bill, by the way, as only a first step. I think that we need a yearly national debate over the future. For example, the Auto Workers have raised a very interesting, profound question for the American society. In their 1976 contract negotiations, the UAW raised the question of the four-day week. I think we ought to have a debate in this society over something as important as that. Do we want to move from the five-day week to the four-day week as, among other things, a way of dealing with unemployment and environmental problems? It would mean we would take our increased productivity not totally in more commodities and goods, but in part in more leisure, which has its own problems but is less of a pollutant. We should have debates over these massive options. What we do in the society now is to back into the options on the basis of

corporate priorities without ever really facing the fundamental issues.

Another proposal, an exceedingly moderate proposal, is endorsed not simply by Ralph Nader but by George Cabot Lodge of the Harvard Business School. George Cabot Lodge comes from the family who talks to God. Lodge and Nader and a lot of other good people have proposed that we have public and employee representatives on the boards of directors of every major corporation in the United States. How long can we kid ourselves that there is a managerial prerogative of secrecy for a company which has as much influence over our lives as IBM or U.S. Steel or General Motors? If people in the United States could elect directors to the boards of the Fortune 500 industrial and financial corporations, it would be more significant than most of the votes cast for members of state legislatures because these corporations are more significant for your life. Why do we say that the introduction of new technology, the location of plants, policies toward women, policies toward minorities, are private matters? Why is it in the United States today that we give corporations that leave New York City a federal subsidy by investment tax credit for leaving? What we need is to democratize and transform the corporation itself.

Related to this, I believe we should aim to democratize work. Most people in this society do not like what they do most of the time. That is a terrible commentary on the society. If you ask most Americans, "Do you like your job?" they will answer yes because they understand that the question you are asking them is, "Do you like your job compared to having no job?" Surely they do. If you ask them the question the Department of

Health, Education and Welfare asked a couple of years back, "If you had to do it over again, would you take that job?" you find that most people in routine jobs, and particularly most blue collar people, do not like what they are doing.

Why do we not begin to change the way we work, for example, to allow workers to decide how to carry out a production process? One of the terrible things in American industry is that there are all kinds of workers who know how to do things better than the company does, but they have to hide it. If an automobile worker figures out a way to do something that is smarter than the way the company has figured it out, and he is quiet about it, he can bank two minutes of time on the production line and smoke a cigarette. But the foreman is walking around trying to figure out whether somebody has doped out a way to get two minutes from the company. So we lock up the productivity of our workers because they are caught in an antagonistic system in which they have to be crazy to give up their productivity so it can be expropriated by their boss. If we could begin to democratize the corporation, democratize work, democratize the economics of the society, perhaps we could get the benefit of some of that creativity.

As another point, I think we should have a Bureaucratic Relations Act in America, on the model of the National Labor Relations Act. The UAW has developed a very interesting institution called the Public Review Board. If a member of the UAW feels that somebody, some officer, some official of that union, has done him wrong, he has the right to appeal to an outside board not under the control of the union—a board which has

been in existence now since the mid-1950's and has on innumerable occasions overruled the president of the union and the international executive board. Every bureaucratic institution of a certain size should be required to have a public review board. I think every university should have one. I think every large corporation should be forced to have one so that whenever the citizen is put into the situation where there is bureaucracy, he has the right of appeal. The bureaucrats would not decide the appeals against themselves, which is what happens in most of American society. These are just a few ideas and examples, not anything like a comprehensive list. I am suggesting that we should democratize the society from top to bottom in all of its institutions. That is the alternative.

I admit that I have omitted an enormous dimension of the problem. I have omitted it because it opens up so many difficulties that could not possibly be dealt with in the space allowed. I refer to the fact that there is a world outside of the United States. I do not believe that it is going to be tolerable much longer for 6 percent of the people of the world to consume 40 percent of the resources. But I leave that aside, precisely because it is so important that I cannot take it up at any kind of length here.

In conclusion, I suggest three propositions. First, capitalism was a magnificent advance for mankind, but a contradictory advance because it was a system of private socialization. The socialization brought enormous successes, but the private socialization has brought us intolerable contradictions. Second, the contemporary manifestation of the contradictions of private socialization are seen in an American system that is not a free enterprise system but a corporate collectivist system in which government honestly, sincerely, and non-conspiratorially follows corporate priorities because they are natural in this society. Third, the alternative, the way to pursue freedom in the late twentieth century, is to democratize economic and social as well as political institutions.

If we ask: "Shall we have free enterprise or shall we have collectivism?" we have asked a meaningless question, because there is no free enterprise today. There can be no free enterprise given the scale of our technology, given the interdependence of our world. Richard Nixon planned as much as Lyndon Johnson. If Ronald Reagan had been elected President of the United States, he would have planned as much as Lyndon Johnson or anybody else. It is not that people sell out. This is the basic thrust of our society.

Therefore, I think the question, as is often the case, is at least as impor-

tant as the answer. I would reformulate the question and say the true question before us today in terms of freedom and social justice is: "Will the collectivist economic and social and political structure, which is emerging right now in front of our very eyes, be bureaucratically run by a united front of corporations and government on the basis of a hidden agenda moving toward a post-capitalist bureaucratic collectivist society run by the grandchildren of the executives?" Or is it possible for the collectivism which is emerging here and now to be democratized, to be subjected to the will of the people instead of its dominating the people? It is that second possibility that I am for, that I pose in terms of ethics and freedom and social justice. I am not sure it can prevail. I am not sure it will prevail. The one thing that I am sure of is that it is the only way for freedom to survive in the modern world.

C O M M E N T S ▪ Q U E S T I O N S

1. Historically, says Harrington, capitalism brought about some very good social changes:

   a. It tended to separate the political, economic, and social orders. Prior to the development of capitalism, in the Middle Ages, a person was born into a station in life that dictated what his or her political, economic, and social position would be.
   b. It tended to produce a society that was democratic and where "surplus wealth" was not produced by

   naked force but by workers who contracted to sell their labors.
   c. It "discovered that allowing people to work together enormously increased their productivity."

   Since the above listed points are clearly things to be said in favor of capitalism, why does Harrington still oppose capitalism so strongly? Does he point out enough bad points about capitalism to outweigh the good points?

2. What Harrington calls *corporate collectivism* has, he says, done a lot

of harm in large part because of unintended and unplanned consequences of government intervention and investment in the economy. For example, government support of the interstate highway system has contributed profoundly to the deterioration of New York City. This happened because the government favored the auto and petroleum industries over "working people, cities, minorities, women, and so on." Would Ayn Rand agree with this point?

3. According to Harrington, the best alternative to capitalism is democratic socialism, a system in which important economic policies should be decided by majority vote. As examples, people should vote on whether or not to have a four-day work week, and people in the United States should be able to elect directors to the boards of the Fortune 500 corporations. "What we need to do is democratize and transform the corporation itself." However, if people in the United States were able to elect the boards of directors of major corporations, is there reason to believe that the people elected would have the business expertise required to effectively run those corporations?

4. The main thing Harrington is attacking is the "trickle down" concept, in which the social policies that encourage corporations to become larger and more successful will eventually benefit everyone. Has Harrington shown that the trickle down concept does not work?

5. Harrington says that he is opposed to socialistic societies (such as the Soviet Union) that are totalitarian rather than democratic. Do you believe that there could be democratic socialist countries that could avoid the abuses of totalitarian ones?

A Y N   R A N D

The Nature of Government

A government is an institution that holds the exclusive power to *enforce* certain rules of social conduct in a given geographical area.

Do men need such an institution—and why?

Since man's mind is his basic tool of survival, his means of gaining knowledge to guide his actions—the basic condition he requires is the freedom to think and to act according to his rational judgment. This does not mean that a man must live alone and that a desert island is the environment best suited to his needs. Men can derive enormous benefits from dealing with one another. A social environment is most conducive to their successful survival—*but only on certain conditions.*

"The two great values to be gained from social existence are: knowledge and trade. Man is the only species that can transmit and expand his store of knowledge from generation to generation; the knowledge potentially available to man is greater than any one man could begin to acquire in his own lifespan; every man gains an incalculable benefit from the knowledge discovered by others. The second great benefit is the division of labor: it enables a man to devote his effort to a particular field of work and to trade with others who specialize in other fields. This form of cooperation allows all men who take part in it to achieve a greater knowledge, skill and productive return on their effort than they could achieve if each had to produce everything he needs, on a desert island or on a self-sustaining farm.

"But these very benefits indicate, delimit and define what kind of men can be of value to one another and in what kind of society: only rational, productive, independent men in a rational, productive, free society." ("The Objectivist Ethics.")

A society that robs an individual of the product of his effort, or enslaves him, or attempts to limit the freedom of his mind, or compels him to act against his own rational judgment—a society that sets up a conflict between its edicts and the requirements of man's nature—is not, strictly speaking, a society, but a mob held together by institutionalized gang-rule. Such a society destroys all the values of human coexistence, has no possible justification and represents, not a source of benefits, but the

---

Ayn Rand, who died in 1982, is best known for her very widely read novels, The Fountainhead *and* Atlas Shrugged, *and for her defense of the philosophy of Objectivism.*

---

deadliest threat to man's survival. Life on a desert island is safer than and incomparably preferable to existence in Soviet Russia or Nazi Germany.

If men are to live together in a peaceful, productive, rational society and deal with one another to mutual benefit, they must accept the basic social principle without which no moral or civilized society is possible: the principle of individual rights. (See Chapters 12 and 13.)

To recognize individual rights means to recognize and accept the conditions required by man's nature for his proper survival.

Man's rights can be violated only by the use of physical force. It is only by means of physical force that one man can deprive another of his life, or enslave him, or rob him, or prevent him from pursuing his own goals, or compel him to act against his own rational judgment.

The precondition of a civilized society is the barring of physical force from social relationships—thus establishing the principle that if men wish to deal with one another, they may do so only by means of *reason*: by discussion, persuasion and voluntary, uncoerced agreement.

The necessary consequence of man's right to life is his right to self-defense. In a civilized society, force may be used only in retaliation and only against those who initiate its use. All the reasons which make the initiation of physical force an evil, make the retaliatory use of physical force a moral imperative.

If some "pacifist" society renounced the retaliatory use of force, it would be left helplessly at the mercy of the first thug who decided to be immoral. Such a society would achieve the opposite of its intention:

instead of abolishing evil, it would encourage and reward it.

If a society provided no organized protection against force, it would compel every citizen to go about armed, to turn his home into a fortress, to shoot any strangers approaching his door—or to join a protective gang of citizens who would fight other gangs, formed for the same purpose, and thus bring about the degeneration of that society into the chaos of gang-rule, i.e., rule by brute force, into the perpetual tribal warfare of prehistorical savages.

The use of physical force—even its retaliatory use—cannot be left at the discretion of individual citizens. Peaceful coexistence is impossible if a man has to live under the constant threat of force to be unleashed against him by any of his neighbors at any moment. Whether his neighbors' intentions are good or bad, whether their judgment is rational or irrational, whether they are motivated by a sense of justice or by ignorance or by prejudice or by malice—the use of force against one man cannot be left to the arbitrary decision of another.

Visualize, for example, what would happen if a man missed his wallet, concluded that he had been robbed, broke into every house in the neighborhood to search it, and shot the first man who gave him a dirty look, taking the look to be a proof of guilt.

The retaliatory use of force requires *objective* rules of evidence to establish that a crime has been committed and to *prove* who committed it, as well as *objective* rules to define punishments and enforcement procedures. Men who attempt to prosecute crimes, without such rules, are a lynch mob. If a society left the retaliatory use of force in the hands of individual citizens, it would degenerate into mob rule, lynch law and an endless series of bloody private feuds or vendettas.

If physical force is to be barred from social relationships, men need an institution charged with the task of protecting their rights under an *objective* code of rules.

This is the task of a government— of a *proper* government—its basic task, its only moral justification and the reason why men do need a government.

A government is the means of placing the retaliatory use of physical force under objective control—i.e., under objectively defined laws.

The fundamental difference between private action and governmental action—a difference thoroughly ignored and evaded today—lies in the fact that a government holds a monopoly on the legal use of physical force. It has to hold such a monopoly, since it is the agent of restraining and combating the use of force; and for that very same reason, its actions have to be rigidly defined, delimited and circumscribed; no touch of whim or caprice should be permitted in its performance; it should be an impersonal robot, with the laws as its only motive power. If a society is to be free, its government has to be controlled.

Under a proper social system, a private individual is legally free to take any action he pleases (so long as he does not violate the rights of others), while a government official is bound by law in his every official act. A private individual may do anything except that which is legally *forbidden*; a government official may do nothing except that which is legally *permitted*.

This is the means of subordinating

"might" to "right." This is the American concept of "a government of laws and not of men."

The nature of the laws proper to a free society and the source of its government's authority are both to be derived from the nature and purpose of a proper government. The basic principle of both is indicated in The Declaration of Independence: "to secure these [individual] rights, governments are instituted among men, deriving their just powers from the consent of the governed. . ."

Since the protection of individual rights is the only proper purpose of a government, it is the only proper subject of legislation: all laws must be based on individual rights and aimed at their protection. All laws must be *objective* (and objectively justifiable): men must know clearly, and in advance of taking an action, what the law forbids them to do (and why), what constitutes a crime and what penalty they will incur if they commit it.

The source of the government's authority is "the consent of the governed." This means that the government is not the *ruler*, but the servant or *agent* of the citizens; it means that the government as such has no rights except the rights *delegated* to it by the citizens for a specific purpose.

There is only one basic principle to which an individual must consent if he wishes to live in a free, civilized society: the principle of renouncing the use of physical force and delegating to the government his right of physical self-defense, for the purpose of an orderly, objective, legally defined enforcement. Or, to put it another way, he must accept *the separation of force and whim* (any whim, including his own).

Now what happens in case of a disagreement between two men about an undertaking in which both are involved?

In a free society, men are not forced to deal with one another. They do so only by voluntary agreement and, when a time element is involved, by *contract*. If a contract is broken by the arbitrary decision of one man, it may cause a disastrous financial injury to the other—and the victim would have no recourse except to seize the offender's property as compensation. But here again, the use of force cannot be left to the decision of private individuals. And this leads to one of the most important and most complex functions of the government: to the function of an arbiter who settles disputes among men according to objective laws.

Criminals are a small minority in any semicivilized society. But the protection and enforcement of contracts through courts of civil law is the most crucial need of a peaceful society; without such protection, no civilization could be developed or maintained.

Man cannot survive, as animals do, by acting on the range of the immediate moment. Man has to project his goals and achieve them across a span of time; he has to calculate his actions and plan his life long-range. The better a man's mind and the greater his knowledge, the longer the range of his planning. The higher or more complex a civilization, the longer the range of activity it requires—and, therefore, the longer the range of contractual agreements among men, and the more urgent their need of protection for the security of such agreements.

Even a primitive barter society could not function if a man agreed to trade a bushel of potatoes for a basket of eggs and, having received the eggs, refused to deliver the potatoes. Visualize what this sort of whim-directed action would mean in an industrial society where men deliver a billion dollars' worth of goods on credit, or contract to build multimillion-dollar structures, or sign ninety-nine-year leases.

A unilateral breach of contract involves an indirect use of physical force: it consists, in essence, of one man receiving the material values, goods or services of another, then refusing to pay for them and thus keeping them by force (by mere physical possession), not by right—i.e., keeping them without the consent of their owner. Fraud involves a similarly indirect use of force: it consists of obtaining material values without their owner's consent, under false pretenses or false promises. Extortion is another variant of an indirect use of force: it consists of obtaining material values, not in exchange for values, but by the threat of force, violence or injury.

Some of these actions are obviously criminal. Others, such as a unilateral breach of contract, may not be criminally motivated, but may be caused by irresponsibility and irrationality. Still others may be complex issues with some claim to justice on both sides. But whatever the case may be, all such issues have to be made subject to objectively defined laws and have to be resolved by an impartial arbiter, administering the laws, i.e., by a judge (and a jury, when appropriate).

Observe the basic principle governing justice in all these cases: it is the principle that no man may obtain any values from others without the owners' consent—and, as a corollary, that a man's rights may not be left at the mercy of the unilateral decision, the arbitrary choice, the irrationality, *the whim* of another man.

Such, in essence, is the proper purpose of a government: to make social existence possible to men, by protecting the benefits and combating the evils which men can cause to one another.

The proper functions of a government fall into three broad categories, all of them involving the issues of physical force and the protection of men's rights: *the police*, to protect men from criminals—*the armed services*, to protect men from foreign invaders—*the law courts*, to settle disputes among men according to objective laws.

These three categories involve many corollary and derivative issues—and their implementation in practice, in the form of specific legislation, is enormously complex. It belongs to the field of a special science: the philosophy of law. Many errors and many disagreements are possible in the field of implementation, but what is essential here is the principle to be implemented: the principle that the purpose of law and of government is the protection of individual rights.

C O M M E N T S ■ Q U E S T I O N S

---

1. Rand's theory of government is based upon a moral philosophy of *rational self-interest*, in which each person ought to pursue his or her own rational self-interest and in which each person can best pursue his or her rational self-interest in a society where the function of government is limited to the protection of basic individual rights. Do you believe that the moral philosophy that underlies Rand's theory of government is correct?

2. Both Rand and Michael Harrington are very much concerned about the abuses to be found in the government of the United States at the present time. Both say in effect that we do not at present live under a system of free enterprise (which Rand favors but Harrington rejects). To what extent would Rand and Harrington be in agreement in their critiques of contemporary society?

3. Is Rand's view of human nature adequate? Specifically, is her emphasis upon the role of reason in human life correct?

B E R T R A N D   R U S S E L L

Control and Initiative: Their Respective Spheres

The *primary* aims of government, I suggest, should be three: security, justice, and conservation. These are things of the utmost importance to human happiness, and they are things which only government can bring about. At the same time, no one of them is absolute; each may, in some circumstances, have to be sacrificed in some degree for the sake of a greater degree of some other good. I shall say something about each in turn.

Security, in the sense of protection of life and property, has always been recognized as one of the primary purposes of the state. Many states, however, while safeguarding law-abiding citizens against other citizens, have not thought it necessary to protect them against the state. Wherever there is arrest by administrative order, and punishment without due process of law, private people have no security, however firmly the state may be established. And even insistence on due process of law is insufficient, unless the judges are independent of the executive. This order of ideas was to the fore in the seventeenth and eighteenth centuries, under the slogan "liberty of the subject" or "rights of man." But the "liberty" and the "rights" that were sought could only be secured by the state, and then only if the state was of the kind that is called "liberal." It is

only in the West that this liberty and these rights have been secured.

To inhabitants of Western countries in the present day, a more interesting kind of security is security against attacks by hostile states. This is more interesting because it has not been secured, and because it becomes more important year by year as methods of warfare develop. This kind of security will only become possible when there is a single world government with a monopoly of all the major weapons of war. I shall not enlarge upon this subject, since it is somewhat remote from my theme. I will only say, with all possible emphasis, that unless and until mankind have achieved the security of a single government for the world, everything else of value, of no matter what kind, is precarious, and may at any moment be destroyed by war.

Economic security has been one of the most important aims of modern British legislation. Insurance against

---

Bertrand Russell, who died in 1970 at the age of 98, was one of the best known and most influential of twentieth century philosophers. He wrote a great many books on a wide variety of topics. Among the many honors which he received were the Order of Merit in 1949 and the Nobel Prize for Literature in 1950.

From Bertrand Russell, "Control and Initiative: Their Respective Spheres," in *Authority and the Individual* (Beacon, 1960). Reprinted by permission of George Allen & Unwin (Publishers) Ltd.

unemployment, sickness, and destitution in old age, has removed from the lives of wage-earners a great deal of painful uncertainty as to their future. Medical security has been promoted by measures which have greatly increased the average length of life and diminished the amount of illness. Altogether, life in Western countries, apart from war, is very much less dangerous than it was in the eighteenth century, and this change is mainly due to various kinds of governmental control.

Security, though undoubtedly a good thing, may be sought excessively and become a fetish. A secure life is not necessarily a happy life; it may be rendered dismal by boredom and monotony. Many people, especially while they are young, welcome a spice of dangerous adventure, and may even find relief in war as an escape from humdrum safety. Security by itself is a negative aim inspired by fear; a satisfactory life must have a positive aim inspired by hope. This sort of adventurous hope involves risk and therefore fear. But fear deliberately chosen is not such an evil thing as fear forced upon a man by outward circumstances. We cannot therefore be content with security alone, or imagine that it can bring the millennium.

And now as to justice:

Justice, especially economic justice, has become, in quite recent times, a governmental purpose. Justice has come to be interpreted as equality, except where exceptional merit is thought to deserve an exceptional but still moderate reward. *Political* justice, i.e., democracy, has been aimed at since the American and French Revolutions, but *economic* justice is a newer aim, and requires a much greater amount of governmen-

tal control. It is held by Socialists, rightly, in my opinion, to involve state ownership of key industries and considerable regulation of foreign trade. Opponents of Socialism may argue that economic justice can be too dearly bought, but no one can deny that, if it is to be achieved, a very large amount of state control over industry and finance is essential.

There are, however, limits to economic justice which are, at least tacitly, acknowledged by even the most ardent of its Western advocates. For example, it is of the utmost importance to seek out ways of approaching economic equality by improving the position of the less fortunate parts of the world, not only because there is an immense sum of unhappiness to be relieved, but also because the world cannot be stable or secure against great wars while glaring inequalities persist. But an attempt to bring about economic equality between Western nations and Southeast Asia, by any but gradual methods, would drag the more prosperous nations down to the level of the less prosperous, without any appreciable advantage to the latter.

Justice, like security, but to an even greater degree, is a principle which is subject to limitations. There is justice where all are equally poor as well as where all are equally rich, but it would seem fruitless to make the rich poorer if this was not going to make the poor richer. The case against justice is even stronger if, in the pursuit of equality, it is going to make even the poor poorer than before. And this might well happen if a general lowering of education and a diminution of fruitful research were involved. If there had not been economic injustice in Egypt and Babylon, the art of writing would never have been invented. There is, however, no *necessity*, with modern methods of production, to perpetuate economic injustice in industrially developed nations in order to promote progress in the arts of civilization. There is only a danger to be borne in mind, not, as in the past, a technical impossibility.

I come now to my third head, conservation.

Conservation, like security and justice, demands action by the state. I mean by "conservation" not only the preservation of ancient monuments and beauty-spots, the upkeep of roads and public utilities, and so on. These things are done at present, except in time of war. What I have chiefly in mind is the preservation of the world's natural resources. This is a matter of enormous importance, to which very little attention has been paid. During the past hundred and fifty years mankind has used up the raw materials of industry and the soil upon which agriculture depends, and this wasteful expenditure of natural capital has proceeded with ever-increasing velocity. In relation to industry, the most striking example is oil. The amount of accessible oil in the world is unknown, but is certainly not unlimited; already the need for it has reached the point at which there is a risk of its contributing to bringing about a third World War. When oil is no longer available in large quantities, a great deal will have to be changed in our way of life. If we try to substitute atomic energy, that will only result in exhaustion of the available supplies of uranium and thorium. Industry as it exists at present depends essentially upon the expenditure of natural capital, and cannot long continue in its present prodigal fashion.

Even more serious, according to some authorities, is the situation in regard to agriculture, as set forth with great vividness in Mr. Vogt's *Road to Survival*. Except in a few favored areas (of which Western Europe is one), the prevailing methods of cultivating the soil rapidly exhaust its fertility. The growth of the Dust Bowl in America is the best known example of a destructive process which is going on in most parts of the world. As, meantime, the population increases, a disastrous food shortage is inevitable within the next fifty years unless drastic steps are taken. The necessary measures are known to students of agriculture, but only governments can take them, and then only if they are willing and able to face unpopularity. This is a problem which has received far too little attention. It must be faced by anyone who hopes for a stable world without internecine wars—wars which, if they are to ease the food shortage, must be far more destructive than those we have already endured, for during both the World Wars the population of the world increased. This question of a reform in agriculture is perhaps the most important that the governments of the near future will have to face, except the prevention of war.

I have spoken of security, justice, and conservation as the most essential of governmental functions, because these are things that only governments can bring about. I have not meant to suggest that governments should have no other functions. But in the main their functions in other spheres should be to encourage non-governmental initiative, and to create opportunities for its exercise in beneficent ways. There are anarchic and criminal forms of initiative which cannot be tolerated in a civilized society. There are other forms of initiative, such as that of the well-established inventor, which everybody recognizes to be useful. But there is a large intermediate class of innovators of whose activities it cannot be known in advance whether the effects will be good or bad. It is particularly in relation to this uncertain class that it is necessary to urge the desirability of freedom to experiment, for this class includes all that has been best in the history of human achievement.

Uniformity, which is a natural result of state control, is desirable in some things and undesirable in others. In Florence, in the days before Mussolini, there was one rule of the roads in the town and the opposite rule in the surrounding country. This kind of diversity was inconvenient, but there were many matters in which Fascism suppressed a *desirable* kind of diversity. In matters of opinion it is a good thing if there is vigorous discussion between different schools of thought. In the mental world there is everything to be said in favor of a

truggle for existence, leading, with luck, to a survival of the fittest. But if there is to be mental competition, there must be ways of limiting the means to be employed. The decision should not be by war, or by assassination, or by imprisonment of those holding certain opinions, or by preventing those holding unpopular views from earning a living. Where private enterprise prevails, or where there are many small states, as in Renaissance Italy and eighteenth-century Germany, these conditions are to some extent fulfilled by rivalry between different possible patrons. But when, as has tended to happen throughout Europe, states become large and private fortunes small, traditional methods of securing intellectual diversity fail. The only method that remains available is for the state to hold the ring and establish some sort of Queensberry rules by which the contest is to be conducted.

C O M M E N T S ■ Q U E S T I O N S

1. Russell says that government should have the following three primary aims because they are things that only government can bring about:
   a. *Security*, which means two things. First, it means the protection of life and property against citizens who break laws, government that abuses its power, and foreign invaders. Second, security means economic protection against unemployment, sickness, and destitution in old age.
   b. *Justice*, which also means two

things. First, in the political sense it means democracy. Second, in the economic sense it means aiming toward equality. This requires a certain degree of socialism since it requires "state ownership of key industries and considerable regulation of foreign trade."
   c. *Conservation*, which means primarily the preservation of the world's natural resources.
   Is Russell correct? Would Michael Harrington agree with Russell?
2. Government, says Russell, may have other functions than security,

justice, and conservation, but in these other spheres the main function of government should be to encourage nongovernmental initiative. Government should especially encourage intellectual initiative and diversity. Government needs to support the publishing by private corporations of books and newspapers and it needs to encourage research institutions such as universities. Is Russell correct about this? Why shouldn't publishing be left wholly to the private sector? What arguments, if any, might be made in defense of the view that all universities should be private?

3. One of the main points that Russell stresses is the very same main point that Ayn Rand stresses. Russell calls it the need in society for freedom of initiative, but he seems to have in mind essentially the same thing as what Rand refers to as the freedom to use reasoning ability and be productive. Is Russell correct in insisting that freedom of initiative requires that government be extremely limited?

4. Would Rand agree with Russell's statement that governmental power should be concentrated as much as possible at the local level? Would Michael Harrington agree?

GERALD DWORKIN

Paternalism

Neither one person, nor any number of persons, is warranted in saying to another human creature of ripe years, that he shall not do with his life for his own benefit what he chooses to do with it. *Mill*

I do not want to go along with a volunteer basis. I think a fellow should be compelled to become better and not let him use his discretion whether he wants to get smarter, more healthy or more honest. *General Hershey*

I

By paternalism I shall understand roughly the interference with a person's liberty of action justified by reasons referring exclusively to the welfare, good, happiness, needs, interests or

Gerald Dworkin is a professor of philosophy at the University of Illinois, Chicago Circle. He has written widely in the areas of social and political philosophy and the philosophy of law.

values of the person being coerced. One is always well-advised to illustrate one's definitions by examples but it is not easy to find "pure" examples of paternalistic interferences. For almost any piece of legislation is justified by several different kinds of reasons and even if historically a piece of legislation can be shown to have been introduced for, purely paternalistic motives, it may be that advocates of the legislation with an anti-paternalistic outlook can find sufficient reasons justifying the legislation without appealing to the reasons which were originally adduced to support it. Thus, for example, it may be that the original legislation requiring motorcyclists to wear safety helmets was introduced for purely paternalistic reasons. But the Rhode Island Supreme Court recently upheld such legislation on the grounds that it was "not persuaded that the legislature is powerless to prohibit individuals from pursuing a course of conduct which could conceivably result in their becoming public charges," thus clearly introducing reasons of a quite different kind. Now I regard this decision as being based on reasoning of a very dubious nature but it illustrates the kind of problem one has in finding examples. The following is a list of the kinds of interferences I have in mind as being paternalistic.

II

1. Laws requiring motorcyclists to wear safety helmets when operating their machines.
2. Laws forbidding persons from swimming at a public beach when lifeguards are not on duty.
3. Laws making suicide a criminal offense.

4. Laws making it illegal for women and children to work at certain types of jobs.
5. Laws regulating certain kinds of sexual conduct, e.g., homosexuality among consenting adults in private.
6. Laws regulating the use of certain drugs which may have harmful consequences to the user but do not lead to anti-social conduct.
7. Laws requiring a license to engage in certain professions with those not receiving a license subject to fine or jail sentence if they do engage in the practice.
8. Laws compelling people to spend a specified fraction of their income on the purchase of retirement annuities. (Social Security)
9. Laws forbidding various forms of gambling (often justified on the grounds that the poor are more likely to throw away their money on such activities than the rich who can afford to).
10. Laws regulating the maximum rates of interest for loans.
11. Laws against duelling.

In addition to laws which attach criminal or civil penalties to certain kinds of action there are laws, rules, regulations, decrees, which make it either difficult or impossible for people to carry out their plans and which are also justified on paternalistic grounds. Examples of this are:

1. Laws regulating the types of contracts which will be upheld as valid by the courts, e.g., (an example of Mill's to which I shall return) no man may make a valid contract for perpetual involuntary servitude.
2. Not allowing as a defense to a charge of murder or assault the consent of the victim.
3. Requiring members of certain religious sects to have compulsory

blood transfusions. This is made possible by not allowing the patient to have recourse to civil suits for assault and battery and by means of injunctions.

4. Civil commitment procedures when these are specifically justified on the basis of preventing the person being committed from harming himself. (The D.C. Hospitalization of the Mentally Ill Act provides for involuntary hospitalization of a person who "is mentally ill, and because of that illness, is likely to injure *himself* or others if allowed to remain at liberty." The term injure in this context applies to unintentional as well as intentional injuries.)

5. Putting fluorides in the community water supply.

All of my examples are of existing restrictions on the liberty of individuals. Obviously one can think of interferences which have not yet been imposed. Thus one might ban the sale of cigarettes, or require that people wear safety-belts in automobiles (as opposed to merely having them installed) enforcing this by not allowing motorists to sue for injuries even when caused by other drivers if the motorist was not wearing a seat-belt at the time of the accident.

I shall not be concerned with activities which though defended on paternalistic grounds are not interferences with the liberty of persons, e.g., the giving of subsidies in kind rather than in cash on the grounds that the recipients would not spend the money on the goods which they really need, or not including a $1000 deductible provision in a basic protection automobile insurance plan on the ground that the people who would elect it could least afford it. Nor shall I be concerned with meas-

ures such as "truth-in-advertising" acts and the Pure Food and Drug legislation which are often attacked as paternalistic but which should not be considered so. In these cases all that is provided—it is true by the use of compulsion—is information which it is presumed that rational persons are interested in having in order to make wise decisions. There is no interference with the liberty of the consumer unless one wants to stretch a point beyond good sense and say that his liberty to apply for a loan without knowing the true rate of interest is diminished. It is true that sometimes there is sentiment for going further than providing information, for example when laws against usurious interest are passed preventing those who might wish to contract loans at high rates of interest from doing so, and these measures may correctly be considered paternalistic.

III

Bearing these examples in mind let me return to a characterization of paternalism. I said earlier that I meant by the term, roughly, interference with a person's liberty for his own good. But as some of the examples show the class of persons whose good is involved is not always identical with the class of persons whose freedom is restricted. Thus in the case of professional licensing it is the practitioner who is directly interfered with and it is the would-be patient whose interests are presumably being served. Not allowing the consent of the victim to be a defense to certain types of crime primarily affects the would-be aggressor but it is the interests of the willing victim that we are trying to protect. Sometimes a person may fall into both classes as would be the case if we banned the manufacture and sale of cigarettes and a given manufacturer happened to be a smoker as well.

Thus we may first divide paternalistic interferences into "pure" and "impure" cases. In "pure" paternalism the class of persons whose freedom is restricted is identical with the class of persons whose benefit is intended to be promoted by such restrictions. Examples: the making of suicide a crime, requiring passengers in automobiles to wear seat-belts, requiring a Christian Scientist to receive a blood transfusion. In the case of "impure" paternalism in trying to protect the welfare of a class of persons we find that the only way to do so will involve restricting the freedom of other persons besides those who are benefitted. Now it might be thought that there are no cases of "impure" paternalism since any such case could always be justified on non-paternalistic grounds, i.e., in terms of preventing harms to others. Thus we might ban cigarette manufacturers from continuing to manufacture their product on the grounds that we are preventing them from causing illness to others in the same way that we prevent other manufacturers from releasing pollutants into the atmosphere, thereby causing danger to the members of the community. The difference is, however, that in the former but not the latter case the harm is of such a nature that it could be avoided by those individuals affected if they so chose. The incurring of the harm requires, so to speak, the active cooperation of the victim. It would be mistaken theoretically and hypocritical in practice to assert that our interference in such cases is just like our interference in standard cases of

protecting others from harm. At the very least someone interfered with in this way can reply that no one is complaining about his activities. It may be that impure paternalism requires arguments or reasons of a stronger kind in order to be justified since there are persons who are losing a portion of their liberty and they do not even have the solace of having it be done "in their own interest." Of course in some sense, if paternalistic justifications are ever correct then we are protecting others, we are preventing some from injuring others, but it is important to see the differences between this and the standard case.

Paternalism then will always involve limitations on the liberty of some individuals in their own interest but it may also extend to interferences with the liberty of parties whose interests are not in question.

IV

Finally, by way of some more preliminary analysis, I want to distinguish paternalistic interferences with liberty from a related type with which it is often confused. Consider, for example, legislation which forbids employees to work more than, say, 40 hours per week. It is sometimes argued that such legislation is paternalistic for if employees desired such a restriction on their hours of work they could agree among themselves to impose it voluntarily. But because they do not the society imposes its own conception of their best interests upon them by the use of coercion. Hence this is paternalism.

Now it may be that some legislation of this nature is, in fact, paternalistically motivated. I am not denying that. All I want to point out is that there is another possible way of justifying such measures which is not paternalistic in nature. It is not paternalistic because as Mill puts it in a similar context such measures are "required not to overrule the judgment of individuals respecting their own interest, but to give effect to that judgment: they being unable to give effect to it except by concert, which concert again cannot be effectual unless it receives validity and sanction from the law."[1]

The line of reasoning here is a familiar one first found in Hobbes and developed with great sophistication by contemporary economists in the last decade or so. There are restrictions which are in the interests of a class of persons taken collectively but are such that the immediate interest of each individual is furthered by his violating the rule when others adhere to it. In such cases the individuals involved may need the use of compulsion to give effect to their collective judgment of their own interest by guaranteeing each individual compliance by the others. In these cases compulsion is not used to achieve some benefit which is not recognized to be a benefit by those concerned, but rather because it is the only feasible means of achieving some benefit which *is* recognized as such by all concerned. This way of viewing matters provides us with another characterization of paternalism in general. Paternalism might be thought of as the use of coercion to achieve a good which is not recognized as such by those persons for whom the good is intended. Again while this formulation captures the

heart of the matter—it is surely what Mill is objecting to in *On Liberty*—the matter is not always quite like that. For example when we force motorcyclists to wear helmets we are trying to promote a good—the protection of the person from injury—which is surely recognized by most of the individuals concerned. It is not that a cyclist doesn't value his bodily integrity; rather, as a supporter of such legislation would put it, he either places, perhaps irrationally, another value or good (freedom from wearing a helmet) above that of physical well-being or, perhaps, while recognizing the danger in the abstract, he either does not fully appreciate it or he underestimates the likelihood of its occurring. But now we are approaching the question of possible justifications of paternalistic measures and the rest of this essay will be devoted to that question.

* * * * *

VI

We might begin looking for principles governing the acceptable use of paternalistic power in cases where it is generally agreed that it is legitimate. Even Mill intends his principles to be applicable only to mature individuals, not those in what he calls "non-age". What is it that justifies us in interfering with children? The fact that they lack some of the emotional and cognitive capacities required in order to make fully rational decisions. It is an empirical question to just what extent children have an adequate conception of their own present and future interests but there is not much doubt that there are many deficiencies. For example it is very difficult for a child to defer gratification for any considerable period of time.

---

1. J. S. Mill, *Principles of Political Economy* (New York: P. F. Collier and Sons, 1900), p. 442.

Given these deficiencies and given the very real and permanent dangers that may befall the child it becomes not only permissible but even a duty of the parent to restrict the child's freedom in various ways. There is however an important moral limitation on the exercise of such parental power which is provided by the notion of the child eventually coming to see the correctness of his parent's interventions. Parental paternalism may be thought of as a wager by the parent on the child's subsequent recognition of the wisdom of the restrictions. There is an emphasis on what could be called future-oriented consent—on what the child will come to welcome, rather than on what he does welcome.

The essence of this idea has been incorporated by idealist philosophers into various types of "real-will" theory as applied to fully adult persons. Extensions of paternalism are argued for by claiming that in various respects, chronologically mature individuals share the same deficiencies in knowledge, capacity to think rationally, and the ability to carry out decisions that children possess. Hence in interfering with such people we are in effect doing what they would do if they were fully rational. Hence we are not really opposing their will, hence we are not really interfering with their freedom. The dangers of this move have been sufficiently exposed by Berlin in his Two Concepts of Liberty. I see no gain in theoretical clarity nor in practical advantage in trying to pass over the real nature of the interferences with liberty that we impose on others. Still the basic notion of consent is important and seems to me the only acceptable way of trying to delimit an area of justified paternalism.

Let me start by considering a case where the consent is not hypothetical in nature. Under certain conditions it is rational for an individual to agree that others should force him to act in ways which, at the time of action, the individual may not see as desirable. If, for example, a man knows that he is subject to breaking his resolves when temptation is present, he may ask a friend to refuse to entertain his requests at some later stage.

A classical example is given in the *Odyssey* when Odysseus commands his men to tie him to the mast and refuse all future orders to be set free, because he knows the power of the Sirens to enchant men with their songs. Here we are on relatively sound ground in later refusing Odysseus' request to be set free. He may even claim to have changed his mind but since it is just such changes that he wished to guard against we are entitled to ignore them.

A process analogous to this may take place on a social rather than individual basis. An electorate may mandate its representatives to pass legislation which when it comes time to "pay the price" may be unpalatable. I may believe that a tax increase is necessary to halt inflation though I may resent the lower pay check each month. However in both this case and that of Odysseus the measure to be enforced is specifically requested by the party involved and at some point in time there is genuine consent and agreement on the part of those persons whose liberty is infringed. Such is not the case for the paternalistic measures we have been speaking about. What must be involved here is not consent to specific measures but rather consent to a system of government, run by elected representatives, with an understanding that they may act to safeguard our interests in certain limited ways.

I suggest that since we are all aware of our irrational propensities, deficiencies in cognitive and emotional capacities and avoidable and unavoidable ignorance it is rational and prudent for us to in effect take out "social insurance policies." We may argue for and against proposed paternalistic measures in terms of what fully rational individuals would accept as forms of protection. Now, clearly since the initial agreement is not about specific measures we are dealing with a more-or-less blank check and therefore there have to be carefully defined limits. What I am looking for are certain kinds of conditions which make it plausible to suppose that rational men could reach agreement to limit their liberty even when other men's interests are not affected.

Of course as in any kind of agreement schema there are great difficulties in deciding what rational individuals would or would not accept. Particularly in sensitive areas of personal liberty, there is always a danger of the dispute over agreement and rationality being a disguised version of evaluative and normative disagreement.

Let me suggest types of situations in which it seems plausible to suppose that fully rational individuals would agree to having paternalistic restrictions imposed upon them. It is reasonable to suppose that there are "goods" such as health which any person would want to have in order to pursue his own good—no matter how that good is conceived. This is an argument that is used in connection with compulsory education for children but it seems to me that it can be extended to other goods which have

this character. Then one could agree that the attainment of such goods should be promoted even when not recognized to be such, at the moment, by the individuals concerned.

An immediate difficulty that arises stems from the fact that men are always faced with competing goods and that there may be reasons why even a value such as health—or indeed life—may be overridden by competing values. Thus the problem with the Christian Scientist and blood transfusions. It may be more important for him to reject "impure substances" than to go on living. The difficult problem that must be faced is whether one can give sense to the notion of a person irrationally attaching weights to competing values.

Consider a person who knows the statistical data on the probability of being injured when not wearing seat belts in an automobile and knows the types and gravity of the various injuries. He also insists that the inconvenience attached to fastening the belt every time he gets in and out of the car outweighs for him the possible risks to himself. I am inclined in this case to think that such a weighing is irrational. Given his life-plans which we are assuming are those of the average person, his interests and commitments already undertaken, I think it is safe to predict that we can find inconsistencies in his calculations at some point. I am assuming that this is not a man who for some conscious or unconscious reasons is trying to injure himself nor is he a man who just likes to "live dangerously." I am assuming that he is like us in all the relevant respects but just puts an enormously high negative value on inconvenience—one which does not seem comprehensible or reasonable.

It is always possible, of course to assimilate this person to creatures like myself. I, also, neglect to fasten my seat belt and I concede such behavior is not rational but not because I weigh the inconvenience differently from those who fasten the belts. It is just that having made (roughly) the same calculation as everybody else I ignore it in my actions. [Note: a much better case of weakness of the will than those usually given in ethics texts.] A plausible explanation for this deplorable habit is that although I know in some intellectual sense what the probabilities and risks are I do not fully appreciate them in an emotionally genuine manner.

We have two distinct types of situation in which a man acts in a non-rational fashion. In one case he attaches incorrect weights to some of his values; in the other he neglects to act in accordance with his actual preferences and desires. Clearly there is a stronger and more persuasive argument for paternalism in the latter situation. Here we are really not—by assumption—imposing a good on another person. But why may we not extend our interference to what we might call evaluative delusions? After all in the case of cognitive delusions we are prepared, often, to act against the expressed will of the person involved. If a man believes that when he jumps out the window he will float upwards—Robert Nozick's example—would not we detain him, forcibly if necessary? The reply will be that this man doesn't wish to be injured and if we could convince him that he is mistaken as to the consequences of his action he would not wish to perform the action. But part of what is involved in claiming that a man who doesn't fasten his seat-belts is attaching an irrational weight to the inconvenience of fastening them is that if he were to be involved in an accident and severely injured he would look back and admit that the inconvenience wasn't as bad as all that. So there is a sense in which if I could convince him of the consequences of his action he also would not wish to continue his present course of action. Now the notion of consequences being used here is covering a lot of ground. In one case it's being used to indicate what will or can happen as a result of a course of action and in the other it's making a prediction about the future evaluation of the consequences—in the first sense—of a course of action. And whatever the difference between facts and values—whether it be hard and fast or soft and slow—we are genuinely more reluctant to consent to interferences where evaluative differences are the issue. Let me now consider another factor which comes into play in some of these situations which may make an important difference in our willingness to consent to paternalistic restrictions.

Some of the decisions we make are of such a character that they produce changes which are in one or another way irreversible. Situations are created in which it is difficult or impossible to return to anything like the initial stage at which the decision was made. In particular some of these changes will make it impossible to continue to make reasoned choices in the future. I am thinking specifically of decisions which involve taking drugs that are physically or psychologically addictive and those which are destructive of one's mental and physical capacities.

I suggest we think of the imposition of paternalistic interferences in situations of this kind as being a kind of insurance policy which we take out against making decisions which are far-reaching, potentially dangerous and irreversible. Each of these factors is important. Clearly there are many decisions we make that are relatively irreversible. In deciding to learn to play chess I could predict in view of my general interest in games that some portion of my free-time was going to be pre-empted and that it would not be easy to give up the game once I acquired a certain competence. But my whole life-style was not going to be jeopardized in an extreme manner. Further it might be argued that even with addictive drugs such as heroin one's normal life plans would not be seriously interfered with if an inexpensive and adequate supply were readily available. So this type of argument might have a much narrower scope than appears to be the case at first.

A second class of cases concerns decisions which are made under extreme psychological and sociological pressures. I am not thinking here of the making of the decision as being something one is pressured into—e.g., a good reason for making duelling illegal is that unless this is done many people might have to manifest their courage and integrity in ways in which they would rather not do so—but rather of decisions such as that to commit suicide which are usually made at a point where the individual is not thinking clearly and calmly about the nature of his decision. In addition, of course, this comes under the previous heading of all-too-irrevocable decision. Now there are practical steps which a society could take if it wanted to decrease the possibility of suicide—for example not paying social security

benefits to the survivors or as religious institutions do, not allowing such persons to be buried with the same status as natural deaths. I think we may count these as interferences with the liberty of persons to attempt suicide and the question is whether they are justifiable.

Using my argument schema the question is whether rational individuals would consent to such limitations. I see no reason for them to consent to an absolute prohibition but I do think it is reasonable for them to agree to some kind of enforced waiting period. Since we are all aware of the possibility of temporary states, such as great fear or depression, that are inimical to the making of well-informed and rational decisions, it would be prudent for all of us if there were some kind of institutional arrangement whereby we were restrained from making a decision which is (all too) irreversible. What this would be like in practice is difficult to envisage and it may be that if no practical arrangements were feasible then we would have to conclude that there should be no restriction at all on this kind of action. But we might have a "cooling off" period, in much the same way that we now require couples who file for divorce to go through a waiting period. Or, more far-fetched, we might imagine a Suicide Board composed of a psychologist and another member picked by the applicant. The Board would be required to meet and talk with the person proposing to take his life, though its approval would not be required.

A third class of decisions—these classes are not supposed to be disjoint—involves dangers which are either not sufficiently understood or appreciated correctly by the persons involved. Let me illustrate, using the example of cigarette smoking, a number of possible cases.

1. A man may not know the facts—e.g., smoking between 1 and 2 packs a day shortens life expectancy 6.2 years, the costs and pain of the illness caused by smoking, etc.

2. A man may know the facts, wish to stop smoking, but not have the requisite will-power.

3. A man may know the facts but not have them play the correct role in his calculation because, say, he discounts the danger psychologically because it is remote in time and/or inflates the attractiveness of other consequences of his decision which he regards as beneficial.

In case 1 what is called for is education, the posting of warnings, etc. In case 2 there is no theoretical problem. We are not imposing a good on someone who rejects it. We are simply using coercion to enable people to carry out their own goals. (Note: There obviously is a difficulty in that only a subclass of the individuals affected wish to be prevented from doing what they are doing.) In case 3 there is a sense in which we are imposing a good on someone since given his current appraisal of the facts he doesn't wish to be restricted. But in another sense we are not imposing a good since what is being claimed—and what must be shown or at least argued for—is that an accurate accounting on his part would lead him to reject his current course of action. Now we all know that such cases exist, that we are prone to disregard dangers that are only possibilities, that immediate pleasures are often magnified and distorted.

If in addition the dangers are

severe and far-reaching we could agree to allowing the state a certain degree of power to intervene in such situations. The difficulty is in specifying in advance, even vaguely, the class of cases in which intervention will be legitimate.

A related difficulty is that of drawing a line so that it is not the case that all ultra-hazardous activities are ruled out, e.g., mountain-climbing, bull-fighting, sports-car racing, etc. There are some risks—even very great ones—which a person is entitled to take with his life.

A good deal depends on the nature of the deprivation—e.g., does it prevent the person from engaging in the activity completely or merely limit his participation—and how important to the nature of the activity is the absence of restriction when this is weighed against the role that the activity plays in the life of the person. In the case of automobile seat belts, for example, the restriction is trivial in nature, interferes not at all with the use or enjoyment of the activity, and does, I am assuming, considerably reduce a high risk of serious injury. Whereas, for example, making mountain climbing illegal prevents completely a person engaging in an activity which may play an important role in his life and his conception of the person he is.

In general the easiest cases to handle are those which can be argued about in the terms which Mill thought to be so important—a concern not just for the happiness or welfare, in some broad sense, of the individual but rather a concern for the autonomy and freedom of the person. I suggest that we would be most likely to consent to paternalism in those instances in which it preserves and enhances for the individual his ability to rationally consider and carry out his own decisions.

I have suggested in this essay a number of types of situations in which it seems plausible that rational men would agree to granting the legislative powers of a society the right to impose restrictions on what Mill calls "self-regarding" conduct. However, rational men knowing something about the resources of ignorance, ill-will and stupidity available to the law-makers of a society—a good case in point is the history of drug legislation in the United States—will be concerned to limit such intervention to a minimum. I suggest in closing two principles designed to achieve this end.

In all cases of paternalistic legislation there must be a heavy and clear burden of proof placed on the authorities to demonstrate the exact nature of the harmful effects (or beneficial consequences) to be avoided (or achieved) and the probability of their occurrence. The burden of proof here is twofold—what lawyers distinguish as the burden of

going forward and the burden of persuasion. That the authorities have the burden of going forward means that it is up to them to raise the question and bring forward evidence of the evils to be avoided. Unlike the case of new drugs where the manufacturer must produce some evidence that the drug has been tested and found not harmful, no citizen has to show with respect to self-regarding conduct that it is not harmful or promotes his best interests. In addition the nature and cogency of the evidence for the harmfulness of the course of action must be set at a high level. To paraphrase a formulation of the burden of proof for criminal proceedings—better 10 men ruin themselves than one man be unjustly deprived of liberty.

Finally I suggest a principle of the least restrictive alternative. If there is an alternative way of accomplishing the desired end without restricting liberty then although it may involve great expense, inconvenience, etc. the society must adopt it.

C O M M E N T S ▪ Q U E S T I O N S

1. Near the beginning of the article Dworkin gives a list of the major sorts of paternalist laws that are presently in effect in the United States or that are actively being proposed for passage. Which, if any, of these laws do you believe is particularly important and ought to be in effect? Which, if any, of these laws do you believe ought not to be in effect at all?

2. Some people have argued that

there are no "pure" cases of paternalism, that is, cases where "the class of persons whose freedom is restricted is identical with the class of persons whose benefit is intended to be promoted by such restrictions." According to Dworkin, laws that require the use of automobile seat belts are examples of pure paternalism; but a counterargument to that is that *everyone* in a society is affected when the extent of serious injuries due to auto accidents is higher than it would otherwise be. Insurance rates go up, greater demands are placed upon police and paramedics, etc. Is Dworkin right to insist upon a distinction between pure and impure cases of paternalism?

3. What arguments would Ayn Rand give in opposition to Dworkin's defense of a limited sort of paternalism?
4. Has Dworkin achieved the best possible balance among basic moral principles in defending his own position?

R E A D I N G S

Ackerman, Bruce A. *Social Justice in The Liberal State.* New Haven, Conn.: Yale University Press, 1971.

Fisk, Milton. *Ethics and Society: A Marxist Interpretation of Value.* New York: New York University Press, 1980.

Friedman, David. *The Machinery of Freedom.* New York: Harper and Row, 1973.

Friedman, Milton. *Capitalism and Freedom.* Chicago: University of Chicago Press, 1962.

Harrington, Michael. *Socialism.* New York: Bantam Books, 1970.

Heilbroner, Robert L. *Marxism For and Against.* New York: W. W. Norton & Co., 1980.

Held, Virginia, ed. *Property, Profits, and Economic Justice.* Belmont, Calif.: Wadsworth, 1980.

Hospers, John. *Libertarianism.* Los Angeles: Nash Publishing, 1971.

Nozick, Robert. *Anarchy, State, and Utopia.* New York: Basic Books, 1974.

Rescher, Nicholas. *Distributive Justice.* Indianapolis: Bobbs-Merrill, 1966.

Rothbard, Murray N. *For A New Liberty.* London: Collier Macmillan, 1973.

Sartorius, Rolf. *Individual Conduct and Social Norms.* Encino, Calif.: Dickenson, 1975.

———. "Paternalism and Restrictions on Liberty." In *And Justice For All*, edited by Tom Regan and Donald Van De Veer. Totowa, N.J.: Rowman and Littlefield, 1982.

Singer, Peter. *Practical Ethics.* Cambridge: Cambridge University Press, 1979.

Sterba, James P. *The Demands of Justice.* Notre Dame: University of Notre Dame Press, 1980.

———, ed. *Justice: Alternative Political Perspectives.* Belmont, Calif.: Wadsworth, 1980.

The World of Business

he most basic issue in business ethics is the question of whether pursuing profits within legal limits is always, or usually, morally good. Three essentially different answers have been given in recent years by well-known writers on business ethics.

The first answer is the affirmative position, taken by John Hospers in a selection from his book *Libertarianism*, which is reprinted in the present chapter. Hospers argues that (1) everyone has a moral right to the legal pursuit of profit and (2) that an economic system that sanctions and encourages the legal pursuit of profit will be more efficient than other systems. In effect, the two arguments given by Hospers appeal to the Principle of Rights and the Principle of the Common Good, respectively. There is another argument that has been widely made and that is a different form of appeal to the Principle of the Common Good. This is the claim that widespread legal pursuit of profit will produce an important social good that cannot be produced in any other way: namely, it will produce a form of pluralism in the power structure of society. It will produce strong businesses competing against each other and a healthy opposition between the power of business, on the one hand, and the power of government on the other.

The second answer is the negative position, which in this chapter is taken by Alan H. Goldman. He rejects both of the arguments given by Hospers. Goldman does not mention the pluralism argument, but it is clear from what he says in his lengthy article (only a part of which is included here) that he would reject this argument on the ground that the harm that is produced by the unrestricted legal pursuit of profit outweighs any benefits—such as social pluralism—that it may also produce. In stating his position, Goldman says that the moral function of a business manager is "not strongly role-differentiated." By this he means that business managers ought to follow the same moral principles as everyone else and cannot defend their actions by claiming that the legal pursuit of profit is moral in itself.

The third answer is what has sometimes been called the "neutral" or "non-moral" position, according to which the legal pursuit of profit is best evaluated from a morally neutral point of view. This position was defended a few years ago by Albert Carr in an article that attracted much attention.[1] In the article, Carr defends what he calls "business bluffing," by which he means the use of deception in business. He claims that deception is very widespread and is, moreover, an essential part of the legal pursuit of profits. Carr says that business bluffing is not ethical, which may make it appear that he is in agreement with Goldman. But Carr's view is actually quite distinct from Goldman's since he believes that even though deception in business is not ethical, nevertheless it should be practiced by people in business.

As Carr sees it, business is best understood as a sort of game, like poker, that has its own rules. Unless the rules are followed, a person playing the game will have little chance at success. The basic rule of the business game is that profit should always be sought as long as no laws are being broken. Therefore, if a person chooses to play the game, but holds back from the legal pursuit of profit because of a moral reservation from his or her private life—for example, regarding deception in advertising—then the person is likely to lose the game. He or she might as well not play at all.

It should be easy enough to see that Carr's position is not *really* morally neutral. A business manager can always ask, why should I play the business game? This is a moral question. He or she can also ask, must I play the game exactly as others—who may believe that they are playing it in a morally neutral fashion—are playing it? This, of course, is also a moral question. The business manager can also ask, should I not attempt, in some small way at least, to reform the game if that appears to be morally desirable? To this question, Goldman would say yes.

While Carr's position is not, after all, morally neutral, it does provide a good illustration of an important fact about business ethics. Namely, that there are two important types of questions that are quite distinct from each other. First, there are questions about *business practices*, procedures that are routinely or commonly followed in the business world. For instance, is it morally acceptable for a business executive to make use of a certain amount of deception in advertising? Is it morally acceptable to sell products such as cigarettes, which are harmful to people's health, as long as people know that the products are harmful and still choose to buy them? Is it morally acceptable to use political influence to obtain contracts, as long as no laws are broken? These and many similar questions have to do with various aspects of the business world today.

In contrast to questions about the morality of business practices, there are questions about what *individuals* should do when faced with the choice between following or not following particular business practices. For example, let us assume that you are a business executive and that a certain type of deceptive advertising practice is widespread in your industry. Should you use the same kind of ads yourself? Your competitors will go on using the same types of ads regardless of what you do. That is, the general practice in question will not be affected by your decision to follow it or not to follow it. Should you take the risk of possibly reducing your company's profits?

It is important to see the extent to which the second question is independent of the first question. An executive may believe that the practice of using deceptive ads is morally wrong, but may also nevertheless believe he ought to continue using such ads. He may give any of several different reasons for believing he is morally justified in using such ads. He may explain that the company cannot afford to stop using them, since its share of the market is slipping, and going out of business means losing a valuable product along with hundreds of jobs; or he may personally be unable to afford to take the risk involved, since he may lose his job and be forced to take his children out of college, etc.

Hosper's intention is to give a moral defense of the general practice of business. He would not, of course, defend every specific business practice; what he would defend is the overall orientation of business practices to the legal pursuit of profit. Goldman is in favor of very significant moral reform of certain general business practices.

A further distinction can be made that will help to clarify what business ethics is all about. The two types of questions to be found in business ethics, which are referred to above, can be distinguished from the type of question to be found in a discussion of the limits and nature of government, which is the subject of the previous chapter. From one perspective, the two chapters deal with many of the same issues, since, to give the most important example, both are concerned with questions about profit making. The primary difference is that chapter 7 treats the issue of profit making in the context of what the best overall type of government should be (capitalist, socialist, or mixed economy), while the present chapter raises questions *within* the perspective of our contemporary society, which is a type of mixed economy.

Needless to say, the basic questions of business ethics would be significantly different if we lived under a different type of economic system such as socialism. Hence, chapter 7 is much more theoretical than the present chapter. Also, chapter 7 has much more to do with questions about what should or should not be made legal, such as private ownership of major corporations. Questions in business ethics may also deal with legal issues, but largely as a matter of fine tuning the present legal system. An example would be the question of whether new laws should be passed to place further restrictions upon deceptive advertising.

What we have, then, are three different types of questions:

1. those pertaining to the morality of the broad structure of society,
2. those pertaining to the morality of practices within a given type of society,
3. those pertaining to the morality of an individual's choice as to whether he or she will go along with a given social practice.

As we have seen, a person can choose to follow, or not follow, a given social practice independently of accepting or not accepting the practice as such. Likewise, a person can approve or disapprove of a practice independently of whether the person approves or disapproves of the broad structure of the society in which the practice is found. Goldman, for example, would like to see certain business practices changed; but it does not follow from this that he would also want to change the basic structure of contemporary society in which the practices in question are to be found. In order for someone to be able to argue as Goldman does, that the legal pursuit of profits is not morally defensible, that person need not have serious objections to the type of competitive mixed economy that contemporary business operates within. It is possible to accept the basic structure of society, but also to maintain that the pursuit of profit needs moral restraints in addition to the presently existing legal ones.

It is also possible to *reject* the basic structure of society on moral grounds, but accept for the most part the legal pursuit of profit. This, in fact, is what Hospers does in his book *Libertarianism*. In that book, Hospers argues against a mixed economy and defends something close to pure laissez-faire capitalism (a definition of which can be found in the introduction to chapter 7).

The final two reading selections in the present chapter regard specific issues in business ethics. The paper by Robert Arrington is a discussion of arguments pro and con regarding contemporary advertising practices. The paper by Gene G. James is an examination of an employee's duty to inform the public of harmful practices carried out by the company or institution for which the employee works.

Notes

1. Albert Carr, "Is Business Bluffing Ethical?" *Harvard Business Review,* Jan.-Feb. 1968, pp. 143–153.

J O H N   H O S P E R S

Profits and Liberty

"He's earning too much—take it away from him!" "A hundred thousand a year while some people in the world are hungry? Nobody ought to be allowed to earn that much!" Such remarks are made, and they have a "humanitarian" sound. Yet, as I shall try to show, they result from ignorance of the function of profits in an economy: and to the extent that the suggestion is followed, the result is poverty for everyone.

In a free economy—one in which wages, costs, and prices are left to the competitive market—profits have a very important function: they help to decide what products shall be made, of what kinds, and in what amounts. It is the hope of profits that leads people to make the products (or

John Hospers, who is a professor of philosophy at the University of Southern California, is very well known for his publications on a diversity of topics in philosophy, especially aesthetics, ethics, and political philosophy. He is editor of The Monist.

From John Hospers, *Libertarianism*. Reprinted by permission of the author. First publication was by Nash Publishing Co., Los Angeles, 1971.

provide the services): if little or nothing can be made from producing them, or not enough to justify the risk of investing the capital, the product will not be made; but the more one hopes to make from it, the more people will bend over backwards to produce it. The hope of profits channels the factors of production, causing products to be made in whatever quantities the public demands. In a state-controlled economy, controlled by bureaucrats, nothing at all may be made of a certain product much in demand, because the ruling decision-makers have decided simply not to make it; and at the same time, millions of other things that nobody wants may be produced, again because of a bureaucratic decision. And the bureaucracy need not to respond to public demand. But in a free-enterprise economy, the producer who does not respond to public demand will soon find his warehouse full of unsalable products and his business bankrupt.

The hope of profits also makes for an enormous increase in the efficiency of production, for, other things being equal, the most efficient producer—the one who can cut out waste and motivate his workers to produce the most and best products—will earn the highest profits. And is there any reason why these profits should not be applauded? To the consumer, these profits mean that the industry producing the goods he wants is healthy and nicely functioning—one that can continue to deliver the goods, and probably for at least as low a price as its competitors, since otherwise more customers would have turned to the competitor. To the workers, profits of their employer mean that the employer is doing a good job for his customers—good

enough so that they keep buying his product—and thus that they, the employees, are more secure in their jobs, and are more likely to receive higher wages in the future than are the employees of a company that is just barely making it. And as for the enterprisers, who can honestly say that they do not deserve the profits they received? First, they are risk-takers: they risked their capital to start the business, and had they lost no one would have helped them. Second, they spent not only their money (and borrowed money) on the enterprise, but, in most cases, years of their lives, involving planning, down to the last detail of production, the solution of intractable problems having to do with materials, supplies, and availability of trained help. Third, they anticipated the market, and did so more expertly than their competitors, for in order to make profits they had to have the right amount of merchandise at the right places for sale at the right time. Fourth, they provided the consumer a product or service (they could not *force* the consumer to buy from them; the consumer voluntarily elected to buy), in quantity—for a price, of course (after all his time and effort, should the enterpriser give it away, or sell it without receiving a return on it?), but nevertheless they provided it at a price which the consumer was willing to pay.

But the public, or a large segment of it, becomes envious and bitter, seeing that the man makes a profit. Perhaps the envious man has tried to start a business himself and lost it; or perhaps he just lost his job or can't pay some of his bills, and sees the employer living in a large luxurious house; in any case, he doesn't understand what side his bread is buttered on, for he doesn't realize that if the employer couldn't keep going, he himself would have no job. For whatever reason, he curses the employer because the man has a larger annual income than he does. Never mind that the employer took the risks, made the innumerable decisions (any one of which could have wrecked the business), and made *his* job possible in the first place: he, the employer, must be brought down to the worker's level. So he curses him, envies him, and votes for higher taxes for his employer, which, if passed, will mean that the employer won't expand his business and hire extra employees, and in fact may even have to cut it down some, even including his (the worker's) job. Officially, his line is that the employer's profits are ill-got. And yet when one examines it carefully, the complaint is groundless and absurd.

Suppose that an enterprise can make a thousand dollars in profits by a certain amount of capital investment; let us call this amount of investment C. Suppose also there is a second enterprise, less efficiently run than the first, which can only make that same amount of profit by investing twice the capital—2C. People will then say that the first, the efficient, manager, is reaping an excessive profit. For on the same investment of capital he can make twice the profits as his sloppy competitor; and for this his profits are branded as "excessive." But this is absurd: the efficient producer who gets more profits has more money to convert into plant expansion, more reserve for research so that he can improve his product, more wherewithal to reduce consumer prices and still make a healthy profit, thus benefiting the consumer with lower costs. The consumer ought to be anxious to have the most

efficient producer possible; for only in that way can he be sure of getting the best possible product at the lowest possible price. By producing efficiently, the producer can undercut his competitors and thus benefit the consumer, while at the same time earning larger profits by capturing a larger share of the market for himself. We should applaud, not condemn, efficient production.

Add to this the fact that our present insane tax laws penalize the producer for his profits, and thus penalize efficiency. "Taxing profits is tantamount to taxing success in best serving the public. . . . The smaller the input (of money) required for the production of an article becomes, the more of the scarce factors of production is left for the production of other articles. But the better an entrepreneur succeeds in this regard, the more he is vilified, and the more he is soaked by taxation. Increasing costs per unit of output, that is, waste, is praised as a virtue."[2]

There would not be any profits but for the eagerness of the public to acquire the merchandise offered for sale by the successful entrepreneur. But the same people who scramble for these articles vilify the businessman and call his profit ill-got.

One of the main functions of profits is to shift the control of capital to those who know how to employ it in the best possible way for the satisfaction of the public. The more profits a man earns, the greater his wealth consequently becomes, the more influential does he become in the conduct of business affairs. Profit and loss are the instruments by means of which the consumers pass the direction of production activities into the hands of

2. Ludwig von Mises, *Planning for Freedom* (South Holland, Ill.: Libertarian Press, 1952), p. 121.

those who are best fit to serve them. Whatever is undertaken to curtail or to confiscate profits, impairs this function. The result of such measures is to loosen the grip the consumers hold over the course of production. The economic machine becomes, from the point of view of the people, less efficient and less responsive.[3]

Many people are so envious of, and bitter against, the man who earns a large salary or makes large profits, that they are unable to stand back impartially and try to understand what the role of profit is in an economy, and how it tends to increase everyone's income, not merely that of the man who receives it.

The man who receives a salary of $100,000 a year from his company— why does he get it? If he rendered no service, or if the company gained $10,000 as a consequence of hiring him, they would never pay him the $100,000. If they did, their costs of production overhead would be that much higher and they would have to charge more for their product (thus causing consumers to buy another brand instead) or absorb the cost somewhere else. Even if the man saved them just $100,000 a year, it would be no gain to them—they would just break even with him. But if his services save them $1,000,000 a year, then paying him the $100,000 is well worth it—and they would gladly pay him more in order to keep him. People who begrudge him the salary should ask, "Am *I* ingenious enough to save the company over $100,000 a year, if it hired me?"

Now the man who does the employing: let us say that his business is successful and through the years he

has become a millionaire. Special venom is reserved by the populace for such men, but this is entirely without justification. If he got a million a year as salary for some tax-supported office, or in graft from the taxpayers' money, then they would have a right to complain; for they would have to work that much harder to make up the difference. But if he gets a profit of a million a year *on the free market*, there is no cause for complaint. I may dislike the latest rock-and-roll singer who gets a million a year, but not one penny of his income comes out of my taxes; and on a free market I am in no way forced to buy (or listen to) his product. I can live in serene independence of his millions; I didn't pay a dime non-voluntarily to put this money into his coffers. I may think the public foolish for buying non-nutritional cereals, thus making the company receive large profits, but this only prompts in me a reflection on the foolishness of much public taste: I do not have to buy the cereal nor contribute to the cereal company in any way. (In fact the shoe is on the other foot: the company, because of its large profits, pays extremely high taxes. Could it be that I pay less tax as a result?) Should I then support a campaign to force people by law *not* to buy the cereal, and thus decimate the company's profits? If I do this— and thus set a precedent against freedom of choice—the next year or the next decade, by the same token, by the same precedent I have set, someone may mount a successful campaign to force people by law not to buy whatever goods or service *I* produce. And if this happens, I shall deserve my fate, since I approved the principle of coercion in the first place. People should be free to make

---

3. *Ibid.* pp. 122, 123.

their own choices—which includes, of course, their own mistakes.

Instead of resenting it when individuals or companies make a million dollars, we should be happy. That million dollars means that there is a prosperous enterpriser who has created many jobs for people and bought equipment and so on (which in turn requires jobs to produce) to keep the product going. A million dollars made on the free market means that a great deal of money has filtered down to a very large number of people in the economy—and that a product is available at a competitive price, else the consumers would not have bought it in sufficient quantity to make our company its million. By contrast, a million dollars earned in government jobs means a million dollars milked from the taxpayer, which he could have spent in other ways.

The future prosperity of everyone—including the needy—depends on *encouraging* persons to become millionaires; to build railroads, houses, and power plants; to develop television, plastics, and new uses for atomic power. The reason is simple: *No man in a free country can make a million dollars through the machinery of production without producing something that we common men want at prices we are willing to pay.* And no man will continue to produce something we want at a price we are willing to pay unless he has the *chance* to make a profit, to become rich—yes, even to become a millionaire.[4]

There is an old saying, "No one should have caviar until everyone has bread." This is, when one examines it, one of the most confused statements

ever made, though it is easily mouthed and chanted and is useful for political campaigns. If the enterpriser were not permitted to have his caviar, he would have far less incentive (perhaps no incentive at all) to produce anything, with the result that in the end fewer people would have even bread. The correct slogan would be, "If no one were permitted to have caviar, finally not many people would have bread."

One of the prevailing impressions, which underlies many arguments in this area but seldom itself surfaces to the level of explicit argument, is that the riches of the rich are the cause of the poverty of the poor. The impression is one of a certain fixed quantity of wealth, and that if some persons have more, this must inevitably mean that others have less.

A little reflection is enough to refute this assertion. If there were only a fixed quantity of wealth, how is it that we have many hundreds of millionaires now, hundreds and even thousands of men with elaborate houses, cars, lands, and other possessions, whereas only a few kings and noblemen had anything like this in bygone ages? Where long ago only a comparative handful of people could live, at the borderline between existence and extinction, in a given area of land, today a thousand times that number live, and live so well that they need spend only 10 to 15 percent of their income on food and all the rest goes for other things, most of which were inconceivable to the population of centuries past.

What people do not comprehend is that wealth is not static, but *grows* as long as people are free to use their ingenuity to improve the quality of their life. Here are deposits of iron, lying in the ground century after

---

4. Dean Russell in *Cliches of Socialism* (Irvington-on-Hudson, N.Y.: Foundation for Economic Education, 1970), p. 186.

century; they do no good to anyone as long as they are just lying there. Now someone devises an economical process for removing the iron from the ground; another devises a means for smelting it, and another for combining it with manganese and other metals to produce steel that can be used in buildings, railroad tracks, and countless other things. When all these factors of production are functioning and the steel is produced, the world's wealth has been increased. Consumers have something to use that they didn't have before, and workers have jobs that didn't exist before. Every party to the transaction is a gainer.

When ten men are adrift on a lifeboat and there is only a certain quantity of provisions, if one person takes more than his share it necessarily follows that others must have less. The example of the lifeboat, or something like it, seems to be the dominating image of those who think in this primitive way about wealth. They apparently believe that because some men are rich, others must therefore be poor, since the rich have taken it away from the poor. Now this *is* the case when a bandit takes away some of your possessions—he has more, and as a consequence you have less. Bandits do not create wealth, they only cause the same amount to change hands. The same happens when the tax-collector takes away by force some of what you have earned; the government too is not creative— it takes away from you to give to others. But the capitalist in a free society is *not* like that: he cannot force the money of you, the consumer, out of your hands; you pay him for a product or a service that did not exist, or did not exist as efficiently or in the same form, prior to his

creative endeavor; his product (e.g., a car) or service (e.g., railroad transportation) is good enough in your eyes so that you voluntarily pay some of the money you have earned in exchange for it. The entrepreneur has brought something into being and offered it on the open market in exchange. He has created something new under the sun, which people may buy or not buy as they prefer.

No, the world is not like a lifeboat. Wealth does increase, and it increases for all as a result of the efforts of a few creative men. The riches of the rich are not the cause of the poverty of the poor: the rich in a free enterprise society can become rich only (1) by hiring workers to produce something and (2) because these consumers on a free market choose to buy what the entrepreneur has offered. They are rich precisely *because* innumerable consumers have, through their purchases, voted for whatever product or service they have to offer. Not one penny of their income on the free market came from the taxed income of anyone else.

One would think that entrepreneurs were armed bandits robbing them by force, to hear the complainers talk, instead of the risk-takers who had the ideas, and, if things went right, benefited the public. But the fallacy persists; many well-meaning people, ignorant of how an economy functions, are trying their best to do them in. In a South American factory, workers agitated, demanded a larger share of the profits, held meetings and finally burned down the factory. "That'll show the filthy profiteer!" they cried. And it is true that they had indeed done him in: his entire life's work and capital were burned to the ground in one night. But they too had lost: they were out of jobs—the jobs that the factory had provided no longer existed. Neither did the products that the factory had made, and consumers had that much less choice in deciding what to buy at the store.

C O M M E N T S ■ Q U E S T I O N S

1. According to Hospers, it is a violation of rights when the profits that a person has made in business are taken away and given to someone else simply for the reason that the second person has fewer goods than the first person. Is Hospers correct in making this claim? Hospers believes that it always—or nearly always—is wrong to violate people's rights. Is he correct in making *this* claim?

2. Making profits, says Hospers, is not getting something for nothing. It involves the risk of capital, planning and running a business, anticipating a market, providing consumers with a product or service at a price they are willing to pay, and providing employees with jobs they are willing to take at the wages offered. The hope of making profits provides the needed incentive for an employer to do all of these things. Hospers concludes that entrepreneurs should be allowed to keep all, or nearly all, of the profits that they make. Is he correct in drawing this conclusion? Is there any reason to believe that entrepreneurs would retain their motivation to make investments even if they were allowed to keep only a *part* of their profits?

3. "The best and only cure for the danger of exploitation is the free market." The free market will offer workers the greatest choice of jobs and thus increase the chances that a worker can find a job at a wage that he or she believes is satisfactory. Evaluate this claim in relation to the Principle of the Common Good.

4. In the long run, says Hospers, the productivity of workers is in direct proportion to the capital investment per worker. Greater capital investment is made possible by greater profits. But is there reason to believe that most profits will be used for capital investment?

5. Hospers opposes any system of taxation—such as the progressive income tax—which taxes individuals or corporations at higher rates when their profits are greater, since, such taxes "penalize efficiency." Are there any moral arguments that can be made in order to justify, to any degree, penalizing efficiency?

6. Is Hospers correct in saying that charity "is a dependent virtue: It rides piggy-back on the primary virtue, namely production"?

7. Are there any possible ways, not mentioned by Hospers, that the pursuit of profit in business could *harm* consumers and employees? (In answering this question you should consider arguments made by Alan Goldman.)

A L A N   H.   G O L D M A N

Business Ethics: Profits, Utilities, and Moral Rights

I

Arguments in favor of the primacy of pursuit of profit generally begin by appealing to classic analyses of the role of profit in a purely competitive free-market system. In this situation, given fluid resources and labor, knowledge of prices and product quality, the pursuit of profit results in the most efficient collective use and development of economic resources. Business people motivated by the prospect of profit, produce what has the greatest surplus of value to the public over cost. Public demand for a good or a service allows prices in that industry to rise. This attracts more producers to develop supplies or substitutes in order to satisfy that demand, until the marginal value of further production falls to that of other goods. At the same time goods or services are distributed to those whose demand, measured in terms of willingness to pay, is greatest. Thus pursuit of profit results in optimal allocation of resources, maximizing the value of economic output to society as a whole. Efficiency is achieved in satisfying demand at a given time, and increased productivity, through minimizing costs relative to output, is encouraged. This generates the economic progress necessary to social progress in satisfying needs and wants. Profits function in this system as incentives to investors or risk takers and as rewards to firms that use economic resources more efficiently than others.

Thus, it is argued, pursuit of profit in a competitive situation best promotes aggregate social good. Profits measure the surplus of the value to society of goods produced over the value of resources taken from the social pool. If the primary social function of business is to achieve the most efficient allocation and use of resources for satisfying the wants of the public, then degree of profit measures degree of fulfillment of social responsibility.[1] When competition reduces costs, reduces prices relative to costs, and attracts resources to satisfy demand, the market

---

1. Compare David Novick, "Cost-Benefit Analysis and Social Responsibility," *Social Issues in Business*, ed. F. Luthans and R. M. Hodgetts (New York, 1976), pp. 561–573.

---

*Alan Goldman is Professor of Philosophy at the University of Miami. He has published two books—*Justice and Reverse Discrimination *and* The Moral Foundations of Professional Ethics*—and many articles in the areas of ethics and epistemology.*

gives the public what it wants most efficiently. Aggregate created wealth is maximized and distributed to those with greatest dollar demand. Pursuit of goals other than maximizing profits will hinder the economic enterprise vital to self-defined aggregate social welfare. Profits of course benefit stockholders and executives, but if pursuit of profit is at the same time pursuit of maximum value to the public, then managers should be wary of the call to sacrifice self-interest to other values.

This defense of placing profit first is thoroughly utilitarian: it provides maximum satisfaction of aggregate demand or wants. But it can also be argued that pursuit of profit in a free market honors rights of free producers and consumers. Fewer rights will be violated in this system than in alternative economies, since here goods will be produced and distributed through a series of voluntary transactions. Parties enter contractual relations only when they view the transactions as benefiting them. Selling an item for a profit extends alternatives to consumers rather than restricting freedoms or rights. In order to make a profit, a business must offer an alternative at least as attractive as others will offer to prospective buyers. Free agreements for mutual benefit will violate rights of neither party (assuming that no fraud is involved). But if the business person tries to place other values over the maximization of profit, he may in effect diminish alternatives and force consumers to pay for products or features of products they might not want or be willing to pay for given the choice. Thus aiming at profits in a free competitive market maximizes satisfaction of wants as well as the possibilities for free trans-

actions. If maximizing alternatives in order to satisfy the demands of consumers maximizes the range of their free choices, then this free economic system appears to be justified in terms of freedom and satisfaction of rights as well as in terms of greatest utility.

The substitution of the values of the business manager for those of the public, expressed through demand as this creates opportunities for profit, appears to limit the choices of consumers and stockholders. Consider, first, arguments on the relative authority of managers and stockholders. As Milton Friedman points out, managers are employees of stockholders; they are entrusted with their money for the express purpose of earning a return on it. But if they sacrifice profits in order to aid what they perceive to be moral or social causes—for example, by contributing to charity or by exceeding legal requirements for safety or anti-pollution devices not demanded by consumers—then they are in effect taxing stockholders without authority to do so.[2] A business manager whose direct application of personally held moral principles makes a difference to a decision is spending the money of other persons, money that is not his own, in a way that these other persons would not choose to spend it. The organization then operates as an extra-governmental institution for selective taxation and public spending. But these functions are better left to the real government. Restraints on

2. See Milton Friedman, "The Social Responsibility of Business is to Increase its Profits," *Ethical Issues in Business*, ed. T. Donaldson and P. H. Werhane (Englewood Cliffs, NJ, 1979), pp. 191–197; see also his *Capitalism and Freedom* (Chicago, 1962), pp. 133–136.

private actions to promote the public good should be generated through the political process, embodying principles of majority rule and proper checks and balances. Public officials can be controlled by the electorate and endowed with the resources to determine properly the effects of taxation and public spending upon the general welfare. Business people lack the same restraints; they are not appointed on the basis of their ability to tax and spend for social welfare. The morally zealous manager assumes power without the accountability of the electoral process. He also is likely to lack the expertise to judge accurately the effects of his presumed moral sacrifice of profits.

Piecemeal decisions of individual managers cannot be based upon accurate prediction of cumulative effects on the economy or on consumer choice. Decisions that negatively affect profits will hurt stockholders, may hurt employees in terms of wages or jobs, may misallocate resources away from production with maximum public value, and may be cumulatively damaging to the economy. The point here is that the individual manager is not in a position, as the well-advised government official presumably is, to assess these cumulative effects. Thus there are good reasons why corporate owners or stockholders do not trust executives to spend their money in accord with personal moral judgments, why they trust them only to maximize returns through most efficient allocation of resources. Other uses of corporate assets, which may be inconsistent with the values of those who own the assets, is a violation of that trust and exceeds the legitimate delegated authority of executives. Or so argues Friedman.

Consider next the argument that claims that managerial decisions which sacrifice prospective profits limit consumer choice. When managers seek to maximize profits by maximally satisfying consumer demand, they allow the public to impose its own values upon business through the market mechanism. When competition exists, consumers need not buy from firms considered to violate the public interest or legitimate moral constraints. Certainly they will not buy products from which they expect harm to exceed benefit to themselves. The market, as reflected in potential profits, appears to be a more sensitive mechanism for satisfying a diverse set of values and preferences than either imposition of managerial values and moral opinions or centralized political decision, even if democratically determined.[3] The reason is that the values of any sizeable minority, even if very small relative to the entire population, can create a potential profit for some astute businessperson. But these values may not match those independently held by business managers, and the minority may not be sizeable or well organized enough to affect centralized decisions of government. An argument for deviating from the profit motive therefore must be an argument for imposing the independent judgments of business managers upon the consuming public, for substituting the values of the former small minority for those of all the various segments of the majority.

Turning more specifically to moral constraints, if a significant segment of the population considers a given moral norm important, the market should

---

3. Friedman, *Capitalism and Freedom*, p. 94.

operate to impose that norm upon business, or at least to make it worthwhile for some business to accept or operate within its constraints.[4] The public's own values are built into the market structure via consumer demand. But if business managers seek to substitute their own moral judgments for the operation of the market—say by adding to a new line of automobiles safety features for which there is no demand rather than more lush interiors for which there is a demand—they either coerce the public into paying for what it would not want given the choice, or else lose out to the competition that provides what the public does want. Once again the managers will have exceeded the authority delegated to them by the public to use resources efficiently to satisfy expressed wants, and that delegated by stockholders to compete for returns on their funds.

The case is totally different when moral commitment contributes to long-range profit by according with the public's values as expressed through the market or as imposed by law. Safety or antipollution devices required by law or for which the public is willing to pay, contribution to programs that improve the community environment and thereby improve employee morale or create effective public relations can all be justified in the name of long-run profit maximization. Here there is no limitation of public choice or taxation of stockholders. The businessperson stays within proper bounds as long as he accepts the public's values, as expressed through projected demand

4. Compare Joseph A. Pichler, "Capitalism in America," *Ethics, Free Enterprise, and Public Policy*, ed. R. T. De George and Joseph A. Pichler (New York, 1978), pp. 19–39.

curves, rather than imposing his own. It is not a question of business managers having a license to be grossly immoral or harmful to consumers. Certainly no serious moral argument could support such license. It is a question only of whose opinion regarding satisfying wants and needs, realizing values, and honoring free choice should prevail— that of the business manager or that of the consuming public. The manager is under moral restraint to subordinate his opinion of what has maximum value to the opinion of the public as expressed through the market. But this restraint is equivalent to the demand to aim first at maximum long-range profits for his corporation. Harmful products or practices may increase short-term profits if they cut costs; but since they generate bad publicity, they are unlikely to be profitable in the long run. Given this moral constraint of the competitive market itself, the primary criterion for business decision must remain profitability, if business is to serve its vital social function rather than usurp that of government or individual free choice.

The argument on sacrificing profits by failing to set prices at maximal profit levels, say from the commendable desire not to contribute to inflation, is somewhat different from that on product features. In the case of prices, by failing to charge full value, the manager may fail to distribute his goods according to greatest demand, and, more importantly, he will encourage overconsumption in the present, create greater shortages of supplies in the future, and fail to encourage the development of more supplies or substitutes to meet real future demand. Thus, once again, well-intentioned sacrifices on the part of managers can have unintended and unfortunate economic effects, effects that derive from failure to conform to market forces.

In this set of arguments for the moral primacy of the profit principle in business, there is a final point suggested earlier that requires some expansion. A single firm or its managers that sacrifices profits to a moral norm is unlikely, in a competitive situation, to succeed in imposing the moral norm. Suppose, for example, that an executive in the automobile industry is convinced, and is objectively correct, that safety in cars is more important than glamour, comfort, or speed, but that cost-benefit market analysis clearly reveals that consumers are not (up to a certain degree—it is always a question of how much safety at what cost). The competition is ready to cater to the public's demand, even though consumer preference reflects only carelessness, ignorance, or failure to apply probabilities. If, under these circumstances, the executive strays too far from consumer preference or the pursuit of profit, he will not succeed in protecting the true public interest. First of all, it is always problematic to assume that interests of others vary from their preferences. In this case it might not be uncontroversially irrational for people to take risks by sacrificing some degree of safety for other values. But the thrust of this final consequentialist argument is independent of the validity of this assumption in particular cases. When consumers can buy from firms that give them what they freely choose to pay for, the firm that attempts to limit their choices by imposing its own values will simply lose out to the competition.

If opposed by consumer prefer-

ence, a manager's personal moral norm may fail to take effect, and his attempt to impose it may well cause him to be replaced by the stockholders or cause his firm to become bankrupt. Then he will have sacrificed not only his own interest and that of his family without positive effect but also that of his employees and the segment of his community dependent on the position of his corporation. Actions that result in so much more harm than benefit are morally suspect even if well intentioned. The imposition of special norms, such as the pursuit of profit principle, that prevent such actions are then supported.

The converse of this argument also seems to follow. That is, the degree to which managers can afford to sacrifice profits to personal moral constraints indicates an unhealthy lack of competition in the industry in question. The luxury of abandoning the profit principle exists only for those who have somehow limited the entry of competitors who will aim to satisfy the public's values and demands.[5] Thus, to the degree that competition for profits exists, the attempt by business managers to impose their own moral principles at the expense of profits is unlikely to succeed in affecting what the public buys, but is likely to produce unintended harm to those dependent on their firms. To the degree that managers can succeed in making stockholders and consumers pay for the moral scruples of their firms, they will have exceeded their legitimate delegated authority to give the public what it wants effficiently, and this will indicate an economic

---

5. See Charles F. Phillips, Jr., "What Is Wrong with Profit Maximization?" in *Issues in Business and Society*, ed. W. T. Greenwood (Boston, 1977), pp. 77–88.

fault in their industry. Business should then aim to satisfy the moral demands of the public as these are imposed by law and reflected in long-range profit potential. But their authority to act directly on personal values in managerial decisions should be limited by the profit principle itself.

This completes the initial case for strong role-differentiation in business according to the primacy of profit principle. Subsequent sections will attempt to expose its weaknesses.

II

The arguments outlined above can be attacked initially by showing that profit maximization need not be efficient or maximize satisfaction of consumer wants. To the extent that maximum profits do not guarantee maximal aggregate utility to the public, the norm of profit maximization lacks even purely utilitarian justification. Counterarguments often begin by pointing out that the rider attached to the initial premise regarding market conditions is never perfectly satisfied in practice. Profit maximization is maximally efficient to the public only when conditions are purely competitive (when each firm is too small to influence prices in the industry single-handedly or to exclude other firms) and when consumers have perfect knowledge of product features, defects, prices, and alternative products. Lack of alternatives under more monopolistic conditions render business decisions inherently coercive in determining what the public must pay for features of products that may be more or less essential. Size generates power over consumers that must be countered by acceptance of moral restraints. To the degree that the market in a particular industry is

noncompetitive, profits might be maximized by lowering quality while raising prices. Business managers in such industries must therefore recognize moral responsibility to the public as a reason for not doing so.

Second, as technological sophistication of products increases, public knowledge of their features decreases. To the degree that businesses can succeed in hiding from the public defects that would be costly to remedy, they can maximize profits at the expense of consumers. It is not always a matter of outright lying or fraud—few businesses would be expected to pay for publicizing every conceivable malfunction or accident involving their products. When relatively few consumers may be harmed by a defect, when consumption of the product is geographically widespread and knowledge of such harm is unlikely to influence consumption greatly, cost-benefit analysis might well call for ignoring the defect in order to maximize profit. If harm to the few is likely to be serious, then ignoring the defect is morally objectionable. In this case, the moral restraint necessary to protect the consuming public is not compatible with profit maximization.

Third, social costs or harm to the public does not always figure in producers' costs or in projected demand for products. Direct harm from products themselves might be expected to influence demand for them (although, as argued in the previous paragraph, not always enough to make it profitable to prevent it); but harm from a production process that does not attach to the product may not influence demand at all. Pollution and waste disposal fall into this category. If such harms are imposed upon neighborhoods in which production is located and not internalized as costs to producers, then production is not maximally efficient to the public. Resources will be overused in relation to net value when full costs are not figured in potential profits. Some restraint, then, on the part of business on moral grounds in the way of refraining from polluting the environment or imposing other neighborhood costs will be a move toward more efficiency to the public. It might nevertheless not be profit maximizing, since consumers far removed from the neighborhood of production will be unlikely to choose products on the normal basis of whether or not neighborhood costs are imposed by the producer. Again we see a gap between profit maximization and public utility, a gap that could be filled by direct acceptance of responsibility for avoiding harm to the public, even at the expense of profits.

Fourth, even creating maximum value in terms of satisfying net dollar demand when social costs are figured will not necessarily create maximum aggregate utility to the public. The reason is that dollar demand is as much a function of the existent distribution of wealth and income as it is a reflection of intensity of wants or needs for the goods in question. Distributing goods to those most willing to pay for them is not necessarily distributing them to those who want or need them most. Thus their distribution does not maximize aggregate utility or satisfaction, unless wealth is distributed equally or the effect of inequalities upon willingness to pay is negligible. For major necessities, unequal distribution will affect not only willingness, but ability to pay. If there is not enough decent housing or medical care to go around, for example, distributing them via a free market will not

maximize satisfaction of want, need, or value—that is, it will not maximize aggregate utility. Those willing or able to pay most will not be those with greatest housing or medical needs. Rights aside, considerations of utility alone would not justify such a method of distribution. If prices are permitted to rise to what the market can bear, important needs and wants, indeed often those most vital and intensely felt, will go unsatisfied. There are many who cannot express their demands through the market. In areas of public decision-making we certainly would not consider it fair to allocate votes according to wealth. Why should we think it fair to allow production and distribution of economic goods to be determined by a system of voting with dollars? Once more, moral restraint in setting prices on the part of producers of necessities, and, in the case of services, on the part of professionals, seems necessary not only to protect rights to necessities, but to maximize utilities by distributing goods to those who need them most or would benefit most from them.

Fifth, there is the problem of the relation of consumer preferences to true interests and needs. In section 1, I argued that opposing preferences expressed through the market to a different conception of interests is often as problematic and objectionable as unwarranted paternalism. But, as Galbraith has argued, when honoring preferences does not seem to lead to long-range satisfaction or happiness, they become suspect as being largely created by those who benefit from satisfying them.[6] The

_____

6. See John Kenneth Galbraith, *The Affluent Society* (Boston, 1958), chap. 2.

satisfaction of wants is utility-maximizing when the wants are given and represent disutilities when unsatisfied. But if the process in question includes creation of the wants themselves, and if their satisfaction results in greater wants or in other harmful side effects, then the whole process may be objectionable from a utilitarian point of view. As the ancient Greeks realized, contentment may be easier to achieve by eliminating superfluous desires than by creating and attempting to satisfy them.

Certainly for many businesses the goal of profit maximization requires the creation of demand as much as its satisfaction. Advertising and salesmanship are not merely informative. The fact that a certain set of desires is created by those who then attempt to satisfy them is not in itself grounds for condemning the desires or the process that creates them. Such cycles are as characteristic of desires for the most exalted aesthetic experience—appreciation of fine opera, for example—as they are of desires for electric gadgets or tobacco.[7] But this shows only that Galbraith's argument is incomplete, not that it is enthymemically unsound. When we have an independent criterion for wants worth fulfilling, then processes can be condemned which create those that fail to satisfy this criterion. One weak criterion that can be adopted from a want-regarding or utilitarian moral theory relates to whether satisfaction of the desires in question increases overall satisfaction in the long run, whether it contrib-

utes to a fulfilled or worthwhile life. Desires are irrational when their satisfaction is incompatible with more fundamental or long-range preferences, either because of harmful side-effects or because of the creation of more unsatisfied desires. Alcoholism is an example of such irrational desire, the satisfaction of which is harmful overall. Processes that create and feed such desires are not utility-maximizing, since even the satisfaction of these desires lowers the subject's general level of utility. The pursuit of profit might well encourage the creation of such wants, especially desires for quickly consumable products. When this occurs, the appearance of efficiency masks a deeper utilitarian inefficiency. The profit motive contributes more to negative than positive utility, creating more unsatisfied than satisfied wants.

It has been argued also against Galbraith that most people are not so influenced by advertisement. They learn to be distrustful of claims made in ads and take them with a grain of salt. But while it is true that consumers become resistant to specific product claims of advertisers, it is not at all so clear that they can easily resist the total life style that bombards them constantly in subtle and not so subtle ways in ads for beer, cars, perfume, clothes, and whatever else can be conspicuously consumed.[8] The desire for this life style may in turn influence particular desires for products or features of products that are irrational and would not arise without this continuous programming. Consumers may desire flashy and fast automobiles more strongly than safe ones;

---

7. For this reply to Galbraith, see F. A. von Hayek, "The Non Sequitur of the 'Dependence Effect,'" in *Ethical Theory and Business*, ed. Tom Beauchamp and Norman Bowie (Englewood Cliffs, NJ, 1979), pp. 508–512.

8. Compare John I. Coppett, "Consumerism from a Behavioral Perspective," in *Social Issues in Business*, pp. 444–454.

but this may be only because safety cannot be conspicuously consumed or because it does not provide the kind of dashing sexual allure that car advertisers attempt to project onto their products. If this preference is suspect in itself, it certainly appears more so when we recognize its source. In some industries there is a natural lack of rational restraint on the part of consumers of which those out for maximum profits can take advantage, for example in the funeral or health-care industries. In others, consumers can be influenced to view certain products as symbols of a glamorous life style and desire them on those grounds. Furthermore, the encouragement of a life style of super consumption by numerous advertisers probably results in overproduction of consumable products and underutilization of resources for public goods that are not advertised, not conspicuously consumed, and less immediately enjoyed—for example clean air, water, and soil, quality schools, and so on. The congruence between free-market outcome and aggregate utility or social good is once more suspect.

Thus the pursuit of profit is efficient to the public only if it operates under certain moral constraints. It is not efficient or utility-maximizing if it results in elimination of competition and hence of alternatives for consumers, in deception regarding product defects, imposition of neighborhood social costs, the creation and exploitation of irrational desires, or the neglect of needs and wants of those unable to express demand from lack of wealth.[9] And it is likely to result in all of these if maximization

of profits is accepted as the principal norm of business ethics. We have also countered the claim (suggested early in the first section) that immorality in business is never profit-maximizing in the long run. Certain immoral practices of a business will hurt its profits, since they will outrage the public, make consumers wary of the products of that business, and reduce demand for those products. Other objectionable practices, such as dishonesty toward suppliers or total callousness toward employees, will be damaging to the production process. The market does impose some moral constraints. But other practices—such as retaining defects in products while hiding them from the public (which is sometimes possible), inadequately servicing products, bribing officials or wholesale buyers, polluting and dumping wastes, or creating desires for harmful products—might maximize profits while being inefficient to the consuming public.

Still other practices might be both profit-maximizing and efficient in relation to consumers and yet morally questionable. This would be the case if a product was desired (or desired at low cost) by many and yet extremely harmful to relatively few. Nuclear power plants or glamorous, yet potentially dangerous, automobiles might be examples. In the former case, aggregate utility might be maximized through cheap production of electricity, given enough customers who benefit, but is it justified to allow considerations of aggregate utility to outweigh the shortened lives of a few plant workers or neighborhood residents? Another example in this category relates to work and working conditions. Total exploitation of workers, even if possible, might not be profit-maximizing, since production suffers when employee morale is low.

---

9. See also Thomas M. Garrett, *Business Ethics* (Englewood Cliffs, NJ, 1966), pp. 25, 144.

But, as Henry Ford discovered long ago, productivity does not vary always with the meaningfulness of work; in fact, in certain contexts it may vary inversely with the interest and possibility for self-realization in work. Nor is consumer demand linked to these variables in working conditions. Profit-maximization and efficiency may sometimes call for reducing work to series of simple menial tasks. But the quality of a people's lives depends substantially upon the type of work they do and their interest in it. Thus we may ask on moral grounds whether gains in efficiency or aggregate utility (up to a certain point), as signaled by increased profit potential, justify reducing work to a menial and dehumanizing level. Numerous other examples in this category involving workers or neighborhoods of production could be produced: questions such as the firing of longtime employees, or the relocation of businesses, in which profit-maximization and even aggregate social utility might not be morally decisive.

This last category of immorality that is potentially profit-maximizing takes the argument to a new level. Prior paragraphs argued within a utilitarian moral framework: the point was to show how profit-maximization may not be efficient in the deeper sense of utility-maximization. But the cases just cited appeal to the notion of moral rights as opposed to aggregate utilities. For our purposes we may define a right as a moral claim to a good that overrides considerations of utility.[10] The fact that others might benefit more than I from my property does not justify transferring it to them against my wishes. In the first section, the proponent of profit-maximization argued that pursuit of profit in a free competitive market results in maximum efficiency—that is, in optimal allocation of resources for satisfying aggregate demand at least overall cost—and also honors rights and preserves freedoms by extending opportunities for free transactions. One who makes this claim might also argue against some of the initial utilitarian arguments in this section by appealing to rights. The argument that unsatisfied wants and low utility from distribution by demand are results of unequal wealth would be countered by appeal to an individual's right to keep or spend what he or she earns and to be rewarded in relation to productivity, which is more nearly approximated in a profit-oriented free market than in other economies.

But appeal to a plausible full theory of rights undoubtedly favors counterarguments to the profit-maximization principle. To the argument that business managers have no right to impose their moral opinions on the majority of consumers or upon stockholders, it can be replied that the majority has no right to maximal utility or the stockholders to maximal profits resulting from violation of the moral rights of even a small minority. Suppose the market reveals aggregate public preference for cheap electricity. Even if the majority of consumers are willing to take the risks involved in generating electricity by unsafe nuclear reactors, do they have a right to impose the risks and resulting severe harms on those who are unwilling to accept them? (The case is different if all are willing to take the risks and are equally exposed to them, or if those unwilling are able to avoid them without undue hardship.)

---

10. For expansion on this definition and defense of the claim that rights always override utilities, see Alan Goldman, "Rights, Utilities and Contracts," *Canadian Journal of Philosophy* 3 (sup. vol., 1977): 121–135.

The market reveals the preferences of consumers (sometimes based on ignorance or deception), as well as their willingness to pay for protection of rights of others. But whether rights ought to be honored does not depend upon the willingness of the majority to bear the sacrifices of honoring them. When buying goods, most consumers are not concerned with whether processes involved in their production impose severe harms or violate rights of others. But the effect of moral norms upon consumer demand is not a measure of the obligations they impose, nor even of their acknowledgment by individuals outside their roles as consumers. The business manager does not have the right to make decisions or retain products or processes that maim, poison, severely deprive, or contaminate even a few individuals unwilling to take such risks in the name of efficiency to the public or profits to stockholders. In general one cannot morally do for others what they would be morally unjustified in doing for themselves.

It is not sufficient that business internalize costs imposed upon the community or compensate victims harmed by their products or processes. This might be sufficient in cases like that of strip mining, where the costs of restoring land can be assigned to coal producers, but not when rights of persons against serious harm or risk are involved. The user of the asbestos-filled hair dryer or the driver of the Pinto that explodes or the infant deformed by chemical waste may not be willing to be harmed and then compensated. Rights are violated precisely when the harms imposed are so severe that we do not allow additions of lesser utilities to override. While rights cannot be overridden by aggregate utility, they can be and sometimes are overridden by other rights. Thus at certain stages of economic development, when scarcity is still the rule and the means for survival of many people depends upon further growth, expansion of gross output spurred by the profit motive may be a reasonable social goal. But in such a case, rights to survival and satisfaction of basic needs are at stake, not utility or efficiency.[11] At later stages of relative abundance, as in our society, whatever efficiency is generated by maximization of profits cannot excuse violations of moral rights in the process. The rights and freedoms exemplified in free-market exchange are only a small subclass of those potentially at stake in economic transactions and decisions.[12] If there are, in addition to rights to earn and spend money as one chooses, negative rights not to be severely harmed and positive rights to have basic needs fulfilled, then the latter will not be adequately protected by free-market exchange when businessmen place profits first.

The profit-maximization principle, then, does not appear to be morally justifiable, except within ordinary moral constraints of honoring rights. It is not a question of business managers imposing purely subjective opinions upon a majority who hold contrary opinions. When moral rights

11. Compare Robert Hay and Ed Gray, "Social Responsibilities of Business Managers," in *Social Issues in Business*, pp. 104–113.

12. See Peter Singer, "Rights and the Market," *Justice and Economic Distribution,* ed. John Arthur and W. H. Shaw (Englewood Cliffs, NJ, 1978), pp. 207–221; also Alan H. Goldman, "The Entitlement Theory of Distributive Justice," *The Journal of Philosophy* 73 (1976): 823–835.

of the kind I have mentioned are violated, the harms imposed are severe. Such cases are relatively easy to identify. When the profit-principle blinder is removed from the eyes of business executives, when consumers outside their roles as consumers are asked, they do not try to justify the imposition of such harms in the name of profit or efficiency. Indeed it is plausible to suppose that neither the public nor the majority of business-persons approve of the maximization of profit principle, not because they are confused about the operation of a free market or ignorant of its virtues, but because a theory of moral rights of the type I am discussing captures significant aspects of common-sense moral consciousness. Rights against being harmed and to satisfaction of basic needs are seen to override considerations of efficiency or utility. When this theory is taken into account, the position of business manager does not appear to be strongly role-differentiated: profits cannot be placed above moral rights that impose constraints in all areas of nonprofessional behavior as well.

C O M M E N T S ■ Q U E S T I O N S

---

1. Goldman's purpose in this article is to defend a negative answer to the following question: Can business managers assume that the pursuit of profit within legal limits will tend toward a moral outcome? It is important to notice that in part 1 Goldman presents major arguments in defense of an *affirmative* answer, and then in part 2 he gives counterarguments to each of them. The counterarguments represent his own view. In order to make entirely clear what the structure of his presentation is, the major arguments and counterarguments will be summarized here:

   a. *Argument.* The pursuit of profit by business managers is the most efficienct way to give to consumers what they want at prices they are willing to pay. Competition in business will force managers to do all they can to give people what they want at the lowest possible price.

   Counterarguments. This need not be so when (1) conditions are not "purely competitive," (2) the technological complexity of products causes consumers to have relatively little understanding of how products work, or (3) people who are harmed by a product are not the ones who buy it. There is also a problem when the people who are able to buy a product are not always the ones who most need it. Lastly, people may choose not to buy what they truly need, but instead may choose to buy products that advertisements influence them to buy.

   b. *Argument.* The pursuit of profit leads to more efficient production techniques, and this in turn helps to maximize the general welfare.

   Counterargument. The most efficient way to run a factory

may be to have people work on assembly lines, doing very simple, menial tasks. "But the quality of people's lives depends substantially upon the type of work they do and their interest in it."

c. *Argument.* The pursuit of profit in a free market honors the rights of both producers and consumers since it allows them free choice in what they will buy or sell.

Counterargument. The majority of consumers may choose to buy products that, when they are used or when they are manufactured, are harmful to other people. The rights of the minority will not be honored by the exercise of free choice by the majority.

2. Goldman does not say the pursuit of profits is wrong, but that the pursuit of profits is wrong unless it is "under certain moral constraints." Do you believe that Goldman is correct in taking this general position?

3. Does Goldman ackowledge sufficiently the extent to which the pursuit of profit by business *does* tend to maximize either the public welfare or the common good? Does he acknowledge sufficiently the extent to which the pursuit of profit tends to support individual rights? (In answering these questions, you should consider arguments made by John Hospers.)

4. Do you believe that advertising is a good thing or a bad thing overall? Does it help us by giving us information about products or does it hurt us by persuading us to buy products that are harmful or unnecessary?

5. Would the United States be better off if everyone had more meaningful jobs (for example, if no one had to work on an assembly line) even if this meant that industry would not be anywhere near as efficient as it is at the present time?

ROBERT L. ARRINGTON

Advertising and Behavior Control

onsider the following advertisements:

1. "A woman in *Distinction Foundations* is so beautiful that all other women want to kill her."

2. Pongo Peach color from Revlon comes "from east of the sun . . . west of the moon where each tomorrow dawns." It is "succulent on your lips" and "sizzling on your finger tips (And on your toes, goodness knows)." Let it be your "adventure in paradise."

3. "Musk by English Leather—The Civilized Way to Roar."

4. "Increase the value of your holdings. Old Charter Bourbon Whiskey—The Final Step Up."

5. Last Call Smirnoff Style: "They'd never really miss us, and it's kind of late already, and it's quite a long way, and I could build a fire, and you're looking very beautiful, and we could have another martini, and it's awfully nice just being home . . . you think?"

6. A Christmas Prayer. "Let us pray that the blessings of peace be ours— the peace to build and grow, to live in harmony and sympathy with others, and to plan for the future with confidence." New York Life Insurance Company.

These are instances of what is called puffery—the practice by a seller of making exaggerated, highly fanciful or suggestive claims about a product or service. Puffery, within ill-defined limits, is legal. It is considered a legitimate, necessary, and very successful tool of the advertising industry. Puffery is not just bragging; it is bragging carefully designed to achieve a very definite effect. Using the techniques of so-called motivational research, advertising firms first identify our often hidden needs (for security, conformity, oral stimulation) and our desires (for power, sexual dominance and dalliance, adventure) and then they design ads which respond to these needs and desires. By associating a product, for which we may have little or no direct need or desire, with symbols reflecting the fulfillment of these other, often subterranean interests, the advertisement can quickly generate large numbers of consumers eager to purchase the product advertised. What woman in the sexual race of life could resist a foundation which would turn other women envious to the point of homicide? Who can turn down an adventure in paradise, east of the sun where tomorrow dawns? Who doesn't

Robert L. Arrington is professor of philosophy at Georgia State University. He has written many articles in the areas of ethics, the philosophy of Wittgenstein, and the philosophy of psychology.

From the *Journal of Business Ethics* 1 (1982) 3–12. Copyright © 1982 by D. Reidel Publishing Co., Dordrecht, Holland and Boston, U.S.A. Reprinted by permission of the publisher.

want to be civilized and thoroughly libidinous at the same time? Be at the pinnacle of success—drink Old Charter. Or stay at home and dally a bit—with Smirnoff. And let us pray for a secure and predictable future, provided for by New York Life, God willing. It doesn't take very much motivational research to see the point of these sales pitches. Others are perhaps a little less obvious. The need to feel secure in one's home at night can be used to sell window air conditioners, which drown out small noises and provide a friendly, dependable companion. The fact that baking a cake is symbolic of giving birth to a baby used to prompt advertisements for cake mixes which glamorized the 'creative' housewife. And other strategies, for example involving cigar symbolism, are a bit too crude to mention, but are nevertheless very effective.

Don't such uses of puffery amount to manipulation, exploitation, or downright control? In his very popular book *The Hidden Persuaders*, Vance Packard points out that a number of people in the advertising world have frankly admitted as much:

As early as 1941 Dr. Dichter (an influential advertising consultant) was exhorting ad agencies to recognize themselves for what they actually were—"one of the most advanced laboratories in psychology." He said the successful ad agency "manipulates human motivations and desires and develops a need for goods with which the public has at one time been unfamiliar—perhaps even undesirous of purchasing." The following year *Advertising Agency* carried an ad man's statement that psychology not only holds promise for understanding people but "ultimately for controlling their behavior."[1]

Such statements lead Packard to remark: "With all this interest in manipulating the customer's subconscious, the old slogan 'let the buyer beware' began taking on a new and more profound meaning."[2]

B. F. Skinner, the high priest of behaviorism, has expressed a similar assessment of advertising and related marketing techniques. Why, he asks, do we buy a certain kind of car?

Perhaps our favorite TV program is sponsored by the manufacturer of that car. Perhaps we have seen pictures of many beautiful or prestigeful persons driving it—in pleasant or glamorous places. Perhaps the car has been designed with respect to our motivational patterns: the device on the hood is a phallic symbol; or the horsepower has been stepped up to please our competitive spirit in enabling us to pass other cars swiftly (or, as the advertisements say, 'safely'). The concept of freedom that has emerged as part of the cultural practice of our group makes little or no provision for recognizing or dealing with these kinds of control.[3]

In purchasing a car we may think we are free, Skinner is claiming, when in fact our act is completely controlled by factors in our environment and in our history of reinforcement. Advertising is one such factor.

A look at some other advertising techniques may reinforce the suspicion that Madison Avenue controls us like so many puppets. TV watchers surely have noticed that some of the more repugnant ads are shown over and over again, *ad nauseum*. My favorite, or most hated, is the one about A-1 Steak Sauce which goes something like this: Now, ladies and

---

1. Vance Packard, *The Hidden Persuaders* (Pocket Books, New York, 1958), pp. 20–21.

2. *Ibid.*, p. 21.

3. B. F. Skinner, "Some Issues Concerning the Control of Human Behavior: A Symposium," in Karlins and Andrews (eds.), *Man Controlled* (The Free Press, New York, 1972).

gentlemen, what *is* hamburger? It has succeeded in destroying my taste for hamburger, but it has surely drilled the name of A-1 Sauce into my head. And that is the point of it. Its very repetitiousness has generated what ad theorists call *information*. In this case it is indirect information, information derived not from the content of what is said but from the fact that it is said so often and so vividly that it sticks in one's mind—i.e., the information yield has increased. And not only do I always remember A-1 Sauce when I go to the grocers, I tend to assume that any product advertised so often has to be good—and so I usually buy a bottle of the stuff.

Still another technique: On a recent show of the television program 'Hard Choices' it was demonstrated how subliminal suggestion can be used to control customers. In a New Orleans department store, messages to the effect that shoplifting is wrong, illegal, and subject to punishment were blended into the Muzak background music and masked so as not to be consciously audible. The store reported a dramatic drop in shoplifting. The program host conjectured whether a logical extension of this technique would be to broadcast subliminal advertising messages to the effect that the store's $15.99 sweater special is the "bargain of a lifetime." Actually, this application of subliminal suggestion to advertising has already taken place. Years ago in New Jersey a cinema was reported to have flashed subthreshold ice cream ads onto the screen during regular showings of the film—and, yes, the concession stand did a landslide business.[4]

Puffery, indirect information transfer, subliminal advertising—are these techniques of manipulation and control whose success shows that many of us have forfeited our autonomy and become a community, or herd, of packaged souls?[5] The business world and the advertising industry certainly reject this interpretation of their efforts. *Business Week*, for example, dismissed the charge that the science of behavior, as utilized by advertising, is engaged in human engineering and manipulation. It editorialized to the effect that "it is hard to find anything very sinister about a science whose principle conclusion is that you get along with people by giving them what they want."[6] The theme is familiar: businesses just give the consumer what he/she wants; if they didn't they wouldn't stay in business very long. Proof that the consumer wants the products advertised is given by the fact that he buys them, and indeed often returns to buy them again and again.

The techniques of advertising we are discussing have had their more intellectual defenders as well. For example, Theodore Levitt, Professor of Business Administration at the Harvard Business School, has defended the practice of puffery and the use of tenhniques depending on motiva-

---

1973), and W. B. Key, *Media Sexploitation* (Prentice-Hall, Inc., Englewood Cliffs, N.J., 1976).

5. I would like to emphasize that in what follows I am discussing these techniques of advertising from the standpoint of the issue of control and not from that of deception. For a good and recent discussion of the many dimensions of possible deception in advertising, see Alex C. Michalos, "Advertising: Its Logic, Ethics, and Economics" in J. A. Blair and R. H. Johnson (eds.), *Informal Logic: The First International Symposium* (Edgepress, Pt. Reyes, Calif., 1980).

6. Quoted by Packard, *op. cit.*, p. 220.

---

4. For provocative discussions of subliminal advertising, see W. B. Key, *Subliminal Seduction* (The New American Library, New York,

tional research.[7] What would be the consequences, he asks us, of deleting all exaggerated claims and fanciful associations from advertisements? We would be left with literal descriptions of the empirical characteristics of products and their functions. Cosmetics would be presented as facial and bodily lotions and powders which produce certain odor and color changes; they would no longer offer hope or adventure. In addition to the fact that these products would not then sell as well, they would not, according to Levitt, please us as much either. For it is hope and adventure we want when we buy them. We want automobiles not just for transportation, but for the feelings of power and status they give us. Quoting T. S. Eliot to the effect that "Human kind cannot bear very much reality," Levitt argues that advertising is an effort to "transcend nature in the raw," to "augment what nature has so crudely fashioned." He maintains that "everybody everywhere wants to modify, transform, embellish, enrich and reconstruct the world around him." Commerce takes the same liberty with reality as the artist and the priest—in all three instances the purpose is "to influence the audience by creating illusions, symbols, and implications that promise more than pure functionality." For example, "to amplify the temple in men's eyes, (men of cloth) have, very realistically, systematically sanctioned the embellishment of the houses of the gods with the same kind of luxurious design and expensive decoration that Detroit puts into a Cadillac." A poem,

a temple, a Cadillac—they all elevate our spirits, offering imaginative promises and symbolic interpretations of our mundane activities. Seen in this light, Levitt claims, "Embellishment and distortion are among advertising's legitimate and socially desirable purposes." To reject these techniques of advertising would be "to deny man's honest needs and values."

Philip Nelson, a Professor of Economics at SUNY-Binghamton, has developed an interesting defense of indirect information advertising.[8] He argues that even when the message (the direct information) is not credible, the fact that the brand is advertised, and advertised frequently, is valuable indirect information for the consumer. The reason for this is that the brands advertised most are more likely to be better buys—losers won't be advertised a lot, for it simply wouldn't pay to do so. Thus even if the advertising claims made for a widely advertised product are empty, the consumer reaps the benefit of the indirect information which shows the product to be a good buy. Nelson goes so far as to say that advertising, seen as information and especially as indirect information, does not require an intelligent human response. If the indirect information has been received and has had its impact, the consumer will purchase the better buy even if his explicit reason for doing so is silly, e.g., he naively believes an endorsement of the product by a celebrity. Even though his behavior is overtly irrational, by acting on the indirect information he

---

7. Theodore Levitt, "The Morality (?) of Advertising," *Harvard Business Review* 48 (1970), 84–92.

8. Phillip Nelson, "Advertising and Ethics," in Richard T. De George and Joseph A. Pichler (eds.), *Ethics, Free Enterprise, and Public Policy* (Oxford University Press, New York, 1978), pp. 187–198.

is nevertheless doing what he ought to do, i.e., getting his money's worth. "'Irrationality' is rational," Nelson writes, "if it is cost-free."

I don't know of any attempt to defend the use of subliminal suggestion in advertising, but I can imagine one form such an attempt might take. Advertising information, even if perceived below the level of conscious awareness, must appeal to some desire on the part of the audience if it is to trigger a purchasing response. Just as the admonition not to shoplift speaks directly to the superego, the sexual virtues of TR-7's, Pongo Peach, and Betty Crocker cake mix present themselves directly to the id, bypassing the pesky reality principle of the ego. With a little help from our advertising friends, we may remove a few of the discontents of civilization and perhaps even enter into the paradise of polymorphous perversity.[9]

The defense of advertising which suggests that advertising simply is information which allows us to purchase what we want, has in turn been challenged. Does business, largely through its advertising efforts, really make available to the consumer what he/she desires and demands? John Kenneth Galbraith has denied that the matter is as straightforward as this.[10] In his opinion the desires to which business is supposed to respond, far from being original to the consumer, are often themselves created by business. The producers make both the product and the desire for it, and the "central function" of advertising is "to create desires." Galbraith coins the term 'The Dependence Effect' to designate the way wants depend on the same process by which they are satisfied.

David Braybrooke has argued in similar and related ways.[11] Even though the consumer is, in a sense, the final authority concerning what he wants, he may come to see, according to Braybrooke, that he was mistaken in wanting what he did. The statement 'I want *x*', he tells us, is not incorrigible but is "ripe for revision." If the consumer had more objective information than he is provided by product puffing, if his values had not been mixed up by motivational research strategies (e.g., the confusion of sexual and automotive values), and if he had an expanded set of choices instead of the limited set offered by profit-hungry corporations, then he might want something quite different from what he presently wants. This shows, Braybrooke thinks, the extent to which the consumer's wants are a function of advertising and not necessarily representative of his real or true wants.

The central issue which emerges between the above critics and defenders of advertising is this: do the advertising techniques we have discussed involve a violation of human autonomy and a manipulation and control of consumer behavior, *or* do

9. For a discussion of polymorphous perversity, see Norman O. Brown, *Life Against Death* (Random House, New York, 1969), Chapter 3.

10. John Kenneth Galbraith, *The Affluent Society*; reprinted in Tom L. Beauchamp and Norman E. Bowie (eds.), *Ethical Theory and Business* (Prentice-Hall, Englewood Cliffs, 1979), pp. 496–501.

11. David Braybrooke, "Skepticism of Wants, and Certain Subversive Effects of Corporations on American Values," in Sidney Hook (ed.), *Human Values and Economic Policy* (New York University Press, New York, 1967); reprinted in Beauchamp and Bowie (eds.), *op. cit.*, pp. 502–508.

they simply provide an efficient and cost-effective means of giving the consumer information on the basis of which he or she makes a free choice. Is advertising information, or creation of desire?

To answer this question we need a better conceptual grasp of what is involved in the notion of autonomy. This is a complex, multifaceted concept, and we need to approach it through the more determinate notions of (a) autonomous desire, (b) rational desire and choice, (c) free choice, and (d) control or manipulation. In what follows I shall offer some tentative and very incomplete analyses of these concepts and apply the results to the case of advertising.

(a) *Autonomous Desire*. Imagine that I am watching TV and see an ad for Grecian Formula 16. The thought occurs to me that if I purchase some and apply it to my beard, I will soon look younger—in fact I might even be myself again. Suddenly I want to be myself! I want to be young again! So I rush out and buy a bottle. This is our question: was the desire to be younger manufactured by the commercial, or was it 'original to me' and truly mine? Was it autonomous or not?

F. A. von Hayek has argued plausibly that we should not equate nonautonomous desires, desires which are not original to me or truly mine, with those which are culturally induced.[12] If we did equate the two, he points out, then the desires for music, art, and knowledge could not properly be attributed to a person as original to him, for these are surely induced culturally. The only desires a person would really have as his own in this case would be the purely physical ones for food, shelter, sex, etc. But if we reject the equation of the nonautonomous and the culturally induced, as von Hayek would have us do, then the mere fact that my desire to be young again is caused by the T.V. commercial—surely an instrument of popular culture transmission—does not in and of itself show that this is not my own, autonomous desire. Moreover, even if I never before felt the need to look young, it doesn't follow that this new desire is any less mine. I haven't always liked 1969 Aloxe Corton Burgundy or the music of Satie, but when the desires for these things first hit me, they were truly mine.

This shows that there is something wrong in setting up the issue over advertising and behavior control as a question whether our desires are truly ours *or* are created in us by advertisements. Induced and autonomous desires do not separate into two mutually exclusive classes. To obtain a better understanding of autonomous and nonautonomous desires, let us consider some cases of a desire which a person does not *acknowledge* to be his own even though he *feels* it. The kleptomaniac has a desire to steal which in many instances he repudiates, seeking by treatment to rid himself of it. And if I were suddenly overtaken by a desire to attend an REO concert, I would immediately disown this desire, claiming possession or momentary madness. These are examples of desires which one might have but with which one would not identify. They are experienced as foreign to one's character or personality. Often a person will have what Harry Frankfurt calls a second-order desire, that is to

---

12. F. A. von Hayek, "The *Non Sequitur* of the 'Dependence Effect'," *Southern Economic Journal* (1961); reprinted in Beauchamp and Bowie (eds.), *op. cit.*, pp. 508–512.

say, a desire *not* to have another desire.[13] In such cases, the first-order desire is thought of as being nonautonomous, imposed on one. When on the contrary a person has a second-order desire to maintain and fulfill a first-order desire, then the first-order desire is truly his own, autonomous, original to him. So there is in fact a distinction between desires which are the agent's own and those which are not, but this is not the same as the distinction between desires which are innate to the agent and those which are externally induced.

If we apply the autonomous/nonautonomous distinction derived from Frankfurt to the desires brought about by advertising, does this show that advertising is responsible for creating desires which are not truly the agent's own? Not necessarily, and indeed not often. There may be some desires I feel which I have picked up from advertising and which I disown—for instance, my desire for A-1 Steak Sauce. If I act on these desires it can be said that I have been led by advertising to act in a way foreign to my nature. In these cases my autonomy has been violated. But most of the desires induced by advertising I fully accept, and hence most of these desires are autonomous. The most vivid demonstration of this is that I often return to purchase the same product over and over again, without regret or remorse. And when I don't, it is more likely that the desire has just faded than that I have repudiated it. Hence, while advertising may violate my autonomy by leading me to act on desires which are not truly

mine, this seems to be the exceptional case.

Note that this conclusion applies equally well to the case of subliminal advertising. This may generate subconscious desires which lead to purchases, and the act of purchasing these goods may be inconsistent with other conscious desires I have, in which case I might repudiate my behavior and by implication the subconscious cause of it. But my subconscious desires may not be inconsistent in this way with my conscious ones; my id may be cooperative and benign rather than hostile and malign.[14] Here again, then, advertising may or may not produce desires which are 'not truly mine.'

What are we to say in response to Braybrooke's argument that insofar as we might choose differently if advertisers gave us better information and more options, it follows that the desires we have are to be attributed more to advertising than to our own real inclinations? This claim seems empty. It amounts to saying that if the world we lived in, and we ourselves, were different, then we would want different things. This is surely true, but it is equally true of our desire for shelter as of our desire for Grecian Formula 16. If we lived in a tropical paradise we would not need or desire shelter. If we were immortal, we would not desire youth. What is true of all desires can hardly be used as a basis for criticizing some desires

---

13. Harry Frankfurt, "Freedom of the Will and the Concept of a Person," *Journal of Philosophy* 68 (1971), 5–20.

14. For a discussion of the difference between a malign and a benign subconscious mind, see P. H. Nowell-Smith, "Psycho-analysis and Moral Language," *The Rationalist Annual* (1954); reprinted in P. Edwards and A. Pap (eds.), *A Modern Introduction to Philosophy*, Revised Edition (The Free Press, New York, 1965), pp. 86–93.

by claiming that they are nonautonomous.

(b) *Rational Desire and Choice.* Braybrooke might be interpreted as claiming that the desires induced by advertising are often irrational ones in the sense that they are not expressed by an agent who is in full possession of the facts about the products advertised or about the alternative products which might be offered him. Following this line of thought, a possible criticism of advertising is that it leads us to act on irrational desires or to make irrational choices. It might be said that our autonomy has been violated by the fact that we are prevented from following our rational wills or that we have been denied the 'positive freedom' to develop our true, rational selves. It might be claimed that the desires induced in us by advertising are false desires in that they do not reflect our essential, i.e., rational, essense.

The problem faced by this line of criticism is that of determining what is to count as rational desire or rational choice. If we require that the desire or choice be the product of an awareness of *all* the facts about the product, then surely every one of us is always moved by irrational desires and makes nothing but irrational choices. How could we know all the facts about a product? If it be required only that we possess all of the *available* knowledge about the product advertised, then we still have to face the problem that not all available knowledge is *relevant* to a rational choice. If I am purchasing a car, certain engineering features will be, and others won't be, relevant, *given what I want in a car.* My prior desires determine the relevance of information. Normally a rational desire or

choice is thought to be one based upon relevant information, and information is relevant if it shows how other, prior desires may be satisfied. It can plausibly be claimed that it is such prior desires that advertising agencies acknowledge, and that the agencies often provide the type of information that is relevant in light of these desires. To the extent that this is true, advertising does not inhibit our rational wills or our autonomy as rational creatures.

It may be urged that much of the puffery engaged in by advertising does not provide relevant information at all but rather makes claims which are not factually true. If someone buys Pongo Peach in anticipation of an adventure in paradise, or Old Charter in expectation of increasing the value of his holdings, then he/she is expecting purely imaginary benefits. In no literal sense will the one product provide adventure and the other increased capital. A purchasing decision based on anticipation of imaginary benefits is not, it might be said, a rational decision, and a desire for imaginery benefits is not a rational desire.

In rejoinder it needs to be pointed out that we often wish to purchase subjective effects which in being subjective are nevertheless real enough. The feeling of adventure or of enhanced social prestige and value are examples of subjective effects promised by advertising. Surely many (most?) advertisements directly promise subjective effects which their patrons actually desire (and obtain when they purchase the product), and thus the ads provide relevant information for rational choice. Moreover, advertisements often provide accurate indirect information on the basis of which a person who wants a certain subjective effect rationally chooses a product. The mechanism involved here is as follows.

To the extent that a consumer takes an advertised product to offer a subjective effect and the product does not, it is unlikely that it will be purchased again. If this happens in a number of cases, the product will be taken off the market. So here the market regulates itself, providing the mechanism whereby misleading advertisements are withdrawn and misled customers are no longer misled. At the same time, a successful bit of puffery, being one which leads to large and repeated sales, produces satisfied customers and more advertising of the product. The indirect information provided by such large-scale advertising efforts provides a measure of verification to the consumer who is looking for certain kinds of subjective effect. For example, if I want to feel well dressed and in fashion, and I consider buying an Izod Alligator shirt which is advertised in all of the magazines and newspapers, then the fact that other people buy it and that this leads to repeated advertisements shows me that the desired subjective effect is real enough and that I indeed will be well dressed and in fashion if I purchase the shirt. The indirect information may lead to a rational decision to purchase a product because the information testifies to the subjective effect that the product brings about.[15]

Some philosophers will be unhappy with the conclusion of this section, largely because they have a concept of true, rational, or ideal desire which is not the same as the one used here. A Marxist, for instance, may urge that any desire felt by alienated man in a capitalistic society is foreign to his true nature. Or an existentialist may claim that the desires of inauthentic men are themselves inauthentic. Such concepts are based upon general theories of human nature which are unsubstantiated and perhaps incapable of substantiation. Moreover, each of these theories is committed to a concept of an ideal desire which is normatively debatable and which is distinct from the ordinary concept of a rational desire as one based upon relevant information. But it is in the terms of the ordinary concept that we express our concern that advertising may limit our autonomy in the sense of leading us to act on irrational desires, and if we operate with this concept we are driven again to the conclusion that advertising may lead, but probably most often does not lead, to an infringement of autonomy.

(c) *Free Choice.* It might be said

15. Michalos argues that in emphasizing a brand name—such as Bayer Aspirin—advertisers are illogically attempting to distinguish the indistinguishable by casting a trivial feature of a product as a significant one which separates it from other brands of the same product. The brand name is said to be trivial or unimportant

"from the point of view of the effectiveness of the product or that for the sake of which the product is purchased" (*op. cit.*, p. 107). This claim ignores the role of indirect information in advertising. For example, consumers want an aspirin *they can trust* (trustworthiness being part of "that for the sake of which the product is purchased"), and the indirect information conveyed by the widespread advertising effort for Bayer aspirin shows that this product is judged trustworthy by many other purchasers. Hence the emphasis on the name is not at all irrelevant but rather is a significant feature of the product from the consumer's standpoint, and attending to the name is not at all an illogical or irrational response on the part of the consumer.

that some desires are so strong or so covert that a person cannot resist them, and that when he acts on such desires he is not acting freely or voluntarily but is rather the victim of irresistible impulse or an unconscious drive. Perhaps those who condemn advertising feel that it produces this kind of desire in us and consequently reduces our autonomy.

This raises a very difficult issue. How do we distinguish between an impulse we *do* not resist and one we *could* not resist, between freely giving in to a desire and succumbing to one? I have argued elsewhere that the way to get at this issue is in terms of the notion of acting for a reason.[16] A person acts or chooses freely if he does so for a reason, that is, if he can adduce considerations which justify in his mind the act in question. Many of our actions are in fact free because this conditon frequently holds. Often, however, a person will act from habit, or whim, or impulse, and on these occasions he does not have a reason in mind. Nevertheless he often acts voluntarily in these instances, i.e., he could have acted otherwise. And this is because if there *had been* a reason for acting otherwise of which he was aware, he would in fact have done so. Thus acting from habit or impulse is not necessarily to act in an involuntary manner. If, however, a person is aware of a good reason to do x and still follows his impulse to do y, then he can be said to be impelled by irresistible impulse and hence to act involuntarily. Many kleptomaniacs can be said to act involuntarily, for in spite of their knowledge that they likely will be caught and their aware-

ness that the goods they steal have little utilitarian value to them, they nevertheless steal. Here their 'out of character' desires have the upper hand, and we have a case of compulsive behavior.

Applying these notions of voluntary and compulsive behavior to the case of behavior prompted by advertising, can we say that consumers influenced by advertising act compulsively? The unexciting answer is: sometimes they do, sometimes not. I may have an overwhelming, TV induced urge to own a Mazda RX–7 and all the while realize that I can't afford one without severely reducing my family's caloric intake to a dangerous level. If, aware of this good reason not to purchase the car, I nevertheless do so, this shows that I have been the victim of TV compulsion. But if I have the urge, as I assure you I do, and don't act on it, or if in some other possible world I could afford an RX–7, then I have not been the subject of undue influence by Mazda advertising. Some Mazda RX–7 purchasers act compulsively; others do not. The Mazda advertising effort *in general* cannot be condemned, then, for impairing its customers' autonomy in the sense of limiting free or voluntary choice. Of course the question remains what should be done about the fact that advertising may and does *occasionally* limit free choice. We shall return to this question later.

In the case of subliminal advertising we may find an individual whose subconscious desires are activated by advertising into doing something his calculating, reasoning ego does not approve. This would be a case of compulsion. But most of us have a benevolent subconsciousness which does not overwhelm our ego and its reasons for action. And therefore

---

16. Robert L. Arrington, "Practical Reason, Responsibility and the Psychopath," *Journal for the Theory of Social Behavior* 9 (1979), 71–89.

most of us can respond to subliminal advertising without thereby risking our autonomy. To be sure, if some advertising firm developed a subliminal technique which drove all of us to purchase Lear jets, thereby reducing our caloric intake to the zero point, then we would have a case of advertising which could properly be censured for infringing our right to autonomy. We should acknowledge that this is possible, but at the same time we should recognize that it is not an inherent result of subliminal advertising.

(d) *Control or Manipulation.* Briefly let us consider the matter of control and manipulation. Under what conditions do these activities occur? In a recent paper on 'Forms and Limits of Control' I suggested the following criteria:[17]

A person *C* controls the behavior of another person *P* if

1. *C* intends *P* to act in a certain way *A*;
2. *C*'s intention is causally effective in bringing about *A*; and
3. *C* intends to ensure that all of the necessary conditions of *A* are satisfied.

These criteria may be elaborated as follows. To control another person it is not enough that one's actions produce certain behavior on the part of that person; additionally one must intend that this happen. Hence control is the intentional production of behavior. Moreover, it is not enough just to have the intention; the intention must give rise to the conditions which bring about the intended effect. Finally, the controller must

intend to establish by his actions any otherwise unsatisfied necessary conditions for the production of the intended effect. The controller is not just influencing the outcome, not just having input; he is as it were guaranteeing that the sufficient conditions for the intended effect are satisfied.

Let us apply these criteria of control to the case of advertising and see what happens. Conditions 1. and 3. are crucial. Does the Mazda manufacturing company or its advertising agency intend that I buy an RX–7? Do they intend that a certain number of people buy the car? *Prima facie* it seems more appropriate to say that they *hope* a certain number of people will buy it, and hoping and intending are not the same. But the difficult term here is 'intend.' Some philosophers have argued that to intend *A* it is necessary only to desire that *A* happen and to believe that it will. If this is correct, and if marketing analysis gives the Mazda agency a reasonable belief that a certain segment of the population will buy its product, then, assuming on its part the desire that this happen, we have the conditions necessary for saying that the agency intends that a certain segment purchase the car. If I am a member of this segment of the population, would it then follow that the agency intends that I purchase an RX–7? Or is control referentially opaque? Obviously we have some questions here which need further exploration.

Let us turn to the third condition of control, the requirement that the controller intend to activate or bring about any otherwise unsatisfied necessary conditions for the production of the intended effect. It is in terms of this condition that we are able to distinguish brainwashing from liberal education. The brainwasher arranges all of the necessary condi-

17. Robert L. Arrington, "Forms and Limits of Control," delivered at the annual meeting of the Southern Society for Philosophy and Psychology, Birmingham, Alabama, 1980.

tions for belief. On the other hand, teachers (at least those of liberal persuasion) seek only to influence their students—to provide them with information and enlightenment which they may absorb *if they wish*. We do not normally think of teachers as controlling their students, for the students' performances depend as well on their own interests and inclinations.

Now the advertiser—does he control, or merely influence, his audience? Does he intend to ensure that all of the necessary conditions for purchasing behavior are met, or does he offer information and symbols which are intended to have an effect only *if* the potential purchaser has certain desires? Undeniably advertising induces some desires, and it does this intentionally, but more often than not it intends to induce a desire for a particular object, *given* that the purchaser already has other desires. Given a desire for youth, or power, or adventure, or ravishing beauty, we are led to desire Grecian Formula 16, Mazda RX–7s, Pongo Peach, and Distinctive Foundations. In this light, the advertiser is influencing us by appealing to independent desires we already have. He is not creating those basic desires. Hence it seems appropriate to deny that he intends to produce all of the necessary conditions for our purchases, and appropriate to deny that he controls us.[18]

Let me summarize my argument. The critics of advertising see it as having a pernicious effect on the autonomy of consumers, as controlling their lives and manufacturing their very souls. The defense claims that advertising only offers information and in effect allows industry to provide consumers with what they want. After developing some of the philosophical dimensions of this dispute, I have come down tentatively in favor of the advertisers. Advertising may, but certainly does not always or even frequently, control behavior, produce compulsive behavior, or create wants which are not rational or are not truly those of the consumer. Admittedly it may in individual cases do all of these things, but it is innocent of the charge of intrinsically or necessarily doing them or even, I think, of often doing so. This limited potentiality, to be sure, leads to the question whether advertising should be abolished or severely curtailed or regulated because of its potential to harm a few poor souls in the above ways. This is a very difficult question, and I do not pretend to have the answer. I only hope that the above discussion, in showing some of the kinds of harm that can be done by advertising and by indicating the likely limits of this harm, will put us in a better position to grapple with the question.

---

18. Michalos distinguishes between appealing to people's tastes and molding those tastes (*op. cit.*, p. 104), and he seems to agree with my claim that it is morally permissible for advertisers to persuade us to consume some article *if* it suits our tastes (p. 105). However, he also implies that advertisers mold tastes as well as appeal to them. It is unclear what evidence is given for this claim, and it is unclear what is meant by *tastes*. If the latter are thought of as basic desires and wants, then I would agree that advertisers are controlling their customers to the extent that they intentionally mold tastes. But if by molding tastes is meant generating a desire for the particular object they promote, advertisers in doing so may well be appealing to more basic desires, in which case they should not be thought of as controlling the consumer.

C O M M E N T S ■ Q U E S T I O N S

1. "There is something wrong in setting up the issue over advertising
and behavior control whether our
desires are truly ours *or* are created in us by advertisements."
According to Arrington, many of
the desires that we acquire as a
consequence of being exposed to
advertisements are desires that *become* our own. We do not repudiate them. There are exceptions,
but they are a small minority of
cases. Does Arrington's experience
conform to your own? Can you
think of *any* desires that you have
acquired from ads that you wish
you did not have? Are there desires
that you have acquired from ads
that you are *glad* that you have?
Are there very many such desires?

2. "Surely many (most?) advertisements directly promise subjective
effects that their patrons actually
desire (and obtain when they
purchase the product), and thus
the ads provide relevant informa-

tion for rational choice." Can you
think of examples of products that
you buy for their subjective effects?
Are you happy with yourself that
you buy such products?

3. According to Arrington, ads sometimes induce us to act on the basis
of "irresistible impulses," to do
things that are clearly not in our
best interest. Has this ever happened to you? If it were to happen
very often to very many people,
then this would be a serious indictment of general advertising practices. Do you believe that it does
happen very often, if not to yourself then to other people? If it has
never happened to you, then what
reason might you have to believe
that it happens to others?

4. Arrington presents what he describes as a "tentative" defense of
advertising. Can his position be
supported by an appeal to basic
moral principles?

G E N E   G.   J A M E S

Whistle Blowing: Its Nature and Justification

histle blowing has increased significantly in America during the last two decades. Like blowing a whistle to call attention to a thief, whistle blowing is an attempt by a member or former member of an organization to bring illegal or socially harmful activities of the organization to the attention of the public. This may be done openly or anonymously and may involve any kind of organization, although business corporations and government agencies are most frequently involved. It may also require the whistle blower to violate laws or rules such as national security regulations which prohibit the release of certain information. However, because whistle blowing involving national security raises a number of issues not raised by other types, the present discussion is restricted to situations involving business corporations and government agencies concerned with domestic matters.

I

It is no accident that whistle blowing gained prominence during the last two decades which have been a period of great government and corporate wrongdoing. The Vietnam war, Watergate, illicit activities by intelligence agencies both at home and abroad, the manufacture and sale of defective and unsafe products, misleading and fraudulent advertising, pollution of the environment, depletion of scarce natural resources, illegal bribes and campaign contributions, and attempts by corporations to influence political activities in third world nations are only some of the events occurring during this period. Viewed in this perspective it is surprising that more whistle blowing has not occurred. Yet few employees of organizations involved in wrongdoing have spoken out in protest. Why are such people the first to know but usually the last to speak out?

The reason most often given for the relative infrequency of whistle blowing is loyalty to the organization. I do not doubt that this is sometimes a deterrent to whistle blowing. Daniel Ellsberg, e.g., mentions it as the main obstacle he had to overcome in deciding to make the Pentagon Papers

Gene G. James is professor of philosophy at Memphis State University. He is co-author of the text Elementary Logic *and author of a number of articles on social and political philosophy and ethics. His current research is focused on technology and human values.*

Gene G. James, "Whistle Blowing: Its Nature and Justification," in *Philosophy in Context*, vol. 10, copyright © 1980, pp. 99–117. Reprinted by permission of the Department of Philosophy, Cleveland State University, Cleveland, Ohio 44115.

public.[1] But by far the greatest deterrent, in my opinion, is self-interest. People are afraid that they will lose their job, be demoted, suspended, transferred, given less interesting or more demanding work, fail to obtain a bonus, salary increase, promotion, etc. This deterrent alone is sufficient to keep most people from speaking out even when they see great wrongdoing going on around them.

Fear of personal retaliation is another deterrent. Since whistle blowers seem to renounce loyalty to the organization, and threaten the self-interest of fellow employees, they are almost certain to be attacked in a variety of ways. In addition to such charges as they are unqualified to judge, are misinformed, and do not have all the facts, they are likely to be said to be traitors, squealers, rat finks, etc. They may be said to be disgruntled, known troublemakers, people who make an issue out of nothing, self-seeking and doing it for the publicity. Their veracity, life style, sex life and mental stability may also be questioned. Most of these accusations, of course, have nothing to do with the issues raised by whistle blowers. As Dr. John Goffman, who blew the whistle on the AEC for inadequate radiation standards, said of his critics, they "attack my style, my emotion, my sanity, my loyalty, my public forums, my motives. Everything except the issue."[2] Abuse of their families, physical assaults, and even murder, are not unknown as retaliation to whistle blowers.

The charge that they are self-seeking or acting for the publicity is one that bothers many whistle blowers. Although whistle blowing may be anonymous, if it is to be effective it frequently requires not only that the whistle blower reveal his or her identity, but also that he or she seek ways of publicizing the wrongdoing. Because this may make the whistle blower appear a self-appointed messiah, it prevents some people from speaking out. Whistle blowing may also appear, or be claimed to be, politically motivated when it is not.

Since whistle blowing may require one to do something illegal such as copy confidential records, threat of prosecution and prison may be additional deterrents.

II

Not only laws which forbid the release of information but agency law which governs the obligations of employees to employers seems to prohibit whistle blowing.[3] Agency law imposes three primary duties on employees: obedience, loyalty and con-

1. See Charles Peters and Taylor Branch, *Blowing the Whistle: Dissent in the Public Interest*, New York, 1972, Praeger Publishers, Chapter Sixteen.

2. Quoted in Ralph Nader, Peter J. Petkas and Kate Blackwell, *Whistle Blowing*, New York, 1972, Grossman Publishers, p. 72.

3. For a discussion of agency law and its relation to whistle blowers see Lawrence E. Blades "Employment at Will vs. Individual Freedom: On Limiting the Abusive Exercise of Employer Power," *Columbia Law Review* 67 (1967), and Philip Blumberg, "Corporate Responsibility and the Employee's Duty of Loyalty and Obedience: A Preliminary Inquiry," *Oklahoma Law Review* 24 (1971), reprinted in part in Tom L. Beauchamp and Norman E. Bowie, *Ethical Theory and Business*, New York, 1979, Prentice Hall; and Clyde W. Summers, "Individual Protection Against Unjust Dismissal: Time for a statute," *Virginia Law Review* 62 (1976). See also Nader, *Op. Cit.*, and David W. Ewing, *Freedom Inside the Organization*, New York, 1977, E. P. Dutton.

fidentiality. These may be summed up by saying that in general employees are expected to obey all reasonable directives of their employers, to not engage in any economic activities detrimental to their employers, and to not communicate any information learned through their employment which either might harm their employer or which he might not want revealed. This last duty holds even after the employee no longer works for the employer. However, all three duties are qualified in certain respects. For example, although the employee is under an obligation to not start a competing business, he or she does have the right to advocate passage of laws and regulations which adversely affect the employer's business. And while the employee has a general obligation of confidentiality, this obligation does not hold if he has knowledge that his employer has committed, or is about to commit, a crime. Finally, in carrying out the duty of obeying all reasonable directives, the employee is given the discretion to consult codes of business and professional ethics in deciding what is and is not reasonable.

One problem with the law of agency is that there are no provisions in it to penalize an employer who harasses or fires employees for doing any of the things the law permits them to do. Thus, employees who advocate passage of laws which adversely affect their employers, who report or testify regarding a crime, or who refuse to obey a directive they consider illegal or immoral, are likely to be fired. Employees have even been fired on the last day before their pension would become effective after thirty years of work and for testifying under subpoena against their employers without the courts doing any-

thing to aid them. Agency law in effect presupposes an absolute right of employers to dismiss employees at will. That is, unless there are statutes or contractual agreements to the contrary, an employer may dismiss an employee at any time for any reason, or even for no reason, without being accountable at law. This doctrine which is an integral part of contract law goes all the way back to the code of Hammurabi in 632 B.C., which stated that an organizer could staff his workforce with whomever he wished. It was also influenced by Roman law which referred to employers and employees as "masters" and "servants," and by Adam Smith's notion of freedom of contract according to which employers and employees freely enter into the employment contract so either has the right to terminate it at will. Philip Blumberg, Dean of the School of Law at the University of Connecticut, sums up the current status of the right of employers to discharge as follows: "Over the years, this right of discharge has been increasingly restricted by statute and by collective bargaining agreements, but the basic principle of the employer's legal right to discharge, although challenged on the theoretical level, is still unimpaired."[4] The full significance of this remark is not apparent until one examines the extent to which existing statutes and collective bargaining agreements protect whistle blowers. As we shall see below, they provide very little protection. Furthermore, since in the absence of statutes or agreements to the contrary, employers can dismiss employees at will, it is obvious that they can also

---

4. Blumberg, *Op. Cit.,* in Beauchamp and Bowie, p. 311.

demote, transfer, suspend or otherwise retaliate against employees who speak out against, or refuse to participate in, illegal or socially harmful activities.

A second problem with the law of agency is that it seems to put one under an absolute obligation to not disclose any information about one's employer unless one can document that a crime has been, or is about to be, committed. This means that disclosing activities which are harmful to the public, but not presently prohibited by law, can result in one's being prosecuted or sued for damages. As Arthur S. Miller puts it: "The law at present provides very little protection to the person who would blow the whistle; in fact, it is more likely to assess him with criminal or civil penalties."[5] All that the whistle blower has to protect himself is the hope that the judge will be lenient, or that there will be a public outcry against his employer so great that he will not proceed against him.

III

There are some laws which encourage or protect whistle blowing. The Refuse Act of 1899 gives anyone who reports pollution one half of any fine that is assessed. Federal tax laws provide for the Secretary of the Treasury to pay a reward for information about violations of the Internal Revenue Code. The Commissioner of Narcotics is similarly authorized to pay a reward for information about contraband narcotics. The Federal Fair Labor Standards Act prohibits discharge of employees who complain or testify about violations of

federal wage and hour laws. The Coal Mine Safety Act and the Water Pollution Control Act have similar clauses. And the Occupational Safety and Health Act prohibits discrimination against, or discharge of, employees who report violations of the act.

The main problem with all these laws, however, is that they must be enforced to be effective. The Refuse Act of 1899, for example, was not enforced prior to 1969 and fines imposed since then have been minimal. A study of the enforcement of the Occupational Safety and Health Act in 1976 by Morton Corn,[6] then an Assistant Secretary of Labor, showed that there were 700 complaints in FY 1975 and 1600 in FY 1976 by employees who claimed they were discharged or discriminated against because they had reported a violation of the act. Only about 20% of these complaints were judged valid by OSHA investigators. More than half of these, that is to say, less than three hundred, were settled out of court. The remaining complaints were either dropped or taken to court. Of the 60 cases taken to court at the time of Corn's report in November 1976, one had been won, eight lost and the others were still pending. Hardly a record to encourage further complaints.

What help can whistle blowers who belong to a union expect from it? In some cases unions have intervened to keep whistle blowers from being fired or to help them gain reinstatement. But for the most part

5. Arthur S. Miller, "Whistle Blowing and the Law" in Nader, *Op. Cit.,* p. 25.

6. Corn's report is discussed by Frank von Hipple in "Professional Freedom and Responsibility: The Role of the Professional Society," in the *Newsletter on Science, Technology and Human Values*, Number 22, January 1978, pp. 37–42.

they have restricted themselves to economic issues, not speaking out on behalf of free speech for their members. Also, some unions are as bad offenders as any corporation. David Ewing has well stated this problem. "While many unions are run by energetic, capable, and high-minded officials, other unions seem to be as despotic and corrupt as the worse corporate management teams. Run by mossbacks who couldn't care less about ideals like due process, these unions are not likely to feed a hawk that may come to prey in their own backyard."[7]

The record of professional societies is not much better. Despite the fact that the code of ethics of nearly every profession requires the professional to place his duty to the public above his duty to his employer, very few professional societies have come to the aid of members who have blown the whistle. However, there are some indications that this is changing. The American Association for the Advancement of Science recently created a standing committee on Scientific Freedom and Responsibility which sponsored a symposium on whistle blowing at the 1978 meeting and is encouraging scientific societies and journals to take a more active role in whistle blowing situations. A sub-committee to review individual cases has also been formed.[8]

Many employees of the federal government are in theory protected

from arbitrary treatment by civil service regulations. However, these have provided little protection for whistle blowers in the past. Indeed, the failure of civil service regulations to protect whistle blowers was one of the factors which helped bring about the Civil Service Reform Act of 1978. This act explicitly prohibits reprisal against employees who release information they believe is evidence of: (a) violation of law, rules, or regulations, (b) abuse of authority, mismanagement, or gross waste of funds, (c) specific and substantial danger to public health or safety. The act also sets up mechanisms to enforce its provisions. Unfortunately, it excludes all employees of intelligence agencies, even when the issue involved is not one of national security, except employees of the FBI who are empowered to go to the Attorney General with information about wrongdoing. Although it is too early to determine how vigorously the act will be enforced, it seems on paper to offer a great deal of protection for whistle blowers.

Although state and local laws usually do not offer much protection, thanks to a series of federal court decisions, people who work for state and municipal governments are also better off than people who work for private corporations. In the first of these in 1968 the Supreme Court ordered the reinstatement of a high school teacher named Pickering who had publicly criticized his school board. This was followed by a 1970 district court decision reinstating a Chicago policeman who had accused his superiors of covering up thefts by policemen. In 1971 another teacher who criticized unsafe playground conditions was reinstated. And in 1973 a fireman and a psychiatric nurse who criticized their agencies

---

7. Ewing, *Op. Cit.,* pp. 165–166.
8. Discussion of the role professional societies have played in whistle blowing can be found in Nader, *Op. Cit.,* von Hipple, *Op. Cit.,* and in Rosemary Chalk, "Scientific Involvement in Whistle Blowing" in the *Newsletter on Science, Technology and Human Values, Op. Cit.,* pp. 47–51.

were reinstated. In all of these decisions, however, a key factor seems to have been that the action of the employee did not disrupt the morale of fellow employees. Also no documents of the organizations were made public. Had either of these factors been different the decisions would have probably gone the other way.[9]

Given the lack of support whistle blowers have received in the past from the law, unions, professional societies, and government agencies, the fear that one will be harassed or lose one's job for blowing the whistle is well founded, especially if one works for private industry. Moreover, since whistle blowers are unlikely to be given favorable letters of recommendation, finding another job is not easy. Thus despite some changes for the better, unless there are major changes in agency law, the operation and goals of unions and professional societies, and more effective enforcement of laws protecting government employees, we should not expect whistle blowing to increase significantly in the near future. This means that much organization wrongdoing will go unchecked.

IV

Whistle blowing is not lacking in critics. When Ralph Nader issued a call for more whistle blowing in an article in the *New York Times* in 1971, James M. Roche, Chairman of the Board of General Motors Corporation responded:

Some of the enemies of business now encourage an employee to be disloyal to the enterprise. They want to create suspicion and disharmony and pry into the proprietary interests of the business. However this is labelled—industrial espionage, whistle blowing or professional responsibility—it is another tactic for spreading disunity and creating conflict.[10]

The premise upon which Roche's remarks seems to be based is that an employee's only obligation is to the company for which he works. Thus he sees no difference between industrial espionage—stealing information from one company to benefit another economically—and the disclosure of activities harmful to the public. Both injure the company involved, so both are equally wrong. This position is similar to another held by many businessmen, viz., that the sole obligation of corporate executives is to make a profit for stockholders for whom they serve as agents. This is tantamount to saying that employees of corporations have no obligations to the public. However, this is not true because corporations are chartered by governments with the expectation that they will function in ways that are compatible with the public interest. Whenever they cease to do this, they violate the understanding under which they were chartered and allowed to exist, and may be legitimately penalized or even have their charters revoked. Furthermore, part of the expectation with which corporations are chartered in democratic societies is that not only will they obey the law, but in addition they will not do anything which undermines basic democratic processes. Corporations, that is, are expected to be not only legal persons but good citizens as well. This does not mean that

---

9. These decisions are discussed by Ewing, *Op. Cit.,* Chapter Six.

---

10. Quoted in Blumberg, *Op. Cit.,* p. 305.

corporations must donate money to charity or undertake other philanthropic endeavors, although it is admirable if they do. It means rather that the minimum conduct expected of them is that they will make money only in ways that are consistent with the public good. As officers of corporations it is the obligation of corporate executives to see that this is done. It is only within this framework of expectations that the executive can be said to have an obligation to stockholders to return maximum profit on their investments. It is only within this framework, also, that employees of a corporation have an obligation to obey its directives. This is the reason the law of agency exempts employees from obeying illegal or unethical commands. It is also the reason that there is a significant moral difference between industrial espionage and whistle blowing. The failure of Roche and other corporate officials to realize this, believing instead that their sole obligation is to operate their companies profitably, and that the sole obligation of employees is to obey their directives without question, is one of the central reasons corporate wrongdoing exists and whistle blowing is needed.

Another objection to whistle blowing advanced by some businessmen is that it increases costs, thereby reducing profits and raising prices for consumers. There is no doubt that it has cost companies considerable money to correct situations disclosed by whistle blowers. However, this must be balanced against costs incurred when the public eventually comes to learn, without the aid of whistle blowers, that corporate wrongdoing has taken place. Would Ford Motor Company or Firestone Rubber Company have made less money in the long run had they listened to their engineers who warned that the gas tank of the Pinto and Firestone radial tires were unsafe? I think a good case could be made that they would not. Indeed, if corporate executives were to listen to employees troubled by their companies' practices and products, in many cases they would improve their earnings. So strong, however, is the feeling that employees should obey orders without questioning, that when an oil pipeline salesman for U.S. Steel went over the head of unresponsive supervisors to report defective pipelines to top company officials, he was fired even though the disclosure saved the company thousands of dollars.

I am not arguing that corporate crime never pays, for often it pays quite handsomely. But the fact that there are situations in which corporate crime is more profitable than responsible action, is hardly an argument against whistle blowing. It would be an argument against it only if one were to accept the premise that the sole obligation of corporations is to make as much money as possible by any means whatever. But as we saw above this premise cannot be defended and its acceptance by corporate executives in fact provides a justification for whistleblowing.

The argument that employees owe total allegiance to the organizations for which they work has also been put forth by people in government. For example, Frederick Malek, former Deputy Secretary of HEW states:

The employee, whether he is civil service or a political appointee, has not only the right but the obligation to make his views known in the most strenuous way possible to his superiors, and through them, to their superiors. He should try like hell to get his views across and adopted within the organization—but *not* publicly, and only until a decision is reached by those superiors. Once the decision is made, he must do the best he can to live with it and put it into practice. If he finds that he cannot do it, then he ought not to stay with the organization.[11]

And William Rehnquist, Justice of the Supreme Court, says "I think one may fairly generalize that a government employee . . . is seriously restricted in his freedom of speech with respect to any matter for which he has been assigned responsibility."[12]

Malek's argument presupposes that disclosure of wrongdoing to one's superior will be relayed to higher officials. But often it is one's immediate superiors who are responsible for the wrongdoing. Furthermore, even if they are not, there is no guarantee that they will relay one's protest. Malek also assumes that there are always means of protest within organizations and that these function effectively. This, too, is frequently not the case. For example, Peter Gall who resigned his position as an attorney for the Office of Civil Rights Division of HEW because the Nixon administration was failing to enforce desegregation laws, and who along with a number of colleagues sent a public letter of protest to President Nixon, says in response to Malek that:

. . . as far as I am concerned, his recommended line of action would have been a waste of everyone's time. To begin with, the OCR staff members probably would have made their protest to Secretary Finch if they had felt that Finch's views were

being listened to, or acted upon, at the White House. . . .[13]

And in defense of sending the public letter to Nixon he states that:

A chief reason we decided to flout protocol and make the text of the letter public was that we felt that the only way the President would even become aware of . . . the letter was through publicity. We had answered too many letters—including those bitterly attacking the retreat on segregation—referred unread by the White House . . . to have any illusion about what the fate of our letter would be. In fact, our standing joke . . . was that we would probably be asked to answer it ourselves.[14]

Even when there are effective channels of protest within an organization, there may be situations in which it is justifiable to bypass them: for example, if there is imminent danger to public health or safety, if one is criticizing the overall operation of an agency, or if using standard channels of protest would jeopardize the interests one is trying to protect.

If Justice Rehnquist's remark is meant as a recommendation that people whose responsibility is to protect the health, safety and rights of the American people should not speak out when they see continued wrongdoing, then it must be said to be grossly immoral. The viewpoint it represents is one that Americans repudiated at Nuremberg. Daniel Ellsberg's comments on why he finally decided to release the Pentagon Papers put this point well:

I think the principle of "company loyalty," as emphasized in the indoctrination within any bureaucratic structure, governmental or private, has come to sum up the

---

11. Quoted in Peters and Branch, *Op. Cit.,* pp. 178–179.

12. *Ibid.*, pp. x–xi.

13. *Ibid.*, p. 179.

14. *Ibid.*, p. 178.

notion of loyalty for many people. That is not a healthy situation, because the loyalty that a democracy requires to function is a ... varied set of loyalties which includes loyalty to one's fellow citizens, and certainly loyalty to the Constitution and to the broader institutions of the country. Obviously, these loyalties can come into conflict, and merely mentioning the word "loyalty" doesn't dissolve those dilemmas. ... The Code of Ethics of Government Service, passed by both the House and Senate, starts with the principle that every employee of the government should put loyalty to the highest moral princples and to country above loyalty to persons, parties, or government department. ... To believe that the government cannot run unless one puts loyalty to the President above everything else is a formula for a dictatorship, and not for a republic.[15]

V

Even some people who are favorable to whistle blowing are afraid that it might become too widespread. For example, Arthur S. Miller writes: "One should be very careful about extending the principle of whistle blowing unduly. Surely it can be carried too far. Surely, too, an employee owes his employer enough loyalty to try to work, first of all, within the organization to attempt to effect change.[16] And Philip Blumberg expresses the fear that "once the duty of loyalty yields to the primacy of what the individual ... regards as the 'public interest,' the door is open to widespread abuse."[17]

It would be unfortunate if employees were to make public pronouncements every time they thought they saw something wrong within an organization without making sure they have the facts. And employees ought to exhaust all channels of protest within an organization before blowing the whistle, *provided* it is feasible to do so. Indeed, as Ralph Nader and his associates point out, in many cases "going to management first minimizes the risk of retaliatory dismissal, as you may not have to go public with your demands if the corporation or government agency takes action to correct the situation. It may also strengthen your case if you ultimately go outside ... since the managers are likely to point out any weaknesses in your arguments and any factual deficiencies in your evidence in order to persuade you that there is really no problem."[18] But this is subject to the qualifications mentioned in connection with Malek's argument.

If it is true, as I argued above, that self-interest and narrow loyalties will always keep the majority of people from speaking out even when they see great wrongdoing going on around them, then the fear that whistle blowing could become so prevalent as to threaten the everyday working of organizations seems groundless. However, Miller's and Blumberg's remarks do call to our attention the fact that whistle blowers have certain obligations. All whistle blowers should ask themselves the following kinds of questions before acting: What exactly is the objectionable practice? What laws are being broken or specific harm done? Do I have adequate and accurate information about the wrongdoing? How could I get additional information? Is it feasible to report the wrongdoing

---

15. *Ibid.*, p. 269.
16. Miller, *Op. Cit.*, p. 30.
17. Blumberg, *Op. Cit.*, p. 313.

---

18. Nader, *Op. Cit.*, pp. 230–231.

to someone within the organization? Is there a procedure for doing this? What are the results likely to be? Will doing this make it easier or more difficult if I decide to go outside? Will I be violating the law or shirking my duty if I do not report the matter to people outside the organization? If I go outside to whom should I go? Should I do this openly or anonymously? Should I resign and look for another job before doing it? What will be the likely response of those whom I inform? What can I hope to achieve in going outside? What will be the consequences for me, my family and friends? What will the consequences of *not* speaking out be for me, my family and friends? What will the consequences be for the public? Could I live with my conscience if I do not speak out?

C O M M E N T S ▪ Q U E S T I O N S

1. Whistle blowing almost always involves a conflict of values: self-interest versus concern for others; loyalty to the company one works for versus a concern for the welfare of consumers who may use a harmful product manufactured by the company; a respect for law versus the need to break a law in order to obtain information that is damaging to an irresponsible organization; and so on. Does James present a properly balanced analysis of the important conflicts of values involved in whistle blowing?

2. A person who blows the whistle on the organization for which he or she works can be harmed in a great many different ways, which James discusses. Because of this, says James, "we should not expect whistle blowing to increase significantly in the near future. This means that much organization wrongdoing will go unchecked." How serious a problem do you believe this is? Does James perhaps exaggerate the need for whistle blowing in contemporary society? Or does he understate the need for it?

3. What arguments do you suppose would be made by John Hospers in defense of whistle blowing? By Alan H. Goldman? What arguments could be made in defense of whistle blowing by applying the basic moral principles stated in chapter 1? What arguments based upon these principles might be made *against* whistle blowing in selected cases?

R E A D I N G S

Acton, H. B. *The Morals of Markets: An Ethical Exploration*. London: Longman Group Limited, 1971.

Bok, Sissela. *Lying: Moral Choice in Public and Private Life*. New York: Pantheon Books, 1978.

Chamberlain, Neil W. *The Place of Business in America's Future: A Study in Social Values.* New York: Basic Books, 1973.

Dworkin, Gerald; Bermanto, Gordon; and Brown, Peter G., eds. *Markets and Morals.* Washington, D.C.; Hemisphere Publishing Corp., 1977.

Edwards, Richard C., Michael Reich, and Thomas Weisskopf, eds. *The Capitalist System.* 2d ed. Englewood Cliffs, N.J.: Prentice-Hall, 1978.

Ewing, David W. *Freedom Inside the Organization: Bringing Civil Liberties to the Workplace.* New York: E. P. Dutton, 1977.

Friedman, Milton. *Capitalism and Freedom.* Chicago: University of Chicago Press, 1962.

Held, Virginia. *The Public Interest and Individual Interests.* New York: Basic Books, 1970.

Lucas, John T. and Richard Gurman. *Truth in Advertising.* New York: American Management Association, 1972.

Millum, Trevor. *Images of Woman: Advertising in Woman's Magazines.* Totowa, N.J.: Rowman and Littlefield, 1975.

Nader, Ralph, Peter J. Petkas, and Kate Blackwell, eds. *Whistle Blowing: The Report of the Conference on Professional Responsibility.* New York: Grossman, 1972.

Packard, Vance. *The Hidden Persuaders.* New York: Pocket Books, 1957.

Rawls, John. *A Theory of Justice.* Cambridge: Harvard University Press, 1971.

Sandage, C. H., and Vernon Fryburger. *Advertising Theory and Practice.* 9th ed. Homewood, Ill.: Richard D. Irwin, Inc., 1975.

Steiner, George A. *Business and Society.* 2d ed. New York: Random House, 1975.

Walton, Clarence C. *Corporate Social Responsibilities.* Belmont, Calif.: Wadsworth Publishing Company, 1967.

Walton, Clarence C., ed. *The Ethics of Corporate Conduct.* Englewood Cliffs, N.J.: Prentice-Hall, 1977.

The Death Penalty

T hroughout much of human history the death penalty has been imposed for a great variety of crimes, including murder, treason, heresy, rape, and even adultery and theft. At the present time in many countries of the world the death penalty is still widely used for criminal and political offenses. But in the United States and other Western countries, the death penalty—when and if it is imposed at all—is imposed almost exclusively in cases of murder. And in recent years the focus of debate regarding the death penalty has been restricted even further. At the present time, the question usually is not: Should the death penalty be imposed for murder cases in general? Rather, the question today is: Should the death penalty be imposed only in certain types of murder cases, such as those involving the killing of police or prison guards or where the killing is particularly vicious? Over the past decade, where state legislatures have considered bills to restore the death penalty in states where it had previously been abolished, almost all of the bills have been restricted to certain "types" of murder.

Opponents of the death penalty would like to see the historical progression in Western countries away from use of the death penalty to continue to the point where it is eliminated completely. At the same time, those who *favor* the death penalty have dug in their heels and insisted that the evolutionary movement away from its use should finally be stopped. They want the movement to be stopped at some point that is short, but not very far short, of total abolition.

During the decade 1967–1977, no executions took place in the United States. In part this was a consequence of general public sentiment, and in part it was because of the appeals of some specific murder cases that were pending before state courts and the United States Supreme Court. The most serious challenge raised by these appeals dealt with the constitutionality of the death penalty: Did it fit the description of "cruel and unusual punishment" prohibited by the Eighth Amendment?

In two important cases, the Supreme Court addressed this issue. First, in 1972 in *Furman vs. Georgia*, the Court declared unconstitutional any law that imposed the death penalty at the discretion of the judge or jury. Such discretionary power had been used arbitrarily and capriciously, said the Court. *Furman vs. Georgia* left undecided the question of whether the death penalty itself is unconstitutional. The second case, *Gregg vs. Georgia* in 1976, did rule on this broad issue. The Court held that the death penalty did not violate the Eighth Amendment's prohibition of cruel and unusual punishment.

Gregg vs. Georgia is worth examining in some detail. The majority opinion, written by Justice Potter Stewart, makes the following points in defense of the death penalty:

1. It is in accord with contemporary "standards of decency." It is consistent with the "basic concept of human dignity" which the Eighth Amendment is intended to protect.
2. It is reasonable to suppose that the death penalty does have some deterrent effect in regard to some cases of murder—those which are premeditated and in particular those committed by someone already sentenced to life in prison.
3. The death penalty is not "disproportionate" to the crime of murder. The death penalty is "unique in its severity and irrevocability," but for this reason it is "suitable to the most extreme of crimes."

In a dissenting opinion to *Gregg vs. Georgia*, which is included in this chapter, Justice Thurgood Marshall rejected the above three claims:

1. The death penalty is excessive, said Marshall, and therefore it is invalid under the "cruel and unusual" clause of the Eighth Amendment. Since the death penalty is not needed to accomplish any of the legitimate purposes of punishment, and since it is a particularly severe punishment, it should be judged to be cruel and unusual.
2. Available evidence does not show that the death penalty is a deterrent to crime.
3. The majority opinion appeals to the concept of retribution. [It does this in saying that the death penalty is proportionate to the crime of murder and that this is a reason for supporting the death penalty. The majority opinion appeals to retribution also when it says that the death penalty is morally acceptable purely for the reason that the murderer deserves it.] But retribution is a "total denial of the wrongdoer's dignity and worth," and thus violates the Eighth Amendment.

It is important to notice that there are two different disagreements between Justices Stewart and Marshall. First, they disagree about a matter of *fact*: is the death penalty a deterrent or not? Stewart says yes, while Marshall says no. Their disagreement here has to do with the consequences of the death penalty—will it tend to lessen the number of future acts of murder or not? Since Marshall believes that the death penalty will have no such beneficial effect, he concludes that its harshness is unnecessary and therefore "cruel and unusual."

Second, Stewart and Marshall disagree about the *moral appropriateness* of appealing to retribution in defending the death penalty. Stewart says it is appropriate, while Marshall says it is not. Their disagreement here is much more difficult to describe than is their disagreement regarding the deterrent value of the death penalty. Deterrence is a relatively easy concept to analyze, in contrast to retribution. It is perhaps easier to say what retribution is not than to say what retribution is.

Retribution is not an appeal to any supposed consequences of punishment. Thus it could never be understood as an appeal to the Principle of the Common Good. Deterrence, on the other hand, does fall under the Principle of the Common Good. Those who accept the death penalty for what they believe to be its deterrent value believe it will help reduce the number of murders that will take place in the future, and thus will make society a safer place.

Those who believe the death penalty is a deterrent can also appeal to the Principle of Rights, since they can say that the death penalty is an effective means to protect the right to life of innocent people who might otherwise become murder victims. But those who accept retribution cannot defend it in this way either. As they see it, a murderer should not be punished in order to protect the rights of innocent people, but instead because the murderer deserves it. Those who accept retribution also sometimes say that the death penalty is right, simply in the "nature of things." For someone who has committed the worst of all crimes, they say, justice requires that the most severe of all penalties be imposed, regardless of whether or not the punishment will have good consequences for other people.

A possible way to analyze the concept of retribution is to consider how the Principle or Rights might be applied, not to the potential victims of murder, but to the murderer. It is sometimes said that a retributive defense of the death penalty respects the human dignity of the condemned person because it is focused on that person, not—in contrast to the deterrence theory—on some use to which the condemned person's death may be put. Some philosophers, such as the German philosopher Hegel, have gone so far as to say that there is a "right to be punished." It should be noted that in *Gregg vs. Georgia* Justice Marshall in effect appeals to the Principle of Rights in order to *reject* the retributive defense of the death penalty. According to Marshall, the retributive view, far from respecting human dignity, is instead a denial of human dignity.

Almost all of the contemporary controversies regarding the death penalty have to do basically with questions about deterrence or questions about retribution. As we have noted, these are the central issues for the majority and dissenting opinions in *Gregg vs. Georgia*. However, not everyone who defends the death penalty would follow Justice Stewart in accepting *both* deterrence and retribution, and not everyone who rejects the death penalty would follow Justice Marshall in *rejecting* both deterrence and retribution. In addition to the positions taken by Stewart and Marshall, several other positions have been taken in recent discussions of the death penalty. Examples of three of them are included in this chapter. First, Steven Goldberg rejects retribution but accepts deterrence as a possible ground for defending the death penalty. Second, George Schedler allows that the death penalty does have deterrent value for certain groups of people, but says that this is not a good enough reason to defend the death penalty. Third, Robert S. Gerstein rests his somewhat tentative case in defense of the death penalty upon retribution but not upon deterrence.

STEVEN GOLDBERG

Does the Death Penalty Deter?

One who opposes the death penalty can terminate all discussion simply by asserting that it is morally unacceptable for a society to take the life of one of its own, and that it would be unacceptable even if it could be demonstrated that the death penalty deters some who would murder if their society did not invoke the death penalty. [1] Likewise, one who supports the death penalty can foreclose further discussion by asserting that an eye must be taken for an eye even if the taking of an eye does not deter anyone any more than would a lesser penalty. Each of these positions is as irrefutable as it is incapable of persuading anyone who does not already accept it.

The question of deterrence is, however, paramount. It is paramount not merely for those whose position would be based on the death penalty's deterrent effect—those who would favor the death penalty if it does deter, but would not if it does not—but also for those who favor and those who oppose the death penalty for any reason and wish to see their view become public policy. [2] For it seems inevitable that public

---

2. Three oft-heard arguments can be seen to reduce, in all respects relevant to this essay, to one or the other arguments referred to in the opening paragraph. (1) The argument that the death penalty is bad because it "creates a climate of violence" or "reduces the value put on life by the members of society" is either (A) arguing that the death penalty does not deter (indeed, that it *increases* the murder rate) or (B) arguing that the death penalty "reduces the value put on life" or "creates a climate of violence" in some sense that is not reflected in the murder rate and that, therefore, it is bad even if it does deter. I must admit that I have never understood in what sense the death penalty could be said to "reduce the value put on life" or "create a climate of violence" if it does deter or why anyone would care if the value put on life were reduced (or if there were an increase in the climate of violence) if this did not mean that there were, in fact, more violence. (2) The argument that the death penalty is good for the retributive reason that it reasserts the moral, social, or legal order is arguing that an eye must be taken for an eye and that the death penalty is good even if it does not deter. I must admit that I have never understood in what sense retribution could be said to reassert the moral, legal, and social order if the retribution does not even deter or why anyone would care

---

Steven Goldberg is an associate professor at the City University of New York. He is author of The Inevitability of Patriarchy.

---

1. This is, of course, the position on torture taken even by most proponents of the death penalty.

From Steven Goldberg, "Does the Death Penalty Deter?" This is a more recent version of a paper which originally appeared in *Ethics*, Vol. 85 (1974), pp 67–74. Copyright © 1974 by the University of Chicago. Reprinted by permission of the author and publisher.

policy will be derived from the assessment of the death penalty's deterrent effect. Therefore, even those who support or oppose the death penalty categorically for purely moral reasons, and for whom the question of deterrence is irrelevant, tend to argue their positions in terms of the ability or lack of ability of the death penalty to deter.[3] This has led to a situation in which the discussion of the death penalty has become—like the discussions of homosexuality, abortion, and pornography—a discussion in which both the proponents and opponents have raised to the level of high art the attempt to bypass logic and invent knowledge in order to make reality congruent with wish.

Those who deny the ability of the death penalty to deter almost invariably invoke a line of reasoning founded on two errors. They argue,

quite correctly, that the murderer often acts out of irrational motivations and conclude, incorrectly, that this somehow indicates that the death penalty does not deter. The two errors are:

(1) concluding that the death penalty does not deter those who have not murdered from the fact that it has not detered those who have murdered. It is not necessary to demonstrate that the death penalty has not deterred the murderer. Of course it hasn't; by definition, the murderer is one who has not been deterred by the death penalty or anything else. *The crucial question is not what deterred the murderer (nothing did—that's why he or she became a murderer), but what deterred those who were deterred (i.e., not the murderer, but the rest of us).* This, incidentally, makes clear the erroneousness of the argument that claims that the fact that many murderers think they will not be caught (so that they do not care what the penalty is) demonstrates that punishment does not deter. Unless one wants to be committed to the silly argument that murderers differ from nonmurderers only in that they think they won't be caught, he or she must ask what deters those who feel that they wouldn't be caught if they did murder, but who *don't* murder.

(2) the assumption that acts motivated by passion are immune to deterrence by the threat of penalty. This assumption is merely *asserted*, despite the fact that it runs counter to all human experience. It is true by definition, as we have just seen, that acts not deterred by the threat of penalty are not deterred by the threat of penalty. But every day millions of people feel anger; something prevents nearly all of them from murder-

---

if the moral, legal, or social order were reasserted if reassertion does not have even the empirical result of deterrence. (3) The argument that the death penalty is good because it supports the desire of a member of the society that, if he is murdered, society will avenge the injustice he suffered by meting out (what he sees as) justice is (in respects relevant to this essay) arguing that an eye must be taken for an eye.

3. Two important points of usage: (1) "deterrence" refers to the ability of a penalty to prevent *others* from taking an action; it does not refer to the deterrence of the person being penalized from taking such action in the future. In this paper I assume that the alternative to the death penalty is life imprisonment under conditions that would preclude the person being penalized from again taking the prohibited action (murder, kidnapping, etc.). (2) I do not like the jargonistic-sounding "positive sanction" and "negative sanction," but the connotations of these terms are more desirably inclusive than are "reward" and "punishment" (which, while arguably denotatively the same as the terms I use, connote relatively more formal sanctions).

ing to satisfy their anger. *There is, in other words, no reason to assume that the penalty for murder plays no role in deterring those who feel murderous feelings but do not murder; nor is there reason to assume that there is no one who is deterred by the threat of execution who would not have been deterred by a lesser penalty.* As we shall see, the increased deterrent effect of increased penalty need not imply any conscious calculation on the part of the potential criminal; the difference between a lesser and greater deterrence may exert its influence over the long term by emphasizing the seriousness of the criminal act and increasing the strength of the internalized resistance to that act.

Until the opponents of the death penalty can offer an alternative theoretical explanation of what deters the rest of us it is not likely that the assertion that the death penalty does not deter will be very persuasive. One need not, of course, accept an element as a "causal" factor simply because he cannot offer an alternative explanation, but when he denies an explanation that is both in accord with common sense and persuasive, it behooves him, if he cannot present an equally persuasive alternative explanation, to demonstrate that the element which is presented as the causal factor he denies cannot be the causal factor.[4] Opponents of the death penalty implicitly acknowledge this when they attempt to demonstrate that the death penalty is not a factor causing a lower murder rate (i.e., when they attempt to demonstrate that the death penalty does not deter).

For example, these opponents have pointed out, quite correctly, that some societies that do not invoke the death penalty have lower murder rates than some that do, and have implied that this fact somehow demonstrates that the death penalty does not deter. It does not, of course. The fact that society A has no death penalty and a murder rate half that of society B (which does invoke the death penalty) can just as legitimately, but no more legitimately, be interpreted as demonstrating that the death penalty does deter and that if society B did not invoke the death penalty it would have a murder rate of, say, four times that of society A. One might, in

---

4. It is, in general, true that, since most empirical variables are not closely "causally" related, the burden of "proof" is on one who claims a close relationship between two variables. This is, however, a rule of plausibility and not a rule of logic. It is important to keep the difference in mind when we consider the argument (made by those who deny that the death penalty deters) that places the burden of "proof" on those who claim that the death penalty deters. It is, it seems to me, most plausible that the death penalty deters. Both common sense and endless amounts of evidence indicate that stronger penalty tends to inculcate a stronger internal resistance to motivation for the penalized behavior, and to thereby reduce the amount of the penalized behavior. It would seem to me that the burden of "proof" is on those who claim that the increase from life imprisonment to death does not have the effect that every lesser increase has. (Subsequent to the writing of this essay and footnote, a number of empirical statistical studies have been published that conclude that the death penalty does deter. If the reader accepts the conclusion indicated by these studies, then he can view this essay as a theoretical explanation of the empirical relationship whose existence is demonstrated by the studies. If he does not accept the conclusion indicated by the studies then he is in the uncertain situation that existed when I wrote this essay. Perhaps the best known of the recent studies is Isaac Erlich's "Participation in Illegitimate Activities" in the May/June 1973 *Journal of Political Economy.*)

other words, argue that the very factors (whatever they are) that generate the high murder rate in society B necessitate the use of the death penalty. This is seen more clearly if we consider what would happen if we invoked the death penalty for all individuals who commit murder, except nuns. We would find that nuns had a far lower murder rate than did the rest of the population, and even though they comprised the only group that was not threatened with the death penalty this can hardly be argued to demonstrate that the death penalty does not deter. (If we had the death penalty only for nuns we would find that nuns had a lower murder rate; this can hardly be argued to demonstrate that it does deter.) Here, in our case, it is obvious that the determinative factor is the internalized social values of the individuals and the strength with which the values have been internalized and not (primarily) the presence or absence of the death penalty. We should note, however, that the fact that another factor (in this case the values that activate or obstruct murderous behavior) is a greater influence on the murder rate than is the presence or absence of the death penalty in no way affects our discussion of the death penalty nor does it indicate that the death penalty does not deter; the question is whether fewer members of the general population commit murder when they are socialized in the presence of the death penalty than when they are not and whether fewer nuns commit murder when *they* are socialized in the presence of the death penalty than when *they* are not and not whether other factors deter. In other words, if the death penalty does deter, the fact that other factors are more effective in inculcating a strong resistance to socially forbidden behavior is irrelevant and will be unless it can be demonstrated that these other factors could reduce the murder rate to zero.

Criminologists have attempted to eliminate the problem of contaminating factors by using statistics on American states, sections of states, and regions for comparisons of every conceivable combination of factors. However, while some comparisons have increased our understanding of the relative importance of various factors to murder rates (as in their demonstration of the immense importance of differing regional values to differing murder rates), I think that they encounter a problem that is insurmountable, particularly if the suggestion of how capital punishment might deter advanced in this essay is correct. All of these American states and areas are in a society that has traditionally emphasized the importance of the prohibition of murder by invoking the death penalty, and this emphasis may well have been internalized even by the populations of those states that have not invoked it. It is likely that the majority of Americans do not even know whether their respective states have the death penalty. What they do know—through movies, television, and stories—is that murder is associated with hanging and electrocution. The crucial question is whether, for a marginal group of people, this association engendered an internal resistance to the emotional and environmental incentives to murder that is sufficient to deter while an association of murder and life imprisonment would not have been sufficient.

The question of whether the death penalty deters, whether execution of the murderer prevents some people from murdering while a lesser punishment of the murderer does not, is an empirical question. I do not think that any of the empirical studies concluding that the death penalty does not deter have avoided the difficulties I have mentioned. I do not wish here to present an empirical argument claiming that the death penalty does deter. I wish to present a theoretical explanation of how the death penalty deters *if* the death penalty does deter. To be sure, if someone does present empirical evidence that overcomes the difficulties I have mentioned and that does indicate that the death penalty does not deter, then these theoretical considerations are worthless. (There is little that is of less use than a theoretical explanation of a nonexistent empirical reality.) But I would suggest that in the absence of such empirical evidence the theoretical considerations do make it seem most plausible that the death penalty does deter and that, for the reason given in footnote 4, the burden of "proof" falls on those who argue that capital punishment does not deter.

A determinative factor affecting the degree to which murder will be committed in any given society may be the strength with which the value prohibiting murder is inculcated in the society's individual members, and this strength may be a function of the penalty with which the society backs up the value. It may be that individuals give values an internal weight concomitant with the weight they perceive the value as being given by their society, and this perception may judge the weight given to the value by the society in terms of—among other things—the weight of the penalty, with which the society backs up the value. This seems a reasonable ex-

planation of why and how most individuals develop an internal resistance to murder that is sufficiently strong to deter them from acting on the basis of the emotional forces (such as anger) and the environmental forces (such as poverty) that encourage murder.

I cannot stress strongly enough that there need be no element of rational calculation on the part of the individual for us to accept the deterrent capacity of the death penalty.[5] The death penalty deters—if it does deter—not because the potential murderer weighs the potential murder against the penalty and decides that life imprisonment would be a cheap price to pay but execution is too high a price. He is deterred by the death penalty—*if* he is deterred by the death penalty—because he has perceived, from childhood on, that murder is the most serious of social offences.[6] He has accepted this assess-

---

5. Those who are temporarily or permanently mentally disturbed have impulses and desires that are, quantitatively or qualitatively, different from those of most people. But there is no evidence against, and much evidence for, the belief that such people are affected by the early internalization of the prohibitions we have discussed. The psychotic murderer, like the normal person who murders, has, of course, failed to sufficiently internalize the prohibition against murder. But, again, this proves only what need not be proved (because it is true by definition); the murderer is one who was not deterred from murdering. The question is: what deters those, psychotic or normal, who *are* deterred?

6. I assume here that we are considering the usual situation (murder for profit, for example) in which the seriousness of the crime as represented by the possible punishment of the death penalty is complemented by the other elements that lead to an individual's accepting the importance of the value and giving it this weight. If other factors tend to counteract this process—if, for example, murder in a particular

ment of the seriousness of murder and has internalized it because (among other reasons) his society has emphasized the importance of this value by penalizing it with a penalty stronger than that which it imposes for any other crime.[7] The death penalty deters—if it does deter—primarily by deterring today's child from becoming tomorrow's murderer; it deters—if it does deter—by engendering in today's child a resistance to murder that prevents him from ever seriously *considering* murder in the

_____

society is punishable by death, but murder of a wife's lover is traditionally considered virtually justified—then the members of the society will not, despite the presence of the death penalty, resist the pressures to commit this crime with the strength with which they resist crimes in which the presence of death penalty is complemented by other factors tending to emphasize the seriousness with which the society views the crime. (In this essay I ignore a number of other considerations that are important in any empirical assessment of the deterrence. For example, it must be remembered that "murder" is socially defined (killing is the act) and one society might define a particular type of killing as "murder" while another will not. Likewise, one society's murder rate might be far more accurately reported than another's. Such considerations are of practical importance in testing the hypothesis that the death penalty deters and in assessing the theoretical points made in this essay, but they are irrelevant to the hypotheses and theoretical points themselves.)

7. It is possible, of course, that this reasoning is all correct, but that one weighs internalized values only in relative terms so that the internal resistance to the emotions that would utilize murder (and to the environmental factors that encourage murder) would be equally strong if life imprisonment were the most severe penalty invoked by the society. Or it is possible that absolute severity is crucial, but that it is so only up to a maximal threshold (ten years' imprisonment, for example) past which the individual's internal resistance no longer increases its strength. However, one is not justified in *assuming* that either of these possibilities in reality obtains.

behavioral calculations he makes as an adult.

There is no reason to believe that the internal resistance is inoperative when the incentive for murder is emotional rather than environmental. When most people feel extreme anger they yell, or punch a refrigerator, or stifle their anger. Most people do not invoke murder in the service of their passions; their internal resistance to murder is sufficient to deflect the passions to a permitted object. In some cases the strong sanction prevents the individual from consciously considering the environmental possibility, or feeling the emotion, that would serve as incentive for murder, while in other cases the sanction channels consciously considered possibility or felt emotion into nonmurderous behavior; in either case the sanction is responsible, in some individuals, for the prevention of murder. If this is all correct, if one develops a stronger resistance to committing murder when there is the death penalty than when there is not, if the additional strength of resistance thus engendered prevents some people from murdering, then we are justified in believing that the death penalty deters, and that it deters crimes of passion as well as rational crimes.

We might see this more clearly if we consider shoplifting, rather than murder: The two-year-old who spies a bit of shiny costume jewelry will "shoplift" without guilt; he is unaware of the negative social sanction on such behavior. The four-year-old child, who is aware from previous observation and experience that shoplifting is considered bad, will consciously weigh alternatives before deciding whether or not to shoplift the jewelry. The twelve-year-old child, who has fully internalized the values and sanctions relevant to shoplifting, will (in most cases and most of the time) not even consider stealing the jewelry. For the twelve-year-old shoplifting is not, as it is for the four-year-old, a question of weighing satisfactions against penalties. In most cases, most of the time, *the thought and possibility of shoplifting do not even enter the twelve-year-old's mind.*

Observation and experience certainly seems to justify the conclusion that the degree to which children internalize the value against shoplifting is, *ceteris paribus*, a function of the severity of the negative sanction (be it formal punishment or a harsh word). Mild sanction, such as verbal parental disapproval, will be sufficient to bring most children to the point where shoplifting does not enter the mind. But there will be some children who will not sufficiently internalize the value if the importance of the value against shoplifting is not supported by physical punishment, while they will sufficiently internalize the value if physical punishment emphasizes the importance of the value.[8] Can this not

all be said of murder and capital punishment as well as of shoplifting and physical punishment and of the adults children become as well as of the children?

It is worth noting that if the death penalty does deter in the manner described here (i.e., if the death penalty increases the strength with which the social sanction is internalized and if rational calculation is of no relevance), then we would not (necessarily) expect the abolition of capital punishment to engender an immediate increase in the murder rate. The increase would not be expected to begin until the new generation (those socialized in the absence of the death penalty) reached adolescence.

If our description of the way in which individuals develop the resistance to emotional and environmental factors encouraging murder is correct, society inculcates in the individual the value prohibiting murder (or any other value) on the basis of its "saying" (through its severe punishment) that the value is a very important one and *not* primarily through the *immediate threat* of punishment. One might argue that threat is always the initiator in the development of the individual's perception of the strength of a value, and this might well be correct, but it is important to note that this is very different from the assertion that threat deters at the time of the act. We who do not murder refrain from murdering because of the strength of the internalized value that one does not murder and not because the present threat of punishment is so great that present

---

8. There is, of course, a third category of children (those who will shoplift whether there is physical punishment or not). There is even a fourth category, children who will shoplift *only* if there is physical punishment (because, for whatever psychological reason in any given case, these children are attracted to the punishment). If the fourth category were larger than the second (i.e., if more were attracted than deterred by physical punishment) this would be identifiable from the fact that shoplifting would be *positively* correlated with physical punishment and no one would argue in favor of physical punishment as a deterrent. However, for the reason given in footnote 9, it is highly unlikely that more are attracted than deterred by an increase in punishment. (In theory, one could impose physical punishment only for category 2 individuals, but this is both

impossible until such individuals can be identified and impermissible in a democratic society.)

fear of punishment precludes our committing the murderous act.

Thus: the fact that some pickpockets picked pockets at the public hangings of pickpockets, a fact often cited as if it demonstrated the inability of the death penalty to deter, demonstrates only that some individuals who have chosen to become pickpockets will not be deterred by the death penalty. It does not even demonstrate that no pickpockets were deterred (but only that not all were, a fact no one doubts). But even if we grant that *no* pickpocket will be deterred by the death penalty we have granted only that the *pickpocket* (i.e., the person who has already chosen to be a pickpocket) has not been deterred. The important point is that the pickpocket story avoids the central question: does the execution of pickpockets, public or private, reduce the number of people who choose to become pickpockets? *If* it does, *if* fewer people become pickpockets when pickpockets are hanged than when they are not, then we can conclude that the death penalty does deter. We can conclude that, *ceteris paribus*, the death penalty caused a marginal group of individuals to develop an internal resistance to pickpocketing that was sufficiently strong to deter them from pickpocketing at all (i.e., from becoming pickpockets), while a lesser penalty would *not* have caused them to develop a sufficiently strong internal resistance. We can conclude that we refrain from committing crimes because (among other reasons) we *feel* that the crimes are too bad to justify our committing them and that the strength of this feeling is a function of the strength of the penalty. (I have no idea whether the number of pickpockets decreases or not when pickpockets are hanged, but neither do the people who invoke this irrelevant fact about hangings and assume, with no justification, the conclusion that they claim to be proving.)

The argument I have presented does not distinguish between the emotional forces that motivate an individual to murder and the environmental forces that encourage murder; I can see no *a priori* reason to assume that the mechanism responsible for the development of the internal resistance to the passions that encourage murder is different from the mechanism responsible for the development of the internal resistance to the environmental forces that encourage murder. I see no reason to assume that the mechanism responsible for one's resisting the impulse to murder out of anger is different from the mechanism that is responsible for one's resisting the incentive to murder for profit. However, if one wishes to treat these separately nothing that I have presented need be altered. The psychiatrist who is interested in the emotions that, as Freud tells us, would "murder even for trifles" must ask why the vast majority of people possess internal resistances to such emotions sufficient to dissuade them from acting on the emotions;[9] he must ask

_____

9. Throughout this essay I have assumed that if the death penalty deters (i.e. if there are some people who will not murder if there is a death penalty but who will murder if there is not), then the number of people who are deterred is greater than the number of people who are *encouraged* (i.e., people who are drawn to the punishment and who will murder if there is a death penalty, but who will not murder if there is not). I think that all human experience indicates that punishment in general deters a greater number of people than it encourages. (Whether the death penalty is, in this respect like all other punishment, is the

whether there exists a marginal group of people who develop an internal resistance that is sufficiently strong to keep them from murdering when the seriousness of murder is societally emphasized by the death penalty, but who do not develop a sufficiently strong resistance when society does not so emphasize the offensiveness of the act.[10] The sociologist, who is more interested in the environmental forces that encourage murder, must ask why most people resist such environmental incentives to murder (why, for example, most poor people do not murder);[11] he must ask whether there exists a marginal group of people equivalent to the one just mentioned.

It is worth noting that the objection to the death penalty that rests on

---

question of the deterrent capacity of the death penalty. However, the psychiatrists are no doubt correct in arguing that there are some people who are encouraged, even if the psychiatrists tend to overestimate the numbers of such people because such people are so overrepresented among the psychiatrists' patients. If such people do equal in number those who are deterred, then, of course, the death penalty does not deter. This will be reflected in the empirical evidence that would demonstrate that the murder rate is not reduced by the death penalty. Thus, this psychiatric argument against the death penalty is, at bottom, an empirical assertion that the death penalty encourages more people than it discourages and that, therefore, the death penalty increases the murder rate. It is on this prediction that the psychiatric argument rests.

10. One could, logically, but most implausibly, argue that all individuals have internal resistances of identical strength and that individuals differ only in the strength of the forces (emotional or environmental) that motivate them to murder. However, logical or not, this view is too implausible to warrant serious consideration; clearly some people have stronger consciences or stronger superegos than others.

11. See "A Theoretical Postscript" for a discussion of the role of environmental pressures leading to murder.

the heinous possibility of the execution of an innocent person can be seen to reduce to the dubious objection against "murder" by the state: those who raise this objection acknowledge that the number of innocent people who are executed is infinitesimal when compared to, say, the sixty thousand people per year we are willing to sacrifice in order to have the automobile. Those who raise this objection distinguish between automobile deaths and the loss of innocent people that, given human fallibility, will accompany the administration of the death penalty, by invoking the fact that only in the latter case does the *state* take the innocent life. But this acknowledges that the objection is not the loss of innocent people (which they accept in exchange for the automobile), but the loss of innocent people in which the state takes an active role. Thus, this objection is, in reality, the objection against "murder" by the state (in this case the "murder" of those mistakenly convicted and executed). This objection is as silly as an objection that the state's incarceration of the kidnapper is "kidnapping" by the state. Certain state acts—such as the execution of political dissidents—are unquestionably *morally* reprehensible, but such acts are not murder if they conform to state laws prohibiting murder; "murder" can have no legal meaning other than "*illegal* killing," so "murder by the state" is a contradiction in terms when the state is legally permitted to execute the person who is executed. (An administration's imposition of execution that ignored legally required mechanisms would, of course, be murder.)

I do not know whether the death penalty deters, but I do know that it makes sense that it would and that the arguments attempting to demonstrate that it does not are unpersuasive. Given the nature of a modern society with its heterogeneity infusing every aspect of social life and its encouragement of diversity and freedom of speech, it does not seem likely that, save perhaps the society in the throes of religious or revolutionary rebirth, any society will ever again be able to count on the strength of a single shared culture and familial authority to maintain even the minimal amount of social control necessary for a society to survive. If we cannot rely on shared values and familial authority as the sole sources of social control it behooves us to understand the mechanisms that serve to permit society to survive. Such understanding is rendered impossible if we categorically assume the correctness of an explanation which may well be incorrect. This is what we do when we assert the inability of the death penalty to deter.

I suspect that we would all *like* to believe that the death penalty does not deter. This relieves us of the weight of a moral decision. The strength of human reaction reflects perceived proximity, and most of us feel the responsibility inherent in supporting the execution of real murderers more intensely than the responsibility for a hypothetical group of victims who—if the death penalty does deter—will be murdered if our opposition to the death penalty prevails but who will not be murdered if our opposition fails and the death penalty is maintained.[12] Our

seeming sympathy may well be an act of moral cowardice, an acceptance of a position that caters to fears of potential guilt rather than to responsibility to real, if unnameable, people. For if the proponent of the death penalty is incorrect in his assumption that the death penalty deters and is successful in his effforts to convince his society to invoke the death penalty, he is responsible "merely" for the deaths of guilty individuals who, if deterrence is the rationale for execution, should not be executed. If the opponent of the death penalty, on the other hand, is incorrect in his assumption that the death penalty does not deter and is successful in his efforts to convince his society to refrain

12. Motivation has, of course, nothing to do with correctness of argument. But it is often the opponents of the death penalty who introduce the issue of motivation—without, I suspect, realizing that an examination of motivation

casts more doubt on the goodness of the motivations of the opponent of the death penalty than on those of the proponent. This becomes clear when we consider the question frequently asked of the proponent by the opponent: would *you* "pull the switch." Now the proponent might well answer that he would not pull the switch; nor would he shoot a man who was about to kill a small child. The fact that he *could not* perform an act is not sufficient to demonstrate that the act *should not* be performed by someone who is capable of performing the act. What the opponent's demand that the proponent pull the switch *does* indicate is the psychological importance (to one's attitude towards the death penalty) of a fear of guilt. For if the proponent is one who would have difficulty pulling the switch (as any human being should), the opponent is often one who does not merely have difficulty, but whose position on the death penalty is determined by the source of this difficulty: the fear of guilt. This is not surprising; a fear of guilt is far more easily elicited by picturing a murderer about to be executed than by trying to picture a statistical group of people who will—if the death penalty does deter—be murdered if there is no death penalty but who will not be murdered if there is a death penalty. Again: none of this has anything to do with whether the death penalty deters or whether—if the death penalty deters—it should be invoked.

from invoking the death penalty, *he* is responsible for the deaths of *innocent* people. Moreover, the number of innocent people who would not have been murdered if the deterrent of the death penalty had been invoked will be far greater than the number of innocent people who could conceivably be executed as a result of the mistaken conviction of innocent individuals for crimes they did not commit in a society that invokes the death penalty and considerably greater, in all probability, than the total number of individuals who will be executed (guilty plus executed by mistaken conviction) in a society that invokes the death penalty. An awareness of this reduces considerably the persuasiveness of the position that argues that since we do not know whether the death penalty deters we should not invoke it.[13]

---

13. One might argue: *(a)* that no matter how great a likelihood we may someday be able to attach to the *hypothesis* that the death penalty deters, the death penalty necessitates the *certain, tangible* deaths of *specific* individuals; *(b)* that *ipso facto*, the lives of these individuals must be given priority over the lives of the members of a *hypothetical* group of *unknown* individuals who will, in all probability, be murdered if the death penalty is not invoked (but who will, in all probability, not be murdered if the death penalty is invoked); and *(c)* that the certainty of the deaths resulting from the death penalty (that is, executions) morally precludes our invoking capital punishment no matter how much larger the *hypothetical* group than the group comprised of the executed, and despite the fact that the hypothetical group is comprised of innocent individuals while the group of the executed is comprised almost entirely of guilty individuals. This argument can be seen to be either irrelevant to this essay or unsatisfactory even if we disregard the distinction between guilty and innocent individuals. For one who so argues will be forced either: *(a)* (if he argues that certainty must *always* take

A Theoretical Postscript

The strength with which values are internalized is a determinant of the degree to which members of a society resist pressures leading to the commission of crime (educational and economic discrimination, for example). It would seem time to discuss the crimes committed by members of oppressed economic and racial groups in more penetrating terms than those utilized in the superficial observation that poverty fathers

---

priority) to deny the acceptability of every military action—in which case his argument is virtually identical with the moral assertion that the state may never take a life, a position that renders irrelevant the question of deterrence, but one that both leaves him responsible for the murders that deterrence would have prevented (if the death penalty does deter) and fails to convince anyone who rejects its moral assertion; or *(b)* (if he is not willing to take the pacifist position and is not willing to argue that certainty always takes priority over probability) to admit that the death penalty will be justified if our future knowledge does enable us to attach to the hypothesis that the death penalty deters a probability equal to that for which he would consider a military action justified even though such an action accepts *certain* deaths as justified by the probability that more lives are ultimately saved. If he takes this latter position he is merely saying that the death penalty is not *now* justified because the evidence does not *presently* allow us to attach to the hypothesis that the death penalty deters a high enough probability to morally justify our invoking the death penalty; he would have to admit that someday we may be able to attach a high enough probability to justify its invocation and that the death penalty is not, *ipso facto*, immoral. This is, incidentally, the position I take. I would not consider the (admittedly very forceful) argument that only God has the right to deny the possibility of worldly redemption (a denial inherent in the invocation of the death penalty) sufficiently strong to justify our ignoring a high probability that by refusing to invoke the death penalty we are condemning innocent people to death.

crime. Poverty does, under certain conditions, father crime, of course, and the pressures leading to the commission of crime are far greater for the members of these groups than they are for members of groups for which the rewards of crime are available through legitimate means, and in whose members the mechanisms that strengthen an individual's internal defenses against the emotional and environmental factors generating crime are more strongly represented. As long as some of the members of oppressed groups feel that they are outcasts in American society, some of the members of these groups will fail to internalize the prohibitions against crime that are inculcated in the other members of the society. But if the commission of murder is the victory of the environmental factors and the emotional forces that encourage murder over the internal forces that reflect social prohibition for every other group, then it is for members of these groups also, and our ignoring this is to treat the members of these groups as irredeemably alien as well as to limit our understanding. Without question the external factors encouraging crime and the internal anger they generate are infinitely greater for blacks than for whites, but other groups in other societies, and blacks in former times in our own, have been equally oppressed, and yet they did not always have high crime rates. Indeed, even now the overwhelming majority of blacks do not commit crimes, despite the fact that they suffer the same outrages as do those who do commit crimes. This all suggests that crimes committed by blacks, like those committed by every other group, reflect not only the external factors encouraging crime and

the anger that such factors engender, but the nature of the values of the group itself and the strength of the mechanisms by which the group inculcates its values in its members— mechanisms that are the same for blacks as they are for every other group. It should be remembered that, whatever the fears and fantasies of the white majority, the overwhelming number of victims of black crime are blacks, and it is they who are suffering as we pretend that it is only factors that are external to the black group that contribute to black crime.

We have done this often: the predictable response to the *Moynihan Report* on the black family was the fallacious attempt at refutation that argued that most black families are not female headed. This is, of course, true, but it misses the point of the report—which is that a far larger number of black families are female headed than are white families. In every society it is an adult male who serves as the threat and the model by which internal resistance to the external and internal pressures encouraging crime is developed in the maturing male. If these pressures are greater for the black than for the white then it is especially important that the methods by which black resistance can be strengthened be discovered. To the extent, and it is a very great extent, that external factors encourage black crime and weaken the development of internal resistance, these external factors must be changed (as, for example, by reducing economic discrimination and those factors that encourage the deterioration of the black family), but to the extent that it is black values that contribute to the weakening of the internal resistance to the pressures encouraging crime in individual blacks it is only blacks who can bring change. It seems to me that only the black nationalists have understood all of this fully and have seen that, for example, to deny the pathological effects of the absence of the father from many black families (that is, the effect of increasing crime by weakening the forces that engender a strong internal resistance to crime) is to argue that blacks develop this resistance in some other way than do all other human beings and that, therefore, they are not human.

A Legal Postscript

One might argue that, even if the death penalty does deter, it is unjust in that, in practice, it is invoked primarily for the lower economic classes or for racial minority groups. If the members of middle- and upper-class groups are executed less often for the commission of the same crimes for which members of the oppressed groups are executed, then this is patently unjust, but it is an injustice that should be corrected not by abolishing the death penalty (it is equally unjust to put the former in prison for ten years while puting the latter in prison for life), but by equalizing the punishment. This seems to be the reasoning invoked by most of the justices of the Supreme Court in the recent decision on the death penalty. Indeed, it would seem the only possible justification for considering as "cruel and unusual" a punishment that was accepted and common when the Eighth Amendment was written and that is still favored, I assume, by a majority of the population. (If it is not so favored, then the legal question is academic; even if the death penalty

does deter, it will not, and should not, be invoked if a majority manifests its moral abhorrence in legislation banning it and the question of whether it is "cruel and unusual" becomes irrelevant.) Thus the Court-imposed moratorium on capital punishment would seem to be justified when the death penalty is unfairly imposed and when there is doubt about where the public stands (though one might argue that the Court must assume that present public opinion is reflected in present laws no matter how old such laws are as long as such laws are fairly applied), but one would be hard put to find a justification for a future Court's ruling the death penalty, fairly imposed and based on recent legislation, was "cruel and unusual."

If members of lower-class groups are executed more often than members of the middle- or upper-class groups, but only in proportion to the greater number of capital crimes they commit, then there are a number of ways in which this fact can be viewed, but, while these views will differ on whether the situation is just or unjust, none is a strong argument for the abolition of the death penalty on theoretical grounds. If the crimes that are punished by death can reasonably be argued to be more serious than those that are not (violent murders as opposed to embezzlement, for example) and if equally serious middle- and upper-class crimes (treason, for example) are also punishable by death—if, in other words, capital crimes are not capital crimes merely because they are crimes committed by the lower class—and if all individuals who commit these crimes are treated equally, then, in a narrow sense, no injustice is present. However, one might argue that this situation is unjust in the wider sense that the groups that commit these crimes do so as a result of environmental forces over which they have no control. To a point this is unquestionably correct. However, such an environmentalist view is sustainable only if carried all the way through to describe all punishment of all types. It is to argue that all punishment is unjust because it assumes free will when there is none. Correct or incorrect, this view is perfectly logical, but no society could predicate its legal system on the central deterministic assumption; for even if all crime is in reality completely determined, i.e., even if there is no free will, the view of crime held by the members of the society (i.e., whether criminal acts are seen as the result of free will or as the effect of only deterministic factors) will be a crucial factor in determining the amount of future crime. Thus, whether or not there is, in reality, free will, the societal view of whether or not there is free will will be a monumentally important factor affecting human behavior and the amount of future crime.

C O M M E N T S ■ Q U E S T I O N S

1. Establishing the causes for a high murder rate in a given society, or a low murder rate in some other society is, says Goldberg, a very complicated matter. For example, it is wrong to conclude that the death penalty is not a deterrent to murder simply from the fact that the murder rate in a society *with* the death penalty is higher than the murder rate in a society *without* the death penalty. There could be other explanations. Do you agree with all of the points that Goldberg makes in his discussion of the complexities involved in attempting to account for different murder rates in different societies?

2. Goldberg's major point is that any deterrent value that capital punishment might have will not come from the fact that a potential murderer will weigh the severity of the death penalty against the severity of life imprisonment and judge the possibility of death too high a price to risk paying. Rather, the presence of the death penalty in a society will impress upon a person from childhood on that murder is the most serious of all offenses. Do you believe that this is the correct way of looking at the matter?

3. If the death penalty *does* deter, then, says Goldberg, if we fail to have the death penalty we are jeopardizing the lives of innocent people—that is, people who will become murder victims if there is no death penalty, but would not have become murder victims had there been a death penalty. Can Goldberg's position on this matter be defended by an appeal to the Principle of Rights? By an appeal to the Principle of the Common Good?

G E O R G E   S C H E D L E R

Capital Punishment and Its Deterrent Effect

I n this essay, I raise doubts of two kinds about the justification of capital punishment. First, I show how a recent argument for capital punishment is unsound.[1] This argument is extremely persuasive insofar as it admits that the relevant statistics do not support the inference that capital punishment is a superior deterrent, but concludes nevertheless that it should be retained because capital punishment runs the risk of the loss of fewer innocent lives than life imprisonment.[2] Secondly, I wish to

raise doubts of a conceptual kind about the relevance of deterence to the justification of capital punishment.

I have divided this essay into seven sections, only the last of which is devoted to this second issue. The first three sections are preliminary ones in which I explain what conditions must be satisfied before we can truly assert that capital punishment has a greater deterrent effect than any lesser penalty. The remaining sections (4, 5, and 6) are devoted to the first point above.

(1) The crucial question about the death penalty is whether we could achieve what it achieves (and avoid

1. Two versions of this argument are: Ernest van den Haag, "On Deterrence and the Death Penalty," *Journal of Criminal Law, Criminology and Police Science* 60 (June 1969): 141–47, and Steven Goldberg, "On Capital Punishment," *Ethics* 85 (October 1974): 67–74.

2. Of course, there are those who believe that within the relevant statistics the deterrent effects can be perceived. It has been argued, for example, that there is a trade-off between the murder rate and the number of executions per conviction, such that a 1.00 percent increase in the execution rate will reduce murders by about .06 percent. See Isaac Ehrlich, "The Deterrent Effect of Capital Punishment," *American Economic Review* 65 (June 1975): 414 ff. For a criticism of this, see Peter Passell, "The Deterrent Effect of the Death Penalty: A Statistical Test," *Stanford Law Review* 65 (November 1975): 62–64. But the criticism I offer in the second part of this essay applies to both these studies. On the other hand, it has been argued that all deterrent theories (that is, those which hold that capital punishment does

have a deterrent effect) must be false, for what they necessarily predict (namely, a decrease in the murder rate) is falsified by available data. See William C. Bailey, "Murder and the Death Penalty," *The Journal of Criminal Law and Criminology* 65 (September 1974): 416–25. But even this argument fails to rule out the possibility that something other than the existence of the death penalty causes the alleged increase in murder rates. That ruling out this possibility is crucial to any such argument is clearly shown in Goldberg's article cited in note 1 above.

George Schedler is professor of philosophy and a J.D. Candidate at Southern Illinois University, Carbondale. He has written articles in the areas of political and legal philosophy.

George Schedler, "Capital Punishment and Its Deterrent Effect," *Social Theory and Practice*, vol. 4 (1976), Department of Philosophy, Florida State University. Reprinted by permission of the publisher.

whatever ill effects it might have) without putting anyone to death. It is not to the point, therefore, to compare what capital punishment would accomplish with what our present practices accomplish, if those practices could be improved. We do not provide a definitive case for capital punishment if some other lesser penalty might yield the same benefits. We must, therefore, compare two hypothetical penal systems: both being similar in *all* respects except that one has capital punishment. Since it is reasonable to suppose that life imprisonment without the possibility of parole has a greater deterrent effect than the present practice of allowing parole, we shall compare the benefits of the former to the benefits of capital punishment *ceteris paribus*.

(2) Secondly, let us examine the group of murderers (or potential murderers) who are deterred by capital punishment but not by this lesser penalty.[3] We can better understand these individuals by imagining a "spectrum of deterrability" for the crime of murder. At one extreme, are individuals who will commit the crime regardless of the penalty; that is, there is no penalty severe enough to deter them. (Let us recall at this point that we are restricting our attention to those who are murderers and could not successfully assert any legal justification, such as self-defense, or any legal defense, such as insanity

or duress.)[4] At the other end of the spectrum are individuals who are deterred by any penalty at all, or perhaps merely by the stigma of conviction itself; they would commit murder only if it were legalized. Obviously, the group of individuals who would be deterred by the death penalty but not by life imprisonment occupy only a small part of this spectrum. We can exclude the following from this group: (a) those who are already deterred by life imprisonment without the possibility of parole, or by any other lesser penalty; (b) those who are deterred by no penalty whatsoever; (c) those who would be deterred only by a penalty *more severe* than (a relatively quick and painless) death, such as a slow or agonizing one.

(3) Let us examine more closely those people who can be deterred only by capital punishment. (We shall call these people "the uniquely deterrable group" or "uniquely deterrable murderers.") Let us ask at this point how it might happen that a penal system with capital punishment might "misfire" in some way so that some members of this group might *not* be deterred even though the death penalty exists in the society of which they are members. At first blush this seems not possible, but let us notice that we have said of this group only that they *can* be deterred by capital punishment. If, for example, the system of mass communication in a society were extremely poor, the deterrent effect of capital punish-

---

3. I am restricting my attention here to the question of the deterrent effect on potential murderers, not potential rapists, hijackers, or any others. What I say here might not apply *mutatis mutandis* to other categories of offenders. (For a discussion of the problems involved in deterring hijackers, see R. Chauncey, "Deterrence: Certainty, Severity, Skyjacking," *Criminology* 12 (Fall 1975): 447–73.

---

4. But see James R. Browning, "The New Death Penalty Statutes: Perpetuating a Costly Myth," *Gonzaga Law Review* 9 (Spring 1974): 656–57, for a discussion of cases in which apparently insane individuals were convicted and executed.

ment may be lost due to poor publicity (that it is prescribed for murder). Some members of this group will of course be deterred once the mass media informs them that the death penalty is so prescribed. But is this sufficient for everyone in this group? Is it not yet conceivable that some other people who are deterred by the death penalty might yet commit murder under these conditions? The answer is affirmative, for it is quite consistent to hold that Jones is deterred from murder by the prospect of capital punishment, but that Jones believes that the chances of actually being executed for any given murder are slim. So, for example, in a society where the death penalty is not mandatory, some individuals might commit murder although they would not if the chances of execution were better. But the mandatoriness of the death penalty is not the only factor here. An exhaustive list would be impossible, but the more important ones are:

(a) mandatoriness of the death penalty;

(b) the possibilities for the appeal of any murder conviction, especially collateral appeals;

(c) the latitude of rights accorded the accused in police interrogations and criminal proceedings;

(d) the efficiency with which police discover that crimes have been committed and carry out subsequent investigation leading to arrest.[5]

To be sure, not all of these factors will be of crucial importance to *each* member of the uniquely deterrable group. Some of them will, of course,

be deterred by even the remotest prospect of death, but others, we must suppose, will not. But it is undeniable that to achieve the maximum deterrent effect, the death penalty should be widely publicized and mandatory, with a minimum of rights for the accused, and so forth. The existence of the death penalty is not sufficient of itself to deter these people—they must believe death will most likely come to *them* if they murder. Any factors which affect the probability of this occurring will be taken into account by potential murderers. (If this were not true, they are not affected by the prospect of death and are not *ipso facto* members of the uniquely deterrable group.)

Before we focus more closely on one of these factors, we should note that this analysis reveals several risks which are "absolute," in the sense that we either lose some deterrent effect of the death penalty, failing to deter some murderer and thus losing the life of an innocent victim, or we maximize the deterrent effect of capital punishment and thereby increase the probability of execution of innocent people. The mandatoriness of capital punishment, for example, is a very important factor in deterrence, but it is also one factor which increases greatly the chances of execution of the innocent. Any society with capital punishment, then, runs some risk of losing the lives of innocent people.[6]

We should note parenthetically

---

5. For a discussion of some of these factors, see pages 64–66 of P. Passell's article cited in note 1 above.

6. I am leaving out of account societies in which the public might be deceived into believing that executions actually take place, even though this does not happen in fact. Such societies avoid the risks under discussion here, but the justification of such a practice raises other moral questions which cannot be pursued here.

here the moral reasons which explain why execution of the innocent is regrettable. There is no reason to suppose that the deterrent effect of the death penalty would be decreased by the occasional discovery that an innocent person had been executed. Thus, execution of the innocent is not regrettable for deterrent reasons, though it is regrettable for the same fundamental reason which makes deterrence *itself* so morally important: minimizing the loss of innocent life. The risk of that loss is increased when capital punishment has greater deterrent effect; when it does not, then the failure to deter also increases the risk that innocent people will be killed by murderers who could have been deterred by the appropriate measures ("a"–"d" above).

(4) *The Effects of Publicity.* By far the single most important ingredient for achieving the deterrent effect is publicity. The publicity need not take the form of public executions. It might mean that the topic of executions occupies a prominent place in daily newspapers. It might not even involve *actual* executions: in some societies, the deterrent effect might be achieved by reminders that the death penalty is prescribed for murder. Although this kind of publicity will be clearly understood by the members of the uniquely deterrable group, we must nevertheless recognize that it may trigger certain irrational responses in certain unbalanced (but not legally insane) individuals. One such group are those who have suppressed self-destructive impulses. These people would be provided with an opportunity for self-destruction that would be absent in a society without capital punishment. For this reason, we can attribute the deaths of both the self-destructive murderers and the murderers' victims to the publicity surrounding capital punishment. In a society without such publicity, the self-destructive impulses might remain suppressed. It is, of course, possible that such individuals might commit suicide if there were no capital punishment, but in that case we would not lose the lives of their potential victims. Furthermore, we must recognize that, although there might be few individuals with these impulses, yet the publicity surrounding capital punishment might increase the numbers through a kind of conditioning process.[7]

There are, in addition, other types of individuals for whom the message the state tries to convey has an entirely different significance. The publicity may nurture the desire to kill *other* human beings. Certain individuals might want to imitate the executioner or the murderers who are executed. These people would probably be more dangerous, since they do not desire to be apprehended, unlike the self-destructive types, and the capture of these people may cost more innocent lives.

It might be said in response that the influence of capital punishment is exaggerated in this regard—except perhaps on an oversimple or outmoded model of human behavior. Actually, however, the possibilities sketched above are quite compatible with widely held theories of human behavior. The Freudian and Jungian theories, for example, allow for various unconscious drives or instincts of

---

7. Aside from the theoretical support for this position which I discuss in note 8 and note 9 below, there is empirical support. See Rudolf J. Gerber, "A Death Penalty We Can Live With," *Notre Dame Lawyer* 50 (December 1974): 266–68.

a self-destructive kind—and in fact such theories give us the impression that such individuals can be found in greater numbers than we might like.[8] On a behaviorist account, too, it is possible that publicity surrounding the death penalty might positively reinforce certain tendencies towards self-destructive behavior.[9] Various theories can easily account for the existence of these tendencies, though they will disagree over how to characterize the tendencies toward this behavior: whether it is innate or learned, whether conscious or unconscious, whether due to instincts, drives, needs, desires, and so on.

How many of these unbalanced individuals will fall into this group (we will call them "irrational" or "unbalanced" murderers) will obviously vary from one society to the next. Various social, genetic, and physiological factors, perhaps too the degree of the society's industrialization, will raise or lower the number. Not enough is known to determine the number of unbalanced murderers in a given population, let alone what factors raise or lower the number.

This is also true of the uniquely deterrable group. It is conceivable that some societies will not have any individuals who fall into that group. Other societies may have a very large number. But if there is to be any advantage to having capital punishment there must be reason to believe that there are some individuals in this group, and we must, in addition, have reason to believe that the number deterred is greater than the number of lives lost by (1) executions of innocents, including unbalanced murderers, and (2) the victims of unbalanced murders. It is crucial to notice that it is not enough to compare the *number* of uniquely deterrable murderers with the numbers in (1) and (2); we must take into account how many in the uniquely deterrable group *will actually be deterred.* This will depend upon publicity and the factors "a"–"d" which we discussed earlier.

(5) *Does Capital Punishment Deter?* An affirmative answer to the question of whether the death penalty deters is not the absolute answer it has often been taken to be. To say the death penalty deters (more than a lesser penalty) is merely to say that in some societies there are individuals who fall into the uniquely deterrable group and that publicity and other factors are right. This is entirely compatible with the claim that the death penalty does *not* deter: in some societies there are no individuals who are uniquely deterrable, or, if so, the

8. Freud discusses this in two places: *Beyond the Pleasure Principle* and *The Ego and the Id.* The discussion in the former can be found on pages 38–41 and 46–47 in volume 18 of *The Standard Edition of the Complete Psychological Works of Sigmund Freud,* ed. James Strachey (London: 1955). The discussion in *The Ego and the Id* can be found on pages 40–46, 53–56, and 159–65. Such self-destructive impulses do not figure as prominently for Jung as they do for Freud, nevertheless, Jung discusses these in the following works: *Psychological Types, The Structure and Dynamics of the Psyche,* and *The Practice of Psychotherapy.* These discussions can be found, respectively, in the following places in *The Collected Works of C. J. Jung* (Princeton: Princeton University Press, various publication dates), volume 6, 341; volume 8, 288; and volume 16, 57.

9. In this regard, see B. F. Skinner's discussion of the following topics in *Science and Human Behavior* (New York: Macmillan, 1953): the causes of aggressive behavior, pages 202f, 302, 372–79 and suicide, 232. See also his discussion of deferred "aversive consequences" of governmental policies in *Beyond Freedom and Dignity* (New York: Bantam Books, 1971), 31ff.

requisite publicity and other factors are not present. Different societies, or different conditions at different times in the *same* society, will warrant different answers to this question. Thus, the question has no general answer—only an answer for a certain society at a certain time.

(6) *Recent Arguments for Capital Punishment.* The state of our knowledge of human behavior, at least in present-day American society, is such that we cannot even make good guesses at how many people, if any, fall into this group. Given this uncertainty, it has been argued recently that we should adopt the minimax strategy: we should choose the policy which will minimize the loss of life should our assumptions about deterrence be incorrect. If we incorrectly assume that capital punishment deters and we retain it, we vainly execute convicted murderers (some of whom may be innocent). On the other hand, if we incorrectly assume it does not deter and we abolish it, then the uniquely deterrable group will kill an indefinite number of innocent people. It has been argued that the former alternative minimizes our losses, for the relative number of executed murderers (who may be innocent) will surely be smaller than the number of innocent victims. Thus, the rational alternative is to retain capital punishment.[10]

Even though this argument avoids the question of the actual numbers involved by estimating only the relative numbers, it does not take into account the (relative or absolute) number of irrational murderers and their victims that may be lost by retention but saved by abolition. Since this number is entirely independent of any deterrent effect the death penalty might have, we could never be sure we lose fewer lives by retaining capital punishment (even though it might not deter) than by abolishing it (even though it might have deterred some). If we retain it, we lose the lives of the unbalanced murderers and their victims; and if we abolish it, we save them. Both these propositions may remain true whether or not it deters. The losses of retention necessarily increase, while the losses of abolition must decrease.

It might even be the case that the number of victims of the uniquely deterrable murderers are as great as the total number of unbalanced murderers and their victims, so that even if capital punishment does deter it may not save any lives. If it did not deter, and this is the possibility relevant to the minimax strategy, the losses would be enormous: we save no innocent victims of the uniquely deterrable group, and we have lost the lives of the unbalanced murderers and their victims. Now, if we compare this to the abolition of the death penalty, even though it would have deterred, we see that we might not have lost anything, for we saved the lives of the unbalanced murderers and their victims although we lost (*ex hypothesi*) the same number of innocent people to the uniquely deterrable group.

Of course, we do not yet know what the numbers in a relative or absolute sense would be. But until we know that, we cannot possibly have

---

10. This is a summary of the argument in van den Haag's paper (see note 1 above). Goldberg's argument (also cited in note 1) is based on the same strategy, but, instead of risks to innocent life, he couches his argument in terms of the respective moral responsibilities for the loss of innocent life that retentionists and abolitionists must bear.

reason to believe that the losses of abolition (if capital punishment would have deterred) are greater than retention (even if it does not deter).

(7) Finally, let us reflect on the reasons why viewing capital punishment in this way (that is, as a way of saving innocent lives) seems so very queer. We begin with the very reasonable position that, if capital punishment is justified at all, it must somehow save more innocent lives than any alternative. But the argument ends with the unreasonable assumption that nothing more is needed to justify capital punishment than a demonstration that fewer lives are risked this way. In other words, the risk of fewer lives is not a sufficient condition for the justification of capital punishment, although it is necessary.

But further reflection on this also leads to odd results, for it leaves open the possibility that a case for the abolition of the death penalty might be made even though abolition would risk more innocent lives. But this is not an irrational risk. For it simply indicates a refusal to save more lives if doing so entails the loss of other fundamental goods, such as civil liberties. And this reveals a defect generally in any argument for—or against—capital punishment based *solely* on its superior—or inferior—deterrent effect: the basic question of the justice or injustice of capital punishment is thereby evaded entirely. Once we restrict the discussion to the probable loss of innocent life, we are treating capital punishment as a sort of tax on a course of conduct, whose justification depends upon how many will find the tax too heavy, how many will not, and how many will try to engage in the conduct

hoping to escape the tax.[11] We raise, so to speak, the "price" of committing murder so high that few are willing to pay it, and, if any chooses to do so, his or her example makes it clear to others that they cannot expect to commit murders without also paying the price.[12] By viewing capital punishment in the context of a price mechanism or taxation scheme, we do not imply that the satisfaction the murderer derives from her or his crime is an absolutely illegitimate satisfaction—we suggest instead that this satisfaction is a scarce commodity of sorts, for which an extraordinarily high price must be paid.[13] But these concerns have nothing to do with the basic justice or injustice of executing those individuals who in society's eyes have committed the most serious

---

11. H. L. A. Hart contrasts punishment with a tax on a course of conduct on page 7 of his *Punishment and Responsibility* (Oxford: Clarendon Press, 1968).

12. John Rawls refers to punishment as a sort of price system in his "Two Concepts of Rules," *The Philosophical Review* 64 (January 1955): 13. The analysis I present here draws upon the conception of justice Rawls presents in his *A Theory of Justice* (Cambridge, Mass.: Harvard University Press, 1971). I also emphasize an aspect of punishment which Joel Feinberg discussed in his "The Expressive Function of Punishment," *The Monist* 52 (July 1965): 397–408.

13. Thus punishment is reduced to a price-posting mechanism. It is worth noting that those theorists who are convinced of the social worth of a "deterrence system" refer to it as a "communication system" which is a more accurate description of what deterrence is. (However, I believe there is more to it than this, since we do not, in a rational penal system, merely post "prices" in a neutral way, as though we are indifferent about the prospect that a large number of people might choose to pay the price.) See Michael R. Geerken and Walter R. Gove "Deterrence: Some Theoretical Considerations," *Law and Society Review* 9 (Spring 1975): 499 and 511.

crime. We are thus left with the conclusion that capital punishment is not justified as a *punishment*, unless, in some sense, those who have been convicted of capital crimes can be said to deserve it apart from any deterrent effects the executions will have on others. There is, then, an inescapable retributive aspect of the justification of capital punishment. The convicted murderer cannot justifiably be used merely as an example to others; what he or she receives as a punishment must somehow be deserved for having committed murder.[14]

With this last point there will no doubt be some who disagree. In

reply, I can only insist that those who discuss the justification of capital punishment solely in deterrent terms cease calling it "capital punishment" and instead refer to it in a neutral way as "the death penalty," since, for them, it is no different from other penalties such as late filing of income taxes or even so-called public welfare offenses. None of these are justified because they are deserved but (usually) because of the favorable effects such fines have on those who might be tempted to commit the offense. It may even be the case that *no* punishment proper can be justified in the way I am suggesting, but we at least should not entertain the false belief that we are seeking to justify a form of punishment when, in truth, if we have justified anything at all, it is some other measure for controlling human behavior.

---

14. I argue that punishment as an institution cannot be justified solely on deterrent grounds in "On Telishing the Guilty," *Ethics* 86 (April 1976): 259–60.

C O M M E N T S ■ Q U E S T I O N S

1. Schedler's article is intended to be quite limited in scope. For example, it is not intended to evaluate retribution or to address the question of whether or not the death penalty is a "cruel and unusual punishment." Do you believe that the issues that Schedler does deal with are the most important ones in a discussion of the death penalty? If not, which issues are most important?

2. Schedler's intention is to attack certain arguments that claim that the death penalty probably has deterrent value. How do you suppose that Steven Goldberg would

respond to the points made by Schedler?

3. According to Schedler, "It is undeniable that to achieve the maximum deterrent effect, the death penalty should be widely publicized and mandatory, with a minimum of rights for the accused." In saying this, does Schedler put too little emphasis on what might be taken to be the central feature of the death penalty, which is to hold out to potential killers the sheer *possibility* of execution—which is not present at all where there is no death penalty?

4. Schedler argues that even if we

suppose that the death penalty has deterrent value, and thus may save some innocent lives, it does not follow that the death penalty is a good thing. The reason why it does not follow is that imposing the death penalty in a way that would achieve deterrence may have undesirable consequences, such as a loss of civil liberties. Do you believe that Schedler is too much concerned about the rights of accused criminals and too little concerned about the rights of potential murder victims? Is he properly concerned about the good of society as a whole?

R O B E R T S. G E R S T E I N

Capital Punishment—"Cruel and Unusual"?: A Retributivist Response

T homas Long, in his article "Capital Punishment— 'Cruel and Unusual'?"[1] canvasses the various arguments made for the view that capital punishment is cruel and unusual punishment and comes to the conclusion that the only argument with substantial merit is that which holds that capital punishment is unconstitutional because the pain and suffering it involves cannot be shown to be justified by its effectiveness as a deterrent. It must therefore be regarded as an irrational imposition of pain and suffering until such time as it can be shown that it is a more effective deterrent than less severe punishments would be. He

then goes on to admit that this argument has its "sinister" aspects: it is probably true that no punishment could meet the burden of proof required by this standard of rationality. The force of the argument then is to undermine the justification for punishment generally.

I would suggest that Long arrives at this surprising result largely because he has chosen to restrict his consid-

---

1. *Ethics* 83 (April 1973): 214–23.

Robert S. Gerstein is a professor of political science at the University of California at Los Angeles and is an adjunct professor of law at Loyola Law School in Los Angeles. He has written many articles in the areas of applied ethics and the philosophy of law.

eration of the legitimacy of capital punishment to utilitarian considerations. The key to understanding this restriction is to be found, I believe, in his decision to disregard the retributivist view because "nonretributive views are today predominant among theoreticians of crime and punishment."[2] Having rejected retributivism, and any consideration of whether people "deserve" certain sorts of punishments or not, he is left with a classic utilitarian calculus in which the pain caused to the criminal is to be balanced against the benefits society would gain from the example his punishment sets to others. The dilemma in which he finds himself at the end of his indecisive calculations serves to underline Kant's warning to the penologist who stops being concerned with giving people what they deserve and instead "rummages around in the winding paths of a theory of happiness"[3] for guidance.

It is true that many judges and scholars simply reject retributivism out of hand.[4] It is also true, however, that there has in recent years been a revival of interest in retributive theory.[5] I would like to suggest that the rejection of retributivism is largely a product of misunderstanding and that, properly understood, the retributive view offers a more plausi-

ble basis for the solution of the problems surrounding cruel and unusual punishment generally, and capital punishment in particular, than do utilitarian views such as Long's.

The most common way of misunderstanding retributivism is to take it to be a fancy word for revenge. Those who assume that it is simply a rationalization for the venting of our passion for vengeance[6] quite rightly conclude that retributivism can offer us little help in deciding what is cruel and unusual punishment. Obviously this passion is not subject to any inherent limits on cruelty: it has been known to lead people to kill not only wrongdoers, but their whole families as well; it has led to boilings in oil and burnings at the stake. Others who connect retributivism with revenge construe it as a kind of utilitarian argument. In this view the retributivist is not one who justifies the urge to vengeance, but one who thinks that punishment is useful because it allows people to vent this emotion in a (relatively) harmless and orderly way.[7] People who see retributivism in this way also quite rightly come to the conclusion that it offers us no help in deciding what kinds of punishments should be ruled out as cruel and unusual.

These misunderstandings have at their heart the equation of vengeance with retribution. The equation is made understandable by the fact that there are connections, historical and conceptual, between these two ideas.

2. *Ibid.*, p. 220, n. 21.

3. Kant, *The Metaphysical Elements of Justice*, trans. John Ladd (Indianapolis: Bobbs-Merrill Co., 1965), p. 100.

4. See *Furman v. Georgia*, 92 S.Ct. 2726, 2779-80 (Marshall, J., concurring 1972), and the authorities cited at 2780, no. 86.

5. See Moberly, *The Ethics of Punishment* (London: Faber & Faber, 1968); Herbert Morris, "Persons and Punishment," *Monist* 52 (October 1968); 475; Jeffrey Murphy, "Three Mistakes about Retributivism," *Analysis* 31 (April 1971): 166.

6. See *Furman v. Georgia*, 92 S.Ct., 2726, 2779 (Marshall, J., concurring 1972).

7. *Ibid.,* at 2761 (Stewart, J., concurring), 2836 (Powell, J., dissenting); Goldberg and Dershowitz, "Declaring the Death Penalty Unconstitutional," *Harvard Law Review* 83 (June 1970): 1773, 1796.

It is mistaken because it misses the enormous and crucial differences between them.

Vengefulness is an emotional response to injuries done to us by others: we feel a desire to injure those who have injured us. Retributivism is not the idea that it is good to have and satisfy this emotion. It is rather the view that there are good arguments for including that kernel of rationality to be found in the passion for vengeance as a part of any just system of laws. Assuming the existence of a generally just legal system, the argument for making retributive punishment a part of it has been succinctly stated in this way:

> In order to enjoy the benefits that a legal system makes possible, each man must be prepared to make an important sacrifice—namely, the sacrifice of obeying the law even when he does not desire to do so. Each man calls on others to do this, and it is only just or fair that he bear a comparable burden when his turn comes. Now if the system is to remain just, it is important to guarantee that those who disobey will not thereby gain an unfair advantage over those who obey voluntarily. Criminal punishment thus attempts to maintain the proper balance between benefit and obedience by insuring that there is no profit in criminal wrongdoing.[8]

It has been seen that some critics of retributivism regard it as a theory that would lead us to use criminals as objects upon which to vent our emotions, as scapegoats to be dealt with without regard to their value as people. In fact, nothing could be further from the truth. It is a major tenet of the standard form of retributivism that "a human being can never be manipulated merely as a means to the purposes of someone else."[9] Punishment is not, in this view, a matter of injuring people because it is useful to us but of dealing with them in the way they deserve to be dealt with. The question for the retributivist is not: what will be the most advantageous way of disposing of this criminal? Rather it is: what is the just way to treat one of our fellow citizens who has willfully taken unjust advantage of the rest of us?

It is especially surprising that critics suggest that retributivism leads to the destruction of all limits on the severity of punishment. Retributivism in its classic form has within it a standard which measures out the severity of the punishment with great care: *lex talionis*.[10] Indeed, if the purpose of punishment is to restore the balance of advantages necessary to a just community, then punishment must be proportioned to the offense: any unduly severe punishment would unbalance things in the other direction.

In fact, one of the great advantages of retributivism over other views is that it serves not only as a justification for punishment but also as a guide to the appropriate kind of punishment and a limit on the severity of punishment. Most other views require us to balance various utilitarian considerations against each other to come to our conclusions. So, for example, a very harsh punishment might be warranted for a particular crime from the point of view of the needs of deterrence, but we might decide to mitigate it because it would simply be too painful to those that would undergo it. Understood from this perspective,

---

8. Murphy, p. 166.

9. Kant, p. 100.
10. *Ibid.,* p. 101.

the problem of deciding whether some particular punishment was cruel and unusual would, of course, be a matter of weighing the social advantages to be derived from it against the pain it would cause the criminal. A variety of policies, including deterrence, security, and rehabilitation, must all be taken into account.

In retributivism, on the other hand, we have a single coherent perspective from which to make a principled judgment as to the punishment appropriate for this offense and this person. Because punishment is justified as the deserved response of the community to a member who has acted unjustly, it is essential that the punishment meted out to him be consistent with his position as a member of the community. He is not to be treated as an object or even as an enemy. Our duty to treat him justly is no less stringent than that which we have toward any other member of the community. The purpose of punishment is to restore the balance of justice within the community, not further to derange it.

What then would retributivism regard as cruel and unusual punishment? Clearly, any punishment the severity of which was out of proportion with the offense. But further, any punishment which would be inconsistent with the criminal's status as a member of the community whose capacity for a sense of justice (a capacity of which he did not make use when he committed his crime)[11] is worthy of our respect. This is not to say that we may not cause him pain, and even very great pain. To say that punishment is justified is to say that a man with the capacity for a sense of justice ought to feel guilty and recognize that he should suffer for what he has done. The line is not to be drawn in terms of the degree, but in terms of the kind of suffering that is inflicted. As Plato pointed out, it can never be the business of a just man to make another man less just than he was.[12] An affliction which undermines a man's self-respect rather than awakening his conscience, which impairs his capacity for justice rather than stimulating it, could not serve as just punishment.

In fact, one of the most widely accepted views of the meaning of "cruel and unusual punishment," that developed by Justice Brennan,[13] fits very well into the retributivist perspective. Brennan argues that cruel and unusual punishments are those which "treat members of the human race as nonhumans, as objects to be toyed with and discarded."[14] He sums up his view in terms of the "primary principle . . . that a punishment must not in its severity be degrading to human dignity."[15] Brennan's position gains both force and clarity when it is seen in the context of retributivism. In this context the distinction between punishments which destroy human dignity and those which do not becomes more plausible because the theory shows us how we can justify the imposition of some afflictive

---

11. The concept of the capacity for a sense of justice is developed in Rawls, "The Sense of Justice," *The Philosophical Review* 72 (1963): 281.

12. *Republic,* trans. Cornford (Oxford: Oxford University Press, 1941), p. 13.
13. Concurring in Trop v. Dulles, 356 U.S. 86, 102 (1958), and *Furman v. Georgia,* 92 S.Ct. 2726, 2742–48 (1972).
14. *Furman v. Georgia,* at 2743.
15. *Ibid.,* at 2748.

punishments on a person while giving full respect to his human dignity. The idea of human dignity is also given content when it is explicated in terms of the capacity for a sense of justice. Just as we justify punishment as a response to those who abuse this capacity, so we shape and limit punishment out of the desire to preserve and stimulate it.

How does capital punishment fit into this scheme? The retributivist view, to the extent it is dealt with at all, is dealt with only as providing arguments in favor of capital punishment.[16] This is, first, because it does offer a justification for punishment in general, and, second, because the *lex talionis* can be seen as a justification for capital punishment in particular: "life for life, eye for eye, tooth for tooth." Of course, this should make it clear that retributivism would almost certainly rule out as cruel and unusual the use of capital punishment for rape, or for any other crime but murder. But is the retributivist committed to the support of capital punishment for murder? Kant argued that because there is "no sameness of kind between death and remaining alive even under the most miserable conditions" only capital punishment can restore the balance of justice where murder has been committed.[17]

The retributive theory contains the foundation of a very different sort of argument, however.[18] It can lead us to

ask how it is possible for us to continue to respect the moral capacity of another while we prepare for and carry out his execution. The answer to this question might depend on attitudes that do change over time. Perhaps the people involved in the ceremony surrounding the public beheading of a nobleman in the eighteenth century could continue to have profound respect for him as a moral being.[19] But ceremonial public executions would not be tolerated among us today. Given our surreptitious and mechanical approach to execution, it is hard to see that the condemned are treated as anything more than "objects to be . . . discarded." The condemned man's physical suffering may be minimized, but that is no more than we would do for a domestic animal to be disposed of. It is not the degree of suffering which might lead the retributivist to regard capital punishment as cruel and unusual, but its dehumanizing character, its total negation of the moral worth of the person to be executed.

I have not attempted here to give a justification of retributivism but only to establish that it would be a serious mistake not to include it among the alternative positions to be considered in gaining a full understanding of the issues involved in declaring the death penalty unconstitutional. Retributivism does offer a coherent and intuitively sound approach to understanding what the phrase "cruel and unusual punishment" can be taken to mean. It is not subject to the difficulties that beset positions like that developed by Long. And if it does not give us an easy answer to the question whether the death penalty is

---

16. See *Ibid.*, 92 S.Ct. 2726, 2779 (Marshall, J., concurring), 2761 (Stewart, J., concurring), 2836 (Powell, J., dissenting).

17. Kant, p. 102.

18. Moberly, on whose view I have drawn extensively here, is one leading retributivist who opposes capital punishment (see *The Ethics of Punishment*, pp. 296–99).

---

19. See Kant, p. 103, where such an execution is used as an example.

cruel and unusual, it does present the question to us in a form which presses us to make a principled judgment of the most serious sort: when, if ever, can we say that a person whom we continue to respect as a fellow member of a community founded on the principles of justice is deserving of death at our hands?

C O M M E N T S   ■   Q U E S T I O N S

1. Does Gerstein argue successfully that retribution is not the same thing as vengeance? Is he correct in claiming that a policy of revenge is an emotional response to crime while a policy of retribution is a rational response to crime?

2. Many parents have had the following sort of experience. They have, let us say, promised to take two children on a picnic. One child becomes ill and cannot go, whereupon he tells the parents: "Don't take my brother either because that would not be fair." The child believes that it is better to have "fairness" even if it means a net loss of benefits overall. Is this case a proper analogy to Gerstein's view of retributive punishment—bringing about justice by *taking away* something of value from the convicted criminal? Why or why not? What might a comparison of the two kinds of cases tell us about retribution?

3. On the question of whether or not a retributive theory of the death penalty upholds human dignity, who is correct, Gerstein or Justice Marshall? Does a consideration of the Principle of Rights support or oppose retribution?

J U S T I C E
T H U R G O O D   M A R S H A L L

Dissenting Opinion in Gregg v. Georgia

I n *Furman v. Georgia* (1972) (concurring opinion), I set forth at some length my views on the basic issue presented to the Court in [the present case]. The death penalty, I concluded, is a cruel and unusual punishment prohibited by the Eighth and Fourteenth Amendments. That continues to be my view.

I have no intention of retracing the "long and tedious journey" that led to my conclusion in *Furman*. My sole purposes here are to consider the suggestion that my conclusion in *Furman* has been undercut by developments since then, and briefly to evaluate the basis for my Brethren's holding that the extinction of life is a permissible form of punishment under the Cruel and Unusual Punishments Clause.

In *Furman* I concluded that the death penalty is constitutionally invalid for two reasons. First, the death penalty is excessive. And second, the American people, fully informed as to the purposes of the death penalty and its liabilities, would in my view reject it as morally unacceptable.

Since the decision in *Furman*, the legislatures of 35 States have enacted new statutes authorizing the imposition of the death sentence for certain crimes, and Congress has enacted a law providing the death penalty for air piracy resulting in death. I would be less than candid if I did not acknowledge that these developments have a significant bearing on a realistic assessment of the moral acceptability of the death penalty to the American people. But if the constitutionality of the death penalty turns, as I have urged, on the opinion of an *informed* citizenry, then even the enactment of new death statutes cannot be viewed as conclusive. In *Furman*, I observed that the American people are largely unaware of the information critical to a judgment on the morality of the death penalty, and concluded that if they were better informed they would consider it shocking, unjust, and unacceptable. A recent study, conducted after the enactment of the post-*Furman* statutes, has confirmed that the American people know little about the death penalty, and that the opinions of an informed public would differ significantly from those of a public unaware of the consequences and effects of the death penalty.

Even assuming, however, that the

Thurgood Marshall has been an associate justice of the U.S. Supreme Court since 1967.

---

428 U.S. 233; 96 S. Ct. 2971 (1976)
Legal references have been omitted.

post-*Furman* enactment of statutes authorizing the death penalty renders the prediction of the views of an informed citizenry an uncertain basis for a constitutional decision, the enactment of those statutes has no bearing whatsoever on the conclusion that the death penalty is unconstitutional because it is excessive. An excessive penalty is invalid under the Cruel and Unusual Punishments Clause "even though popular sentiment may favor" it. The inquiry here, then, is simply whether the death penalty is necessary to accomplish the legitimate legislative purposes in punishment, or whether a less severe penalty—life imprisonment—would do as well.

The two purposes that sustain the death penalty as nonexcessive in the Court's view are general deterrence and retribution. In *Furman*, I canvassed the relevant data on the deterrent effect of capital punishment. The state of knowledge at that point, after literally centuries of debate, was summarized as follows by a United Nations Committee:

"It is generally agreed between the retentionists and abolitionists, whatever their opinions about the validity of comparative studies of deterrence, that the data which now exist show no correlation between the existence of capital punishment and lower rates of capital crime."

The available evidence, I concluded in *Furman*, was convincing that "capital punishment is not necessary as a deterrent to crime in our society. . . ."

. . . The evidence I reviewed in *Furman* remains convincing, in my view, that "capital punishment is not necessary as a deterrent to crime in our society." The justification for the death penalty must be found elsewhere.

The other principal purpose said to be served by the death penalty is retribution. The notion that retribution can serve as a moral justification for the sanction of death finds credence in the opinion of my Brothers STEWART, POWELL, and STEVENS. . . . It is this notion that I find to be the most disturbing aspect of today's unfortunate [decision].

The concept of retribution is a multifaceted one, and any discussion of its role in the criminal law must be undertaken with caution. On one level, it can be said that the notion of retribution or reprobation is the basis of our insistence that only those who have broken the law be punished, and in this sense the notion is quite obviously central to a just system of criminal sanctions. But our recognition that retribution plays a crucial role in determining who may be punished by no means requires approval of retribution as a general justification for punishment—in particular, capital punishment—that we must consider.

My brothers STEWART, POWELL, and STEVENS offer the following explanation of the retributive justification for capital punishment:

The instinct for retribution is part of the nature of man, and channeling that instinct in the administration of criminal justice serves an important purpose in promoting the stability of a society governed by law. When people begin to believe that organized society is unwilling or unable to impose upon criminal offenders the punishment they "deserve," then there are sown the seeds of anarchy—of self-help, vigilante justice, and lynch law.

This statement is wholly inadequate to justify the death penalty. As my Brother BRENNAN stated in *Furman*, "[t]here is no evidence whatever that utilization of imprisonment rather than death encourages private blood feuds and other disorders." It simply defies belief to suggest that the death penalty is necessary to prevent the American people from taking the law into their own hands.

In a related vein, it may be suggested that the expression of moral outrage through the imposition of the death penalty serves to reinforce basic moral values—that it marks some crimes as particularly offensive and therefore to be avoided. The argument is akin to a deterrence argument, but differs in that it contemplates the individual's shrinking from antisocial conduct, not because he fears punishment, but because he has been told in the strongest possible way that the conduct is wrong. This contention, like the previous one, provides no support for the death penalty. It is inconceivable that any individual concerned about conforming his conduct to what society says is "right" would fail to realize that murder is "wrong" if the penalty were simply life imprisonment.

The foregoing contentions—that society's expression of moral outrage through the imposition of the death penalty pre-empts the citizenry from taking the law into its own hands and reinforces moral values—are not retributive in the purest sense. They are essentially utilitarian in that they portray the death penalty as valuable because of its beneficial results. These justifications for the death penalty are inadequate because the penalty is, quite clearly I think, not necessary to the accomplishment of those results.

There remains for consideration, however, what might be termed the purely retributive justification for the death penalty—that the death penalty is appropriate, not because of its beneficial effect on society, but be-

cause the taking of the murderer's life is itself morally good. Some of the language of the opinion of my Brothers STEWART, POWELL, and STEVENS . . . appears positively to embrace this notion of retribution for its own sake as a justification for capital punishment. They state:

[T]he decision that capital punishment may be the appropriate sanction in extreme cases is an expression of the community's belief that certain crimes are themselves so grievous an affront to humanity that the only adequate response may be the penalty of death.

They then quote with approval from Lord Justice Denning's remarks before the British Royal Commission on Capital Punishment:

The truth is that some crimes are so outrageous that society insists on adequate punishment, because the wrongdoer deserves it, irrespective of whether it is a deterrent or not.

Of course, it may be that these statements are intended as no more than observations as to the popular demands that it is thought must be responded to in order to prevent anarchy. But the implication of the statements appears to me to be quite different—namely, that society's judgment that the murderer "deserves" death must be respected not simply because the preservation of order requires it, but because it is appropriate that society make the judgment and carry it out. It is this latter notion, in particular, that I consider to be fundamentally at odds with the Eighth Amendment. The mere fact that the community demands the murderer's life in return for the evil he has done cannot sustain the death penalty, for as JUSTICES STEWART, POWELL, and STEVENS remind us, "the Eighth Amendment demands more than that a challenged punishment be acceptable to contemporary society." To be sustained under the Eighth Amendment, the death penalty must "compor[t] with the basic concept of human dignity at the core of the Amendment;" the objective in imposing it must be "[consistent] with our respect for the dignity of [other] men." Under these standards, the taking of life "because the wrongdoer

deserves it" surely must fail, for such a punishment has as its very basis the total denial of the wrongdoer's dignity and worth.

The death penalty, unnecessary to promote the goal of deterrence or to further any legitimate notion of retribution, is an excessive penalty forbidden by the Eighth and Fourteenth Amendments.

C O M M E N T S ■ Q U E S T I O N S

1. One of the claims made by Justice Marshall is that the American people—if they were fully informed—would consider the death penalty as morally unacceptable. Have developments since 1976, when Marshall's opinion was written, helped to substantiate his position or to undermine it?

2. Marshall does not consider the matter of what is called a *discretionary* death penalty, to be applied only in a very few select cases such as murder committed by someone who is already convicted of murder and is serving a life sentence for it. Assuming that Marshall is essentially correct in

his opposition to retribution and in his claim that the death penalty is not a more effective deterrent than life imprisonment, could a case still be made in defense of a narrowly applied discretionary death penalty?

3. Does Marshall adequately respond to the arguments made by Steven Goldberg? If in your opinion he does not do so, do you suppose that he *could* do so by further developing his (Marshall's) arguments?

4. Do you believe that Marshall is correct in his rejection of retribution (the claim that murderers "deserve" the death penalty)?

R E A D I N G S

Andenaes, Johannes. *Punishment and Deterrence*. Ann Arbor: The University of Michigan Press, 1974.

Bedau, Hugo Adam, ed. *The Death Penalty in America*. New York: Doubleday and Co., 1967.

Berns, Walter. *For Capital Punishment*. New York: Basic Books, 1979.

Black, Charles L., Jr. *Capital Punishment*. New York: W. W. Norton & Co., 1974.

Cairns, Huntington. *Legal Philoso-*

phy from Plato to Hegel. Baltimore: Johns Hopkins Press. 1967.

Camus, Albert. *Reflections on the Guillotine: An Essay on Capital Punishment.* Translated by Richard Howard. Michigan City, Ind.: Fridtjof-Karla Press, 1959.

Ewing, A. C. *The Morality of Punishment.* Montclair, N.J.: Patterson Smith, 1970.

Ezorsky, Gertrude, ed. *Philosophical Perspectives on Punishment.* Albany: State University of New York Press, 1972.

Feinberg, Joel, and Hyman Gross. *Philosophy of Law.* Belmont, Calif.: Wadsworth Publishing Co., 1980.

Hart, H. L. A. *Punishment and Responsibility: Essays in the Philosophy of Law.* Oxford: Oxford University Press, 1968.

Honderick, Ted. *Punishment: The Supposed Justifications.* New York: Harcourt Brace Jovanovich, 1969.

Menninger, Karl. *The Crime of Punishment.* New York: The Viking Press, 1968.

Murphy, Jeffrie G., ed. *Punishment and Rehabilitation.* Belmont, Calif.: Wadsworth Publishing Co., 1973.

—————. *Retribution, Justice and Therapy.* Boston: D. Reidel Publishing Co., 1979.

Van den Haag, Ernest. *Punishing Criminals.* New York: Basic Books, 1975.

Nuclear Deterrence

he subject of this chapter is not nuclear war since there is nothing really controversial about it. Every reasonable person agrees that nuclear war of the kind that could be waged given present levels of nuclear weapons would be an extremely bad thing for the countries that participated in it, and indeed for the entire world. No one knows for sure exactly what would happen, but nearly everyone agrees that there would be a very large number of deaths, extremely widespread and lingering suffering, major disruptions of industry, trade, government, etc. Not enough is known about the effects of nuclear war to answer what is no doubt the ultimate question about it; but the fact that this question cannot be answered is very frightening in itself. Would nuclear war between the United States and the Soviet Union destroy the human race once and for all?

The subject of this chapter is not nuclear war, but the prevention of nuclear war and especially the morality of policies intended to prevent it through nuclear deterrence. By "nuclear deterrence" is meant the threatened use of nuclear weapons for the purpose of deterring foreign aggressors. It is well known, and a source of very great anxiety to many people, that both the United States and the Soviet Union have a foreign policy that rests heavily upon a strategy of nuclear deterrence. The general question of whether or not nuclear deterrence is moral is an updated version of an age-old moral issue: when, if ever, is it morally justifiable to use force, or the threat of force, against a foreign country?

Those who oppose *any* use of force, or any threat of force, are called pacifists. They are opposed to all wars. They do not accept any of the arguments that have been made in defense of the so-called just war—such as that a war is just if it is the only possible way to stop a foreign power that has attacked first and if the force used to stop the foreign power is no greater than is needed. Some pacifists argue that violence and the threat of violence are wrong *in principle*, that is to say, wrong in themselves to such a degree that they cannot ever be justified. Other pacifists insist that wars are always wrong because of their bad consequences—most importantly, the unavoidable killing of innocent people. The reading selection in this chapter by Cecil John Cadoux is a discussion of the major arguments for pacifism. The paper by William Earle is an attempt to defend war against such arguments.

Must a pacifist be opposed to nuclear deterrence? Since nuclear deterrence is the threat to use an extreme measure of force, it might appear that a pacifist would necessarily be opposed to it. However, some defenders of nuclear deterrence would argue that it is compatible with pacifism since, they would say, the threat to use nuclear weapons in an all out nuclear war is not a *bona fide* threat. No one intends ever to have to carry it out, since doing so would invite retaliation by the other side of such a magnitude that the country that struck first would be devastated. This is the reasoning behind the policy of mutually assured destruction (MAD for short), which is intended to preserve peace. Opponents argue that if the nuclear weapons exist then it is inevitable that someday they will be used.

Both the United States and the Soviet Union have a two- or possibly three-tiered defense system. This consists, first, of land-based missiles. Second, it consists of submarine-based missiles that could destroy the other country if that country made the first move in a nuclear war that resulted in the destruction of land-based missiles (along with the cities and most of the people of the country). Air based weapons are a possible third tier in American and Russian defenses.

The fact that nuclear weapons can, before they are launched, be destroyed by other nuclear weapons very much complicates the strategy of nuclear deterrence. If country A fears that country B will actually use some of its nuclear weapons against country A, then country A has an incentive to strike first, and in very great force, with the hope of destroying a great many of country B's nuclear weapons before they can be used. One consequence of this is that any strategy for the limited use of nuclear weapons becomes very problematic. In recent years some military strategists have proposed the limited use of nuclear weapons, as for example in defense of West Germany if it were invaded by the Russians using conventional forces that couldn't otherwise be stopped. Opponents have argued that rapid escalation of the conflict would be inevitable or at least very likely.

Hence, we are brought back to the claim mentioned earlier that threats to use nuclear weapons must somehow not be counted as true threats. However, it can also be claimed that a threat that people believe has no realistic expectation of being carried out can have no effective force. Clearly, therefore, there is something very puzzling about the concept of nuclear deterrence. One contemporary writer, Jonathan Schell, goes so far as to say that the doctrine of nuclear deterrence is contradictory. It is contradictory, says Schell, to threaten to perform acts that could result in the extinction of the human race for the very purpose of seeking to *prevent* the extinction of the human race.[1] Other writers, who do not go as far as to say that nuclear deterrence is contradictory, do say that there is a deep moral problem in threatening to do something the actual doing of which would be unquestionably immoral. This point is made, for example, by Trudy Govier, whose paper is reprinted in this chapter.

In the 1960s motion picture *Dr. Strangelove* (directed by Stanley Kubrick) an ultimate deterrent device is produced called a "Doomsday Machine." This was a nuclear weapon that if activated was guaranteed to destroy the earth. It was built in such a way that once it was armed and set up, even the country that produced it (Russia in the movie) could never make it inoperative. Any tampering would set it off. Also, a nuclear attack by the other side would set it off. This was supposed to make it an "absolute deterrent." However, in the movie an American general who had not yet heard of the Doomsday Machine had a mental breakdown and ordered a nuclear attack on Russia—with the inevitable catastrophic effect on the world.

Dr. Strangelove was intended to satirize the use of deterrent nuclear forces. It was also intended to raise a very troubling question about the psychological stability of the people in charge of our nuclear defenses. Clearly, the possibility that unstable individuals may control nuclear weapons intensifies the dangers that they pose.

Because of the moral ambiguities that are inherent in a policy of nuclear deterrence, and also because of the terrible dangers that are inherent in the existence of nuclear weapons, some writers have concluded that the only hope for the human race lies in the abolition of nuclear weapons altogether. One of the recent writers who has defended this position is Helen Caldicott.[2] What is needed, she believes, is a popular worldwide movement that would eventually become powerful enough to bring about total disarmament. Caldicott is also opposed to the nuclear power industry because it shares a great deal of technology with weapons-producing nuclear industries and also because she believes its dangers even in peacetime far outweigh its benefits.

Caldicott's views are strongly opposed by those who defend the doctrine of "peace through strength," as it has been called. The speech from President Reagan that is included in this chapter expresses this point of view. Reagan's basic argument is that "real arms control" cannot be achieved unless the United States will first strengthen its nuclear defenses. President Reagan's position is, of course, opposed to the *nuclear freeze* movement, which advocates that the United States cease immediately from increasing its supply of nuclear weapons and then endeavor to have the Soviet Union do the same. Those who support the nuclear freeze position, in contrast to President Reagan, are not concerned with the question of whether or not at the time the freeze goes into effect the United States is militarily at least as strong as Russia. They believe that the two countries at the present time are more or less equal in strength, and that that is good enough.

President Reagan's position is also in opposition to the view of Leon Wieseltier, who argues that nuclear deterrence *by itself* is immoral and irrational. He defends a policy of nuclear deterrence that is to be combined with a partial disarmament, on the ground that the deterrent effect of nuclear weapons would still be present even if the United States and the Soviet Union had far fewer weapons. Each could still threaten to damage the other country to a degree that would be completely unacceptable, but which would fall far short of the damage to the United States, the Soviet Union and the entire world that present levels of nuclear weapons could bring about.

Notes

1. See Jonathan Schell, *The Fate of the Earth* (New York: Avon Books, 1982), part 3.

2. See Helen Caldicott, *Nuclear Madness* (New York: Bantam Books, 1978), chapter 6.

C E C I L   J O H N   C A D O U X

Christian Pacifism

History, indeed, provides us with a number of instances in which, so far as we are able to judge, the cause of human progress, freedom, enlightenment, and culture has been promoted, or at least protected against a very damaging set-back, by a successful appeal to arms. One might mention in this connexion the resistance offered by Greece to Persian expansion early in the fifth century B.C., the Maccabaean revolt against the Seleucid empire of Syria in the second, Pompeius the Great's suppression of the Mediterranean pirates in the first, the long drawn-out conflict waged for many centuries by the Roman Empire against the nomadic peoples from the north and east, the tense struggle between Christian Europe and Islam—a struggle which lasted for nearly a millennium, the wars of King Alfred against the Danes, the armed protection given by the Protestant princes of Germany to the Lutheran movement, the opposition offered by the Netherlands under William the Silent and his son and by England under Elizabeth to the bigoted tyranny of Philip the Second of Spain, the Puritan revolt against Charles the First, Cromwell's threat to the persecutor of the Vaudois, the Scottish Covenanters' resistance to Claverhouse and the Stuarts, the com-bination of Europe against the insufferable pride and greed of Napoleon, the campaigns of Cavour and Garibaldi for the emancipation of Italy, the Civil War in America—which preserved the union of North and South and abolished negro-slavery, the British Government's protection of north-western India against the murderous tribesmen beyond the frontier; and—many would add—the Allies' vindication of the violated neutrality of Belgium in 1914, and of the outraged decencies of international conduct in 1939.

The foregoing survey of the various forms in which, and the various occasions on which, injurious coercion has apparently had to be employed for the protection of real human values, and has therefore been justifiable, constitutes a very damaging criticism of our tentative ethical theory. One can indeed hardly be surprised that for many serious-minded persons this body of evidence furnishes an unquestionable and absolutely final refutation of the view that all coercion involving injury to others is an infringement of the Christian standard of conduct. I do

Cecil John Cadoux, who died in 1947, wrote many books on Christian history and theology.

From *Christian Pacificism Reexamined* (New York: Garland Publishing, Inc., 1972, pp. 102–110), which was originally published in 1940 by Basil Blackwell. Reprinted by permission of the estate of Cecil John Cadoux.

not wish to deny or undervalue the formidable strength of such an objection to Christian pacifism. It is, in fact, this close interrelation between coercion and social security which makes pacifism the most controversial of all Christian ethical ideals. For you can abolish institutions like slavery, torture, private wealth, and capital punishment, you can even advocate celibacy and voluntary poverty, without seeming to imperil the normal peace and well-being of society. But you cannot wholly abstain, and persuade others to abstain, from all exercise of injurious coercion, without apparently opening the door to "red ruin and the breaking-up of laws." Before, however, we conclude that the test of expediency tells quite decisively against the theory we are subjecting to it, account has to be taken of several other considerations. Some of these, if studied in isolation, might seem inconclusive; but cumulatively they are not without great weight. For the sake of completeness, and at the risk of creating prejudice against my case, I propose to include them all—the less strong along with the more strong—in the following enumeration.

[Note: The present selection includes seven out of the ten considerations to be found in the original.]

(1). The superficially plausible assumption that a state cannot function properly unless it is strong enough successfully to resist foreign aggression by main force is a curious instance of the liability of the obviously true to turn out on inspection to be quite false. Let us cast our eyes down the list of the independent states of the world, and ask, how many of them are strong enough to resist successful and determined attack from one of the handful of states which we usually designate as "the Great Powers." Why, the world is full of states which have virtually no power to withstand aggression from a strong neighbour, but are nonetheless safe because they do not invite aggression. The fact is so palpable that there is no need to specify examples. If it be said that they need only to be able to resist such neighbours as are *likely* to attack them, the case under criticism is not mended: for there is no means of measuring this likelihood; and whether aggression be likely or not, clearly many states succeed in functioning notwithstanding the risks they run. If, on the other hand, it be said that states *ought* to be prepared to resist any likely aggression, I reply that that is a different question—the very question, in fact, which we are investigating. Whatever be the right answer to it, the fact remains that a State's capacity and willingness to resist a foreign aggressor stand on quite a different footing, so far as concerns the necessity of its successful functioning, from capacity and willingness to restrain law-breakers within its own borders.

(2). In many, though we may not say in all, of the instances we have noted of apparently righteous wars, the aggression that had to be repelled was not entirely unprovoked. Even the nomadic invasions to which the Roman Empire was subject need to be studied in the light of the ruthless barbarity with which Rome had treated, first the Gauls and then the Germans, and the bad faith with which she later treated the Goths. Erasmus thought that the Turks kept up their attacks on Christendom because they believed that Christendom was aiming at dominion over them. There have been extremely few wars in which the faults have been wholly on one side, and the issue at stake has been one between pure white and pure black. Even in those cases in which our sympathy and our sense of justice are very definitely enlisted on one side as against another, we can usually see that the side in the wrong was yet contending for some positive principle of value. This was ably pointed out by Mr. G. F. Bridge in 'The Hibbert Journal' for October 1917 (pp. 50–52): among his instances is Italy's war against Austria in 1859 (in which an international court of law, had one existed, could hardly, he thinks, have done otherwise than give a verdict in Austria's favour). I do not want to lay much stress on this point, since there clearly have existed cases of purely unprovoked aggression (a pathetic example is narrated in Judges 18: 7–10, 27–29); and it is not inconceivable that such might occur again. I have nevertheless felt it worth mentioning, as a useful check to exaggeration on the other side. Moreover, caution is in any case necessary in linking too closely the beneficial effects of certain wars on civilization generally with the ethical justifiability of those wars. It might, for instance, be pleaded that Joshua's conquest of Canaan, Alexander's conquest of Persia, and Rome's destruction of Carthage, proved ultimately to have benefited humanity, though ethically unjustifiable. One is tempted to digress at this point into a discussion of the right and the good: but it is not necessary; for no Christian today would advocate or defend an ethically unjustifiable war on the ground that it might ultimately prove beneficial to civilization.

(3). The apparent continuity of the series of situations which might be claimed as unquestionably justifying the use of coercion (pp. 100–103), and the difficulty of designating any point in it at which a new ethical principle is palpably introduced, do not of themselves prove that the way of coercion is equally justified at both ends of the scale. I have already given reasons (pp. 64 f.) for insisting that, in practical ethics, a difference of principle, on which the judgment as to what is right and what is wrong may turn, is not infrequently a difference of degree, despite the fact that we do not possess the means of determining the precise point at which moderation becomes excess, just as the existence of pools and moisture make it impossible for us to draw a sharp line between land and water, palpably different as these are.

(4). I move to yet stronger ground in proceeding to meet the objection that no other means than war (or some other form of injurious coercion) exists whereby certain intolerable evils can be adequately met. It is very often tacitly assumed that, if the way of injurious coercion be abjured, nothing is left but purely negative passivity, a futile laissez-faire-policy which allows the evil thing to run its course unchecked. Now the refusal to use injurious coercion *may* in certain circumstances deserve to be so regarded. When a man or nation refuses to strike because of cowardice or parsimony or unconcern, the choice of peace is worthy of reproach as negligent, inactive, and therefore disastrous. But what if the refusal to strike arises from some quite different motive? What if it rests on the conviction that there is, in love and gentleness, showing itself in forgiveness and service, an alternative method of grappling with the evil thing? No Christian, having before his eyes the Apostolic injunction to "conquer evil with what is good" (Rom. 12:21), can afford to deny that such an alternative exists, and has a claim on our attention. Doubtless there are difficulties and complications to be cleared up, before the reader can be expected to admit that in the existence of this alternative policy of love and gentleness we have a sufficient warrant for discarding all injuriously coercive methods; and these difficulties and complications we shall face and discuss all in good time. At the moment let us keep to this single point: does there, or does there not, exist—in the Christian ethic as we know it from the New Testament—a clear and effective method of meeting and overcoming evil? I submit that the only possible answer is in the affirmative. There is certainly no doubt as to the character of that method; nor is there any doubt regarding the faith of the New Testament teachers and writers in its general effectiveness. There is furthermore ample proof from history and human experience that this faith was justified (see above, pp. 17f., and below, pp. 107–112). It is important that this general affirmation of the positive efficacy of Christian love should be accepted as it deserves, and should not be hastily set aside as irrelevant because of some objection or other which we have not yet examined, and to which it is often prematurely supposed that there is no answer.

(5). Probably the foremost difficulty which will occur to a Christian nonpacifist, who feels obliged to concede *in the abstract* our plea that gentleness and love have positive value, will be the serious risk in many cases that this particular policy of gentleness and love may fail, and that the victory will then remain with evil. But if pacifism may fail, so too may war. Most of the arguments used for the purpose of justifying war on behalf of a righteous cause tacitly presuppose as certain the success of such war, *and are valid only if its success can be counted on as certain*. Yet nothing is more uncertain than the outcome of an armed struggle between two powers which are at all evenly matched. If the test of expediency can be used to discredit pacifism, on the ground that pacifism may fail, it can be still more cogently used to discredit war, on the ground that war may fail, as it quite obviously and frequently does. Incidentally, it is also worth observing at this point that the military victory of the wrong side is not always the unrelieved calamity it seems to be, and does not therefore always stand in such urgent need of being forcibly prevented as its opponents feel: the historian Fyffe, for instance, doubted whether mankind's permanent interests might not have been better served by Napoleon's success in 1812 than by his defeat. Be that as it may, I would again plead here with the reader not to repudiate this argument by prematurely summoning *other* difficulties to his aid. There are admittedly several points to be met, and I shall endeavour to meet them all honestly: but clearly they can be dealt with only one by one; and the answer to this one is that, since there is a risk of failure in all human policies including war, risk of failure in particular cases does not constitute a valid refutation of pacifism.

(6). One of the commonest means used to show that pacifism completely fails to answer the test of expediency is to frame an hypothesis positing the universal adoption of it and then to picture the terrible social and political chaos that would result. "If we all did as you" (so the nonresister is frequently told), "what would become of the security of life and property in the community?" or "If we all did as you, we should have the Germans landing here, massacring the population, and annexing our country to their Reich." To this hypothesis-criticism there is more than one answer to be made, and we shall need to recur to it later (see below, pp. 132–134). But let me at this stage point out its inherently self-contradictory character, when couched in this simple form. What is the value of an hypothesis which first posits that *all* the members of a society are so good that they will not return evil for evil, and then (in order to have a real grievance to put forward) arbitrarily withdraws some of the "all" to play the part of wrong-doers?

A similar, but less vulnerable criticism of the pacifist argument might be framed on the ground that, while in individual cases the efficacy of returning good for evil had been proved, we have no sufficient exemplifications of it on a large communal scale to show its feasibility as a national policy; and it is, of course, as a national measure that war has to be considered.

But if the historical examples of the practical success of pacifism are less numerous and impressive than we should like, consider whether the reason may not be the fewness of pacifists rather than the ineffectiveness of pacifism. Seeing that only a small fraction of the population has at any time attempted to practise it, we cannot reasonably demand instances of its success when taken up on a nationwide scale. We are not, however, without a number of examples of its success when followed by individuals or groups of individuals in their dealings with communities of considerable size; and these instances leave us in no doubt but that the same success as attends this method when followed by individuals would also attend it if it were followed by a whole community.

The pre-Constantinian Christian Church offered no violent resistance to the often brutal ill-will of the pagan populace and the ruthless repression often attempted by the Imperial government. Yet it lived down the hostility and, by meeting cruelty and hatred with patience and kindness, it eventually became so large and influential that Constantine found the toleration and protection of it the only practicable policy. It is sometimes said—and I think with truth—that the Roman Empire never did its best to crush the Church, and that, had it done so, it could easily have succeeded. That, however, does not alter the fact that the hostility both of government and populace was severe and long drawn out, and that it was overcome by the Christian method of turning the other cheek. The pacifying influence of the Christian clergy in the post-Constantinian days is acknowledged to have considerably mitigated the calamities resulting from the barbarian invasions.

The power of patient endurance to wear down persecution has often been illustrated since Constantine's days. The English Puritans (after the Restoration) and the Scottish Covenanters are cases in point. The Quaker colony in Pennsylvania (1682–1755), unlike all the other European colonies in America, made no arrangements to defend itself, with its women and children against the wild tribes of Red Indians with whom everywhere else the colonists were at war. The Quakers made a point of dealing with the Indians in just and generous ways; and as long as they refrained from injustice and armed conflict, they were immune from molestation. To suggest that this policy succeeded only because defencelessness was an impressive novelty to the Indians is surely a mistake: if it had done so, why did it not promptly fail as soon as the novelty of it wore off?

In the latter part of last century, the United States Government spent a huge sum and lost numerous lives in an endeavour to subdue the Modoc Indians. At length the difficulty was solved by the conversion of the whole tribe to Christianity through the efforts of a Quaker woman-missionary.

Theodore Pennell travelled alone for several years among the warlike Afghan tribes on the northwest frontier of India, armed with nothing but his medicine chest, and engaged in healing the sick. The value of his work as a power for peace, in a quarter where military operations for the defence of civilization are usually held to be specially necessary, may be judged from the opinion of a British General in India, who declared that Theodore Pennell was worth to the British Government more than two regiments of soldiers. Another instance is the opinion of one who knew the facts that, had Mary Slessor

the missionary been settled in the Aro country in Calabar, the Government would not have needed to send a punitive expedition thither in 1902 in order to suppress the slave trade. It is, in fact, widely maintained by well-informed persons that practicable alternatives to punitive bombing (in the form of civilizing missions, promotion of agriculture, etc.) exist as a means of dealing with dangerous primitive tribes. The records of the various missionary societies are full of instances of this kind, demonstrating the power of Christian love and service to check the savage instincts of imperfectly civilized peoples.

The well-known work of Mr. Ghandi, both in India today and earlier in Africa, exemplifies rather the power of noncooperation than of Christian love on the part of a group; but even so, it calls for mention at this point as another manifestation of the efficacy of nonviolent methods of restraint. Incidentally, there are, of course, numerous cases on record of rival communities, even rival nations, replacing conflict and the risk of it by friendly mutual understanding.

While, therefore, for the reason stated, we cannot produce an historical instance of a *whole nation* overcoming evil with good, history furnishes us with plenty of testimonies as to the positive power of Christian love and gentleness as a counter-blast to violent wrongdoing. Such facts as we have illustrate indeed the fewness of pacifists, but vindicate rather than discredit the practical usefulness of their pacifism.

C O M M E N T S ▪ Q U E S T I O N S

1. Do you agree with the following statement (written by Cadoux in 1939 but perhaps as true today as it was then): "The world is full of states that have virtually no power to withstand aggression from a strong neighbor, but are nonetheless safe because they do not invite aggression." Assuming that this statement is true, is Cadoux correct in using it as a premise in his general defense of pacifism?

2. In many apparently righteous wars throughout history, says Cadoux, "The aggression that had to be repelled was not entirely unprovoked." In other words, it would be difficult to find a truly just war. Again, is this a reason for believing in a general pacifism, or a pacifism for all possible cases?

3. What is your assessment of the "policy of love and gentleness" that Cadoux is advocating?

4. Critics of a policy of pacifism argue that it may fail. Cadoux's response to this argument is to point out that a policy of war may also fail. Is this a good response?

5. How strong an argument in defense of pacifism can be constructed from Cadoux's somewhat lengthy discussion of historical examples?

W I L L I A M   E A R L E

In Defense of War

* * * * *

T he justification of war aims at showing both its morality and its rationality; if therefore there are occasions when a moral and rational man must fight, then a proscription of war in principle must be itself irrational and ethically deplorable.

In a word, the justification of war is existence; to will to exist is to affirm war as its means and condition. But

William Earle is professor of philosophy (emeritus) at Northwestern University. Among his books are The Autobiographical Consciousness, Public Sorrows and Private Pleasures, Mystical Reason, *and* Evanescence.

William Earle, "In Defense of War," reprinted by permission of *The Monist* from Vol. 57, No. 4 (1973) of *The Monist*.

perhaps the term "existence" puts the matter too abstractly. In the present context, and in its most abstract sense, existence is a synonym for life, and nonexistence for death. And yet little has been said; the life and death of what? Bare life measured by the beating of the heart, is hardly life at all; it would be prized only as the supporter and condition of a life *worth living.* Obviously men have always thought it justifiable to fight not merely to preserve their physical being, but also for those additional things which make that life worth living, fertile lands, access to the sea, minerals, a government of their choice, laws and customs and religions, and finally peace itself. Existence then is hardly bare survival but an existence in the service of all those concrete values which illuminate and glorify existence. They too must exist; it is almost by definition that values, in and of their intrinsic meaning, *demand existence.* Justice would misunderstand itself if it were content to remain abstract and merely ideal.

So much might easily be granted until another reflection arises, that perhaps the goods of existence could be shared by all men. This utopian notion is much beloved of *philosophers* or *art critics* who look upon the diversities of thought and cultural style as so many advantages and opportunities for spiritual growth. And indeed they are; but then those values are not exactly what war is about. If the library can house every book in peaceful coexistence, or if the museum can calmly exhibit the styles of the world, why must men themselves fight? Could the world not be like an international congress of philosophy or perhaps a quieter meeting of UNESCO: would this not be the civilized thing? Would it not be better if nations conducted themselves according to the model of a general conversation, where views are advanced and withdrawn without anger, and where men say "excuse me for interrupting"?

But elementary reflection is sufficient to dispel these dreams. Existence or life individuates itself; when it can speak it says "I," and what it possesses, "mine." Nothing is changed logically in this respect when the I becomes a we, and mine, ours. That I am not you, or we are not they, is the ineluctable ground of war; individuation is essential to existence. That which is not individuated does not exist, but subsists as a universal or abstract meaning. Consequently the meaning of a book or cultural artifact can be shared by all; but the existent book or existent painting can not, and could supply a ground for conflict. No wonder philosophers or scientists or critics, accustomed to living in the domain of abstractions and ideal meanings which are not, like quantities of matter, diminished progressively by each man who partakes of them, find something scandalous and primitive about war or anything else appropriate in the domain of existence and life. Nothing is easier than for the spirit to neglect the conditions of its own existence, or indeed be outraged by them.

I have used the term, "existential" intentionally in spite of its abstractness to avoid at all costs what might seem to be its more common equivalent, "material." Some sentimental pacifists think it sufficient to prove that a nation has gone to war for "material" interests to conclude, with cheers from their audience, that such a war is *immoral.* That idealism should find itself opposed to "matter," or its equivalent, life and existence, would certainly not have surprised the Buddha or Nietzsche, both of whom accurately perceived that the only surcease of war and public sorrow is in nothingness, Nirvana or eternity. And, as President Truman remarked, those who can not stand the heat should get out of the kitchen.

But, of course, what the sentimental pacifist wants is nothing so radical as the genuine alternative of Buddha; he wants an *existent* heaven, perpetual peace-on-earth, a mishmash which has never been or never will be seen, violating as it does patent ontological differences subsisting between existence and the abstract. The exposure of this error is not difficult. At what precise point do material interests become ideal? Is the health of a nation "material" or "ideal"? But its health depends, of course, upon its wealth; is the pursuit of that wealth ideal or materialistic and crass? Is the culture of a nation an ideal or a material value? and is its culture dependent or not upon the wealth available for education and leisure? Is the wealth devoted to such tasks materialistic or idealistic? Money versus human life! All these false contrasts need not be multiplied to perceive the vacuity of any argument against war based upon "idealistic" as opposed to "materialistic" principles.

Functioning according to the same false logic is another simplistic contrast, also beloved of pacifists: that thought to exist between egoism and altruism. The high-minded rhetoric poured out against "selfishness" is laughable indeed when not taken seriously. Is it "selfish" for me to protect my own life, or those of my family, friends, or compatriots? And, moreover, not merely our physical existence, but our human life with its wealth, customs, laws, institutions, languages, religions, our autonomy? Or to protect the "material," i.e., economic conditions which support all these values? To affirm any form of life at all is at the same time to affirm the means to it; what *could* be more confused than to will our life and also to will the life opposed to it? The ultimate pacifist who would do nothing even to protect his own life for fear of killing another, is simply a case of self-hatred; but both nature and logic combine to guarantee that this particular illness never becomes widespread. Has or could there ever be a defense for the idea that everyone else's life is preferable to my own, particularly when adopted in turn by everyone else? To be bound together in friendship is certainly preferable to being torn apart by hostility; but is it not clear that neither the friendship of all nor the hostility of all is possible; the line to be drawn which assures the provisional existence of any state is to be drawn by practical statesmanship judging in its time for its time, and not by abstract, would-be idealistic principles, which by hoping to be valid for all times are pertinent to none.

Excursus on Equality. No doubt it will have been noted that war here has *not* been justified as a means of securing justice or equality. It has been justified as a means necessary to any nation to secure or preserve its own social good, and as such, is held to be eminently reasonable and honorable. However, the social life of a nation is not itself to be further judged by means of abstract categories such as justice or equality. Hasty thought frequently identifies justice with equality, particularly since justice is elusive and protean in its applications, whereas the notion of equality, being mathematical and abstract, is within the grasp of all. I either do or do not have as much as another; if I do not, am I not wronged? Cannot anyone see this? Indeed they can, but what cannot be so immediately seen is whether such inequality is also ipso facto unjust.

These confusions pour into those discussions which, for example, would justify any war at all against the United States; since we have more than anyone else, we could never have a right to defend that more. To have more is to be guilty before the abstract bar of Equality. But this last gasp of the French Revolution, amplified by Marxist bellows, blows against certain existential realities. Those realities are simply that the earth itself is differentiated by rivers, climates, flora and fauna, mountains, valleys and plains. Not all can live everywhere nor is this an injustice to them. And, to belabor the obvious, men are not equal, having very different temperaments, tastes, ideals, and histories. Not merely are men not equal, they are not unequal either, the category of "equality" being quantitative whereas a man or a nation is not a quantity of anything, but rather an individual or communal person aiming at a definite form of excellent life. Since nations and men are always already in a differentiated possession of the goods of the world, differentiated forms of excellence, differentiated histories and memories, the desire to equalize all is equivalent to the desire to obliterate history as well as the individuated free choices of nations and men. Computerized thought might delight in such simplicities, but is there any a priori reason why a truly just mind must accept it?

If I have not used the notion of justice in any abstract form to justify war, again, it is for the simple reason

that it leads nowhere. Wars are fought *over* differing notions of justice; does any party to war ever think itself unjust? Justice in the abstract therefore is useless for purposes of condemnation or justification. Victory in war, again it is for the simple reason abstractly just, but which form of justice will prevail.

Objections to War

(a) *What the "people" think of war.* I shall use this title for a slippery mass of appeals increasingly popular in the mass media. Reporters, seemingly getting the "objective" facts, can always ask some fleeing peasants: "do you want war?" Of course, the bewildered peasant replies that he only wishes to live in peace, that war has destroyed his family, his rice fields, that it is caused by "government," that he could live equally well under any regime, that in fact he does not know the enemy, or does, having relatives among them, etc., all of which is pathetic as much for the sufferings of the peasant as for the mindlessness of the reporter who imagines himself to be presenting an ultimate argument based upon "humanity."

Television, since it cannot picture any thought about war, is confined to showing what can be shown: the dismembered, burned, legless, eyeless, as if to say: this is what war really is. And when the dead or wounded are little children, women, or old men, the very heart recoils; the argument is decisive. But not yet: the soldiers must be asked; have they not seen it firsthand, fought it with their lives, seen their comrades fall before their very eyes? Any number can be rounded up to swear they haven't the faintest idea what all the killing is about, that it must be immoral or absurd, probably conducted by munition makers or politicians seeking reelection, in a word, by all that "establishment" in which they never had much participation even during peace. Their own virtue is to be resigned or, if they "think," to wearing peace symbols.

As for the ideal component in war, the honor and courage of the soldier, that too is immediately debunked. "There's nothing heroic about war" says the soldier who may just yesterday have risked his life to save a comrade. War is nothing but living in the mud and rain, with poor food, disease, fatigue, danger and boredom; is that heroic? His reticence about "heroism" is admirable; but we need not believe what he says. Since heroism is doing one's duty or going beyond it under extreme conditons, it is difficult to see how the difficulties diminish the accomplishment; without those difficulties, genuine heroism would be nothing but parade-ground heroics. But let us look in more detail at these arguments of the people.

The "People": who are they? They are either citizens of their country or not; if not, they have no political right to complaint. If so, then their government is indeed theirs, and they have every political duty to observe its decisions or try to alter them legally. In any event, the people are all the people, not merely the peasants, and they are in their collective capacity *already* represented by their government, whose decisions they must respect as made by their legal representatives. If the people are in no way represented by their government, then the question shifts itself away from war to that of forming a representative government. In any event, war and peace are decisions which

obviously fall to the national government and not to miscellaneous groups, random interests, or ad hoc political rallies. Nor, least of all, to the private opinions of reporters interviewing a few people, usually those with the least opportunity to consider and weigh what is at stake. To suggest opinion polls or referenda on these questions every month or so, simply offers us the idea of another form of government altogether, an unheard-of populism which in effect negates representative government altogether and substitutes for it the ever-shifting voice of the street. And since that in turn clearly reflects the overwhelming influence of propaganda, immediate "democracy" of this order shifts the decision from government to the directors and voices of "news" media. It is hardly surprising that this prospect delights the media, but it is surprising that so many otherwise sensible citizens wish to shift their allegiance from their own duly elected representatives to the directors of news media whom they have not elected and for the most part hardly know, all the while imagining that this offers them an opportunity themselves to direct the course of events.

The truth is, unwelcome as it may be, that the "people," ordinary housewives, factory workers, farmers, etc., as fine as they may be personally, are in no position whatsoever to consider the wisdom of that very politics upon which their own lives depend. It is, naturally, for this reason that very few nations at all, and none of any importance, are run on any such scheme. It is precisely the responsibility of representatives of the people to occupy themselves with such questions, inform themselves and circumspectly weigh the possibilities. The limits of experience and political habits of thought which more or less make the ordinary private citizen private, at the same time warn us against encouraging any immediate or undue influence of his opinions on matters of state. What the people think is simply the repetition of slogans derived either from campaigning politicians or their favorite newspaper. For some researchers, the popular mind is a pool of infinite wisdom and goodness; the truth is it is nothing but an ephemeral reflection of popular songs, sandwich-board slogans, newspaper headlines and cliches. For the popular mind, "thought" is what can be written on a placard or shouted at a rally; for the reflective, thought is precisely what eludes this form of expression. Who has the wind to shout a *qualified* thought?

Nothing could be more dangerous than the enthusiasms of the people. Mad joy at the beginning of hostilities; and rage when the bodies are brought in, the expenses reckoned up. But of course this is precisely what is to be expected from the people, suggestible, flighty, and unused to either foresight or circum spection. As for the shallow notion that the people want only peace, that all peoples love one another as brothers, and that war therefore is imposed upon them from above— could one find any stretch of history or any segment of the world where these notions are significantly illustrated? The natural brotherhood of man? The natural goodness of the people? Indeed! One could far better argue that there is nothing whatsoever "natural" in man; the natural is exactly what man *decides*.

When we substitute for the people, the common soldier, all the same applies. Their experience is always

tempting to novelists, looking for the "reality" of war. The reality in question, it should be remembered, is the one they are best equipped to express with vividness: the day-to-day life in the foxhole, or in the pouring rain, the mudholes, the terror, the sickness, ambiguities of fighting life. It is easy for novelists to enter into the mind of the G.I. who is presented as seeing only what lies before his eyes: a dead friend. *That* is the reality of war; meanwhile at headquarters, the colonels are arrogant, incompetent, not really suffering but instead well provided with booze and whores, no doubt profiteering from the PX, and in cahoots with the government, known to be corrupt. No doubt all this is true enough from time to time, and no doubt anyone at all can sympathize with the sentiments involved. And no doubt at all, the same structure can easily be found in any civil society that ever was in peacetime as well. The question however concerns the exact pertinence of such considerations, to the justification or lack of it for any given war. Since wars are not fought in the first place to make common soldiers comfortable, nor to make generals live the same lives as privates, nor to remove corruption in the armies involved, the only pertinence of such observations when true would be to improve the army, not to stop the war. And that a platoon leader does not know the whole strategy from his experience, that a general cannot perform his legitimate functions in the same state of exhaustion as the G.I., nor carry his maps and codes into the foxholes, nor subject himself to the same risks as the ordinary soldier, is all obvious but no doubt at times escapes the full approval of the G.I., which is why the G.I. is not a general.

Related, is the curious popular objection that war is immoral because the soldier does not know his enemy *personally*. A German soldier of World War I in *All Quiet on the Western Front* receives a shock when after killing a Frenchman, he realizes he never knew him personally. However he would have received a greater shock upon recovering his wits when he realized that if he *had* known him personally and acted out of personal rage, his act would be radically transformed in meaning. From being a soldier doing his *duty*, he would be transformed into a *murderer*. But no doubt this distinction is too fine for those who love to talk of war as "mass murder," oblivious to all distinctions between on the one hand the legitimate duties of the police and soldiers, and on the other punishable murder. This essential distinction is obliterated in that higher pacifistic fog where all "taking of human life" is immoral. There could hardly be anything more obscurantist than the desire to obliterate all distinctions of roles and offices of men into that warm, personal, brotherly unity of "the personal." Generals receive criticism for not taking a "personal" interest in each of their troops; I, for one, would demote any who did. If some such thing is the philosophy of the best seller, it is easy to predict that of the worst seller: the wise general and the stupid G.I. In all of this, it would hardly take a Nietzsche to perceive the influence of that old, popular motive, the resentment of authority. In the present instance it feeds pacifism.

Popular thought loves to "psych" its political leaders. In this, has it not been aided and abetted by the rise of psychological novels where the plot sinks into insignificance and the psychological analysis of motives occupies the stage, usually a popular version of Freud. Psychologizing has, undoubtedly, a limited relevance to political decision; national policies are at the same time policies of leaders, whose characters and temperaments are significant factors in their actions and reactions. Roosevelt and Churchill both considered the personalities of Hitler and Stalin in this fashion, and if their judgments left something to be desired, at least the pertinence of the question is undeniable; political personality is unquestionably a factor in objective policy. Which items in announced policy are sticking points, and which negotiable? Which remarks made to the inner constituency, and which to the outer world? Generals also try to sense the temperament of their opponents, as one factor in the whole.

On the other hand, what could be more ludicrous than the popular effort to assess policy through a judgment of the character and assumed private motives of the initiators of that policy? Antiwar finds nothing but reprehensible private motives at the root of the matter; prowar finds nothing but heroic strength; reflection finds both irrelevant. Wars are neither justifiable or unjustifiable in terms of the private motives of the leaders; wars are not personal acts of rage and revenge, but as von Clausewitz showed, an extension of policy by other means. Policies are measured by their probable costs and effects, and not by the motives of the agents.

The weighing of policy properly belongs in the hands of those responsible and thoughtful men who are experienced in such matters. It is not in any conspicuous sense the experience of pastors in their morality, poets with their sensitivity, the young with their "idealism," psychoanalysts with their probings of emotions, or news reporters with their "scoops."

The distressing thing about popular psychologizing is its confidence; it *knows* the black heart inside the political leader, and is certain that anything more complex or even favorable is "naive." All of which reflects the failure of both psychology and the psychological novel to make their point; should not popular wisdom at least be sensitive to the difficulties and ambiguities of searching out the motives of the human heart? If I can only seldom if ever be confident I know my own motives, how can I be so sure I know those of others?

I conclude that the "people" must take their chances in war, do not represent a pool of persons separate from the organized body of citizens with a government, and that their perception, judgment and analysis of public policy is sound only by accident. Public policy is beyond the scope of private people; since it is, the common people revert to something they imagine themselves to be expert in, the psychological motives of leaders; but alas, even that is beyond their or anyone else's proper grasp. At which point we have nothing to do but return to where we should never have left, the objective consideration of policy by those competent to consider it.

(b) *The Sufferings of the People.* A final set of criticisms against war again purports to rest upon humanitarian or idealistic grounds: its argument is the simple exhibition of death, injuries, disease, poverty, destruction, the ravaging of both countryside and cities. Television makes it as vivid as

possible, and the color photographs in *Life* magazine are almost enough to sicken the heart of the bravest and to shake the firmest judgment. Indeed this is their overt intention, and it is not long before they end up on pacifist posters as ultimate arguments. But of course arguments they are not, at best facts to be considered; but then who hasn't already considered them? Is there anyone who imagines war to be anything but killing? The decision to fight is the decision to kill; such a decision, needless to say, is never easy although it may frequently be justified. *If justified*, what service is performed by such direct appeals to vital instinct and sentiment? At best they would enfeeble our powers of judgment, never too strong, so that we would choose the unjustifiable rather than the wise course.

These images thought to be decisive, are in reality nothing but kicks below the belt and from behind; reasonable moral judgment can never be a simple reaction to our emotions and sentiments; the emotions and sentiments themselves are more than enough for that; but it is the role of policy and judgment to judge *over* these forces. The job is no doubt the most difficult man faces; it is hardly made easier by the daily flood of images of suffering in the media.

The image in itself is no argument against anything. It would be easy indeed by vivid color photographs, accompanied by recordings of screaming, wailing and crying, to sicken anyone of the very project of living. Surgical operations would never be undertaken, women would be afraid to give birth to children; images of the old, sick and senile would convince us that life itself is folly; and some such thing is the conclusion of transcendental ascetics.

But then such an ethic, by intention, is not pertinent to public policy, necessarily committed to not merely life, but the good life.

The humanitarian argument drawn from ruins and suffering, aims at a higher idealism; but with a suddenness which would have delighted Hegel, turns into its opposite, a crass materialism. If human life is justifiable in terms of its excellence, where is the idealism in locating that excellence in a clinging to cities and fields? Or finally, in clinging to mere life itself as our highest value? The founder of Western philosophy, Socrates, disdained to use arguments resting upon such sympathies in his own defense, and did *not* bring his wife and children to court to plead for him. Nor did he conjure up imaginative pictures of his own suffering. No doubt, this is old-fashioned. . . .

Since one dies anyway, the sole question would seem to be *how* one dies, with honor or not. There is no moral obligation to live at all costs and under any conditions; there is no moral obligation to live at all; there is a moral obligation to live honorably if one lives at all. What that obligation dictates under specific historical concrete circumstances clearly cannot be decided for all and in general; but it can dictate that under some circumstances, some men must find their honor in defending unto death what they take to be more valuable than sheer existence, namely a human life dedicated to excellence and dignity. Human lives whose chief moral defense is that they have kept themselves alive, have at the same stroke lost *all* moral defense. Such is the age-old paradox of life.

Traditionally, the man who chose life and personal safety under any conditions was regarded as a coward, and his condition that of a slave. Do we now have new reasons for reversing this decision? Which is not to say that some have not tried; what other judgment could be pronounced upon the current rash of movies and novels all celebrating the *antihero* as a new form of excellence; sometimes it is even thought to be "authentic" or "existential"! What is it but mediocrity and cowardice? It follows that some are authentic cowards, but need we admire them? A footnote to the present confusion is the argument that war "brutalizes" the troops. The brutalization is rarely spelled out although hovering around the attack is the suspicion that troops are brutalized in their coarse speech, their terms of contempt for the enemy, their failure personally to consider the "justice" of every order, to bring their superiors before the bar of their own private conscience, their fondness for booze and camp followers above lectures and the opera. Well! But if brutalization means a willingness to kill the enemy, I for one fail to perceive the fault; that's what they are there for in the first place, and who is closer to the brute, a man afraid to kill the enemy, or one who will kill and die to preserve the freedom and dignity of himself or his compatriots?

There will always be occasions when human freedom and dignity are threatened; there will always be occasions then for a justifiable war, and the pacifistic argument fails. To attack the very idea of war is to attack something fundamental to the preservation of any honorable life, and to offer under the flag of idealism or humanitarianism, the very substance of cowardice. Having already denounced Soviet injustice, what could be a worse capitulation than Bertrand Russell's slogan: "Better Red than dead"?

C O M M E N T S ■ Q U E S T I O N S

1. "The justification of war is existence; to will to exist is to affirm war as its means and condition." Earle is arguing that if something is valuable (and one's own life or existence is fundamental to other values), then it is worth fighting for as affirmation of its value. What pacifist arguments, if any, could be used to oppose this point of view?

2. It may be objected that Earle's position is selfish. His response is the following: "Is it 'selfish' for me to protect my own life, or those of my family, friends, or compatriots?" Is Earle's response a defensible one?

3. Earle's position presupposes a certain inevitability to conflicts among human beings. Is such a view realistic?

4. Earle's position appeals to the values of honor and courage. Among all the things in life that are valuable, how would you rank honor and courage? Are there any things of greater worth that are jeopardized by war?

5. What would Earle say about Cadoux's "policy of love and gentleness"? Would Earle accept Cadoux's claim that a policy of love and gentleness can be quite a different thing from a policy of cowardice or unconcern?

T R U D Y   G O V I E R

Nuclear Illusion and Individual Obligations

I f we ask why philosophers as such should contribute to public understanding of nuclear problems, answers are readily forthcoming. Fundamentally, the danger of nuclear war is the most pressing problem of our time. If there is a global nuclear war most (if not all) of the other human problems will entirely disappear. Any which remain will appear in a radically different context. Global nuclear war would, in all likelihood, end human social life as we know it. It could end the human race altogether and might

Trudy Govier is a Canadian philosopher who has written articles in the areas of ethics and logic.

From the *Canadian Journal of Philosophy*, vol. 13 (1983), pp. 483–492. Reprinted by permission of the author and the publisher.

even result in the death of virtually all mammalian life on the planet.[22] A discussion of moral values and political structures which ignores this pervasive threat is in a sense absurd, for the threat could eliminate all those things we value. And it is a real one. There is a genuine persistent risk of nuclear war and virtually all adult citizens are at some level aware of this risk. To 'apply' ethics to such problems as abortion, sexism, and capital punishment and ignore the nuclear arms race is to suggest that these less cosmic problems are more real and pressing than the problem of global peace or war. It may also suggest to students and the public at large that philosophers who have studied moral theory, competing ideologies, and principles of probability and strategy, condone the nuclear status quo.

Secondly, if we do not discuss the nuclear arms race and related dangers, we contribute to the suppression of thought about the issue which has been such a dominant feature of the nuclear age. Public silence through much of the period between 1945 and the present has enabled the super-powers to move from a position where there were three nuclear weapons in 1945 to one where there are more than 50,000 today. Now, that silence is ending; awareness is increasing. And philosophers, especially in their role as educators, can play their part in ending the silence.

---

22. The grizzly details are amply described in Schell's *The Fate of the Earth*. Precise predictions are obviously not possible, due to possible variations in numbers of weapons used, reliability of weapons, performance of weapons over a North-South route, weather conditions, and pertinent gaps in scientific knowledge.

An additional point is that the nuclear arms race and the enormous accumulations of conventional arms weapons are important forces behind the economies, technologies, ideologies, and scientific research programs of our time. These military developments (said by some to occupy forty percent of the scientists and engineers on the earth) contribute to the world political and social scene in many ways. By ignoring them, we risk an analysis of social reality which is seriously distorted and inaccurate.

Obviously the reason for philosophers as people to become knowledgeable about nuclear problems is that their very survival is at stake. But the reason for philosophers as philosophers to do this is that they have special opportunities to educate people on the topic, and they have special obligations to do so, especially insofar as they teach ethics, applied ethics, and political philosophy.

To show that issues pertaining to nuclear arms are related to other matters which are already recognized to be legitimate topics of philosophical study, we go on to mention some specific topic areas.

(a) Occupational Ethics: Defence Production

In the American Catholic bishops' pastoral letter on nuclear weapons, a very conditional endorsement of (strict?) nuclear deterrence is given. Maintaining a nuclear arsenal for deterrence is allowed to be morally acceptable for some period of time provided that all efforts are made to eliminate reliance on this arsenal for national defence. The bishops conclude that the traditional just war theory could not justify the use of nuclear weapons, for just war theory requires a strict distinction between combatants and civilians in war. The distinction cannot hold up when nuclear weapons are used. Their conclusion, then, is that it could never be morally acceptable to detonate nuclear weapons against targets in populated areas. Nuclear weapons can never be used.

Given this conclusion, some bishops (notably Archbishop Hunthausen of Seattle) went much further, developing the following argument: If it is not right to use nuclear weapons, then it is not right to threaten to use them. If it is not right to threaten to use them, then it is not right to possess them; possession itself might be said to constitute some kind of implicit threat or implicit intention to use. If it is not right to possess nuclear weapons, then it is not right to manufacture them. On this analysis those participating in the design, manufacture or testing of nuclear weapons are participating in immoral activities, and have an obligation to change their occupation. Hunthausen's view went further than that of the majority of bishops; many disagreed with him as to the soundness of the inference 'if doing X is wrong, then threatening to do X is wrong.' The argument raises some important and fascinating problems which should certainly be discussed by philosophers interested in occupational ethics.[23]

23. For some discussion of the bishops' debate, see R. G. Hoyt, 'The Bishops and the Bomb,' *Christianity and Crisis,* August 9, 1982; Michael Novak, 'Nuclear Morality,' *America,* 147 (1982) 5–8; J. A. O'Hare, 'One Man's Primer on Nuclear Morality,' *America,* 147 (1982) 9–12; Francis X. Winters, 'Catholic Debate and Division on Deterrence,' *America,* 147 (1982) 127–31. Also relevant is Walter Wink, 'Faith and Nuclear Paralysis,' *Christian Century,* 99 (1982) 234–7.

(b) Nation States

In *The Fate of the Earth,* Jonathan Schell argues that the only way to eliminate the risk of nuclear war is to eliminate nation states. He says that the knowledge of nuclear weaponry is now a permanent feature of the human condition, and given this, any war will retain the potential for becoming a nuclear war. Thus nuclear weapons make *all* war obsolete as a means of resolving disputes. Yet, Schell claims, the ability to wage war in pursuit of its interests and in its own self-defence is an intrinsic feature of the sovereign nation state. For nuclear security to be possible, national sovereignty must go.[24]

There are many issues central to the appraisal of this argument. Among them are conceptual issues as to how we understand the nation state and national sovereignty. Also involved are evaluative issues. What is the value of nation states, as such? If they possess real cultural and social/psychological value, is the preservation of this value worth some attendant risks? Could it be worth the risk of global nuclear war? Of limited nuclear wars? Schell's instinct—shared by the present author—is to think that the nation state is a comparatively transient historical entity which does not possess a value worth preserving at jeopardy to the very survival of mankind as a whole. The question is arguable, however; if the risk of nuclear war is believed to be very small and the value of nation states very large, a different judgment would likely be made. A number of reviewers reacted with great hostility to Schell's conclusion that the

24. Schell, *The Fate of the Earth,* part 3. This part of the book has been strongly criticized.

world—the international order, in particular—would have to be 'reinvented' in order to eliminate the risk of nuclear war. Suggestions of the necessity of some kind of world government struck them as utopian at best; Orwellian at worst. Yet the issues raised clearly bear thinking about, and should be central topics in political philosophy.

(c) Future Generations

Philosophers have discussed the question of what kind of moral status people who do not yet exist, but will or may exist, should have. How should they count in our moral decision-making, when we come to weigh the consequences of our actions? Equally with existing people? Or not at all, since they are not real at the time that a decision is made? Neither answer seems quite right, and compromise positions tend not to work very well.[25] Philosophers have also discussed reproductive morality: whether the interests of a prospective child should be taken into account when he or she is still nonexistent and an agent is deciding whether or not to produce him or her.

These topics are important and difficult to resolve, but the questions raised avoid yet another question. Will there be any future generations of humans? It is not certain that even a global nuclear war would end the era of human beings on the planet earth, but there is a very good chance that it would. There are indications that a large number of nuclear detonations would destroy the earth's protective ozone layer. If this were to happen, human and animal life could be entirely destroyed. Part of the problem about the moral status of future generations, then, is whether we have any obligation to work to ensure that they *can* persist on our globe. If there is such an obligation, it is rather different from others which have been discussed in the context of the moral status of future people. These have fallen into two categories: obligations to take into account the interests of people who will (or likely will) exist; and obligations pertaining to reproductive decision-making. Obligations to ensure that some future people can exist on this globe would be another subject.

Would the annihilation of the human species be a tragedy? If so, to whom? If it were a tragedy would this be so only because those who were already alive wanted to live longer and (in some cases) suffered greatly in dying.[26] Or would there be a less person-related tragedy: the death of the species as a whole? To the last question most of us would probably give an instinctive affirmative answer. But we might not know just why. Such an answer is not easily made coherent with the individualistic ontology of such common moral theories as utilitarianism and contractarianism. Ecologically minded philosophers have

---

25. This comment applies to my own paper, 'What Should We Do About Future People?', *American Philosophical Quarterly*, 16 (1979) 105–13. An indication as to just how complex these problems have become may be gleaned from Derek Parfit, 'Future Generations: Further Problems,' *Philosophy and Public Affairs*, 11 (1982) 113–72.

26. Schell dwells on these questions in a manner quite metaphysical in Part II of his book. They have also been addressed by John Leslie in 'Why Not Let Life Become Extinct?', a paper presented at the Canadian Philosophical Association meetings in Montreal, June 1980. See also John Leslie, *Value and Existence* (Totowa, NJ: Rowman and Littlefield 1979).

reflected on whether and why it would be a bad thing for such species as the whale and the whooping crane to become extinct. The same questions can, alas, be extended to our own species.

(d) The Meaning of Life

Discussions of the meaning of life have largely ignored the constant possibility that human life on this planet could simply end. The real possibility of a nuclear catastrophe at any time can cast a dark shadow of meaningless over all mundane activities which have a future orientation. For many, that simply means all mundane activities. (It need not, if one interprets and values activities in terms of their internal actions rather than in terms of their goals and results, but such an attitude is not common in western culture.) The prospect of the extinction of our social world is more radically disruptive psychologically than the prospect of our own individual death. Individual death is inevitable; social or (worse yet) species death is not. Individual death permits the survival of descendants and of valued projects; social or species death does not. All future-oriented meaning is in jeopardy when the very survival of our social world is at risk. Psychiatrist Robert Lifton has long argued that the pervasive and unspoken threat of nuclear disaster has been profoundly damaging to the psyche of post-war generations.[27] He believes that it is responsible for hedonistic and self-interested attitudes, for irresponsibil-

ity to the biosphere, and for the low birth rate in many industrialized countries.

Lifton's claims would be extremely difficult to verify. Yet there is a basic sense in which the nuclear threat does undermine the meaningfulness of many human activities and forces into new relief old questions about the very meaning of human life itself. Many philosophers are still willing to acknowledge that reflection on the meaning of life is a fundamentally philosophical task. If this is so, then a central part of this task is to acknowledge the nuclear threat and try to make sense of it. For the time being, this is a fact about our world, and one which we cannot will away.

(e) Self-Deception

Intricate articles have been written trying to make logical and psychological sense of self deception. Traditionally, philosophers argued that self-deception was morally wrong, for all people in all circumstances. Recently some have revised this stance, contending that self-deception can be excusable or even admirable in some circumstances.[28] The nature of nuclear arms and the risks and nature of nuclear war are topics on which we may well have society-wide self-deception. The psychological need to repress information and to highlight any optimistic prospects is very great. For several decades between the early nineteen sixties and the present time, the arms race accelerated, billions were spent, accidents occurred, nuclear threats were made, and scarcely

---

27. See R. J. Lifton and Richard Falk, *Indefensible Weapons* (Toronto: CBC Publications 1982). Lifton's discussion of psychological effects of nuclear weapons comprises Part I of this work.

---

28. This view has been defended by Béla Szabados in 'Self-Deception,' *Canadian Journal of Philosophy*, 4 (1974) 41–9.

anyone thought much about it. Looking back, this hardly seems possible. Was this a case of society-wide self-deception? Does that idea make sense? What are the social, political, and linguistic strategies which a society employs in order to deceive itself? If we decide that societies have in fact deceived themselves about the role of nuclear weapons and the threat of nuclear war, this may make us want to re-examine the recent more charitable view of self-deception which allows that it can sometimes be a good thing. Public illusions and ignorance about the nature and role of nuclear weaponry have been a necessary condition of the perpetuation of the dangerous nuclear arms race.

Individual Responsibility in the Face of a Global Threat

Many people believe that no ordinary individual has a chance to make any difference to the unfolding of global events. If this is so, then individuals would have no obligation to try to affect the course of such events. They would not be morally responsible, either, when things go wrong. The traditional principle of 'ought implies can' will give us these comfortable conclusions, provided of course that it is true that an individual cannot make a difference. In an obvious sense whether this principle is true will depend on which individual you are. Mohatma Gandhi, Bertrand Russell, Albert Einstein, and (more recently) Helen Caldicott and Rosalie Berthell *have* made some difference. But then we do not all have their special abilities and opportunities.

A more general point is that whether an individual can make a difference to the prospects of nuclear peace or nuclear war depends on

how many other individuals are trying to make a difference. To say that a single person cannot make a difference may be true. But to say that a very large number of single persons cannot is obviously false. An energetic peace movement of 50,000,000 people within the United States could certainly do a very great deal to reduce the risk of nuclear war. A peace movement of 1,000,000 dedicated people in that country would have some chance of doing this, as would a movement of 100,000 dedicated people in Canada or another allied country.[29] Three or four hundred people would have a very limited chance of having any influence, unless they were in positions of special power and importance. In general, the impact of one person's actions will depend on how other people act. He or she will be impotent alone, but powerful as one of a number.

What we are able to do will depend, then, on what others do. Following on the 'ought implies can' principle, it appears that what we are obliged to do will depend on what others do. How are we obligated to act when we do not know what others will do?

At this point we have reached an impasse familiar in moral philosophy. The problem is a dramatic version of that which arises whenever an agent questions an obligation to act at

---

29. Moral perspectives on nuclear issues, and potential for political action to alter the status quo, vary considerably depending upon whether one is a citizen within a super-power or a citizen within an allied country. The difference in perspective is often blurred by uses of 'we' which fail to make it clear whether the point of view taken is that of the U.S., of Canada, or of any country within the NATO alliance.

possible personal cost in a moral community which can offer no guarantee that all or most of its members will abide by moral rules. Though interest may be foregone to no avail unless a sufficient number of others abide by the rules, this does not appear to be an excuse for ignoring the obligation. At least, from the moral point of view it is not commonly taken to be an excuse. Plato, Hobbes, Gauthier and many others have wrestled with this problem, trying to show how a commitment to moral principles can be made rational in the sense of being in an agent's ultimate self-interest.

In a beautifully expressed essay entitled 'Secular Faith,' Annette Baier approached the problem differently. She made no attempt to justify moral action on the basis of reason alone: whether it be reason understood as enlightened pursuit of self-interest, or on some other model. Rather she argued that an individual's commitment to a project whose success requires the actions of a number of other individuals requires, in the end, *faith* in other people.

Baier wrote:

If everyone insisted on knowing in advance that any sacrifice of independent advantage which they personally make, in joining or supporting a moral order, will be made up for by the return they will get from membership in that moral order, that moral order could never be created, nor, if miraculously brought about, sustained.[30]

For social life to continue we need to have a secular faith—the faith that enough other people will have the moral concern to make our own moral commitments practically significant.

It is such faith in other people that is needed in order to vindicate the individual sacrifices of time and valued projects which will be necessary for individuals to work to reduce the risk of nuclear war. The work is bound to go slowly and the task will be accomplished (if at all) only in many small stages. A large part of this work consists in seeking very basic changes in public attitudes toward nuclear weapons and their historical and present role. The illusion that these weapons have kept us safe, serve only to deter, and are being well-managed by people who know what they are doing has made the nuclear arms race possible. This illusion must be eliminated, and this is no easy task. No one person can do this alone; yet all are obliged to do their part.

Baier does not discuss the problem of global war but she makes a number of remarks which seem very appropriate to it.

. . . the alternative, giving up on that crucial part of the moral enterprise which secures co-operation, must eventually lead to an outcome disastrous to all— although those with a taste for gun-running may make a good profit before doomsday dawns.

A morally serious person has no alternative to trying in such contexts, though he has no guarantee that a sufficient number of others will make the effort. Although his action *can* succeed only if a substantial number of other people act in similar ways, he *ought* to undertake the action in any event. It is faith in other people which bridges the gap. It replaces the faith in God which played an analogous role for earlier generations. Instead of

30. Annette Baier, 'Secular Faith,' *Canadian Journal of Philosophy*, 10 (1980) 131–148.

believing in a god who will reward the virtuous and punish the wicked (thus making morally good actions which turn out to be futile on earth 'pay off' for the individual in heaven), we are to believe in the capacity of other people for those virtuous actions which we ourselves undertake, so that our own moral commitments may lead to the desired goals right here on this earth. We do not *know* that enough other people will abide by the moral code for this goal to be realized. No deductive or inductive argument can prove this either, given the nature of the problem. Our faith in other people is not rational in the sense of being warranted by proof or evidence. Yet it is rational in the broader sense of serving an overall purpose: it is the foundation of the social and moral order.

If secular faith is, as Baier argued, the necessary foundation for much moral action, then there is no special basis for denying the responsibility of individuals for the global nuclear situation. Although we cannot, as individuals, control what happens, collectively people do have an impact. And this collective capacity is a sufficient basis for individual commitment. Any single action taken by an individual toward the goal of reducing risks of

nuclear war is likely to appear solitary and futile, the means seeming grotesquely disproportionate to the end. The action needs to be set in a context where many other people act in similar and related ways. In this context, it appears in a framework where people are working to do something they can do: stop the nuclear arms race and reduce the risks of nuclear war.

We need hope and a will to believe to remain within the moral order. So far as nuclear peace or war is concerned, we have had both. But they have been sadly misused. We have placed our hope in the political and military leaders whose sanity and responsibility we have trusted beyond all evidence. And we have willfully ignored the risks of nuclear disaster, while failing to place our confidence and trust in the moral capacities of our fellow human beings. Those of us who are students and teachers of moral philosophy can play our own small part in changing this situation, and should now be convinced that we have a special obligation to do so.*
April, 1983

*An earlier version of this paper was presented at the annual meeting of the Society for Women in Philosophy, London, Ontario, October 1982.

C O M M E N T S ■ Q U E S T I O N S

1. One of Govier's purposes is to state several different arguments regarding nuclear deterrence, which she maintains very much need to be thought about and discussed. Examples:
   a. If it is wrong to use nuclear weapons (which, she says, it clearly is), then it is wrong to *threaten* to use them.
   b. Only the final elimination of nation states will eliminate the threat of nuclear war; therefore, nation states should be eliminated.
   c. The threat of nuclear war is

much worse than ordinary threats to a person's own life because it threatens all the things we value (social goods, our descendants) in addition to our own lives. It has therefore been "profoundly damaging to the psyche of post-war generations."

d. Some philosophers have argued that self-deception can be a good thing. But it would appear that there has been society-wide self-deception regarding the dangers of nuclear weapons. Therefore, it may be that self-deception is a worse thing than has been believed.

Govier does not necessarily endorse the conclusions of all of these arguments. But she very much wants the arguments to be given serious consideration. Which do you believe are the most important? Do you believe that some or all of the arguments can be shown to be sound?

2. We face a sort of dilemma, says Govier, regarding what we as individuals should do as a moral response to nuclear dangers. Our own actions will count for little or nothing unless a great many other people act as well. But we don't know how many other people will act. Likewise, they cannot know whether or not *we* will act. To break this impasse, according to Govier, "We need to have a secular faith—the faith that enough other people will have the moral concern to make our own moral commitments practically significant." Do you share Govier's point of view on this matter?

P R E S I D E N T
R O N A L D   R E A G A N

Arms Control Policy: A Plea for Patience

L ast week, I spoke to the American people about our plans for safeguarding this nation's security and that of our allies. And I announced a long-term effort in scientific research to counter some day the menace of offensive nuclear missiles. What I have proposed is that nations should turn their best energies to moving away from the nuclear nightmare. We must not resign ourselves to a future in which

Ronald Reagan is president of the United States.

President Reagan's speech as made available by the White House. Delivered to the Los Angeles World Affairs Council, Beverly Hills, California, March 31, 1983.

security on both sides depends on threatening the lives of millions of innocent men, women and children.

And today, I would like to discuss another vital aspect of our national security: our efforts to limit and reduce the danger of modern weaponry.

We live in a world in which total war would mean catastrophe. We also live in a world that's torn by a great moral struggle between democracy and its enemies, between the spirit of freedom and those who fear freedom.

In the last 15 years or more, the Soviet Union has engaged in a relentless military buildup, overtaking and surpassing the United States in major categories of military power, acquiring what can only be considered an offensive military capability. All the moral values, which this country cherishes, freedom, democracy, the right of peoples and nations to determine their own destiny, to speak and write, to live and worship as they choose, all these basic rights are fundamentally challenged by a powerful adversary which does not wish these values to survive.

This is our dilemma, and it's a profound one. We must both defend freedom and preserve the peace. We must stand true to our principles and our friends while preventing a holocaust.

The Western commitment to peace through strength has given Europe its longest period of peace in a century. We cannot conduct ourselves as if the special danger of nuclear weapons did not exist. But we must not allow ourselves to be paralyzed by the problem, to abdicate our moral duty. This is the challenge that history has left us.

We of the 20th Century who so pride ourselves on mastering even the forces of nature—except last week when the Queen was here—we are forced to wrestle with one of the most complex moral challenges ever faced by any generation. Now, my views about the Soviet Union are well known. Although, sometimes I don't recognize them when they're played back to me. And our program for maintaining, strengthening, and modernizing our national defense has been clearly stated.

Today, let me tell you something of what we are doing to reduce the danger of nuclear war. Since the end of World War II, the United States has been the leader in the international effort to negotiate nuclear arms limitations. In 1946, when the United States was the only country in the world possessing these awesome weapons, we did not blackmail others with threats to use them, nor did we use our enormous power to conquer territory, to advance our position, or to seek domination.

Doesn't our record alone refute the charge that we seek superiority, that we represent a threat to peace. We proposed the Baruch Plan for international control of all nuclear weapons and nuclear energy, for everything nuclear to be turned over to an international agency. And this was rejected by the Soviet Union. Several years later, in 1955, President Eisenhower presented his "open skies" proposal that the United States and the Soviet Union would exchange blueprints of military establishments and permit aerial reconnaissance to ensure against the danger of surprise attack. This, too, was rejected by the Soviet Union.

Now, since then, some progress has been made, largely at American initiative. The 1963 Limited Test Ban Treaty prohibited nuclear testing in the atmosphere, in outer space, or under water. The creation of the "Hot Line" in 1963, upgraded in 1971, provides direct communication between Washington and Moscow to avoid miscalculation during a crisis. The Nuclear Non-Proliferation Treaty of 1968 sought to prevent the spread of nuclear weapons. In 1971, we reached an agreement on special communication procedures to safeguard against accidental or unauthorized use of nuclear weapons, and on a seabed arms control treaty, which prohibits the placing of nuclear weapons on the seabed of the ocean floor. The Strategic Arms Limitation Agreements of 1972 imposed limits of anti-ballistic missile systems and on numbers of strategic, offensive missiles. And the 1972 Biological Warfare Convention bans—or was supposed to ban—the development and production and stockpiling of biological and toxin weapons.

But while many agreements have been reached, we've also suffered many disappointments. The American people had hoped, by these measures to reduce tensions and start to build a constructive relationship with the Soviet Union.

Instead, we have seen Soviet military arsenals continue to grow in virtually every significant category. We have seen the Soviet Union project its power around the globe. We have seen Soviet resistance to significant reductions and measures of effective verification, especially the latter. And, I'm sorry to say, there have been increasingly serious grounds for questioning their compliance with the arms control agreements that have already been signed and that we've both pledged to uphold. I may have more to say on this in the near future.

Coming into office, I made two promises to the American people about peace and security: I promised to restore our neglected defenses, in order to strengthen and preserve the peace, and I promised to pursue reliable arguments to reduce nuclear weapons. Both these promises are being kept.

Today, not only the peace but also the chances for real arms control depend on restoring the military balance. We know that the ideology of the Soviet leaders does not permit them to leave any Western weakness unprobed, any vacuum of power unfilled. It would seem that to them negotiation is only another form of struggle. Yet, I believe the Soviets can be persuaded to reduce their arsenals—but only if they see it's absolutely necessary. Only if they recognize the West's determination to modernize its own military forces will they see an incentive to negotiate a verifiable agreement establishing equal, lower levels. And, very simply, that is one of the main reasons why we must rebuild our defensive strength.

All of our strategic force modernization has been approved by the Congress except for the land-based leg of the TRIAD. We expect to get congressional approval on this final program later this spring. A strategic forces modernization program depends on a national bipartisan consensus. Over the last decade, four successive administrations have made proposals for arms control and modernization that have become embroiled in political controversy. No one gained from this divisiveness; all of us are going to have to take a fresh look at our previous positions. I pledge to you my participation in such a fresh look and my determination to assist in forging a renewed bipartisan consensus.

My other national security priority on assuming office was to thoroughly re-examine the entire arms control agenda. Since then, in coordination with our allies, we've launched the most comprehensive program of arms control initiatives ever undertaken. Never before in history has a nation engaged in so many major simultaneous efforts to limit and reduce the instruments of war. Last month in Geneva, the Vice President committed the United States to negotiate a total and verifiable ban on chemical weapons. Such inhumane weapons, as well as toxin weapons, are being used in violation of international law in Afghanistan, in Laos, and Kampuchea.

Together with our allies, we've offered a comprehensive new proposal for mutual and balanced reduction of conventional forces in Europe.

We have recently proposed to the Soviet Union a series of further measures to reduce the risk of war from accident or miscalculation. And we are considering significant new measures resulting in part from consultations with several distinguished Senators.

We've joined our allies in proposing a Conference on Disarmament in Europe. On the basis of a balanced outcome of the Madrid meeting, such a Conference will discuss new ways to enhance European stability and security.

We have proposed to the Soviet Union improving the verification provisions of two agreements to limit underground nuclear testing, but, so far, the response has been negative. We will continue to try.

And, most importantly, we have made far-reaching proposals, which I will discuss further in a moment, for deep reductions in strategic weapons and for elimination of an entire class of intermediate-range weapons.

I am determined to achieve real arms control—reliable agreements that will stand the test of time, not cosmetic agreements that raise expectations only to have hopes cruelly dashed.

In all these negotiations certain basic principles guide our policy: First, our efforts to control arms should seek reductions on both sides—significant reductions. Second, we insist that arms control agreements be equal and balanced. Third, arms control agreements must be effectively verifiable. We cannot gamble with the safety of our people and the people of the world. Fourth, we recognize that arms control is not an end in itself but a vital part of a broad policy designed to strengthen peace and stability. It's with these firm principles in mind that this administration has approached negotiations on the most powerful weapons in the American and Soviet arsenals—strategic nuclear weapons.

In June of 1982, American and Soviet negotiators convened in Geneva to begin the Strategic Arms Reduction Talks, what we call START. We've sought to work out an agreement reducing the levels of strategic weapons on both sides. I proposed reducing the number of ballistic missiles by one-half and the number of warheads by one-third. No more than half the remaining warheads could be on land-based missiles. This would leave both sides with greater security at equal and lower levels of forces.

Not only would this reduce numbers—it would also put specific limits on precisely those types of nuclear weapons that pose the most danger.

The Soviets have made a counter proposal. We've raised a number of serious concerns about it. But—and this is important—they have accepted the concept of reductions. Now, I expect this is because of the firm resolve that we have demonstrated. In the current round of negotiations, we have presented them with the basic elements of a treaty for comprehensive reductions in strategic arsenals. The United States also has, in START, recently proposed a draft agreement on a number of significant measures to build confidence and reduce the risks of conflict. This negotiation is proceeding under the able leadership of Ambassador Edward Rowny on our side.

We're also negotiating in Geneva to eliminate an entire class of new weapons from the face of the earth. Since the end of the mid-1970's, the Soviet Union has been deploying an intermediate range nuclear missile, the SS-20, at a rate of one a week. There are now 351 of these missiles, each with three highly accurate warheads capable of destroying cities and military bases in Western Europe, Asia and the Middle East.

NATO has no comparable weapon; nor did NATO in any way provoke this new, unprecedented escalation. In fact, while the Soviets were deploying their SS-20's, we were taking a thousand nuclear warheads from shorter range weapons out of Europe.

This major shift in the European military balance, prompted our West European allies themselves to propose that NATO find a means of righting the balance. And in December 79, they announced a collective two-track decision.

First, to deploy in Western Europe 572 land-based cruise missiles and Pershing II ballistic missiles, capable of reaching the Soviet Union. The purpose, to offset and deter the Soviet SS-20's. The first of these NATO weapons are scheduled for deployment by the end of this year.

Second, to seek negotiations with the Soviet Union for the mutual reduction of these intermediate-range missiles.

In November of 1981, the United States, in concert with our allies, made a sweeping new proposal: NATO would cancel its own deployment if the Soviets eliminated theirs. The Soviet Union refused and set out to intensify public pressures in the West to block the NATO deployment, which has not even started. Meanwhile, the Soviet weapons continue to grow in number.

Our proposal was not made on a take-it-or-leave-it basis. We are willing to consider any Soviet proposal that meets these standards of fairness:

An agreement must establish equal numbers for both Soviet and American intermediate-range nuclear forces.

Other countries' nuclear forces, such as the British and French, are independent and are not part of the bilateral U.S.-Soviet negotiations. They are, in fact, strategic weapons and the Soviet strategic arsenal more than compensates for them.

Next, an agreement must not shift the threat from Europe to Asia. Given the range in mobility of the SS-20's, meaningful limits on these and comparable American systems must be global.

An agreement must be effectively verifiable.

And an agreement must not undermine NATO's ability to defend itself with conventional forces.

We've been consulting closely with our Atlantic allies and they strongly endorse these principles.

Earlier this week, I authorized our negotiator in Geneva, Ambassador Paul Nitze, to inform the Soviet delegation of a new American proposal which has the full support of our allies.

We are prepared to negotiate an interim agreement to reduce our planned deployment if the Soviet Union will reduce their corresponding warheads to an equal level. This would include all U.S. and Soviet weapons of this class, wherever they're located. Our offer of zero on both sides will, of course, remain on the table as our ultimate goal. At the same time, we remain open—as we have been from the very outset—to serious counter-proposals. The Soviet negotiators have now returned to Moscow where we hope our new proposal will receive careful consideration during the recess. Ambassador Nitze has proposed and the Soviets have agreed that negotiations resume in mid-May, several weeks earlier than scheduled.

I am sorry that the Soviet Union, so far, has not been willing to accept the complete elimination of these systems on both sides. The question I now put to the Soviet Government is: If not elimination, to what equal level are you willing to reduce? The new proposal is designed to promote early and genuine progress at Geneva. For arms control to be truly complete and world security strengthened, however, we must also increase our efforts to halt the spread of nuclear arms. Every country that values a peaceful world order must play its part.

Our Allies, as important nuclear exporters, also have a very important responsibility to prevent the spread of nuclear arms. To advance this goal, we should all adopt comprehensive safeguards as a condition for nuclear supply commitments that we make in the future. In the days ahead, I will be talking to other world leaders about the need for urgent movement on this and other measures against nuclear proliferation.

Now, that is the arms control agenda we have been pursuing. Our proposals are fair. They are far-reaching and comprehensive. But we still have a long way to go. We Americans are sometimes an impatient people. I guess it is a symptom of our traditional optimism, energy, and spirit. Often, this is a source of strength. In a negotiation, however, impatience can be a real handicap. Any of you who have been involved in labor-management negotiations or any kind of bargaining know that patience strengthens your bargaining position. If one side seems too eager or desperate, the other side has no reason to offer a compromise and every reason to hold back, expecting that the more eager side will cave in first.

Well, this is a basic fact of life we cannot afford to lose sight of when dealing with the Soviet Union. Generosity in negotiation has never been a trademark of theirs. It runs counter to the basic militancy of Marxist-Leninist idealogy. So it is vital that we show patience, determination, and above all, national unity. If we appear to be divided, if the Soviets suspect that domestic, political pressure will undercut our position, they will dig in their heels. And that can only delay an agreement, and may destroy all hope for an agreement.

That is why I have been concerned about the nuclear freeze proposals, one of which is being considered at this time by the House of Representatives. Most of those who support the freeze, I am sure, are well-intentioned, concerned about the arms race and the danger of nuclear war. No one shares their concern more than I do. But however well-intentioned they are, these freeze proposals would do more harm than good. They may seem to offer a simple solution. But there are no simple solutions to complex problems. As H. L. Mencken once wryly remarked, he said,"For every problem, there's one solution which is simple, neat, and wrong."

The freeze concept is dangerous for many reasons. It would preserve today's high, unequal, and unstable levels of nuclear forces, and, by so doing, reduce Soviet incentives to negotiate for real reductions.

It would pull the rug out from under our negotiators in Geneva, as they have testified. After all, why should the Soviets negotiate if they've already achieved a freeze in a position of advantage to them?

Also, some think a freeze would be easy to agree on, but it raises enormously complicated problems of what is to be frozen, how it is to be achieved and, most of all, verified. Attempting to negotiate these critical details would only divert us from the goal of negotiating reductions for who knows how long.

The freeze proposal would also make a lot more sense if a similar movement against nuclear weapons were putting similar pressures on Soviet leaders in Moscow. As former Secretary of Defense Harold Brown has pointed out—the effect of the

freeze "is to put pressure on the United States, but not on the Soviet Union."

Finally, the freeze would reward the Soviets for their 15-year build-up while locking us into our existing equipment, which in many cases is obsolete and badly in need of modernization. Three-quarters of Soviet strategic warheads are on delivery systems five years old or less. Three-quarters of the American strategic warheads are on delivery systems 15 years old or older. The time comes when everything wears out. The trouble is, it comes a lot sooner for us than for them. And, under a freeze, we couldn't do anything about it.

Our B-52 bombers are older than many of the pilots who fly them. If they were automobiles, they'd qualify as antiques. A freeze could lock us into obsolesence. It's asking too much to expect our service men and women to risk their lives in obsolete equipment. The two million patriotic Americans in the armed services deserve the best and most modern equipment to protect them and us.

I'm sure that every President has dreamt of leaving the world a safer place than he found it. I pledge to you, my goal—and I consider it a sacred trust—will be to make progress toward arms reductions in every one of the several negotiations now underway.

I call on all Americans of both parties and all branches of government to join in this effort. We must not let our disagreements or partisan politics keep us from strengthening the peace and reducing armaments.

I pledge to our Allies and friends in Europe and Asia—we will continue to consult with you closely. We're conscious of our responsibility when we negotiate with our adversaries on conditions of—or issues of concern to you and your safety and well being.

To the leaders and people of the Soviet Union, I say, join us in the path to a more peaceful, secure world. Let us vie in the realm of ideas, on the field of peaceful competition. Let history record that we tested our theories through human experience, not that we destroyed ourselves in the name of vindicating our way of life. And let us practice restraint in our international conduct, so that the present climate of mistrust can some day give way to mutual confidence and a secure peace.

What better time to rededicate ourselves to this undertaking than in the Easter season, when millions of the world's people pay homage to the One who taught us peace on earth, good will toward men?

This is the goal, my fellow Americans, of all the democratic nations— a goal that requires firmness, patience and understanding. If the Soviet Union responds in the same spirit, we're ready. And we can pass on to our posterity the gift of peace—that and freedom are the greatest gifts that one generation can bequeath to another.

Thank you. And God bless you.

C O M M E N T S   ■   Q U E S T I O N S

1. According to President Reagan, the Soviets will not agree to a mutual reduction in nuclear weapons unless they believe that, without such an agreement, the United States will increase its own military strength in order to be as strong or stronger than the Soviets. This is the basis for Reagan's rejection of an immediate nuclear freeze. What response to this view would Leon Wieseltier give? What response do you suppose would be given by someone who accepts the pacifist views of Cecil Cadoux?

2. According to Reagan, "The Western commitment to peace through strength has given Europe its longest period of peace in a century." He is referring to the years since World War II up to the present. Is Reagan's statement misleading in light of the fact that during this period of time non-European nations have engaged in many wars—in Korea, Vietnam, the Middle East, Afghanistan, etc.? Is there reason to believe that the existence of nuclear weapons in the world will reduce the number, or the severity, of nonnuclear wars in the world?

L E O N   W I E S E L T I E R

The Great Nuclear Debate

The great nuclear debate, then, has consisted mainly in the trashing of deterrence. It is trashed on the right and trashed on the left. There is arresting agreement on this matter. In 1973, for example, the present Undersecretary for Policy in the Department of Defense, Fred C. Iklé, published an article called, "Can Nuclear Deterrence Last Out the Century?" which helped inaugurate the right-wing revisionism that has come to rule; and in 1981 E. P. Thompson published "Deterrence and Addiction," a lecture given before the British Association for the Advancement of Science. These texts must be read together if our full fall from our senses is to be understood. The planner and the professor concur that it is the dogma of deterrence that stands in our way. They think it is immoral. According to Iklé, it is really "mutually assured genocide," and "Tomas de Torquenade, who burned ten thousand heretics at the stake, could claim principles more humane than our nuclear strategy"; and according to Thompson, it is "inducing nuclear war," and is "carrying us towards the Final Solution." And they think it is irrational. According to Iklé, "there exists no rational basis" for deterrence, because "those calculated decisions which our deterrent seeks to prevent are not the sole processes that could lead to nuclear war. . . . We are making survival depend on the rationality of all future leaders in all major wars"; and according to Thompson, deterrence "proceeds by attributing a rationality to states which can rarely be found in History . . . untroubled by those nonrational surges (of panic or of national self-assertion) which mark the historical record. . . . What if the Russians are playing a different game from the Americans, and each ignores or misunderstands the other's rules?" Then the planner and the professor part company. The one takes to the Pentagon, to find ways to win with nuclear weapons. The other takes to the streets, to find ways to abolish them. Many follow both. And the only idea that has so far come between us and these weapons, and equilibrated this evil world, is left almost friendless.

There is a sense in which deterrence is certainly immoral. It is a promise of murder. We prevent them from using their weapons by threatening to kill millions of people, and by making them believe that we mean it; and they do the same. If the deed cannot be called moral, the threat

Leon Wieseltier is Literary Editor of The New Republic.

cannot be called moral. This is the objection that is made in the pastoral letter on nuclear weapons drafted for the National Conference of Catholic Bishops. Drawing upon the congressional testimony of Cardinal Krol of Philadelphia against SALT II, a pronouncement that marked an important moment in the politicization of the Catholic clergy, the pastoral letter states that "not only the *use* of strategic nuclear weapons, but also the *declared intent* to use them involved in our deterrent policy, are both wrong." The bishops continue that "the nature of the deterrent in the nuclear age has raised the most severe moral questions for Catholic teaching on warfare," and proceed to detail what they call "the negative dimensions of deterrence." They conclude that "under no circumstances may nuclear weapons or other instruments of mass slaughter be used for the purpose of destroying population centers. . . . Our condemnation applies especially to the retaliatory use of weapons striking enemy cities after our own have already been struck." What their condemnation applies to especially, in other words, is the second strike. While the second strike certainly poses a shattering moral difficulty, it (or the plausible threat of it) is the essence of deterrence. The bishops have done much, then, to bring deterrence into disrepute, though they conclude rather correctly by accepting it as "the lesser of the two evils." It must be said to the credit of the bishops that their reservations about the Administration's strategic agenda are not crazy, that they have correctly decoded the Pentagon's present counter-political plans, which is the slaughter of innocents by another name; and it must be said to the discredit of the Pentagon

that its plans for the fighting of a nuclear war have been so deceitfully disguised as deterrence that doubts about the one have led to doubts about the other. Still, the disparagement of deterrence in the present intellectual and political climate is more than a little irresponsible.

There is a sense, too, in which deterrence is irrational. It is irrational to think highly of human nature. Our intelligence has placed intercontinental ballistic missiles at the disposal of our instincts. Nothing in the past can have been so attractive to the aggressive drives of men, so seductive to their desire for self-destruction, as nuclear weapons. "Men have gained control over the forces of nature to such an extent that with their help they would have no difficulty in exterminating one another to the last man": Freud made this observation a full fifteen years before the explosion at Almagordo. No policy on nuclear weapons, except for the immediate unscrewing of every one of them, can guarantee against an accidental war, but there is something even worse to consider. Who can say with any certainty that there will never be somebody to push it? The world may one day pay dearly for somebody's experience of his or her parents. This is the happiest time in history for sick minds.

Deterrence, moreover, is not peace. It is a condition of crisis. Indeed, deterrence is another word for danger, a brief expression for the first stage of nuclear confrontation, for the fact that what we fear most may have already begun. Deterrence is often said to have "worked," and if anything has "worked," it has; but we cannot be sure. Even if it "worked" in the past, we cannot be confident that it will "work" in the future. (Deterrence must be the only public arrangement that is a total failure if it is successful only 99.9 percent of the time.) Thompson is correct that deterrence is "a counter-factual proposition that does not admit of proof." To be a little more precise, deterrence is a proposition that may be known to be false, but not to be true. When it fails, we will know that it was false, or a few of us will. Until then we will persist in believing that it is true, and not entirely without reason. Deterrence is probably more than a necessary fiction and probably less than a law of history.

The criticism of deterrence, then, is not quite groundless. But many of the conclusions drawn from this criticism are. The alternatives to deterrence that have been proposed are no more moral or rational; they are in fact less so. The razing of Moscow known as "decapitation" is ethically no more satisfactory than the razing of Moscow known as "mutual assured destruction." Nor is it particularly moral to place our populations in still greater peril simply by taking back the threat, or taking back the weapons. The only thing more menacing to our security than nuclear strength is nuclear weakness. Any scheme for dealing with the nuclear danger that would disarm only one side, or upset the balance between the two sides, would leave us more exposed, not less. It is just as irrational to invite a war with ICBMs as it is to fight a war with ICBMs.

The proper conclusion to be drawn from the shortcomings of deterrence is, rather, that deterrence is not enough. It must not be rejected. It must be completed. And it is completed by disarmament, in the form of arms control. Deterrence and disarmament are complementary con-cepts. The proper policy for the nuclear powers may be put this way: no deterrence without disarmament, no disarmament without deterrence. But this is a slogan, whose meaning must be spelled out.

The need of deterrence for disarmament is pretty plain. The existence of such weapons means that we already exist in a state of emergency. They simply cannot be left to the pacific tendencies of people in power. They must be controlled, limited, reduced, and abolished—that is, they must be more than deterred. It follows from the nature of the emergency, furthermore, that all this must happen bilaterally. Anybody who is sincerely concerned about the nuclear danger will agree that the world will be no safer if cuts are made in only one arsenal. Nuclear superiority does not lessen the possibility of nuclear use; the United States dropped the bomb on Hiroshima when it had a nuclear monopoly. (It is worth noting, too, that if Japan had had the bomb, Hiroshima would not have been hit, because the United States would have been deterred.) The only real disarmament, then, is mutual disarmament. It is the only form of disarmament that will not advance the national interests of one side at the expense of the other's, and the only form of disarmament that will advance the higher interests of both.

The need of disarmament for deterrence is perhaps less plain. Put simply, deterrence serves as the proper regulating principle for arms control. It determines how many weapons, and of what kind, may be limited or reduced without upsetting the balance—without tempting either side to think that there would be a greater advantage in using force than in controlling it. There follows from deterrence the ideal for disarmament, which is the ideal of stockpiles shrinking more or less symmetrically. They continue to deter each other as they are diminished; and if they did not deter, they would not be diminished. This is not very rousing—unlike, say, Schell's summons to "rise up to cleanse the earth of nuclear weapons"—but it is very responsible.

Some say that the reliance upon negotiations to rid us of the risk is a counsel of despair. As anybody knows who has read Gerard Smith's comfortless account of the SALT I talks, there is some truth to this. Arms control talks have almost always smothered their purpose with the political ends of the parties. In such critical areas as strategic nuclear weapons they have not been able to agree even upon the definition of the reality that they have been mandated to modify; different measures of nuclear strength are proposed in order to disguise advantages that nobody is prepared to give away. The effort at the table has often been not to renounce, but to retain, as many weapons as possible. To be sure, SALT I and SALT II were not exactly futile; there are fifty thousand nuclear weapons alive in the world, and every cut counts. The symbolic significance of nuclear negotiations, furthermore, should not be sacrificed. But arms control is not the solution to the nuclear problem, at least not for a long time to come. Ronald Reagan has called for the reduction by a third of the nuclear warheads in the land-based and sea-based missiles of both superpowers, to be followed by an "equal ceiling" on the number of land-based warheads. George Kennan has called for "an across-the-board reduction by fifty percent of the nuclear arsenals now being main-

tained." Both are fine proposals, and both would leave intact the power to destroy the world. That is the most pressing reason for preserving the doctrine of deterrence—these missiles and warheads are not going away. If you do not believe that we should unilaterally disarm, and you do not believe that we should fight a war, and you do not believe that the arms race should forever be run, then you must believe in deterrence.

This last point should be clarified. The relationship of deterrence to the arms race is a matter of dispute. It is true that there has been no military buildup in the atomic age that has not been made in the name of deterrence, and in many cases (the "bomber gap" and the "missile gap") its name was taken in vain. Deterrence has become an idea behind which a major sector of the American economy frequently hides. This is the version of deterrence that does not include a principle of limits. It is, in this version, a purely relative idea—we must have whatever they have. And if they have more, then so must we. Such a doctrine of keeping up is a perfect rationale for an arms race. Strategic stability is a worthy goal, but strategic stability applies also to the most swollen arsenals, which is exactly the present predicament. The other side is allowed to raise the ante, and to dictate the size and style of our forces. It is not on the basis of this version of deterrence, then, that the arms race may be restrained.

There is another version of deterrence, however, which flies in the face of the arms race. This version originates not in the idea of strategic stability, but in the idea of mutual assured destruction, which it takes very seriously. The strategic criterion for the research, development, and production of nuclear weapons is taken to be simply the capacity to inflict an unacceptable degree of damage upon any aggressor. During the McNamara administration at the Pentagon, when the idea of mutual assured destruction was adopted as American policy, such unacceptable damage was deemed to be 20 to 33 percent of the Soviet population and 50 to 75 percent of Soviet industry. Obviously a lower level of damage would be equally unacceptable. The point is that whatever the definition of unacceptable damage, the capacity to inflict it already exists. It existed twenty years ago. For this version of deterrence the numbers are not relative but absolute. The manufacture of nuclear weaponry beyond the requirements of assured destruction is redundant, and so is its research and development; and according to this version of deterrence, the arms race is exactly that—an exercise in redundancy.

There is a kind of redundancy, of course, that deterrence requires. The United States must ready itself with the ability to strike at the Soviet Union after it has itself been struck, and so its forces are structured in a "triad" of land, sea, and air forces, each of which can do the deadly work of the other. But the arms race is a redundancy not of structure, which is necessary for security, but of numbers, which is necessary for business. "And the result," as Kennan remarked, "is that today we have achieved, we and the Russians together, in the creation of these devices and their means of delivery, levels of redundancy of such grotesque dimensions as to defy rational understanding." Kennan then scoffs at "something called deterrence," again from the perfectibilian point of view, but it is precisely

the technological and military situation to which he points that is deterrence's reason for being. Unless a weapon must be made it must not be made. This is what is known as "minimal deterrence." In the early Nixon years it was known as "sufficiency." It would lead to a kind of selective freeze, with some projects of research and development properly frozen.

Deterrence, finally, is more than a military dispensation. It is a political dispensation, too. It permits nations that have the power to kill each other to prosecute their interests without killing each other. This is part of its offense to many in the peace movement, who want everything called off until the nuclear problem is solved. The most prominent spokesman for the suspension of politics due to the nuclear peril is George Kennan. In a recent speech in Frankfurt, Kennan succinctly delivered his well-known views on the way in which American policy toward the Soviet Union must adapt to the nuclear condition. "We must immediately stop every type of economic warfare . . . these are means for preparing a new war, not the means for preventing one." And "we have to put an end to the often systematic condemnation of another great people and its government—a condemnation which if not stopped will really make war inevitable by making it seem inevitable." And we must "exercise restraint in the tragic question of human rights and national independence," bearing in mind always "that a new war would not help those who are considered victims of Communist arbitrariness." The argument is simple. Because of the possibility of nuclear war, the United States may do nothing, in words or in deeds, to express its profound philosophical differences with the Soviet Union. It may challenge Soviet influence, and the Soviet ideal of life, only in ways that will not matter.

To "put an end to the systematic condemndation" of the Soviet Union, however, is to put an end to the telling of the truth. (Kennan disagrees. In 1976 he told an interviewer that "I can see very little merit in organizing ourselves to defend from the Russians the porno shops in central Washington. In fact, the Russians are much better in holding pornography at bay than we are." They certainly are.) Furthermore, to "exercise restraint in the tragic question of human rights" is to deprive the victims of "Communist arbitrariness" of their only hope. The course that Kennan counsels is the compromise of America's deepest convictions. It is also political paralysis. A "tragic question" is a question you can do nothing about. Kennan is a man unnerved by a nightmare. He would unnerve his countrymen, too. He would have them believe that the tightening of credit to the Russians, or the public support of Soviet dissidents, or the linkage of Jews and others from the Soviet Union, will lead to war. This is especially odd in a man who denies that the Soviets are "aggressively disposed."

There is a part of politics, to be sure, that must never be linked to the rivalry between the superpowers, and that is nuclear politics. Arms control must not be a pawn in the game. It must be recognized as a different dimension, and dissociated from the ordinary political world. But ordinary politics must go on. Just as the bomb must not become a tool of political principle, political principle must not become a tool of the bomb. It is the divorce of the two that deterrence

accomplishes. Deterrence does not depart from the consideration of the Soviet Union as an enemy—as an enemy of which the United States may be proud. Deterrence and arms control are quite compatible with the cold war. Their objective is simply to keep the cold war cold.

That is not to say that deterrence is incompatible with détente. Obviously it is not. But if détente is to be defended, it must be on its own grounds. The military relationship of the United States with the Soviet Union must not be confused with its political relationship. (Détente, in its first try, did not change the pace of Soviet weapons production, as it was hoped it would.) The management of the military relationship has a single objective, the avoidance of war. For this a stalemate will suffice. The management of the political relationship is considerably more complicated. It must not be conducted, therefore, in Geneva. Unfortunately arms control has been laden with too heavy a political burden. Many of its advocates look to it not merely for the terms of our national security policy, but for the terms of our foreign policy, too. This is a mistake. It will make agreements on arms more difficult to achieve; and the full panoply of differences between the superpowers cannot be adequately addressed within the narrow framework of such negotiations, which must be narrow if they are to succeed. Arms control may lead to a lessening of tension, and it may not. If it does not, it must still stay on course, tension and all. Before it is anything else, then, arms control is "a managerial concept," in Freedman's words. That may not seem like much, but if you are serious about reducing the nuclear danger, you will not mind. There is no contradiction between anti-Communism and arms control. But it works both ways. If anti-Communists must not be daunted by arms controllers, arms controllers must not be daunted by anti-Communists. For the ultimate reason for the absence of a contradiction between anti-Communism and arms control is the grotesque size of the nuclear arsenal itself. The United States has 1,052 intercontinental ballistic missiles, on which there are 2,152 warheads; and 520 submarine-launched ballistic missiles, on which there are 4,768 warheads; and 316 long-range bombers. In this decade, furthermore, the United States will deploy air-launched cruise missiles, making its strategic triad into a strategic pentad. The requirements of deterrence, then, are well satisfied. This means that a good deal of arms controlling may take place before this country, and the campaign against totalitarianism, is put in jeopardy. Because the numbers are so great we have room in which to move. Let us,

to show that we are serious about arms control, volunteer to take apart some of what we have, because the gesture may make a change in the hearts of Americans and in the hearts of Russians; and let us default on the Polish debt. These actions will cost us nothing in security. They will profit us much in morality.

This, then, is the situation. There is the party of peace, and the party of war, and the party of deterrence. The party of deterrence is too little esteemed by the public. This is not surprising; no masses ever marched in the name of realism. But the public must be made to see that freedom's immediate future lies with this party, and that there is much work to be done. "It is not for you to finish the work," said a rabbi of the second century, "but neither are you free to desist from it." The rabbi was martyred by the Romans, but he spoke like a man who knew he would be survived.

C O M M E N T S ■ Q U E S T I O N S

1. Nuclear deterrence, says Wieseltier, is in a sense both immoral (because it is a "promise of murder") and irrational (because it places too much trust in fallible human nature). Nevertheless, nuclear deterrence is a better policy than to have the United States disarm while the Soviet Union remains armed. "The only thing more menacing to our security than nuclear strength is nuclear weakness." Do you agree? To what

extent would President Reagan agree (assuming that his response is to be judged from the speech of his which is included in this chapter)?

2. "Deterrence is a proposition that may be known to be false, but not to be true." What Wieseltier means is that, if present policies of deterrence are not sufficient to keep the peace then they will be proven to be so by a nuclear war; but if present policies of deterrence *are*

sufficient to preserve the peace, we can still never have enough evidence to show in any strong way that this is the case. At best, we can only *suspect* that it is the case—which in fact is Wieseltier's own position. Would you say that Wieseltier is correct in his assessment of the strength of the evidence supporting nuclear deterrence? If he is correct, would you say that this is the single most worrisome aspect of nuclear deterrence?

3. The position that Wieseltier advocates is a combination of nuclear deterrence and partial, but very significant, disarmament. Nuclear weapons on both sides, he says, could be reduced drastically while the United States and the Soviet Union would still maintain sufficient strength for each to inflict an unacceptable degree of damage upon the other. What would President Reagan say in response to such a proposal?

R E A D I N G S

Fallows, James. *National Defense.* New York: Vintage Books, 1981.

Ground Zero. *Nuclear War.* New York: Pocket Books, 1982.

Kahan, Jerome H. *Security in the Nuclear Age.* Washington, D.C.: The Brookings Institute, 1975.

Mandebaum, Michael. *The Nuclear Question.* Cambridge: Cambridge University Press, 1979.

Marrin, Albert. *War and the Christian Conscience.* Chicago: Henry Regnery Co., 1971.

Mayer, Peter, ed. *The Pacifist Conscience.* Chicago: Regnery/Gateway Inc., 1967.

Shaffer, Jerome, ed. *Violence.* New York: David McKay, 1971.

Stanage, Sherman M., ed. *Reason and Violence.* Totowa, N.J.: Littlefield, Adams & Company, 1974.

Thompson, W. Scott. *From Weakness to Strength.* San Francisco: Institute for Contemporary Studies, 1980.

Watkin, Malham M., ed. *War, Morality, and the Military Profession.* Boulder, Colo.: Westview Press, 1979.

Wasserstrom, Richard, ed. *War and Morality.* Belmont, Calif.: Wadsworth, 1970.

Walzer, Michael. *Just and Unjust Wars.* New York: Basic Books, 1977.

Act morality A moral theory or a moral principle that has to do with making moral judgments about the kinds of acts that a person does. To be contrasted with *agent morality*.

Act utilitarianism See *utilitarianism*.

Active euthanasia See *euthanasia*.

Affirmative action programs Programs intended to lessen the extent of racism, sexism and other forms of objectionable discrimination, the essential feature of which is that they do pay some attention to whether or not a person is black or white, male or female, etc. Blacks and women, for example, will in some way be given special or *preferential treatment*. This may be in the form of more aggressive recruitment, preferences given among equally qualified candidates for employment or admission to professional schools, the establishment of numerical quotas for admissions or hiring policies, etc.

Agent morality A moral theory or a moral principle that has to do with the question of whether or not a person is moral. To be contrasted with *act morality*. The distinction between agent morality and act morality is implied when it is said that a person who is morally good has (on occasion) done something that is morally bad.

Altruistic ethics Ethical theories that have as their basic principle the claim that one should not, overall in one's life, put concern for oneself above concern for others. To be contrasted with *ethical egoism*. In the history of ethics there have been many altruistic ethical theories. Some of the most important of them are to be found in the Biblical story of the Good Samaritan, in Plato's theory that the interests of the individual should be subordinated to those of society, in Immanuel Kant's *universalization principle*, and in the basic principles of *utilitarianism*.

Autonomous decision making Deciding all moral questions in such a way that all or most adult human beings are treated as capable of deciding for themselves the important questions that affect their well-being. Opposed to *paternalistic decision making*.

The Categorical Imperative (From Immanuel Kant) "I ought never to act except in such a way that I can also will that the maxim of my action be universal law." What Kant means, approximately, is that it is wrong for one person to do something unless that person is willing to have everyone else in similar circumstances do the same thing. See also *deontological ethics*.

Civil disobedience Breaking the law for a moral purpose, most commonly in order to have the law tested against some higher law. Perhaps the best-known examples of civil disobedience are ones from the civil rights movement of the 1960s, when racially biased laws were purposefully broken on many occasions.

Conventional rights Rights that human beings are said to possess as a consequence of legislation, social conventions, or social practices. To be distinguished from *natural rights*.

See also *rights*.

Deontological ethics A family of ethical theories according to which the rightness or wrongness of an individual act is to be determined primarily by something other than the consequences of the act. One of the best-known deontological theories is that of *Immanuel Kant*, who held that an act is morally right if and only if it conforms to a special rule that he called the *categorical imperative*. Another deontological theory is that of W. D. Ross, who held that an act is right if and only if it conforms in the proper way to all of our *prima facie* duties. Deontological ethical theories are to be contrasted in general with *teleological ethical theories*.

Deterrence One of the major goals of the criminal justice system. When criminals are punished for the sake of deterrence it is believed that the example of their punishment will decrease the incidence of crime in general, or at least will decrease the incidence of the particular sort of crime in question. See also *prevention, retribution, rehabilitation*, and *restitution*.

Distributive justice Justice that has to do with the distribution of things that have value in life. According to some theories of distributive justice, the good things in life should be distributed as equally as possible. Other theories place emphasis on the question of who is entitled to receive benefits. To be contrasted with *procedural justice* and *retributive justice* (for which see *retribution*).

Divine command morality The view that everyone ought to follow certain moral principles because God, or some supernatural being, has told us that we ought to. Classical defenders of divine command morality are St. Augustine, St. Thomas Aquinas, and Martin Luther.

Due process of law See *procedural justice*.

Duty When used broadly, any moral obligation. The expression "duty-based ethics," which is a narrower use, usually means *deontological ethics*.

Egoism See *ethical egoism, psychological egoism*, and *rational self-interest*.

Equal consideration Treatment that is adjusted, using morally defensible criteria, to the differing needs and capacities of those being treated, but which is intended to be equal within the scope of this adjustment. For example, equal consideration of humans and animals dictates that their respective needs for food and comfort be given equal weight morally even though in actual practice animals need different kinds of food, security, and so on than do humans. To be distinguished from *equal treatment*.

Equal treatment The very same treatment, as for example feeding human beings and animals the very same types of food. To be distinguished from *equal consideration*.

Ethical absolutism The view that certain moral principles apply equally to everyone under circumstances that are relevantly similar. The opposite of *relativism*.

Ethical egoism The view that everyone ought to be selfish, or in other words that everyone ought always, or usually, to act for the sake of self-interest regardless of the needs or supposed rights of others. According to ethical egoism, a person should take into account the rights and needs of others only when it is in the person's self-interest to do so. To be contrasted with *psychological egoism* and also with *altruistic ethics*. See also *rational self-interest*.

Ethical hedonism The position that pleasure is the only thing that is good in itself and pain is the only thing that is bad in itself. There are two versions of ethical hedonism: (1) hedonistic egoism—each person has a duty to seek pleasure and avoid pain for himself or herself only; (2) hedonistic utilitarianism—each person has a duty to seek pleasure and avoid pain for the greatest number of people. Ethical hedonism in general is to be contrasted with *psychological hedonism*.

Ethical relativism The position that values are relative either to (1) individuals—*personal ethical relativism*, or (2) the dominant beliefs of cultures—*cultural ethical relativism*. Opposed to *ethical absolutism*. Both versions of ethical relativism make claims about what values a person ought to follow. According to personal ethical relativism a person ought to follow his or her own values, and according to cultural ethical relativism, a person ought to follow the values of

his or her culture or society. The latter position is to be contrasted with *sociological value relativism*.

Euthanasia Ending the life of someone who is severely incapacitated by either (1) taking positive steps such as giving a lethal injection (*active euthanasia*) or (2) by failing to do some of the things required for the prolongation of life, as when an ill person is not put on a needed life support system (*passive euthanasia*). The distinction between active and passive euthanasia is not always clear and is a cause of much philosophical controversy. In all cases of euthanasia there is a presumption that a life has been ended for a reason that at least in itself is morally praiseworthy, such as the alleviation of suffering.

Fair employment practices legislation Laws that make it illegal to hire, fire, promote, etc., in a way that is biased in regard to race, sex, age, and some other factors.

Free market An economic system whereby the market forces of supply and demand are the primary economic determinants. In a free market the following regulative functions of government (among others) are very minimal or nonexistent: the imposition of tariffs or trade quotas, the setting of prices or wages, the redistribution of wealth for the sake of achieving *distributive justice*, the government ownership of business. A free market is the defining characteristic of *laissez-faire capitalism*, which is opposed to *socialism*. The classical defense of a free market is to be found in Adam Smith's *The Wealth of Nations*.

Greatest happiness principle The claim that the most basic moral obligation is to bring about the greatest good for the greatest number. See *utilitarianism*.

Hedonism See *ethical hedonism* and *psychological hedonism*.

Hypothetical consent The consent that a person *would* have given had the person been able to give it. Hypothetical consent is appealed to,

for example, in the defense of euthanasia for a seriously ill and comatose patient when it is said that the person *would have* expressed a desire to die if the person had been able to.

Implied consent The consent that is implied by a person's actions. For example, if a person drives his car on the public roads, this may be taken to imply that he has consented to obey the traffic laws.

Instrumental good Something that is not good in itself but is good because it will lead to something else that is good. An example would be disagreeable labor that pays well. To be distinguished from *intrinsic good*.

Intention Reason for acting, or the final goal of one's action. An intention is specified in answer to the following sorts of questions: Why did you do that? What were you really trying to accomplish in doing that?

Intrinsic good Something that is good in itself. To be distinguished from *instrumental good*.

Justice See *distributive justice*, *procedural justice*, *Plato's theory of justice*, and *retributive justice* (which is discussed under *retribution*).

Laissez-faire capitalism See *free market*.

Lifeboat ethics Ethical decisions or principles that are addressed to, or reflect, the features of emergency situations. For example, "If you were in an overcrowded lifeboat in the frigid Atlantic, who would have to be sacrificed?" Very often philosophers make reference to lifeboat situations in order to validate moral principles that they claim are applicable also to everyday situations.

Mixed economy An economic system that combines features of both a *free market* and *socialism* and that thus could be thought of as being a kind of compromise between them. There are many varieties of the mixed economy, such as those to be found in the United States, Great Britain, and some Scandinavian countries.

Natural rights Rights that all people are said to possess because of their natures as human beings. Natural rights are held independently of anyone's voluntary agreement to recognize them. Some theories of natural rights place special emphasis on the claim that the natures that we have as human beings were given to us by God. (See also *divine command morality*.) Classical defenses of natural rights are to be found in St. Thomas Aquinas and John Locke. To be distinguished from *conventional rights*. See also *rights*.

Normative A normative judgment or statement is one that tells people what is good or what they ought to do, as opposed to a descriptive judgment or statement, which tells the way things are. For example, *ethical relativism* is normative, while *sociological value relativism* is not normative but rather is intended to be descriptive.

Passive euthanasia See *euthanasia*.
Paternalistic decision making (paternalism) Deciding certain moral questions in such a way that one group of persons will act in the role of a parent toward another group of persons. For example, a paternalistic view of government would lead to this type of decision making. Opposed to *autonomous decision making*.
Plato's theory of justice Holds that the most important thing in life is achieving a balance or harmony among all of the conflicting aspects of a person's own self and all of the conflicting aspects of society. The most complete statement is to be found in Plato's *Republic*, which contains a discussion of what Plato calls the "parts of the human soul" and a discussion of how the ideal state should be organized.
Preferential treatment programs See *affirmative action programs*.
Prevention One of the major goals

of the criminal justice system: for example, a criminal may be prevented from committing further crimes during a period of incarceration. To be contrasted with *deterrence*, which is the use of punishment for the intended purpose of making it less likely that *anyone* (not just the person who is actually being punished) will commit crimes, or a particular type of crime. See also *retribution, rehabilitation*, and *restitution*.
Procedural justice Propriety or fairness in a set of rules, laws, or procedures; or propriety or fairness in following some set of rules, laws, or procedures. For example, whether or not a person receives a fair trial is a question of procedural justice that has nothing to do with the person's actual guilt or innocence. Also referred to in some contexts as *due process of law*. To be contrasted with *distributive justice* and *retributive justice* (for which see *retribution*).
Prima facie duty A moral obligation that everyone in a certain circumstance has and which must be followed unless it conflicts with a more important prima facie duty. "Prima facie" means, roughly "on the face of it." Ethical theories based upon prima facie duties (such as that of W. D. Ross) place special emphasis upon the idea that one prima facie duty can *override* another. See also *deontological ethics*.
Psychological egoism The view that all human beings do everything they do for selfish reasons. To be contrasted with *ethical egoism*. The classical defense of psychological egoism is to be found in Thomas Hobbes. The classical rejections of psychological egoism are to be found in Bishop Butler and David Hume.
Psychological hedonism The position that everyone by nature seeks only pleasure and the avoidance of pain, or in other words, that people cannot help doing everything that they do in order to gain pleasure and to avoid pain. To be contrasted with *ethical hedonism*.

Racism An attitude of bias towards members of a particular race, usually

one's own. Actions, policies, and social circumstances that reflect such an attitude are racist.
Rational self-interest Self-interest that is understood in the broadest and most defensible way to include everything that is of benefit to a person, especially self-interest that is understood to include within it the need to live in society, have friends, conduct business, and in general to cooperate with other people. The classical defense of an ethics of rational self-interest is to be found in Aristotle. See also *ethical egoism*.
Rehabilitation One of the major intended goals of the criminal justice system; namely, to reform the character or enhance the socially useful skills of persons convicted of crimes. See also *deterrence, retribution, prevention*, and *restitution*.
Relativism See *ethical relativism* and *sociological value relativism*. Compare to *situation ethics*. To be contrasted with *ethical absolutism*.
Restitution One of the goals of the criminal justice system. Restitution is achieved when someone convicted of a crime is made to pay the victim (or heirs of victims) of the crime compensation that, to the degree that this is possible, is equal to the amount of loss incurred as a result of the crime. See also *deterrence, prevention, retribution*, and *rehabilitation*.
Retribution Punishing someone simply because the person has done something wrong and not for any other reason such as *deterrence* or *prevention*. Also (and what may mean the same thing) punishing someone simply because the person is said to deserve the punishment. The concept of retribution is often associated with *deontological ethics*; it is not consistent with *teleological ethics*. Retribution is a controversial goal of the criminal justice system. Also called *retributive justice*. See also *restitution, deterrence, prevention*, and *rehabilitation*. The classical defense of an ethics of retribution is to be found in the Old Testament notion of an "eye for an eye, a tooth for a tooth." The classical rejections of an ethics of retribution are to be found in the New Testament

"Sermon on the Mount" and in Plato's *Republic*.

Reverse discrimination This occurs when, for example, whites are discriminated against in the job market as a mechanism for decreasing, or as a consequence of decreasing, discrimination against blacks. When reverse discrimination occurs, there is a presumption that it is intended to be for the sake of a morally praiseworthy end; thus reverse discrimination in the case of whites and blacks is to be distinguished from "white backlash," which is a form of retaliation that has a racist motivation.

The reversibility of roles test A procedure for making moral judgments that requires that a person place himself or herself imaginatively in the roles of everyone else who would be affected by the act in question.

Rights Ethical theories based upon the concept of rights emphasize the protection or enhancement of each and every individual human being, or of certain groups of human beings, and are to be contrasted with theories that emphasize justice, the common good of all, or other values that in principle could jeopardize certain individuals or groups. Examples of rights that are said to pertain to every person are the rights to life and liberty; examples of rights that are said to pertain to certain groups are the rights of women and students. An important characteristic of rights is that they entail duties; thus, if I have a right to own property, others have a duty to respect my legitimate ownership claims. In recent years the concept of rights has been extended to nonhumans in discussions of the rights of animals. See also *natural rights* and *conventional rights*.

Rule utilitarianism See *utilitarianism*.

Sexism An attitude of bias towards members of one gender, usually one's own and very often associated with the attitudes of men toward women. Actions, policies, and social circumstances that reflect such an attitude are sexist.

Situation ethics Broadly, the view that the rightness or wrongness of an action varies from one situation to another. More specifically, it is the view that no abstract moral principles are absolutes (such as "always keep promises"), but that the rightness or wrongness of an act will be determined by the moral quality of one's attitude or intention directed toward a given situation (having a loving or concerned attitude in contrast to a selfish attitude, for example). The situation will determine exactly how one's concern ought to be manifested. The meanings of *situation ethics* are similar to, but should not be confused with, some of the meanings of *relativism*.

Socialism An economic system in which all or most businesses are owned or run by the government, or in other words, an economic system in which most decisions regarding wages, prices, what will be produced, and so on, are the consequence of central planning and not a *free market*. The classical defense of socialism is to be found in Karl Marx's *Das Kapital*.

Sociological value relativism The theory from sociology or anthropology that different cultures or societies in fact have differing fundamental ethical beliefs or practices. As a theory that does not say what values anyone should actually follow, it is to be contrasted with *cultural ethical relativism* (defined under *ethical relativism*).

Summum bonum The highest good. According to some philosophers, that for the sake of which all other things that are good are good.

Teleological ethics A family of ethical theories according to which the rightness or wrongness of an individual act is to be determined primarily by the consequences of the act. *Utilitarianism* and *ethical egoism* are examples of teleological ethics. To be contrasted with *deontological ethics*.

Utilitarianism An ethical theory that has several different versions. In association with the names of Jeremy Bentham and John Stuart Mill, it is the view (sometimes called *hedonistic utilitarianism*) that everyone should always act so as to bring about the greatest amount of pleasure and least pain for the greatest number of people. In association with the name of G. E. Moore and others it is the view—sometimes called *ideal utilitarianism*—that everyone should always act so as to bring about the greatest good for the greatest number, whatever the good might be, whether pleasure or something else.

Rule utilitarianism is the view that everyone should follow those rules that—if all or most people obeyed them—would bring about the greatest good for the greatest number of people.

Act utilitarianism is the view that everyone should seek to perform those individual acts that, when all of their consequences are considered, will or most probably will bring about the greatest good for the greatest number of people.

Because all the versions of utilitarianism stress the consequences of moral actions, utilitarianism, like *ethical egoism*, is an example of *teleological ethics*. In contrast to ethical egoism, utilitarianism requires more than the good of the agent to be considered.

Victimless crimes Crimes in which it is alleged that the person who has committed the crime is the only one who is harmed by it. As an example, personal use of harmful drugs has been called a victimless crime.

Virtue A moral excellence. Specifically, a disposition or capacity for doing the morally right thing. Temperance, for example, is the disposition to avoid moral excess in eating or drinking. The classical formulation of an ethics of virtue is to be found in Aristotle's *Nicomachean Ethics*.

Women's autonomy The right that is defended by some philosophers that allows decisions regarding the use of a woman's own body to be made by the woman herself (for example, whether to continue a pregnancy).